HOSPITAL COMPUTER SYSTEMS

BIOMEDICAL ENGINEERING AND HEALTH SYSTEMS:

A WILEY-INTERSCIENCE SERIES

Advisory Editor: JOHN H. MILSUM, University of British Columbia

L. A. Geddes and L. E. Baker
Principles of Applied Biomedical Instrumentation

George H. Myers and Victor Parsonnet
Engineering in the Heart and Blood Vessels

Robert Rosen
Dynamical System Theory in Biology

Stanley Middleman
Transport Phenomena in the Cardiovascular System

Samuel A. Talbot and Urs Gessner
Systems Physiology

Morris F. Collen
Hospital Computer Systems

Israel Mirsky, Dhanjoo N. Ghista, and Harold Sandler
Cardiac Mechanics: Physiological, Clinical and Mathematical
Considerations

Richard S. C. Cobbold
Transducers for Biomedical Measurements:
Principles and Applications

Marshall M. Lih
Transport Phenomena in Medicine and Biology

HOSPITAL COMPUTER SYSTEMS

Edited by

DR. MORRIS F. COLLEN

Director, Medical Methods Research
The Permanente Medical Group
Oakland, California

A WILEY BIOMEDICAL-HEALTH PUBLICATION

JOHN WILEY & SONS, New York · London · Sydney · Toronto

Library of Congress Cataloging in Publication Data:
Main entry under title:

Hospital computer systems.

(Wiley-Interscience series on biomedical
engineering)
"A Wiley-Interscience publication."
Includes bibliographical references.

1. Electronic data processing—Hospitals—
Administration. I. Collen, Morris Frank, 1913-
ed. [DNLM: 1. Computers. 2. Hospitals. WX26.5
H828 1974]

RA971.H59   362.1'1'02854   73-17140
ISBN 0-471-16510-7

Printed in the United States of America

10 9 8 7 6 5 4 3 2 1

Series Preface

"To love
is not to gaze steadfast
at one another:
it is to look together
in the same direction"

St. Exupery, *Terre des Hommes*

The provision of good universal health care has only just become a social imperative. Like such other interlocking systems as transportation, water resources, and metropolises, the recognition of the need to adopt a systems approach has been forced upon us by the evident peril of mutual ruin resulting if we do not. The required systems approach is necessarily interdisciplinary rather than merely multidisciplinary, but this always makes evident the very real gulf between disciplines. Indeed, bridging the gulf requires much more time and patience than necessary just to learn the other discipline's "language." These different languages simultaneously represent and hide the whole gestalt associated with any discipline or profession. Nevertheless sufficient bridging must be achieved so that interdisciplinary teams can tackle our complex systems problems, for such teams constitute the only form of "intelligence amplification" that we can presently conceive.

Fortunately the existence of urgent problems always seems to provide the necessary impetus to work together in the same direction, using St. Exupery's thought, and, indeed, as a result of this to understand and value each other more deeply.

This series started with its emphasis on biomedical engineering. It illustrates the application of engineering in the service of medicine and biology. Books are required both to educate persons from one discipline in what they need to know of others, and to catalyse a synthesis in the core

v

subject generally known as biomedical engineering. Thus one set of titles will aim at introducing the biologist and medical scientist to the quantitatively based analytical theories and techniques of the engineer and physical scientist. This set covers instrumentation, mathematical modelling, signal and system analysis, communication and control theory, and computer simulation techniques. A second set for engineers and physical scientists will cover basic material on biological and medical systems with as quantitative and compact a presentation as is possible. The omissions and simplifications necessitated by this approach should be justified by the increased ease of transferring the information, and more subtly by the increased pressure this can bring to bear upon the search for unifying quantitative principles.

A second emphasis has become appropriate as society increasingly demands universal health care, because the emphasis of medicine is now rapidly shifting from individual practice to health care systems. The huge financial burden of our health care systems (currently some 6% of GNP and increasing at about 14% per year) alone will ensure that engineers will be called upon, for the technological content is already large and still increasing. Engineers will need to apply their full spectrum of methodologies and techniques, and, moreover, to work in close collaboration with management professionals, as well as with many different health professionals. This series, then, will develop a group of books for mutually educating these various professionals so that they may better achieve their common task.

This book has developed from the experiences of the notable pioneering operation in computer information systems at the Kaiser Foundation Research Institute. Since the cost of information handling is commonly estimated at around 25-30% in typical institutions such as hospitals, there is now great interest in the use of automation and computer techniques. Indeed it may be plausibly argued that one practical justification for proceeding to computer systems in health care is to ensure the latter's present quality can be maintained, given the continually increasing demands, and given improvements in available techniques. In this sense the difficult issue of demonstrating greater economy may largely be bypassed in practice. In any case the important practical result of implementing this technological innovation will be, as always in such cases, that the greater quality now potentially available will in fact be demanded. This book then should prove valuable to a wide spectrum of health care professionals.

Vancouver, British Columbia   JOHN H. MILSUM

Preface

A variety of computer applications in medical care has been developed within many hospitals in the U.S. and Europe over the past ten years. In the first half of 1973, there was not yet in existence a single completely computerized hospital information system, although considerable progress has been achieved in utilizing the computer for many inpatient and out-patient services. Therefore, it appears worthwhile to take stock of the current status of hospital computer systems and their component modules; to review their objectives and requirements, the important causes of failure, and the factors necessary for success; and to describe those existing projects which appear to be leaders in the field.

This book does not discuss all computing applications in medicine but is limited to those applications which already have some utility to hospital inpatient and outpatient medical care functions. Special attention was directed to medical computing applications rather than administrative and business computing since the greatest potential for the use of computers is in direct patient care, an area still in the developmental stage.

It is hoped that this book will encourage medical and hospital professionals to realize that a vast amount of experience has already been accumulated in this difficult, expensive, and complex technological systems field. The door is already more than half-way opened to exploit computers for direct patient care in hospitals. It can be predicted that, in the 1980's, every patient and every doctor in any hospital in the U.S. with more than 200 beds will directly interface a computer almost daily.

Great appreciation is expressed to all the contributors to this book in recognition of the time taken from their very busy work schedules and for their ability to surmount the difficulties of an international cooperative publication attempting to provide a broad representation of the state of the art and science of Hospital Computer Systems in the U.S. and Europe.

Oakland, California   MORRIS F. COLLEN

Contributors

John Anderson, M.D., F.R.C.P., F.B.C.S.
   Professor, Department of Medicine
   King's College Hospital Medical School
   (University of London)
   Denmark Hill
   London, S.E.5, England

G. Octo Barnett, M.D.
   Associate Professor of Medicine
   Harvard Medical School;
   Director, Laboratory of Computer Science
   Massachusetts General Hospital
   32 Fruit Street
   Boston, Massachusetts 02114

Morris F. Collen, B.E.E., M.D.
   Director, Medical Methods Research
   The Permanente Medical Group, and
   The Kaiser Foundation Research Institute
   3779 Piedmont Avenue
   Oakland, California 94611

Lou S. Davis, M.A.
   Manager, Computer Center
   Department of Medical Methods Research
   The Permanente Medical Group
   3779 Piedmont Avenue
   Oakland, California 94611

Charles D. Flagle, D. Eng.
   Professor of Public Health Administration
   School of Hygiene and Public Health

x   Contributors

The Johns Hopkins University
601 Broadway
Baltimore, Maryland 21205

Sidney R. Garfield, M.D.
Founder, Kaiser-Permanente Medical Care Program
3779 Piedmont Avenue
Oakland, California 94611

Paul F. L. Hall, M.D.
Professor of Clinical Medicine, Head Physician
Department of Medical Information
Karolinska Sjukhuset
104 01 Stockholm 60, Sweden

Donald A. B. Lindberg, M.D.
Professor of Pathology
Director, Medical Center Computer Program
School of Medicine
University of Missouri-Columbia
Columbia, Missouri 65201

Gwilym S. Lodwick, M.D.
Professor and Chairman
Department of Radiology
University of Missouri Medical Center
Columbia, Missouri 65201

Peter L. Reichertz, M.D.
Professor, Department of Biometrics and Medical Information Science
Medical School Hannover/Germany
Roderbruchstrasse, 101
D 3 Hannover-Kleefeld, German Fed. Rep.

Robert H. Richart, Ph.D.
Senior Health Systems Analyst
Department of Medical Methods Research
The Permanente Medical Group
3779 Piedmont Avenue
Oakland, California 94611

Robert E. Robinson III, M.D.
Assistant Director, Hospitals and Clinics
The Center for the Health Sciences
University of California, Los Angeles
Los Angeles, California 90024

Krikor Soghikian, M.D., M.P.H.
Chief, Division of Preventive Medicine and Health Center
The Permanente Medical Group
3779 Piedmont Avenue
Oakland, California 94611

William A. Spencer, M.D.
Director, Texas Institute for Rehabilitation
and Research in the Texas Medical Center
1333 Moursund Avenue
Houston, Texas 77025

Joseph F. Terdiman, M.D., Ph.D.
Biomedical Information Scientist
Department of Medical Methods Research
The Permanente Medical Group
3779 Piedmont Avenue
Oakland, California 94611

Carlos Vallbona, M.D.
Professor and Chairman
Department of Community Medicine
Baylor College of Medicine
Texas Medical Center
Houston, Texas 77025

Edmund E. Van Brunt, M.D.
Project Chief, Medical Data System
Department of Medical Methods Research
The Permanente Medical Group
3779 Piedmont Avenue
Oakland, California 94611

Douglass Williams
Vice President, Administrative Services
Permanente Services, Inc.
1924 Broadway
Oakland, California 94612

George Z. Williams, M.D.
Research Institute of Laboratory Medicine
Pacific Medical Center
Institute of Medical Sciences
2200 Webster Street
San Francisco, California 94115

Robert L. Williams, B.S.
    President, Computer Medalytics Corporation
    6 Granada Drive
    Corte Madera, California 94925

Contents

Section II   CURRENT STATUS OF HOSPITAL COMPUTER SYSTEMS

HOSPITAL COMPUTER SYSTEMS

Section I

IMPLEMENTING HOSPITAL COMPUTER SYSTEMS

CHAPTER ONE

General Requirements

by Morris F. Collen

A. INTRODUCTION

We are currently in an era of technological revolution. In contrast to the period of the industrial revolution, which was directed to the use of machines and factories to exploit natural resources and improve goods and materials output, the current technological revolution is directed towards improving our way of life by better communications, education, health services, and environmental control.

Computer technology will have an increasing impact on society through important evolving innovations in hospital care, outpatient care, and organized systems for delivery of health care.[1-7] Since several studies[8,9] have shown that 25–40% of a hospital's costs are related to information handling (see Chapter Thirteen), there is an increasingly urgent need to use modern computer technology for a more efficient hospital information system. A significant change in data flow and communication within a hospital will have important effects on every hospital subsystem, procedure, and person.

Over the past ten years, a number of hospitals in the U.S. and Europe have been implementing hospital computer systems; however, by early 1973, there was not yet a single successfully completed total hospital computer system.

To analyze the problem, we must determine the reasons for the failures that occurred and identify the factors which will tend to insure success. It is important first to define carefully the components, functional requirements, and objectives of such a system.

3

B. DEFINITIONS

A Hospital Computer System (HCS) as herein defined is one which utilizes electronic data processing and communications equipment to provide on-line processing with real-time responses for patient data within the hospital and its outpatient department, including ancillary services such as clinical laboratory, x-ray, electrocardiography, pharmacy, etc.[10,11] (See Figure 1–1.)

A hospital administrative computer system is a subcomponent of HCS, which handles its administrative and business functions including admission procedures, bed census, menu planning, and patient schedules for departmental services such as x-ray, surgery, outpatient visits, etc.

A laboratory data system is a subcomponent of HCS which handles the clinical laboratory data for inpatient and outpatient services, including generation of laboratory work lists and test quality control programs; it may even include limited bed census files or input/output terminals at nurses' stations.

C. IMMEDIATE OBJECTIVES OF HCS

The usual objectives of a HCS are to:

(1) Improve quality, quantity, utility, and speed of medical data communication while at the same time containing costs.

(2) Communicate individual patient data from the professionals providing medical care (doctors, nurses, technicians, etc.) into the computer medical record and then to other professionals (e.g., dietitian) and hospital service departments (e.g., radiology).

(3) Communicate patient data from subsystem components (e.g., automated multiphasic screening laboratory or intensive care unit) into the patient's computer medical record.

(4) Communicate between clinical services (i.e., nursing stations) and ancillary services (e.g., ECG or radiology).

(5) Establish scheduling and booking files and communicate such information for patients, personnel, and medical care services.

(6) Establish a data base for administrative and business functions.

(7) Establish a medical data base which can support clinical and health services research.

(8) Assist in the teaching of medical staff and medical students and in the health education of the lay public.

(9) Provide data necessary for projection of health care needs and planning for hospital and medical services, not only for the hospital itself but also for the community.

	Health care services						
Clinical	Ancillary	Scheduling	Administrative	Computer center	Medical research	Medical teaching	Community services
Medical	Laboratory	Hospital admissions	Insurance eligibility	Data base	Clinical	Medical students	Health resources
Surgical	X-ray ECG	Bed census	Accounting	Patient files	Epidemio- logical	Medical staff	Health facilities
Pediatrics	Pharmacy	X-ray procedures	Personnel	Schedule files	Health services research	Allied health personnel	Vital statistics
	Dietary		Payroll				
Obstetrics	Multiphasic screening	Hospital staffing	Supplies	Special data sets		Patient health education	Planning
Intensive care	Medical records	Office visits	Inventories				
Emergency		Home visits					Evaluation
Outpatient							

Figure 1-1. A hospital computer information system.

D. FUNCTIONAL REQUIREMENTS

To achieve the above objectives, a HCS must be capable of fulfilling the following requirements: [12,13]

1. Provide data quality control programs and procedures to reduce errors of patient identification and minimize instrumental and human errors throughout all HCS subsystems. It must be able to provide more complete data and/or more selective data for each user's needs, increasing the utility and legibility of printouts by employing human engineering factors. It should increase the speed of communication of data between data sources and data users. (See Chapter Three.)

2. For each patient, on a continuous, 24-hour-day basis, capture at the source, on-line if necessary, all inpatient and outpatient service data, and store in the patient computer record[14,15] the following essential information (see Chapter Four): (a) selected history, physical examination, and progress report data which is quantitated or susceptible to some standardization of terminology and formatting of input; but the system must be capable of handling natural language as necessary; (b) all diagnoses; (c) all diagnostic interpretations from x-ray (see Chapter Nine), ECG, EEG, pathology, and other physician-reported examinations (see Chapter Ten); (d) doctors' orders (see Chapter Six); (e) all procedures, including operations, deliveries, etc.; (f) all clinical laboratory test results (see Chapter Seven); (g) essential summarized patient monitoring data from intensive care areas; (h) all drugs administered in the hospital and dispensed in the outpatient pharmacies; and (i) ancillary services provided to patients (for example, physiotherapy, dietary, etc.). (See Figure 1-2.)

Patient Data	Scheduling & Administration
Selected history	Hospital admissions
physical exam	Bed census
progress notes	Ancillary services
Medical diagnoses	Hospital staffing
X-ray, ECG, pathology data	Inventory control
Laboratory test data	Menu planning
Hospital & pharmacy drugs	Laboratory test log
Surgical procedures	Laboratory quality control
Ancillary services	Outpatient appointments
↓	↓
Integrated patient computer medical record	Individual special data sets

Figure 1–2. Functional requirements for HCS.

3. To provide any appropriate part or all of this data, on demand when necessary, in the form of printouts or visual displays to (1) the physicians for patient care, and (2) the administrative and business offices for patient accounts.

4. To provide administrative communicative functions, such as (1) scheduling of patients and procedures, including outpatient appointments and registration; hospital admissions, bed census, and scheduling; and scheduling for ancillary services (e.g., laboratory, radiology, dietary, surgery, etc.); (2) to provide scheduling and control functions for personnel, supplies, and equipment; including hospital staffing, inventory control, menu planning, automated equipment quality control, etc.; (3) to provide message switching functions to multiple departments (e.g., laboratory test orders to and from nursing station to laboratory, to medical chart room, and to computer center); and (4) provide business functions, including posting of charges, billing, payroll, etc. (See Chapter Five.)

5. To provide a data base useful for (1) investigators needing both patient and statistical files for clinical, epidemiological, and health services research;[16] (2) administrators for hospital services evaluation, simulation, projection, and planning (see Chapter Fourteen); and (3) medical education (see Chapter Fifteen).

6. To satisfy confidentiality, security, and legal requirements.[17]

E. PERSONNEL REQUIREMENTS

Since there are not yet "turn-key" HCS packages available (many turn-key subsystem modules are now commercially available for clinical laboratory, automated multiphasic testing, ECG processing, intensive care monitoring, business functions, etc.), the hospital will have to consider its HCS to be a developmental project; it will need to modify any available software to fit its own needs. When turn-key systems do become available, large hospitals will still need to consider carefully the disadvantages of a rigid commercial system versus a flexible self-serving, self-designed system.

The development of a large medical-technological system such as HCS will require a large "in-house" staff.[2] In addition to medical and data processing personnel, the following qualified specialists should be included:

1. Project Chief

A project chief will be essential for a developmental HCS. He should be a "physician-engineer" (i.e., an M.D. with training also in engineering, biophysics, or computers) who has the confidence and support of hospital management. The great difficulties associated with interdisciplinary communications between physicians and engineers require at least one key person to have adequate expertise in both fields of technology. It is advisable to support the project chief with several physicians who also have some background in the physical sciences and who devote themselves at least part-time to the project. Once a HCS is routinely operational, it is desirable but not essential that the project chief be a physician.

2. Systems Supervisor

The systems supervisor is preferably someone with a background in the life sciences.

3. Computer Center Manager

This manager should be an administrator trained as a computer scientist, with adequate knowledge of the biological sciences to communicate effectively with physicians, to be responsible for selection and implementation of the hardware and modification of software for the central computer and its satellite processors and terminals. A good manager of programmers is not necessarily a good manager of a computer service center where the primary need is to satisfy the user. He must be a business-oriented administrator capable of evaluating performance of hardware, software, programming personnel, budget, and user requirements.

4. Information Engineer

The information engineer should be someone qualified in information science and the life sciences to supervise the data base and develop procedures for high-quality medical information processing.

5. Medical Systems Analysts

Required here are personnel trained in analysis of medical subsystems, to define needs and problems and to recommend alternative approaches. Good medical systems analysts are required if HCS is to be used innovatively rather than for the mechanization of existing manual methods. To facilitate interdisciplinary communication and maximize the user acceptance, it is necessary to orient physicians, nurses, laboratory technologists, etc., in methods of systems analysis.

6. Applications Programmers

These programmers will write computer programs for the medical functions. It is desirable to train a pharmacist, laboratory technician, nurse, and physician to function as or work with a programmer for their particular applications to facilitate communications with those programmers not trained in the biological sciences.

Maintenance applications programmers are evolving as an important continuing requirement for an operational HCS. Most applications programs in medicine are dynamic; they are constantly being modified due to the need to assimilate new information or new methods.

7. Systems Programmers

These programmers will design and implement the complex computer central control system and its related service programs to store, retrieve, and process patient data for the medical application programs. The systems programmers are also responsible for installing and monitoring the vendor's computer operating system software.

8. Equipment Engineers

Equipment engineers will work out problems of interfacing hardware from different manufacturers and maintaining the terminal equipment. Although the manufacturer usually maintains the major components of data processing equipment, it is usually necessary to have a resident maintenance engineer trained on the selected terminal equipment.

9. Orientation and Training Personnel

It is necessary to develop standard operating procedure manuals and to orient and train HCS users in its operations. The successful achievement of these objectives requires use of middle management hospital personnel in planning and implementing HCS subsystem components. To obtain user compliance for data input terminals as an operational part of a hospital service, be it a nursing station, laboratory, or pharmacy, it is necessary to evolve the planning and the implementation of the terminal systems as an integral part of that hospital department's development. To develop data outputs with content and format of high utility to physicians requires careful planning. Regular meetings must be held at which the project chief meets with representatives of the departments affected. Intradepartmental orientation sessions should then follow.

Good departmental supervisors can be a great help when implementing a new subsystem. Often a host of minor problems appears because the systems analysis did not identify procedures previously handled on an informal basis but which now require formal definition. Good middle management personnel will adjust readily to the new system and minimize the number of such secondary problems.

F. DATA BASE REQUIREMENTS

A prime concept of HCS is the requirement to serve as the central register and medical data repository for all patients receiving care from the hospital, including its outpatient department. The most essential requirement for HCS is an integrated computer record for all data for each individual patient for every hospitalization and outpatient visit.[14,15] Small collections of patient data for subsystem components (e.g., blood banks, laboratories, bed census, etc.), will never satisfy clinical services requirements.

Accordingly, to satisfy the requirements for handling many forms of medical information for many visits through time, it is necessary to provide an integrated, variable length, variable format, computer-stored medical record. Each datum should be stored once in its most fundamental unit of information. At any time it can then be extracted according to many criteria and grouped with other data or classified to satisfy the needs of any user. It is necessary to store data in a structure which permits retrieval of all or any specified portion of that individual patient's records[18] in (1) time-oriented sequence, in chronological order by patient visits; or (2) source oriented sequence, by services (e.g., ophthalmology, radiology, laboratory, pharmacy, etc.); and/or (3) patient medical problem-oriented sequence. Inverted files of data can best be generated for users on a scheduled basis.

G. PATIENT IDENTIFICATION REQUIREMENTS

Identification of each patient must be established for each visit to the health services system (hospital or clinic). Positive identification of the patient requires agreement on four identifiers: (1) encoding of each patient by a unique number,[18] which may be a governmental assigned number (e.g., the Social Security number), or a locally assigned patient medical record number which will never be re-assigned; (2) patient's name; (3) sex; and (4) birthdate. Any identification procedure using less than all four of these patient identifiers will probably have a significant error rate in record linkage for multiple data entries. When medical record numbers are manually entered, a check-digit procedure should be added.

Entry of patients' identification data by embossed or punched paper, plastic or metal cards is essential to minimize the transcription and transposition errors arising from multiple manual entries. However, since people accidentally exchange identification cards, it is mandatory that at each registration the four identifiers be checked to verify that the encoded card does in truth identify the patient for whom the data is being entered.

H. EQUIPMENT AND SOFTWARE REQUIREMENTS

Improvements in new hardware and new software will continually be developed, but management must make a decision at some point in time to "freeze" the system configuration for a number of years in order to devote its programming resources to the users' needs rather than to the system's needs. Then, perhaps in five to seven years, the expense of another iteration of system improvement will be acceptable in order to take advantage of interim innovations.

Considerable controversy exists as to whether a HCS is best served by a shared large-scale central computer, by several dedicated small computers, or by both.[11,19] If one accepts the basic concept of the integrated patient computer record continuing through time, then the central data base computer becomes the core of HCS, and the integration of all other subsystem modules into HCS permits the use of the central computer or an integrated minicomputer if the latter best suits the needs of that module. (See Chapter Three.)

1. Central Equipment

An equipment configuration must be developed to permit patient data to be stored in and retrieved from the patient computer record and from remote terminals in the inpatient and outpatient departments.

The central processing unit and its core storage must be of sufficient size and speed to perform simultaneous multiple on-line tasks with an acceptable response time to the users.

A basic requirement of HCS is that it should provide reliable service to physicians, 24 hours a day, seven days a week. Accordingly, sufficient redundancy of equipment must be allowed to provide continuing service despite equipment breakdown. Until improved economy in equipment is developed, complete redundancy of equipment to provide full 24-hour service may not be economically practical.

Storage devices for the large central data base must be of sufficient size and speed to permit access to the data for any patient in the health services system within an acceptable response time. Two levels of storage devices appear to be required for the data base itself:

(1) Mass direct-access storage, with less than one-second random access time for all active medical files for personnel eligible to use the HCS.[20]

(2) Magnetic tape drives for archival storage of inactive patient files, for backup records of transactions of patient data, and for batch-processing of data.

Large direct-access storage files are also necessary for reference data sets (drug compendia, dictionaries, thesauri, etc.) and programs not located in core storage.

2. Peripheral Equipment

a. *Terminals:* Selecting suitable terminals acceptable by professional users is a critical requirement for HCS. Physicians and nurses must be able to enter patient data directly into the computer via acceptable terminals. For example, instantaneous response is necessary for on-line monitoring of patients in intensive care units. At nursing stations, physicians may enter medical orders by selections from visual displays[21] of multiple choice formats (see Chapter Six); this seems to be acceptable to the physician if the displayed response appears within one second. Laboratory technicians and pharmacists may accept a slightly longer response time, but certainly not longer than three seconds. Printouts of patient data on demand in the record room may take several minutes. Routine reports may be batch-processed off-line. It is advisable to consider the necessary response time for each application to avoid establishing unnecessary requirements for the system.

The requirement to collect data at the point of origin reduces error due to transcription and eliminates use of clerks as intermediaries between professional personnel and terminals.

Terminals must be ample in number to avoid an intolerable amount of queuing; 50–100 terminals may be required in a 200–300 bed acute general hospital. Terminals must be tailored to the user's needs. Physicians will not accept typewriter keyboards; but they will accept voice communication to medical transcriptionists and touch-wire or light-pen visual displays; hopefully the future will also bring visual phones into use. Pharmacists will accept typewriter keyboards, and laboratory technicians will accept a push-button keyboard input device for certain functions.

b. *Dedicated minicomputers:* A small peripheral computer will usually be required as a satellite to the central computer for operation of terminals, storage of display formats, maintenance of local hospital patient and specimen schedules and status, laboratory quality control processing, etc. Small dedicated computers will also be required for high-density data generators such as for intensive care units and quality-control monitoring of large automated chemical analyzers. Compatibility between computers is an essential requirement to permit the transfer of data between the central and satellite computers.

When a HCS considers a "turn-key" system in which a commercial vendor installs and maintains a dedicated automated subsystem (e.g., clinical laboratory), it is critical that the turn-key system be integrated into HCS and interface directly with the central data base.

3. Software Requirements

Systems programs must be developed to handle multiple medical functions (subsystem components) simultaneously, permit teleprocessing between the central and peripheral processors, enter and integrate the data into a specific patient computer record in the central data base, and then retrieve the data from the same patient computer record almost immediately in accordance with different clinical needs.

The software requirements for an integrated medical data base are described by Davis and Terdiman in Chapter Four. It thus becomes a requirement to develop a general programming system to store, process, and retrieve all kinds of patient data. This has to include routines for the handling of direct access storage, remote terminal and input/output devices, and on-line in real time in addition to off-line batch-processing. It is necessary to treat various separate medical applications or functions in a modular fashion, integrating these functions into the system as added.

Programs may need to be written in low-level (assembly) languages for the purpose of maximum economy of computer time for routine repetitive real-time procedures performed many times each day. In programs which require frequent changes, higher-level languages which permit programmers readily to write, enter, and debug applications programs directly from remote terminals, using a relatively small number of program statements, should be used.

Error correction, recovery, and restart programs must be developed. Error-checking programs should include checks for missing data, check digits for patient identification numbers, validity limits for laboratory and other digital data, etc.

Post-installation programming will be required continually to improve operational and control procedures, file maintenance, backup system maintenance, and unanticipated problems.

A voluminous documentation of procedures and programs will be necessary to facilitate maintenance programming, reprogramming, and transferability to other systems. Documentation should also be provided for users as manuals to guide them in system operation and in the event of system failure.

I. SYSTEM RELIABILITY REQUIREMENTS

It is a critical requirement that HCS perform with almost 100% reliability (dependability). That is, the system must be available so that a physician can enter and retrieve patient data any time of day, seven days a week. To the user, reliability means the percentage of time the terminals are operating satisfactorily. Equipment and equipment components integral to HCS should perform with more than 98% individual reliability, or an equivalent "down" time of less than 1 hour in 50. It is therefore essential to have a proper mix of backup equipment, modules, parts, and corrective maintenance capability to maintain operations despite failure and breakdown. A periodic preventive maintenance program is required.

Alternative backup procedures for each subsystem component provide a second means for maintaining continual system operation. When the computer goes down, nursing stations, pharmacy, laboratory, and all other users must be able to continue to operate and collect data in a manner which permits ready entry into the patient computer record when the system goes back up. A backup or degraded mode of operation must always be available to continue critical operations.

It is required that the system provide backup capabilities for both hardware and software. Thus, the central computer and peripheral terminal equipment ideally should be duplicated, comprising two paired systems which functionally support one another; by circuit switching, one unit provides backup in case of failure of the other, providing a "fail-soft" system. All terminals should be paired at each user station to insure that one-half of the terminals are active in case one system fails. Paired remote terminals should use independent phone lines to the computers so that, if one phone line is interrupted, at least one terminal always remains active at each user station. Terminals should be "plug-in" movable modules so they can be easily repaired or replaced by a stand-by terminal.

A noninterruptible power supply is necessary in case of an electric power failure. Such a system requires a constant voltage battery charger, storage batteries, static inverter, and a diesel engine generator. One method of operating is for the ac line to supply power to the static battery charger, which in turn "float" charges the battery and supplies dc power to the static inverter, which supplies ac power to the ac load. If normal ac power failure occurs, the battery continues to supply power to the inverter in order to sustain the ac load without any interruption. Because of the limited time the battery can power the total hospital system, the battery system is supplemented by the diesel engine generator. When normal ac supply is restored, automatic transfer of the load back to normal power occurs.

The air-conditioning system for the computer central and peripheral processes must be so designed that it is composed of at least two independent units. Thus, if one unit fails, the second is capable of fulfilling minimal cooling requirements to maintain temperature control at a safe level to prevent computer failure.

J. UTILITY REQUIREMENTS

User acceptability is enhanced if the HCS is capable of smooth integration into the professional activities. Terminals which are acceptable to each user category must be selected. HCS procedures must be developed with and by the users themselves to increase acceptability and decrease required orientation and training. Key physician personnel must be required to participate in planning and implementation. A well-planned period of training of users will greatly enhance acceptability of HCS.

For visual display users, three different levels of programs will be useful: (1) orientation displays for first users, with detailed instructions and a small amount of information in each display sequence; (2) routine user displays for experienced users, with fully loaded displays and only minimal essential instructions; and (3) personalized displays for frequent high-volume or high-priority users, with custom-tailored displays which permit entering full pages of routine orders at high speed. (See also Chapter Six.)

It has already been emphasized that all users of HCS shall enter their patient data directly into the computer. On-line verification of data entered into the patient computer record by the one who generated the data minimizes errors and insures highest quality data.

An adequate number of terminals must be available to satisfy the demand for services. Costs for hardware are clearly related to percent demand satisfaction of users.[3]

K. CONTROL REQUIREMENTS

1. Privacy and Confidentiality

All data within the patient computer record must be subject to the same regulations of privacy and confidentiality as is data in a hospital record room.[17] This concept requires controls for protection of the computer records to specified degrees of user-imposed privacy—controls whereby a physician is required to identify himself by key, card, or password to insure that a specific patient's data will be released only to the physicians responsible for the care of that patient. Psychiatric data requires that additional special controls be released only to the specific psychiatrist responsible for the patient. In some communities, venereal disease data may require special privacy controls. (See also Chapter Four.)

Research data require identification of the principal investigator; epidemiologic research on groups of patients requires maintaining privacy of individual patients so that only data in aggregate form are distributed.

Programmers who have access to the data base must be required to sign a statement that they will never give medical data to unauthorized persons, and they should note in a log book each time they use the data base programs.

2. Data Quality Control

Much of the quality control for HCS involves editing of incoming data for validity at the input level (e.g., automatically checking a patient's identifying data against his existing computer record at time of office visit registration or hospital admission; checking validity limits of laboratory tests against standard definition tables at the time of entry of test value, etc.).

On-line data entry permits immediate error detection and correction at source. The detection of an error at a later time is usually difficult to correct when the professional user who generated the input no longer has the relevant source data readily available. As included under software requirements, programmed error surveillance procedures should scan all data at input for missing or logically invalid data and notify the operator and/or user when such errors are found.

A prime concept of HCS, therefore, is that all data should be entered directly into the computer from source. By avoiding the use of intermediary personnel, one decreases errors and information loss. Physicians should enter their medical orders directly into the computer. The use of clerk technicians to enter into a hospital information system the medical orders handwritten by doctors merely mechanizes a traditional manual operational mode. Similarly, pharmacists should enter prescriptions directly into the computer and verify the label printout without working through clerk typists. Physicians should enter their diagnoses directly into the computer by selecting the best fit from a structured terminology; this avoids coding by record librarians. Only when the physicians are able to retrieve useful data from the HCS data base will they be careful, selective, and accurate as to the data they enter into the data base.

L. COST REQUIREMENTS

Consideration of the total costs of implementing a HCS should include three components: (a) the monetary costs necessary to develop and implement the system; (b) the resource costs for the manpower and nonfinancial resources which will be needed; and (c) the opportunity costs—that is, what other projects will have to be abandoned or not undertaken if the HCS is pursued? And also, what are the costs of not undertaking a HCS? In this chapter, opportunity costs will not be considered.

The special needs of HCS result in costly requirements for computer terminals, which usually eventuate in more expenditures for peripheral than for central equipment. Also, the increasing requirements for time sharing and real-time processing usually result in more costs for software than for hardware.

It is essential to plan for obsolescence. New hardware and new software will continually be developed; but to achieve an economical cost/performance ratio, management must make a decision at some point in time to "freeze" the system design for a number of years in order to devote its resources to the users' needs rather than to the system's needs. Then, perhaps in four or five years, the expense of another iteration of system improvement will be acceptable in order to take advantage of interim innovations.

Costs must be determined for (a) implementation of HCS hardware and software and (b) its operations, including cost of HCS per hospital day per patient. It is generally anticipated that if a hospital day in 1972 costs $100 and if about $30 of this is involved in information processing, then a cost of $10 per day for HCS will be reasonable. It will be important to establish a cost evaluation center with the hospital accounting services in order to assess HCS costs.[22,23]

It is generally projected that, by 1978, the average hospital day in the U.S. will cost a patient about $200. If one assumes the same proportion (30%) will be spent for information processing in 1978 if we continue current manual modes, the cost will be $60 per day. If only one-third of all the information processing can be taken over by a HCS[21] and if $10 per patient day is reallocated to a HCS, the result would be a net saving of $10 per patient day, or about one million dollars savings per year for a 300 bed hospital.

Cost effectiveness may be difficult to demonstrate in 1973–1974 for a HCS because software is still in a developmental stage and developmental costs always are greater than subsequent routine operational costs. As a minimum, the computer should improve efficiency by making a larger information load manageable at these costs. It is also evident that medical data can be transmitted faster via a computerized system, thereby decreasing personnel waiting time. Furthermore, the computer should help nurses and technicians to avoid errors.

It is likely that technology may not decrease the number of hospital personnel, but it will definitely change job content and increase productivity, effectiveness, and quality.

M.   TIME PLANNING REQUIREMENTS

The planning schedule for HCS must fit into the planning schedules for the hospital organization as a whole. For example, if a schedule of five years completion is projected for a HCS and if the hospital board plans only one-, two-, or three-year budgets, it will be very difficult to convince such a board to embark on a five-year program. In such instances, the HCS project can be divided into smaller modules, such as the clinical laboratory or the admission and bed census, which can be completed and cost-justified on a one- or two-year basis. Presented to a board in this way, approval usually can be more readily obtained.

The HCS module that is the most costly and difficult to cost-justify (but is absolutely indispensable for the long-term success of a HCS for a hospital which has a continuing obligation for care to a growing population) is the patient computer file and medical data base. Even if approval cannot be obtained to implement this at the onset, the HCS project leader must conceptually plan ahead for the central integration of all HCS subsystem modules into this common computer medical file.

A hospital of sufficient size (300 beds or more—see Section L.—Cost Requirements) to cost-justify its own independent HCS should develop its own in-house staff rather than depend upon outside consultants or contractors. Consultant designed or off-the-shelf turn-key systems may often be installed faster (saving perhaps 6–12 months implementation time), but they will be less flexible and more costly to change in the future than in-house developed systems since consultant contracts will be initially more rigidly defined and later will cost more for changes as new requirements develop.

In any case, a complete HCS will require several years to implement. Accordingly, it is prudent to establish attainable objectives with realistic time tables. Therefore, a HCS is always installed in a modular fashion. Hospital business functions, hospital admission and bed census, clinical laboratory or pharmacy services are usually initiated first, then other subsystem components are added. This requirement for an integrated, modular implementation results in a long lead-time in achieving an operationally complete HCS.

Assuming the project staff has been acquired, *each* modular function subsystem will require a time-plan schedule which will: (1) define precise objectives of the total HCS; (2) conduct functional analyses of information load (volume and characteristics) and personnel information handling (output specifications and time responses); (3) determine subsystem configuration; (4) establish subsystem priorities and set time tables for implementation of each module; (5) select project team leader and his project team; (6) obtain management approval for the selected configuration and implementation schedule and secure funding commitments; (7) order equipment; (8) write and test programs; (9) prepare facility for equipment installation; (10) install, test, and debug equipment and programs; (11) prepare users' manuals and conduct training of personnel; (12) conduct pilot operational test; (13) implement manual backup mode; (14) implement operational subsystem; (15) conduct evaluation of performance; and finally (16) revise, modify, and improve as needed. (See Figure 1-3.)

1. Define total system goals	10. Order equipment
2. Establish subsystem priorities	11. Write programs
3. Set module time tables	12. Prepare facility
4. Define precise requirements	13. Install equipment
5. Select project leader	14. Conduct user training
6. Acquire project team	15. Pilot test
7. Conduct subsystem analysis	16. Implement backup mode
8. Define configuration	17. Implement computer mode
9. Obtain funding commitments	18. Evaluate and revise

Figure 1-3.   Check list for planning for HCS.

It is important to emphasize the great value often found by first implementing a manual backup mode of operation before going on to implement the automated operating mode. This tends to separate systems benefits from computer benefits and to train users thoroughly in the backup mode when the computer systems go down.

If any HCS modules are to be transferred from another HCS, a successful transfer requires first a transfer of concepts, second a transfer of the methods and procedures for manual backup with any modifications necessary to satisfy the needs of the new users, and last a transfer of the automated system with necessary interfacing to integrate the module into the new HCS and its computer patient record file.

Time schedule plans should be provided for both management and the project staff in sufficient detail for each subsystem component, so all can check progress against projected dates and permit review of accomplishments at critical points to be certain the system will achieve its desired objectives and meet schedule, functional, and performance specifications.

N. REASONS FOR FAILURE OF HCS

An analysis of why past efforts to implement hospital computer systems (as herein defined) in the U.S. have failed[24] yields the following reasons:

1. A suboptimal mix of medical and computer specialists was the most common cause of failure. Generally, the project staff consisted of (a) well-motivated physicians who had little experience with computers and (b) computer and systems experts with little experience in medical applications. The extreme difficulty with inter-communicating between the highly technical and complex aspects of these two disciplines resulted in the computer staff usually underestimating vast medical needs. They planned a system adequate perhaps for the hospital administrative subsystem but totally insufficient for the medical functional requirements such as computer processing of natural language information. By the time the medical staff became aware of the deficiencies of the system, the investment in time and money had already been so heavy that the result was either termination or severe reorganization of the project. Usually, the contractual relations between the hospital and the computer systems group were terminated and the hospital then reorganized its approach to start again.

2. Inadequate commitment of capital for long-term investment was the second most frequent cause for failure. Most organizations grossly underestimated the large amounts of money and time involved in implementing an HCS. Several projects in the U.S. were terminated after three to five years because several million dollars had already been spent and the HCS was still far from completion.

3. A suboptimized systems approach was frequent. Several HCS projects failed because they had successfully implemented one or more subsystem components for the administrative, laboratory, bed census, patient scheduling, or pharmacy units and now desired to integrate them all into a HCS. At this point, they discovered serious incompatibilities between the various modules which would require major reprogramming at prohibitive costs to achieve an integrated patient file. These projects usually continued the individual subsystem modules as independent computerized units.

At the other extreme were some projects which began with the global systems approach to implement a total HCS; the sheer enormity of such an approach has not yet found anyone with the vast resources capable of successfully following this course.

4. Many of the early HCS projects were never implemented because of unacceptable terminals. The first systems required physicians and nurses to use keyboard terminals such as typewriters. It was soon established that physicians would not accept such means for communicating with the computer, and clerical-type personnel had to take over the process of data entry. As a result, current HCS projects all use visual display-type terminals, since physicians will accept touch-wire or light-pen methods of selecting data from a display.

5. An occasional cause of failure was inadequate management organization. Several projects in the U.S. were initiated in smaller hospitals with inexperienced medical management and terminated after having completed one or two HCS subsystem modules, usually an administrative-business type of HCS.

O. FACTORS FOR SUCCESS

Since there is as yet no completely successful HCS, we can only suggest those factors which will tend to avoid the past reasons for failure.

1. Optimal mix of medical and computer personnel is essential. Those projects in the world which appear to be moving steadily toward the successful implementation of a total HCS all have a large "in-house" staff of medical, systems, and computer personnel supervised by a "physician-engineer," that is, an M.D. who also has experience with computers. The great difficulties associated with interdisciplinary communications between physicians and engineers require at least one key person who has adequate expertise in both fields of technology.

2. Large investments of capital for long-term commitments are required. The hospital management must recognize that the more complex the technology, the greater the lead time from outset of planning to completion of system. They must be prepared to commit several million dollars for three to five years before they are likely to see an operational system.

3. An integrated, modular systems approach is fundamental. It is absolutely essential to plan from the beginning to integrate the various operational modules into the eventual total HCS. The best way to insure compatibility of all modules, with or without small dedicated computers, is to require one common central data base file containing an integrated, continuing computer record for all data from each individual patient for every hospitalization and outpatient visit. Small collections of patient data for subsystem components on dedicated small computers for the laboratory,

blood bank, hospital admissions, or discharges will never satisfy medical service requirements.

A complete HCS will require many years to implement. It is such a large, complex technological system that it will not be possible to implement a complete HCS at any one point in time. Accordingly, a HCS can only be successfully installed in a modular fashion. Hospital business functions, hospital admission and bed census, clinical laboratory or pharmacy services are usually initiated first, then other subsystem components are added. This requirement for modular implementation results in a long lead time in achieving an operationally complete HCS.

4. A hospital (or group of hospitals) of sufficient size is required, with effective organization and management by technically sophisticated men who can make reliable decisions after considering technological alternatives. Management needs to understand enough about computers to avoid being sold a faulty proposal and be able to decide when a system is good enough—and then agree to that. Large technological systems tend to commit an organization to a relatively fixed goal for a number of years. Since a total HCS does not yet exist, great uncertainties result in large unanticipated costs in time and manpower. Flexibility in committing capital and other resources is required to meet the inevitable deficiencies not foreseen in early planning of a large project conducted over a long period of time. Since an investment in HCS is usually a very heavy one, a poor technical judgment can be disastrous.

REFERENCES

1. Collen, M. F. et al. Proceedings of a Conference on Medical Information Systems NCHSR&D, H. E. W. Government Printing Office, January, 1970.
2. World Health Organization Symposium on the Development of Hospital Computer Systems. Toulouse, France, June 28, 1971. Copenhagen: WHO Publication, 1972.
3. Ryan, G. A., and Monroe, K. E. "Appendix G." *Computer Assisted Medical Practice: The AMA's Role.* Chicago: American Medical Association, 1971.
4. Ontario Department of Health, "Health Care Delivery System, Role of Computers in the Health Field." Suppl. 9 (1970).
5. Ontario Council of Health, "The Role of Computers in the Health Field." Suppl. 9A (1971).
6. Harmon, L. D. "Some Problems and Priorities in Health-Care Technology." *Proceedings, Conference on Technology and Health Care Systems in the 1980's,* January, 1972. San Francisco: Government Printing Office.
7. "The Computer and Hospital Information Systems." *Inquiry* 5 (September, 1968): 3–69.

8. Jydstrup, R. A., and Gross, M. J. "Cost of Information Handling in Hospitals." *Health Services Research* 1 (1966) : 235–260.

9. Richart, R. "Evaluation of a Medical Data System." *Conference on Medical Information Systems, San Francisco, January, 1970.*

10. Van Brunt, E. E.; Collen, M. F.; Davis, L. S.; Besag, E.; and Singer, S. J. "A Pilot Data System for a Medical Center." *Proc. I.E.E.E.* 57 (1969) : 1934–1940.

11. Van Brunt, E. E. "The Kaiser-Permanente Medical Information System." *Comp. and Biomed. Res.* 3 (1970) : 477–487.

12. Flagle, C. D. "On the Requirements for Information Systems in Hospitals." *Proceedings in ADP in Hospitals.* Elsinore, Denmark, 1966.

13. Collen, M. F. "General Requirements for a Medical Information System." *Comp. and Biomed. Res.* 3 (1970) : 393–406.

14. Davis, L. S.; Collen, M. F.; Rubin, L.; and Van Brunt, E. E. "Computer Stored Medical Record." *Comp. and Biomed. Res.* 1 (1968) : 452–469.

15. Davis, L. S. "Prototype for Future Computer Medical Records." *Comp. and Biomed. Res.* 3 (1970) : 539–554.

16. Collen, M. F.; Davis, L. S.; Van Brunt, E. E. "The Computer Medical Record in Health Screening." *Meth. Info. Med.* 10: (1971) : 138–142.

17. Curran, W. J.; Stearns, B.; and Kaplan, H. "Privacy, Confidentiality and Other Legal Considerations in the Establishment of Centralized Health-Data Systems." *New Eng. J. Med.* 281 (1969) : 241–248.

18. Acheson, E. D. *Medical Record Linkage.* London: Oxford Univ. Press, 1967.

19. Greenes, R. A.; Pappalardo, A. N.; Marble, C. W.; and Barnett, G. O. "Design and Implementation of a Clinical Data Management System." *Comp. and Biomed. Res.* 2 (1969) : 469–485.

20. Terdiman, J. F. "Mass Random Storage Devices and Their Application to a Medical Information System." *Comp. and Biomed. Res.* 3 (1970) : 528–538.

21. Singer, S. F. "Visual Display Terminals in a Hospital Information System." *Comp. and Biomed. Res.* 3 (1970) : 510–520.

22. Richart, R. H. "Evaluation of a Medical Data System." *Comp. and Biomed. Res.* 3 (1970) : 415–425.

23. Flagle, C. D. "Evaluation Techniques for Medical Information Systems." Conference on Medical Systems, San Francisco, January, 1970.

24. Collen, M. F. "Reasons for Failure and Factors Making for Success in Public Health in Europe." *Health Planning and Organization of Medical Care.* Copenhagen: WHO, 1972.

CHAPTER TWO

The Computer and New Health Care Systems

by Sidney R. Garfield

This book is concerned with only one important component of today's medical care system: computers in hospitals. Effective planning requires that proposed changes to one part of a system be carefully viewed in proper perspective to its effect on other parts and on the system as a whole. This does not mean that the entire system must be changed at one time, but it does mean that a model of the entire system should be examined before finalizing and implementing changes in any of its parts. Such systems thinking assures the integrative compatibility of the change and serves to optimize its effect on the total economics and efficiency of the system.

All of the above particularly holds true with the introduction of computers to medicine. The acquisition and processing of information and knowledge is extremely important to medical care; the computer is the most powerful machine ever developed for information technology. Their union creates a uniquely potent force for change, the potential impact of which transcends the mere improvement of the function and management of the existing medical care process, its hospitals, and other components. It even transcends the improvement of today's medical care product—the care of the sick. Actually, the great promise of computers for medicine lies in making an entirely new medical care system possible.

Such a new system is just now beginning to take form and emerge from the old. It is a product of the fusion of computer information technology with new medical care methods, a fusion sparked by the inexorable spread of free medical care (free to the user) throughout this country. This chapter will conceptualize a model of that new medical care system and describe the causes and methods of its evolution, its goals, and its opportunities, providing a realistic frame of reference for computer planning in hospitals.

To begin with, let us examine the traditional fee-for-service medical care system. The input (demand) is not a clear-cut binary sick, not-sick situation. Health is a spectrum consisting of well, worried-well, early-sick, and sick states, with people constantly changing from one state to another and with a great many of them concerned and uncertain about their exact location in that spectrum. That uncertainty creates a tremendous potential demand for medical care which ordinarily is regulated by the fee mechanism of the marketplace. When people have to pay fees, they tend to put off seeing the doctor until they are definitely sick. They have other uses for their money. This keeps out most of the "uncertainty demand": the well, the worried-well, and the early-sick. Conversely, it admits the definitely sick who seek relief regardless of fee. Thus, fee-for-service demand is predominantly sick demand. The delivery system that has evolved under two centuries of fee-for-service to match that sick demand is a sick-care system; doctors are at the point of entry and remain deeply involved in every step of that sick-care process. Likewise, our medical schools have evolved teaching sick-care technics. In this sick-care system, the fee is the regulator of flow, keeping out "uncertainty demand" and admitting the sick. In general, it is the mechanism that keeps the system demand and supply in balance.

With those facts in mind, let us follow what happens when we eliminate personally paid fees. Our objective, of course, is to help the sick who cannot afford today's excessive costs. When we eliminate fees, we lose the regulator of flow into the delivery system. This immediately converts the entire potential "uncertainty demand" into real demand, which begins to compete with the sick to get into the delivery system on a first-come, first-served basis. The impact of this flood of demand on the delivery system has some serious adverse effects:

(1) It overloads the relatively inelastic sick-care system, causing a serious demand for unavailable services.

(2) The large number of well people who actually get into the system by usurping doctor time act as a barrier to the entry of the sick—the reverse of what we are trying to accomplish by eliminating fees.

(3) With this altered demand, instead of caring for the sick, the doctors are spending a large portion of their time trying to find something wrong with well people, and they are doing this with technics taught them to diagnose sickness. This reverse use of sick-care technics, searching for illness in well people, is extremely wasteful of doctor time and is irritating and frustrating to him as well.

(4) The impact of the relatively unlimited amount of "uncertainty

demand" on the limited supply of physicians inevitably creates inflationary costs.

These are the urgent problems facing medicine today—not only in this country but in many countries of the world. They have all fallen into the same trap of eliminating the fee-regulating mechanism and then trying to funnel the resulting tremendous "uncertainty demand" through the existing sick-care system. Not only is this physically impossible, but "uncertainty demand," with its large component of well people, is incompatible with direct entry through sick-care physician services—incompatible because it does not match the technics of sick care and, consequently, seriously dissipates and wastes medical manpower. Sick-care diagnosis is a clue-directed, step-by-step search for patterns of illness, which can be performed efficiently by the physician. The more definite the clues, the more effective he is. "Uncertainty demand" has vague, misleading, or absent clues, requiring a different approach. Here the diagnostic procedure becomes a meticulous checking out of systems, a countdown process that is most efficiently performed by automation and paramedical personnel, not by the doctor.

The incompatibility between "uncertainty demand" and the existing sick-care physician technics has not been recognized by the medical world. That recognition is extremely important since it warns us that merely increasing the number of doctors will not solve today's unavailability of services. Providing more doctors will only use up an enormous amount of doctor time in searching for the relatively few people who need doctor time and thus will leave little time for care of the sick—a truly self-defeating procedure.

It should be clear that the basic cause of our medical care problems has been the increasing spread of free user care throughout our population. The effect is an expanded and altered demand that is largely incompatible with the existing sick-care system, wasting its medical manpower and rendering the system unbalanced and seriously defective. Understanding that cause-and-effect relationship leads us to a solution.

Our analysis has demonstrated that the elimination of personally paid fees creates a dichotomy of demand: a "definitely sick demand" vs. an "uncertainty demand." The existing medical care system, designed to care for the sick, matches only the "sick demand." Balancing the system necessitates that "uncertainty demand" be similarly matched with a suitable service. This requires two things:

1. A method of entry that can separate "uncertainty demand" into its basic components—the well, the early asymptomatic sick, and the sick.

2. An adequate service to receive each of those components.

The new method of entry beginning to emerge is Health Testing. The services are a new Health Care Service for the well, a new Preventive Maintenance Service for the asymptomatic sick, and the existing Sick Care Service for the sick.

This new system has four divisions (Figure 2-1), coordinated by computer services:

1. *Health testing,* the heart of the new system, combines a detailed automated medical history with comprehensive panels of physiological and laboratory tests administered by paramedical personnel, a nurse physical examination, computer processing of results, and a doctor review. Health testing is ideally suited as a new method of entry into medical care since it can effectively separate "uncertainty demand" into its components with a minimum of physician involvement.

2. *Health care* is a new division of medicine that does not exist in this country or any country. Its purpose is to improve health and keep people well. To date, health care has been an elusive concept and understandably so, since it has been submerged in sick care—the primary concern of doctors. Doctors trained in sick care have been much too busy to be involved with well people.

This clear definition of the Health Care Service is a first step in creating a positive program for keeping people well. Whether or not one believes this can be done is beside the point. This service is essential to meet the increasing demand for health care and to keep these people from using sick care services.

3. *Preventive maintenance* is a service for the early asymptomatic sick and high-prevalence chronic illnesses such as hypertension and diabetes, conditions that require monitoring and surveillance. This type of care, performed by paramedical personnel, programmed and guided by computerized advice rules with followup printouts of pertinent data to the patient's doctor, can relieve the physician of many routine visits.

4. *Sick care,* with its high-level decisions on diagnosis and therapy, becomes clearly the realm of the physician. Here he becomes the manager of patient care rather than the man-of-all-work and is aided in this by the three other divisions.

There are several important features to be emphasized in this new delivery system:

First: It is designed specifically to match the entry mix of free care. All other existing systems, including Great Britain's, unload the entire free care entry mix into sick-care physician service and thus dissipate and waste manpower.

Second: Three of the divisions—Health Testing, Health Care, and Preventive Maintenance—are primarily automated, existing paramedical serv-

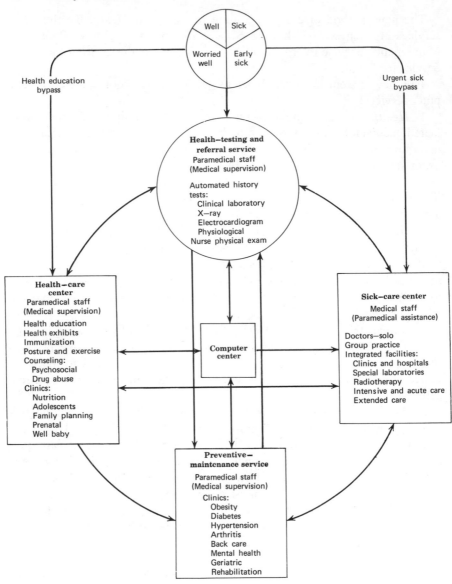

Figure 2–1

ices. Therefore, they are relatively easy to staff and relatively inexpensive.

The use of paramedical personnel with limited knowledge and skills to relieve the physician of routine and repetitious tasks requires that such tasks be clearly defined and that patient input be structured. The existing delivery system with its unstructured heterogeneous entry mix is almost the exact antithesis of those requirements and, therefore, has never permitted effective and safe use of such personnel. For this reason, Health Testing and the clear separation of services, automatically defining tasks and patient structure, becomes the key to paramedical manpower effectiveness. This effectiveness is greatly enhanced by the guidance made possible by the computer in the handling of data and issuing of advice rules.

Third: This new system requires no basic modification of sick-care services. It can function with either solo practice or group practice. All we need do to sick care is remove from it the extraneous portion of the entry mix produced by free care, where it did not belong in the first place. Sick care relieved of that considerable load of well, worried-well, and asymptomatic sick people thus develops a greatly increased capacity for the care of the sick.

Adequate medical care for all who need it is an admirable concept which has been accepted by the medical profession; yet until now there has been no way of reaching that objective. Health testing and computer technologies have evolved as an amazingly effective team for achieving that goal. Health testing is a well-suited, extremely thorough process for handling the patient uncertainty and concern that is such a large part of free-user demand. In addition, it has the unique capability of transforming patient wants into patient needs—not as a means test but as an ideal nonmonetary process that establishes each individual's specific health appraisal with minimum physician involvement. Furthermore, entry through health testing provides an important new opportunity for medicine. The same health testing process that identifies the need for sick care is concurrently identifying the need for health care, automatically elevating preventive medicine to equal status with sick care, a new first in medical history.

All this leads us into an evolving concept of programmed continuing care. Once a patient enters the health care system through health testing services and his needs are identified, he remains in the system with appointments to either health care, preventive maintenance, or sick care and always has a return appointment to health testing services for updating his medical profile. Thus, medical care is programmed and continuing rather than episodic, and much of illness becomes a trend rather than a crisis. Patients with acute problems occurring between scheduled profiles may receive care through problem-directed health testing programmed for specific panels of tests for common conditions. Their problems then can be evaluated and diagnosed against their own background of updated profiles.

The effect of such programmed continuing care on the health of the individual, upon medical-care resources, and upon the diagnostic process itself is today purely speculative. The system holds great promise for the provision of truly preventive care. We need no longer generalize, but instead we can instruct each individual about what he should do for optimal health on the basis of his own updated profile. Such personalized instruction should lead to maximum motivation and cooperation on the part of patients.

This change from episodic crisis sick care to programmed total health care forces a new look at the recording and processing of medical information. Traditionally, such information has been based on the personal medical record of the individual; however, these records have been largely fragmented and disconnected, with each spell of illness a separate happening and with records scattered randomly among many doctors' offices, hospitals, and other components of the medical care system. Obviously such fragmented and episodic information is grossly inadequate to serve the needs of this new medical care system. Continuing total health care requires a continuing life health record for each individual. That expandable record must include a basic health testing appraisal followed consecutively by periodic updating profiles collating all the pertinent data that flows out of health care, preventive maintenance, and sick care. The content of that life record, now made possible by computer information technology, will chart the course to be taken by each individual for optimal health. The proper function and survival of biological systems depends on predictability. This life health record makes possible the feedback necessary to remove uncertainty and achieve such predictability within the limits of existing medical knowledge.

Though this lifetime health record of the future will no doubt function with defined populations at a level above that of the individual hospital, e.g., at a health plan or community level, it will be mandatory that the hospital computer system have ready access to this data bank for prompt receipt and input of patient information. Failure to plan for that requirement can lead to a profusion of small systems designed to meet today's local hospital needs but perhaps end up incompatible with future vital linkage to a central record bank. It is, therefore, important in the planning of the hospital information system that we raise our sights from purely hospital needs to the total health care needs of the individuals to be served. To that end, it becomes an imperative that computer planners give due consideration to the new medical care system now emerging and the health information system that goes with it.

REFERENCES

1. Garfield, S. R. "The Delivery of Medical Care." *Scientific American* 222 (1970): 15–23.

2. Garfield, S. R. "Multiphasic Health Testing and Medical Care As A Right." *New Eng. J. Med.* 283 (1970): 1087–1089.

3. Garfield, S. R. "Prevention of Dissipation of Health Services Resources." *American Journal of Public Health* 61 (1971): 1499–1506.

4. Feldman, R. "Multiphasic Screening and Medical Group Practice." *Early Disease Detection*, Florida: Halos and Associates, 1970, pp. 48–52.

5. Collen, M. F. "Periodic Health Examination Using an Automated Multitest Laboratory." *Journal of American Medical Association* 195 (1966): 830–833.

CHAPTER THREE

Data Processing Facilities

by Lou S. Davis

A. ORGANIZATION

1. General

The clearest common denominator of medical data processing facilities is their atypicalness. The data processing alternatives to a medical organization are many and complex. Even after the administrative functions of the medical computing systems are separated out (see Chapter Five) the staffing arrangements and hardware configurations are highly varied. There are many factors responsible for this. The priorities and long-term requirements of each hospital and medical complex, the medical staff interests, the resources available for data processing costs, and the level of computer science knowledge of the programming and medical staff are only a few of the factors that have had a bearing on the organization of medical data processing facilities and their objectives. Future organizational variations will be forthcoming, as it has only been recently that much of the work in applying computers to medical applications has begun to move from research, development, and trial basis to everyday standard operation.

Some medical data processing facilities are run like service bureaus, each having a large computer, but the medical user, who uses the facility primarily for research, uses it either in time-sharing mode from a terminal or batch mode. Each user has his own research project with little incentive for communication of data to other researchers or to the clinical staff for patient care. He has his own data base and structure, his own encoding, his own retrieval requirements, etc.

In other medical organizations, computing configurations have been set up independently in separate medical clinics or application areas for limited and specific purposes. Here each medical application area has been approached individually to solve problems within the application only. The application generally keeps records solely for the application area and only for the length of time needed by the application. Hence, the benefit of the computer is felt primarily in the department served with usually only computer hardcopy output, leaving the boundaries of the department via the facility mail distribution system. Most of the efforts to date in the application of computers to medicine have been this "small" application area approach. There have been several different programs developed for clinical laboratory, ECG analysis, admission/census, pharmacy, etc.

There are a few organizations where efforts are being made in medical information and control systems to combine and interface separate application services. These attempts to develop hospital information systems and other research leading towards helping the clinician care for his patient are forcing medical data processing development to be approached more systematically. The machine resources for these data processing facilities vary from use of single large computers to combinations of large computers and mini-computers.

There are fundamental reasons, though, why more broad scope and extensive system efforts have not been started. Medical practice today is a highly skilled art and is subject to broad professional interpretations in the practice of the art. Physicians make decisions on the basis of their personal experience and subjective judgment. When we ask to apply data processing to medicine, we are asking physicians to specify an objective system and a set of standards which can be programmed. Physicians generally have not had the experience or training to do a good job of defining information requirements and information flow in an objective and standardized way. For example, common agreement is lacking among physicians for many medical definitions and for medical terminology. What is stated to be important medical data will vary from physician to physician, specialty to specialty, hospital to hospital, clinical service to research, short-term use to long-term use, one part of the country to another, etc. Part of the insufficiencies and criticism of current medical records is undoubtedly related in part to these problems.

Limiting data processing development to a given application area or specialty makes it easier to come to agreement about terms, definitions, and standards. Interface and communication problems with other departments and services are minimized. It is easier to set and achieve goals and objectives for the system when it is completely local. Still, there are many problems of enormous magnitude left for each of these "small" facets of medicine. It is easy to understand the slowness with which progress has been made—not only for the individual application areas but even more so for larger comprehensive systems.

Because of the problems and because medical data processing is still so young, there is little theory or experience for making hard recommendations as to the organization, the services, the hardware configurations, and the software for medical data processing facilities. Questions of centralization vs. decentralization, mini-computer networks vs. large computers, direct-access medical records vs. magnetic tape storage, single-episode data availability vs. lifetime data, easy interpretive medical languages for application programming vs. many other programming approaches, are all in such early formative and research stages that conclusions based on production experience and performance are left for the future.

It would not be possible to report in a single chapter on the details of organization of the many existing data processing facilities, the equipment, the software, the programming, the staffing, etc., for all the alternative ways of attacking medical data processing problems. Such a report would be difficult to summarize, would contain a lot about what is now obsolete equipment and undocumented programs, and would likely be a report on "how it was."

However, some generalized opinions, concepts, and reflections about medical computer system requirements can be related. These are based on long-term experience with a large research project aimed at a systems approach to the handling of medical information. Hence, these remarks are oriented to the systems approach. The reader can select, choose, discard, compare, contrast, or expand these requirements, depending on his own experiences, needs, and resources.

2. Staffing

As medical data processing moves from the research and development stages to everyday service operation, the staffing and management requirements of the computer and programming systems also change. For many years to come, data processing centers will be under the coercion of two diametrically opposed requirements: (1) the need to continue development, add new applications, and modify in-service applications and (2) the need to keep the in-service applications going on an ultrareliable day-to-day basis. Under these requirements, a continual parade of new programs, modified programs, upgraded systems programs, all with new computer and terminal operating procedures, is injected into the data processing network. Real-time computer operators have been likened to airline pilots in that as long as things go smoothly the system flies along with only moderate attention;

but when there is a component failure or other emergency, they are expected to act with the most expeditious and judicious dispatch. However, the airlines rarely schedule an airplane for passenger service while it is being maintained or while a new tail or a new motor is replaced. Because of the exorbitant expense of complete duplication of all equipment, the data processing system has to be planned in such a way that the software and even parts of the hardware can be maintained and replaced while continuing service. The applications and systems programmers, in the real-time environment, are expected to maintain programs and insert new major features without crashing the system. Operators are expected to know the new changes to the procedures for running the modified system.

In a real-time computer system, every user at each data input or other terminal device knows instantaneously when the system has crashed. Often as not, many users call simultaneously to the data processing center to inquire when the system will be back up. Because of the variety and complexity of failure problems, it is often impossible for the operators to give precise or accurate estimates as to when the system will be back in service. In these cases, difficult decisions of whether to wait for the system or go to a backup mode of operation must be made by the medical application personnel.

The planning, control, scheduling, documentation, programming, and operation of a computer system is largely a technical execution requiring technically trained, highly competent personnel. The programming staff must contain creative personnel for new development and extremely methodical and accurate personnel for program implementation, documentation, and maintenance. The amount of detail that must be carefully executed and controlled in a coordinated manner by both the programming and computer operations staff transcends that of most other occupations. These sometimes contradictory skills of creativity and strict attention to detail often lead to difficult supervisory and management relationships.

a. Management/administrative personnel. In the environment discussed above, the effective guidance of the data processing team requires successful blending of managerial and technical abilities. The data processing director preferably should be a computer scientist with sufficient experience or training in the biological sciences to enable him to communicate meaningfully with the medical and paramedical staff. He is the interface to the medical application project chief(s) and is responsible for the final design and implementation of the hardware and software for the total data processing system. He is responsible for estimating what goals and implementation schedules are obtainable within the constraints of budget, state of the technology, programming and engineering resources, and hardware delivery schedules.

Depending on the size of the staff, a systems programming supervisor, applications programming supervisor, systems engineering supervisor, computer operations supervisor, and project or team programming leaders are needed to manage their respective personnel (as discussed below). An administrative assistant, preferably a programmer, is valuable for handling administrative matters including computer usage accounting. He can provide an enormous timesaving service in coordinating all calls from vendor sales representatives and maintaining an organized current hardware equipment literature reference library. A secretary and typing clerks are needed to handle the correspondence and heavy documentation needs of the staff.

b. Systems programmers. The systems programmers are responsible for installing, monitoring, and maintaining the vendor's supervisor programming system and other supplied software services programs. They are responsible for routines to monitor the performance and efficiency of the computing system as well as monitoring file space as related to the efficiency of direct-access data sets, growth needs, etc. They are involved in software and hardware configuration planning for future data processing needs. Primarily, they are responsible for the design and implementation of the overall medical information control program and its related service programs to store, process, and retrieve patient data for the medical application programs.

c. Application programmers. Application programmers design and write the programs for the various medical application areas. They are expected to help in the implementation of programs and to train medical and paramedical personnel in the new data processing procedures. We have found it helpful to train individuals, such as a pharmacist, a lab technician, etc., from the application areas to at least the junior programmer level of skill. They then work with the programming staff in the design and development of their respective application area programs. It is also desirable that the application programmers themselves have experience and training in the biological sciences.

d. System engineers. As the data processing system grows larger and networks of terminals and mini-compuers stretch out from the central system, the kinds of equipment, the number of different vendors' equipment in the network, and the numerous communication lines magnify the interface problem. A staff of qualified computer and equipment engineers to maintain equipment, aid in diagnosing difficult problems, and help in evaluating new configurations is a necessity. They also provide technical assistance in recommending, implementing, and maintaining environmental necessities such as air-conditioning, backup power supplies, etc.

e. Computer operators. In addition to the usual operator duties. the operators in the medical real-time environment use the medical supervisor program's command language to start and stop application programs, monitor the status of the system, interchange terminals when necessary, direct output to local or remote terminals, and effect backup and recovery procedures.

Often the operations group also has a section for data control. We have a section, called Computer Records Library (CRL), which serves as the entry and exit point of all submitted programs for batch background execution. CRL also has responsibility for executing planned schedules of periodic production jobs. They also maintain the magnetic tape library including the master programs, medical data base, and backup tapes.

f. Documentation personnel. The general poor state of program documentation is a well-known and much discussed phenomenon. Not only are programmers reluctant and poorly motivated to document, but pressure to document by management declines as higher and higher priorities are given to getting the programs written, debugged, and implemented to meet schedules. This, of course, is costlier in the long run, as it increases difficulties in program maintenance. Also, lack of operating and user documentation for a program can lead to costly errors via misused and unused program features. A documentation specialist(s) on the staff can alleviate this difficulty and should be a requirement for every data processing center. He is responsible for monitoring documentation schedules for all required pre- and post-program documentation, aids the programmers in documentation, edits all documentation for adherence to documentation standards, and is directly responsible for preparing general user service information manuals. Anyone funding a data processing system, whether it be management, a granting agency, or a contracting agency, should insist that the personnel roster explicitly include programming documentation personnel.

B. EQUIPMENT REQUIREMENTS

1. General

Selection of a computer depends not only on its capabilities to accomplish the estimated work load but also on the availability and sophistication of the supervisory or monitor programming system needed to handle the work. The availability of the level or specific programming languages desired can also limit hardware selection. The more one relies on specific available systems and application programs, the more one is restricted to particular manufacturers and particular equipment within one manufacturer's range. Because these available programs often represent significant man-years of programming effort, continual compromises must be made between complete freedom of equipment selection vs. programmer costs, completion of schedules, equipment overspecification, and future incompatibilities.

2.   Central Equipment

A systems approach to medical information and control leads to modularity of hardware. Phased software development schedules for applications (according to priorities) over time are necessary, as an entire medical system cannot be programmed and implemented at once. As the additional applications are added, additional hardware capabilities will be required. To minimize costs, not only must an equipment configuration for the medical control system and its first applications to be implemented be specified, but it must be possible to add additional hardware capabilities modularly in such a way that the software does not have to be redone.

One of the primary requirements for the central processing unit is that it be of sufficient speed to handle the on-line and interactive terminals within defined response times which are acceptable to the professional users—even at peak loads. The central processing unit should also have interrupt schemes to allow the supervisory system to schedule input/output devices and supervisor calls effectively and to allow a priority scheme for multiprogramming. This latter is especially important to enable the different on-line medical application programs priority to maintain adequate terminal response times. Memory size must be sufficient to handle the supervisory system, root segments, and executing segments of the multiple on-line application programs as well as background, low-priority programs. If there is to be only one main computer in full-time operation, the memory size must allow for a test program scheme system so that new applications and maintenance for current applications can be tested safely before being transferred to the real system memory region.

Decisions regarding combinations of auxiliary storage devices for the central computer system for storage of program sets, work space, various inverted files, etc., while nontrivial, are less difficult to make. Selection of magnetic tapes for linear retrieved data sets vs. disk files for direct-access retrieval are relatively straightforward decisions. Extensive consideration should be given to all peripheral equipment from vendors other than the central processing unit vendor. Considerable savings can be realized. A more difficult decision is to ascertain the equipment required for storage of continuing patient computer medical records. It is generally unreasonable to sort and merge medical records on magnetic tape—or mount numerous tapes in real time—for large numbers of records in an environment where patients appear for return visits over long periods of time. Direct-access storage is generally required although very fast files are not needed. (This assumes that, on the first request for a record, the record can be moved off a large, slower direct-access device to a standard fast disk for the rest of the time the patient is active in the medical system.) To date, no hardware exists or has been announced that meets the criteria of moderate speed, high reliability, and add-on modularity that are required to store very large numbers of patient medical records on a direct-access basis at a reasonable cost.

Estimating needs for input/output equipment such as card readers, card punching equipment, and printers is relatively easy. Data preparation equipment such as keypunch devices, verifiers, sorters, collators, reproducers, etc. are also needed to varying degrees. Consideration should be given to key-to-tape devices for data preparation as well as on-line interactive terminals for programmer use. The latter can have a significant effect in reducing the programming time necessary to complete projects.

3.   Telecommunication and Telecommunication Control

In a large medical complex it becomes inevitable, as the applications expand, to have remote terminals connected to the computer system via communication channels that require modems (modulation/demodulation devices). These devices connect to telecommunication control units adjacent to the central processing unit. These control units vary in capabilities and costs. Proper selection of a control unit and the subsequent programming to operate it can cause large differences in overall computer system costs. For example, one large computer vendor charges an overtime rate for each hour of usage over the 176 hour-per-month prime shift as measured by meters on each device and the central processing unit. These mechanical (nonelectronic) meters continue to run for up to 400 milliseconds after the central processing unit has stopped. The selection of the manner in which the terminals operate (polling/addressing vs. contention) or the wrong type of telecommunication control unit may cause all the meters to run continuously even though the central processing unit is busy only a fraction of the time. Additional charges of all equipment up to 20–25% over the prime shift rental may result.

Programmable telecommunication control units are highly desirable. They give more control and flexibility for terminal alternatives to the programming staff, resulting in less reliance upon hardware engineers or the vendor.

Telecommunications programming is one of the most difficult areas in systems programming. The number of permutations of problems and unexpected errors that can occur in the network is fantastically large. Each of these problems must be anticipated in the programming. Proper procedures, including resend and recovery, must be provided for.

Telecommunications problems and errors are also among the most difficult to diagnose. The various components—the terminal, the communication channel, the modem, the telecommunication control unit, and the central processing unit—may all belong to different vendors. The engineers from each of the separate vendors are quick to assume that problems are in some other vendor's equipment or in the software. Your own programmers blame the hardware. Often it takes extraordinary coordination efforts to get the engineers from each of the vendors, together with your own hardware and software experts, to diagnose and resolve persistent problems.

4.   Terminals

The requirements for any medical information control system should include that each class of data be as accurate, valid, reliable, and timely as necessary and feasible within the economies allotted. The achievement of these criteria rests not only on the terminal hardware itself but also on how, when, and why the data is entered, who enters it, and under what conditions it is input. The closer one can get to the original source of generation of data for input, the more likely the data will meet these criteria. For example, given the proper terminal, a diagnosis recorded directly by the physician to the system is likely to be more accurate than later entry by a clerk transcribing (or deciphering) the physician's notes. On-line real-time systems can, under program decision rules, respond to input terminals with reminder or error messages to facilitate and monitor data input.

Therefore, the selection of suitable terminals acceptable to medical professionals requires in-depth consideration. Each application and each type of user will have different requirements in terms of response time, ease of entry, type of entry, amount of input information, hard-copy output, multiple copies, etc. Visual display units will be required for more and more applications. Physicians, using visual display units, may directly enter orders and diagnoses by light-pen selection from multiple choice displays. The visual display response time in moving from one display page to the next in succession to build a complete order should not be significantly longer (and will hopefully be shorter) than the time it takes the physician now to write in the chart. Longer response times for display of retrieved data may be satisfactory because of the longer time it takes a physician to search through a chart. Further, with proper programmed, preformatted selections of data, the physician will be able to display patient care data within seconds of its input in other application areas—data that heretofore would not be received for several hours. There must be a sufficient number of terminals in each application area to avoid unacceptable amounts of queuing of users waiting access to the system.

In very large systems, terminal response times may be improved by having small or mini-computers handling subsets of terminals; e.g., the terminals in a clinical laboratory. Each such computer would have its own direct-access files for worklist information for the application area. These computers would then be connected to the large data base computer for patient computer medical record storage, retrieval, and transmission of data to other terminals in other application areas. Mini-computers will also be necessary to handle automated devices such as automated chemical analyzers, intensive care units, ECG analysis, etc. These small systems will also be considered as terminals to the data base system for storage, retrieval, and transmission of data. Careful consideration should be given to the selection of the mini's for on-going hardware and software compatibility and standardization of maintenance problems.

5. Backup and Reliability

Ideally, a medical information control system should operate with 100% reliability. Even with complete replication of all equipment, combinations of hardware failures will cause unanticipated downtime. In addition, system and application programming errors will cause all or parts of the system to fail occasionally. Because of the continual entry of modified systems programs and new application programs to service the dynamic changes in medical requirements, the on-line system is continually changing. In spite of rigorous program pretesting, program errors will surface, resulting in a continuing residual software failure rate. Expectations, therefore, for complete system reliability are unrealistic. Each application area must have backup procedures to follow when the system is down.

A high reliability rate can only be obtained with the most rigorous efforts and consideration in many areas.

a. Equipment replication. While it is too expensive to replicate all equipment, our experience indicates that duplication of certain critical equipment can have significant results in reducing system downtime. The expensive central processing unit itself, once installed and operated through a shakedown period, has a low frequency of failure. This is especially true for the latest generation of equipment where more and more hardware error recovery mechanisms are being built in. The most frequent cause of downtime is centered about highly mechanical equipment. During the calendar year 1971, the typewriter console on our previous (older generation) central processing unit failed, causing system downtime, twice as often as the entire processing unit itself. Thus, duplication of the console type-writer, a very small fraction of the computer cost, would have led to a noticeable increase in system reliability.

In the remote application areas where there is more than one terminal of the same type, separate communication channels to the central processor (or local multiplexor processor) may be desirable. If one line is inter-rupted, at least the other terminals remain active and available for use.

b.   Spare parts inventory.   An ample spare-parts inventory should be accessible within a sufficient time interval. The highly mechanical mass storage devices used in our previous system failed frequently. In the early history of our installation, the vendor's customer engineers occasionally had to send to Dallas or Los Angeles for the part that had just failed in the device. Long lead times, even with special air shipment handling, for delivery of these parts caused our on-line system to be down for long periods of time—up to 24 hours. Duplication of this expensive equipment was prohibitive. It took considerable effort on our part to convince the vendor's local management and they in turn their distribution management to keep an adequate spare parts inventory in the local district.

Spare terminal units at remote application areas are highly desirable if they can be moved to and plugged in to replace malfunctioning devices.

c.   Corrective maintenance.   Insist on timely vendor response to re-solve unanticipated failures in equipment servicing the real-time system. Be more flexible for equipment that has lower use priority. Vendors' field engineers are generally very responsive. The level of response is reflected in the amount of effort made to keep the vendor apprised of the critical-ness of your on-line medical system.

Timely on-line repair of malfunctioning remote terminals can be a severe problem in those cases where they are located in an area served by a differ-ent branch office than the office serving your central facility. It is difficult to motivate the other office personnel concerning your problems and diffi-cult to schedule coordinated efforts in telecommunication troubleshooting.

It should be possible to operate and test any terminal device while it is disconnected from the system. There should be diagnostic test programs in the system to drive and test terminals to aid in repair.

In addition, a test application program to try out a terminal in its envi-ronment should be available as a final test before putting the terminal back in the on-line system.

d.   Preventive maintenance.   A strong preventive maintenance pro-gram reduces the unanticipated failure rate. Periodic inspection and exercise of all components under controlled procedures and test programs will disclose many incipient problems. Do not expect the vendor, on his own, to be consistent in exercising a maintenance program. He will need periodic reminders.

The vendor's computer operating system should furnish a daily engineering log of all transient failures in the computer system, including the central processing unit, the input/output units, auxiliary storage devices, and the telecommunication control units. This log can provide valuable information in pointing to early or marginal device malperformance. Preventive maintenance can then be scheduled to fix the problem before a hard failure occurs.

e. Trouble reporting system. A formal trouble-reporting system is highly recommended to improve reliability. In our installation, it has improved communication about problems and has pinpointed repetitive troubles. Each computer operator and terminal user is required to fill out a simple form relating the time, date, and problem experienced. For hardware problems, other information, such as time (vendor) engineer was called, time arrived, time fixed, etc., is also noted. These forms are forwarded to the computer operations supervisor, who reviews them. Hardware problems are forwarded to the responsible vendor customer engineer. Software problems are in turn forwarded to the responsible programming supervisor. The forms must be completed by the responsible person, stating the cause of the problem and the action taken for correction. The forms are returned to the computer operations supervisor for review at a weekly "trouble" meeting held by the computer center manager. In attendance are the appropriate vendor engineers—those whose equipment failed during the week—and the responsible programmers and their supervisors. The problems are discussed with relation to the errors or failures affecting the reliability of the medical system and their future prevention. These discussions often lead to general improvements in the software, especially in relation to additional aids for error recovery and operator control.

6. Air-Conditioning and Power Supply

The succeeding generations of computers over the years have lessened requirements for air conditioning for given levels of computer capability. However, data processing facilities experience gradual increases in computing needs so that the total level of heat removal often stays constant or increases. In addition, some new equipment such as large disk file units produce large increases in cooling requirements. These units are often sensitive to overheating. We have experienced increases in transient errors when operating disks at the upper limit of the recommended temperature range.

Air-conditioning units, like anything else mechanical, fail. As with other equipment, a preventive maintenance program to lubricate, clean filters, etc., will prevent some breakdowns. When air-conditioning failures occur, the computer operators must begin the process of stopping the computer system. Depending on many factors (climate, time of day, load on the computer, etc.), the shutdown process proceeds component by component in an effort to reduce the heat output in the room to keep the on-line system active as long as possible. If the air-conditioning system is composed of modular units, this process can often be arrested at the stage where only components nonessential to the on-line system need be shut down. Thus, if a unit fails, the remaining units are capable of supplying minimal cooling to maintain temperature control for the on-line system. A sufficient number of units should be connected to a backup power generator. If the computer system is on a backup power system and the air-conditioning system is not, long power outages would still mean no computer use because the air-conditioning units would be inoperable.

Several backup noninterruptible power systems are on the market and are readily available. Establishing backup power requirements for the obvious but infrequent extended periods of ac power outages is routine. What is not so obvious is the effect of transient power surges and short power interruptions. These events are normally transparent to humans because they do not cause problems with usual equipment such as motors and may not even cause lights to flicker. But many computers are subject to failure when power interruptions of only a few milliseconds in duration occur. These interruptions occur frequently and may cause lengthy recovery and reinitialization procedures to restart the computer system. Our backup power system has the outside ac line supply power to a static battery charger, which in turn "float" charges a set of batteries and at the same time supplies dc power to a static inverter. This inverter supplies ac power to the ac computer load. If normal ac power failure or transient surges occur, the batteries continue to supply power to the inverter in order to sustain the ac load without interruption. In the first three months following installation of our backup power system, we experienced at least six failures on the ac lines that should have caused computer failure. In each case, the inverter continued to supply power smoothly and the computer system ran without interruption. Some power system manufacturers claim that power surges on the ac lines can also cause transient hardware errors. It is claimed that the continuous power systems prevent these problems. Our experience tends to corroborate these claims.

C. SOFTWARE REQUIREMENTS

1. General

The need to define goals, objectives, and the amount of systems analysis needed before programming are favorite discussion topics in computer literature. It is not possible to state accurately *all* long-term goals and objectives for complex organizations. Goals and objectives change during organization evolution. A completely *thorough* analysis of any complex organization may be possible but is not usually practical or beneficial beyond a modest return for the investment. Analyses are often aimed at developing complete design implementation specifications for new procedures. When implemented, the effects of the change by any one of the new procedures may be contrary to what was expected and upset the balance of the design. Systems have been carefully designed, programmed, and put into use and still have failed. (At the other extreme, starting programming with insufficient analysis, specification of goals, and design also leads to unacceptability and a likely higher failure rate.) Changes to be initiated because of availability of new techniques offered by data processing exacerbate the difficulty of doing the proper amount and kind of preanalysis. Too often, the system being studied is not what it will be after data processing is introduced. The introduction of data processing tools to the medical environment is already altering current medical procedures and will bring lasting changes to the delivery of health care.

The actual effort of programming an application is, unfortunately, the ultimate way to find out what is really effective. In our own experience, it has been consistently observed that, in spite of the amount of preanalysis and design specification during programming of a new application, the medical staff working with the programming staff learned much about the capabilities of data processing and the programmers learned much about what the medical personnel really wanted. The program was usually partially written, implemented, and tried in the actual application environment before this learning process was completed. Hence, the first implementation of an application was usually inefficient and not completely satisfactory for the medical activity. Therefore, the ability to modify, change, and adapt programs to the new experienced requirements easily becomes necessary for acceptance and viability. Undoubtedly, the same type of experience will hold true for the development of medical information control systems. Different systems will have to be tried and the experience from these trials will lead to new specifications. The more modular and flexible the programs, the greater the chance of evolvement to highly usable and cost-effective medical information control systems.

Perhaps the fundamental requirement for any medical program is that it be open-ended; i.e., it should be designed so that it can develop in a modular fashion in order to be flexible enough to handle the daily changes in requirements and to meet the evolving long-term objectives of the medical organization.

2.   Systems Approach

A medical information control system must consider the interface of the application areas and optimization of overall organizational goals. Very little experience, and that by only a few institutions, has been gained to date with the development of systems for complete information flow, availability of medical data, and overall optimal use of medical resources.

Much experience has been reported in several smaller application areas of medicine. Work has been reported by many in ECG analysis, clinical laboratory systems, admission office and census systems, appointment systems, etc. These application areas have been developed relatively independently of one another and have largely ignored the complex problems of integrated information flow throughout the medical organization. While not minimizing the value or importance of the very good work done in these areas, these applications should not continue to develop without some effort to integrate the information. For example, a clinical laboratory system should not exist just to solve the problems internal to the laboratory but should also serve the overall clinical service, research, and administrative needs of the total medical organization. These multiple needs are often beyond the scope, interest, and resources of any one application area director and consequently are not integrated into the total system when designed independently. Typically, each department director optimizes in accordance with his needs rather than those of the parent entity. This procedure leads to a future suboptimization for a medical information control system in the parent organization. If in any medical organization each application area uses data processing tools independently of other areas and optimizes on local needs only, it may be extremely difficult and expensive to combine them in the future for an integrated medical information control system. To superimpose a coherent and controlled programming system after independent application development may not be feasible.

A programming system with the organization and fundamental programs necessary to support an organized, integrated, and controlled medical system optimizing overall goals and information flow is needed. The individually, separately programmed medical applications could be added modularly to the system as they are developed, allowing an orderly phase-in of the various medical application areas according to priorities and needs.

Because of the reasons stated previously, it may not be possible to analyze, design, and specify (in light of current experience) a complete medical information control system. It is possible, however, to do a broad scope analysis and specification statement for requirements and long-range goals for the medical organization as related to an overall programming system. A medical information control programming system could be specified with emphasis on modularity to minimize future problems due to lack of sufficient foresight today. With such a programming system conceptually developed, the various medical applications could then be designed with the overall goals well in mind. The first applications could be developed either concomitantly with the overall programming system or subsequently in accordance with these integrated goals.

3. System Programming

Whether the application programs exist in mini-computers linked to the central computer system or whether they exist in the central computer, it will be necessary to control them in a real-time environment where they will be operating essentially simultaneously. Often the central system will have the additional requirement of running a background batch system for administrative and research jobs. These requirements, along with the handling of multiple terminals, telecommunications, and medical data storage and retrieval for multiple applications, will require a sophisticated and comprehensive supervisor program. The extent of the supervisor requirements can, in effect (as discussed in B.1.), determine the hardware requirements for the central computer system. Unless one decides to write his own such supervisor program (which may put an enormous drain on the programming resources and extend the development lead time), a thorough study of available operating systems from the various computer manufacturers is required. The limited availability of supervisor systems sufficient to meet requirements may constrain eventual hardware selection more than the available hardware to do the job.

While the vendor's supervisor system will handle the priority and multiple programming requirements, there are additional processing requirements needed for the medical information control system. Much of the control of information flow between the medical data terminals, mini-computers, medical application programs, and the medical data base is unique and not controllable by the vendor's supervisor. A master medical supervisor program to accomplish this control is necessary. It can operate under and in conjunction with the vendor's supervisor program. The medical supervisor program should have a command language for the computer operators' use to keep surveillance over the entire medical information control program system. Some of the features of this language are noted in A.2.e.

A medical application program inputs, stores, processes, retrieves, and outputs data. Application programmers should not have to be concerned with the minute details of input, output, storage, and telecommunication hardware. The medical-supervisor program should provide several types of data management services for the application programmers' use. A few examples are:

a.   Telecommunication.   As discussed in B.3., telecommunication programming with all its technical vagaries of communication lines and remote terminal "hello/goodbye" line requirements is difficult. A medical-supervisor program service should be supplied to allow the application programmers to state various data transmission requirements, in a simple command or parameter list, to handle the sending and receiving of messages to and from terminals and other application programs automatically. Such a data control service will be the communication center of the medical information control program system and should be designed with care and extreme forethought.

b.   Medical data base.   The various application programs will be accessing the computer medical record for storage and retrieval of patient data. Many applications, especially for essential medical information summary reports to physicians, require access to data collected across many other applications. A standardized central computer medical record data base would facilitate this communication. Given this requirement, only one updating program should be allowed to change, modify, correct, or post new data to the record. This restriction would prevent any application program—new or old—from erroneously damaging any record. For data input, the application program would send a formatted standardized stream of data to the updating service. If the stream violates any rules, the data is rejected with an error message redirected to the application program. This required service offers enormous savings in programming and debugging time of application programs.

c.   Retrieval.   Another medical supervisor program service would provide capabilities of data retrieval by simple commands of parameter lists. Requested data would be returned to the application program in standardized formats.

d.   Work tables.   Many applications require, for their own use, to keep track of processed data. For example, the clinical laboratory must keep account of specimens and daily work for internal laboratory control. These worklists are generally kept in the form of tables; the capability of table look-up is based on an index such as medical record number, accession number, transaction number, etc. A system service which automatically stores and returns data filed under an index furnished by the application program is desirable.

The choice of programming language with which to implement the medical information control program may be limited. There are few higher-level languages which allow the multiprogramming necessary to operate the system with its many applications. Higher-level languages are also generally inefficient of either computer processing time or memory space. Since the medical supervisor program itself is largely memory resident and participates in so much of the processing, it is desirable for it to be carefully programmed for efficiency. Often assembly-type languages are necessary for implementation of large parts of this program and its service routines.

Some medical installations have provided an overall higher-level interpretive type of language in which all application work is programmed. These have the advantage of conserving memory space for the application programs but generally suffer in degradation of execution time. This may lead to severe terminal response time problems in systems with large numbers of terminals. Other alternatives have also been implemented. In our installation, a variety of methods were tried. Our hospital information system had terminals controlled by two small computers which, in turn, were connected to the central data base computer. That part of the hospital application controlled by the small computers was programmed in a high-level interpretive language. Application programs resident in the central computer were largely written in assembly language with many system services, in the form of macros, available to the application programmer. Over 150 service macros were supplied for the application programmer's use. These allowed the application programmer to be more concerned with the logic of his application and less concerned with the actual coding techniques and hardware requirements; hence, programming and debugging time was reduced, but we still had the efficiencies of assembly language coding. Mandatory usage of many of the service macros resulted in improved standardization.

4. Application Programming

A well-designed programming system should be able to handle the modular addition of application programs. As new application areas become of interest either for clinical or administrative priorities or research needs, it should be possible to analyze, define, program, and implement the new application easily into the medical information control system. With the mandatory system services, especially for data entry into the medical record, patient data from new applications would integrate easily into existing records.

With modular software add-on capability, hardware requirements to handle additional medical applications are also largely additive. This is usually in the form of additional mini-computers or other terminals only, as all the system hardware would already exist to support the application. If care had been exercised in the original choice of central hardware, upwards software compatibility would also exist to expand into more powerful processing units. This will be necessary when the number of applications grow to the point where the current hardware system is no longer supplying sufficient response time or is otherwise inundated.

The difficulty of implementing many application areas, even with the support of the programming system services, is not to be underestimated. All the difficulties that exist today in developing such applications independently still exist. Progress has been slow. In addition, we are now asking that these programs be developed within the standards and rules of a system. Fundamental problems, such as discussed in A.1. and C.1., will still exist to increase the difficulties.

Relevant, comprehensive, and timely information is needed by the medical professional in the delivery of health care service to the patient. The efforts to build medical information control systems to improve these services hopefully will help significantly in the accomplishment of *the* primary requirement of the system—the high-quality fulfillment of the health care needs of the individual citizen.

REFERENCES

Aron, J. D. "Information Systems in Perspective." *Comp. Surveys 1* 4 (1969): 213–236.

Asherhurst, R. L. "Systems Analysis and Design." *Computers and Crises* Edited by R. W. Bemer. Association for Computing Machinery, Inc. (1971) 80–88.

Collen, M. F. "General Requirements for a Medical Information System." *Comp. and Biomed. Res.* 3 (1970): 393–406.

Davis, L. S.; Collen, M. F.; Rubin, L.; and Van Brunt, E. E. "Computer-Stored Medical Record." *Comp. and Biomed. Res.* 1,5 (1968): 452–469.

Davis, R. M. "The Role of the Computer." *Computer and Crises.* Edited by R. W. Bemer. Association for Computing Machinery, Inc. (1971) 192–204.

Dodd, G. G. "Elements of Data Management Systems." *Comp. Surveys 1* January, 1969, pp. 117–132.

Eyres, R. R., and Howe, J. M. "Building a Hardware Maintenance Team." *Datamation 18* 11 (1972): 92–95.

Harmon, L. D. "Some Problems and Priorities in Health-Care Technology." *Proceedings, Conference on Technology and Health Care Systems in the 1980's.* January, 1972. Government Printing Office.

International Business Machines Corporation. "Organizing the Data Processing Installation." *Data Processing Techniques,* Form C20-1622.

Kehl, T. H., et al. "A Reexamination: Centralized versus Decentralized Computers in Biomedical Environments." *Proceedings, 1971 Annual Conference ACM* pp. 357–366.

Martin, J. *Telecommunications and the Computer.* New Jersey: Prentice-Hall, 1969.

Murphy, J. A. "Part II—UPS and Regulator Devices." *Modern Data* 5 5(1972):33–36.

Ontario Department of Health. "Health Care Delivery System, Role of Computers in the Health Field." Suppl. 9 (1970).

Reilly, N. B. "Computers in Medicine." *Datamation* 15 46(1969).

Rosen, S. "Programming Systems and Languages." *Comm. ACM* 15 7(1972):591–600.

Rosin, R. F. "Supervisory and Monitor Systems." *Comp. Surveys* 1 1(1969):35–54.

Sanders, D. H. *Computers and Management.* New York: McGraw-Hill, 1970.

Saunders, M. G. "Computers and Medical Practice." *Computers and Crises* Edited by R. W. Bemer. Association for Computing Machinery, Inc. (1971): 366–373.

Saunders, M. G. "Computers and Medical Research." *Computers and Crises* Edited by R. W. Bemer. Association for Computing Machinery, Inc. (1971): 374–379.

Singer, J. P. "Computer-Based Hospital Information Systems." *Datamation* 15 38 (1969).

Terdiman, J. F. "Mass Random Storage Devices and Their Application to a Medical Information System." *Comp. and Biomed. Res.* 3(1970):528–538.

Theis, D. J. "Communications Processors." *Datamation* 18 8(1972):31–44.

U.S. Department of Labor. "Occupational Analysis of Computers in Medical Sciences." (June, 1969).

Van Brunt, E. E. "The Kaiser-Permanente Medical Information System." *Comp. and Biomed. Res.* 3(1970):477–487.

Vander Noot, T. J. "Systems Testing . . . a Taboo Subject?" *Datamation* 17 22(1971): 60–64.

Waterman, J. J. "Part I—Uninterruptible Power Systems." *Modern Data* 5 5(1972): 30–33.

Wilson, C. R. "How to Live Happily with Vendors." *Datamation* 18 5(1972):62–65.

Wood, F. A. "Letters to Editor, UPS: A Rebuttal." *Modern Data* 5 10(1972):6–7.

World Health Organization. "The Development of Hospital Computing Systems." *Report on a Symposium.* Copenhagen, 1970.

Yoder, R. D. "Management of Computer Failures in Clinical Care." *Datamation* 18 10(1972):78–80.

Yourdan, E. "Reliability of Real-Time Systems, Parts 1–6." *Modern Data* 5 (January-June, 1972).

CHAPTER FOUR

The Medical Data Base

by Lou S. Davis & Joseph F. Terdiman

A. INTRODUCTION

As more information/communication needs have been identified as basic storage and retrieval problems, attempts to develop computer-processing methods to solve these problems have increased. General data base problems have been receiving attention in the past few years.[1-4] It has gradually become apparent that many individual application-oriented data files are not sufficient for the information flow and control needed by an overall organization.[5] Hence, there is a trend toward common data bases that serve many of the application areas in the organization. The many failures and few successes of these efforts have gradually resulted in the beginnings of a data base science.[6-8] Extensive literature on the subject is beginning to appear. Two large groups, the GUIDE-SHARE group and the CODASYL Systems Committee, have issued reports on data base systems.[5,8-10] The GUIDE-SHARE report defines long-range requirements for data base management systems. The CODASYL report is a proposal for data definition and data manipulation-language specification to extend COBOL to work with data bases.

Unfortunately, because of the extensive work that has been done on application data files, the growing recent work on data bases, and the many independent workers in the field, data base definitions and design requirements are overburdened with conflicting ideas and redundant terminology.[11-13] This chapter will generally use the terminology defined by the GUIDE-SHARE group.[10,14,15]

In the sense of the GUIDE-SHARE definition, a *data base* is a named collection of units of physical data which are related to each other in a specified manner.[10] The data base has the prime function of conditioning, storing, and making available the data required by the management system.[5] The GUIDE-SHARE report states, "The data base is conceived as the fundamental repository of relevant data not only for the retrieval of information but also for the operational and strategic planning and control of an economic unit (corporation, division, university, government body, etc.). To serve these fundamental needs effectively, it is essential that a common and controlled approach be used in the introduction of new data and the processing of existing data within the data base."[10]

The problems of information communication are not unique to medicine. From an information science standpoint, the problems are very similar to those in other disciplines. *The timely delivery of relevant needed information to the appropriate user remains the goal.* Data processing can provide the mechanization of the information flow within the organization via a management system to and from a common data base. The data base cannot stand alone since it requires a management or control system to collect and distribute information. (See Chapter Three for a discussion of the control system.)

B. HISTORY OF MEDICAL DATA BASE AT KAISER-PERMANENTE

Several medical data processing problems were experienced during the first Kaiser-Permanente Automated Multiphasic Screening (AMS) program after its first implementation in 1964.[16-21] We experienced the dynamic changes in medical requirements and the resultant long-term problems of a simple, fixed-field, fixed-format (although highly efficient) approach to storage of medical data in a comprehensive computer system. We learned how difficult it becomes to sort and merge records on a magnetic tape system for large numbers of records in an environment where patients appear for return visits over extended periods of time. We learned of difficulties in data errors and the value of on-line checking and immediate correction of errors by medical personnel vs. off-line batch input and later attempts to correct medical data errors by data processing personnel. We began to obtain insight into the need for standardization of terms describing the data variables being input to a computer medical record— particularly for subsequent research use. Tests and test conditions *do* change. Simple strategies for medical record storage simply do not handle these changes well over long periods of time, greatly increasing the amount of additional programming required in data analysis.

It also became obvious that, despite widespread interest in medical information systems, only subsets of systems (such as a multiphasic laboratory, clinical laboratory, business and administrative data subsystems, etc.) had been implemented. Even today, it is possible to observe, in a single medical institution, researchers working on several medical applications, using the same computer, yet each with his own independent programs and application medical data file. The programs and data files are usually incompatible as to encoding, definitions, standards, etc., so that even though one patient's data may be in the same single computer system, there is little possibility of collating it to study the patient or provide comprehensive service to the clinician about his patient.

From these experiences and with increasing requirements to collect, store, retrieve, and analyze additional clinical information, we began to develop the concept of an overall control system for collecting and distributing medical data and coordinating information flow. A common data base for storing and retrieving needed data was to be at the center of the system. This system would not only furnish computer medical record storage service analogous to the traditional medical chart room, but also provide the facilities for getting data into storage and retrieving selected data for an individual requester. More important was the essential idea of developing an information system that would assist in the integration of the subsystems (the various medical and ancillary clinics) in the medical complex. Others have stated the need for systems approaches in the medical field.[22-27]

The Kaiser-Permanente medical data base and control system was originally conceived in 1965. The strategy and structure were defined during 1966.[28]

The design of the system was based on the premise that the medical record is the fundamental repository and basic source of patient information in the medical environment. It would be necessary for each patient record to have the capability of being a continuous lifetime record containing all essential present and future inpatient and outpatient data. The record would also contain each patient's data from any facility in any location. It was decided to keep all data for a given patient together in one addressable "bucket" in computer storage to reduce risk of losing pointers and linkages and consequently to make recovery and backup procedures easily and also to eliminate involvement in complicated time-consuming record retrieval strategies. This "bucket" is, in effect, the record. The strategy for data storage inside each "bucket" is basically a tree structure, with data items stored at various levels in medically meaningful relationships. The record would also have to keep data not normally stored in the conventional chart; for example, outpatient pharmacy prescription data. Furthermore, to avoid the impossible task of accessing, sorting, merging, and mounting hundreds of tapes on a daily basis, it would be necessary to store the record on a direct-access storage device.

It must be stressed that this continuous integrated record concept was a major undertaking. It increased the complexity of the programming and extended the initial development time. However, once the system for supporting and updating a continuing integrated record was available, adding application subsystems became a much easier task. Only recently have others in this field begun to consider the necessity of the continuing integrated medical record.[24-26]

A strategy evolved which was medically satisfactory, which the programming staff felt could be efficiently implemented, and which would meet the requirements stated above. The detailed description of the strategy of this record structure has been published.[28,29] A summary follows below in section D.6. This data base management program was implemented in 1968, and over the following four years a number of representative medical applications (functions) were phased into operation under the system.[28,30-35]

The Kaiser-Permanente Data Base was in operation from August 1968 through August 1973. Due to the curtailment of research funds (as discussed in Chapter Twenty-one), the system was discontinued on August 31, 1973. At that time the data base had records for 1.5 million patients. Of these records, 437,475 contained medical data acquired from the various clinics where data processing had been implemented. These records varied from under 50 to over 48,000 characters in length.

Data was successfully input from the automated multiphasic laboratories, the San Francisco Medical Center pharmacies, and outpatient clinics.

The San Francisco clinical laboratory application was partially implemented, with bacteriology scheduled for input. An essential medical information retrieval capability was installed in the San Francisco emergency room and pediatric non-appointment clinic for real-time medical record inquiry.

By August 1973, office visit data in the data base was being incremented by approximately 1,000 prescriptions, 300 multiphasic examinations, and diagnoses for approximately 2,000 outpatients each day. Laboratory work for inpatients and outpatients was being added at the rate of about 2,100 tests each day. The successful experiences we had with this very large data base have proven the fundamental soundness of many of the original concepts, especially for the timely supply of needed information in a real-time medical response environment.

Even though this project met and solved many data base and data base related problems to various degrees, several problems continue to exist. These problems, partially recognized at the beginning of the project, now remain as the significant ones to solve in the further evolution of the data base and data base management system. (While this chapter primarily discusses the medical data base, the strong interface between it and the management or control system in certain areas precludes restricting the discussion to the data base alone.) These problems are:

(1) The failure of hardware technology to supply modular direct-access storage devices at a reasonable cost for storage of large amounts of medical data.[36]

(2) Medical practice is diverse, dynamic, and often nonstandard. Consequently, medical opinion as to data relationship varies significantly. A better method of expressing the complex logical relationships and dependencies of medical data, independent of the physical structure of the record, should be developed to attempt to minimize extensive reprogramming when the relationships are respecified.

(3) A need exists for specification of generalized and standardized methodology in medical data collection. The differences of interpretation and specification for data input presentation to the data processing system from medical application to application and one facility to another create severe problems in data storage as well as retrieval, processing, summarization, and output presentation of the data.

(4) A need exists for specification of generalized and standardized reporting capabilities. While various categories of medical users will always require output reports from the data processing system to be tailored in many different ways for each specialty, the lack of general guidelines precludes general storage rules and the development and use of the report generator type of medical output program. This greatly increases lead times to implement needed information system services.

With the advances in data base science and new hardware technology and in light of our practical experience over the past several years, we can now crystallize and formulate recommendations with regard to medical data base requirements and the needs and constraints we can expect in the future.

C. MEDICAL DATA BASE GOALS AND REQUIREMENTS

As a minimum, two major goals of a data base within a medical care delivery system should be:

(1) to maintain clinically and administratively relevant, readily accessible medical data for each patient served in the health care delivery system, and

(2) to provide a source for the systematic retrieval of medical data, across large numbers of patients, for any desired administrative and research studies.

There are many objectives and requirements that must be satisfied to obtain these goals. The GUIDE-SHARE report lists several objectives for a data base management system.[10] Some of these objectives, as well as others we have added, are discussed below in terms of requirements for a medical data base.

1. Data Independence

"The tremendous cost of seemingly trivial change has had an increasingly severe effect on the ability of data processors to perform well."[10] As discussed above, medical opinion related to data relationships varies. These opinions differ from specialty to specialty, as well as from individual to individual within specialties, and change by individual over time. When data relationships are expressed by the way variables are physically stored, severe reprogramming problems can arise to change application programs that process data when the relationships are changed.

The physical structure of data within the data processing system is a complex computer science problem. Strategies relating to performance (discussed in C.2 below) as well as to relationships require extensive evaluation. Storage of variable-length, variable-format data in a tree structure proved to be an effective strategy for our medical data base. Data was stored in reverse chronological order and was grouped by computer-defined visits. Within each visit, data was further subdivided into medically meaningful parts, and in each part data was stored in the form of logical tree structures. These structures allowed for both association and membership type relationships of the data. However, these relationships have often been defined physically via the tree structure as well as being physically grouped in parts. In many ways, physically defined relationships of the data in storage is desirable and efficient if it could be directly appropriate to the reporting of any particular clinical report. However, reports for other clinics may depend on different relationships of the same data in the storage structure. For example, the data could be physically stored as a problem-oriented record (i.e., problem-oriented for a given specialty). If it became necessary to report-out the data in problem-oriented format for a different specialty, or if different orientation was necessary such as time-oriented, or source-oriented, or any of several inverted file arrangements, the original physically specified relationships may not only be inefficient but may preclude reformatting. Because of these conflicting requirements—the expression of medical relationships for a set of data and the impact of those relationships physically expressed in the structure—it is essential to develop strategies to separate the definitions of logical relationships from the physical storage of the data. These logical expressions would be more amenable to change and could allow for greater independence of data storage vis-a-vis the application programs. We are currently researching the independence problem as related to a medical data base. Complete independence may not be feasible.

2. Performance

The medical data base must be able to respond in a timely manner to requests for information either on a recurring or one-time basis. Performance must be consistent, measurable, and adjustable to satisfy various categories of medical users.

As stated above, the original design of the Kaiser-Permanente medical data base began with the premise that the medical record was the fundamental repository and basic source of patient information in the medical environment and would be an integrated lifetime record for storing all inpatient and outpatient medical data. Even though the system was designed and implemented with this flexibility (including the ability to store natural language), we were very selective as to which data was stored in the data base. Only subsets of data which we considered to be essential for medical care or for specific research studies were stored. Even so, it has become increasingly evident that the resultant amount of "essential" medical data will surpass acceptable storage costs on currently available direct-access devices in a system with a large number of patients. It is doubtful that technological developments will improve the situation in the very near future. Even with low-cost devices, the computer processing of long records may be undesirable. Therefore, it is questionable whether it will be feasible to maintain indefinitely even such limited medical information in a dynamic direct-access system.

Consequently, storage of data on lower-cost devices, at slower access time capabilities, will be required. This in turn affects the performance level of the system. Our data storage strategy was, in effect, an open-ended one. Medical data selected for acquisition through the computer medical data system stored in one mass direct-access storage device in a single hierarchy, without further regard to relative clinical utility, or other characteristics of the data. As previously discussed, within this single level, the data was clustered basically by episode or visit in the form of a tree structure.[36] The objective of this approach was to be able to provide a requested report from a patient's computer medical record in real-time to a physician at any location served by the medical data system (i.e., within seconds of the request). Because it was not possible to predict *a priori* what data a physician might request, it was decided, at least for the initial phase of development, to provide the physician with real-time access to virtually all medical data in the data base. The result of this approach was that all data in a given visit were given equal weights in retrieval access priority for a given request. In view of the direct-access storage cost problems for the growing size of a medical data base, this strategy concept will have to be reexamined.

The desired performance of the system in retrieving classes of stored medical data and the elements within them depends on their utility to various outpatient and inpatient clinical services. Attributes of data utility include their reliability and accuracy, elapsed time since collection, type or specialty of user, and the real-time environmental needs or problems that determine the data priorities. Medical importance is most readily measured by actual usage and clinical significance; for example, a patient's weight is frequently used and a drug sensitivity is of high clinical significance. A day-old hematocrit value is of high clinical utility, whereas there will be little interest in a value obtained ten years previously. Measures of data utility can be obtained by examining by category the frequency of requests for computer-stored data from various clinical services. Our storage strategy provided a means for monitoring the utilization of computer-stored medical data by the physicians. By measuring the frequency of requests by various users for specific kinds of medical data and determining parameters of the data that affect this frequency, it was possible to determine the probability of utilization for a specific datum. These measures will help to establish criteria for maintaining acceptable system performance in establishing priority access for levels of storage across different devices. The number of levels and types of hardware used in the total storage system will depend on the speed of access required for data at different priority levels. At the highest level, real-time accessibility is required; this data will be stored on fast direct-access devices. Lower priority data without real-time access requirements can be stored on slower and less-expensive devices. By providing the capability for reassignment of priorities, data can be shifted between levels. The kind and volume of data in each level should be amenable to change according to medical or other data processing criteria. If certain data in lower levels are frequently requested, they can be shifted to lower levels.

3. Compatibility

As the hardware and software technology and data base science evolves, the steps to the new generations must have minimum impact on the existing data base manipulation software. New, lower-cost storage devices will appear in time. Not only must the software be such that minimal reprogramming is necessary to use the new devices, but as costs are reduced it should be possible to eliminate or collapse priority levels of storage originally needed simply because of hardware cost considerations.

4. Data Integrity

The medical data must be protected against accidental or deliberate invalidation. Because the data base responds to many application areas, many users in various clinics, laboratories, etc., have access to the records for entry of data, correction of data, and/or removal of data. Decision rules must be established for right of entry, correction, and removal of data. These rules should be program directed and controlled where possible by the data base management system.

Data integrity problems overlap those of backup and recovery, as it must be possible to reestablish records that have been changed erroneously.

5. Security

There is a long tradition of confidentiality in communications between patient and physician and the records arising from medical care.[37,38] This tradition is reflected in the Hippocratic Oath and is recognized to some extent in the law. Many states have privileged communication statutes that apply to physician-patient communications and to the disclosure of medical records, while other states have no clear-cut laws protecting confidentiality.[39-44] Very few states have, as yet, specific laws regarding the privacy of computer medical records. Despite a lack of uniformity in the law, most physicians, nurses, and other health professionals are aware of ethical and legal responsibilities in this area and continue to maintain high standards of confidentiality. For example, the Joint Commission on Accreditation, a group of health professionals that gives accreditation to hospitals and other medical facilities that meet certain standards of health care, requires that medical records be confidential, current, and accurate. Furthermore, it singles out certain portions of the psychiatric record as requiring extraordinary measures to preserve privacy. Since these requirements apply, in essence, to medical information regardless of its form, it is logical to extend the regulations governing the confidentiality of the traditional medical chart to the computer medical record and to require the various data processing personnel who may have access to these records to share in the responsibility of protecting the confidentiality of that information.

a. Security violations. In describing the measures required to preserve confidentiality, it is instructive to contrast the environment and accessibility of the computer record with that of the medical chart. Patient charts are usually stored in a central record room under the general supervision of a medical record librarian. Charts can be called for by an authorized individual, usually a staff physician or nurse. They are forwarded to the location of the requester by a messenger. When a patient is admitted to the hospital, his chart is transferred to the appropriate ward, where it is stored in a restricted file at the nursing station. Psychiatric records are traditionally stored in separate files, and special permission is required for their use. Confidentiality of these records can be violated in two ways: by accidental disclosure of information to unauthorized individuals, or by deliberate interrogation or removal of charts from restricted areas by unauthorized individuals.

Medical records in a computer data base are written on machine-readable storage media such as magnetic tape or disk. A set of programs on the central processor provides access to the data base for both storage and retrieval of data. Inputs and retrievals are often made from geographically remote communication terminals linked to the central processor via a data communication network. In such a system, data security can be threatened in three basic ways: accidental disclosure, deliberate passive monitoring, or deliberate active interrogation.[45,46]

Accidental disclosures of confidential data may occur through hardware, software, or human failure. Disclosure through hardware failure may be avoided by various memory protection schemes and by improvements in hardware reliability. Thorough debugging and testing of programs and incorporation of "fail-soft" features can reduce the risk of disclosure due to software failure. With the development of computer medical records, programmers, computer and terminal operators, technicians, and other data processing personnel will have access to all or part of individual patient records and must share in the responsibility to protect the confidentiality of the automated medical record. Frequent causes of accidental disclosure are careless handling or disposal of computer printouts or routing privileged information to the wrong terminal or individual.

Passive monitoring refers to wire-tapping of digital transmission between the central processor and a remote terminal. Most digital communication networks use telephone company lines for transmission. Dial-up lines are the most susceptible to this type of infiltration. Leased or private lines are less vulnerable.

The most serious threat to the confidentiality of the computer medical record is deliberate active interrogation. Such infiltration of the system may be done overtly or covertly. Overt infiltration may occur through normal access procedures. An individual authorized to retrieve specific portions of a record may attempt to obtain unauthorized parts. An unauthorized individual may masquerade as a legitimate user after having obtained the proper identification or key for retrieving data. Personnel employed by the computer center who are familiar with retrieval procedures and programs may employ this knowledge to retrieve medical records without authorization or "need to know."

Covert active infiltration involves the unauthorized access to medical records by means of by-passing control and protection programs that monitor normal access routines. This is the most sophisticated type of system security violation and may involve either software modification or the use of special terminals. Covert program modifications or unsuspected entry points discovered by the infiltrator may permit him to access the data base, by-passing control routines designed to protect security. Special terminals tapped into communication channels may permit the infiltrator to obtain entry to the system at the same time as a legitimate user and gain access to confidential files.

b. Protective measures.   There are a number of protective measures that can reduce the threat to data security. These include the use of private communication lines, central allocation of remote terminal functions, access control and monitoring, processing restrictions, and privacy transformations. The use of private or leased telephone lines between central computer and remote terminal makes it much more difficult for an infiltrator to tap into a communication channel. Central allocation of computer terminal functions places control of general terminal retrieval capabilities in the hands of a computer operator rather than the terminal user. The advantage of this operating mode is that the input and output of data from a terminal can be restricted according to the specific medical activity performed. For example, a legitimate user of a terminal in a hospital admissions office generally will not require access to medical portions of a patient's computer record. The terminal user cannot override this restriction; only the computer operator can, and he must first receive proper authorization.

Access control involves the authorization, identification, and authentication of legitimate users. Authorization is a one-time procedure to identify an individual to the system as a legitimate user who may gain access to certain files and request certain types of information. To enter the system, the user must first identify himself and then (where deemed necessary) authenticate his identification. Machine-readable user identification cards with punched holes or magnetic strips that are read by a badge reader attached to the terminal are frequently employed. Where authentication of the user's identification is required, the user generally enters a password into the terminal keyboard.

If a terminal is connected to a dial-up line rather than a leased or private line, transmission of terminal identification may be required. This may involve transmission of an internally-generated or user-entered code. Terminal access control procedures may require a system initiated call-back before data will be accepted from the terminal. Monitoring identification of terminal user, specific files accessed, rejected attempts to enter restricted files, and attempts to perform restricted operations may reveal possible misuse or tampering. Monitoring must be able to continue under various contingencies such as system failures and recovery periods, and start-up and shut-down of parts of the system.

Scrambling devices that automatically encode data for transmission and decode it at the other end of the communications link are available. Other more complicated coding schemes called "privacy transformations" may be used by the central processor on individual characters of an information record or on sets of such records.

Processing restrictions may be imposed on the data base management system to require that all accesses to computer medical records for input or output of data be handled by specific programs whose operations are monitored. This reduces the ability of an infiltrator to access the data base without detection.

Finally, physical access to data base files must be controlled. This problem is compounded by the usual practice of maintaining backup files. Preparation, transport, and storage of these files present opportunities for copying, theft, or an off-line printout. Physical security of the files, including locked storage vaults for files, should be provided.

c. Confidentiality of research data. Another aspect of data base security is related to the unique ability of the computer to scan large number of records in a relatively short time. In addition to retrieving individual patient computer medical records, many data base management systems also provide the ability to scan the data base, retrieving from each record only information specifically requested. This type of retrieval is extremely useful for statistical and epidemiological investigations of the patient population in the data base, from which specific variables may be selected for study. However, it also raises the danger that an investigator, by chance or design, may retrieve, analyze, and publish results based on data belonging to another investigator. In order to protect the data base against this type of violation, the use of retrieval programs should be strictly controlled, and all retrieval requests should receive specific authorization by the data base administrator and those individuals with overall responsibility for the use of clinical data and for the activities of the investigator (for example, the physician-in-chief of the medical facility).

In summary, the confidentiality of the medical record must be protected.

The data should be viewed or processed only by users who have the proper authority and/or the need to know. Several access authorization levels must be defined for different sensitivity levels of the data. Even programmers, who in the course of writing new application programs frequently have to examine actual records, only need to know about certain data in the records. Programming debugging aids for examining records should require passwords for progressively larger parts or sensitive parts of the record. An automatic logging system should be provided for examination of data requests.

6.   Checkpoint and Backup

Checkpoint procedures for active records in the update process to prevent loss of on-line data are necessary. Procedures for data generation from backup of the complete data base are imperative.

7.   Data Quality

In any system, quality control is defined as the set of procedures required to insure the accuracy of data generated by the system. There are two basic aspects of data quality control. The accuracy of the data itself must be checked, and the data must be routed to the proper location. Since the common destination of medical data in a data base management system is the computer medical record, quality control procedures require verification of the record linkage.[47,48] There are several steps in common to most quality control systems. They include standardization and calibration (where applicable), data monitoring, error detection, error recovery, and reporting. Depending on the application, quality control can be performed during data input, storage, or output.

a.   Input quality control.   Quality control of data at the input source is often the most effective form of control. Each medical application is responsible for its internal quality control procedures, which are conducted by its own personnel. All data originating in a facility should be verified for accuracy and record linkage before it is entered into the computer system. Source documents, completed by the patient or health professional, must be screened and edited for accuracy, completeness, and legibility of both identification and medical data. If errors are detected prior to data entry, the source document should be returned for correction to the originator of the data. In a multiphasic or clinical laboratory, a quality control program includes periodic maintenance of test instruments, calibration against known standards, and frequent testing of quality control standards during regular operation.[49,50] If on-line or off-line quality control programs are available, both patient data and quality control standards should be monitored for baseline drift or unusual distributions of test results, indicating possible instrument malfunctioning or improper operation. Quantitative data should be compared against upper and lower validity limits. All data should be checked for logical inconsistencies (such as entering a pregnancy test result for a male or a change in blood group) and invalid entries (e.g., a qualitative result where a quantitative result is required). Internal accession numbers assigned to patients or samples must be carefully controlled to insure the correct record linkage of data.

b. Data base quality control. Data that has been checked for accuracy at the input source is now ready for storage in the data base. All information to be entered must be associated with a primary identifier (such as a medical record number), which provides the linkage to the corresponding computer record, and optionally, with secondary identifiers (such as patient's name, sex, and date of birth). The accuracy of the linkage may be verified by a comparison of secondary identifiers on the input document with corresponding identifiers in the computer record. Various degrees of correspondence may be found from complete agreement (correct linkage) to total disagreement (incorrect patient). Suitable algorithms can be programmed to distinguish with a high degree of reliability between a correct linkage with a minor discrepancy and an erroneous linkage.

If erroneous data is discovered in a computer medical record, it is necessary to indicate that the data is invalid. A general philosophy of error correction is that modification to a computer medical record is analogous to modification to a chart. An erroneous result is not removed from the chart, but is crossed out and dated and the correct result is inserted. Similarly, erroneous data in the computer record should be flagged and dated, but not deleted. The new value, if any, should be inserted at the same point. Standard flagging and error correction procedures should be developed for each medical application; and whenever possible, corrections should be performed by applications personnel.

Data base quality control should also include periodic random sampling of newly stored data for each medical application. Comparison of data in the computer medical record with the corresponding source documents found either in the patient's chart or in the facility's records will provide a measure of the error rate of data entry.

c. Output quality control. Portions of a computer medical record may eventually be printed out as a clinical report. Provision should be made for receiving feedback from the recipient of the report regarding his estimate of the accuracy of the data. Frequent reports of erroneous blood pressure measurements, for example, may indicate an inaccurate or unstable blood pressure instrument requiring more frequent calibration or poor measuring techniques.

8. Nonredundancy

The removal and prevention of redundant data, where possible and economical in relation to processing costs, must be considered.

D. REVIEW OF DATA BASE SYSTEMS

1. Introduction

A computer data base consists of an ordered collection of data elements. Information is stored in the data base in two ways: in the content of data elements, and in the relationship between these elements. For example, the statement "hematocrit = 40%" contains three informational units. Two units, hematocrit and 40%, are data element values. The third unit, the equals sign, is a relational statement. Relationships between data elements are usually defined in a data base by a hierarchical ordering of elements. The most primitive relationships between data elements can be represented by a linear list or array of elements. An example of a linear list is a set of blood pressure measurements. The most recent measurement is inserted at the top of the list, while the bottom of the list contains the oldest measurement. The only relationship defined by this list is a chronological one. Data bases with this type of structure are limited in utility and can handle only the simplest kinds of data.

A more complex data structure that can represent the hierarchical branching relationships of medical information is called a tree structure. In this type of structure, relationships between data elements are explicitly or implicitly defined by pointers between elements. For example, an element that contains the name of a specimen may point to a set of elements that describes the tests performed, which in turn point to test results.

More complex multi-linked structures are possible but have not yet been used with a medical data base. This type of structure may be useful in representing such concepts as the problem-oriented medical record, in which a single data element may contain information relating to more than one problem and, therefore, may receive pointers from several data elements and point to several more.

Most successful attempts at developing a medical data base have been variants of the tree structure approach. Among these attempts, which will be reviewed here, are those at Massachusetts General Hospital, Hannover, Danderyd, Karolinska, and Kaiser-Permanente. Since each of these systems is constantly evolving, the data base descriptions presented here, which were compiled both from personal communications and the literature, may lag behind their current status.

2. Massachusetts General Hospital

One of the earliest efforts to develop a medical data base was carried out by the Laboratory of Computer Science in Massachusetts General Hospital.[51] (See also Chapter Seventeen.) A compact time-sharing system called MUMPS (MGH Utility Multi-Programming System) was developed, dedicated to clinical data management applications. MUMPS provides a high-level interpretive language for applications programming, with a flexible input/output monitor that permits conversational dialogue from a variety of terminals, and an extensive data management facility.

Within the MUMPS system, data is characterized as either local or global. Local data files are defined only within the domain of a particular program. Global data files can be referenced by all programs and, therefore, provide a common data base for the system. Each variable in a data file has a symbolic name (e.g., "AGE," "GLUCOSE," etc.) and may be given either a numerical value or a variable-length string value. The variables in global data files are organized hierarchically in a branching tree structure. Each node may possess a numeric value, string data value, or a pointer to a lower-level node in the tree. The structure is dynamic; the node content and/or structure may vary during usage. A given element of data is located within a structure by giving the symbolic names of the structure and variable. In MUMPS language, the structure is represented as a subscripted array where each subscript is a variable name at a different level in the tree and the hierarchical ordering of variables is represented by the order of the subscripts. The organization of data within a tree structure is both topical and chronological. The data hierarchies used in the MGH are, in order from highest to lowest levels: patient ID number, major data category (patient identification, chemistries, review of systems, etc.), data sub-category (name, glucose test, cardiovascular system, etc.), date of event (if appropriate), additional data referenced by the date. Dated sub-trees are stored in reverse chronological order.

Physically, global data files are stored on a fixed head disk. The many records belonging to a given file are not physically contiguous, but their structure and content are mapped into directories that contain all data values stored at a given level and all pointers to directories at the next lowest level. When a file is updated or a record deleted, the directories are modified to optimize both average access time and space utilization.

3. Hannover

The Medical System Hannover (MSH) is designed to provide a hospital information and data base management system for 1 million patients.[52]

(See also Chapter Nineteen.) The data base of this system contains both on-line and off-line (archival) files. The data management system chosen was DATA LANGUAGE/1, an IBM-developed program (now called IMS/360).

The on-line data files are divided into two categories: files for rapid access, and slower access hierarchical files. The principal rapid access file is the Status Summary File, which contains a brief summary of the status of each patient as well as references to other files. Other rapid access files contain data linkages and administrative data and provide intermediate files for data storage and backup.

There are two on-line hierarchical files, CONPAT and APAT. When records from these files are no longer relevant, they are permanently stored off-line on corresponding archival magnetic tape files, DOKPAT and ARCHPAT.

CONPAT contains brief information on all treatment episodes of the patient. The file is organized into nine data categories at three hierarchical levels. At the highest level, the "root segment," is stored identification and administrative and essential medical data (blood group, medical summaries, etc.). Data categories at the next level include diagnosis, problem treatment, etc. In each category containing dated information, data is stored in reverse chronological order. Only formatted data is stored in CONPAT. Diagnoses are coded in one of the standard coding systems. An additional storage level is provided for data subcategories.

APAT contains detailed information on all treatment episodes. The file is organized into 16 categories on 4 hierarchical levels. At the highest level the root segment includes administrative data and a set of summary bits that describe the contents of the remainder of the record. Within a data category, structures with a maximum of eight levels are possible. Categories include hospital admissions, medical history, physical findings, laboratory, etc. As in CONPAT, the data are stored in reverse chronological order by episode.

4. Danderyd

The Medical Information System for Danderyd Stockholm (MIDAS) is designed to serve about 1.5 million patients in the Stockholm area.[25,26] The system provides a data base for storage and retrieval in real-time from remote terminals throughout the region.

The "main file" (HR) is an on-line direct-access disk file that contains identification, administrative and essential medical data for all patients. Active patient data is stored in the "active patient file" (PR). A record is created in the PR when a patient makes an appointment or is admitted to a medical facility. The PR handles most of the information flow from daily hospital work. The PR record is formed from the HR and from an archival "medical history tape file" (MHR). The MHR is the archival counterpart of the HR and contains medical data of a noncritical nature. When a patient is discharged from the facility, the HR is automatically updated with essential data from the PR, and remaining data is stored in the MHR. Additional work files stored on disk include a resource file (used by the appointment system), social care and insurance files. The data in each patient record in the HR file is divided into five categories: (a) personal data (ID number, name, occupation, etc.); (b) critical medical information (blood group, critical diagnoses, etc.); (c) information from previous inpatient visits (location, dates, diagnoses, operations, etc.); (d) information from previous x-ray examinations (location, date, type of exam, organ diagnoses); and (e) information from previous outpatient visits (location, date, diagnoses, operations, anesthesia).

HR is divided into three physical files: personal data file (except name), name file, and medical information file. The personal data file is further divided into two parts: patients over 18 years of age, and patients 18 years or younger. The contents of the HR are available for direct-access via remote terminals to authorized users in the region.

Medical data are stored in the various files in the form of variable-length, variable-format records arranged in a tree-structure. The tree is limited, however, to three levels. At the highest level are patient record identifiers and data common to all subrecords. At the next level, there may be up to six subrecords, each of which may contain up to six segments. At the lowest level, each segment may contain multiple data elements. Elements are of variable length and format. It may be a binary number, a 6-bit internal code number, or a character string. Each element is given a symbolic name by which it can be addressed. The name, type of data, lengths, and format of each element are defined in file description tables. All variables used must have an entry in this table.

Patients are identified to the system by a ten-digit identification number, including a six-digit birthdate, a three-digit serial number, and a check-digit. A cross-reference file permits patient identification by name, sex, age, and other variables. A patient record in the PR contains basic patient data and pointers to addresses that contain data for various hospital functions (laboratory, scheduling, etc.).

File security is provided by requiring a terminal operator to identify himself by a unique password. It is possible in this system to store data which cannot be retrieved by anyone without the password. Psychiatric and venereal data is available only for statistical studies and cannot be retrieved for specific patients.

5. Karolinska

The hospital computer system developed at the 2000 bed Karolinska Hospital in Stockholm will perform a variety of clinical, educational, communication, and scheduling services for the institution.[53] The current system, known as J5, provides a data base for the storage and retrieval of patient records. (See also Chapter Eighteen.)

The primary file, the "Computer Medical Record Library" (CMRL), is stored on magnetic tape and is not available for direct-access by remote terminals. All information for a patient is stored in a physically contiguous record. The file is updated periodically from disk files in the various hospital subsystems called "Computer Records" (CR). A patient may have one or more CR's. A portion of each record containing administrative and hospital admission data is kept in direct-access storage on disk. Each CR contains data associated with one registration point. Patients are identified to the system by a ten-digit identification number including a six-digit birthdate, a three-digit serial number, and a check-digit. In the CMRL, data for each patient is organized by type; within type by date; and within date by source location. Medical information is stored as variable-length, variable-format elements in a branching tree structure. Symbols and coded data are translated via dictionaries resident in the system.

In the CR, each record is divided into two parts called the "header segment" and "data segment," respectively. The header segment is a fixed-length, fixed-format record that contains an identification number and administrative data (location, clinic, ward, date, etc.) and a code for the type of data contained in the data segment. The data segment is a variable-length, variable-format record consisting of an arbitrary number of data elements arranged in sequences called "code groups." A code group can be mapped directly into a tree structure. At each node in the tree, a series of data elements are stored, beginning with a positive integer code that identifies the type of data stored on that level, and a level label (except for the root node). Data elements stored at lower-level nodes in a subtree are considered to modify the data contained in the node to which they are attached. The identifying code of the root node is colled the "major code" of the tree. Following each identifying code in a code group is a sequence of one or more paired data elements called "terms." The first term of a pair is a "label." A label is a negative integer which identifies the type, length, and format of the second term, the data value. A data value may be a number, character string, code representing a phrase, data, time, etc.

Data may be retrieved from the CMRL for individual patients or for a population subset. Clinical reports of all or part of a patient's record can be printed. For research purposes, it is possible to scan the entire CMRL for a set of conditions and retrieve only those records that satisfy the search criteria. Since the CMRL is stored off-line on magnetic tape, retrievals are not available in real-time and must be scheduled as necessary.

6. Kaiser-Permanente

The data base of the Kaiser-Permanente medical information system provided a continuing integrated medical record for over 1 million patients in the Kaiser Health Plan.[28-29] The data base was a computer file of patient identification, administration, and medical data. A patient computer medical record (PCMR) existed for each patient in the Health Plan and for any private patient who had attended a Kaiser facility. (See also Chapter Twenty-One.)

a. File structure.   The primary file for the data base consisted of 1.2 billion bytes of on-line direct-access disk storage. Each PCMR formed a physically contiguous record in the file. When a PCMR was updated with new medical data, the entire PCMR was rewritten on disk, with the new data inserted in its proper place. This file then contained all medical data and current essential identification and administrative data. Non-essential or obsolete identification and administrative data, which were not needed for real-time applications, were stored on magnetic tape and constituted an off-line data base in a lower hierarchy than the on-line file. A more complex problem, the hierarchical classification of clinical data based on data utility, is under study.

b. Storage requirements.   The data base resided on 12 IBM 3330 Disk Drives, each of which had a storage capacity of 100 million bytes. The effective maximum capacity of this file was about 1.2 billion bytes, and some 750 million bytes of data had been stored in this volume. In 1972, over 60 million bytes were added to the data base; the estimated increment for 1973 was 140 million bytes. Of 1.5 million PCMR's in the data base, about 1.0 million contained only identification and administrative data. Of the remaining 500,000 records, the average PCMR had an average length of 1,600 bytes and contained seven visits.

c. Data structure.   (1) General. The PCMR is a logical branching tree structure in which information is represented at each branch point (node) by data elements, and in the hierarchical structure by the relationship between nodal points (Figure 4-1). Data is stored at the nodes in two different forms: fixed-length, fixed-format indices and variable-length, variable-format definitions and values. Relational data between nodes is implicitly represented by the tree structure itself: data elements within a

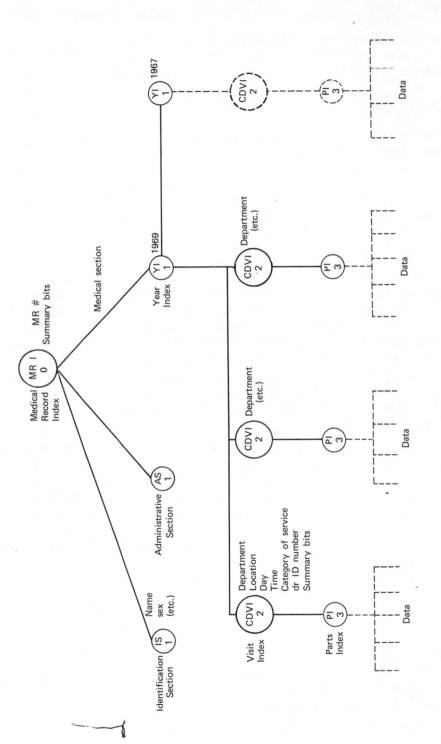

Fig. 4-1. Schematic diagram of first four levels of PCMR.

node or subtree modify the higher level nodes from which they branch. There may be as many as 13 node levels in a PCMR.

(2) Indices. The indices, which are of fixed length and format, serve primarily as pointers to specific portions of the PCMR. They also contain certain types of identification and visit data.

(a) Medical record index—Level 0. This index contains the patient's seven-digit medical record number, which is the primary identifier of the PCMR, summary bits, various counters and field lengths.

(b) Year index—Level 1. This index is in the Medical Data Section, and contains the year of visit or visits, a count, and a field length. All visits in a given year are logical branches of a single year index.

(c) Computer defined visit index—Level 2. This index is in the Medical Data Section, and contains five visit parameters and time. The five parameters are Julian day, location, department, category of service, and personnel identification number. All visit parameters except identification number are required to identify the visit. If any visit parameter is changed, a new visit is created. The index also contains summary bits, a field length, and a key.

(d) Parts index—Level 3. This index specifies the parts into which medical data from a visit has been stored. It contains the number of parts, part number, and field length.

(e) Summary bits. Summary bits are a series of 56 binary flags that are set whenever certain data are stored. There are bits corresponding to general and specific data categories, procedures, and laboratory specimens. Definitions of summary bits are given in Table 1. Summary bits are found in the PCMR at Level 0 in the medical record index and at Level 2 in every computer defined visit index. Bits set at Level 0 represent the logical "or" of the bits in each Level 2 index. The principal function of summary bits is that they are easily and rapidly tested by retrieval programs to determine whether the data of interest are present in that record.

(3) Data node definition and values. In the Medical Data Section, data nodes begin at Level 4; in Identification and Administrative sections, data nodes begin at Level 1. Each node contains three elements: an item, a format, and a value.

(a) Item. The first element of the node is the item. It specifies the definition of the third element of the node—the value. For example, "diagnosis" and "glucose" are item definitions. They indicate that the values to follow will be the name of a diagnosis or the result of the glucose test. To conserve storage, an item is physically represented in the PCMR by a four hex-digit number called a Cataloged Item Identifier of Data (CIID). The collection of CIID's and their corresponding item definitions comprise a separate data set called the Item Catalog.

Table 1.   Summary bits—56 bits

Bit no.		Bit no.	
0	Part 0	28	Part 3 other
1	Part 1	29	Drugs
2	Part 2	30	Surgical procedure
3	Part 3	31	Part 8 other
4	Part 4	32	Anthropometry (incl. Ht. & Wt.)
5	Part 5		(Part 3)
6	Part 6	33	Clinical microscopy (see also
7	Part 7		B16, B17, B19, B20)
8	Part 8	34	Blood specimen (see also
9	Part 9		B18, B35)
10	Part 10	35	Specimen other (see also B18,
11	Part 11		B34)
12	Part 12	36	
13	Part 13	37	
14	Part 14	38	
15	Reserved for computer use	39	
16	Chemistry (see also B17, B19,	40	
	B33, B20)	41	
17	Bacteriology (see also B16, B19,	42	
	B33, B20)	43	
18	Urine specimen (see also	44	
	B34, B35)	45	
19	Hematology (see also B16,	46	
	B17, B33, B20)	47	
20	Part 2 other (see also B16,	48	
	B17, B19, B33)	49	
21	X-ray contrast study	50	
22	X-ray chest	51	
23	X-ray other	52	Reserved for computer use
24	ECG	53	
25	Surgical pathology	54	
26	Autopsy	55	PSI update bit*
27	Cytology		

*Identification (ID) and/or Administrative Sections (AS) that come from Permanente Services Inc. (PSI) tapes.

   (b) Format. The second element of the node is the format code. It specifies the format of the third element. There are format codes representing date, time, integers, fixed point numbers, floating point numbers, upper and lower bounds, EBCDIC characters, and encoded English words. The latter format refers to words that are stored in a special data set called the English Text Dictionary. Each word in the dictionary is assigned a unique four hex-digit code, which is stored in the PCMR in place of the word.

(c) Value. The third element of the node is the value. The value is a conclusion or test result that corresponds to the item definition and format specification. For example, if the item is "diagnosis" and the format is encoded English words, the stored value might be the hexadecimal code for the English word "influenza." If the item is "serum glucose" and the format is the code for a fixed point number, the stored value might be "100.5."

(d) Data content—general. Each patient is assigned a unique seven-digit medical record number which serves as the primary identifier of his PCMR. An eighth digit, computed by an algorithm from the other seven, may be used as a check-digit for errors in entering and transmitting the medical record number. Last name, first name, middle initial, sex, and month and year of birth serve as secondary identifiers for verification of the primary. All identifiers are embossed on Health Plan cards that are carried by each patient but are also available to medical facilities by telephone through the Patient Identification Department.

Within a PCMR, data can be stored into one of three main sections: identification, administrative, or medical.

Identification Section. The Identification Section contains all secondary identifiers and other information characteristic of the individual patient. This section may include social security number, address, telephone number, medical record, numbers of relatives, maiden name, blood group, skin color, and special study classification. To conserve on-line storage volume, however, only name, sex, date of birth, place of birth, and study group code were stored in the PCMR. The average identification section requires 63 bytes of storage.

Administrative Section. The Administrative Section may contain information on Health Plan coverage, Medicare, and other data of a nonmedical nature. However, only group and coverage were stored on-line. The average administrative section requires 20 bytes of storage. Periodically, Identification and Administrative Sections were updated and new PCMR's were created from tapes supplied by Kaiser Health Plan administration. An average of 1000 new PCMR's per week were created in this manner.

Medical Data Section. The Medical Data Section contains medical data for each patient visit, indexed and stored in reverse chronological order. Medical data has been further subdivided for storage purposes into 10 parts. Each part represents a general category of medical data. For example, history data is stored in Part 0, laboratory data in Part 2, etc. Complete part definitions are given in Table 2. Medical data from a given visit may be stored in one or more parts. Within each part, data is stored in the tree structure described above.

Table 2. Medical Data Section Part Definitions

Part 0: Will contain any information reported by any means (word, phone, correspondence, etc.) from any source outside of the Kaiser-Permanente (KP) medical entities. Examples include the following: information from patients, referring doctors, schools, agencies, lawyers, etc.; all parts of the classical medical history such as chief complaint, present illness, past history, family history, occupational history, etc.; laboratory results when reported from an outside laboratory.

Part 1: Includes any and all observations currently made by KP physicians on either the patient as a whole or that portion of the patient which the physician in question customarily and usually examines in lieu of total patient examination. Examples of data to be included in this part are: results of the physical examination, results of those tests customarily done on the patient by physicians such as Romberg and Weber tests, observations of MD physiatrists (but not physical therapists), observations of neurologists and the office tests they perform, blood pressures taken by physicians, observations of anesthesiologists.

Part 2: Contains the results of all tests of body fluids (urine, blood, cerebrospinal fluid, bone marrow examinations, etc.) currently customarily performed in the laboratory, usually by technologists or automated equipment.

Part 3: Contains the results of a specified list of observations generally comprising those tests done by physicians or technologists on the body as a whole for the purpose of testing a specific organ or organ system. This list will include, but not be limited to: radiological examinations, all observations of pathologists, EEG, ECG, EMG, photomotogram, thermography, anthropometry, etc.

Part 4: Will contain but not be limited to those observations not categorized above. Nurses' notes and other observations of paramedical personnel will be included here.

Part 5: Will contain provisional diagnoses and impressions and other notes by physicians, intended as reminders, but not to be considered firm diagnoses at the time. These impressions are to be of the "consider" or "rule-out" variety and are not to be included in insurance reports. Impressions by any PMG physician, including radiologists, are to be stored here.

Part 6: Includes firm diagnoses at the time, made by PMG physicians, including pathologist's diagnoses.

Part 7: Will contain prognoses and information consisting of estimates of future events. This includes rehabilitation potential.

Part 8: Includes information concerning therapeutic procedures and diagnostic studies involving drug administration either ordered and/or performed by physicians, nurses, and other personnel. It does not include referral for consultation. (Includes drugs, operative procedures, diet, appliances, occupational therapy, physical therapy, etc.)

Part 9: Includes all recommendations not primarily therapeutic in themselves and not included in the treatment section. For example, return appointments, referral to another physician or optometrist, ordering of tests, physician suggestions.

(e) Retrieval. The Kaiser-Permanente medical data base satisfied the objectives and requirements defined in this chapter. It provided a repository for clinical, identification, and administrative data in computer-accessible form for each patient in the health care delivery system, and it provided a source for the systematic retrieval of medical data both for individual patients and across the data base population.

Three types of data base retrievals were provided. They were directed at clinical, statistical, or programming requirements. First, the system provided clinicians with medical reports for individual patients. The data for this type of report were derived from individual PCMR's. Second, health services research and epidemiological studies usually required retrieval of several variables from the data base across a defined population. In this case, data were retrieved from hundreds or thousands of PCMR's and presented in a form suitable for statistical analysis. This type of retrieval has provided both medical data for epidemiological studies of the Kaiser Health Plan population and administrative data for utilization studies. Third, the system provided listings of individual PCMR's as they appeared in computer storage. This type of output was useful to programmers and systems analysts for debugging of programs, error correction, and interpretation of PCMR discrepancies.

REFERENCES

1. "Trends in Data Management." *EDP Analyzer*. Canning Publications Inc., Part I, May 1971; Part II, June 1971.

2. Patterson, A. C. "Data Base Hazards." *Datamation 18*:48 (July 1972).

3. Schubert, R. F. "Basic Concepts in Data Base Management Systems." *Datamation 18*:42 (July 1972).

4. Fries, J. F. "Time Oriented Patient Records and a Computer Databank." *Journal of American Medical Association 222*(1972):1536–1542.

5. CODASYL Systems Committee. Introduction to "Feature Analysis of Generalized Data Base Management Systems." *Comm. of ACM.* 14(1971):308.

6. Dodd, G. C. "Elements of Data Management Systems." *Comp. Surveys 1* (June 1969).

7. Lyon, J. K. *An Introduction to Data Base Design.* New York: John Wiley & Sons, Inc., 1971.

8. CODASYL Systems Committee. "Feature Analysis of Generalized Data Base Management Systems." *ACM.* (April 1971).

9. Data Base Task Group. *Report to the CODASYL Programming Language Committee.* October 1969; April 1971 reports.

10. Joint GUIDE-SHARE Data Base Requirements Group. *Data Base Management Systems Requirements.* November 11, 1970.

11. "The Debate on Data Base Management," *EDP Analyzer.* Canning Publications Inc., 10, March 1972.

12. Cotterman, W. W. Review of Reference 7, above. *Computing Reviews.* 13, April 1972.

13. "News in Perspective, Standards." *Datamation 18:82* (July 1972).

14. Patterson, A. C. "A Data Base Management System." *Proceedings of the 1971 Annual Conference.* ACM: August 1971.

15. Patterson, A. C. "Requirements for a Generalized Data Base Management System." *AFIPS Conference Proceedings.* 39 (1971) : 515.

16. Collen, M. F.; Rubin, L.; and Davis, L. "Computers in Multiphasic Screening," in Stacy, R. W. and Waxman, B. D.: *Computers in Biomedical Research.* Vol. 1. New York. Academic Press, 1965.

17. Collen, M. F. "Computers in Preventive Health Services Research." *7th IBM Medical Symposium,* October 27, 1965, Poughkeepsie, N.Y.

18. Collen, M. F. "Periodic Health Examinations Using an Automated Multitest Laboratory." *Journal of the American Medical Association* 195 (1966) : 830–833; Editorial in *Arch. Environ. Health* 12 (1966) : 275.

19. Collen, M. F. Automated Multiphasic Screenings and Occupational Data. *Arch. Environ. Health* 15 (1967) : 280–284.

20. Collen, M. F., and Davis, L. S. "The Multitest Laboratory in Health Care." *J. Occup. Med.* 11 (1969) : 355–360.

21. Collen, M. F., and Davis, L. S. "The Multitest Laboratory in Health Care." *Occup. Health Nursing* 17 (1969) : 13–18.

22. Singer, J. P. "Computer Based Hospital Information Systems." *Datamation* 38–45 (May 1969).

23. Jackson, G. G. "Elements of Data Management Systems." *Comp. Surveys 1* (June 1969.)

24. Ontario Dept. of Health, "Health Care Delivery System, Role of Computers in the Health Field." Suppl. 9 (1970).

25. Abrahamsson, S.; Bergstrom, S.; Larsson, K.; and Tillman, S. "Danderyd Hospital Computer System II. Total Regional System for Medical Care." *Comp. and Biomed. Res.* 3 (1970) : 30–46.

26. Abrahamsson, S., and Larsson, K. "Danderyd Hospital Computer System. Basic Software Design." *Comp. and Biomed. Res.* 4 (1971) : 126–140.

27. World Health Organization. *Symposium Report: The Development of Hospital Computing Systems.* Copenhagen: June 1971.

28. Davis, L. S.; Collen, M. F.; Rubin, L.; and Van Brunt, E. E. "Computer-Stored Medical Record." *Comp. and Biomed. Res.* 1 (1968) : 452-469.

29. Davis, L. S. "Prototype for Future Computer Medical Records." *Comp. and Biomed. Res.* 3 (1970) : 539–554.

30. Van Brunt, E. E.; Collen, M. F.; Davis, L. S.; Besag, E.; and Singer, S. J. "A Pilot Data System for a Medical Center." *Proc. IEEE* 57 (1969) : 1934–1940.

31. Collen, M. F. "General Requirements for a Medical Information System." *Comp. and Biomed. Res.* 3 (1970) : 393–406.

32. Richart, R. H. "Evaluation of a Medical Data System." *Comp. and Biomed. Res.* 3 (1970) : 415–425.

33. Van Brunt, E. E. "The Kaiser-Permanente Medical Information System." *Comp. and Biomed. Res.* 3 (1970) : 477–487.

34. Singer, S. J. "Visual Display Terminals in a Hospital Information System (HIS)." *Comp. and Biomed. Res.* 3 (1970) : 510–520.

35. Collen, M. F.; Davis, L. S.; and Van Brunt, E. E. "The Computer Medical Record in Health Screening." *Meth. Info. Med.* 10 (1971) : 138–142.

36. Terdiman, J. F. "Mass Random Storage Devices and Their Application to a Medical Information System (MIS)." *Comp. and Biomed. Res.* 3 (1970) : 528–538.

37. Westin, A. F. "Legal Safeguards to Insure Privacy in a Computer Society." *Comm. ACM* 10 (1967) : 533–537.

38. Westin, A. F., and Baker, M. A. *Databanks in a Free Society.* New York: Quadrangle Books, 1972.

39. California Legislature, *A Final Report of the California State Assembly Statewide Information Policy Committee.* Sacramento, 1970.

40. Curran, W. J.; Stearns, B.; and Kaplan, H. "Privacy, Confidentiality and Other Legal Considerations in the Establishment of a Centralized Health-Data System." *New Eng. J. Med.* 281 (1969) : 241–248.

41. Freed, R. N. "Legal Aspects of Computer Use in Medicine." *Law and Contemporary Problems* 32 (1967) : 674–706.

42. Gotlieb, C. C. "Regulations for Information Systems." *Computers and Automation,* 14–17 (September 1970).

43. McNamara, J. J. "Legal Aspects of Computerized Medical Records." *Journal of the American Medical Association* 205 (1968) : 18–19.

44. Miller, R. I. "Computers and the Law of Privacy." *Datamation,* 49–55 (September 1967).

45. Hoffman, L. J. "Computers and Privacy: A Survey." *Computing Surveys* 1 (1969) : 85–103.

46. Springer, E. W. *Automated Medical Records and the Law.* Pittsburgh: Aspen Systems Corporation, 1971.

47. Wagner, G. "Record Linkage: Its Methodology and Application in Medical Data Processing." *Meth. Info. Med.* 9 (1970) : 121–138.

48. Acheson, E. D. *Medical Record Linkage.* London: Oxford University Press, 1967.

49. Hanson, D. J. "Suggested Definitions for Clinical Laboratory Standards and Reference Materials." *Am. J. Clin. Path.* 54 (1970) : 451–453.

50. Raymond, S. "Laboratory Verification of Patient Identity." *Proc. SJCC* (1971) : 265–270.

51. Greenes, R. A.; Pappalardo, A. N.; Marble, C. W.; and Barnett, G. O. "Design and Implementation of a Clinical Data Management System." *Comp. and Biomed. Res.* 2 (1969) : 469–485.

52. Sauter, K.; Reichertz, P. L.; and Zowe, W. "The Integrated Patient Data Bank of a Hospital Information System." Presented at *Symposium on Medical Data Processing,* Toulouse, France, 1972.

53. Hall, P. "J5—A Data Processing System of Medical Information." *Meth. Info. Med.* 6 (1967) : 1–6.

CHAPTER FIVE

The Administrative System

by Douglass A. Williams

A. A REVIEW OF EARLY ADMINISTRATIVE SYSTEMS IN THE HOSPITAL

While the early use of computing was for mathematical and scientific problem solving, the computer was also the logical successor to unit record equipment which dominated the commercial and business applications in the 1950's. Early administraive applications, such as payroll and inventory control, were developed by major electronics and aerospace companies, often using computers designed primarily for scientific computing (e.g., fixed-word length with limited editing and character handling instructions). With the introduction in 1960 of IBM's moderately priced 1401 general purpose business computer, a substantial market developed in the United States for business data processing.

In most hospitals throughout the U.S., the hospital administrator is the chief operating executive responsible for maintaining a center for the more intensive forms of medical care. He also determines computer applications and cost-effectiveness. Therefore, the first steps in applying computers to hospitals were in the Administrative System area.

In the early 1960's, administrators began to apply computers to the problems of collecting bills (patient billing, accounts receivable), paying employees (payroll), knowing who is in the hospital (census, admitting), keeping the hospital solvent (general ledger, accounts payable, etc.), and managing the hospital resources (nurse staffing, diets, operating room scheduling, maintenance scheduling, etc.).

One of the pioneers in such applications was the Sisters of the Third Order of St. Francis in Peoria, Illinois.[1] Unit record equipment was installed in 1961 in support of accounting and payroll applications. In 1963, a small IBM 1401 computer replaced the unit record machines; and programs were developed in the areas of inpatient billing, accounts receivable, accounts payable, payroll, and financial reporting.

Data processing in the hospital during the early 1960's was oriented to ledger card systems, master files stored on the familiar 80-column punched card, and equipment consisting of mechanical card reproducers, sorters, collators, and calculating printers. As a variety of low- to medium-priced business-oriented computer systems became available, they began to replace the slower less reliable unit record devices. The punched card remained the basic media for data storage, giving way to magnetic tape units and magnetic disk files as users became more sophisticated. With improved reliability and speed of processing afforded by higher-speed storage units and larger computer memories, data communications (teleprocessing) over standard telephone lines with appropriate modems were added, providing the means for attaching various low-speed devices such as teletype printers, paper tape readers, low-speed card readers, and data transceivers to move data to and from hospital facilities and the data processing center.

By the mid-1960's, there were several hospitals applying this evolving technology to administrative support of hospital operations. Loyola University Hospital and Monmouth Medical Center[2] both installed computer systems with terminals to various hospital departments and developed more comprehensive applications than previously possible.

The State University Hospital of Downstate Medical Center, New York,[3] opened in 1966 with a computer installation planned as an integral part of hospital operations; this system supports a teleprocessing network throughout the hospital which operates between 8:00 AM and 12:00 PM, at which time the computer system is placed in a batch processing mode and processes the data collected during the prior 16 hours to yield a variety of operational and administrative reports.

Most hospitals continued to process their administrative applications through clerical departments with the aid of small accounting machines. The costs of computer systems and the short supply of qualified data processing personnel were initial barriers to the early application of administrative computer systems in the hospital setting; however, the possibility of sharing this new technology between several hospitals emerged as an alternative.

B. SHARED HOSPITAL COMPUTER SYSTEMS

As early as 1966, Rikli, et al.,[4] discussed the potential value in shared hospital computer systems. The term "shared computer systems" in its broadest sense connotes two or more users sharing data processing resources in any or all of the categories of computer equipment, applications programs, and technical personnel. Hammon and Jacobs[5,6] discuss some of the various types of shared systems currently in use and estimate that over 75 such systems were in operation by 1970. They cite many of the advantages and disadvantages encountered with shared computer systems and conclude with suggested criteria for evaluating these systems.

The trend toward shared hospital computer systems can be traced from the mid-1960's to the present. The Sisters of the Third Order of St. Francis, mentioned earlier,[1] continued their developments into an extensive shared hospital system serving ten outside hospitals in addition to their own.[7] Various administrative applications supported in this system are charged out to participating users on a transaction or account basis. Some typical rates given are: 30¢ per patient day for hospital billing, 25¢ per check for payroll or accounts payable, 15¢ per active account for accounts receivable, and $250 per month for general ledger, financial statements, and cost allocation reports.

Shared hospital computer systems can be considered on almost any scale. Gillette, et al.[8,9] review the planning and development of a shared system for two 350-bed hospitals, while Owen[10] describes an extensive statewide shared system sponsored by the New Jersey Hospital Association (147 member hospitals), in which 10 hospitals representing 3,000 beds currently participate; 35 other member hospitals are considering adopting the system.

Several Blue Cross Associations have also developed various forms of shared computer systems in support of claims processing/patient billing and other accounting applications. Hill and Laybourn[11] discuss a system shared by 14 hospitals and 6 medical clinics. One of the largest and earliest (1966) on-line shared hospital systems was developed by Minnesota Blue Cross. Planning for this system began in early 1963, with study completion in 1964. Systems design, applications development, and equipment installation were completed by late 1965. In February 1966, the system was implemented with on-line patient billing.[12] By late 1971, approximately 100 state hospitals were sharing the use of the application program, while 19 hospitals were on-line to a central computer facility.[13]

Another approach to sharing of data processing resources is described by Anthoney.[14] The Daughters of Charity of St. Vincent de Paul Hospitals planned and coordinated their computer program for 14 hospitals located in 7 states and the District of Columbia. A central data processing staff assisted with the development of hospital application programs, documentation, and training of hospital staff while computer support was provided by small computer systems located in each hospital.

C.   KAISER-PERMANENTE SHARED COMPUTER SYSTEM

The evolutionary development of a shared computer system for the Kaiser-Permanente Medical Care Program in northern California was a natural progression occurring from within the administrative framework established in 1953.

In that year, a separate division of administrative service functions was organized to provide centralized regional support to all Northern California Kaiser-Permanente Medical Centers. Rapid growth of the Kaiser-Permanente program in northern California to its present level of more than one million members (whose medical care is delivered in 15 clinic/hospital facilities staffed by approximately 1,000 physicians and 9,000 medical center and administrative personnel) brought an attendant growth in data processing development from unit record equipment to a small computer to a major computer center. The present administrative data processing shared-computer facility supports a library of more than 600 programs operating in a multi-programmed batch processing mode and an on-line communications network of cathode ray tube (CRT) terminals and printers which connect the 15 medical centers and the administrative offices to a membership/patient data base.

1.   Administrative Data Processing

Administrative data processing at Kaiser-Permanente is significantly influenced by the organizational structure of a prepaid, group practice form of medical care delivery. A unique membership system has been developed, avoiding the usual emphasis toward hospital patient billing. This system maintains a basic administrative record for each individual, which is linked to a family account. A majority of family accounts are associated with employee benefit programs, and thus the billing of prepaid dues is affected through a cyclic billing system to approximately 2,500 employer groups; a separate billing subsystem for individual family accounts completes the process, through which some 80% of the total revenues (prepayment) are collected. A separate Medicare reimbursement system coupled with a patient billing system for the collection of private patient charges, third-party payments, and supplemental charges account for the remaining 20% of revenue.

The membership system also provides the basis for a comprehensive series of statistical reporting systems covering both inpatient and outpatient services. Reports showing the distribution of the membership population to medical center service areas with corresponding utilization statistics provide both current information and trend patterns for future planning of facilities and staffing.

Administrative programs in the areas of payroll, personnel, general accounting, property accounting, pharmacy operations, purchasing, and stores inventory are also specific to the Kaiser-Permanente Medical Care Program.

2.   Membership/Patient Administrative Data Base

In recognition of the importance of member/patient identification in the medical centers and the necessity for support of administrative and operational services, in 1967 a major development effort was established to design and implement an administrative data base system oriented to the individual member/patient. Prior to this time, records were maintained manually and on punched cards with the attendant data errors common to this type of procedure. The need for special software to manage a membership/patient file containing basic administrative information (i.e., name, address, sex, birthdate, health plan contract coverage, and benefits, etc.) became evident as new application programs were considered. Design requirements included: (1) fast inquiry-response via CRT terminal to any one of 1,000,000 plus member/patient records; (2) the ability to link members of a family together for family retrieval; (3) the ability to update data base information on a daily basis; and (4) capability to operate a number of separate application subsystems to and from the data base.

a.   Record linkage.   Particular attention was given to the record linkage method to be employed. Since the early 1950's, when random access devices (e.g., UNIVAC File Computer, Model 1, general storage drums) were first available to the users of business data processing, there has been the need to link data records together in some logical sequence or relationship. For the Kaiser-Permanente membership/patient data base system, two types of record linkage were defined: linkage between records of a family unit (e.g., subscriber-to-spouse-to-dependents), and linkage across data sub-files (e.g., Medicare, Accounts Receivable, etc.).

Generally, the linkages required in an administrative system and its data files are not complex because the processing rules and constraints associated with these data are normally well defined. In this case, the *medical record number* of the individual is used as the linkage key and is the basis for developing the basic file search algorithms. Medical record numbers are issued sequentially to new member/patients and uniquely maintained over time without reassignment (i.e., a lifetime medical record number). This medical record number assignment has no bearing on demographic characteristics or other data content factors related to the membership/patient population.

In the membership/patient data base, a family linkage is maintained in order to associate the subscriber's record with all members of the family and to retrieve the entire family unit upon request. This is done by placing in the subscriber's record the medical record number of the first dependent in the family unit. As each dependent record is created, both the subscriber medical record number and the next adjacent family member medical record number in the chain are placed in the dependent record. The last number of the family carries only the subscriber number and a zero-indicator identifying this as the last member of the family unit. This technique is commonly referred to as a modified ring structure.

The second class of record linkages involves associating particular records in one or more data subfiles with a basic record in the membership/patient data base. Data subfiles linked through the data base could include Medicare records, accounts receivable account, appointment schedule, etc. For example, only 4% of the total Kaiser-Permanente membership population have a Medicare record; thus, a separate Medicare data file is maintained with only an "indicator bit" shown in the individual's data base record signifying that this member/patient is also covered by Medicare. The medical record number again provides the key for accessing the correct subfile data records signified by the indicator bits contained in the data base.

A special feature of this data base system is the alphabetic retrieval program. Two distinct techniques are used to search this large file for a specific member/patient record by using the individual's name and secondary identification information. First, the Computable Name Table provides the means for searching the data base given the spelling of last name, first name, and sex; it also matches middle initial and birth year ($\pm 10\%$), if given. Slight variations in spelling (e.g., Neil, Niel, or Neel) are accepted by the system due to frequent misspellings encountered in processing such data. A second technique based upon "Soundex" codes with a complex homonym structure uses the same input data as the computable name method to produce CRT displays of all names which "sound" or "look like" the search name given. After two years of name retrieval to the 1 million member/patient data base, these techniques have proven very effective; typically, a name search and retrieval function provides a proper response in 4–10 seconds.

Once these linkages and special search algorithms were defined and the applications software written, usage of the membership/patient data base was extended into the operational departments.

b. Present status. In 1970, CRT terminals were installed in the Kaiser-Permanente administrative offices and the chartroom of each medical center to provide communications to the shared-computer membership/patient data base. Through the system, users may access information concerning patient identification, membership status and benefits, medical record number assignment, and medical chart location (by chartroom facility). Studies are currently being made in applying the membership/patient data base in the areas of computer-assisted patient registration, collection of utilization data, and appointment scheduling.

c. Future development. As continued growth and change are experienced in the Kaiser-Permanente Medical Care Program, the data processing services to the regional medical centers will be adapted to meet new needs. A direct management and physician involvement in policy decisions and long-range planning is an essential contribution to maintaining a responsive and evolutionary computer development program.

D. ADMINISTRATIVE SUBSYSTEMS IN PATIENT CARE SERVICE

As data processing was gaining wider acceptance in both individual hospital and shared-hospital computer systems supporting the general administrative applications of patient billing, payroll, and financial reporting, this technology was also being applied to several of the hospital's patient-care needs through government-supported research programs. While most of these pioneering programs were developed as dedicated (stand-alone) systems, they can also be considered as parts of a larger health-care delivery system; in this context, they represent *subsystem applications* which must eventually be integrated into an overall functional system to serve the needs of patients effectively and at an acceptable cost.

Computer application developments in the areas of admissions/bed census, pharmacy, dietary, outpatient appointment scheduling, and medical records management are briefly reviewed.

1. Admissions/Bed Census Subsystem

One of the early administrative computer applications directly related to patient care activity was the hospital admissions and bed census subsystem. The first computer-based patient location control system was developed at the Children's Hospital Medical Center, Boston, Massachusetts[15,16] and implemented in March, 1966. Utilizing a small computer with communications to 16 nursing station CRT devices, an admitting office input/display terminal, and four teletype printers (admitting, housekeeping, inpatient accounting, central reception), this system creates an administrative patient record and updates it throughout the patient's stay. Upon admission, a clerk enters patient name, phone number, birthdate, sex, medical record number, admission number, admission date, and hospital division to which the patient is assigned; this information is stored in the computer for subsequent reference. When the patient arrives at the proper hospital division, the admission number and a function key "patient admitted" are entered at the nursing station terminal; the computer responds with a CRT display of the patient record previously created in the admitting department. After verification, the bed number is then entered which identifies the patient's location. During the patient's stay, bed transfers, anticipated discharge date, patient condition (special function keys), and final discharge notification can be entered as appropriate. In addition to providing accurate and current patient location information to all concerned hospital departments, a series of census summary and inpatient statistical reports are routinely produced by the computer system.

An early grant-supported research program was developed by Barnett, et al.,[17,18] at the Massachusetts General Hospital. The patient census application was selected for early implementation in 1966 for three primary reasons: (1) patient location data for 1000 beds was necessary for other planned hospital research applications; (2) the patient census application would be minimally affected by computer down-time; and (3) data entry could be done by the clerical staff. Teletypes were installed in the three admitting departments to process patient admissions, transfers, and discharges. The system produced census lists for 38 individual care units; these lists were distributed and reviewed by the evening nursing staff. Changes were entered the following day by the admitting office, and a bed availability list was produced. An inquiry capability was programmed to allow the admitting office to locate any patient upon request; early experience with this system indicated several inconsistencies, time delays, and communications problems between the several nursing care units and admitting departments which affected census accuracy by 1 to 2%

These two early patient census programs and several similar systems provided the basis for computer application research and development into other hospital departments.

2. Pharmacy Subsystem

The pharmacy is an integral component of the medical care delivery system for both the inpatient and outpatient. The responsibility for dispensing drugs on an order from a physician rests primarily with the pharmacist. For the outpatient, the point of service is the pharmacy; it is here that the patient receives his prescribed medications. The application of data processing techniques to pharmacy operations has provided the means whereby drug monitoring can be accomplished. It is now possible to study drug utilization, detect adverse drug reactions, provide drug information service, and implement inventory control techniques on an ongoing basis with the aid of computer processing.

One of the most highly developed outpatient pharmacy computer programs at this time is that of the Los Angeles County General Hospital, described by Seibert[19] and Maronde.[20] Through research grant support, a pharmacy computer system which accepts 2500 prescription orders per day was designed and implemented in late 1967. CRT terminals are used to enter coded data carefully edited by the computer programs. The CRT display provides several operator conveniences, including display of the coded input character string, special operator instructions and error designations, and display of the final prescription label for verification before printing of the label. The system also provides for multiple prescriptions for the same patient; only the new information such as drug name and instructions for use need be entered since the system has retained the previously entered data (i.e., date, patient name, doctor name, etc.). The CRT display also provides certain operator conveniences such as a sequential count of the number of prescriptions entered that day and inquiry of drug names in the formulary. A trained pharmacist or clerk can enter a prescription and produce the finished label in one minute.

Several reports produced by the L.A. County General Hospital system support detailed analysis and research concerning physician prescribing patterns, frequency distributions by drug, prescription cost analysis, controlled drug utilization, and potential drug interaction.

In a separately supported research program, the department of Medical Methods Research of Kasier-Permanente developed a pharmacy data acquisition subsystem as part of a larger "Medical Data System" program implemented in the Kaiser Medical Center, San Francisco.

Utilizing five typewriter terminals connected by phone lines to a central computer facility located eight miles from the medical center, the pharmacy subsystem time-shares the computer resources with many other application programs. Since 1968, pharmacists have entered approximately 1200 prescriptions per day through this subsystem. In this system, patient identification data are entered; this entry initiates a search and retrieval of the patient's computer medical record from mass storage. An encoded character string representing the prescription order is entered and verified by the computer system. A finished label is output by the pharmacy subsystem and verified by the pharmacist prior to being affixed to the filled prescription. Because this application is part of a comprehensive medical data system oriented to the patient's chart, drug profile information is available to the physician. Over 300,000 prescriptions annually are being entered into the system; of these, 37% are refill prescriptions which require only a limited data entry by the pharmacy to produce the prescription label.

Special report programs are used periodically to analyze the prescription orders, evaluating potential changes and improvements in the drug formulary, package sizes, and drug inventory. The major emphasis of this pharmacy subsystem is the collection of pharmacy prescription orders for entry into a comprehensive medical data base for use by both physician in individual patient care and medical researcher in longitudinal studies of a large patient population.

3. Dietary Subsystems

Significant research in computer-assisted menu planning has been conducted by Balintfy.[21,22] As early as 1962, menu planning was recognized as a linear programming problem, i.e., the problem of determining optimum combinations of menu items which meet specified criteria of nutritional value, production constraints, and cost considerations. Early studies were conducted by Balintfy at Tulane University with Public Health Service grant support. A prototype menu planning system was developed and installed at four participating hospitals. Using the Tulane central computer system, programs were written to support the planning of both selective and nonselective menus for regular and modified diets. Mathematical modeling to optimize the menu planning and related food service operations (e.g., purchasing, inventory) in the study hospitals was included. As newer computer equipment supporting communication terminals became available, the study objectives were expanded to include on-line menu planning capability utilizing man/machine communication in the dietary decision process.[23]

The Tulane dietary program research studies led to a second generation development of Computer-Assisted Menu Planning (CAMP) in 1968;[24] principal parts of the Tulane system were reprogrammed with the support of IBM to produce the CAMP system. The CAMP system is divided into three sections: (1) the basic off-line data processing programs; (2) the on-line information retrieval programs; and (3) the off-line menu planning programs. The basic programs create the nutrient data file, the food item data file (including cost data), and the menu item master file which provides for the computer input of the recipes used. The on-line retrieval programs provide the dietary department with a direct communications capability to the computer for menu planning activity. CAMP provides programs for recipe yield, food usage, and nutrient tally, which allow food service personnel to plan in advance for food purchasing, to schedule food preparation, to reduce food inventories, and to effect cost savings in the range of 5%–20% over manual methods. Finally, the menu planning programs provide for both selective and nonselective menu generation. A matrix generator program provides for varying parameters on nutrients, food-item substitution, meals per day, and portion sizes. A multi-stage menu planning program provides the means for generating menu plans for several months in advance. McNabb[25] discusses the use of the CAMP system in a very large institutional complex serving more than 30,000 meals per day. Beginning in August 1968, a two-week course in dietary management and menu planning was offered at Tulane, followed by an eight-month period of food service data collection, analysis, coding, and transcription to prepare the basic CAMP data files and finally by the implementation of the system with 90-day menu plans produced in August 1969.

Since implementation in several hospitals of computer-assisted menu planning, studies have been performed to evaluate approaches and cost benefits. Cost comparisons have been conducted between the traditional menu planning approaches and the CAMP system. With the computer-assisted menu planning, nutrient levels consistently met hospital specifications; manual planning was often in excess of established criteria or below the standard requirements for calories, protein, and thiamin. Computer-assisted menu planning showed consistent cost reductions over conventional methods. Both through patient surveys and interviews with dietary staff, it was established that no significant statistical difference existed in acceptance of menu plans under either manual or computer-assisted approaches.[26]

Two companies, Trans Tech, Inc., Kansas City, and Management Optimization Systems, Inc., New Orleans, now offer commercial services to institutions providing food service to a defined population (e.g., hospitals, regional school districts, etc.). The CAMP system is available to a growing number of hospital dietary departments as this important cost center seeks improved methods for providing consistent nutritional standards in a more cost effective environment.*

4.   Outpatient Appointment Scheduling Subsystem

The hospital outpatient department as well as the general clinic provide medical services for a variety of patient needs. Balancing patient waiting

---

* A series of 13 articles is published in *Hospitals, J.A.H.A.* beginning with Vol. 43, September 1, 1969, on the subject of dietary planning and the use of computer systems.

time with physician availability has been and still is a problem in need of an improved approach. There are many human factors (both patient and provider) and resource allocation problems to consider in the outpatient scheduling subsystem. The Kaiser-Permanente Medical Care Program provides outpatient care to more than one million members who generate over 4 million doctor-office visits annually. Due to the magnitude of the appointment scheduling activities associated with this large outpatient practice, a statement of goals and objectives (Figure 5–1) was prepared as a guideline

1. *Proper matching of patient needs and physician resources*
   The selection of a personal physician is a primary step; the physician's medical judgment and knowledge of his schedule should be used to provide optimum utilization of his services.
2. *Quality and continuity of care*
   A system must support quality and continuity of care. Delivery of medical care will be further enhanced by proper routing of patients based upon appropriate referral decision rules and availability of chart, laboratory, and x-ray results.
3. *Flexibility for handling contingencies and future changes*
   An appointment system must allow for appropriate exceptions—in advance. A flexible design should be impervious to day-to-day contingencies while allowing for change and improvement as the delivery system evolves.
4. *A climate in which the patient is seen as a total human being with many needs*
   Attention to continuity of care recognizes the patient's wholeness over time. Also at any given instant he must be seen as a human needing care rather than an interesting case, an "appointment," an injured limb, or a disease.
5. *Effective liaison with appointment-related functions*
   While any system will have a defined scope, it must consider activities outside the system proper, recognizing both its dependence and effect upon those activities. Minimum drop-ins (nonappointment), no-shows, and cancellations should result.
6. *Optimum alignment of personal and organizational goals*
   A mechanized (computer-assisted) appointment system must take into account the personal career goals and day-to-day involvement of physicians and non-M.D. personnel as well as organizational requirements.
7. *Economic feasibility*
   The design of an appointment system will be evolutionary and constrained by appropriate cost/benefit criteria. The balance of patient needs with physician resources requires new and innovative methods to support future medical services.
8. *Equity of workloads*
   A new appointment system should increase the potential for achieving equity of workload among all physicians.

Figure 5–1.   Goals of the Kaiser appointment-making function.

for further study and possible definition of a computer assisted appointment system.

Several research studies have been undertaken to examine the environment surrounding the outpatient care delivery system.

Studies by Rockart, et al.,[27] have explored various methods for pre-screening patients' needs in the large multi-specialty Lahey Clinic. A patient questionnaire provides essential medical history and current symptom information; the patient answers approximately 200 questions and mails the completed form to the Lahey Clinics. The information is key-punched and entered to a computer system for special processing and compilation of two reports. The first report provides a positive patient/medical history and current symptoms printout for the physician. A second report provides a list of specialty assignment scores or rankings based on the computer analysis of the patient symptom information. Using a pre-defined series of scheduling rules which considers physician referral and chief complaint as primary factors, a patient schedule is established to assure that applicable specialists will see the patient. Rockart states that significant improvement in clinic scheduling has occurred as a result of this system approach.

In a separate study, Rockart and Hoffman[28] investigated various scheduling methods involving block appointment times vs. individual appointment times. Patient waiting time was found to be not only a function of scheduling method used, physician availability, and patient availability (late or no-shows), but was positively influenced in those clinics where patients were assigned to specific physicians. As greater recognition of the patient was given through individual appointment times with specific physicians, improvement in patient waiting time, reduction in patient no-show rate, and early arrival of patient and doctor was reported. It was concluded that an improved attitude and feeling of responsibility between patient and physician were created through a basic change in scheduling approach.

Mathematical modeling of outpatient appointment scheduling has been reported by several authors;[29-31] a common observation made in each of these studies was that a best outpatient scheduling algorithm consisted of a hybrid system using a modified block appointment scheme with interspersed individual appointments. Lane[31] examined 2000 patient visits and modeled several appointment plans to arrive at an optimal schedule for his specific practice and patient mix. The results indicated a shorter patient waiting-time average, while total patients seen and percentage of physician time spent with patients were substantially increased when compared to the prior appointment scheduling method employed.

Two computer-assisted appointment scheduling systems, developed with research grant support, are briefly discussed to indicate the current direction of automating this activity.

Computers have been applied directly in the appointment-making process at Childrens Hospital Medical Center, Boston, Massachusetts. Cronkhite[32] describes this scheduling system, which serves 54 separate clinic departments providing over 150,000 patient visits annually. Based upon their earlier work on inpatient scheduling and development of a patient location control system, Childrens Hospital designed and implemented this clinic appointment scheduling system to support more efficient processing of patients through the facility, improve continuity of care through improved scheduling and access to the same physician, and to provide a master patient record accessible from any clinic floor. On-line computer terminals support the process of booking appointments and providing information regarding patient schedules between clinics. A series of batch programs support this system by producing various work-lists including chart requests for tomorrow's appointments, a total appointment list for central reception, and appointment lists by clinic.

A detailed account of the Peter Bent Brigham Hospital automated appointment system is given by Jessiman and Erat.[33] Beginning in 1961, a paper-based (manual) appointment system was instituted to support an outpatient load of 50,000 visits annually. This system contained many features to provide for flow of information to all departments supporting patient care services. Appointment lists, chart requests, cancelled appointments, and statistics regarding no-shows and cancellations were manually prepared. In 1964, with the experience gained from this manual system and recognition of several limitations, a decision was made to automate the appointment scheduling process. Peter Bent Brigham Hospital elected to use a commercial time-sharing service bureau to provide both software and hardware support for this application. An employed systems analyst/programmer wrote the appointment system programs, which: (1) create patient identification record, (2) print patient identification record, (3) delete patient records no longer required on-line, (4) generate doctor or clinic basic schedule and delete outdated schedules, (5) search for available appointments in the schedule, (6) make appointments or cancel appointments, (7) print daily clinic schedules, and (8) print daily medical record request slips. Teletype terminals were installed and clinics gradually phased into the system beginning October 1967. Approximately 50% of all appointments are scheduled through the automated system. With over two years of system experience, a record of 98% availability of the system (with one day the maximum outage) has been maintained; a schedule of three months advance appointments is kept, and no information loss due to system failure has been experienced. The automated system offers several advantages over the manual approach, including an inquiry capability which prints a patient's appointment schedule, advance schedule of patients by doctor or clinic which can be used to evaluate physician patient load, and identification of high utilization patterns for special review. Backup procedures are employed, using appointment schedule printouts to locate available openings until the system is functioning properly; any booked appointments are then entered to update the computer appointment schedule files. The automated system requires one minute to confirm an existing appointment, two minutes to schedule an appointment, and three minutes to cancel an appointment.

Jessiman and Erat conclude with an analysis of system cost; personnel required to support the automated appointment-making process were unchanged from the previous manual approach. On-going costs are estimated to be $1.00 per kept appointment (excluding the estimated $60,000 one-time system development costs). While the automated system provides several improvements, the present costs are excessive in terms of justification for operational use; further hardware improvements and research based on such projects should change this situation.

5. Medical Records Administrative Subsystem

A significant application of computers and data processing has developed over the past ten years in the field of abstracting and reporting medical records. Two basic hospital reporting requirements are included: the recording of various routine statistics such as admission/discharges, patient days by type of service, length of stay, etc., and case abstracts for discharged patients indexed by diagnosis, operation, and physician. The information contained in these reports can be used to satisfy hospital accreditation requirements and provide information required by local or state officials, for medical audits by the professional staff of the hospital, for staff education and research programs, and, finally, for hospital management and planning.

The first computerized system for compiling hospital reports was developed in 1952 by Slee and associates from the Southwestern Michigan Hospital Council.[34] A standardized case abstract form containing basic information about the patient, coded information identifying hospital and physicians, and provisions for recording multiple diagnosis and procedures related to the patient's hospitalization was developed.

Beginning its first operation in early 1953 with a group of 13 participating Michigan hospitals, the system was so successful that, by 1955, an independent nonprofit corporation, the Commission on Professional and Hospital Activities, was formed with the support of the American College of Physicians, American College of Surgeons, the American Hospital Association, and a private foundation. The system, now known as the Professional Activity Study (PAS), has experienced steady growth from its inception; at the end of 1971, there were 1,560 hospitals participating in this shared computer service.[35] These hospitals account for over 12 million abstracts annually. During the past decade, the PAS system has processed over 60 million abstracts and thus represents the largest single resource for computer-stored medical record information in existence.

Over 70% of the PAS member hospitals also participate in a supplementary program, the Medical Audit Program (MAP). The MAP reports, prepared quarterly, utilize the same basic case abstract prepared for PAS; however, more elaborate and detailed information is reported for use by the professional staff in performing internal medical audits. This activity is discussed in more detail by Slee[36] and Williams.[37]

A separate development in the field of hospital medical record reporting was initiated by the California State Department of Public Health. Known as the CHIPS project (California Health Information for Planning Services), a series of 12 computer produced reports were designed in 1966 and implemented by three hospitals in early 1967.

As reported by Derry, et al.,[38] the project has several objectives: to provide comprehensive institutional reports for use by professional and hospital management; to compile area planning reports for better planning of health care facilities in the State; and to support a health information exchange through which participating agencies could benefit through improved information relating to health services, manpower, and community planning. In December 1967, California Health Data Corporation (CHDC) was formed as a nonprofit organization to establish a health information exchange. Supported by the California Medical Association, California Hospital Association, and the CHIPS advisory group, CHDC continued the development of medical record reporting programs which presently support over 200 California subscriber hospitals.

Both the PAS and CHDC systems charge their member hospitals between 30¢ and 40¢ per abstract for the standard series of reports produced. Additional income is derived from special research studies utilizing these information data bases.

E.   COMMERCIALLY DEVELOPED HOSPITAL COMPUTER SYSTEMS

As the information processing needs of the hospital (estimated to range anywhere from 25% to 40% of operating costs) were recognized, there followed the development of several general purpose computer systems for the hospital. These evolutionary developments are characterized by a diversity of systems approaches, which include: (1) general administrative software for use by the hospital on its computer system; (2) availability of hospital applications through communications terminals to a shared hospital service bureau; (3) dedicated hospital computer systems oriented to more comprehensive order entry and information retrieval capabilities; and (4) contractual arrangements among several hospitals to develop user-tailored or customized systems.

Several of the commercially developed hospital computer systems are briefly described. Each systems approach offers certain advantages and disadvantages; all require careful study and evaluation by the prospective hospital user whose particular requirements and needs should be defined in detail before selection of any system is anticipated.

1. MISP/SHAS

IBM has devoted major resources in their research and development efforts relating to computer systems for the hospital and medical applications. By the mid-1960's, IBM was developing the Medical Information Systems Programs (MISP) in cooperation with Monmouth Medical Center. MISP is a series of executive and control programs which perform various functions including terminal polling and line control, data management, general system control, and user application program initiation. Implemented in late 1967, MISP has been improved upon and adopted by more than 24 hospitals. Most of the application programs developed by MISP user hospitals (e.g., admitting/bed census) have been shared by others through a user-group organization.

IBM evolved their hospital applications program through a series of developments leading to the Shared Hospital Accounting System (SHAS). The SHAS system supports a supervisory control and teleprocessing executive program which provides for a shared centralized computer facility available to several hospitals through telephone communications and remote terminals. SHAS offers application programs in the areas of patient billing (both inpatient and outpatient), accounts receivable, and general ledger. A number of features are available to user hospitals to provide for customizing of SHAS applications to meet specific needs or standard practices for each shared hospital. These include patient identification procedures; report format controls; Medicare reporting options; selective printing and scheduling of reports; insurance proration; and a hospital profile feature which provides SHAS with information on hospital name and address, accounts receivable parameters, census summary data requirements, and control parameters for hospital billing procedures.

The SHAS application subsystems are oriented to hospital management. The patient billing subsystem processes patient accounts from preadmission to final billing; a number of related data files are updated and maintained throughout the patient's hospital stay, providing for charge collection, pricing, patient account inquiry, and billing (with provision for insurance proration and Medicare invoicing). A census subsystem provides various reports on preadmissions/admissions/discharges/transfers, and census summary reports by nursing station, service, and doctor. Another byproduct of the billing subsystem is the reporting of management statistics regarding hospital census, percent of occupancy and days of care by service.

The accounts receivable subsystem operates in conjunction with the patient billing application by accepting the final billing at the time of patient discharge and maintaining the accounts receivable until the account is closed. This subsystem provides for recording of payments from the patient of third party (Medicare, insurance, etc.), accounts receivable inquiry, and management of accounts (bad debt write-off, statement consolidation by family, statement cycle billing). A series of reports provide for aged trial balance, insurance accounts receivable, delinquent accounts, bad debt write-off, current account status, and several cross-indexed directories. The accounts receivable subsystem also produces entries to the third SHAS subsystem application, the general ledger.

The general ledger application provides a series of financial reports to hospital management. A daily process accepts transactions from both the patient billing and accounts receivable subsystems as well as other user-provided application programs (e.g., cash disbursements, payroll, purchasing) and posts these entries to a general ledger file. The reporting programs produce a variety of accounting and financial journals, trial balance, operating statements, balance sheet, and cost allocation summary.

SHAS was first implemented at the Loyola University Hospital and has since been adopted by more than 100 hospitals. This system combines both remote terminal communications between the hospital and the SHAS central computer and batch processing of the more voluminous reports on a scheduled basis. The user can provide for alternative choices of terminal device types including typewriter, card reader, and line printer.

2. MEDINET

MEDINET is the designation given to an autonomous section of the Information Services Business Division of the General Electric Company. After a two-year study of hospital information systems needs, MEDINET adopted a general approach termed "cycle processing," which combines on-line computer processing with off-line batch processing methods. The

MEDINET system was designed as a general purpose, shared-hospital service bureau operation with subscriber hospitals contracting for various application services. MEDINET operations began in August 1968, and the system presently services a number of hospitals from Maine to Florida.

Early emphasis was placed on application programs to serve the needs of hospital management. These include the areas of census and utilization, patient billing, personnel accounting, accounts receivable/payable, and general ledger.

MEDINET provides for four distinct modes of operation; subscriber hospitals can select from these in meeting their particular needs. In the *Communications Processing* mode, MEDINET terminals can be located throughout the hospital providing direct communication between departments. A communications computer processes and routes message traffic in addition to collecting data for subsequent applications processing.

A second mode is *Remote Entry Batch with Cycle Processing.* Using leased telephone lines and appropriate terminal devices, the subscriber hospital enters daily operating data; on a scheduled basis, MEDINET application programs process this data and produce reports which can be transmitted back to the hospital or, if not time-critical, printed at a MEDINET site for subsequent delivery to the hospital.

A third mode is *Batch Processing,* in which input data is keypunched and processed by MEDINET in application areas not requiring rapid service (e.g., medical record statistics).

Finally, a fourth mode, *Time-Sharing,* provides for sophisticated application developments using real-time terminal communication between the subscriber hospital and a series of MEDINET application programs in such areas as cash flow analysis, budget analysis, nurse/staff allocation, and cost allocation. This mode also provides the means for developing specific user application programs utilizing the MEDINET software system.

A five-phase approach is used by MEDINET to implement an application for a subscriber hospital. An orientation phase introduces the MEDINET concept and systems approach to hospital management and staff personnel concerned with the application. This is followed by a site analysis phase to review hospital procedures, suggest changes, and arrange for equipment installation. A file development phase follows, in which necessary data are collected and assembled to form the particular data base for the application being installed. A training and file conversion phase prepares the hospital and concerned personnel for implementation. Actual conversion to the MEDINET system from prior operations varies between applications, usually involving some overlap for several days or weeks. Finally, a followup phase assures the hospital management that the application has been successfully installed and is considered operational.

MEDINET has approached the total hospital information system as a collection of application modules or subsystems, with early emphasis concentrated in the areas of hospital management. Each application is designed as a functional unit which can "stand alone," allowing subscriber hospitals to choose from a variety of applications; however, program interfaces are also provided so that applications can be linked together (i.e., data can be passed through from one application to the next). Having established a "bottom up" design based upon accepted hospital applications, MEDINET expects to expand their system, as cost justification can be established, into all areas of the hospital and into medical data collection and reporting.

3. Medelco

Medelco Incorporated, a subsidiary of the Riley Corporation, designed their T*H*I*S (Total Hospital Information System®) as a dedicated hospital communications and data collection system. A special purpose central processing unit controlled by a Medelco furnished software system provides for a communications network of special card reader and teletype printer devices directly connected to the system. A unique edge-punched card is used to identify each hospital service which can be ordered through the system.

The first Medelco system was installed in September 1967; since that time, a total of 24 T*H*I*S® systems have been placed into operation by hospitals ranging in size from 112 beds to over 900 beds. Medelco, Inc. recommends that a prospective hospital perform a detailed study of hospital departments to be included in the system, including their information needs and their present operating costs. An equipment configuration is then designed for the hospital based upon their specifications. Multiple files of special edge-punched cards representing the hospital's standard operating practices and chargeable services (i.e., medication orders, laboratory requisitions, purchase orders, etc.) are prepared and verified prior to delivery of the system.

After installation of the central computer system, a complement of card readers, teletype printer devices, and appropriate punched card files are placed in the various hospital departments. A complete staff-training and system-testing program is provided to insure proper system use. Typically, a card-maker unit is used by the admitting department to prepare a patient card for each admission. The admitting clerk places the patient card and the bed assignment card in a card reader, which reads the information and transmits it to the central computer. Special credit-card-sized patient cards are available for outpatient clinic use. The computer system maintains a perpetual patient location bed census file for real-time inquiry by physician, admitting office, business office, or information desk. The system also relays the patient location information to other affected departments such as dietary and housekeeping. Each transmission of information includes the date, time, and identification of the person sending the data. A special "Results Reporter" mark-sensing input station provides a means for the hospital laboratory to transmit test results back to the nursing floors; both the laboratory order and the test result include the time of entry to the system providing useful statistics on the elapsed time from request to result.

The Medelco system is normally placed in a data output mode at midnight without affecting its communications and data collection ability. The day's orders and service charges are summarized to a "Patient Ledger" or computer generated "Daily Billing Summary." Information can be formatted and recorded on an appropriate data file for subsequent processing by the hospital's patient billing system. Upon patient discharge, the business office has a patient invoice current through midnight; by inquiry to the system, any charges accumulated since midnight are printed on the teletype and can be added to the invoice to complete the billing.

The Medelco system is oriented to data collection and rapid communication of orders throughout the hospital. The edge-punched card provides a simple means to catalog and enter the various hospital orders, services, and charges. A perpetual file of patient location and charge information is maintained; a 24-hour computer storage file maintenance run allows the system to purge itself of patient charge information on a routine scheduled basis without disturbing the bed census/patient location file. Special employee cards are available so that employees may "clock in" at their assigned work stations. Medelco provides for interfacing to other computer systems by formatting the data to an appropriate media (e.g., magnetic tape or paper tape); this then becomes the input to various application programs such as patient billing, inventory control, and hospital statistics.

4. REACH

The REACH Corporation, a subsidiary of National Data Communications, Inc., has developed one of the most comprehensive hospital information systems commercially available. REACH, an acronym for Realtime Electronic Access Communications for Hospitals, is designed as a patient-oriented system supporting both medical and administrative information storage, retrieval, and processing.

REACH utilizes a fast general purpose computer with special communications interface equipment connecting the central processor to a network of specially designed CRT (cathode ray tube) terminals. The CRT terminal is a unique feature of the REACH system; its design includes a badge reader which accepts a coded plastic card identifying the user to the system and allowing access to only that information defined by the code. The various user identification cards (e.g., nurse, physician, pharmacist, administrator, etc.) coupled with the terminal identifier code establishes authorized access to the REACH system and those system programs available to that user. A second unique feature is the use of 20 microswitch select buttons located on the left side of the CRT screen; these 20 buttons are associated with the 20 lines of information available on the CRT console.

In a typical medication ordering sequence, a physician would place his personal badge in a REACH terminal and the system would respond with a list of his patients. He would then depress the appropriate "line select button" opposite the relevant patient's name. A "paging system" displays to the physician a selection of categories which would include, for example, medication orders. By depressing that select button, the doctor continues through a series of CRT displays providing drug name, dosage, and frequency of drug administration. Printer units supply a hard copy of the order where required (for example, in pharmacy, a printed gummed label is produced for use in dispensing the medication). The example medication order would normally be entered in 15 to 20 seconds.

The REACH system maintains a complete computer patient chart reflecting all orders and services applicable to the patient during his hospitalization. Upon discharge, the patient chart is removed from the real-time system and recorded on magnetic tape for subsequent reference or use in statistical reporting. Charge information is also accumulated as patient orders are placed throughout the system, providing a running account for each patient.

An extensive software system designed by the REACH technical staff controls the total operation of the computer and terminal network. A dual processor configuration is normally employed to provide for backup of the real-time process. The second computer functions as a batch processor when not needed for backup and is used to support the various application programs producing reports for hospital staff and management. Applications software supports a "Business Office Subsystem" including hospital billing, cost accounting, payroll function, purchasing and inventory function, outpatient accounting, accounts payable/receivable, and general ledger. The "Patient Care Subsystem" contains application programs for admitting, patient transfer, service scheduling, dietary planning, laboratory test results recording and display, nurses' notes recording, physician orders, physician display function, and medical records maintenance.

The REACH Corporation began development of their system in early 1967 and installed the first test site system at the 275-bed Baptist Hospital,

Beaumont, Texas. This configuration included 40 CRT terminals (16 in nursing units, 2 in admitting, 3 in radiology, 2 in clinical laboratory, 5 in chartroom, 1 in pharmacy, 1 in doctors' lounge, and 10 in administrative offices). A second REACH system was installed in the 324-bed St. Francis Hospital, Miami Beach, Florida, in 1970. The initial configuration included 35 CRT consoles; however, after three months of REACH operation, the equipment configuration was increased both in storage capacity and by the addition of 15 CRT's. The REACH Corporation has signed contracts for three more systems, including their most recent agreement for a 625-bed hospital system.

The REACH system is a major technological development in the application of computers and communications equipment to hospital operations. Supported by an extensive software executive program and a broad range of application programs, REACH provides a fast response, CRT-based order entry system. While early experience indicates a user reluctance to discard the "paper chart" in favor of the computer patient chart, the system does provide rapid electronic access to all hospital patient information including nurses' notes, laboratory results, standing orders, etc. Hard copy printout from the system provides a uniform record of the patient's stay for permanent storage in his chart.

5. Technicon

Technicon Medical Information Systems Corporation (formerly a division of Lockheed) initiated studies of hospital information needs in 1965. After three years of study by a physician/engineering team, a joint arrangement was established with the 440-bed El Camino Hospital, Mountain View, California, to develop an extensive medical information system. An additional three years of research and development activity produced the Technicon MIS-1 system.

The MIS-1 system is based upon a central computer located in the Technicon facility with dedicated broad-band phone lines connecting this computer center to the hospital. The system uses a special CRT terminal equipped with keyboard and light-pen for selection of items displayed on the video screen; companion printers are used wherever printed output is required. The system was designed for direct physician man/machine communications. The physician enters his identification number through the keyboard, and the MIS-1 system displays his list of patients in the hospital. Using the light-pen, the physician selects a patient's name, and a new display for that patient is furnished; he may wish to receive the computer-stored patient's chart (initiated upon the patient's admission to the hospital) before placing any orders. The video display contains a Physician Master Guide, providing a list of functions or choices available to him. The physician might elect to review current orders for his patient as well as laboratory results before entering any new orders. Basically, then, the physician is interacting with the MIS-1 system by using either or both light-pen selection and keyboard entry to indicate his requests for information stored in the computer and to place any medical orders appropriate for his patient.

An extensive software system provides for the logical processes and terminal communications control required for MIS-1 to record the physician's order. The system automatically prints the new orders at the nurses' station for verification and signature. At the beginning of each work shift, the system initiates the printing of a Patient Care Plan for each hospital ward. Medications Due lists are printed for the nursing staff as both a reminder notice and a worksheet available for recording medication administration for subsequent entry by the nurse through the video terminal and for recording in the computer patient chart. MIS-1 terminals located in other hospital departments provide for both authorized data entry and inquiry of patient census, laboratory, radiology, pharmacy, dietary, and patient charge information. Each morning, a 24-Hour Summary by patient is printed, including cumulative medication, laboratory, and input/output reports. These summaries, coupled with an afternoon Interim Summary and manually prepared clinical reports (not entered in MIS-1 due to extensive narration or signatory requirements), constitute the patient's medical chart for this hospitalization.

In June 1971, Technicon announced that a five-year operational service contract had been negotiated with El Camino Hospital. A complement of 48 CRT terminals and 28 printers were placed in the hospital, and system testing began in December 1971. During 1972, the MIS-1 system was being phased into the hospital's operational functions of admitting, patient transfer, discharge, automatic charging, automatic cash posting, laboratory, radiology, EKG, EEG, dietary, inhalation therapy, physical medicine, and pharmacy, including unit dose medications. Technicon projects that their MIS-1 Regional Center system configuration should support an indefinite number of beds depending upon the number and size of central processing units utilized. The Department of Health, Education, and Welfare has awarded El Camino Hospital a study contract to produce a definitive evaluation of MIS-1. Columbus Laboratories of Battelle Memorial Institute will provide professional assistance in their extensive evaluation of the physician as a principal MIS-1 user, the effect of system costs vs. benefits in hospital operation and patient care, medical staff and hospital staff acceptance, and the potential of the system approach for supporting new trends (e.g., Health Maintenance Organizations) in health care organization and delivery.

Technicon has also developed a Hospital Business Office Services applications system, which provides a comprehensive reporting system to subscriber hospitals in the areas of patient billing, accounts payable/receivable, payroll and personnel, general ledger, and inventory control.

6. MediData

In April 1966, representatives of three Charlotte, North Carolina, hospitals (Charlotte Memorial, Presbyterian, and Mercy) met to discuss the development of a shared-computer system based upon several design criteria which included: (1) direct involvement of hospital staff personnel in system definition; (2) improvement of patient care and hospital communications through a CRT terminal-based computer system; (3) use of ward clerks for data entry to conserve professional staff time; and (4) as a byproduct of system operation, production of the necessary administrative reporting (patient billing, accounting, general ledger, medical records statistics, etc.). In November 1966, MediData, Inc. was formed by the participating hospitals as a nonprofit corporation whose purpose was to provide the systems design and specifications for the planned shared-hospital computer system. Burroughs Corporation was selected to work with MediData, Inc., to furnish computer programming, data processing equipment, communications terminals, and a data center facility for on-going computer service support to the hospitals.

The overall systems design consisted of two major segments: an on-line real-time processing system and an off-line batch processing system.[39] To facilitate development and implementation, the program was defined in five phases: (1) off-line accounting, administrative and medical records system; (2) on-line reservations, admitting and surgery scheduling; (3) on-line doctor order entry and department requisitions; (4) on-line nursing care plans, medication plans, and service department results; and (5) various departmental statistics, on-line nurses staffing, and doctor's office communications. Hospital nursing personnel and departmental coordinating committees worked directly with MediData in the early definition and design review activities to assure their participation and gain user confidence in the system as it was developed.

The MediData/Burroughs system was first installed at the 876-bed Charlotte Memorial Hospital in June 1969 and became fully operational in October 1971. The system supports 85 hospital cathode ray tube (CRT) terminals and companion teletype printers connected to the Burroughs data center on a 7-day, 24-hour service arrangement. The Presbyterian and Mercy hospitals utilize the off-line applications portions of the system.

In their presentations, Rankin[40] and Somers[41] discuss the experience in using this system at Charlotte Memorial. The doctor's handwritten orders are given to a specially trained ward clerk (data processing technician) for entry into the computer system via CRT device. After appropriate display, entry, and confirmation, a verification copy of medical orders is printed at the nursing station, checked by the nurse in charge, and signed. The computer compiles patient care and medication schedules by shift in advance of the change in shifts. The computer maintains work-to-be-done files (outstanding orders); as patient care is administered, the data processing technicians enter the completed orders, which are removed from the work-to-be-done file and placed into the computer patient record. The on-line nursing care portion of this system required a significant effort to define formally and standardize the over 200 "initiators" of nursing service (a patient experience which initiates the giving of nursing care) and their corresponding "components" of care (the procedures normally followed in providing the nursing care). A *Components of Care* manual was published as a guideline for nursing and the design of the computer nursing care phase.

MediData conducts monthly presentations and demonstrations of the hospital computer system for interested hospitals.

7. User-Hospital Associations

The formation of data processing hospital user associations, sponsored nonprofit corporations, and special contract agreements between hospitals and computer service companies is now introducing additional opportunity for further selection and flexibility to meet the hospital users' special needs, both technically and financially.

In January 1972, a new organization, Health DataNet, was formed with the sponsorship of City of Hope National Medical Center, Duarte, California, and University Computing Corporation, Dallas, Texas. Health DataNet plans to establish geographical regional centers to provide data processing services and expertise to associated member hospitals participating in this organization. Member hospitals take an active role in defining information processing needs and priorities; Health DataNet evaluates these needs and supports a multi-phased development program to furnish new applications systems. The City of Hope acts as the pilot test center to exercise and prove out each hospital application before it is offered to associated member hospitals for their use.

Health DataNet had plans for implementing a five-phase program as follows: 1972—hospital management/accounting support system; 1973—patient care services (nursing station order entry); 1974—medical applications; 1975—geographic area-wide health datanet; and 1976—nationwide (linked geographic regions) health datanet.

In another recent development, IBM has announced a new Medical Information Communications and Processing System through their Custom Contract Services Department. Under this arrangement, the fixed-price costs for development and installation of programs provided by IBM are shared by a group of six hospitals; one hospital is designated as the Development Hospital, while the remaining five are Participating Hospitals. IBM provides for liaison between all contracting hospitals to assure that each installs an appropriate equipment configuration for their hospital and receives a system which will meet the needs of that institution.

Functionally, this custom system is designed as a dedicated hospital computer system utilizing CRT terminals located throughout the hospital. As patients are admitted (or pre-admitted), a Patient Master Record is created in the system via an admitting office CRT. Nursing station CRT's and printers provide for the entry and display of patient care information; order entry/cancellation, order acknowledgment, patient summaries, notes, and observations are processed by the system. Terminal devices located in the clinical laboratory, radiology, dietary, and pharmacy support the related patient medical services. The system also connects to other hospital departments including central supply, housekeeping, business office, and medical records.

Normally, three days after discharge, the Patient Master Record is purged from the computer system to a tape file for transfer to microfilm or hard copy. The system also interfaces to either the IBM Shared Hospital Accounting System or the established accounting system in use by the hospital.

This systems concept is based upon an order entry system supported by CRT display terminals. Controlled entry and use of the system is provided by issuing user identification badges with encoded ID numbers; the user badge is inserted into the CRT device and is used both to control access to information and identify data entered through the terminal. The system uses item lists (or menu display) from which the operator selects the appropriate item or function by using a light-pen. The system also provides for establishment of standard sets of orders which a physician might define for a given patient diagnosis; this minimizes the item selection for that diagnosis by creating a hierarchy of orders as predefined by the physician. When such a predefined order is selected, the system issues appropriate orders to the various service departments involved. A Shift Change Summary report is produced prior to nursing shift changes. A schedule of patient activity is produced providing both a work guide and reminder notices for orders requiring confirmation.

The prospective hospital users of these commercially developed hospital computer systems are encouraged to evaluate their hospital information processing needs carefully and to then consider the several choices available to them.

F. STATUS OF ADMINISTRATIVE DATA PROCESSING IN THE HOSPITAL

With an increasing variety of hospital systems approaches being developed and implemented throughout the United States, some measure of the current status is appropriate.

Recent estimates of the hospital computer market[42,43] range from a present level of $160 million to a projected level as high as $1 billion by the mid- to late-1970's.[44] These optimistic forecasts are supported by two major factors: (1) the inflationary spiral of health care costs and the expectation that improved utilization of data processing technology will reduce this trend; and (2) the research and development programs in the application of computers to a broad spectrum of medical service areas. While Johnson[45] states that the labor-intensive hospital should consider machine systems in carefully selected hospital areas where potential cost/benefit studies support it, he also cautions that estimates of the potential hospital market for computers are overstated and that more judicious selection will reduce these expenditures. Another factor which may affect the future hospital computer market is the rapid growth of shared hospital systems.

In their article "Computers in Medicine," McCarn and Moriarty[46] cite a study conducted by International Data Corporation. This study indicates that in 1970 over 1,300 computers were being applied in the U.S. health industry with the majority of these installed in hospitals. A frequency distribution of the hospital computer applications shows that most of these systems are used almost exclusively for administrative support. The four highest ranking entries were: (1) hospital patient billing; (2) payroll; (3) accounting (receivables, payables); and (4) general applications (non-medical).

The remainder of the list showed a preponderance of administrative functions. The authors concluded that only 19.3% of computer applications were related to patient care and, as a result, few computer functions have at this time become a routine part of direct provision of health care.

During the next decade, however, many changes are expected; Howell[47] suggests that computers have been accepted as an integral part of hospital operations and that data processing has shifted from the controller's office to the administrator's broader responsibilities.

1. Current Problems

Several authors have identified certain mistakes and problems associated with developing a rational data processing support activity for the hospital. Hospitals are generally separate and quite unique from other business concerns. While there has been some success in developing individual administrative applications such as patient billing, payroll, inventory, and more recently the commercial development of more integrated hospital computer systems (e.g., MediData, REACH, Technicon, Medinet, Medelco, etc.), to date there has been limited success across any large number of hospitals to develop comprehensive administrative and medical applications which are complementary, sharing common resources of personnel and computer equipment and utilizing a common set of files (data base). Perhaps the most significant reason for the lack of integrated hospital information systems is the considerable difficulty in defining medical system procedures which can be programmed and supported at a cost acceptable to hospital administration.

Humpherey[43] discusses some of the current problems in hospital computer systems, including a lack of adequate planning for computer utilization, inadequate organizational (management) support, and breakdowns in human communications relating to development of computer systems. He cites a case in point—a patient billing system which was developed with insufficient systems definition and planning, resultant computer programs which were incomplete and poorly tested, a lack of parallel operation during transition from manual billing to the computer billing system, and finally, project schedules and costs which were underestimated. Humpherey suggests that longer-range planning (2 to 3 years) is necessary and should include definition and review of hospital management objectives, project identification and priority, feasibility studies, consideration of outside computer consulting, definition of schedules, and anticipated costs by project. He also emphasizes the importance of involving all concerned hospital departments in the review of proposed new programs, the need for adequate training, and the importance of parallel operations until any new system is finally in place.

Singer[48] emphasizes the need for the hospital to define its role in the community and the evaluation of proposed computer applications in terms of patient care objectives and cost-to-benefits analysis; as computer systems become more complex, they become more difficult and expensive to change. Singer concludes that hospital computer systems must be compatible with patient needs and that significant planning must be done to ensure systems which will be responsive to the hospital's operating philosophy.

Improved understanding of computer systems' development costs and the expected benefits to be realized from these systems is needed. Several authors[47,49,50] suggest that present hospital costs can be reduced by careful selection of applications with favorable cost-to-benefits ratios. Hospital computer system costs range from $1 to $7 per patient day, with administrative applications comprising between $1 and $2 per patient day.[48] Very little is known about the accuracy of cost data and the effects of computer applications in reducing direct hospital costs; it has been generally recognized that very few computer system applications have significantly reduced personnel costs. However, there is evidence to suggest that an increased volume of clerical processing with more accurate cost controls has been accomplished through data processing without concomitant increase in personnel staffing.

G.   THE FUTURE OF ADMINISTRATIVE DATA PROCESSING IN HOSPITALS

During the past decade, a multi-billion dollar computer industry has developed in the United States. A variety of general- and special-purpose computer systems are available to the hospital community. A significant barrier in applying this technology to hospital administration and operation has been the need for highly qualified data processing personnel, both technical and management. Not only is a competent staff of professional systems analysts, programmers, and computer operations personnel necessary; but more importantly, there is the need for hospital management to be intimately involved in the planning, implementation, and evaluation of data processing applications. This is not unique to the hospital industry; the rapid development of a complex technology and its application to a vast spectrum of business and industry has not been without its setbacks, high costs, and major investments of resources to overcome a constantly changing technology. It is perhaps fortuitous that the hospital community has been generally slow in accepting and usefully employing computers to their operations.

In their excellent report[51] entitled *Health Care Delivery Systems*, the Ontario Council of Health eloquently states the case as follows: "For efficiency and economy, computer technology must be embodied in a total system. . . . A conceptual model of the entire system must be examined prior to the development and implementation of any part thereof. It is ineffective to develop the system randomly, even by priority need, without considering the relationship of the areas developed to other areas and the system as a whole." They also reference Baruch,[52] who suggests that the medical information facility must serve three rather divergent user needs. "The patient-care system [would incorporate] a collection of small, fast-access systems, with great attention paid to the human engineering for each group using the system. No exceptional files, great long-term record stores, complex programming languages, or extensive processing capability seems required." Baruch continues, "For the administrator, on the other hand, the image we get is one of a large business system very similar to those now used in the more cost conscious industries." He concludes, "For the researcher, the picture that comes through is one of a massive long-term memory to provide for records of large populations, coupled with very high level programming and record configuration language in order to provide for the essential modifiability. The extensive processing capability needed is reminiscent of the scientific machines used in other disciplines, one capable of dealing with matrices of high order, long programs and complex displays." Baruch summarizes by noting the importance of providing communications between such systems with the long-range hope of evolving toward a single unified system.

A general theme is observable; it perhaps best fits the needs of the hospital community in applying the computer to administrative and operational functions. Success is more likely through the combined efforts of regional hospital associations willing to discipline their operational requirements, define standards, and analyze their present and future needs through careful study and planning. The "total hospital information system" remains an elusive and somewhat doubtful target; therefore, the definition of subsystem applications, planned in the context of a long-range evolutionary development of data processing, should produce meaningful results. The approach outlined by Gillette, et al.,[8,9] represents a good model. Shared computer systems offer sufficient advantages over the individual hospital computer approach to suggest that this be carefully evaluated. If hospitals in a community can adopt standard procedures for processing information, they can organize to develop a competent management/technical team to implement efficient and cost beneficial data processing systems to meet their collective needs.

REFERENCES

1. IBM Application Brief. *Centralized Hospital Accounting with the IBM 1401 at the Sisters of the Third Order of St. Francis*, K20-0015-0.
2. IBM Application Brief. *Rx for Hospitals*. GK 20-0393-1.

3. Geisler, Robert. "The Thomis Medical Information System." *Datamation* (1970) 133–136.

4. Rikli, A. E.; Allen, S. F.; and Alexander, S. N. "Study Suggests Value of Shared Computer." *Modern Hospital,* 106 (1966) : 100–108.

5. Hammon, Gary L., and Jacobs, Stanley E., PhD. "Shared Computer Systems— Part 1." *Hospitals, J.A.H.A.* 44 (1970) : 50–53.

6. Hammon, Gary L., and Jacobs, Stanley E., PhD. "Shared Computer Systems— Part 2." *Hospitals, J.A.H.A.* 44 (1970).

7. Huff, Walter S., Jr. "Shared Computer Time: Big Benefits for Small Hospitals." *Modern Hospital,* 113 (1969) : 88–91.

8. Gillette, Philip J.; Rathburn, Philip W.; and Wolfe, Harry B., PhD. "Hospitals Information System—Part 1." *Hospitals, J.A.H.A.* 44 (1970) 76–78.

9. Gillette, Philip J.; Rathburn, Philip W.; and Wolfe, Harry B., PhD. "Hospitals Information System—Part 2." *Hospitals J.A.H.A.* 44 (1970).

10. Owen, Jack W. "Co-op EDP." *Hospitals, J.A.H.A.,* 43 (1969) 65–68.

11. Hill, Charles H., and Laybourn, Hale. "North Dakota Blue Cross and Blue Shield Shared Computer Program." *Inquiry* 5 (1968) : 64–69.

12. *Honeywell Application Summary: Minnesota Blue Clue—Honeywell EDP Hospital Computer Sharing Program.*

13. Bride, Edward J. "Minnesota Hospitals Share DP for Business, Lab Work." *Computerworld* November 17, 1971, p. 38.

14. Anthoney, James M., Jr. "Data Processing in a Community of Hospitals." 50 (1969).

15. Smith, Robert M. "How to Automate a Hospital." *Management Services* (1966) 48–53.

16. "The Patient Location Control System." *The Childrens Hospital Medical Center,* Public Relations Department.

17. Barnett, Octo G., M.D., and Hoffman, Paul B. "Computer Technology and Patient Care: Experiences of a Hospital Research Effort." *Inquiry* 5 (1968) : 51–57.

18. Hoffman, Paul B., and Grossman, Jerome H., et al. "Automated Patient Census Operation: Design, Development, Evaluation." *Hospital Topics* 47 (1969) : 39–41.

19. Seibert, Stanley, et al. "Utilization of Computer Equipment and Techniques in Prescription Processing at Los Angeles County General Hospital." *Drug Intelligence* 1 (1967) : 342–350.

20. Maronde, Robert F., M.D., et al. "A Study of Prescribing Patterns." 9 (1971) : 383–395.

21. Balintfy, J. L. "Menu Planning by Computer." *The Communications of ACM* 7 (1964) : 255-259.

22. Balintfy, J. L., and Nabel, E. C. "Experiments with Computer-Assisted Menu Planning." *Hospitals* 40 (1966) : 88–96.

23. Balintfy, J. L., et al. *Computerized Dietary Information System.* Vols. I-III. Monography. Computer System Research: Tulane University, 1967.

24. Balintfy, J. L. "System/360 Computer-Assisted Menu Planning." *Contributed Program Library 360D-15.2-013, IBM Corporation, PID,* New York: Hawthorne, 1969.

25. McNabb, M. E. "90-Day Nonselective Menus by Computer." *Hospitals, J.A.H.A.* 45(1971):88–91.

26. Balintfy, J. L. "Computer-Assisted New Planning and Food Service Management." *Report from Center for Business and Economic Research.* School of Business Administration, University of Massachusetts, 1971.

27. Rockart, J. F., et al. "A Symptom-Scoring Technique for Scheduling Patients in a Group Practice." *Proc. IEEE* 57(1969):1926–1933.

28. Rockart, J. F., and Hoffman, P. B. "Physician and Patient Behavior Under Different Scheduling Systems in a Hospital Outpatient Department." *Medical Care* 7(1969):463–470.

29. White, M. J. B., and Pike, M. C. "Appointment Systems in Outpatient Clinics and the Effects of Patients Unpunctuality." *Medical Care* 2(1964):133.

30. Villegas, E. L. "Outpatient Appointment System Saves Time for Patients and Doctors." *Hospitals* 41(1967):52.

31. Lane, W., M.D. "The Last Word in Appointment Systems." *Medical Economics* (1967):96–101.

32. Cronkhite, Leonard W., Jr., M.D. "Computer Brings Order to Clinic Scheduling System." *Hospitals, J.A.H.A.* 43(1969):55–57.

33. Jessiman, A. G., M.D., and Erat, K. "Automated Appointment System to Facilitate Medical Care Management." *Medical Care* 8(1970): 234–246.

34. Slee, Vergil N., M.D. "Measuring Hospital Effectiveness: Patterns of Medical Practice." *The University of Michigan Medical Center Journal* 35(1969):112.

35. Kinkaid, William H. Editor, "PAS Reporter." *Commission on Professional and Hospital Activities* 10(1972).

36. Slee, Vergil N., M.D. "The Medical Audit." *Hospital Progress,* 46(1965):106–108.

37. Williams, Kenneth J., M.D. "Practical Applications of the Medical Audit." *Hospital Progress* 46(1965):109–111.

38. Derry, John R., et al. "California Health Information for Planning Service." *Inquiry* 5(1968):58–63.

39. Burroughs/MediData. "Hospital Information Systems: Executive Information."

40. Rankin, J. W. "Four Carolina Hospitals Go On-Line with Computers." *Modern Hospital* 110(1968).

41. Somers, J. B., R.N. "A Computerized Nursing Care System." *Hospitals, J.A.H.A.* 45(1971).

42. *Computer Digest.* Vol. 6, 1971.

43. Humpherey, Mitchell O. "A Reappraisal of Computer Utilization." *Hospital Progress* 51(1970):88.

44. Courtney, Sister Dorothea. "Information Processing." *Hospitals, J.A.H.A.* 45 (1971).

45. Johnson, Richard L. "Systems/Over-Automating" *Hospitals, J.A.H.A.* 44(1970).

46. McCarn, Davis B., and Moriarty, David G. "Computers in Medicine." *Hospitals, J.A.H.A.* 45(1971).

47. Howell, John P. "Data Processing." *Hospitals, J.A.H.A.* 44(1970).

48. Singer, J. Peter "Hospital Computer Systems: Myths and Realities." *Hospital Topics* 49(1971):28.

49. Blanco, Jose, Jr. "Streamlined Billing for Medicare Outpatients." *Hospitals, J.A.H.A.* 43 (1969) : 50.

50. White, Wilma L., et al. "Low Cost Laboratory Reporting System Uses Business Computers." *Hospitals, J.A.H.A.* 43 (1969) : 83.

51. Ontario Department of Health, "Health Care Delivery Systems, Role of Computers in the Health Field." Suppl. 9 (1970).

52. Baruch, Jordan J. "The Generalized Medical Information Facility." *Inquiry* 5 (1968) : 17–23.

CHAPTER SIX

Nursing Station Subsystems

by E. E. Van Brunt & M. F. Collen

A. DEFINITIONS

1. The hospital nursing station is fundamentally a communication center and is the point of focus for the bulk of those activities which are collectively termed patient management. Work measurements have shown that the major activity of physicians, nurses, and clerks at nursing stations is communication, by one mode or another.[1] Communications take place between personnel (e.g., physician-nurse), between persons and agencies (e.g., nurse-clinical laboratory), and between persons and the medical record (e.g., physician recording a diagnosis, or physician review of the dose of an administered medication). The substance of these communications consists essentially of physician orders, physician and nursing records or activity statements, and a variety of patient and ward management processes. A nursing station data subsystem consists primarily of a set of data (computer) terminals to be used by health professionals for communication to and from other hospital nursing stations, ancillary service subsystems (e.g., clinical lab), and a central patient data base.[2]

Special medical process applications, such as monitoring of physiological functions (Chapter Ten) are not covered in this chapter—we will discuss only those considerations that relate to the communication aspects of nursing station functions.

While so-called "administrative" functions are reviewed separately (see Chapter Five), it is worth noting that there are workers experienced in the field of medical data processing who, from the standpoint of implementation, consider that there is merit in *not* separating administrative from patient care computing because many functions or applications involve data that is essential to both interests, e.g., clinical laboratory, hospital census, pharmacy, etc.[3]

B. REQUIREMENTS FOR NURSING STATION DATA SYSTEMS

When viewed as a whole, the complex communication functions of the nursing station create the most difficult requirements for any of the hospital subsystems, particularly with reference to hospital system interrelationships, terminal characteristics, and software sophistication.[4] (See also Chapter One.) An extensive analysis of information needs of nursing stations has been published[5] and has served as the basis for development of one of the most advanced prototype hospital computer systems of today.

At this point, one must pause to consider the basic issues: Why are computer-supported communications and computational capabilities desirable in the nursing station environment? What general objectives seem appropriate in a given hospital or medical center?

The first question has been addressed often and from several points of view.[6-8] The costs of hospital care have been progressively rising, seemingly out of proportion to some other public services. An important part of the costs has to do with the processing (including communication) of medical and medical "administrative" data. Coupled with these measurable costs are the variable and immeasurable but potentially very high costs of communications and computational errors, including loss of data, adverse effects of medications (e.g., drug interaction), and unnecessarily prolonged hospital stays or other excessive patient exposure to the medical care process. That there are severe limitations to the effectiveness of the medical care process there is no doubt; but that there exist serious defects in the quality of medical care due to want of an improved capacity to make needed information available is equally certain. These defects are sometimes large and, while not quantifiable or suitable for anlysis by the usual accounting methods, are costly in the extreme in terms of increased morbidity and possibly mortality and prolonged and unnecessarily redundant investigative and therapeutic interventions.

The second question must be addressed to rationalize any discussion of data system requirements. The information uses of the data system, as well as the communication capabilities required to support the desired applications, must be known. Dissertations on "medical" data processing often reflect considerable knowledge about data processing but little attention to, or possibly understanding of, the medical process.[9]

All hospitals operate data systems. Most are manual. A few are reliable, acceptably efficient, accurate, and relatively cheap; but they usually exist only in small, well-controlled hospitals having alert and well-motivated personnel. Experience thus far suggests that, as institutional size (numbers of patients, personnel, procedures, etc.) increases, the data processing problems increase exponentially. Such a statement cannot properly be quantified; however, little exposure is required to realize that the data handling problems of a 115-bed hospital in an affluent suburb are much less complex than those in a 400-bed teaching hospital. The problems loom even larger as one views the nationwide trend toward larger medical centers, grouping of facilities, pooling or sharing of selected services (including fiscal data processing services), and managing ever larger numbers of patients in and out of the hospital.

A glance at the administrative and direct medical care uses of data affords some insight to requirements as far as the communications aspects of data handling are concerned.

In the hospital, a large amount of data is stored in the individual patient's medical record; the purpose and utility of this record have been variously discussed.[10-13] In general, the record constitutes a reservoir of information for subsequent use. Much of the data has transient, day-to-day utility; other data are, for all practical purposes, forever important to the patient's subsequent care and are of sufficiently high potential utility—[frequency of use] × [relative importance to future care]—that it is desirable to have access to the data at any time. Summaries of records are therefore made (hopefully containing the latter class of data) concerning nursing station care, and they constitute a first approximation of "essential" medical information.

One must not confuse frequency of data need with relative importance. Knowledge of a blood test in progress may be required at a nursing station, but only for a brief period. A test result of high immediate importance may be of no further use two weeks later. But an answer to a question denoting "allergy" to penicillin carries high potential utility for the lifetime of the patient.

Thus, it is important to determine how, and to what extent, a data-processing application relates to the local system of medical records. Is it completely extraneous, e.g., a subsystem designed to handle nursing station drug inventory? Is it additive, e.g., a machine-produced laboratory test report to be included in the paper chart? Is it substitutive in the sense that the new data system stores the data and is capable of communicating it upon demand at a later point in time?

It is obvious, then, that a medical data management and communication system must, in addition to parochial application needs, be viewed in terms of the relation of the functional aspects of the individual hospital applications to the many functions of the system of medical records, and of the utility of the processed information. It follows that the functional requirements for a nursing station data subsystem must be so considered. They should include some or all of the following capabilities:

(1) Data Entry.

(a) Patient movement or location data–check-in, transfers, discharge, check-out. [Assumes the existence of a controlled patient identification and census mechanism (usually in the admitting office)].

(b) Physicians' orders—tests, medications, general nursing orders.

(c) Diagnoses, procedures performed.

(d) Nursing data—medications administered, selected measurements such as vital signs.

(2) Data Retrieval/Communication.

(a) Provide visually displayed or printed representations of data entered for verification by those responsible for data entry. On demand, provide periodic reminders to health care personnel of medical schedules and procedures to be carried out (e.g., ambulate patient with assistance, withhold next meal). Provide local station drug/narcotics inventories, staff schedules, patient schedules for special procedures, etc.

(b) Provide, on demand, individual patient care data which facilitate physician, nurse, clerk, etc., in decision-making. (Includes current diagnoses, medications, test results, etc.; and also selected *prior* medical record information—the "essential medical data" from prior hospital and outpatient care.)

(c) Communicate patient care orders to appropriate ancillary service departments (e.g., lab test requests to the clinical laboratory, drug orders for nonward stock to the pharmacy, special diet requirements to dietary).

(d) Control user access to data entry routines and access to stored medical data, based upon individual user category, need to know, etc. All current methods of user identification are imperfect; the best thus far that is amenable to program control and user convenience is a machine-readable coded card, either punched or magnetic strip.

(3) Terminals/Software.

(a) The terminals in the nursing stations must be acceptable to a variety of health professionals for both data entry and retrieval.

(b) Electric typewriters were originally used as nursing station data entry devices, but it was quickly established that physicians and nurses would not accept such terminals. Keyboard terminals with plastic overlay keymats (e.g., IBM 1092) were tested in several hospitals for entry of medical orders and procedures by medical professionals at nursing stations, but they also were found to be slow and too inflexible. By training nurses in the use of a restricted number of coded drug names and procedures, a few such limited operating systems were implemented. This is conceptually similar to another system whereby prepunched cards representing encoded drug orders and procedures can be entered into card readers at each nursing station (see Chapter Five). Cost considerations aside, such modes of terminal entry are generally rather inflexible and limited.

(c) Visual display terminals used at nursing stations employ computer-generated displays rather than the photographic type of displays that are often used for generating automated patient histories.[14] Computer-refreshed displays generally utilize cathode ray tubes (CRT) with character generators. The alpha-numeric characters displayed are usually generated in a 5- by 7-point dot matrix or by a stroke system which forms symbols by drawing short straight lines between specified coordinates. The usual display size is 4–6 inches by 8–9 inches and may be horizontally or vertically oriented. The capacity of a display may vary from 240 to 2080 characters. Raster scan television (TV, video) type monitors are beginning to replace CRT displays due to the lower cost of TV tubes and the capabilities for transmitting pictures (see Chapter Five). Color TV monitors are being used for special functions (for example, Spectra Medical System uses color video terminals to provide red-colored error or warning messages—e.g., a drug dose has been ordered which violates preset limits).

Visual display terminals have a variety of auxiliary devices for data entry. Almost all terminals include typewriter-like keyboards for entry of natural language or "free" text. All display units use a cursor or entry marker to indicate where the next character will be displayed when entered. Supplemental "function" or "edit" keys facilitate manipulation of displays and displayed data. Light-pens direct a light beam from a hand-held pen-shaped device onto a matrix of photo cells; upon closing a switch with the finger, the coordinates of the light beam signal the data item which was selected. Surface capacitance "touch" cross wires similarly permit the user to indicate (by touching the screen with his finger) the data item he wishes (e.g., Control Data Corporation's Digiscribe). Crossed beams of light parallel to the surface of the display and directed onto photo cells can also be intercepted by the finger. Alternatively, microswitch push buttons located around the perimeter of the display can be depressed to select corresponding items from the display (see also Chapter Five). In general, the light-pen permits considerably higher density of displayed data, theoretically resulting in a reduction in the number of displays required for a given set of selections. Some terminals have associated card readers to permit user identification. (For example, Sanders Associates— see Chapter Twenty-one.)

(d) Data retrieval devices at the nurse stations generally include visual displays and associated printers to provide "hard" copy documentation for user signature and filing in manual charts. Electric on-line typewriter terminals are slow and noisy and are generally being replaced with higher speed (30–100 characters per second) impact printers provided with insulated sound muffling covers. A variety of electrostatic printers which are less noisy are available; but these require special (more expensive) paper, do not permit multiple-copy printing, and some are not permanent, fading after a relatively short time. High-speed ink jet printers are almost noiseless and provide highly readable characters, but they often require frequent servicing to maintain ink flow and produce single copies only.

(e) Whatever data terminals are used, the design and software must permit frequent, rapid, and inexpensive changes to applications programs.[15,16] In the case of visual displays, both format and content will vary with continued use and growth of the system. From a functional standpoint, many workers today feel that maximum flexibility is achieved by defining a terminal as comprised of a visual display, light-pen, keyboard, and printer. Costs are currently relatively high, but decreasing.

C. COMPUTER SYSTEM CONSIDERATIONS

The nursing station terminal displays can be generated from a large central hospital computer, from a dedicated mini-computer, or from built-in refresh units in so-called "intelligent" or "smart" terminals.

A large number of terminals linked by telephone directly to a central time-sharing computer generally increases communication line costs, slows down response times between displays, and competes with high-priority data base management functions for central computer time.

Response time between displays is often a subject of some controversy. In general, experience reveals that the need for rapid or less rapid response time varies with the type of terminal-user interaction. When entering data to the computer "medical record," or "worktables," the user is anxious to proceed as rapidly as possible; when searching for or retrieving information, he often will tolerate considerably longer wait periods. In the former case, the user has *already made his decision*: he wishes to enter an order for a laboratory test or a diagnosis statement. Once the user is familiar with the display logic employed for entering such data, he will find delays of more than one-half to one second unacceptable. In the latter case, he is anxious to retrieve a blood test result or search for information concerning the administering of a given drug dose. Here he will tolerate longer periods (several seconds between a reasonable number of displays) for three reasons: first, he needs the information; second, the alternative search methods (paper record, telephone, etc.) are much slower; third, as he scans displayed data, he will often be stimulated to modify his original requirements, to seek more data, or to abort his search.

A dedicated mini-computer with associated disk drives for the storage of the displays for nursing station terminals may minimize some of the above problems, but care must be exercised to avoid establishing a second "computer center" within the hospital with its associated increased unit maintenance and operator costs.

A new generation of "intelligent" terminals is evolving; these have their own buffer storage and control logic circuitry to regenerate displays and may well become one of the best alternatives for nursing station systems.

Hardware reliability cannot be overemphasized. It is advisable to have more than one terminal at each nursing station, both for backup purposes and to minimize queuing. It would be ideal, at least in the functional sense, to have a duplex data system with paired terminals at each nursing station so that one-half of the terminals remain active when one of the systems fails. As the scope of data processing functions increases, this will become a progressively less negotiable consideration.

D. ALTERNATIVE USER-TERMINAL APPROACHES

To avoid the high costs of physician-acceptable terminals (meaning sufficiently sophisticated software running on high performance hardware) and the difficulties of training doctors to use computer terminals, some nursing station subsystems employ clerks to operate the terminals and act as intermediary between the computer and the health professionals. The physician writes his patient care orders on a traditional order form, a nurse edits and encodes the orders, and the clerk enters the coded messages into the computer by on-line card reader, electric typewriter, or visual display-keyboard terminals (see Chapter Five).

An alternative is for the doctor (or nurse) to dictate, directly or by telephone, the patient care orders to a trained terminal operator, who enters the orders into the computer system. One approach has been to allow the physician, while telephoning, to monitor the direct entry of his orders by the terminal technician via a "slave" visual display so that he can verify the accuracy of orders as they are stored in the computer (see Chapter Two). Whoever is using the terminal and whatever his purpose, the relation of the data function to the medical and other nursing station record procedures must be considered. It is in this area that costly redundancies must be minimized, error-recovery facilitated, and user-acceptability nurtured. In general, the demands of high-quality medical care are that investigative, therapeutic, and other actions be recorded somewhere, often including supporting data. If blood transfusion is the action, its order, administration, and justification must be discernible in the record. Thus, whether in a computer file or paper chart, the important nursing station actions must be held for future reference, both short- and long-term.

Many nursing station actions and observations are important for subsequent care. Thus, the extent to which such "essential" data is available at time of follow-up, ambulatory care, or re-hospitalization determines the extent to which significant savings can be made in utilization of medical services, including repeat testing, re-hospitalization, inappropriate or delayed treatment, and physician time, and, therefore, in patient morbidity. It has been established that the current, purely manual systems of recording, storing, copying, and disseminating important medical information are largely inadequate. It follows that isolated electronic data processing applications, which rely ultimately upon the same manual communication system for their integration into the mainstream of the medical care process, make but small inroads into the body of the problem.

Thus has evolved the concept of an integrated "lifetime" medical record, containing data of different levels of clinical and administrative importance, stored in accord with strategems yet to be optimized and managed by a sophisticated data management and communication system. Some workers have arrived at advanced stages of achievement in this regard.[17] (See Section II.)

The underlying philosophy cannot be overemphasized; the separation of hospital care, ambulatory care, and related services is a convenient "administrative" artifact. Medical and medical-administrative information needs transcend such a boundary. The medical data systems which will prove beneficial in the support of medical care will have broken through this boundary and will be capable of providing integrated patient management information when needed at the nursing station, as well as in the laboratory, emergency room, or in the physician's or administrator's office.

E. VISUAL DISPLAY INTERACTIONS

Most nursing station subsystems which are at an advanced stage of development employ interactive visual display (CRT or TV) terminal devices for many input-output operations. The advantages of these devices (other factors being equal) are size, speed, silence, and relative ease of user interaction, particularly error detection and correction.

The basic methodology employed is multilevel indexing of branched files. It is felt that use of a high-level re-entrant interpreter language best facilitates the programming requirements alluded to earlier,[16] although some systems successfully employ a lower-level "assembly" language, e.g., Lockheed's Technicon. Depending upon the complexity of the individual application, the higher-level languages usually permit the inevitable programming modifications to be made more rapidly and with greater flexibility, but often at the expense of reduced overall efficiency (in terms of central processor time, numbers of disc accesses, response time, etc.).

There are several logical steps to be considered in user-terminal interactions:

1. *User identification.* The system must be capable of controlling user access to data entry programs and level of access to stored medical data as a function of the user's identification code. Such functional restrictions may be guided by local or more general rules and ethics; for example, an admissions clerk may not enter a drug order; a physician may not have access to admission files except for review, i.e., he may not change the spelling of the patient's name or other identification data. Similarly, only a psychiatrist may retrieve psychiatric data; a hospital maintenance engineer may have access to message routing functions or patient location, but not medical data, etc. These types of restrictions are usually accomplished under program control at time of "sign-on" to a terminal.

2. *System acknowledgment.* The user must be made aware that he or she has been properly recognized (the first of many error detection mechanisms) and presented with action options.

3. *User indication of primary intent.* This step of data entry, data retrieval, or message routing bypasses the stored medical record.

4. *Patient identification and selection.* Positive patient identification, a keystone to error minimization, is critical to the patient himself. This would be the first priority consideration in any data system supporting medical care. Real-time system "acknowledgment" of proper patient identification, including secondary and tertiary identifiers, is one approach to this requirement.

5. *Selection of desired data.* Different terms and symbols indicating diagnoses, signs or symptoms, medication orders, procedure names, etc., are selected. Drug names may be generic, proprietary, or chemical. The same clinical conditions may have alternative word orders, spellings, even different terms. Multiple listings and indices must be available to minimize the time required to identify and select data both for entry and retrieval. In the case of medication orders, for example, there must exist an alphabetic index to drug names and forms, followed by a detailed scheme of selection options permitting the "construction" of special drug orders. However, one

must also consider "common" order listings (by service, or individual) and pharmacodynamic (functional) and other indices to drug names.

6. *Verification*. Data selected for entry must be in accord with the user's intent. Verification may take place at several levels of interaction. At any level, detection of errors must be facilitated, in addition to easy deletion of selections where desired. Rapid re-entry to multiple sublevels of various routines must be possible in order to minimize imposing redundant data entry steps on the user. The newer visual display units and the more sophisticated software permit several approaches to these goals, such as color-coding, blinking symbols or words, use of dual intensity displays, and multilevel re-entry to programmed routines.

Most visual displays appear to have similar properties from a general viewpoint but in fact differ remarkably in both the formatting of displayed data and the logic of the underlying applications programs. Often, these are determined less by physical constraints than by the compromise reached by the medical advisors and the programmers who together are responsible for the way in which the data entry and data retrieval functions "behave." Standardization of both the terminology and content of displays has been suggested,[18] and attempts have been made to formulate guidelines for display design based upon the number of steps required to identify a particular item, branching ratios, response time, etc.[19]

A frequent format for visual displays, whether used for data entry or retrieval, consists of four sections; (1) a 1–3 line part for displaying user or patient identification, dates, times, perhaps error messages. (2) a 2–6 line part, sometimes referred to as a "status" area, for displaying items selected for verification, error messages, and instructions to the user. If information entered exceeds the capacity of the status area, the data may "roll off" onto a stored verification page which can be displayed by selecting a control function, shown when appropriate at the bottom of each display. The status area thus always contains the last several lines of information entered. (3) The bulk of the display, or "body," contains fixed and variable data items which constitute the indices and data lists from which specific items are compiled for entry. Items selected may be transferred to the status area and/or "drive" the user directly to another display. (4) A group of several lines containing selectable "control functions'" which permit such operations as: forward or back page, "drive" to a named index or data page, identify an error, switch from light-pen to keyboard mode, verify, print, etc.

To illustrate some of these considerations a sample series of data entry sequences is presented in Figure 6–1. The following goals are assumed: entry of a clinical condition (hyperkalemia due to drug intolerance) followed by entry of three physician orders (increase in frequency of blood

DR. A. SMITH   30 MAR 73
                                                      1401

>>NO MESSAGES FOR DR. A. SMITH

LOCAL CENSUS<   SEND MESSAGE

CENSUS INDEX   DONE

Figure 6–1a

                      * CENSUS   4E   1/3 ·

402A   DOE, JANE   0123456   DR. JONES
  A—21 OCT 72

402B   BROWN, BILL   7890123   DR. SMITH<
  A—19 OCT 72

403   GREEN, MARY   4567890   DR. BLACK
  A—22 OCT 72

404A

404B

405

406A

406B

LOCAL CENSUS   FRWD PAGE   SEND MESSAGE

CENSUS INDEX   WORKPAGE

GENERAL INDEX

Figure 6–1b

pressure and pulse monitoring and an intravenous solution order with a drug additive).

Figure 6–1a appears when Dr. "Smith" inserts his identification card into the terminal identification card reader; at the top of the visual display are his name, the date, and the time of his interaction with the terminal. If the system has a message routing capability, then any outstanding messages might be viewed at this time. In the control function portion of the display, he selects "Local Census" and is "driven" to a displayed listing of patients and their bed locations "local" to his terminal address (Figure 6–1b). If we assume the patient in question is the patient in Room 402B, then, upon selection of that name, the physician user is driven to Figure 6–1c, entitled "Physician Index."

The name of the patient selected appears in the verification area. The display consists of a title and two subtitles, both nonselectable (as might be indicated by the center dot brackets), and various items which indicate the user's intent—data entry or retrieval. In the event of error in selection of patient's name, the user may use one of the control functions to branch back to the local census or to a general index to all terminal locations in the hospital. Upon selection of the term "Diagnosis," he is driven to display 6–1d. He then selects "Endocrine Metabolic" and is confronted automatically with an appropriate subindex. Selection of the term "Fluid Electrolyte" drives the user to display 6–1f, where he selects "Hyperkalemia." It is to be noted that, as the user progresses from one display to another, the control functions change in order to permit re-entry at a higher level to the logical sequences in which the display may be found. The user is, in this example, automatically driven to a "modifier" display where he may expand the diagnostic statements with chronological or other modifier terms, as shown in Figure 6–1g. He indicates "New," "Severe," and "Possible Drug Reaction," the latter selection branching him to a new logical subset as shown on display 6–1h. Selection of "Intolerance" drives him to display 6–1i, where he is asked to indicate the specific drug suspected, if known, and to 6–1j and 6–1k, where he may identify the agent. As on display 6–1f, the display 6–1k also permits selection of the term "Other" which puts the user in keyboard entry mode. This feature would permit entry of data not included in the prestructured lists. Following drug name identification, the user branches back to the "Physician Index" (Figure 6–1l) and indicates his readiness to enter a "General Nursing" order. He is confronted with the general nursing order index 6–1m; he selects "Special Vital Signs" and is driven to 6–1n. Display 6–1n illustrates the use of multiple light-pen selections in order to construct one or more orders on a single data page. The light-pen sequences are indicated in the circled numbers. The user returns to "Physician Index" (display 6–1o), selects "Medi-

402B   BROWN, BILL   7890123   23 OCT 72
DR. A. SMITH   1401

* PHYSICIAN INDEX •

DIAGNOSIS<   WARD PROCEDURES

SIGNS AND SYMPTOMS   CONSULTATION REQUEST

• ORDERS •

    COMMON ORDERS
    DISCHARGE
                            DIRECTORY—PATIENT
    GENERAL NURSING   —STAFF
    MEDICATIONS   REVIEW PATIENT'S COMPUTER
    TRANSFER   MEDICAL RECORD

• TESTS •

    ECG
    ISOTOPES

    LABORATORY
    NEUROLOGICAL

    X-RAY
    OTHER (KEY)

LOCAL CENSUS   SEND MESSAGE

GENERAL INDEX   WORKPAGE

CENSUS INDEX

Figure 6–1c

402B   BROWN, BILL   7890123   23 OCT 72
DR. A. SMITH   1401

· DIAGNOSTIC INDEX ·

ALLERGY DRUG SENS   HEMATOLOGY

AUTOIMMUNE COLLAGEN   MUSCULOSKELETAL

CARDIOVASCULAR   NEUROLOGY PSYCH

CHEST BREAST   OBSTETRICAL

ENDOCRINE METABOLIC<   SKIN

ENT   NEWBORN

EYE   PEDIATRIC

GI ABDOMEN   INFECTIOUS DISEASE

GENITOURINARY   SURGICAL COMPLCTN

KIDNEY URETER

LOWER TRACT

GYNECOLOGY

SIGNS—SYMPTOMS

PHYSICIAN INDEX   WORKPAGE

Figure 6–1d

402B BROWN, BILL 7890123 23 OCT 72
DR. A. SMITH 1401

· ENDOCRINE METABOLIC ·

ENDOCRINE

ADRENAL—GONAD

PANCREAS
DIABETES

PARATHYROID—THYROID

PITUITARY

METABOLIC

FLUID ELECTROLYTE<

OTHER

DIAGNOSES

SIGNS—SYMPTOMS

PHYSICIAN INDEX WORKPAGE

Figure 6–1e

402B   BROWN, BILL

1   HYPER–KALEMIA

                        · ENDOCRINE METABOLIC 3/3 ·

· FLUID ELECTROLYTE DISORDER ·

ACIDOSIS–METABOLIC   HYPO–CALCEMIA
         –RESPIRATORY   –CHLOREMIA
                                      –KALEMIA

ALKALOSIS–METABOLIC   –NATREMIA
          –RESPIRATORY   –MAGNESEMIA

DEHYDRATION
                                WATER INTOXICATION
HYPER–CALCEMIA
      –KALEMIA<
      –NATREMIA

HYPEROSMOLAR SYNDROME

                   · OTHER ENDOCRINE METABOLIC ·

HIRSUTISM   OBESITY–CENTRIPETAL
METABOLIC BONE DISEASE   –GENERALIZED

OTHER . . [KEY]

ENDOCRINE METABOLIC

DIAGNOSES

SIGNS—SYMPTOMS   BACK PAGE   WORKPAGE

Figure 6–1f

402B   BROWN, BILL

1   HYPERKALEMIA —N SEVERE

          N—NEW DIAGNOSIS OR FINDING<
          R—RECURRENCE

          C—CONTINUING—ESSENTIALLY UNCHANGED
          I—IMPROVED

          W—WORSENING OR EXACERBATION
          O—OLD—NO LONGER PRESENT

          D—DELETE—CONDITION NO LONGER VALID
          P—PROVISIONAL

              MILD   LEFT   ANTERIOR

              MODERATE   RIGHT   POSTERIOR

              SEVERE<   BILATERAL

COMMENTS—[KEY]

                    POSSIBLE DRUG REACTION<

                         ERROR

                         WORKPAGE

                    Figure 6–1g

402B   BROWN, BILL

1   HYPERKALEMIA –N SEVERE
          POSSIBLE DRUG REACTION

               • POSSIBLE DRUG REACTION •

• TYPE OF REACTION •

DRUG INTERACTION   –SIMULTANEOUS EFFECT OF
                     TWO OR MORE DRUGS

HYPERSENSITIVITY   –ALLERGIC MANIFESTATION

IDIOSYNCRASY   –UNUSUAL RESPONSE

INTOLERANCE   –EXCESSIVE PHARMACOLOGIC
                     EFFECT FROM USUAL DOSE

OVERDOSE   –EXCESSIVE PHARMACOLOGIC EFFECT
                     FROM LARGER THAN USUAL DOSE

UNKNOWN

RETURN TO DX–SX

                              ERROR

Figure 6–1h

402B   BROWN, BILL

1   HYPERKALEMIA –N SEVERE
          POSSIBLE DRUG REACTION: INTOLERANCE

          SPECIFIC DRUG SUSPECTED<

          DRUG NOT KNOWN

                                    ERROR
                    Figure 6–1i

402B   BROWN, BILL

1   HYPERKALEMIA –N SEVERE
                POSSIBLE DRUG REACTION: INTOLERANCE
                DRUG SUSPECTED—

INDICATE FIRST TWO LETTERS OF DRUG NAME:

· ALPHABETICAL DRUG INDEX ·

A	F	K	P	U
B	G	L	Q	V
C<	H<	M	R	W
D	I	N	S	X
E	J	O	T	Y
				Z

DIAGNOSIS—SX INDEX   ERROR

Figure 6–1j

402B   BROWN, BILL

1   HYPERKALEMIA –N SEVERE
        POSSIBLE DRUG REACTION: INTOLERANCE
        DRUG SUSPECTED—CHLOROTHIAZIDE TAB

   · C—ALPHABETIC DRUG LIST PAGE 1–2 ·

      CAFERGOT   TAB
      CALADRYL   LOTION

      CALCIUM CARBONATE   TAB
      CARBENICILLIN   INJN

      CELESTONE   TAB
      CHERACOL   CAP

      CHERACOL D   SYRUP
      CHLORTRIMETON   TAB

      CHLORAL HYDRATE   CAP
      CHLORAMBUCIL   TAB

      CHLORAMPHENICOL   CAP
      CHLORAMPHENICOL   INJ

      CHLOROQUINE   TAB
      CHLOROTHIAZIDE   TAB <

      CHLORPROMAZINE   TAB
      CODEINE   TAB

    OTHER [KEY]   FRWD PAGE

    ALPHA DRUG INDEX   BACK PAGE

    DIAGNOSIS INDEX

    PHYSICIAN INDEX

Figure 6–1k

4028   BROWN, BILL   7890123   23 OCT 72
         DR. A. SMITH   1245

· PHYSICIAN INDEX ·

DIAGNOSIS   WARD PROCEDURES

SIGNS AND SYMPTOMS   CONSULTATION REQUEST

· ORDERS ·

    COMMON ORDERS
    DISCHARGE ORDERS

                          DIRECTORY–PATIENT
    <u>GENERAL NURSING</u> <   –STAFF
    MEDICATIONS
    TRANSFER   PCMR REVIEW

· TESTS ·

    ECG
    ISOTOPES

    LABORATORY

    NEUROLOGICAL

    X-RAY
    OTHER [KEY]

LOCAL CENSUS   SEND MESSAGE
CENSUS INDEX   WORKPAGE
GENERAL INDEX

Figure 6–11

402B   BROWN, BILL

1   HYPERKALEMIA –N SEVERE
         POSSIBLE DRUG REACTION: INTOLERANCE
         DRUG SUSPECTED—CHLOROTHIAZIDE TAB

         · GENERAL NURSING ORDERS ·

     VITAL SIGNS AND OBSERVATIONS—ROUTINE

         SPECIAL VITAL SIGNS <
         NEUROL SIGNS
         TEMPERATURE CONTROL
         WARD TESTS—URINE AND FECES
         WEIGHT—I/O

ACTIVITY—UP AD LIB

         ACTIVITY LIMITS
         ISOLATION
         RESTRICTIONS (VISITORS, TV, ETC.)

DIET—REGULAR FOR AGE

         SPECIAL DIETS   INFANT FORMULAS
                                TUBE FEEDINGS

· TREATMENTS ·

         ENEMAS
         RESPIRATORY (OXYGEN, IPPB, ETC.)
         SKIN CARE—COMPRESSES-DRESSINGS
         TUBES, -DRAINS, -SUCTION
         TRACTION

· MISCELLANEOUS ·

         EQUIPMENT REQUESTS
         PATIENT/PARENT INSTRUCTION
         PHYSICAL THERAPY

PHYSICIAN INDEX   ERROR

                            WORKPAGE

Figure 6–1m

402B   BROWN, BILL

POSSIBLE DRUG REACTION: INTOLERANCE
DRUG SUSPECTED—CHLOROTHIAZIDE TAB
PULSE—APICAL   Q2H
BLOOD PRESSURE   Q2H

· VITAL SIGNS · ¼

· NUMBER PANEL ·

TEMPERATURE–ORAL   1   3   <u>2</u> <   3
            –RECTAL   6
                           4   5   6

        –AXILLARY
                           7   8   9

PULSE–PERIPHAL
   1   –<u>APICAL</u> <   0

RESPIRATIONS   ML (/) DEGREES

4   <u>BLOOD PRESSURE</u> <

CVP   ROUTINE

        ABOVE
IF——BELOW——CALL MD   5 2 Q——HR <
                               Q——MIN

LEVEL OF CONSCIOUSNESS Q——HR

PUPIL SIZE/REACTIVITY Q——HR

SPECIAL INSTRUCTIONS [KEY]

7   <u>PHYSICIAN INDEX</u> <   FRWD PAGE   ERROR

                                   WORKPAGE

Figure 6–1n

402B   BROWN, BILL   7890123   23 OCT 72
         DR. A. SMITH   1245

· PHYSICIAN INDEX ·

DIAGNOSIS   WARD PROCEDURES
SIGNS AND SYMPTOMS   CONSULTATION REQUEST

· ORDERS ·

    COMMON ORDERS
    DISCHARGE ORDERS
                                   DIRECTORY–PATIENT
    GENERAL NURSING   –STAFF
    MEDICATIONS <
    TRANSFER   PCMR REVIEW

· TESTS ·

    ECG
    ISOTOPES

    LABORATORY
    NEUROLOGICAL

    X-RAY
    OTHER [KEY]

LOCAL CENSUS   SEND MESSAGE

CENSUS INDEX   WORKPAGE

GENERAL INDEX

Figure 6–1o

402B   BROWN, BILL

POSSIBLE DRUG REACTION: INTOLERANCE
DRUG SUSPECTED—CHLOROTHIAZIDE TAB
PULSE—APICAL   Q2H
BLOOD PRESSURE Q2H

INDICATE FIRST TWO LETTERS OF DRUG:

ALPHABETIC DRUG INDEX

A	F	K	P	U
B	G	L	Q	V
C	H	M	R	W
D	I	N	S	X
E	J	O	T	Y
				Z

IV FLUIDS AND DRUG ADDITIVES <

BLOOD AND BLOOD PRODUCTS

PHYSICIAN INDEX   WORKPAGE

LOCAL CENSUS

Figure 6–1p

cations," and is confronted with display 6–1p. Here he may indicate the
type of drug order he wishes to enter and selects "IV Fluids." Note that in
the "Status" part, the items selected on prior data pages have been displayed and "rolled-off" as each new selection or set of selections is added
to the bottom line. On display 6–1q, he indicates the desired "IV Solutions"; on 6–1r, he qualifies the "Volume," "Start" time, and rate of

402B   BROWN, BILL

B   POSSIBLE DRUG REACTION: INTOLERANCE
              DRUG SUSPECTED—CHLOROTHIAZIDE TAB
              PULSE—APICAL   Q2H
              BLOOD PRESSURE   Q2H

IV SOLUTIONS

NUMBER PANEL

②	①	2	3
		4	5	6

① BOTTLE NUMBER: —

		4	5	6
		7	8	9
			0	

③ 5%/DW

2½% D/W

10% D/W

20% D/W

25% D/W

50% D/W

5% D/NS

FRWD PAGE

Figure 6–1q

402B   BROWN, BILL

PULSE—APICAL   Q2H
BLOOD PRESSURE   Q2H
BOTTLE #1 5% D/W 1000 ML TO START
AT 1300 HR TO RUN FOR 6 HR

IV SIG PAGE

VOLUME   NUMBER PANEL

① 1000 ML   3   1   2 ④ 3

   500 ML   4   5 ⑧ 6

   250 ML   7   8   9

   - - - ML   ⑤ ⑥ 0

TO START   TO RUN

STAT   7 TO RUN FOR—HR <

② AT- - -HR <   - - - ML 1ST HR

ON CALL   - - - ML 2ND HR

TO FOLLOW IV BOTTLE   - - - ML 3RD HR
   NUMBER:

                                KEEP OPEN AT - - - ML HR

IV APPARATUS   ERROR

⑨ DRUG ADDITIVES   WORKPAGE

SPECIAL INSTRUCTIONS

PHYSICIAN INDEX

Figure 6–1r

402B   BROWN, BILL

PULSE—APICAL   Q2H
BLOOD PRESSURE   Q2H
BOTTLE #1 5% D/W 1000 ML TO START
AT 1300 HR TO RUN FOR 6 HR

DRUG ADDITIVES

ANTIBIOTICS
   AMPICILLIN
   KEFLIN
   METHICILLIN
   PENICILLIN

ANTIHISTAMINES
   BENADRYL

CORTISONES
   ADRENAL CORTICOTROPHIC
     HORMONE
   SOLUCORTEF

ELECTROLYTES
   KCL <
   SODIUM BICARBONATE
   SODIUM CHLORIDE

VASOPRESSORS
   LEVOPHED
   ARAMINE
   ISUPREL

VITAMINS
   FOLBESYN
   BERROCCA

OTHER

AMINOPHYLLIN
ETHRACRYNIC ACID
HEPARIN
REGULAR INSULIN
XYLOCAINE

IV SOLUTIONS   ERROR

ALPHA INDEX   WORKPAGE

PHYSICIAN INDEX

Figure 6–1s

402B   BROWN, BILL

          PULSE—APICAL   Q2H
          BLOOD PRESSURE   Q2H
          BOTTLE #1 5% D/W 1000 ML TO START
          AT 1300 HR TO RUN FOR 6 HR ADD KCL 40 MEQ

               IV DRUG ADDITIVE SIG PAGE

          AMOUNT   UNIT

     1   2   3   AMP   UNIT

     <u>4</u><   5   6   <u>MEQ</u> <   ML

     7   8   9   GM   MG

            <u>0</u><   GRAIN
          [.]   000

SPECIAL INSTRUCTIONS [KEY]

IV SOLUTIONS

ALPHA INDEX   ERROR

PHYSICIAN INDEX   <u>WORKPAGE</u> <

                    Figure 6–1t

administration and indicates the desire to add a drug to the intravenous
solution. He is driven automatically to display 6–1s, where he initiates the
"Drug Additive" statement; he completes it on display 6–1t. At this point,
he has finished his entry sequences and now wishes to review all selected
data on a single display. For this purpose, he chooses the term "Workpage," which drives him to such a review or verification display (Figure
6–1u). Upon selecting the function "Verify All," the data is entered into
the patient's computer record in appropriately designated parts for diagnoses and physician orders and is printed locally (at the nursing station
terminal printer) in two parts, shown in Figure 6–1v, for inclusion in the
patient's chart.

402B   BROWN, BILL   7890123   23 OCT 72
DR. A. SMITH   1245

· WORKPAGE ·

1. HYPERKALEMIA −N SEVERE
    POSSIBLE DRUG REACTION: INTOLERANCE
    DRUG SUSPECTED—CHLOROTHIAZIDE TAB
2. PULSE—APICAL   Q2H
3. BLOOD PRESSURE   Q2H
4. BOTTLE #1 5% D/W 1000 ML TO START AT
    1300 HR TO RUN FOR 6 HR ADD KCL 40 MEQ

VERIFY ALL <
─────────────

DELETE ALL

PHYSICIAN   INDEX

Figure 6–1u

─ ─ ─ ─ ─ ─ ─ ─ ─ ─ ─ ─ ─
402B   BROWN, BILL   7890123   23 OCT 72
                                              1245

CONDITION: HYPERKALEMIA −N SEVERE
             POSSIBLE DRUG REACTION: INTOLERANCE
             DRUG SUSPECTED—CHLOROTHIAZIDE TAB

                                      A. SMITH, M.D.

─ ─ ─ ─ ─ ─ ─ ─ ─ ─ ─ ─ ─
402B   BROWN, BILL   7890123   23 OCT 72
                                              1245

ORDERS: 1. PULSE—APICAL   Q2H
          2. BLOOD PRESSURE   Q2H
          3. BOTTLE #1 5% D/W 1000 ML TO START AT
              1300 HR TO RUN FOR 6 HR ADD KCL

                                      A. SMITH, M.D.
─ ─ ─ ─ ─ ─ ─ ─ ─ ─ ─ ─ ─
Figure 6–1v

Studies have suggested that, after several hours of training, the entry of medical data by physicians using visual displays with light-pens may become comparable in speed to the traditional manual mode and requires no new skills.[20,21] The further development of standard care plans, common orders, and "favorite" lists of medical orders for specialty departments, even for individual or small groups of physicians, may actually speed up order entry by permitting the physician to make only a few necessary modifications to a long list of standard orders to fit his individual patient's needs. He then may enter the entire list into the computer file with but a few strokes of the light-pen.

It is likely that, with sufficient file space, 95% of medical orders can be structured for visual display presentation so that only a few special or unusual orders need be entered by the keyboard mode.

Doctors' orders entered via nursing station data systems generally include instructions for general nursing care, medications, laboratory, ECG, x-ray procedures, consultations, patient transfer, and discharge.

Doctors also use the nursing stations terminals to transmit messages to one another and request consultations (see, for example, Chapter Twenty-one).

The use of visual display terminals for the entry of patient histories, physical examination data, and patient progress notes is also evolving but is not yet at a sufficiently advanced stage of development in any hospital to be of general use.

Routine data printouts are sometimes generally filed in the manual chart for physician review on his regular rounds. The legality of "signatures" and other computer-stored medical data has not yet been established.

In time, one of the more important uses of visual display terminals will be for the continuing education of physicians. For example, when entering medication orders, drug-interaction information may be displayed to him and may perhaps suggest alternate therapeutic regimens for his patient based upon medication data already stored in the specific patient's computer medical record.

In intensive care monitoring stations, nurses soon become proficient at using visual display terminals. Nurses often need to enter medical orders as agents for the physician (e.g., following a phone call from the doctor at night). Nurses enter relevant data for drugs administered, procedures completed, and notices of patient transfers and discharges. Some attempts to enter short, structured nursing notes have been tested.

Printed output for the nurses might include active patient lists by specific procedures and regularly scheduled medication reminder lists.

One of the immediate results of nursing station computer supported data systems is an improvement in nurses' "goal achievements."[22,23]

F. CONCLUSION

It is clear that the many capabilities of electronic data processing and communications technology together have the potential of greatly improving some of what may be termed the information support-communications-record-keeping functions of hospital nursing stations. Some prototype systems, developed on a limited scale, simultaneously confirm this estimation and point up many complex problems. Traditional nursing station operations are not well systematized. In many hospitals, even within the same hospital, there exists a lack of concordance on the part of medical professionals and administration as to what are the basic functions of a nursing station and what are the functions of the personnel working in that environment, not only for nursing procedures *per se* but also for nurse station data acquisition, recording, and communications functions.

A deeper understanding and systematization of direct patient care and related nurse station procedures is needed. It appears that efforts to apply modern data processing and communication techniques to this area of medical care may eventually permit the realization of these needs.

REFERENCES

1. Richart, R. H. "Evaluation of a Medical Data System." *Comp. and Biomed. Res.* 3 (1970) : 415–425.
2. Collen, M. F. "General Requirements for a Medical Information System." *Comp. and Biomed. Res.* 3 (1970) : 393–406.
3. Lamson, B. G. "Managing of Medical Records Automation." *Proceedings: Medis-International Symposium on Medical Information Systems.* Osaka, Japan, September 1972.
4. Ontario Department of Health, "Health Care Delivery System, Role of Computers in the Health Field." Suppl. 9 (1970).
5. Lockheed Missiles and Space Company. "Medical Information Systems." *Technical Report (No. LMSC-682684, May 1969): Analysis of Information Needs of Nursing Stations.*
6. Jydstrup, R. A., and Gross, M. J. "Cost of Information Handling in Hospitals." *Health Services Research* 1 (1966) : 235–271.
7. U.S. Department of Labor, *Technology and Manpower in the Health Service Industry, 1965–1975.* Manpower Research Bulletin 14 (1967).
8. Cluff, L. E. "Adverse Drug Reactions: The Need for Detection and Control." *Am. J. Epidemiology* 94 (1971) : 405–408.
9. White, W. C. et al. "An Experimental Computer Network for Medical Data Processing." *Meth. Inf. Med.* 8 (1969) : 113–120.
10. Weed, L. L. "Medical Records that Guide and Teach." *N. Engl. J. Med.* 279 (1968) : 593–600, 652–657.

11. Murnaghan, J. H., and White, K. L. "Hospital Patient Statistics—Problems and Prospects." *N. Engl. J. Med.* 284 (1971) : 822–828.

12. Goldfinger, S. E. "The Problem-Oriented Record: A Critique from a Believer." *N. Engl. J. Med.* 288 (1973) : 606–608, 629–630.

13. Brook, R. H. et al. "Effectiveness of Inpatient Follow-up Care." *N. Engl. J. Med.* 285 (1971) : 1509–1514.

14. Ball, M. J. (a) "E.D.P. Terminals: Speed, Legibility, Control." *Modern Hospital* (Aug.) 1971; and (b) "An Overview of Total Medical Information Systems." *Methods Info. in Med.* 10 (1971) : 73–82.

15. Singer, S. J. "Visual Display Terminals in a Hospital Information System." *Comp. and Biomed. Res.* 3 (1970) : 510–520.

16. Barnett, G., and Greenes, R. "High-Level Programming Languages." *Comp. and Biomed. Res.* 3 (1970) : 488–494.

17. Davis, L. S. "Prototype for Future Medical Records." *Comp. and Biomed. Res.* Res. 3 (1970) : 534–554.

18. Weed, L. L., et al. "Background Paper for Concept of National Library Displays." *The Problem-Oriented System,* Edited by J. W. Hurst and H. K. Walker. New York: Medcom Press, 1972.

19. Young, D. W. "Organization of Information into Displays." *Comp. and Biomed. Res.* 5 (1972) : 148–155.

20. Siekert, R. G.; Hwey, B.; Williams, P.; and Uber, G. T. "A Video Terminal-Light-Pen Device for Ordering Medical Tests." *Journal of the American Medical Association* 206 (1968) : 351–356.

21. Juergens, J. L., and Kieley, J. M. "Physician Entry of Cardiac Physical Findings into a Computer-Based Medical Record." *Mayo Clinic Proceedings* 44 (1969) : 361–366.

22. Beggs, S. et al. "Evaluation of a System for On-line Computer Scheduling of Patient Care Activities." *Comp. and Biomed. Res.* 4 (1971) : 634–654.

23. Simborg, D. A. et al. "Ward Information Management System—An Evaluation." *Comp. and Biomed. Res.* 5 (1972) : 484–497.

CHAPTER SEVEN

Clinical Laboratory Subsystem

by George Z. Williams & Robert L. Williams

A. EARLY EXPERIENCE

First attempts to employ computers in the clinical laboratory were imitations of the applications developed for business and industry on the assumption that laboratory operations are standardized, stable, and definable. It was soon discovered that, although the single analytical instrument is readily coupled to a computer for simple processing of raw data, the entire laboratory operation, including collection and identification of specimens, preparation, aliquoting, multiple testing, varied processing of results in differing terms, sorting and collation of data, and printing of medically meaningful reports, is a complex matter. Furthermore, the processing of all specimens cannot be identical because of dependence on each patient's state and other unpredictable variable factors.

Thus, the past 10 years of pioneering efforts saw some false starts, failures, and much redesign. From these years of accumulated experience in development of equipment, programs, and computer-compatible laboratory work flow methods, several guiding principles for computerizing a clinical laboratory have emerged:

(1) Laboratory tasks should be carefully divided between humans and computers to take advantage of their respective capabilities.

(2) The computer programs should include self-checking features.

(3) Utilizing computers for repetitive data handling where speed and accuracy are important yields the most benefits.

(4) High development costs can be avoided by fitting the laboratory to a predesigned system.

One of the first limitations to become obvious was the inherent rigidity of digital computers and their inability to perform certain tasks done easily and quickly by human workers. Computers respond mechanically to a rigid set of internally stored instructions and are capable of making choices of action only between situations which can be predicted and predefined by the programmer. Confronted with a new situation which does not exactly match one of these predefined events, a computer responds incorrectly or not at all, rendering it useless; or if it does act in error, it will do so at lightning speed before a human can intervene. These drawbacks hampered early attempts to utilize computers in real-time processing of laboratory operations, but now the more experienced programmers provide built-in safeguards in the programs. Such safeguards cause the computer repeatedly to check the validity of its processing steps and to halt and await a human "go-ahead" concerning any action which is not defined in the program. For instance, most current systems will not accept out-of-limits test result data unless authorized to do so after alerting the human operator that the data is unacceptable by program rules. A similar "alarm flag" can be included to warn that the sequence of incremental standards is out of proper order in the sample tray.

The capacity of humans to respond correctly to a variety of new or unpredicted situations is still far beyond the most cleverly programmed computer. On the other hand, humans are notoriously slow and error prone in performing repetitive routine tasks.

Therefore, the most successful early laboratory systems utilized off-line batch processing of data from a few standardized analytical instruments and merely captured, stored, retrieved, and printed test results identified by order of sequence.[1] Several attempts to develop large systems encompassing the entire laboratory operation failed. Two or three other attempts succeeded by developing the system slowly one step at a time. Current interest has been spearheaded by a more hardheaded attitude. Experience has proven there are real benefits in utilizing the power of computing equipment primarily in the areas where it excels—repetitive tasks requiring speed and accuracy.

Early fears that computers might replace laboratory technologists or that the laboratory director's position and prerogatives would be somewhat usurped proved entirely unfounded. The computer is being accepted, instead, as another laboratory machine to lessen drudgery and improve efficiency. In cases where these two benefits were realized, the laboratory staff productivity was increased significantly.

In common with new developments of any sort, the initial cost of laboratory computer equipment and programs has been very high. Until recently, laboratory computers have been difficult to justify on the basis of cost effectiveness alone, even in the largest laboratories.[2,3] Equipment costs are now decreasing as more systems are being marketed and the impact of electronic miniaturization is more fully realized.[4]

The pioneering developments have stimulated industry to produce systems which include laboratory applications programs. These predesigned and packaged systems are intended to relieve the laboratory director of employing additional staff for programming and operating the computer system. By contrast, the necessity either to self-generate a system or hire a medically ignorant manufacturer to invent a system at great expense characterized the pioneering era of laboratory computer systems during the 1960's. Pioneering will continue, but for those who do not mind "fitting" their laboratory to one of the fixed design systems now available, the extra high costs of new development can be avoided.

B. FUTURE POTENTIAL

Past experience has proven the computer to be a valuable laboratory tool. Although currently available systems are largely limited to test data collection, retrieval, and report printing by small machines of fixed design and limited application, development of modular hardware and software has started. Soon these building blocks can be put together at reasonable cost in different configurations to fit the specific requirements of different laboratories. Trends now indicate improvements in the area of higher-level computer languages designed ultimately to relieve the laboratory staff of dependence on programmers to modify or update laboratory computer programs. These languages or "specialty compilers" will allow laboratory staffs to make certain changes in the computer programs after only a few hours of training.

The second phase of computer application will vastly improve laboratory cost-effectiveness and information content. Improved operating efficiency and high-speed reporting can save hospitalization days. By intelligent design of programs, correlations of only the pertinent physiologically related tests will reduce the number of different tests needed; and computer conversion of complex multiple data into rationalized medical information with decision guides should permit physicians to make more accurate diagnoses and initiate more effective treatment. The future will witness development of the computer as the most powerful single tool in medicine and preventive health care.

C. LABORATORY ENVIRONMENT AND CONSTRAINTS

One of the earlier lessons of laboratory computerization led to the current practice of first carefully defining the specific goals and functions of any particular laboratory before selecting the computing equipment. By this means, one can hope to avoid "bad fit" or expensive "white elephant" experiences, the point being that, before a computer system can be effectively put to work, one must know exactly how to define its tasks and which tasks already being done manually should be computerized.

1. Service Demands on the Laboratory

Depending on the size of laboratory workload, organization, medical requirements, and administrative requirements, the most suitable processing system may vary from a minimal desk-top calculator and coupled typewriter to a large computer with sophisticated programs, on-line control of automated assay instruments, and multiple communications terminals on each hospital ward. Although systems are available which cover this wide range, the largest number of laboratories will require medium systems utilizing one or more minicomputers. Therefore, emphasis will be given to the utility of these equipments.

To be economical and productive and to avoid operating bottlenecks in utilizing a computer processing system to full advantage, the work flow and organization of preparative and analytical procedures must be suitably designed.

In planning automation, the first step is a detailed review and definition of all demands on the laboratory for analytical services. These include:

Volume of specimen load, number of specimens, types of tests, number of tests per specimen;

Identification of the "high-volume" tests—those for which automation would save time and cost;

Requirement for immediacy—or short turn-around time from test requests to delivered report;

Proportion of emergency work, *real* emergencies;

Requirement for storage and retrieval of test results longer than one day, short-term storage during patient's hospital stay, long-term storage for future reference;

Level and complexity of quality control procedures;

Current desirability of future expansion to include medical use reporting such as periodic cumulative summary reports, flagging of abnormal or changing results, correlations of test groups, calculation of clearances, and on-demand interim query for partial test results during day;

Inclusion of blood bank inventories and transfusion records;

Periodic statistical reports of workload by categories of specimens and tests;

Billing system procedures.

For each laboratory there will be other specific demands due to particular desires of physicians or administration. Some examples are: special correlations, retrieval of data for clinical research, comparison of current results with patient's previous results, etc.

2.   Laboratory Organization and Work Flow

The sequence of operations, the manner of performing each task, work habits of the technical staff, and the interdependence of these operations should be studied in detail and preferably charted for repeated reference in relation to planning and implementing computerization. These daily operations include:

Specimen collection and delivery procedure, accumulation in batches or continuous flow, time of peak load, control of collection;

Test request and sample accessioning procedure, identification, date requested, collection lists with sample amounts and labels, batch accessioning or continuous all day, numbering system cycle—one day, two weeks or longer, *serial* samples (glucose tolerance) ;

Sample preparation steps and aliquot distribution, centrifuging, serum or plasma, identification of aliquots;

Functional organization of laboratory test stations, test groups by technique, "sharing" of samples, automated instruments (12/60, DSA, Model S, etc.), manual methods and inter-relation of analytical procedures—routine tests, special tests, automated test groups;

Procedures for recording results, calculations, report preparation and format;

Result validation—quality assurance;

Report delivery.

3.   Quality Control Requirements

Although the maximum achievable quality assurance of every test is desirable, some lesser degree is practical or necessary depending on local circumstances. In any case, two types of control are necessary: continuous control of assay procedures with immediate indication of errors, equipment failures or results of control materials outside acceptable limits; and indication of daily, weekly, and monthly drifts.

Automated periodic calibration of instruments and validation of methods are advisable, but the cost and feasibility must be examined.

4.   Use of Laboratory Data

The primary and traditional service of the clinical laboratory is to provide acceptable test results. Demands are growing, however, for expanding information content and medical utility of laboratory reports.[5] Medical use is facilitated by daily or weekly cumulative summary reports. Asterisks or other pointers can alert the physician to abnormal results or medically significant changes compared to previous results. Correlations in the results of related tests such as electrolyte balance, enzyme groups, etc. may be noted. These are functions ideally suited to computer processing, but unless programs are already available with a contemplated system to suit specific local needs or preferences, development and writing of such programs becomes expensive. The hardware necessary to implement such processing is more complex and costly than the simpler, limited systems. Therefore, these needs must be carefully examined and evaluated for priority planning.

Most laboratories must indulge in accounting practices to maintain a billing function or provide billing data to the hospital or clinic business office. These requirements must be reviewed to determine the specific types of information and timing needed. Inventory of equipment and supplies, purchasing projections, and work load statistics for budgetary purposes can be valuable contributions of the more sophisticated computer systems. This potential should be evaluated for possible efficiency and economy of operation. In some hospitals, the improved efficiency of these functions can help to cost justify the computer system in the laboratory.

5.   Relation to Other Hospital Functions

Depending on the size of the hospital and the need for computer processing of other functions such as bookkeeping, admissions, bed census data, and inventories, the sharing of a central computer may be thought desirable. Unless particularly favorable circumstances exist, the laboratory cannot efficiently share a central hospital computer except for long-term storage and statistical reports. The type of computer most suited to business systems and related functions is not designed for on-line, process control of analytical functions. Experience in such systems shows that billing operations usually take priority over laboratory operations, frequently interfering with completion of laboratory work. Whenever work load justifies the advantages and economy of computer processing, the *computer should be considered a laboratory instrument.* The recent advent of mini-computers programmed for laboratory processing makes this economically feasible.

6.   Process Plan

The foregoing analysis of laboratory organization and operating procedures must be translated into a functional plan of processing with specific identification of those steps best accomplished by a computer. Detailed flow diagrams serve this purpose exceptionally well. A flow diagram of "function boxes" (specimen accession booth, manual test station, data input console, automated assay instrument, computer, etc.) and connecting lines with arrows indicating direction of work flow will visually clarify the detailed operating steps and facilitate identification of those steps best done by computer.[2]

It is usually most convenient to flow-diagram blood chemical analyses, urinalysis, hematology procedures, and emergency and special purpose laboratories separately. Large complex laboratory systems may require flow charts for each division and a coupling diagram to show interrelations. The system should be planned so that breakdown of any part can be immediately and effectively substituted by other equipment and/or manual performance. The ideal but infrequently feasible method is a completely duplicate stand-by system. Between this and stark manual backup are many options. One of the great advantages of a system employing several small, low-cost computers is the feasibility of one backing the other in emergency breakdown.

The charted and listed specifics should include at least the following detailed steps:

Input of basic new patient data into the system (admissions);
Test requesting procedure;
Charge items to business office;
Specimen collection (preparation of specimen collection lists and
    labels);
Specimen accessioning in laboratory and identification to the computer;
Generation of work sheets and loading lists;

Specimen aliquoting and sample distribution to analytical stations (automated on-line and manual);

Quality control reference materials and identity;

Monitoring of operation of each on-line assay instrument and error detection;

Acquisition of raw data by computer from on-line instruments;

Input of manual test data to computer;

Computer processing steps for reduction of raw data to results in terms of medically useful units;

Generation of reports:

Desired types of reports of patients' test results—format of each;

Cumulative reports—chronologic for several weeks for each patient, results for all patients by test category;

Statistical reports; workload reports;

Handling of test requests, data, and reporting of tests requiring several days;

"Housekeeping" procedures (transfer of data to long-term files, updating or rearranging files, preparing core programs and disk for next day, etc.).

Identification of the specific processing needs and functions of the laboratory is very important if the most suitable system is to be selected. This step is imperative as a basis for writing a well-defined invitation to bid or a purchase order to the suppliers of commercially available systems.

The specification should clearly depict each requirement in functional terms and label connecting operations (accessioning, sample identification, centrifuging samples, raw data transfer to computer, generation of work lists, manual operations, printing of reports, etc.). Such a chart should be made for each operating area of the laboratory: specimen receiving, accessioning and distribution, chemistry, hematology, microbiology, urinalysis laboratories, and blood bank.

7. Staff Acceptance

Although computers are commonplace and affect our lives in many ways, there remains much resistance by both physicians and technical staff to interference in their "proven" work habits by computers. Even with initial enthusiasm, the debugging period and problems of changing procedures and delays occasioned by introduction of computer processing are discouraging and sometimes are the primary factors in failure of a laboratory system to operate satisfactorily. Therefore, acceptability to physicians and technicians of changed reports, test requesting procedures, and necessary changes in their work habits must be anticipated and dealt with.

D. LABORATORY COMPUTERIZATION

1. Philosophy

The excellence of modern electronic computers in speed and precision is well beyond the best human ability. Even the smaller machines are now capable of feats such as correctly adding 1 million multiple-digit numbers per second. It is not too surprising, then, that properly programmed computers are capable of high performance when it comes to well-defined and highly repetitive data handling. Regarding this type of computer utility in the laboratory, Krieg et al.[7] present a survey estimating the equivalent human labor costs of 10 laboratory data handling tasks which can be performed by computers.

Converted to percentages, the table reveals 80% of the labor saving value to be in preparation and maintenance of duplicate report files in alphabetic order (instead of hand transcription of results), preparation of interim ward reports, preparation of cumulative reports and listing of patient tests for billing purposes, another 12% are in "bad data" messages to technicians, collection schedules, and work sheets; and the remaining 8% are in daily reports of incomplete results, daily reports of abnormal results, display of frequency distribution on test results, and printing quality control results.

At 1970 labor rates, the yearly range for manual performance of all 10 tasks in a medium to large laboratory was estimated at $50,000 to $80,000.

There is no longer any question that properly applied computer technology can perform most of the above data handling tasks more speedily and accurately, but there is still a question as to whether laboratory computers can be more economical than manual labor.

Although the less tangible benefits of laboratory computerization are difficult to assess, laboratory directors most experienced in the use of data processing systems agree on the primary benefits of a properly implemented computer system:

(1) Improvement in turn-around time from test request to reported result.

(2) Efficient storage and retrieval of vast quantities of data useful to research correlation and statistical studies.

(3) Improved "visibility," accuracy, and timeliness of data which allows the laboratory director and staff to improve their advisory service to the medical community.

(4) Improved quality control by the judicious application of the computer capability for rapid and accurate mathematic manipulations.[8]

It is valid to consider the computer as a versatile laboratory instrument and to measure its contribution to overall laboratory productivity and accuracy as a means of judging its utility.

2.   Patient and Specimen Identification

Nothing is more crucial to the reliability of laboratory information than precise matching of patient specimen identity to test results. All manual methods are vulnerable to multiple errors due to frequent specimen handling by different individuals, the necessity to relabel various specimen containers manually, match sample tray sequence numbers to patient numbers, transcribe identification data and results from one document to another, etc.

Although no foolproof manual or automatic method has been devised to track specimen identity, it is worthwhile to examine the requirements and compare some practical attempts.

In the ideal situation, some unique characteristic of a patient should be an inseparable part of his specimen, recognizable by both humans and machines. Chromosomal patterns, retinal images, voice prints, fingerprints, and such may be uniquely characteristic of individuals but are impractical to retain with the specimen or be read by apparatus. No other distinguishable attribute of individuality has yet been isolated which meets the requirements of practicality. Therefore, efforts have centered on identification items which can be artificially added to the specimens or the specimen containers. A number of intriguing ideas have been suggested, ranging from the addition of chemically inert compounds or radioactive isotopes to differing levels of electromagnetic resonance of specific additives. So far, the only practical success has been with numbering procedures akin to the customary practice of manually scribbling a name and hospital number on a piece of tape attached to the specimen container. Number coding systems of this type have been designed at various levels of sophistication.

In the Clinical Pathology Department, National Institutes of Health, laboratory computerization was initiated in 1964.[1] Although several alternative identification mechanisms were tested for improved efficiency and reliability, the original specimen identity system proved preferable and has remained essentially unchanged. Mark-sense cards are used for test requesting. Each new patient's name and hospital number are preprinted and code-punched on 25 mark-sense test request cards at the time of admission. The cards are placed in the patient medical record jackets at the nursing stations so that physicians may mark the tests desired on the cards. The cards then accompany the collected specimens to the laboratory. In order to reduce errors as much as possible and to provide automatic positive identification of specimens, an accessioning station is utilized to provide the computer with a list of specimen identities matched with accession numbers and specimen rack code numbers. The computer refers to this list as it reads each code number off of racks holding specimens during automated testing.

The photograph of Figure 7-1 depicts a plastic specimen rack moulded to a semicircular shape. The pie shape allows a train of such racks to fit around a turntable. Each of four positions on each rack is marked by a human and machine readable number. Vertical columns of holes code the

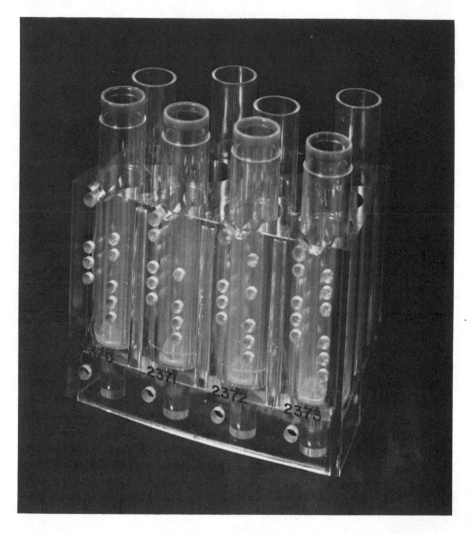

Figure 7–1. Specimen rack.

position numbers into computer readable binary format. These racks are also made of stainless steel sheet metal. Automatic specimen identification proceeds as follows: At the accessioning station, a turntable carries empty specimen racks under an insertion guide. Specimen tubes are inserted one at a time through the tube guide into the next empty place in a rack which has been automatically positioned directly under the guide. The accessioner generates a separate incremental accession number as each specimen is inserted. The rack position carrying the specimen is assigned an accession number corresponding to that particular position code, and at the same time the patient identification and test-request information on the accompanying card are read by an attached mark-sense card reader.

The computer receives all necessary information to identify specimens automatically during analysis as long as they remain in their respective rack positions. The conventional sample trays on analytical machines are replaced with a large turntable to accommodate as many as 30 racks. The turntable is equipped with a rack code reader and sample aspirating probe. When the aspirator probe dips into a specimen, the rack number code is read automatically into the computer. The computer refers to its list of matching accession numbers and patient names to identify the particular specimen being sampled. Accession numbers are used because they are time-oriented and identify the specimen even though it is often divided into a number of aliquots in different racks for different tests. Racks are used over again and the permanent rack code numbers would not reliably serve this purpose. The order in which racks are placed on the turntable is immaterial. Any rack not being sampled at the moment may be moved to a different position, and a rack containing stats may be put in its place. Although this system remains a prototype, no other positive identification device has yet equalled its operating efficiency and reliability. The high cost of production has prevented commercial marketing of this proven method.

Several other means of mechanical specimen identification have been developed and marketed with marginal user acceptance.

One technique is based on the use of plastic tabs attached by split collars to large specimen tubes. The tabs are coded with rows of embossed points at the time of specimen collection. A unique code identifying the patient is mechanically transferred from his wrist band to a blank specimen tab by the use of a portable hand press. There is room on the tabs to write the patient's name so that the tabs may be both human and machine readable. As long as the tabs are not removed from specimen containers, the specimens are positively identified. Code readers may be placed at assay stations; and for the Autoanalyzer, a turntable sampler with attached tab reader is available.

The majority of laboratory computer systems presently in operation do not use automatic specimen and patient identification. Some method of positive identification must become better proven before there will be wide acceptance. Where no automatic tracking is available, it becomes necessary to record sample tray sequence numbers manually and to enter them with matching patient identifiers into the computer manually via keyboards or card readers. It follows that there are more opportunities for error when automatic identification is not utilized. Errors can be reduced somewhat by programming the computer system to print adhesive-backed specimen labels with patient names and identification numbers which match specimen collection lists.

3. Signal Processing

Laboratory instruments and input keyboards transmit two types of electrical signals to the computer. Digital signals consisting of discrete voltage levels usually can be captured and stored as is. Analog signals consisting of continuously varying voltages require conversion to digital representation before storage and final processing.

The two aspects of analog signal processing are digital curve representation and curve analysis. Curve representation consists of translating a continuously varying electrical quantity into a sequence of discrete numbers which mathematically represent the original curve. Taking the Autoanalyzer chart as an example and dividing a portion of the baseline into a series of equidistant vertical measurements to the curve would result in a table of numbers representing the height of each vertical above the baseline (Figure 7-2).

The analog signal is produced by a potentiometer attached to the pendrive of a chart recorder. The electrical power ratio at the terminals of the potentiometer will follow the excursions of the chart pen, creating an electrical analog of the chart curve. The electronic process equivalent to measuring curve-height verticals manually is to time-slice the analog signal and convert the different electrical power levels at the time-slices into digital units.

Conversion of these discrete electrical energy levels to digital numbers is accomplished by an electronic analog-to-digital converter. The basic principle of this device involves the energizing of a special circuit by the discrete signal level presented to it at each time-slice. A high-speed counter is automatically reset at the beginning of every time slice and runs until the energy in the circuit is depleted. The greater the curve height at any particular time slice, the greater the energy represented and the higher the related count. This count is stored in computer memory as a measure of

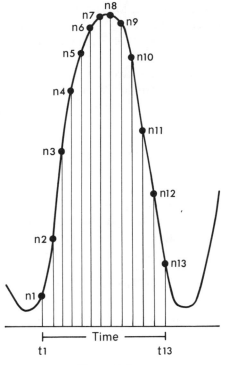

Figure 7-2

curve height above baseline at a particular point in time. A repetition of this process yields the desired table of curve-height numbers.

Resolution (how finely the curve is represented) is a function of conversion repetition frequency. Put another way, resolution is dependent on the number of times the curve is "sampled" (sliced) per unit of time.

Accuracy (how closely the numbers represent the actual vertical heights) is a function of laboratory instrument accuracy, electronic equipment accuracy, and the number of digits in the analog-to-digital conversion. Since each value of the final number table is the result of an electromechanical and electronic reaction chain the overall accuracy is cumulative and can be no better than the least accurate link in the chain.

Since Autoanalyzer curves change relatively slowly with time and because of the accuracy limitations inherent to the laboratory chemical and instrument processes, a curve sampling rate of 10–500 times per second and an analog-to-digital conversion precision to .1% is generally considered quite adequate. Fortunately, these magnitudes in no way tax the electronic state of the art. Given that the electronic parts of the chain are operating properly, unacceptable low accuracy is usually due to extrinsic factors such as electrical noise.

Electrical noise or false signal levels imposed by the environment can cause gross inaccuracy. The 60-cycle power lines running throughout all modern facilities radiate enough electromagnetic influence to be picked up by inadequately protected instrument signal wires or connections. Effective safeguards include either passive or active electrical components for filtering out 60-cycle noise.

Repeatability of assay results is affected by environmental changes such as temperature, chemical process variables, mechanical linkage wear, aging of instrument components, variance in quantities of diluent or reagent ("pipetting errors"), and human errors. Frequent calibration of instrumentation and the inclusion of standards spaced among specimens provide references for detection of system drift. Appropriate computer programs can calculate drift rates and adjust readings to compensate for drift deviations.

Since analog-to-digital converters and digital signal conditioners are normally an integral part of computer systems supplied to laboratories, the necessary details of impedance matching, choice of analog noise filtering methods, use of isolation amplifiers or signal conditioning circuits and amplifiers, proper ground reference, compensation for thermo-electric effects, etc. should be the responsibility of the vendor's engineers. It is well, however, to be sure these engineers are thoroughly cognizant of the electrical specifications and output signal characteristics of every laboratory instrument which is intended to be directly connected into the system. This is especially important for instruments with electrical outputs not within the ranges considered standard for the supplier's equipment. It is also essential that the systems engineers and programmers have correct information regarding the timing and control signal specifications of the laboratory instrumentation.

Single or multiple channel Autoanalyzers, chromatographs, flame photometers, and atomic absorption photometers are the instruments with analog outputs most commonly connected directly for computer processing. Analog signals from most laboratory instruments are essentially similar, and their processing techniques are applicable to any continuously variable electrical signal which is smoothly variable and not pulsed. Other assay instruments provide digital or fixed level outputs. Pulsed, "square wave," and binary-coded signals are handled by the regular digital channels of the computer interfacing circuitry.

Unwanted electrical noise mentioned so far has been primarily of the cyclic type (alternating continuously between the same maximum and minimum power levels at some fixed frequency or resonant harmonic thereof). This type of noise is susceptible to electronic filtering by the nature of its periodicity. Another kind of electrical noise consists of random spikes or false peaks in a slowly varying analog signal. Such random and abrupt deviations, however, are not so easily dispatched by analog filtering without the danger of distorting the underlying signal itself.

Digital computers are fast enough to perform digital filtering to sift out false peaks in real-time (while the curve is being generated and analyzed). Mathematical techniques are available to detect values of curve verticals which change too abruptly. Once these values are detected, they can be tested and rejected if they fall outside predetermined limits for rate-of-change. This technique is sometimes referred to as "low-pass digital filtering" because it acts as if only low-frequency components of the signal are allowed to pass through to acceptance. When the foregoing signal conditioning (curve smoothing) has been accomplished, the true analog output signal of a laboratory instrument will have been "reproduced" in tabular form to the closest practical approximation. Curve analysis may then proceed at high speed within the computer entirely by the use of mathematical program routines. For curve analysis, the two main ingredients are peak recognition and base-line drift compensation.

If electronic and digital filtering has already smoothed the curve, a true peak is then simply the maximum curve height value in any one sampling interval. To arrive at appropriate timing for sample intervals, the computer program examines the stored tabular values for curve heights in sequence. Timing between successive "waves" will then serve to index sample intervals. (Alternately the mathematical differentiation of values to provide slopes may be used to detect peaks.) Standards having been identified to the computer by the technologist for any particular analysis, the computer knows what peaks correspond to sets of standards at the beginning and end of the run, respectively.

Theoretically (all other things being approximately equal), the values of standards at the end of a run should be the same as those at the beginning of the run. If they are not, the factor by which the two sets differ is assumed to be caused by a steady drift. A correction may then be calculated by the computer and applied to each sample peak value as a compensation for drift.

The computer stores a revised table of peak values which it converts into the milligrams percent or other unit language appropriate to the test. Various mathematical expressions for computation of final results related to calibration standards are available as processing algorithms for the computer.

4.   Data Conversion and Reporting

a.   Data entry.   Before detailing the test reporting procedures, it is pertinent to consider raw data entry modes and devices. Ideally, manual input errors can be best avoided when data is entered only once (without human retranscription) and preferably by the originator of that data, the laboratory technologist.

In many laboratories, the technologist records test results in a workbook. The same information is then transcribed into a master log book and also onto a report slip. The report slips are collected and either keypunched on cards for computer entry or typed into the computer system via a keyboard. This procedure involves a maximum of manual transcription. Minimal transcription may be achieved by full automation of patient and specimen identification and by using laboratory instruments directly connected to the computer. Since both identification and test results are transmitted directly over wires into the computer, no manual transcription is necessary.

Most available systems compromise between these two alternatives with a mixture of manual tests and automated assays and with provision for the entry of manual test results and appropriate specimen identification. Depending on the requirements of the particular laboratory and the style of computer system, nonautomatic result entry may take one or more of the following forms:

(1) Results are written on work sheets and later transcribed to punched cards or entered via keyboard;

(2) Results are written on the same work sheets produced by the computer and entered later by keyboard;

(3) Results are marked directly on preprinted mark-sense cards and read into the computer via a card reader;

(4) Results are entered directly by the technologist by special keys or switches on special purpose laboratory consoles or via a full alphabetic keyboard (Consoles have indicator displays or typewriter print-outs for verification of entered data.) ;

(5) Results are entered directly by the technologists via one or more teletypewriters.

b.   Special-purpose consoles.   Some of the consoles for laboratory use do not have a full alphabetic keyboard. Their keys are labeled to suit the functions of a particular test or set of tests. These consoles can handle only one numeric result at a time. Consoles with more elaborate key layouts may be used to designate a limited vocabulary of descriptive words pertinent to the test result (differential leukocyte descriptive phrases, stylized bone marrow descriptive sentences, etc.).

In surgical pathology or bacteriology where narrative phrases are necessary to record results, there are three alternatives. One is the traditional handwritten or dictated narrative which must later be keyed into the computer via a full alphabet keyboard; a second is to select by mark-sense or special keyboard the codes or names for sets of standard phrases to be combined by the computer and printed in full on the report; a third is to have the full report typed by an assistant directly into the computer while performing the examination.

With a few exceptions, the laboratory consoles that are specialized by function differ only in the number and function names of the keys. The general physical size and shape remain the same for any one manufacturer. The method of entry verification also remains unchanged within any particular system. Verification is either by means of a typewriter-like printing device, a CRT screen, or a series of illuminated numerical digit displays.

One exception is a small analyzer signal box with a few buttons and numerical switches for communicating START, CONTINUE, PAUSE, and STOP instructions to the computer. The manufacturer suggests that "time-consuming trips to the computer or a central teletype are eliminated" by placing this box adjacent to each instrument which is on-line to the computer.

Some manufacturers offer more elaborate consoles with a large number of keys in columns corresponding to the columns on a typical work sheet, and others group their keys into separate numeric, alphabetic, and special function sections of the keyboard panels. In either, it is the number and names of the special function keys which vary for application to one operation or another. The principle of operation is simple. The technologist merely selects whichever numeric and special function keys represent the test result that is to be reported and presses only those keys. The system will respond by printing or displaying the fully spelled-out entry for verification. If the technologist validates the display, an "enter" or "verified" button is activated, telling the computer to accept the entry. The special function key method avoids a necessity to spell out words character by character on a general-purpose keyboard or teletypewriter but requires different key configurations for different analytical procedures. A few manufacturers offer consoles with both general purpose and special function keys.

Some operatives are common to most keyboards. These include functions such as: "Verify," "Test Number," "Date," "Clear," "Increment," "Stat," "Routine," "Inquiry," "Delete," "Repeat," "Limits," etc. Special function keys unique to the various classes of laboratory analyses for chemistry, serology, and hematology include designations such as: "BUN," "SGOT," "BILI," "GLU" . . . "CA," "CL," "HGB," "HCT," "RBC,". . . .

Special code keys are available for bacteriology to produce standard phrases such as: "many, moderate, less than 10,000," etc. Various manufacturers provide individual keyboards to designate types of organisms.

Accurate identification of donors and recipients, accurate blood type records and reporting, and accurate records of blood units received, stored, or distributed constitute the vital information necessary to safeguard blood bank operation properly. Traditionally this paperwork has taken the form of specimen labeling, blood type examination requests, and result reports, and master log books to record donor/recipient information, blood unit status, and delivery logs.

Mark-sense cards are adaptable as request, result, or inventory records for these operations. The laboratory computer can be programmed to produce the required blood type records, inventories, and reports.

Blood unit inventory utilizing mark-sense or prepunched cards requires that, whenever a unit is received or distributed, appropriate information be marked and written on the card so that the computer system may compile accurate records of the inventory and transactions. If a small line printer, a teletype, or a CRT console with attached hard copy device is available at the blood bank location, transactions may be logged on paper by the computer as they occur.

c. **Program functions.**   Whatever way test results are entered, the computer program must categorize and sort the information and match results, accession numbers, and specimen numbers with patient names and the names of requesting physicians. The program performs the necessary calculations (dilution factors, conversion factors, etc.) , assembles information into appropriate report formats, and prints out the paper copies as scheduled or demanded. Confidentiality of patient data requires that access authorization codes are provided only to appropriate persons. The medicolegal implications of this problem are not yet resolved. Therefore, all patient data files stored in computers must be protected from unauthorized access, as are patient charts on the hospital unit. Permanent storage, if desired, is best done on magnetic tape stored in security cabinets.

Individual patient tape records can be updated periodically as new data is acquired. Results should always be reviewed by knowledgeable laboratory staff to validate plausibility and quality control and detect errors before being released via any method such as CRT, telephone, or written report.

Results may be stored temporarily in various forms of computer memory (disc, tape, or drum) from which they may be retrieved on demand and transferred via tapes, punched cards, or directly over phone wires to other computers. Most often, only enough information is transferred to allow billing to be done by a separate accounting office system. To assure correct communication, the most desirable and legally valid report of laboratory test results is the printed report.

d.   **Consolidated reports.**   Computer-generated reports may have a wide variety of formats. The information content and the frequency of generation are controllable by the program, but some limitations are imposed by the data storage capacities of the particular system and the speed of its printing devices.

In addition to the immediate reporting of individual test results to the patient's chart ("daily patient report"), various consolidated listings of results have proved so useful that most packaged laboratory computer systems marketed today include a basic set as stock in trade. Depending on the systems supplier, these reports include some or all of the following types:

(1) Patient directory. An alphabetical listing of patient name, specimen accession number(s), and tests ordered. The list is updated as test requests come in. It is most efficient in answering telephone inquiries. The list becomes a handy index to asking the computer for status of results on any particular patient.

(2) Abnormal or incompatible results. A list of all results not meeting predetermined criteria for acceptability, such as results which are off scale, in too much disagreement with a previous result, or internally incompatible. This list may have a section separating out those tests requiring a report.

(3) Incomplete results. A compilation of incomplete results for a particular time period.

(4) Daily patient report. For patient care staff.

(5) Interim ward reports. Reports by ward of test results for all patients in a particular ward. Abnormal results are usually starred. When appropriate data are in the computer files, room numbers, bed numbers, specimen accession numbers, hospital numbers of patients, attending physician names, and special comments may be included.

(6) Cumulative reports. Cumulative results on particular patients are presented in a format indicating a time sequence of test results so that trends may be distinguished as aids to diagnosis and therapy. These may cover periods of one week or longer and can be updated daily. Reports may also show "normal ranges" for comparison. Some reports show ranges as sex specific and age stratified. One form of cumulative report is especially convenient for inclusion in the patient's chart. Each new test printout for a particular patient automatically includes all data on any prior tests. As each new report is added, the old one may be discarded to avoid the necessity for "shingling" reports in the chart.

(7) Billing report. A periodic report of patients by hospital number (or outpatient identification) with dates and tests to be billed.

e. Statistical reports. Statistical reports can provide information useful to quality control, laboratory operations monitoring, economic planning, and research and technical development. When properly defined to the computer, statistical reports are far easier to assemble automatically than manually. In fact, the prodigious manual labor involved has probably inhibited the full exploitation of statistical techniques until the recent advent of computerization. Compared to manual labor, the speed and mathematical accuracy of computers are exceedingly efficient in statistical analyses.

The following examples represent only a part of what will no doubt be available in the future:

(1) Test summary. A periodic summary of all tests done in a laboratory reporting period, including types of tests and total number of tests performed in each category.

(2) Quality control. One of the more common approaches to quality control is the assay of standardized control samples along with patient specimens. The computer prints a cumulative list of results on these control samples to indicate precision. The program may include built-in statistical techniques such as calculation of means, standard deviations, ranges, etc. More sophisticated programs should be developed for on-line quality control utilizing appropriate routines for continuously checking laboratory instrument performance and system operation during every test run.

(3) Statistical correlations. Correlation, cluster analysis, and other statistical analyses can be programmed to produce desired correlation information from stored patient data.[6] One such available program computes blood electrolyte balance information. Correlations of results of groups of organ- or tissue-specific enzyme tests would be clinically useful. There is almost unlimited opportunity for development and utilization of even more sophisticated test group interpretation and model building of physiological and chemical functions in health and disease.

E. AVAILABLE TECHNIQUES AND SYSTEMS

When functional specifications have been completed, selecting the most suitable computer system will require objective screening of available equipment to match the particular functional and economic requirements of the laboratory. To clarify description of the final selection process, it is pertinent first to examine the laboratory utility of computer system components and different configurations.

Figure 7-3 illustrates conventional practice for the application of computer technology to a typical laboratory. The computer system is indicated by shaded blocks in the diagram. It is a network of electronic and electro-

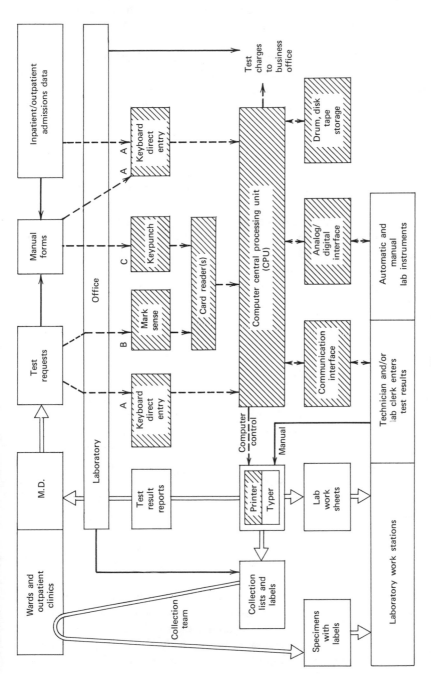

Figure 7-3

mechanical apparatus guided by computer programs that collect, manipulate, collate, store, and report test data. Control remains in the laboratory office whether or not a computer system is present. To indicate an appropriate ability to do without the computer system either entirely or during computer breakdown, double-line arrows delineate essential document flow produced either manually or with computer aid. The solid thin-line arrows indicate information paths usable as alternates or adjuncts to the dotted-line computer data paths. The dotted-line paths for computer input information passing through the laboratory office imply that an option should be open to the laboratory for monitoring the inflowing test requests and patient information as well as the outgoing test result records.

When data input is via an interposed medium such as cards or keyboards and the data is accepted in convenient groups, the system may be considered in an "off-line batch" processing mode of operation. "On-line real-time" operations utilize analog and digital interfacing equipment for direct electronic coupling of laboratory instrument outputs to computer input circuitry with no arbitrarily interposed time delay in related functions. When appropriate equipment and programs are available, the two modes of operation may be intermixed.

In Figure 7–3, alternates "A," "B," and "C" illustrate methods most commonly used singly or collectively to enter data into the computer.

1.   Off-line Batch Mode

Alternate "B" makes use of Hollerith cards imprinted with lists of laboratory tests with spaces to mark indicating the desired selections. Since it is too cumbersome to mark-sense alphabetic names, the patient name must be prepunched, handwritten, or typed. Alternatively, the name may be matched with the patient's identification or laboratory accession number via keys or punched cards in parallel with the mark-sensed test request. Some installations preprocess a set of cards at admissions so that test selection cards are already prepunched with the patient identification when the doctor receives the new patient file jacket. Data from manual forms already in use for both patient identification and tests requested can be keypunched in one operation for input method "C." The cards may be saved as permanent records of the input.

Both card methods "B" and "C" require card reading equipment peripheral to the computer central processor. The card readers may be either exclusively for punch cards or of the type which will accept punched and mark-sense cards. High-speed photo-electric readers are now marketed for general use. Older style readers employ metal finger contacts to sense card holes and are slower. If test result information is also keypunched, the computer may be a general purpose device entirely separate from the laboratory and used only to compile worklists and reports. Some advantages of this "batch mode" operation are:

(1) It lends itself to easy conversion from all manual operations and has been employed as an interim step in the development of on-line real-time systems.

(2) It is not necessary to own the computer. Provided an appropriate program is available, keypunching and processing services can be rented on a use-time basis from service bureaus or similar computer facilities.

Some disadvantages of off-line batch mode are:

(1) Necessity for a large amount of keypunching.

(2) Potential for human error in handling and rehandling documents and cards and in the transcription of data from manual forms to punched cards.

(3) Computer utility is limited to some calculations, worksheet preparation, and result report generation.

(4) Longer turn-around times.

(5) Laboratory instruments are not connected directly to the computer, which obviates immediate quality control.

2.   On-line Real-time

Experience has proven that the least errors and greatest efficiency derive from entering data only once, directly from the source into the computer. On-line real-time modes of operation provide equipment configurations and programs for direct entry of data from external sources, such as patient identification, test request, and raw analytical data from machines electronically coupled to the computer.

The keyboard direct entry of method "A" employs typewriter keyboards attached either to television-style cathode-ray tube screens or mechanical printing devices. Each character key produces a unique code transmitted electrically to temporary storage, allowing material to be reviewed on screen or print-out and verified or edited before the computer is permitted to accept the data.

An admissions or nursing station terminal may be wired directly or through phone lines to the computer. This method is not yet popular, however, because of high cost, physician and nurse resistance to the use of keyboard input consoles, and the expense of printing copies on-site for signature, verification, computer failure back-up, etc.

However, the keyboard direct entry method has been accepted in situations where similar devices are already used in a general hospital information and medical record computer system.

Once test request information and patient identification data are in the computer, preparatory schedules and lists can be provided immediately by an appropriately programmed machine. These include specimen collection schedules, specimen labels, and worklists for the different laboratory work stations. Blood collection teams place the adhesive labels on specimen containers at sample collection to avoid errors. Labels are usually printed in sets of 4 or 6 to provide enough extras for additional identification of aliquots in distributing specimens for analysis.

3. Test Data Acquisition

The capture of analytical test results, sample identity, and test identity is usually accomplished by a combination of on-line and off-line operations. A useful low-cost off-line device is the mark-sense Hollerith card. A field of 12 rows by 40 columns is available per card for the technician to mark boxes which identify sample numbers, test results, and other data. This information is read directly into the computer via a mark-sense card reader.

Ordinary teletypewriters or general purpose CRT/keyboard units have been used, but both have certain drawbacks. Although less expensive than CRT consoles, the teletypewriters are very slow and quite noisy. Several special 2-way devices are marketed for entering test results from instruments or from manual methods with provision for limited communication back to the technologist from the computer. These devices are usually obtained only as a component of the system for which they were designed.

The ideal solution would be a number of reasonably priced keyboard console modules with feedback error signals which could be used separately or combined to fit the requirements of any laboratory and which could interface to any laboratory computer. Several consoles now marketed as part of ready-made systems display test result data keyed in by the technologist for verification before acceptance by the computer. The more sophisticated devices permit entering the numbering sequence and content nature of Autoanalyzer tray cups, calibration data, result limit settings, and test type identity. In turn, the computer can alert the technologist via display lights or printout devices to out-of-order standards, out-of-range values, various instrument malfunctions, certain types of human errors, etc., depending on the sophistication of the program.

Those laboratory instruments which produce either continuously variable electrical signals (analog) or discrete electrical number codes (digital) as test result quantities can be connected directly (on-line) to the central processor analog/digital conversion and multiplexing interfaces. The multiplexer is a high-speed electronic switching device which under computer control accepts signals from one instrument after another in such rapid sequence that no information is lost even though this signal input path to the computer may be shared by several analytical instrument data sources.

4. Processing

The list of instructions to be performed by a laboratory computer is referred to as a "program." In reality, the "program" consists of a group of subprograms called "routines." Each routine is designed to perform a specific task or part of a task. Tasks which are repeated often, such as Auto-analyzer peak detection, use the same set of instructions, over and over. The number of separate routines necessary for the variety of tasks and subtasks can be numerous, and it is obvious that, in order to juggle these routines with appropriate timing and orderly dovetailing, an overall manager program is necessary.

This set of management instructions is appropriately called an "executive" or "monitor." It keeps continuous account of data entering and leaving the computer system and sorts out priorities for calling into play the various task routines in proper sequence. The executive, therefore, must reside in the fastest access memory available to the computer, the "core" memory. Core memory is relatively expensive per unit of storage capacity and is usually integral to the central processor. Task routines, being less immediate, are often stored on peripheral mass memory devices such as magnetic drum or disk; the executive program transfers these routines to core memory from drum or disk storage as needed.

The magnetic drum or disk memory is much larger in capacity than core. A medium-size disk pack can store millions of "bits" of information. One type in wide use is the disk pack, which utilizes removable sets of 10 magnetic platters. This mass storage capacity is also essential for patient test data files and other information accumulated during laboratory operation.

Magnetic tape transports are not necessary for the daily operation of a laboratory computer system, but they are quite useful for economic storage of very large quantities of old data in compact form. It is common practice to transfer all data from disk to tape at the end of each operating day for duplicate storage as protection against inadvertent loss by damage or improper handling.

The system principles diagrammed in Figure 7–3 indicate that, when properly implemented, the computer system can fail (shaded parts in the diagram) without stopping any significant data flow. Parallel manual operations are available which can be immediately implemented in an emergency to avoid breakdown of services. To this end, there are advantages in using computer input devices which can independently generate paper information or read information already on paper. It would thus be handy when exclusively using CRT/keyboard entry consoles to have at least one console capable of operating and producing paper records independently of the computer.

F. EQUIPMENT EVALUATION AND SELECTION

1. Preliminary Preparation

Certain information is needed before comparing available systems and selecting the most suitable computer for local needs:

(1) Comparison of specific advantages and disadvantages of computer processing in the particular laboratory.

(2) Measurement of the data processing (paper work) load.

(3) Detailed listing of the time spent daily by technical staff for paper work which could be done by computer in order to salvage human effort for more creative tasks.

(4) Estimation of potential improvements in efficiency.

(5) Shortening of turn-around time.

(6) Increasing specimen workload capacity.

(7) Reduction in laboratory transcription and calculation errors.

(8) Comparison of merits and necessity of batch and on-line processing of raw test data.

(9) Determination of backup in instrumentation and processing equipment which is mandatory. Can laboratory obligations tolerate an occasional day when the system is completely "down"? Can the staff manually turn out necessary (stat) work and delay routine analyses until the computer is "up" again?

For each component of a system, there is a variety of equipment available from different manufacturers either as individual items or a part of a packaged system.[9,10] In all cases, the machines are electronically complex and of varied internal design although their functional specifications may be remarkably similar. Selection of the most suitable equipment for a particular laboratory requires a detailed comparison of alternatives and knowledgeable evaluation of component characteristics. Marketing propaganda and written material foreign to the medical buyer can be misleading. An organized evaluation and selection process is essential to avoid later disappointment and costly changes.

Descriptive brochures and operating specifications can be obtained from each vendor. Salesmen will provide ready marketing propaganda, but it must be remembered that such information and claims are rarely objective, frequently inadequately documented, and often understandably biased. There is a tendency to understate the limitations and deficiencies. Therefore, selection must be based on a knowledgeable survey of specified and proven performance characteristics, and these should be evaluated according to relative importance to the operating goals of the laboratory.

2. Selection Filters

Figure 7–4 represents the criteria of system selection as three screens or "filters": the cost limitations as imposed by the particular budget resources, "cost filter"; the required technical features of the system as determined by the laboratory functional specifications, "technical filter"; and the supplier support as determined by common-sense safeguards against poor quality, irresponsibility, etc., "supplier filter."

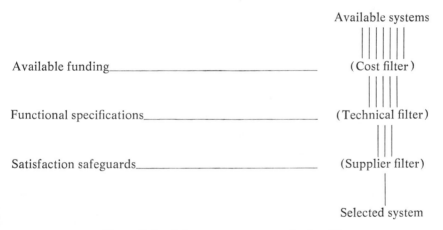

Figure 7–4.   Laboratory computer selection filters.

Since choice of the supplier depends initially on the system's technical features selected as most suitable, the "supplier filter" is logically applied last. The computer equipment finally selected is the system which passes through all filters with the highest score.

a. Cost filter. The cost constraints will immediately screen-out certain manufacturers. If consultant services are to be employed in the evaluation and selection process, the consultant should be informed of budget limitations.

b. Technical filter general criteria. The considerable variety of computing equipment and systems suppliers in the present-day market can make comparative evaluation and objective selection a rather tedious process unless the field of choice is narrowed by applying general criteria based on functional requirements common to most laboratories. Typical of these common criteria are:

(1) Flexibility and "forward compatibility." Equipment should fit the task at hand, yet be flexible enough to handle expansion of laboratory functions without replacement or major modification of hardware and software.

(2) Programming and interfacing efficiency. Unless all required programs for the laboratory operations are provided in the supplier's "standard" system, software development can be very costly. Some computers possess more convenient standard software than others. Changes in laboratory procedures will require that the system be efficient to program and that the peripheral interfaces be flexible and modular enough to readily accept additions or changes in laboratory instrumentation or communications terminals.

(3) Real-time and priority interrupt capability. To justify a computer system, any laboratory must perform a fairly large workload. The resulting data collection and communication functions require a computer capacity for interleaving tasks. A "priority external interrupt" capability is mandatory to guarantee highest priority tasks the necessary attention.

(4) System operating speed. The system must have sufficient operational speed to handle priority interrupt sorting routines for every interrupt, to service multiple input/output channels for data flow, and properly to interleave "background" activities which can be done on a time-available basis with "foreground" activities requiring processing of information while the data is coming in (real-time).

At first glance, it may appear that slow laboratory instruments and relatively infrequent data sampling input to the system do not require central processor speeds in microseconds. Experience has convincingly demonstrated, however, that the number of varied simultaneous tasks require considerable speed to handle the complex of randomly occurring multiple testing events and data processing tasks in real-time. The executive program should have sufficient speed and interrupt efficiency to monitor lab instruments continually for the capture of results when ready while "simultaneously" performing data search, data retrieval, and the transfer of blocks of data between the Central Processing Unit and mass storage files or input/output devices. Processors with memory cycle times on the order of one microsecond or faster are most likely to meet this requirement.

(5) Expandable core memory. The system should be so designed that additions of core memory capacity to 32,000 words or more can be made

with a minimum of cost and no rewriting of the major system programs. An operating systems program for laboratory applications usually requires at least 4000 words of core memory and can run as high as 8000 or 12,000 words for very sophisticated programs.

(6) Word length. The number of binary integers (bits) handled as a group (word) by computer circuitry is "word length." The mathematical precision per word of 24-bit or longer word machines is not required for laboratory applications, and the high cost of such machines is not justified. Eight-bit-per-word machines cannot achieve the 10-bit accuracy convenience *per word* of analog to digital conversion for the laboratory instruments. Eight-bit machines are efficient for character communications but are inefficient for addressing large sizes of core memory. To designate a memory address number greater than 255, an 8-bit machine must use indirect addressing methods. A 16-bit word, on the other hand, may designate any number up to 65,535. Thus, depending on how many bits of a 16-bit word are available for addressing, thousands of memory locations can be addressed directly by one 16-bit word. Furthermore, 16-bit machines are able to combine two 8-bit bytes per word and have sufficient word length to handle 10-bit A/D conversion in a single word. These features of 16-bit machines provide efficiency advantages in the laboratory where input events demand immediate computer attention. Information must be handled fast enough that results of this processing can be used to control, modify, reject, or otherwise respond to input data from varied parts of the system. For laboratory applications this cost performance ratio of trade-offs between memory capacity and execution times favors 16-bit machines.

c. **Technical filter specific criteria.**   Although the CPU is only part of any system and must be evaluated in relation to the real-time instrument interfaces and the human/computer communication equipment, specific CPU internal characteristics important to the efficiency of a laboratory computer system are listed under "Specific Hardware Comparison" of Table 1. The first group of criteria are applicable to any computer systems being considered for laboratory use, while the second group of factors include additional criteria related particularly to packaged systems intended primarily for laboratories.

The final group of specific hardware feature comparisons is divided into details of the computer central processing unit, the laboratory instrument and technician consoles, direct-coupled input/output channels, and the peripheral equipment required for data storage and human/computer communications.

If weighted ranking points are assigned to each of the characteristics, a convenient numerical evaluation score can be obtained for each supplier

Table 1. Technical Filter Factors

Criteria applicable to any laboratory system
Flexibility, modularity and expandability
Degree of instrument independence
Compatability with manual backup
Maximum core memory size available
Capacity to handle external priority interrupts
Memory cycle time in microseconds
Data-word-length in bits

Packaged system criteria (systems specifically sold for laboratories)
Central processing unit type
Does standard software include higher-level languages?
What are core residency requirements for these languages and what peripheral
    drivers are included?
Is applications software available for:
    Chemistry?
    Hematology?
    Urinalysis?
    Microbiology?
    other?
What are memory requirements (core and disk) for these programs?
Interface to other computer?
Turnkey system?
Typical system cost
Data inputs available:
    Human generated—
        Paper to keypunch?
        Mark-sense cards?
        Direct keyboard?
        Technician consoles?
    Direct from lab instruments—
        Autoanalyzer?
        SMA-12?
        other (such as Coulter)?
Data outputs available
    Technician console
        Input verify?
        Alarm and status?
        Hard copy audit?
Printer outputs
    Teletype?
    Line printer?
    Collection lists?
    Specimen labels?

Table 1.   Technical Filter Factors (continued)

Lab worksheets?
Incomplete results?
Abnormal results?
Cumulative reports?
Alphabetical patient/I.D. number and requested tests listing?
Billing?

Hardware comparisons
Central processing unit (type and base price)
 Memory cycle time in microseconds
 Maximum core size and price per 4096-word unit
 Number of standard interrupt levels
 Number of external interrupts available
 Number of addressing modes available
 Number of hardware index registers
 Number of additional hardware registers
 Is multiple indirect addressing available?
 Real-time clock, standard or option, and price for option
 Parity check, standard or option, and price for option
 Memory protect, standard or option, and price for option
 Power failure protect, standard or option, and price for option
Input/output channels
 Number of addressable digital inputs and price per word
 Number of words of 10-bit A/D input and price per word
Peripheral equipment
Disk memory with controller, maximum capacity and price per increment
Magnetic tape with controller, number of tracks, packing density, ins/sec.,
    price, speed
Line printer with controller, number of columns, lines/minute, price
CRT units with controller, number of characters per page, price/unit
Punched card reader with controller, cards/minute, price
Mark-sense card with controller, cards/minute, price

---

system. Technical ranking can then be either separate from or combined with price ranking. This facilitates picking the best technical system in any particular price range. Weighting of ranking points is arbitrary. The example given in Table 2 attempts to delegate emphasis appropriately to the general needs of most laboratory systems.

Speed and core expandability are two of the most crucial characteristics of the CPU hardware. In the example of Table 2, the product of the maximum core size (in number of words) and the reciprocal of its respective memory access time in microseconds was used as a basic comparison figure of merit. If a feature was optional, it was assigned zero points since the

Table 2.   Scaled Ranking Point Method Example

Characteristic	Points
Parity check a standard item	5
Memory protect a standard item	5
For each hardware register (in addition to index)	1
For each index register	1
For each available addressing mode	1
Standard interrupt priority levels, per level	1
For multi-level addressing	5
Real-time clock a standard item	5
Power failure protect a standard item	5

System features	Supplier A	Pts	Supplier B	Pts	Supplier C	Pts
Maximum core size and cycle time	32/0.80	40	65/0.96	67	32/1.60	20
Standard interrupt levels	16	16	8	8	16	16
Addressing modes	8	8	2	2	4	4
Index registers	2	2	1	1	None	(2)
Additional hardware registers	10	10	6	6	7	7
Multiple indirect addressing	Yes	5	None	(5)	Yes	5
Real-time clock	Optional	0	Optional	0	Optional	0
Parity check	None	(5)	Optional	0	Optional	0
Memory protect	Optional	0	None	(5)	Optional	0
Power failure protect	Optional	0	Standard	5	Standard	5
Subtotals		76		79		55

extra price would tend to offset the advantage of the option. However, if a feature was missing entirely, it was assigned negative points (indicated by parentheses). For the sake of brevity, the example includes only a few of the Table 1 features. In practical use, the ranking point method would be applied to the entire table.

d.   Programming efficiency and computing power.   Comparative evaluation of programs provided by the vendor and particularly of the programming efficiency of a computer is difficult but worth the effort where long-term use of the system and expansion of applications are anticipated. If new programming is necessary to customize the system, the difference in the cost of programming efficient and less-efficient systems can be significant. A meaningful comparison of today's computer products depends on the intended application. To quantitatively compare the programming efficiency of computer candidates for laboratory systems it is necessary to test each machine with the same actual program. The test program ought to include certain functions peculiar to laboratory applications and should be written for each machine in the assembler language peculiar to that brand. This type of program is often called a "bench mark" routine written for each of the machines to be compared. One example of a laboratory bench mark program including subroutines for the interleaved performance of three representative tasks is given below:

(1) Monitor twelve asynchronous Autoanalyzer channels containing 30 cups each, filter noise, determine true peak values to a repeatable accuracy of one part per thousand or better; determine and compensate for baseline drift and store each peak value for matching with identity numbers and reporting.

(2) Monitor sixteen independent channels of variable height square waves, each of whose horizontal portions may occur with a frequency of between one a minute and one every two minutes. Store values as in task 1 above.

(3) Service random human queries through CRT (Cathode Ray Tube) keyboards or teletypewriter keyboards for any of the above stored values and print these on demand along with identifying patient name and patient hospital number.

The common program design charts are coded for each machine under consideration. The actual task performance duration times may then be obtained by summing the times for each instruction for each machine. The required words of core memory can also be totaled for each machine. These two quantitative expressions of performance can reveal differences between machines of similar price range and similar hardware characteristics. While coding the bench mark program for each machine, the analyst can also rank them according to the programming time required and comment on the ease of programming.

e. **Supplier filter.** The "supplier filter" of Table 3 compares reputations and abilities of vendors to support the user. Each manufacturer should be willing to provide well-documented performance data, commit a rea-

Table 3. Supplier Filter Factors

1. Supplier years of experience in laboratory systems
2. Number of installations, locations and user comments
3. Degree of acceptance by user laboratory personnel
4. System on-time delivery reputation
5. Type of acceptance procedures agreeable to supplier
6. Types of warranty and maintenance agreements available and cost
7. Nearness and dependability of service personnel
8. Availability and cost of orientation training
9. Quality and accuracy of system hardware/software documentation
10. Software completeness, quality control method and support

sonable amount of programming support, and provide training of laboratory staff. A supplier's background in laboratory computer systems is important. His history of prompt and effective repair service should be examined closely. The cost of preventive maintenance and repair services should be considered. Another important characteristic is the willingness of a supplier to sign a written system acceptance test agreement which adequately protects the purchaser.

The selection methods described are applicable to both the package systems which have total capability including laboratory oriented software and the do-it-yourself type of systems put together from separate pieces of equipment obtained from different manufacturers.

G. PURCHASE PROCEDURE

After obtaining a sale, the salesman's job requires him to move on to the next potential customer. Some manufacturers of small- and medium-sized computers and some suppliers of packaged laboratory systems obtain a few customers and then withdraw when they find this market is not profitable because of the major investment required in programming and the necessary special engineering. The pathologist may be left with a good piece of hardware but no support. For the laboratory director to avoid acquiring an expensive, nonoperative, or otherwise inadequate system, he needs to know what he is buying and what it will do. Therefore, an exact specification for equipment and software is most helpful when soliciting proposals from suppliers. Each interested supplier should be required to submit a proposal in writing which specifies in detail the exact and warranted capabilities of each piece of hardware, each package of computer programs, and the performance of the entire system.

Each supplier proposal should include answers to the specific customer questions as well as a copy of an operating manual for the equipment, a systems instruction manual for laboratory personnel who will use the system, and copies of actual daily patient test reports and worklists produced by the system during a normal production operation in a clinical laboratory (not from a demonstration). Each proposal should be signed by a responsible executive of the supplier company. While selecting the most desirable of these proposed systems, it is essential that as many of the contender's systems as possible be examined in daily operation in a routine laboratory setting.

Do not sign a salesman's order. The order should be written by the purchaser. Include hardware specifications taken from applicable sections of the specification or proposal, required operational characteristics of each item, the system interfaces, size, type, model, and operating characteristics of the computer, the memory size, all accessory processing equipment, electrical specifications, and the *exact* functional specifications of the programs to be included.

Do not omit the expansion capabilities required for more tests. If the selected vendor has offered programming assistance, specify the desired service in terms of either man years or named programs which are to be successfully operational by a certain date. The purchase order should also include an agreement concerning installation costs, evaluation period of satisfactory operation without significant failure, terms of acceptance, and provision for continuing maintenance of equipment and programs by the system supplier. Before making any deposit payment, the purchaser should demand a letter of acceptance of the order signed by a responsible executive of the supplier. A proper acceptance agreement will protect the laboratory from any failure to comply with specifications and assure satisfactory installation and performance of the system before final payment. Beware of a supplier-generated acceptance statement which can be expected to read somewhat as follows:

"PURCHASE PAYMENT SHALL BE DUE OR RENTAL PAYMENTS SHALL COMMENCE UPON WRITTEN CERTIFICATION BY BITWHACKER CORPORATION TO BUYER/ LESSEE THAT THE ACCEPTANCE TEST WAS SUCCESSFULLY COMPLETED. THE ACCEPTANCE TEST SHALL BE THE ACCEPTANCE TEST PROCEDURE PROVIDED BY BITWHACKER CORPORATION FOR THE EQUIPMENT."

This type of agreement offers no real protection to the laboratory. Note that it is the manufacturer alone who not only specifies the nature of the acceptance tests but also determines when they have been "successfully completed."

A supplier should either accept in writing all detailed acceptance testing requirements written by the purchaser or quote any additional charges for incorporating those particular features specified which he does not customarily provide. The following statement illustrates a better wording to protect the buyer.

"PURCHASE PAYMENT SHALL BE DUE OR RENTAL PAYMENTS SHALL COMMENCE UPON *WRITTEN CERTIFICATION BY BOTH PARTIES HERETO* THAT THE EQUIPMENT ACCEPTANCE TEST HAS BEEN SUCCESSFULLY COMPLETED. THE ACCEPTANCE TEST SHALL BE *THE ACCEPTANCE TEST AGREED TO IN WRITING BY BOTH PARTIES* AND IS ATTACHED HERETO AS EXHIBIT 'A'."

It is possible, of course, to require such stringent acceptance tests that no vendor can meet the demands. A realistic set of acceptance test requirements takes time to generate but is well worth the effort. An example of an appropriate acceptance agreement is included in Section H. Payment of the final installment of the agreed prices should not be made until the system has met all acceptance specifications.

1.   Purchase, Lease, or Rent Factors

A few leasing companies in the U.S. today specialize in laboratory instruments. At least one of these (Telco Leasing, Chicago), also provides "true" rental plans. There appears to be an accelerated trend recently for medical institutions to lease or rent equipment rather than to purchase outright. Most computer systems suppliers lease but do not rent. However, where both leasing and renting are possible through an appropriate third party, the decision whether to purchase, lease, or rent becomes a real consideration. Some definitions of terms are adopted here for clarity:

1. *Lease.*   A contract for the use of equipment in which there is no buildup by the lessee (user) of equity in the property (generally for a specified time period).

2. *Lease-Purchase.*   A contract with provisions for purchase options or renewals and a build up of equity.

3. *Rental.*   A contract with no build up of equity and no low-cost purchase options (generally for an unspecified time period and uniform monthly payments per unit of equipment).

In practice, the word "lease" is used loosely. Most so-called lease contracts are in reality lease-purchase contracts. In a true rental, the user may ultimately acquire title to the equipment but only at a fair market value. In this sense, a true lease and a true rental are practically synonymous and can be considered so in the remainder of this discussion. Depending on the specific terms and conditions available from a particular leasing company, it can be seen from Table 4 that under *some* circumstances rental can be advantageous. This may be particularly true for institutions where the productive use of the equipment and its monthly cost of use are more significant than ownership of title to the equipment. Most of the information in Table 4 was derived from an article in the June 1972 issue of *Laboratory Medicine* titled "Should You Rent or Lease Laboratory Equipment Instead of Purchasing It?" by Martin E. Zimmerman. The table may appear slanted in favor of renting. Lest this be misleading, consider that, in practice, rental agreements must usually cover a longer period than 3 years to get the monthly rent figure down to an amount which begins to meet the competitiveness implied by the table.

Table 4.

Purchase	Lease-Purchase	Rental (true lease)
1. Depreciation usually can only be written off over a longer period (8 or 10 years).	1. Monthly payments tax deductible only to the extent of depreciation and interest.	1. Monthly payments deductible in full. Entire cost of equipment can be written off during the term of contract.
2. Reimbursement of depreciation not allowed under government grant funds.	2. Only "nonequity" portions of payments possibly applicable to overhead.	2. Rentals reimbursable as "overhead" by government grant funds.
3. Cash tied up in depreciating equipment (representing a steady loss).	3. More cash available for profitable investment than in purchase.	3. Purchase cash equivalent (less rental) may be invested at a profit.
4. High risk of obsolescence. Full impact of economic penalties from depreciation (often up to 50% after first three years for computer systems).	4. Medium risk of economic penalties for obsolescence. (Depending on purchase option discounts or equity buildup versus fair market value.)	4. Minimum penalty for obsolescence, since user's commitment during first 3 years usually totals less than purchase price.
5. Full price amortized over useful life of equipment plus losses from non-investment of equivalent case can sometimes result in higher monthly amount than rental.	5. Cost of equipment plus overhead and interest must be paid by lessee.	5. Renter retains ownership and theoretically can re-rent or sell equipment. Renter has retained a major portion of obsolescence risk.

H. CONTRACTUAL AGREEMENTS

The following paragraphs are an example of appropriate contractual agreement terms and conditions a final selected supplier could be asked to sign.

Please note: If meeting any of the terms or conditions stated herein will necessitate special prices or charges not already provided for by the blank spaces below, supplier is requested to note these extra charges and the reasons for them in a reply document referred to this sample agreement.

This equipment acceptance agreement is entered into this_____ day of_____, 197 , by and between_____ _____(hereinafter referred to as Supplier), and _____(hereinafter referred to as Purchaser), and is applicable to all items covered by the following Purchase Orders

1.   Equipment Delivery, Installation, and Penalty Terms

All shipments are F.O.B. Supplier's plant in_____, _____ , at full valuation, and freight collect, unless otherwise agreed to. All equipment remains the property of the Supplier until delivered and installed at Purchaser's site and shipment will be at the risk of the Supplier. Supplier will provide the necessary qualified personnel who are thoroughly experienced with this system and undertake the necessary tasks to install the said computer and peripheral equipments in the laboratories of Purchaser at_____ _____and to attach the necessary power lines to the equipment from the electrical breaker box provided by Purchaser as specified in Supplier site preparation requirements dated_____. Purchaser will supply any necessary building electrical conduits and will be responsible for pulling the required cables through these conduits. Cabling for primary system peripherals will be supplied by Supplier. Cabling for each laboratory terminal set entry console in excess of fifty (50) feet will be paid for by Purchaser at the rate of_____per foot. Supplier will provide the mechanical and electrical work necessary to connect all components and peripheral equipment specified in the system and to attach laboratory instruments, consoles, mass storage devices, printers, card readers, CRT's, and such other equipments as included in the laboratory computer system according to the terms and conditions herein and as specified in purchase orders_____. Supplier will use its best efforts to deliver the equipments and available software and complete the installation tasks as stated above so that hardware acceptance testing shall begin on or before

The system software, including special changes to the software specified in "AMENDMENTS TO SPECIFICATIONS," shall be installed no later than _____ or be subject to the penalty of paying to_____the equivalent rental price per month of the total system and equipment listed in the final purchase orders dated_____, for each and every 30-day period following_____, 197___, for which the terms of equipment delivery and installation have not been met. Otherwise Purchaser may exercise the option to cancel, and all prior payments shall be immediately refunded in full. Upon completion by Supplier of the equipment installation tasks as stated above, Supplier shall so inform Purchaser in writing and allow Purchaser the prerogative for the purpose of determining to the satisfaction of Purchaser that the installation requirements have been met in full. Installation terms shall not be considered met in full by Supplier until Supplier has received confirmation in writing signed by an authorized representative of Purchaser that in the opinion of Purchaser the installation requirements as set forth herein have been met in full by Supplier. Such confirmation or denial in writing shall be delivered by Purchaser to Supplier not later than five (5) working days after the date of receipt by Purchaser of written notification from Supplier that delivery and installation are complete. Should such written confirmation or denial not be supplied by Purchaser within the specified five (5) day period, then the installation requirements shall be considered automatically met in full.

2. Warranty

All Supplier manufactured and OEM hardware is guaranteed to perform to specification during the acceptance period and for ninety (90) days following the certified completion of the hardware system acceptance tests. Defective components will be replaced or repaired by Supplier at no cost to Purchaser for parts. Replaced or repaired elements of equipment are subject to the same overall guarantee for ninety (90) days after replacement.

All software installed by Supplier and not modified by Purchaser is guaranteed to perform to specification as defined by acceptance test procedure for eighteen (18) months following certified completion of acceptance testing.

3. System Documentation

Supplier will provide complete maintenance level documentation of the laboratory system. This includes equipment schematics, cable charts, and maintenance manuals. All software will be documented with flow charts, program listings, and a written functional description including internal description manuals, user's manuals, and programmer's manuals. All operating systems and applications programs shall be supplied thus:

1. A human readable listing in the source language in which they were originally written.

2. Magnetic tape copies of the programs in source and machine language.

3. Any compilers, assemblers, loaders, etc., used to convert source programs to machine language shall be supplied according to 1 and 2 above.

4. Magnetic tape and documented copies of all maintenance and diagnostic programs shall also be provided.

Copies of manufacturer's specifications, service manuals, and operating manuals will be supplied for each Supplier system component supplied by an OEM vendor.

All software documentation provided by Supplier which is so specified will be considered proprietary and will be used only by Purchaser personnel or Purchaser contractor personnel in conjunction with the subject system.

4. Orientation Training and Software Support

Supplier shall provide an orientation course on the selected equipment and software for individuals on Purchaser's staff. The course will be designed to train laboratory personnel in use of the laboratory terminal sets and acquaint them with the operational features and capabilities of the computer system. This training shall commence no later than_____, after announcement of contract award and shall be conducted for_____ people at _____.

Supplier shall also make available by prearrangement computer operator's and programmer's training courses for_____ members of the Purchaser's staff to be conducted at_____and to commence no later than_____after announcement of system contract award. The operator's course will have sufficient content and "hands on" training to provide students the necessary understanding and skills for operating the computer system while it is performing the laboratory tasks described in this Request for Proposal. The programmer's course need not be a fundamentals course, but rather should assume that students already have a basic knowledge of programming principles and need orientation to Supplier's system. This orientation must provide students with knowledge of sufficient detail to enable them to make repairs to or changes in the laboratory computer operating system software and utility and applications programs.

In addition to providing all necessary programming and program installation support to insure that the system meets the requirements described and passes acceptance tests, Supplier shall make available by prearrangement competent analysts and programmers to generate special programs either at a fixed fee quoted per program at the time of definition or at an hourly rate of $_____per hour for systems analysts and $_____ per hour for programmers.

Supplier agrees to provide to Purchaser at maximum fee of $_____ source tapes for all future updated, modified, and newly developed programs applicable to this system and whose updating, modification, and development are made at Supplier's expense for general use by all Supplier customers.

5. Acceptance Conditions

Upon certified completion of equipment installation according to the terms stated above, Supplier shall provide appropriate software programs and qualified personnel necessary for the laboratory computer hardware system to perform the system performance check as described herein.

Prior to acceptance testing, there shall be up to ten (10) consecutive working days during which Purchaser personnel may perform system validation/familiarization. This may be performed at the Supplier facility or the Purchaser facility as mutually agreed. Supplier shall be responsible for system maintenance during this period.

The duration of acceptance testing for hardware components shall be ten (10) consecutive eight (8) hour working days and accomplished in two (2) consecutive weeks. During the times allowed for maintenance (10 hours outside the laboratory day shift in each 24-hour period), the system shall not be required to perform any tasks except to save any and all laboratory data gathered during active performance check periods. All components and programs of the system shall be tested by appropriate diagnostic procedures designed to validate the full capability of the component or program and the results documented to assure full compliance with the manufacturer's specifications and where appropriate by using the attached Systems Performance Check Procedure. During acceptance testing, and prior to confirmation of acceptance, the laboratory will not be dependent on the system, except as provided herein, and in no event shall the system or its outputs be used for purposes other than system validation and operating performance check. Supplier shall provide all necessary maintenance support for the system during the acceptance testing period.

Supplier will provide appropriate readiness check procedures and programs for locating the hardware component responsible for system malfunction or failure. Supplier will provide a Daily Start-up Readiness Check program for testing the system each day for an indication that components are in satisfactory working order.

Performance will be considered acceptable if failures or interruptions of continuous operations are minor and occur no more frequently than one (1) time in five (5) consecutive days of eight (8) hours per day operation. Duration of such failure must not exceed one (1) hour and must not result in loss of data already acquired and stored.

At any time prior to completion of the acceptance test that such accumulated system down-time exceeds the above described amount, Purchaser may elect to consider the entire acceptance test period to start anew timewise, and may demand that all acceptance tasks already performed be repeated. If Supplier fails to complete the ten (10) day acceptance test within sixty (60) days after initiation of the acceptance test, Purchaser may exercise the option to cancel and all prior payments shall be immediately refunded. Following the completion of the ten (10) day acceptance test, system reliability test will be conducted for thirty (30) successful operational days. As a part of the thirty (30) day reliability test, the system shall be operated in parallel mode with manual operation of the laboratory during the last five (5) days.

Satisfactory completion of the ten (10) day acceptance test and the thirty (30) day reliability test must be certified in writing by personnel authorized by Purchaser and will constitute proof of performance of the tasks specified in this document.

6.   Payment

Payment for the amounts in the above referenced purchase orders shall be made as follows:

(1) A portion of the total system price ($_____) shall be due and payable prior to Supplier shipping said system to Purchaser upon inspection and conditional acceptance of the system components at the Supplier plant in_____, _____;

               city   state

(2) additional ($_____) dollars shall be due and payable upon successful completion of the ten (10) day hardware acceptance test as described in this agreement; and

(3) the balance, ($_____) dollars, shall be due and payable when the thirty (30) day reliability testing as described in this agreement is completed.

7. Maintenance Agreement

Continued maintenance and repair of both hardware and software components of the entire system as encompassed by equipments listed in purchase orders_____dated_____after the warranty period stated above is over shall consist of the following schedule and terms:

a. **Preventive maintenance.** Supplier shall conduct preventive maintenance procedures on all pertinent components of the system as recommended by manufacturer's and supplier's written specifications. Such maintenance shall be performed not less than once every_____ on_____(day of week) between the hours of_____ and_____. This preventive maintenance shall be provided by system Supplier for the equipments specified above for a fixed price of $_____ per month *including* all expenses of Supplier's maintenance personnel.

b. **Emergency service.** Should an emergency malfunction of the system occur after installation and acceptance which in the judgment of responsible Purchaser personnel cannot be readily corrected by those present and the malfunction will cause unacceptable degradation of laboratory operations, Supplier must provide assistance over the telephone within one (1) hour regardless of time of day; and if this is not adequate, Supplier must have a competent repairman at the Purchaser's computer room no later than twelve (12) hours after requested.

Supplier agrees to pay Purchaser a portion of system lease or purchase price for every twenty-four (24) hour period following an emergency system breakdown that Supplier fails to meet the above emergency service commitments and for every day following the first forty-eight (48) hours of repair that the system is still not completely laboratory functional. This refund shall be $ per day.

8. System Performance Check

Tasks to be performed by the laboratory computer system *during acceptance testing* are categorized into groups of similar tasks by function, but this is not meant to imply that these tasks are done separately or one at a time. The continued acquisition of laboratory data with no degradation while producing scheduled printed reports and/or servicing random on-demand requests for stored information is required. The laboratory computer system shall perform the following performance check tasks in parallel with the on-going manual operation of the laboratory during the acceptance testing.

a. **Input tasks.** The system will accept data from on-line laboratory instruments via appropriate analog and digital interfaces and shall accept input from laboratory personnel via appropriate consoles and mark-sense readers. Several times during the acceptance testing, data shall be entered by laboratory personnel via keyboards and card or page readers. Demands will then be made for the system to print out sufficient information to indicate that all data input was accurately acquired and stored by the system. Such output will be checked against the manual records used in parallel during the acceptance testing. This comparison is to be performed by Purchaser staff members or directly under their supervision.

Real or dummy input data shall be of such nature as to check the system capability to accept either by manual alpha-numeric (α-n) keyboard or by mark-sense/punched media:

Patient name (including spaces) up to	24 characters
Patient hospital chart number	7 digits
Patient home address (provision for)	40 characters
Medical service	4 characters
Patient age	2 digits
Patient sex	1 character
Patient status (inpatient/outpatient)	1 character
Inpatient ward location	4 α-n
Doctor name (including spaces) up to	24 characters
Doctor code	3 digits
Test urgency (emergency/routine)	1 character
Tests requested by abbreviation	8 characters
Test requested by test code	4 digits
Specimen accession numbers	5 digits
Specimen body source	4 characters
Date and time of collection	10 digits

The system shall accept at any time the insertion through the system input devices: patient identification data, test-request data, and test-result data. Alternately or in addition, the system shall accept sets of dummy test-request data and test-result data specially prepared by authorized personnel of Purchaser, and up to, but not exceeding in quantity per unit of time, the amounts for which the system was originally specified and designed. Test requests will be entered through the appropriate system entry devices during the acceptance performance check tests.

b. Output tasks.   Information displayed and/or printed shall be activated on demand by entering an appropriate code via any of the terminal sets or operator console keyboards. System programs shall not respond to improper codes except for displaying or printing a message that the code is in error.

Information normally printed on the character printers shall also be displayed on demand by CRT. In addition, CRT's shall be able to display at any time by demand the stored information concerning the status and results of tests on any patient in the system. The system shall respond to a given patient name with all names in the system which are the same (if any) and the corresponding hospital numbers. Operator may then select the desired patient by number. System will respond to a given hospital patient chart number with the patient name corresponding to that number and the appropriate test information. If no number matching the given one is found in the files, the system shall so state.

Printed output formats and exact contents shall be as designated in a separate document at the time of "system definition" but will be similar to examples given in section_____of the Request for Proposal.

REFERENCES

1. Williams, G. Z. "The Use of Data Processing and Automation in Clinical Pathology," *Military Medicine* June 1964.

2. Brecher, G., and Loken, H. "The Laboratory Computer—Is It Worth Its Price?" *American Journal of Clinical Pathology,* 55 (1971) : 527.

3. Lamé, K. D. "Can An Automated Laboratory System Be Cost Justified?" *Laboratory Medicine* November 1970.

4. Pollycove, M. "An Economic Projection of Clinical Lab Automation," *Laboratory Management* June 1971.

5. Department of Health, Education and Welfare. "The Mechanization, Automation and Increased Effectiveness of the Clinical Laboratory." *A Status Report by the Automation in the Medical Sciences Review Committee of the National Institute of General Medical Science.* Publication No. (NIH) 72–145, 1971.

6. Robinson, R. *Clinical Chemistry and Automation* London: Charles Griffen & Co., 1971.

7. Krieg, A.; Johnson, T. J.; McDonald, C.; and Cotlove, E. *Clinical Laboratory Computerization* Baltimore: University Park Press, 1971.

8. Riddick, J. H. Jr. "Automated Quality Control With An IBM 1800 Computer." *American Journal of Clinical Pathologists* 53 (1970) : 176–180.

9. *Clinical Laboratory Computer Systems—A Comprehensive Evaluation.* Illinois: J. Lloyd Johnson Associates, 1971.

10. Department of Health, Education and Welfare. *A Study of Automated Clinical Systems.* Publication No. HSM 72-3004.

11. Williams, G. Z.; Young, D. S.; Stein, M. R.; Cotlove, E. "Biological and Analytic Components of Variation in Long Term Studies of Serum Constituents in Normal Subjects." *Clinical Chemistry* 16 (1970) : 1016.

12. Williams, G. Z. "Laboratory Automation Systems Availability and Procurement." *Bulletin of the College of American Pathologists* 21 (1967) .

CHAPTER EIGHT

Pathology Subsystem

by Robert E. Robinson, III

A. INTRODUCTION

The pathologist's two principal narrative text reports are surgical pathology and autopsy. The surgical pathology report is a description of the macroscopic and microscopic characteristics of a surgically obtained tissue specimen and an interpretation of the pathologist's findings. The autopsy report is similar in nature except that it is a detailed description of the postmortem examination of multiple organ systems. Ten to fifteen thousand surgical pathology and three to five hundred autopsy reports are typical yearly volumes for a five-hundred-bed hospital.

The conventional approach to surgical pathology and autopsy reporting is for the pathologist to dictate his findings at the time of tissue examination. The dictation is transcribed and the resulting document is stored within the patient's medical record and other paper-based files. The report provides information of value to the immediate and continuing care of the patient, medical research, and education.

This chapter describes some of the computer-based techniques which have been developed to assist report generation and information retrieval operations.

B. DATA ACQUISITION

Pathology report information may be acquired for computer processing through use of a coding system, the entry of narrative text, or as part of an interactive report generation process.

1. Coding

The Systematized Nomenclature of Pathology, SNOP, is one of the primary systems which has been developed for classifying pathology findings.[4,11,18] Classification is based on a description of the pathology at specific anatomical locations. Coding can be accomplished by manually scanning a conventional narrative text report for the phrases of interest and locating the corresponding code in the code book. The codes are entered for computer processing by keypunching the information onto standard 80-column cards, through use of other off-line entry techniques, or by an interactive terminal.

A coding method has several advantages: data are presented to the computer system in a compact and consistent format and classification and cataloging are facilitated. The disadvantages are that the abstracter must be familiar with the code system; codes have a tendency to reduce and stereotype information, and they require frequent revision or become obsolete.

2. Narrative Text

Part or all of the narrative text of a report may be acquired for computer processing at the time of original transcription, through use of optical scanning techniques, or by retyping the conventional typewritten report. An important and currently unresolved question is which parts of a pathology report should be processed through the computer system. Opinions range from the interpretation section to the text of the entire document. The advantage of including a minimum amount of information is that processing time and storage requirements are decreased. The disadvantage is that less information is available through the computer system, increasing the need for reference to paper-based files.

From the standpoint of quality control and editing, the most desirable approach to narrative data acquisition is the transcription of the dictated report directly into the computer system by use of an interactive terminal.[1,7,14] The computer system can scan the information at the time of entry, check format and content, and assist with the editing process. The disadvantages of this approach have been the relatively high expense and poor reliability of time-sharing computer systems. These disadvantages are, however, rapidly disappearing as a result of improved technology. A second approach is the use of an off-line key-to-tape or key-to-disk system for transcription of the dictated material.[2,13,14,15] This approach retains some of the advantages of an interactive terminal in that limited format control and editing are possible. The IBM Magnetic Tape/Selectric Typewriter (MT/ST) is an example of a good keyboard-to-tape system. It consists of a high-quality office typewriter which is interfaced to a pair of magnetic tape drives. Errors noted during typing are easily removed by backspacing and retyping. "Tape-to-tape" operations are possible, allowing any amount of data to be added to or deleted from a tape record. One tape may be used to generate standard headings which can be simultaneously printed and recorded on the second tape, thus lightening the burden of the secretary while at the same time prompting replies which might be inadvertently omitted. Individual documents may be located on a tape by means of a coded search system. The advantages of this approach are that the information is acquired for computer processing at the time of normal transcription, some editing capability is provided, and the user is not dependent on a time-shared computer system. The cost is moderate. The primary disadvantage is the lack of sophisticated editing capability.

An optical character reader may be used for entry of a typewritten report in its original format. These readers have been significantly improved in recent years and are used successfully for scanning airline ticket stubs, finance vouchers, and a variety of other documents. The primary advantage of this approach is that a conventional, inexpensive office typewriter can be used for preparation of reports for entry into the computer system. There are, however, some significant limitations to this technique.

In single-spaced documents, page registration can be a very critical factor. It is not unusual for small amounts of horizontal skew to cause the optical reader to jump incorrectly to the line above or below the one being scanned. It is difficult to maintain the required page alignment even with the use of sprocket-fed paper. The printed characters must be distinct; smudges, partial erasures, and other distortions can cause read errors. Some optical character readers cannot handle colons, semicolons, equal signs, and other standard characters. Many readers require the use of nonstandard characters or special document formats. Finally, this approach to narrative text data acquisition typically provides little, if any, editing capability at the time of preparation of the source document.

Narrative text may also be acquired by manually abstracting part or all of the text of a typewritten report.[2,8,9] The abstracted text is entered for computer processing using either interactive terminals or "stand-alone" data acquisition systems. The advantages of this approach are that the format and content of the original document can be less restrictive. The disadvantage is that this is a secondary transcription process which costs time and effort and has the potential for introducing errors.

Limitations are imposed on the entry of narrative text for computer processing regardless of the specific data acquisition system. The text must be accurate, concise, consistently worded, and in accordance with the rules of English grammar. These same criteria apply to conventional typewritten reports; however, their observance is more critical when the data are to be processed by a computer system.

At one medical center where the full texts of approximately 25,000 pathology reports are processed each year, detailed studies revealed a 20 to 30% increase in transcription time as a result of more stringent document criteria.[14,15] Significant time was expended in locating missing information and in looking up words when a transcriptionist was uncertain about their correct spelling. Time was also increased by the necessity of correcting errors which were detected by the computer-based data screening operations. For example, approximately 15% of the reports being scanned were found to contain one or more spelling errors.

3.   Interactive Report Generation

A final data acquisition technique which should be considered is the use of interactive techniques to produce both the original narrative text report and a coded equivalent.[3,5,11,12,19] The physician generates the report directly by entering a combination of shorthand and multiple-choice selections which the computer system translates to a narrative text report. The advantages to this approach are that the transcription step is eliminated, the input is checked at the time of entry, the computer system can provide reminders to reduce accidentally omitted information, decision assistance is possible, and the features of a coding system are retained. The disadvantages are that the physician is required to do his own typing, and the classification scheme may reduce the information content of the report.

The major pathology data systems now in use include manual and computer-assisted coding of the pathology interpretations, the abstracting of the interpretations in natural language, and the acquisition of the entire narrative text at the time of original transcription. For the future, the optimum approach appears to be the direct entry of information through use of an interactive terminal. The primary question regarding this approach is whether the report information will be entered by the physician or by a scribe. The use of a typewriter keyboard will continue to be necessary until such time as computer-based voice analysis is practical. Innumerable studies confirm the difficulties of requiring the physician to type. The disadvantages of typing may, however, be outweighed by the benefits obtained through use of an interactive report generation system. Also, good shorthand and coding techniques can reduce the quantity of information which must be typed to a practical level.

C.   DATA SCREENING

Data screening is best carried out coincident with the entry of the information. When off-line data acquisition techniques are used, the screening should be the first step of the batch data processing operation. The first items of information to be screened are the patient, document, and reporter identification. The latter two items may be confirmed through use of look-up tables.

1. Patient Identification

Patient identification is best screened by comparing the data in the report with that contained within a computer-based Master Patient Identification File (MPIF). Such files typically contain a patient's hospital identification number, full name, birthdate, sex, and other data. Items of identification which are common to a report and the MPIF are compared and any inconsistencies are flagged. Studies have shown that one or more items of identification can be in error in as high as 5% of the reports being processed.[15] Many of these errors are minor variations in the spelling of a patient's name or changes in his birthdate, but a significant number of potentially serious identification errors are also detected.

2. Content Analysis

Screening of the remainder of the report depends on whether the information is coded or in natural language. Individual codes can be checked for validity and the overall completeness of the document evaluated. More sophisticated checking is also possible; for example, an analysis of a pattern of codes to determine the probability of descriptive findings being related to specific interpretations. This operation can be carried out in an interactive mode and may be of value in assisting the physician in developing his interpretation.

Natural language data screening operations include checks of format, completeness, adherence to the rules of English grammar, and content analysis.

No known general computer program provides automatic screening for either syntactic or semantic errors. It is practical, however, to confirm that each word in the text is correctly spelled. This is achieved by sorting the words contained in the incoming reports in alphabetical order. This alphabetical list is then matched against a computer-based master vocabulary. The procedure identifies new words and misspellings but not words which are correctly spelled but incorrect within context.

A number of investigators have compiled medical vocabularies, and their scope is of interest. In the field of surgical pathology, one investigator[8,9] found approximately 10,000 different words in the interpretation section of 110,712 surgical pathology reports. Another investigator[13,14,15] reported approximately 9,000 different words in scanning the same report section. An analysis of ten million words contained within a consolidated medical record file revealed 40,000 unique words, many of which were proper nouns.[14] A study of the medical terminology contained in articles in the *Journal of the American Medical Association* over a one-year period revealed a total medical vocabulary of approximately 7,500 words. In contrast, a standard medical dictionary contains over 500,000 different terms. The limited size of operational medical vocabularies is unexpected but does greatly facilitate natural language data processing operations.

It is not feasible to review the content of a natural language document to the extent possible with coded information;[16,17] however, there are some practical data screening operations. One is to determine whether or not selected paragraph titles are followed by appropriate responses. The exactness of the check depends on the complexity of the data. For example, the identification information can be screened accurately whereas more descriptive information can only be checked for omissions and certain very obvious inconsistencies. More sophisticated analyses are theoretically possible by comparing the descriptions and interpretations with textbook information.

D. REPORT COMPACTING

Each document record normally includes a label which identifies the document type, date, identification of the patient and author, indexing data, and the identification of internal sections of the document. The body of the document is stored as originally encoded in natural language or in a coded equivalent of natural language. Information which is coded at the time of entry has already been compacted and requires no further discussion.

Natural language data may be handled in one of several ways. First, it may be retained in its original narrative format. No compacting step is required but it is difficult to search clear text and significant space is required for its storage.

Second, blanks can be removed and each term preceded by a character count. The storage space is approximately the same as for clear text, but searching is facilitated by having identified the lengths of the terms.

Third, each term may be replaced by a code word. This greatly compacts the text; for example, a 19-bit code can handle all the terms in a standard medical dictionary. The codes can be arranged to have a fixed relationship with computer word boundaries, facilitating highly efficient binary searching. That the codes can form the basis of a classification system is an additional advantage.

The disadvantages are that a code table is required for conversion between natural language and the codes, and it is impractical to encode some items of information. With a large-sized vocabulary, the encoding/decoding process requires a significant amount of computer time. It is true, however, that the time is usually not critical because the volume of new documents which must be processed each day is small, as is the information printed for most information retrieval operations. One method which may be used for circumventing the decoding process is to maintain separate files of both the original narrative text and its coded equivalent. In this system, searching is carried out using the coded file, but the information of interest is printed from the text file. The decoding step is eliminated, but there is the necessity for maintaining two separate files.

There is no easy solution to the problem of encoding numeric values. It is obviously impractical to develop a coded equivalent for every possible number. There are two alternatives. One is to describe the number in natural language; for example, "one hundred" rather than "100." Second, the number may be retained in its original format but preceded by a special code and appropriate pointers to identify the beginning and end of a clear text numeric field.

Another type of compacting is an actual reduction in the number of words in the original text. This is achieved by deleting "a," "the," and other terms which may not be essential to the meaning of a paragraph. Storage space is reduced, but there are the potential hazards of making the document less readable or of changing the sense of a sentence or paragraph.

E.   DATA ABSTRACTING

Data abstracting is of value for generating subfiles or for transferring critical items of information to an integrated data base. These operations are facilitated when a classification system has been used for the interactive generation and storage of the report or for encoding the original natural language terms; however, limited abstracting is also feasible with clear text. For example, selected sections of reports can be automatically screened for a series of words and phrases which indicate a diagnostic interpretation of malignant disease.

The abstracting of "significant" medical information is difficult with a coding scheme and almost impossible with natural language. The problem is that there are few clear-cut definitions of medically significant information and the data must usually be understood within context. This latter operation is particularly difficult to automate when processing natural language information.

F.   FILE MAINTENANCE

On completion of the final editing, the reports are stored in one or more files. Three common files are: the document type file (e.g., pathology); an integrated patient data file; and special subfiles (e.g., a tumor registry).

The items in the document label can be used as an index for inserting the new report into a file which is maintained in "sort sequence"; for example, a pathology file ordered by patient identification number and date.

The techniques for adding the new information depend on whether sequential or direct access files are used. Magnetic tape or other sequential access files are updated by first sorting the incoming documents in the desired sequence. The resultant file is then merged with the original master, creating a new master. Direct access files which are maintained in sort order through use of index sequential or other techniques can be updated directly.

Natural language vocabularies must be updated with the new words encountered in incoming reports. It is of value to maintain a current tabulation of the frequency of occurrence of each word as part of the vocabulary.

Code tables must also be updated. A particularly complex updating process is the addition, modification, or deletion of information contained within a computer-based classification table. When a code is changed, appropriate modifications must be made to all codes to which linkages occur.

G. INFORMATION RETRIEVAL

Retrieval of individual documents is easily achieved when they are stored on a direct access device and the label information is indexed in sort sequence. Options typically include the ability to locate documents by patient number, individual dates, or ranges of dates.

Retrievals based on information contained within the body of a document involve sequential file searching, the nature of which is dependent on whether or not a coding/classification scheme has been employed.

1. Coded Data

The first step in searching a coded data base is locating the appropriate code numbers in a catalog. This may be done manually or through the use of an interactive terminal. Second, the logical associations of the information retrieval request are formulated. For example, report years 1970–1971, males over the age of 40, with a given series of interpretation codes and not others. The search strategy should permit scanning specific sections of the document, including the label, for items of information which have definite logical relationships.

2. Natural Language Data

Natural language reports, whether in clear text or a coded equivalent, are retrieved by locating a series of words or phrases which have the requested logical associations.

A typical search request is entered by stating first which section of the document is to be scanned; for example, the microscopic findings or interpretation. The keywords or phrases are then entered. Retrieval may be based on the location of a single word or one word in a series—the OR option. It is possible to specify that two or more words or phrases be located—the AND option. Any word or phrase may be made synonymous with any other word or phrase. A report may be retrieved only if it contains one or more words or phrases and not certain other words or phrases —the NOT option. This option is useful in reducing "false positives" which may result when words of interest are preceded by negatives.

Options may be required to control the degree of separation that is permitted between a group of words, all of which are to be located. Fixed order specifies that one word must directly follow another. This is useful in those instances in which there are two or more words which always occur together in a fixed sequence—for example, a phrase. The option may be modified so that one or more intervening words are permitted. When fixed order is not specified, any word order is accepted; however, the options can provide that the series of words to be located must occur together within the same phrase, sentence, or paragraph.

It is important to be able to search for numeric data. One method of achieving this with natural language is to scan the text for numeric fields which appear adjacent to specific search arguments. When a numeric value is located, a comparison is made to determine if it is lower, equal, or higher than a specified value.

Output options include the reproduction of one or more sections of the documents of interest or the generation of statistical tabulations.

3. Retrieval Problems

Finally, there is the problem of success of the information retrieval operations. Ideally, none of the desired reports should be missed nor should any documents be retrieved that fail to meet the search criteria. Such error-free operation is rarely achieved in practice for a number of reasons.

Retrieval is dependent on the identification of a series of words or phrases that occur in some prescribed pattern. Reports will be missed if the requester fails to enter the appropriate search words or synonyms, if there are misspellings either in the data or in the request, or if search options are inappropriate to the data being scanned.

The requester is required to have sufficient knowledge of the subject material so that he understands the ways in which the items of interest might be phrased. For example, if he is searching for a particular diagnostic impression, he must be aware of all the ways in which this might be stated.

This problem can be partially reduced by encouraging the originators of the material to use standard terminology and by maintaining synonym tables within the computer system. Both of these approaches have been found to be of value; however, the requester still has the final responsibility for formulating the search argument.

The problem of misspellings can be handled either by attempting to eliminate misspelled words or by the use of techniques which compensate for spelling errors. "Soundex" and other techniques for word matching based on the successful comparison of patterns of characters within a word are possible. Unfortunately, these techniques approach cryptographic analysis in complexity and consume prohibitive amounts of computer time. As an alternative, every effort must be made to ensure that all documents contain correctly spelled words.

A variety of search options may be selected. These have a direct effect on the retrieval operations. For example, a search for the diagnosis "mitral stenosis" could be made by requesting the phrase "mitral stenosis" or by stating that the search argument is satisfied if "mitral" and "stenosis" appear within the same sentence or phrase, regardless of their order. If the phrase option is selected, documents which contain statements such as "stenosis of the mitral valve" will be missed and if the option is selected in which "mitral" and "stenosis" can appear in any sequence, reports which contain "aortic stenosis and mitral insufficiency" may be erroneously retrieved. Problems of this nature are extremely difficult to resolve; for this reason, natural language retrieval operations are subject to some inaccuracies.

Failure to retrieve a document is a much more serious problem than is retrieving too many, as the latter mistake is immediately evident to the requester. It is thus desirable to design the system so that the absolute minimum number of documents will be missed, even if this is at the expense of retrieving a certain percentage of "false positives."

It is difficult to evaluate search errors in the general case, as they are dependent on both the nature of the text and the search arguments which have been selected. Experience has demonstrated that, with carefully worded natural language search requests, the "false positive" error rate will be in the range of 2–10%.

H. COST

Surgical pathology reports vary in size from one-half to two typewritten pages, with an average length of three-quarters of a page. In one study, the cost of transcribing an average-sized document, using a conventional office typewriter, was 35¢. This cost includes the transcriptionist time and typewriter but not overhead expenses. The cost of transcription using a stand-alone data acquisition system, the IBM Magnetic Tape/Selectric Typewriter (MT/ST), was 70¢ per document. The cost differences result from the equipment and the more stringent editing requirements which are imposed on reports prepared for computer processing.

The same study revealed the data processing cost to be 84¢ for an average length narrative report. This cost includes data screening, editing, abstracting, and file maintenance. The approximate cost of storing one surgical pathology report for one year on a direct access device is 25¢. The cost of retrieval of one report by direct access is in the range of 3¢. A sequential search of a natural language file requires approximately 0.1 second per report.

No good estimates are available as to the cost of encoding pathology reports. It is estimated that most of the data processing costs would be significantly less than those of a natural language system, due to the reduced size of the records.

I. BENEFITS

The primary benefits of using computer-based techniques for processing pathology report data are assistance with report generation and quality control, abstracting, information retrieval, and administrative functions.

The report generation assistance provides a means for reducing omissions, inconsistent data, and a variety of other errors. An additional benefit is that the reports are rapidly made available to users.

The computer-based data screening operations also contribute significantly to a reduction in omissions and other report errors.

The automatic abstracting of information—for example, the data which are required for a tumor registry—is more accurate than a corresponding manual system and results in a saving of the time and effort which the medical staff must devote to this task.

Information retrieval operations provide immediate access to specific reports and make possible the scanning of large files to find documents that contain a series of items of interest. This latter function is essential to both research and medical education.

Finally, the information system can provide data for patient billing, the distribution of cases, workload statistics, and other administrative purposes.

REFERENCES

1. Barnett, G. Octo; Greenes, R. A.; and Grossman, J. H. "The Capturing of Medical Text Information." *Meth. of Infor. in Med.* 8 (1969) : 117–182.

2. Barnhard, H. J., and Long, J. M. "Computer Autocoding, Selecting, and Correlating of Radiologic Diagnostic Cases: A Preliminary Report." *American Journal of Roentgenology* 96 (1966) : 854–863.

3. Brolin, I. "MEDELA: An Electronic Data Processing System for Radiological Reporting." *Radiology* 103 (1972) : 249–255.

4. Cohen, M., et al. "Coded System for Computer Retrieval of Pathology Diagnoses." *Military Medicine* 135 (1970) : 1028–1033.

5. Greenes, R. A., et al. "Recording, Retrieval and Review of Medical Data by Physician-Computer Interaction." *New Eng .J. of Med.* 282 (1970) : 307–315.

6. Jacob, W. "Processing of Basic Data in Pathology." *Meth. of Info. in Med.* 6 (1967) : 166–173.

7. Korein, J. "The Computerized Medical Record: the Variable-Field-Length Format System and its Applications." *Information Processing of Medical Records. Proceedings of the IFIPS TC4 Conference, Lyon, France,* 1970.

8. Lamson, B. G., and Dimsdale, B. "A Natural Language Information Retrieval System." *Proceedings of the IEEE* 54 (1966) : 1636–1640.

9. "Storage and Retrieval of Uncoded Tissue Pathology Diagnoses in the Original English Free Text Form." *User's Manual 1, A Natural Language Information Retrieval System.* Los Angeles: IBM Corporation, 1966.

10. Myers, J.; Gelblat, M.; and Enterline, H. T. "Automatic Encoding in Pathology Data." *Archives of Pathology* 89 (1970) : 73–78.

11. Pratt, A., and Thomas, L. B. "An Information Processing System for Pathology Data." *Pathology Annual* 1966.

12. Reichertz, P. L. "PIRS (Personal Information Retrieval System), A Multi-Purpose Computer Program for Storage and Retrieval of Reference Files." *Methods of Information in Medicine* 7 (1968) : 165–172.

13. Robinson, R. E.; White, J.; Shore, A.; and Kwok, G.-Y. "Medical Record Acquisition, Screening and Retrieval Using Natural Language Data Processing Techniques." *The Sixth Annual Colloquium on Information Retrieval.* Philadelphia: Medical Documentation Service, 1969.

14. Robinson, R. E.; White, J.; Shore, A.; and Kwok, G.-Y. "Acquisition and Analysis of Narrative Medical Record Data." *Comp. and Biomed. Res.* October 1970.

15. Robinson, R. E.; White, J.; Shore, A.; Kwok, G.-Y.; and Meschan, I. "Computerized Radiologic Reporting with Word Retrieval Using MT/ST." *Radiology* October 1971.

16. Simmons, R. F. "Answering English Questions by Computer: A Survey." *Communications of the ACM* 8 (1965) : 53–70.

17. Simmons, R. F. "Natural Language Processing." *Datamation* 12 (1966) : 61 Passim.

18. Smith, J. C. "Anatomic Pathology and Data Processing." *Archives of Pathology* 81 (1966) : 279–280.

19. Templeton, A. W.; Reichertz, P. L.; and Paquet, E. "RADIATE—Updated and Redesigned for Multiple Cathode-Ray Tube Terminals." *Radiology* 92 (1969) : 30–36.

20. Van Brunt, E. E. "The Kaiser-Permanente Medical Information System." *Comp. and Biomed. Res* 3 (1970) : 477–487.

CHAPTER NINE

Information Management in Radiology

by Gwilym S. Lodwick

A. INTRODUCTION

It has been said that there are three professional health care delivery systems within the hospital structure, any one of which can make or break the quality of the total health care delivery system.[1] These three systems are pathology, anesthesiology, and radiology. A poorly functioning department of radiology can delay the extensive process of patient care, estrange patients from the system, infuriate the referring physicians, endanger the stability of the unit economic system, and generally spread poor morale throughout the institution. In a properly functioning department of radiology, the patients move through smoothly and without stress, the physicians receive their reports without delay, radiologists are available for consultation and their opinions are respected, bills are rendered promptly and accurately, films are available in the file room when needed, special procedures are handled smoothly and competently, essential statistics are collected, and schedules are met. Efficient radiological services can build spirit for the entire institution. A strong case is to be made for adequate institutional support and attention to the requirements for good radiological services.

Many factors enter into the structure of a smoothly functioning radiology department. One is proper departmental design, which guarantees that the flow of patients and internal operational flow—including technologists, radiologists, flow of films through the darkrooms, quality check, file room, and interpretation mechanisms—are not intermixed.

Second, radiology does not exist in a vacuum but is part of a highly

206

complex interrelated series of mechanisms. In an institution assembled as a series of health care islands, each functioning individually and separately from the whole, even a well-organized department of radiology can be made to look bad because of the uncontrolled flooding of patients into radiology waiting rooms. This phenomenon can overwhelm and break the morale of even a unit with strong internal integrity.

Third, the relationship between the numbers of staff and the size of the demand must be appropriate. A rough rule of thumb relates numbers of technologists to numbers of examinations, but in any institution this ratio must be individualized, within limits, because of different ratios of patients.

In another instance, there is an acceptable ratio between the number of radiologists and the number of examinations; in teaching institutions, this generally is one radiologist for every 6,000 to 8,000 examinations. It seems that, as the size of the program increases, so does the number of examinations that each radiologist can handle.

However, since the usual hospital department of radiology is a high production unit, with patient flow, courier and technologist flow, film flow, and radiologist function all needing to be tightly integrated, internal communication is an extremely important element (Figure 9–1). To cite a few examples: When the patient returns for a repeated gastrointestinal examination, effective use of professional personnel and space requires that the previous examination be instantly available. The patient who requires a colon series, an intravenous pyelogram, and a thyroid uptake requires an exact order of sequence; otherwise, substantial delay is incurred. The physician seeing an outpatient who has come 25 miles for an examination requiring radiological consultation needs an immediate response so that the patient does not need to return unnecessarily. The charges for radiological services should be available when that patient leaves so that a financial settlement can be made. Patient A on surgery has taken a sudden turn for the worse, and his films are somewhere in the routine flow pattern within the department. They are needed immediately. Or Dr. X from Medicine has just appeared at the file room, wanting three cases of a certain syndrome for this afternoon's ward rounds. How can they be found? The last example: radiologist Y, interpreting a routine set of films, is preoccupied because his oldest son totaled the family car the night before and misses an obvious coin lesion which is partially obscured by the clavicle.

These examples are typical of the many information requirements and demands placed on our special kind of health delivery organization, which often handles several hundred examinations and exposes several thousand films a day. It is apparent that excellent internal communication, external communication, and quality control are absolutely essential.

We can see that there are certain goals which are critical to the effective

INFORMATION MANAGEMENT IN DIAGNOSTIC RADIOLOGY

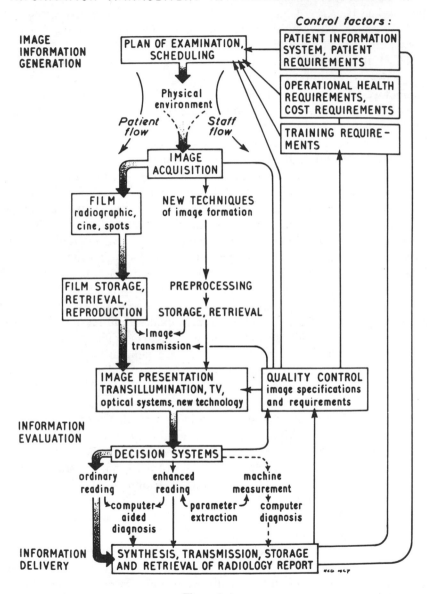

Figure 9–1

delivery of radiological health services in the hospital environment. By order of precedence, these are:

(1) The through-flow of patients
(2) Accuracy of diagnosis
(3) Reporting on time
(4) File room control
(5) Billing on time
(6) Retrievability of cases and reports
(7) Keeping of necessary statistics
(8) Space savings
(9) Personnel savings

These are the kinds of problems that every radiologist faces and wishes that he had adequate solutions for.

Within any given environment, the order of precedence may change. However, as we move into the mid–1970's and prepare for the 1980's, each of these important problems in radiological health care must be resolved to its optimum. From our experience, we find that a highly integrated computer information system specially designed for radiological health care needs offers a major resolution to these problems. To exemplify how an integrated computer information system can be used in delivering radiological health care, we shall refer to our department and its long, various, and successful experience with this type of system.

In our Department, the Missouri Automated Radiology System (MARS),[2,3] a computer-mediated time-sharing teleprocessing information system has been on-line for more than two years and has made substantial contributions to improving information flow. MARS I is mediated through a centrally based IBM 360/50 computer which supports multiple programs in addition to the radiological service. MARS II is a stand-alone midi-computer version, modular in concept, which employs a PDP-15 computer that is based in the department and is dedicated to radiological function.

Our efforts to use a computer to handle problems of radiological health care began in the mid–1950's when punched data cards were used to provide flexibility in handling large amounts of information collected in an intensive study of the x-ray patterns of neoplastic bone disease. Later, the computer proved useful in statistical analyses of data to determine whether some of our startling findings were real or the result of random distribution. Similarity of punched cards which recorded data from similar images naturally led to the thesis of using a computer for pattern recognition, a thesis which was awarded NIH support (CA 06263, Computer Analysis of Tumor Roentgenograms) by the beginning of 1962. One cannot work with a computer without learning many new things. Consequently, by the mid–

1960's, our efforts had multiplied to include not only computer-assisted diagnosis in a number of different dimensions[4-9] but also modeling of radiological systems[10-12] with the initiation of our work on MARS (Missouri Automated Radiology System),[13,14] the collection and publication of extensive bibliography of computer health related subjects,[15-17] and some very early conceptions related to automation of image analysis.[18] Our earliest work at Missouri was done on a Burroughs 205, then on an IBM 1620, IBM 7040, IBM 1410, and eventually on a complex of IBM 360/50's and an IBM 360/65. The IBM 1410 and a 360/50 were consecutively installed as the central data processing and information system for the Medical Center. Our initial activation of an IBM 2260 terminal for MARS was accomplished early in the spring of 1967, and MARS went on-line full time as of April 1, 1970. Our systems modeling began early in 1956 and was completed several years later. We have now gone around the clock to initiate an entirely new system study of departmental function in greater detail.

One by-product of the use of many different computers, particularly in respect to on-line applications in support of a health care facility, has been the recognition that the individual vested with responsibility for managing a radiological health care delivery system apparently must be in control of that computer or segment of the computing system which supports the health care system. As will be shown later in our detailed discussion of MARS, the man-machine (physician/computer) interface is almost directly dependent upon the reliability of the computer in maintaining its end of the interface. In the state of the computer arts currently available at Missouri, a number of health care systems are dependent upon the central computer in addition to the off-line batch operations. Inevitably, the demand of some systems must take precedence over others, which means that some services must wait. The demands for radiological health services are such that they cannot wait. As the manager of a radiological health care system, this author has experienced his department immobilized because an elective action by a computer operator brought the support system down. Seemingly none are as impressed with the urgency of need for medical support as those who are on-line using a support system. Our departmentally based small computer version of MARS is in response to the urgency of need for a stand-alone radiology information system.

Finally, after many years of attempting to achieve an interface between radiology and the engineering disciplines, we have been successful in conjoining significant elements of medicine and engineering to form an image analysis laboratory, which is now supported by a number of research projects. Our bioengineering program now includes elements of industrial engineering, electrical engineering, bioengineering, statistics, information sciences, radiology, and involves work with pattern recognition, automated image analysis, computer-assisted diagnosis, small computer interface, image transmission, storage retrieval, and measurement of intelligence content in radiant images. Our goals for the future include the welding of all of the many facets of this program together into a modular management system for diagnostic radiology.

B. MISSOURI AUTOMATED RADIOLOGY SYSTEM

A variety of information management systems have been designed to improve quality and efficiency of radiological practice.[19-31] A few have been tested with varying degrees of rigor. Each has its own advantages and compromises. These range from a system where a secretary inputs dictated reports into the computer that reduces each report to its significant elements which are stored and can be retrieved, to systems that employ branching logic trees which lead the radiologist into more and more specialized tables as he narrows the range of his differential diagnosis. Although each of these systems provides improvements which are desirable for radiological health care delivery, additional incentives are provided by the social and political pressures to deliver care to more patients without substantial increases in manpower or money. For nearly two years, the Department of Radiology at the University of Missouri-Columbia has centered clinical practice around an on-line computer system. Our experience with this system has convinced us that such a system can improve health care delivery; it therefore seems likely that computers will be widely used by radiologists for this purpose.

We began developmental work on an automated radiology system in 1965. The basic concept was to interface the radiologist directly with the computer by using a high-speed cathode ray terminal (CRT). The physician, by means of a "dialogue" with the system, would create x-ray consultations which would be not only suitable for incorporation into a patient's chart but also well designed for computer processing. The strategy was to store "dictionaries" of phrases which were available for use in reports in the computer. The radiologist, employing a modified key-word approach, could retrieve and incorporate any of these terms into his report. For example, if the examinations performed were posteroanterior and lateral chest, the radiologist would type into his keyboard "CHES." The computer program would then display on the cathode ray terminal all phrases in the examination dictionary which contained any word beginning with "CHES" (Figure 9–2). The radiologist would then type the appropriate letter heading ("A" in this instance) to select the term he wished to incorporate into his report. In addition to examinations, tables of anatomic sites and diagnoses were

A   CHEST, PA AND LATERAL

B   CHEST, PA

C   CHEST, AP UPRIGHT

D   CHEST, LATERAL

E   CHEST, SUPINE

F   CHEST, DECUBITUS

G   CHEST, LORDOTIC

H   CHEST, MULTIPLE VIEWS

Figure 9–2

constructed beginning with all terms in the American College of Radiology Index supplemented by suggestions from our own radiologists. The hope was that this terminology would be reasonably complete and would provide standardization of terminology while allowing the radiologist enough flexibility to give an adequate consultation.

The concept of an interactive system was somewhat in advance of the computer hardware available at the time so that the initial prototype ran on an IBM 1620 computer, required punched card input from the radiologist, and responded by means of the console typewriter. The advent of third-generation computers and high-speed cathode ray terminals made possible the implementation of a second prototype system, RADIATE (Radiologic Diagnoses Instantly Accessed and Transmitted Electronically),[28] which used an IBM 2260 display station to link the radiologist to an IBM 360/50 computer. During 1967, the system underwent a major software redesign in order to allow several radiologists to use the program simultaneously; in 1968, programs to make computer-aided diagnosis[4-6] available on-line to the radiologist were added, and the system became known as ODARS (On-line Diagnostic and Reporting System). During 1969, clinical testing of ODARS began, and numerous modifications were made in order to fit the program into the complex operation of a department of radiology. Finally, on April 1, 1970, the system was renamed MARS (Missouri Automated Radiology System) and adopted as the means to process all radiologic consultations.

1. Operation of the System

To understand how we use MARS, it is useful to follow the progress of a typical consultation through the department (Figure 9–3). A patient accompanied by a consultation request completed and signed by the refer-

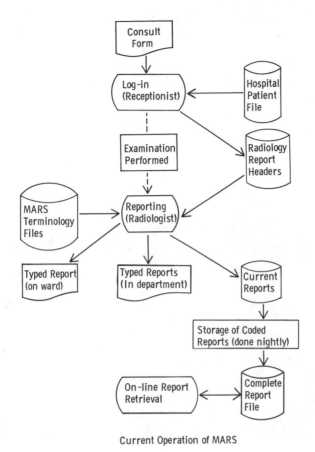

Current Operation of MARS

Figure 9–3

ring physician is presented for examination at the reception area. The receptionist informs the computer of the patient's arrival by entering the patient's unit number via an IBM 2260 television display station terminal. The computer searches the hospital master disk file for this number and responds by displaying the information stored there, including the patient's name, date of birth, sex, race, and hospital ward or outpatient clinic code. If the information is not on file (as, for example, in the case of a patient not previously seen at the hospital who requires emergency care), it is entered by the receptionist manually. The receptionist then types in the referring physician's name as well as the clinical history which has been provided. Finally, the examination requested is entered, and the computer stores all of this information in a temporary holding file. A three-digit number indicating the location of the record within this file is displayed to the receptionist who writes it on the request form.

Next, the patient is examined and his roentgenograms, along with his previous x-rays and the request form, are brought for interpretation to a radiologist at one of the 2260 terminals (Figure 9–4). The radiologist begins by typing the three-digit address of the header previously entered by the receptionist. The computer retrieves this data and displays it on the screen. The radiologist corrects any errors in this data and then completes the report by adding his findings and impressions.

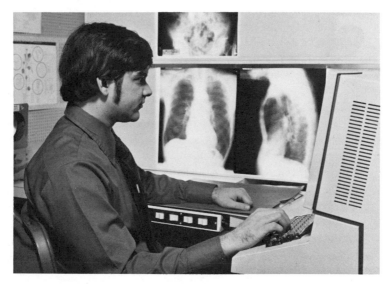

Figure 9–4

In addition to incorporating phrases retrieved by key word as illustrated above, the radiologist has additional options in preparing his report. He may select any of a list of commonly employed phrases, such as "there has been essentially no change in findings since the previous examination." Since this particular phrase is the fourth in the list, the radiologist may simply type "P4" to add it to the report. If he does not remember the number, he may simply type "P" to request display of the entire list from which he then makes his selection. Another option available is the incorporation of a precoded sequence of statements which are retrieved by typing a three-letter abbreviation, or mnemonic. For example, if the radiologist types "CAD," the computer will incorporate into the report a series of statements describing a geriatric chest with calcification in the aortic arch, tortuosity of the descending aorta, and degenerative changes in the thoracic spine. These pre-coded statements frequently make it possible to complete an entire report by typing only a few letters. The approach is obviously quite similar to the use of "canned" reports generated by semi-automatic typewriters. However, the computer does have an advantage in that the radiologist reviews the report on his CRT immediately and, if he wishes, he may easily edit it. For example, if the changes in the spine are unusually marked, he might add an appropriate modifier to the report. Finally, if the radiologist is unable to express himself fully by the options provided, he may type any additional remarks which he feels are necessary.

After the radiologist has proofread the entire report and made appropriate corrections, the computer immediately types out a copy of the report (Figure 9–5) on an output terminal located on the patient's ward; three

```
***** RADIOLOGY REPORT *****


PT:  PETER HAUGWITZ                      UNIT #:  96-42-00
   AGE:  24 YEARS      SEX:  M     RACE:  C     WARD:  E5
   EXAM:  03/03/72 AT 8:42 AM     REPORTED:  03/03/72 AT 10:12 AM
REF. PHY:  H. JONES      CL. DATA:  PNEUMONIA.     ANY CHANGE?


EXAMINATION:  CHEST, PA AND LATERAL
      SITE:  LOWER LOBE
                LEFT
   FINDING:  INFILTRATE
               DECREASED
AS COMPARED TO THE EXAM OF 2-27-72


IMPRESSION:  PNEUMONIA


              JAMES L. LEHR, M.D.
```

Figure 9–5

copies are produced simultaneously in the department of radiology. One of these copies is affixed to the jacket containing the patient's radiographs; the second is sent to the referring physician for his convenience; and the third is attached to the request form, presented to the radiologist for signature, and returned to the patient's medical record.

All the reports transmitted during the day are kept on a random access disk file. Any of them can be reviewed instantly by entering the patient's unit number via a 2260 display terminal. At night, each report transmitted is permanently stored on a numerically coded form on a large direct access file. From this file, any report for any patient can be retrieved for review within a matter of seconds. In addition, it is possible to retrieve all cases with any combination of examination, site, and/or diagnosis at a CRT. The user employs the same key word scheme as that used in reporting to specify what class of cases he wishes to retrieve. Those reports are then located, translated from numeric codes into English, and displayed one at a time beginning with the most recent one. Retrieval time is essentially independent of the total number of reports on file and averages about 15 seconds per case retrieved. The program is used to gather material for radiology teaching conferences as well as for the lecture series given to medical students. It is also employed to retrieve examples of uncommonly performed examinations for use in the technology training program and to locate cases for research projects.

MARS I has been implemented on an IBM 360/50. The interactive programs all operate under the control of the Baylor Message Handler which, in turn, operates under the IBM Operating System. All programs are written in FORTRAN (H-Level) using BAL routines to support direct access I/Q and some data conversion operations. The on-line reporting program handles up to eight users simultaneously and executes in a partition of 74K bytes. Multiple special purpose on-line utility programs are also available for tasks such as updating the MARS displays, rearranging terminology files, adding "pet" phrases, or creating "canned" reports. Updating of the terminology tables is on-line and available to the radiologist as a part of the reporting routine. Seventeen direct access files are used by MARS. All but one reside on a 2314 disk and occupy a total of 20 cylinders. The remaining file, which contains the coded radiology reports along with the information needed for on-line retrieval, is located on a 2321 data cell and requires, with indexing, an average of 77 bytes per report.

2. Evaluation

Use of MARS as the primary means to process all consultations in the department has permitted us to accumulate some quantitative data relating to its performance. Since additional steps are required to enter patient identification information when a patient arrives at the department, we were concerned that the total time spent by patients in the department would increase. Accordingly, this time was measured for each patient entering the department for a week with MARS in use and compared to similar data obtained prior to the use of MARS. In the week without MARS, 439 patients were processed in an average time of 59.8 minutes; with MARS, 474 patients were processed in an average time of 59.3 minutes. The additional steps clearly did not increase patient time in the department.

Another concern was that the radiologist would be slowed down by being required to type into a computer terminal rather than simply speaking into a dictaphone. Radiologist time to report with dictation was measured for 327 cases and compared with time per report in 325 randomly selected cases reported over MARS. The average for each group was 2.7 minutes. It should be noted that the dictated reports require proofreading at a later time and that this additional effort is not reflected in the averages. On the other hand, the MARS reports are proofread by the radiologist as they are reported so that this time is included in the average for MARS reports.

An important factor in the delivery of radiological health care is the delay in making the radiologist's interpretation of an examination available to the referring physician. Certainly the radiologist's opinion, no matter how accurate, is of little importance if it is available only after the important decisions regarding patient care have been made and a course of action already embarked upon. The time delay between a patient's arrival in the department and transmission of a report (via a tube system) was measured in 805 cases prior to the use of MARS. The time delay between patient arrival and transmission of the report using MARS was collected in 8,515 cases. These results are shown in Figures 9–6 and 9–7. The delay in delivery of dictated reports is not significantly different from similar data collected in other institutions.[19,20] It is apparent that a marked improvement was experienced with MARS. Whereas 70% of the dictated exams were not available until the next day, 75% of our reports now go out the same day and 93% by the end of the second day. Many factors contribute to the remaining delays. For example, fluoroscopic examinations are held for the radiologist performing them and reported in a group, generally in the afternoon. Another factor is that examinations may be performed on patients whose previous films are on loan, and reporting is generally delayed until the old films can be secured for comparison. Finally, a few films are simply misplaced for variable periods.

However, a critical measure of any automated system is its reliability. Beginning in August 1970, we began keeping a careful record of the time, expressed as a percentage of our working day, during which the computer was "down" (Figure 9–8). The causes of failure were multiple and sometimes never determined. Failures could generally be ascribed to systems software, hardware, or MARS software, in descending order of frequency. For

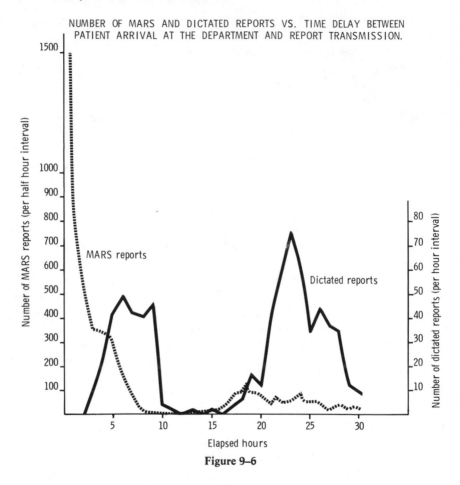

NUMBER OF MARS AND DICTATED REPORTS VS. TIME DELAY BETWEEN
PATIENT ARRIVAL AT THE DEPARTMENT AND REPORT TRANSMISSION.

Figure 9–6

example, during October 1970, a new version of the IBM operating system was installed; and in June 1971, a major hardware catastrophe occurred. The most common type of problem is a failure in the system's programs which govern the flow of jobs through the computer. Such failures generally require roughly a 15–20 minute lapse in operations while the system is restarted and provide unscheduled breaks in reporting. For more prolonged failures, we employ dictaphones in reporting. The relationship between down-time and reports dictated is shown in Figure 9–8.

Another important measure of a reporting system is its cost. Certain costs, such as rental of terminals, are easily estimated and should be comparable for many systems. Other costs, such as the charge for computer memory occupied by the program and its supporting software (e.g., the Baylor Message Handler), are more difficult to estimate. Their value may

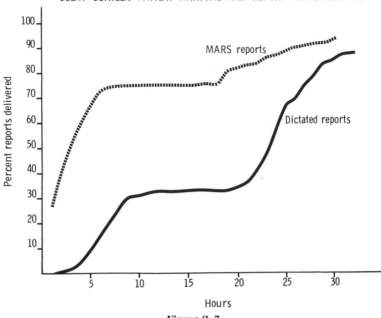

CUMULATIVE PERCENTAGE OF MARS AND DICTATED REPORTS VS. HOURS DELAY BETWEEN PATIENT ARRIVAL AND REPORT TRANSMISSION.

Figure 9–7

vary considerably depending upon the system configuration. At our computer center, there are multiple teleprocessing jobs, all supervised by the Baylor Message Handler and executing from "slow" core memory. In this configuration, MARS uses roughly 400 interactive terminal hours and 7 GPU hours (two of which are consumed by the off-line program which updates the retrieval file) a month. The estimated cost of these services is about $35,000 per annum. In addition, we rent eight IBM 2260 terminals, a 2848 control unit, and a 1053 output device for a total of about $15,000 a year. Since we process roughly 50,000 reports annually, the average cost of an examination is about $1.00.

Our experience with MARS has proved that it is possible to handle the flow of medical information through a reasonably large department of radiology by means of an on-line computer system. The most impressive change by far has been the great improvement in the speed with which a written consultation is made available to the referring physician. We feel that good patient care requires this service. The immediate production of a written report also improves the radiologist's situation. Interpretations of previous examinations are nearly always available to the reporting radiologist, even if the previous examination has been done earlier the same day. Furthermore, since a written consultation is on the film jacket when the

AVERAGE NUMBER OF MARS AND DICTATED REPORTS PER WEEK,
PLUS PER CENT DOWN TIME BY MONTH.

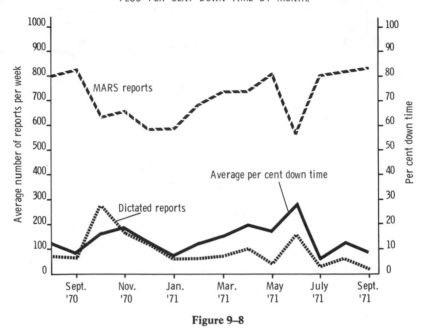

Figure 9–8

referring physician comes to review his patient's film, we avoid the awkward and wasteful situation of having one radiologist deliver an oral consultation while another renders the official written one. If the referring physician wishes to discuss the case in greater detail, he has the name of the consulting radiologist to whom he should turn.

Our major problem in operating MARS has been the poor reliability of the computer. When the machine functions properly, work flows smoothly through the department; when it fails, operations are severely disrupted. Radiologists lose the reports on which they are working at the time of the failure and must begin them again when the system revives. The receptionist is not able to enter patient information, which must be typed in later by the radiologist. Reports which were awaiting print-out are taken out of the print queue and must be retransmitted from disk files individually by clerks. Finally, if the failure is prolonged, reports must be dictated, and, since we no longer have a pool of stenographers, our secretarial staff has the added burden of transcribing reports. Basically, however, the problem is a technical one which presumably can be solved by improved programs and machines.

A more nebulous and more difficult problem is the somewhat restrictive form of the computerized reports themselves. MARS was developed around a philosophy of reporting in which the emphasis was placed upon listing the radiologist's conclusions rather than describing the findings in detail. Not all radiologists in all cases, including some within our own department, are comfortable with this philosophy.

For example, confronted with a difficult case which requires discussion, the radiologist using MARS has several options. He may type in as much text as he wishes; he may list only his impressions on the MARS report and refer to a dictated addendum; or he may simply request that the referring physician discuss the case further in person. Of these options, the first is the most frequently used, for two reasons. First, typing into the terminal is not very objectionable to a radiologist experienced in its use. Second, the radiologist is assured that his observations will be immediately available for patient care if he enters them himself.

Although the ability to include prose in reports is necessary to insure that the radiologist can say whatever he wants in an individual case, the development of MARS has been directed toward reducing the number of cases in which free text is required. To some extent, this can be accomplished simply by adjusting the terminology data base—for example, by adding more "pet" phrases or pre-coded reports or even entirely new dictionaries, such as a table of recommendations. At another level, the reporting program itself can be altered. For example, since the heading "diagnosis" did not seem appropriate to some radiologists, the program was altered so that the radiologist could label the entry as a "finding" or an "impression" instead. Finally, it is possible to adjust both the terminology and the programs within broad limits to suit the needs of individual radiologists. This seems desirable since it is the radiologist, not the system, who bears the responsibility for the quality of his consultation.

3. Transfer to Department Stand-alone Computer—MARS II

One of the advantages of automated systems is the availability of a continuous record of system performance. Unfortunately, our use of a central hospital computer has been plagued with an average 10% downtime. Problems have arisen with both hardware and systems software. Our current philosophy is based on the concept that the person responsible for health care must also be directly responsible for the means by which it is delivered. Furthermore, the use of our software and graphics will now be exportable to other users. Also, independence of a large central CPU allows use of any of the MARS modules with a minimal hardware configuration keyed to the user's environment and needs. For these reasons we have implemented the transfer of the current MARS system to a PDP-15 department computer.[3] The MARS system was transferred from FORTRAN coding to interpreter language (MUMPS) in less than 6 months (with considerable additions), with the aid of the MUMPS operating system. The new system is currently in the final debugging stage. Extensive use of statistics on frequency of usage from clinical operation was made in assembling the terminology tables of the new system.

The MUMPS system developed at Massachusetts General Hospital and documented and augmented by Digital Equipment Corporation is an interpretive language system with extensive string manipulation and file structure ability. We have observed approximately a 3:1 efficiency factor in programmer output compared to FORTRAN coding. The system allows protected time-shared use of core; our current hardware allows up to 16 simultaneous users (28K–18 bit core, two 8 port, 2,400 baud terminal scanners, a total of 20 million words of disk storage).

We are combining many of the management information systems with the current clinical reporting system. Currently available with the report generation program are teaching file programs, coded report look-up programs, mnemonic "canned" reports with allowance for mnemonic use of individualized pet phrases, day sheet enquiry, patient scheduling, terminology table updating, and a referring physician's patient summary. These options are displayed in menu form to the user who signs in with the MARS program, if he replies with a "?" to the options interrogation. The system allows simultaneous developmental programming from remote CRT's; as modules are completed, they are integrated under the MARS program. This is implemented easily with the call, overlay, and protective features of MUMPS. Each user of a terminal has a choice of slightly over 1000 words of core. The resident system utilizes approximately 12K of core depending on the number of device handlers.

A typical example, Figure 9–9 will serve to indicate how the file struc-

```
EC/S UP LB L LNG/FCM=5.5 MSS "WITH SHAGGY BORDERS" /NCLC/ICA



        EXAMINATION:  CHEST, PA AND LATERAL
        SITE:  UPPER LOBE OF THE LEFT LUNG
        FINDING:  5.5 CM, MASS WITH SHAGGY BORDERS
                  NO EVIDENCE OF CALCIFICATION
    IMPRESSION:  CARCINOMA
```

Figure 9–9. Example of coding used to construct report. Most reports are constructed and transmitted by typing a single line. The slash is used to force a new line in the output. If a physician does not remember a mnemonic code he types the first four letters (or more) of any word in the desired phrase. If the tables contain more than one such phrase all possibilities are displayed for the user choice of the correct phrase. The bottom five lines result from entry of the top line.

ture and coding of the MARS system serve to offer the radiologist aid in quickly constructing a report. Combination of command and phrase codes allows most reports to be constructed and displayed from a single line entry. Maximal use is made of the physician's active memory, and "menus" are displayed for passive memory selection only when he uses a four-letter (or greater) mnemonic for which a terminology table search indicates there is more than one use of the term. In this case, all phrases using the term are displayed for choice with the one-, two-, or three-letter code designators which could have called the term or phrase to aid the active memory of the user for future use. Any report can be retrieved, in particular, by using the patient's name or identification number or, in general, by a Boolean combination of the key words of which the report is constructed. Hence, one can search for any Boolean combination of diagnosis, site, or examinations; this search is specified using the mnemonic codes. Retrieval is fast because the *code* for the text is stored, not the text proper. Free text is allowed in constructing a report, but it is stripped when the report is permanently stored so that all such reports contain only vocabulary from basic tables. These tables are extensive but need to be stored only once. Reports are held in a work file in full format during the period in which they are actively used in the department and automatically converted to coded form after a fixed time interval from their inception. The MUMPS language allows fast recovery using only the pointers to the information. The MARS system is constructed so that neither the tables nor the reports need to be searched, but the report and the terminology contained are assembled as the Boolean search is satisfied.

Scheduling of patients presently utilizes only a simple computer-mediated appointment book. A module expediting the handling of patients which involves computer checking of proper sequencing of examinations, the ability to block schedule use of particular facilities, and integration of emergency requirements is currently in the planning stage. Planning is based on an extensive Industrial Engineering analysis of our Department and its relation to total hospital patient flow.[11] Using the basic structure of the MARS system, it will be a straightforward exercise to expand patient scheduling algorithms as soon as systems needs and terminal locations to monitor patient flow are evident.

Fiscal management programs are not yet functioning under the MARS program but are being developed and tested as submodules. They rely more heavily on menu selection and the ability of the user to call for a menu with a question mark whenever his active memory fails. The basic charges accrued to each patient are kept with the stored report. The use of a common data base for all programs allows testing of developmental programs (which do not modify the data base) on-line simultaneous with clinical operation.

C. COMPUTER-AIDED DIAGNOSIS

Research in computer-assisted diagnosis from x-rays was initiated in the Radiology Department in 1961 and has been supported by the National Cancer Institute since 1962 (CA-06263). In computer-aided diagnosis, the radiologist performs as an image scanner and feature extractor. In our limited Bayes Program for the diagnosis of bone tumors, the radiologist and the computer interface through a CRT. The radiologist searches the film and finds the information requested by the computer to compare with stored data to arrive at a differential diagnosis. This process is not quite so simple as it might seem; in order for the radiologist to recognize features and to provide accurate information, there must be a descriptive language or image "set" by which the radiologist can consistently recognize features. An example of such a set designed for bone tumors is shown in a recent publication.[9] The development of an adequate descriptive language is the problem, for this requires that the radiant image of a disease system be extremely carefully analyzed and as large a number of cases as possible be used to assure that all kinds of features can be recognized and that each feature is indeed a separate entity. The language must also be such that radiologists can learn to recognize each of the features with an acceptable level of consistency. Our method of developing a parameter recognition system (or a language for communicating features by radiologists and computers) has been to model the system. If we have developed our language to the extent where it is possible to reconstruct the original image from a set of features provided to a radiologist, we feel reasonably certain that the model represents the real world. So far, our modeling has been confined to disease systems such as bone disease, gastric ulcer, cardiac disease, and pulmonary disease. Theoretically, it should be possible to create a single model to represent the radiant image aspects of all disease systems. We have seen this attempted in an embryonic way; however, if we are to arrive at a stage of sophistication where we can attempt directly to recognize the reflections of disease in any x-ray, a universal model will be necessary. This appears to be a problem for the future; at present, we are completely absorbed with the difficulty of developing relatively simple models for only a few parts of the anatomical system.

Once we have developed the model, we apply it to extract features in a large number of cases, build a probability matrix from the data which prove to be statistically significant, and use a mathematical scheme such as Bayes' rule of inverse probability to compare the features the radiologist has extracted from a new case with the same features in the probability matrix. Our early results with bone tumors proved successful in separating and identifying the correct kind of tumor with about 85% accuracy when only nine different types of bone tumors were being considered.[32] Similar excellent results were obtained by workers in our department for the differential diagnosis between benign and malignant gastric ulcers;[21] somewhat less accurate results were obtained for congenital and acquired heart disease[6] and pulmonary nodules.[7] In each instance, the range of numbers of possibilities was relatively limited. More recently, we have had occasion to modify our bone tumor program into a system which would differentiate between more than 30 diagnostic possibilities. This modification increases the magnitude of the problem by a considerable degree. The solution to this larger problem has been the development of a "Limited Bayes Concept"[33,34] which first employs a Boolean decision tree, formalizing the natural rules of diagnosis for bone tumors, and permits sharp reduction of the number of disease possibilities. This Boolean stage of data reduction is followed by straightforward Bayesian analysis using the residual data, which are more probabilistic in nature than Boolean. This method has evolved over a period of many years and is now available on-line for both the IBM 360/50 and the PDP/15 systems, where it is applied in conjunction with our automated radiology system. The decision tree has solved a number of problems for us in accomplishing preliminary data reduction so that only a relatively small number of possibilities is considered for the Bayesian analysis. At the same time, it has eliminated most situations where powerful predictors can be over-ridden by combinations of weak predictors, permitting the computer to make a misdiagnosis where the human intuitive approach would have made the correct diagnosis. Our Limited Bayes approach to the diagnosis of bone neoplasms is now a useful clinical instrument used as a matter of course in considering the differential diagnosis of bone lesions which routinely pass through our department. The overall accuracy of diagnosis for a series of more than 200 cases, specially selected to illustrate patterns ranging from the typical to the very atypical, has been correct in three cases out of four, or one of the first three choices correct in 95 out of 100 (Table 1). This is an accuracy rate which prob-

Table 1. Computer Evaluation of Primary Tumors of Bone (231 Cases)

First diagnosis—correct	154 cases	71.3%
One of the first three diagnoses—correct	216 cases	93.5%

ably would exceed that of most humans in performing this same task. Because of our special diagnostic facility and our interest in the subject, our department is the base for the Mid-America Bone Diagnostic Center and Registry, where problem cases are reviewed from all over the nation and where our Limited Bayes program for Bone Tumor diagnosis has consistent application.

While computer-assisted diagnosis has been very helpful in the clinical situation to a limited extent, it has certainly been the source of much new knowledge regarding the diagnostic process itself. One cannot approach the detailed kind of analysis of any disease system required for image modeling without learning new information. Furthermore, one cannot teach diagnostic principles to a computer without having the concepts clear and precise.

Surely the educational and teaching benefits of using a computer for diagnosis have been worth the effort. We have come to regard diagnosis as a process of data reduction where data treatment is either Boolean or probabilistic (or combinations of both), and we understand that, in decision-making, one uses the most powerful predictors first, reserving the less powerful predictors for lower orders of priority. We have also observed that it is better not to use a doubtful sign than to make an incorrect guess. Our research in computer-aided diagnosis also has set the stage for attacking the difficult problem of direct computer diagnosis (see below). In short, the applications of computer-aided diagnosis to the analysis of radiant images inevitably brings all aspects of the problem into crystalline focus.[35,36]

In spite of the existing achievements, a nearly insurmountable amount of work remains to be done in systems modeling and improvement of the diagnostic process for radiant images.[11] Some high-priority areas are dysplasias of bone and chest diseases. However, if one were to explore the future usefulness of computer-aided diagnosis for a department of radiology, perhaps the most useful of all would be an application to improve control of the number of consultation requests from referring departments. Radiology examinations are costly, yet they are often misused. This misuse occurs in a number of ways. For example, the diagnosis may be sufficiently proven when the request is submitted, or the radiological examination may be of help only in a few instances. Furthermore, when one already has several strong predictors pointing toward a diagnosis, the radiologic examination may be a weak predictor and relatively useless. Often the examination may actually have been unnecessary. Such improper usage can be very costly to both patient and hospital and can overload already stressed radiological facilities. We suggest that probability standards be set to achieve certainty in common diagnostic situations and, when these probabilities have been met through other studies, that therapeutic action be taken without further laboratory investigations. If on-line computer facilities equipped with good decision-making routines for the common diagnosis can be provided to perform this task for clinicians, we believe that a more rational basis for ordering radiology tests can be established. This is an important concept for future investigation.

1. Direct Computer Diagnosis

For many, it has been difficult to accept the role of the computer in direct diagnosis from radiant images because of the virtuosity of humans in doing the same task. Whoever could imagine a computer scanning and analyzing a film and thinking through a diagnosis with greater effectiveness than a well-trained human?

Certainly this is not possible now except on an experimental basis and probably will not be widely possible for some time; however, in some situations, the computer is technically capable of better image analysis than humans. These situations are those in which the examination is represented by a standard image taken in a standard projection, produced in large numbers, and with dependable diagnostic quality. Computers can be trained to find themselves in standard images and to perform measurements with great accuracy and repetitive tasks without fatigue. The so-called production or assembly line mode is a situation where humans have difficulties.[37,38]

In medical diagnosis, humans are demonstrated to have an ROC (Receiver Operating Characteristics) curve with false-positives on one side and false-negatives on the other. The human has his own setting on the ROC curve representing his balance for under-diagnosis or over-diagnosis. It may be difficult for him to manipulate his setting on the curve. Because of this fact, diagnostic accuracy is never much better than about 90% and is generally much lower; however, with computers, we can set the point on the ROC curve to meet any specific requirement.

In our image analysis studies, we are concentrating on radiant image systems which best fit the requirements. This selection should permit us to optimize our efforts and to produce substantial results in a reasonable time.[37,44] To this end, we have selected several radiant image classes: one with low information content, that is, brain scintiscans;[39] one with high information content and demand for large volume, the chest film;[40,41] and another image system with high information content but relatively low volume production, the knee,[42,44] but which is especially valuable because of its sharp, well defined, easily recognizable features. Each of these three systems has something special to offer in the development of algorithms for direct computer diagnosis.

With the brain scan, we first solved the problem of the computer finding itself in an image system.[39] With the chest, we have been successful in getting the computer to find the heart and measure its size, area, and configuration; to establish normal–abnormal classes; and to classify abnormals into one of the four classes of acquired heart disease with the same or greater accuracy than humans.[35-38] Our results with the knee are impressive but incomplete.[42-44]

In general, we needed to establish certain characteristics desirable in a scene to be analyzed by an automated system. Not all of these are necessary for analysis to be successful; however, the more of these characteristics are applicable to a scene, the more feasible the scene is for computer analysis. These include the following: first, scenes must be simple; second, a class of scenes should contain a vast number of pictures; third, the pictures should contain important information; and fourth, pictures must have a standard view.[40,42,45–48]

This particular image analysis system has five interrelated segments (Figure 9–10):

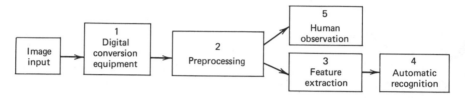

Figure 9–10.   Schematic of an image analysis system.

(1) Image input and digital conversion—the camera and associated analog-to-digital conversion equipment required to convert the images into an $n \times n$ array of points whose entries give the brightness value of the image.

(2) Preprocessing—programs used to suppress the noise put into the image data by the digital conversion equipment and also programs used to emphasize certain properties in the image that are more important than others for the later stages of analysis.

(3) Feature extraction—removal from the image information to be used in the automatic recognition of objects in the image. The data emitted from this stage of processing should be reduced greatly from that of the preprocessing stage.

(4) Automatic recognition—the automatic recognition of important objects in the image by the computer.

(5) Human observation—a human interpretation of an improved image on the display unit. This can occur following preprocessing and is not an integral part of the automated system.

No scene analysis system or algorithm is so general that it can recognize a particular object in any given scene. For certain picture classes, however, several characteristics of the scene are similar for all pictures in that class. In the algorithm we use, we incorporated the ability to change the picture class while retaining the ability to recognize the objects in the scene. We can achieve this generality in radiographic images—for example, chest x-rays, knee x-rays, or brain scans—because several characteristics of the scene hold for each of the picture classes.

The approach we advocate is linguistic in nature but tends to be more semantic or descriptive in practice.[46,47] The picture class description that guides the feature extraction phase of processing pattern recognition is incorporated within the feature extraction phase. The following are the assumptions behind our method:

(1) The analysis of the scene should be vertical or topdown. One should first analyze the large objects in the scene at a low resolution and later the finer objects in the scene as details of the large objects. We have self-adjusting programs on the System/360 that describe the object to be analyzed in a tree structure. Moreover, we can examine the image at six levels, starting with the overall x-ray (for example) and then examining the primary subject area at higher and higher resolution.

(2) Feature extraction and pattern recognition must be combined into a reinforcing system (a system with feedback). Feature extraction is the most difficult stage in implementing an automated system. One must know that each relevant feature to be extracted has been recognized.

(3) A description of the class of scenes to be analyzed must be contained within the program.

(4) Region enumeration rather than contour tracing should be used in primitive object identification. In the region enumeration method, a point x (i,j) in the picture array is located, perhaps by a raster scan; and one desires to identify the points that lie in the same region with x.

(5) All parameters in the program must be self-adjusting to increase the generality of the algorithm by minimizing the effect of external factors such as type of film used, exposure time, and the lighting variations.

(6) The concept of "field of vision" is important in locating the true boundaries of objects. This concept implies that there is a fixed number of objects in the picture and that these objects fit together in jig-saw fashion and completely fill the area of the picture. The concept is important to the location of boundaries. An example is a chest x-ray, where the exact contour of the heart is needed to diagnose certain kinds of heart disease.[40,46-48]

The actual scanning procedure is as follows: The image to be analyzed, such as an x-ray plate or a large transparency of a printed circuit board, is placed on a light-box below the image dissector camera, developed as an early satellite scanner. The light box is illuminated by a series of fluorescent tubes that operate on direct current with separate control circuit for each tube, for stability. From 10 to 18 tubes may be illuminated, depending upon the degree of light required. Those at the edges are more brightly lit to compensate for the nonlinearity of the cathode scanner.

The camera records the transmittance of light through the x-ray and accepts the control voltages of the analog input signal whose average value is proportional to the intensity of light of the selected points. Most images are scanned as a 256×256 point array. This produces 65,536 points, all of which can be stored in the System/360 core memory at one time during processing. The system can scan an array of up to 1,024×1,024 points. However, more than one million total points produced constitute an unwieldy storage problem.

Next, the camera scans each point for one millisecond; it can handle material ranging from 35 mm half-frame to 14 by 17 inch x-ray plates. The size of the scan can be changed either electronically or by moving the image closer to the camera lens.

The output signal from the camera is sent through a low-pass filter, an integrator, and a logarithmic amplifier that calculates the logarithm of the transmittance of light through the film. Then the analog-to-digital converter changes the analog signal into an integer that is stored on magnetic tape or disks.

In the preprocessing stage, filtering and enhancement algorithms may be applied. However, we use only simple averaging to change the resolution of the array from 256×256 to an $n \times n$ array. Typically, n equals 8, 16, 32, 64, or 128. The values in the array are then scaled linearly into the 0 to 63 range to represent the intensity of the gray shade at each point.

The picture is now ready for analysis. Two paths can be taken: One involves feature extraction and pattern recognition to implement automated analysis; the other is simply human observation. The automated procedure is applied to chest x-rays—for example, as follows: The first task of feature extraction is to isolate the area of the film that contains the cardiac silhouette. This is difficult because of the substantial range of anatomical differences of normal and abnormal anatomy. For instance, each individual exhibits a different diaphragm height and thoracic width. We also encounter a wide range of film exposures. But since computer classification depends solely on the size, contour, and shape of the heart outline as seen on a standard chest plate, the goal is to extract only this information from a background of irrelevant data in the chest x-ray. We accomplish this by an algorithm that constructs a cardiac rectangle (Figure 9–11) around the heart. The rectangle is variable in size, dependent upon the heart size.

Once the cardiac rectangle has been located, the problem still remains of selecting the technique for obtaining the closed cardiac surface necessary for the cardiac measurement to be taken. This entails outlining the edge of the left and right cardiac boundaries. The technique developed for this purpose involved thresholding of a gray level histogram to produce a 1-bit (2-level) representation of the chest image within the cardiac rectangle into a 2-bit representation (black-and-white) image of the heart.

The next step is to outline the cardiac contour from the black-and-white

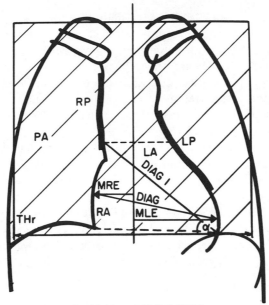

ANATOMICAL FEATURES MEASURED

Figure 9–11

representation. The left and right heart boundary values are found by detecting two consecutive black (zero) values to the right and left of the midline, respectively, on each horizontal line within the cardiac rectangle.

Next, the intersection of the right cardiac edge and the diaphragm is determined and a line is drawn from this point across to the intersection of the left cardiac edge with the diaphragm. A line also is drawn to connect the right and left top of the heart outline so that the entire heart and portions of the pulmonary arteries are enclosed. Area and extent measurements are now easily made from this closed contour.

Nearly all information needed for the diagnosis and classification of heart disease has been extracted at this point from the standard chest radiograph. The next step is measurement of the heart. This involves 11 measurements, one angular measurement, and two polynomials. The polynomials are mathematical expressions of specific heart contours.

All these cardiac measurements are normalized to obtain a ratio figure. The linear measurements are divided by the thoracic width, and the area measurements are divided by the thoracic area. This allows correction for variation in heart sizes related to the patient's overall size. The same algorithm can be used for different film input sizes—the standard 14 by 17 inch. 35 mm reduction, or chest photofluorograms.[35]

Once these heart measurements and polynomials have been extracted from the cardiac rectangle, the information is used as a basis for first classifying the case normal or abnormal. If abnormal, the classification goes further by placing the case into the correct group of rheumatic heart disease. The diagnoses are divided into five classes, and the 16 possible combinations of heart valve disease considered are divided into four separate groups. Computer classification is accomplished through the use of linear and quadratic discriminant functions, a method selected because of its relative simplicity and speed (Figure 9–12).

It would be difficult to judge the value of this automated feature extraction and classification algorithm unless its accuracy could be compared to the diagnostic accuracy of radiologists. For this reason, the following study was instituted.

Ten radiologists were asked to individually diagnose 135 representative cases of the cases evaluated by the computer. This group of radiologists consisted of 7 board certified academic radiologists and three third-year residents whose training was nearly completed. Each radiologist was given

Computer Aided Diagnosis

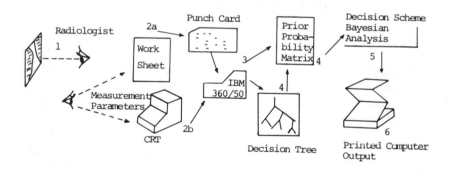

Direct Computer Diagnosis

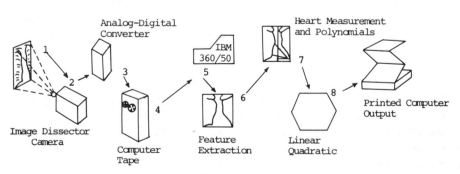

Figure 9–12

the PA and lateral views and told that each case was either normal or indicative of rheumatic heart disease. He was asked to make a complete radiological diagnosis and record his answers on a form designed for the study.
Each case diagnosed was counted as one physician's observation. Information on the forms was then transferred to punched cards and computer
programs were written to separate the 639 physician observations collected.
Not all of the physicians completed the task of reading all 135 films. Overall accuracy was 78% for the computer and 62% for the group of radiologists. The overall accuracy was computed from the following equation:

$$\text{Overall accuracy} = \frac{\text{Total number of correct diagnoses}}{\text{Total number of cases in test group}}$$

This example illustrates that, although automatic computer diagnosis is
quite different from the other methods, it is competitive and may out-
perform radiologists.

Our methods have been thus far applied to the analysis of the AP chest
x-ray in order to diagnose abnormality in the heart and lungs, to the AP
x-ray of the knee, and to nuclear medicine images. However, other medical
applications are also under investigation. For example, intensive effort is
now underway to train the computer to recognize the various kinds of congenital heart disease, a task somewhat more difficult than acquired heart
disease because of the anatomic disproportions encountered in infant chest
films which are not present in adults and because of the need to recognize
hypo- and hyper-vascularity in the lung fields. Solving this last problem has
led us into attempting textural analysis of the lung fields.[49] Efforts to recognize pulmonary nodules are underway.[50] We see these latest developments
as having significant application in the early diagnosis of lung cancer[51] and
for the detection and staging of coal miners' pneumoconiosis or black lung
disease.[52] Some preliminary work has been done on thyroid scans.[53]

The goal of automated image analysis is not to replace the radiologist; it
more realistically relates to making the radiologist's task easier by screening
large numbers of films, identifying the normal and the obviously abnormal,
and earmarking and referring problems unsolvable by the computer for the
radiologist's analysis. Industrial applications of these techniques, particularly for assembly line inspection and quality control, are being developed
locally and with cooperation of industry.

D. RADIANT IMAGE TRANSMISSION, STORAGE
AND RETRIEVAL

At the University of Missouri-Columbia, we believe that we are demonstrating the direction for improving radiological health care for the future
of our nation through the development of information systems to speed

the flow of information and through the use of the computer in the diagnostic process. A very substantial gap yet remains to be filled: that of
efficient transmission, storage, and retrieval of radiant images within the
medical environment. With this problem solved it would become possible
to speed the delivery of radiological health care to the small community
unmanned by radiologists and to expedite the delivery of radiological health
care within hospital and community units with a satisfactory degree of
cost effectiveness. A major impediment to the development of adequate
image transmission systems has been the lack of a standard for measuring
the loss of intelligence content in any radiant image so transmitted, stored,
and redisplayed.[54]

Directed towards solving this problem, a test file of some 5,000 cases
has been established, cases specially selected to reflect graded ranges of
difficulty of perception and difficulty of diagnosis. The test file contains
20% of normals. We are currently using this test library to determine
whether images reproduced on special 35 mm film, mounted in aperture
cards, and displayed with an extraordinarily high-quality commercial display device contain the same intelligence content as the original large films.
This is being attempted by a double blind study using 10 radiologist teams,
each alternately examining large and small film examinations, with no
radiologist ever seeing the same examination in both large and small film
format. It would be impossible to accomplish such an effort in a clinical
contest if the storage and retrieval of information were not automated. The
terminology tables of MARS were used and the data base modified to allow
this project a special subset of storage for completion of separate statistics
and records. Performance and grading statistics for the 35 mm library will
soon be available. Initial results show little difference between the large
and the microfilm images. However, we plan to initiate a clinical test for
further evaluation. It is certain that, without the organization and communication offered by computer graphics, such a study would be impossible. One can easily imagine the difficulties of manually selecting such a
library, much less those of getting physicians to code their diagnoses manually for research in a clinical context. Even an infinite clerical staff would
have difficulty coping with the problem of deciphering physician's handwriting. The practical value and impact of developing such a test library
is enormous.[54]

Through our test library it now becomes possible to test the quality of
any microfilming system or to manipulate radiant images in any manner
and be able to determine whether the original intelligence content is still
present. We have found, based on our experience with the 35 mm storage
and redisplay system, that the weakest link in the diagnostic chain is the
human link, the human diagnosis. Our present effort to move vigorously

toward automation of the diagnostic process is justified by observed human inaccuracy. That humans are inaccurate is not new, but our direct evidence of this phenomenon provides the strongest kind of motivation.

The special computer techniques and programs that have been developed to motivate radiologists to participate and give correct (or their best) responses are becoming excellent teaching programs as well as programs which may serve in the future to test radiologist ability to analyze radiant images. We are also gaining extensive experience with each of the cases in the test library and are beginning to know which cases will be most useful in challenging a high-quality imaging system and which cases can be used for less demanding problems. We look forward to future years of testing other important imaging systems.

An impact of this research project for determining intelligence content, although not complete, has been to create confidence in the usefulness of quality 35 mm images as the future means of presenting and storing images for clinical radiology. A number of film manufacturers are designing 35 mm cameras for the initial capture of radiant image information on less expensive small films.

We see much future effort to develop the interface between the Missouri Automated Radiology System and 35 mm film storage and retrieval management systems. It seems that the day is not too far away when it will be possible not only initially to produce the film in 35 mm format but also to transmit it inexpensively on an ordinary telephone wire by digital techniques and to record the image in 35 mm format with flying spot scanning techniques without significant loss of intelligence content. Also, it should be possible to evaluate a substantial percentage of such images by automated diagnostic techniques, possibly using a small computer. A future function of MARS will be to print out and deliver diagnostic opinions automatically and to store, retrieve, or reproduce miniature images under computer control. This entire technology is feasible at this moment; there is merely the requirement to develop systems which will operate in a cost effective manner.

E. THE FUTURE

From the experiences of the past and the present, it seems inevitable that the future of radiology is to be tied to computers and their applications. A major goal is the development of physical space for a new kind of department designed for effective use of the new tools currently under development and in the process of being tested. This department of the future will emphasize rapid screening processes, fast, but comfortable services for patients, and maximum integrity, retrievability, and reproducibility of its information files, including the radiant images themselves.

As we develop greater experience with computers, it becomes apparent that they are ultimately destined to be of great help to us. An immediate and unexpected benefit of using computers in diagnosis has certainly been to show a way of improving teaching. The computer requires crystal-clear instructions and hard data; when these are provided, the computer offers direct feedback by demonstrating the desired results. These computer-proved techniques have already proved impressive in human learning situations. Such unanticipated benefits are becoming commonplace; for example, in our immediate experience, from data routinely collected by MARS we can assess who carries the work load and the relative efficiency of human performance. In our assessment of intelligence content of image systems, we have also discovered a mechanism for measuring individual human performance in diagnosis, and, by successive measurements, to assess the rate of learning. Apparently we have unexpectedly created a new teaching tool in the same program.

The new radiology department will be a teaching department which will maximize the use of these new techniques for evaluating both rate of learning and accuracy of decision-making, hopefully to individualize the length of graduate training.

It seems certain that in the future practice of radiology we will be heavily dependent on computers for the intra-departmental management of information. We may expect further improvements in reporting techniques and probably will become dependent upon the computer for the routine screening of certain kinds of examinations, particularly the chest film. At a time when rising costs of medical care threaten to challenge our dream of providing good health care for everyone, the computer offers us greater efficiency and better cost effectiveness. Through new transmission techniques, radiological health care of good quality will be offered to the small community where primary radiological health care had previously been unavailable.

It is reassuring that these new advances will be of great help to radiologists but will probably never replace them. Luckily, the virtuosity of the well-trained human brain in coping with specific problems can probably never be duplicated. For the management of routine tasks, the computer has nevertheless much to offer. The technology for the computerized department and the computerized hospital is here; it merely needs to be exploited from almost any perspective. A timely revolution in techniques for managing and improving health care delivery is underway; it is gratifying for us to know that our department is making a major contribution in bringing about these advances.

REFERENCES

1. Lepper, M., M.D. Personal Communication. Executive Vice-President of Professional and Academic Affairs, Rush Medical School. Chicago, Illinois. 1972.

2. Lehr, J. L.; Lodwick, G. S.; Nicholson, B. F.; and Birznieks, F. B. "Experience with MARS (Missouri Automated Radiology System)."*Radiology,* in press.

3. Manson, D. J.; Lehr, J. L.; and Lodwick, G. S. "MARS—Missouri Automated Radiology System, Computer Graphics in an Automated Department." *Proceedings, Association for Computing Machinery, Special Interest Group for Graphics, Symposium on Computer Graphics in Medicine, Pittsburgh, Pennsylvania, March 1972.*

4. Lodwick, G. S.; Haun, C. L.; Smith, W. D.; Keller, R. F.; and Robertson, E. D. "Computer Diagnosis of Primary Bone Tumors: A Preliminary Report." *Radiology* 80 (1963) : 273–275.

5. Wilson, W. J.; Templeton, A. W.; Turner, A. H.; and Lodwick, G. S. "The Computer Analysis and Diagnosis of Gastric Ulcers. *"Presentation, 13th Association of University Radiologists Meeting, Seattle, Washington, May 14–15, 1965.* Also, *Radiology* 85 (1965) : 1064–1073.

6. Templeton, A. W.; Lehr, J. L.; and Simmons, C. "The Computer Evaluation and Diagnosis of Congenital Heart Disease, Using Roentgenographic Findings." *Radiology* 87 (1966) : 658–670, 682.

7. Templeton, A. W.; Jansen, C.; Lehr, J. L.; and Hufft, R. "Solitary Pulmonary Lesions." *Radiology* 89 (1967) : 605–613.

8. Lodwick, G. S. "Solitary Malignant Tumors of Bone: The Application Predictor Variables in Diagnosis." *Seminars in Roentgenology* 1 (1966) : 293–313.

9. Lodwick, G. S. *The Bones and Joints: An Atlas of Tumor Radiology.* Chicago: Year Book Medical Publishers, Inc., 1971.

10. Lodwick, G. S., and Convert, R. P. "A Generalized Simulation Model for a Diagnostic Radiology Department." *Digest of the 7th International Conference on Medical and Biological Engineering, Stockholm, 1967.*

11. Lodwick, G. S. "Principal Investigator: A Systems Model for an Operating Radiology Department; Final Progress Report." Grant #HM 00477. Department of Radiology, University of Missouri-Columbia. Columbia, Missouri, March 1971.

12. Lodwick, G. S. "Computer Simulation and Information Systems in Radiologic Departmental Operations (I, II, III)." *EDV in Medizin und Biologie* Vol. 2, Nos. 2, 3, 4. Stuttgart, Gustav Fischer and Eugen Ulmer. 1971.

13. Templeton, A. W.; Lodwick, G. S.; and Turner, A. H., Jr. "RADIATE: A New Concept for Computer Coding, Transmitting, Storing, and Retrieving Radiological Data." *Radiology* 85 (1965) : 811–817.

14. Templeton, A. W.; Lodwick, G. S.; Sides, S. D.; and Lehr, J. L. "RADIATE: A Project for the Synthesis, Storage, and Retrieval of Radiologic Consultations." *Digest of the 7th International Conference on Medical and Biological Engineering, Stockholm, Sweden, 1967.*

15. Wilson, V. E.; Lodwick, G. S.; Schmidt, D. A.; Lehr, J. L.; Computers in Medicine Bibliography." Edited by A. H. Turner. Department of Radiology and Medical Center Library, School of Medicine, University of Missouri. Columbia, Missouri. September 1965.

238   Gwilym S. Lodwick

16. Wilson, V. E.; Lodwick, G. S.; and Lehr, J. L. "Computers in Medicine Bibliography." Edited by A. H. Turner, Jr. and D. A. Schmidt. Department of Radiology and Medical Center Library, School of Medicine, University of Missouri. Columbia, Missouri. August 1966.

17. Schmidt, D. A. and Reichertz, P. L. eds. "Computers in Medicine Bibliography." Department of Radiology and Medical School Library, University of Missouri, School of Medicine, Columbia, Missouri. July 1968.

18. Lodwick, G. S. "Recommendations for Obtaining the Maximum Benefit of Radiation Exposure in Diagnostic Radiology Through Improved Production and Utilization of Image Information." *Report to the National Center of Radiological Health on a Study of X-Ray Image Analysis and Systems Development, July 1968.*

19. U.S. Department of Health, Education, and Welfare; Public Health Service; Food and Drug Administration; and Bureau of Radiological Health, "An Information and Communication System in Hospital Diagnostic Radiology." Prepared by Kelly, D. P., and Sprawls, P., Jr. June 1971.

20. U.S. Department of Health, Education, and Welfare, Public Health Service, Bureau of Radiological Health, "Automatic Data Processing System Study for Massachusetts General Hospital Diagnostic Radiology Department." August 1970.

21. Wilson, W. J. "An Automated System for Coding Radiology Reports." *Proceedings, Conference Computer Applications in Radiology, University of Missouri, September 1970.*

22. Meschan, I., and R. Robinson. "Computerized Radiologic Reporting with Work Retrieval Using MTST." *Proceedings, Conference Computer Applications in Radiology, University of Missouri, September 1970.*

23. Barnard, H. J.; Jacobson, H. G.; and Nance, J. W. "ACR Diagnostic Radiology Information System (DRIS)." *Proceedings, Conference Computer Applications in Radiology, University of Missouri, September 1970.*

24. Kricheff, I. I. "Narrative Processing of Radiologic Reports." *Proceedings, Conference Computer Applications in Radiology, University of Missouri, September 1970.*

25. Brolin, I. "Experience With an Automated Reporting System." *Proceedings, Conference Computer Applications in Radiology, University of Missouri, September 1970.*

26. Bauman, R.; Pendergrass, H. P.; Greenes, R. A.; and Kalayan, R. "Further Development and Initial Use of an On-Line Computer System for Radiology Reporting." *Proceedings, Conference Computer Applications in Radiology, University of Missouri, September 1970.*

27. Margulies, S. I. "Development of an Automated Reporting System." *Proceedings, Conference Computer Applications in Radiology, University of Missouri, September 1970.*

28. Templeton, A. W.; Reichertz, P. L.; Paquet, E.; Lehr, J. L.; Lodwick, G. S.; and Scott, F. I. "RADIATE—Updated and Redesigned for Multiple Cathode-Ray Tube Terminals." *Radiology* 92(1969):1:30–36.

29. Brolin, I., M.D. "MEDELA: An Electronic Data-Processing System for Radiological Reporting." *Radiology* 103(1972):249–256.

30. Koeppe, P., and P. Schaefer. "ORVID—An On-Line Roentgen Diagnosis using

Video-Display and Including Documentation." *Computers in Radiology.* Edited by R. DeHaene, Bruxelles, Basel: A. Wambersie, 1970.

31. Lodwick, G. S.; Reichertz, P. L.; Paquet, E.; and Hall, D. L. "ODARS, A Computer Aided System for Diagnosing and Reporting, Part I, Clinical Problems." *Computers in Radiology. Proceedings, International Meeting, Brussels.* (1969), pp. 279–282.

32. Lodwick, G. S.; Turner, A. H. Jr.; Lusted, L. B.; and Templeton, A. W. "Computer-Aided Analysis of Radiographic Images." *J. of Chron. Dis.* 19(1966): 485–496.

33. Lodwick, G. S., and P. Reichertz. "Computer Assisted Diagnosis of Tumors and Tumor-Like Lesions of Bone: The Limited Bayes' Concept." *Proceedings, Symposium Osseum, London, April 1968.*

34. Lodwick, G. S., and P. L. Reichertz. "Computerunterstutzte Diagnostik von Tumoren and tumorahnlichen Veranderungen des Knochens: Das begrenzte Bayes-Konzept." *Röntgenblatter Heft* 4(1969):22. Jahrgang F55935 E.

35. Kruger, R. P.; Dwyer, S. J.; Hall, D. L.; and Lodwick, G. S. "Computer Processing of Radiographic Images." *Technical Report, Image Analysis Laboratory, Departments of Electrical Engineering and Radiology, University of Missouri-Columbia, Columbia, Missouri. May 1971.*

36. Kruger, R. P.; Hall, D. L.; Lodwick, S. G.; and Dwyer, S. J., III. "Computer-Aided Diagnosis of Radiographic Cardiac Size and Shape Descriptors." *IEEE Proceedings* April 1971.

37. Hall, D. L.; Lodwick, G. S.; Kruger, R. P.; Townes, J. R; and Dwyer, S. J. III. "Direct Computer Diagnosis of Rheumatic Heart Disease." *Radiology* December 1971.

38. Kruger, R. P.; Townes, J. R.; Hall, D. L.; Dwyer, S. J. III; and Lodwick, G. S. "Automated Radiographic Diagnosis Via Feature Extraction and Classification of Cardiac Size and Shape Descriptors." *IEEE Transactions on Bio-Medical Engineering* 19(1972) 174–186.

39. Harlow, C.; Lehr, J.; Parkey, R.; Garrotto, L.; and Lodwick, G. "Computer Algorithms for the Detection of Brain Scintigram Abnormalities." *Radiology* 97(1970).

40. Harlow, C., and S. Eisenbeis. "The Analysis of Radiographic Images." *Proceedings, Two Dimensional Digital Signal Processing Conference, University of Missouri-Columbia, Columbia, Missouri, October 1971.* Also, *Technical Report IAL TR 11-72, Image Analysis Laboratory, Departments of Electrical Engineering and Radiology, University of Missouri-Columbia, Columbia, Missouri, April 1972.*

41. Harlow, C. A.; Levin, W. M.; Dwyer, S. J. III; and Elder, D. M. "Computer Analysis of Chest X-Rays." *IEEE 1971 International Conference on Information Theory, Pacific Grove, California, January-February 1972.*

42. Harlow, C. A.; Henderson, S. E.; and Lodwick, G. S. "Feature Extraction of Knee X-Rays." *1971 IEEE Decision and Control Conference, Miami, Florida, December 1971.*

43. Ausherman, D. A.; Dwyer, S. J. III; and Lodwick, G. S. "Feature Extraction for Computer Diagnosis of Primary Bone Tumors." *Proceedings, Two Dimensional Digital Processing Conference, University of Missouri-Columbia, Columbia, Missouri. October 1971.*

44. Ausherman, D. A.; Dwyer, S. J. III; and Lodwick, G. S. "Extraction of Connected Edges from Knee Radiographs." *IEEE Transactions on Computers July 1972.*

45. Harlow, C. A.; Otto, J. L.; Hall, D. L.; and Lodwick, G. S. "Feature Extraction in Images." *Joint National Conference on Major Systems, Los Angeles, California, October 1971.*

46. Dwyer, S. J., III; Harlow, C. A.; Ausherman, D. A.; and Lodwick, G. S. "Computer Diagnosis of Radiographic Images." *Proceedings, AFIPS Conference.* 40 (1972) : 1027–1041.

47. Dwyer, S. J., III; Harlow, C. A.; and Lodwick, G. S. "Keys to Computerized Image Analysis." *Research/Development* April 1972.

48. Dwyer, S. J., III; Harlow, C. A.; and Lodwick, G. S. "Computer Analysis of Radiographic Images." *IEEE Proceedings.* To be Published, September 1972.

49. Hall, E. L., and R. N. Sutton. "Texture Measures for Automatic Machine Recognition and Classification of Pulmonary Disease." *Proceedings, Two Dimensional Digital Signal Processing Conference, University of Missouri-Columbia, Columbia, Missouri, 1971.*

50. DeGroot, J. M.; Hall, E. L.; Dwyer, S. J., III; and Sutton, R. N. "Computer Simulation of Lesions in Radiographs." *Proceedings, 24th Annual Conference on Engineering in Medicine and Biology, Las Vegas, November 1971.*

51. Kahveci, A. E. "Lesion Detection in Chest Radiographs." *NEC National Electronics Conference, Chicago, Illinois, Fall 1972.*

52. Sutton, R. N.; Hall, E. L.; and Lodwick, G. S. "Texture Measurements of Pulmonary Disease." *Radiological Society of North America* November 1971.

53. Otto, J. L., and Harlow, C. A. "Automated Analysis of Thyroid Scans." *Technical Report, Image Analysis Laboratory, Departments of Electrical Engineering and Radiology, University of Missouri-Columbia, Columbia, Missouri. August 1972.*

54. Braaten, M. O.; Dwyer, S. J., III; Farrell, C.; and Lodwick, G. S. "The Development of an Image Library." *Technical Report IAL-TR 3–72, Image Analysis Laboratory, Departments of Industrial Engineering, Electrical Engineering, and Radiology, University of Missouri-Columbia, Columbia, Missouri, January 1972.*

CHAPTER TEN

Physiological Monitoring Systems

by Joseph Terdiman

A. INTRODUCTION

The goal of physiological monitoring is the measurement and display of physiological signals that characterize the functioning of a biological system. Certain types of physiological signals, such as bio-electric activity, can be directly sensed and recorded; others, such as arterial blood pressure, are usually transduced to an electrical form for display; other variables, such as cardiac output, must be derived from indirect measurements. The functions of the simplest monitoring systems are only to sense and display these signals; more advanced systems analyze the measurements and generate appropriate responses, which may be either passive or active in nature. A passive response is one in which the analysis results are displayed and alarms triggered if a physiological measurement exceeds a specified limit. An active response is one in which the monitoring system is used to control a physiological input variable, and forms, therefore, part of a feedback loop for the biological system. An example of the latter case is a system in which the rate of infusion of an intravenous solution depends on the volume of urine output and central venous pressure; the infusion pump rate is controlled by the monitoring device.

The components of a monitoring system can be divided grossly into five categories. These are: sensor, signal conditioner, display device, logic module, and controller (see Figure 10–1). Each monitoring system receives one or more inputs through its sensors and may produce a variety of outputs for display. A minimal monitoring system must contain a signal detector, signal conditioner, and a display device. Optionally, a monitoring system may contain a logic module, and, in certain instances, a controller.

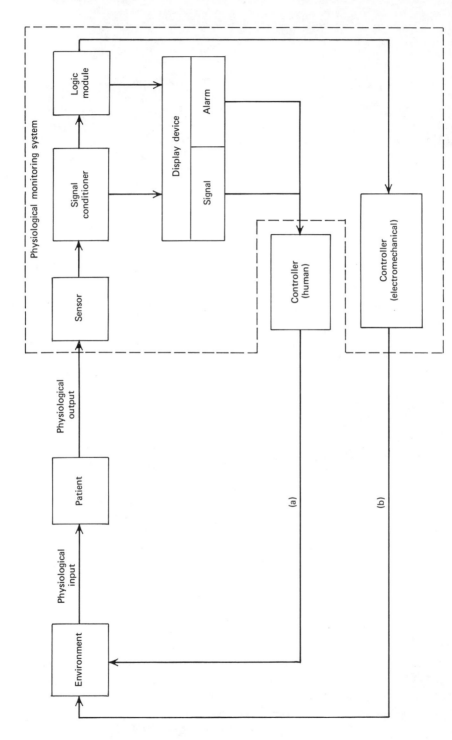

Figure 10–1. Schematic representation of physiological monitoring system showing basic system components and signal flow pathways. Pathway (a) contains a human interaction in the feedback loop. Pathway (b) contains an electromechanical controller in the feedback loop.

1. Sensor

The properties of various electrodes and transducers used to detect physiological signals are well described in the literature.[1-3] The ones most commonly used in physiological monitoring systems are large and small surface area contact electrodes for electrocardiography and electroencephalography, intravascular and respiratory pressure transducers, ultrasonic and electro-magnetic flow rate detectors, chemical and pH electrodes. The outputs of these sensors are electrical signals which are functions of the measured physiological input signal.

2. Signal Conditioner

This component includes detector, amplification, filter, and other signal transformation circuits, which extract information of interest from the input signal and condition it for display, recording, or analysis.

3. Display Device

This component receives an electrical signal from the signal conditioning module and displays the signal in the medium of the display device. Various types of displays include: dial indicators, digital displays, cathode-ray tubes, signal lights, audible alarms, and hard-copy displays. The latter include strip-chart and XY recorders, photographs, microfilm, and computer printouts.

4. Logic Module

This module may consist entirely of electronic hardware or a combination of electronic hardware and a digital computer. A logic module may be used simply to compare a signal to a reference level, as in the case of a limit check, or to perform more complex analyses. A common example of the former is a cardiac monitor that compares heart rate to preset upper and lower limits. The latter includes computation of cardiac output, respiratory parameters, Fourier transforms of signal waveforms, analyses of electrocardiograms, etc. The use of hardware vs. software to perform a particular analysis depends on the nature and complexity of analysis required. Advantages of each approach will be discussed with the specific application described below.

5. Controller

The type of control used, if any, is dependent on the application. A passive control system, which is essentially a feedback control system that includes a human interaction in the feedback path, usually operates by means of visual and/or auditory alarms that are triggered whenever a physiological signal falls outside a preset range. When an alarm occurs, the intended response is that a human observer attempt to bring the physiological signal back within its normal range by exerting some direct or indirect controlling action on the physiological system through, for example, drugs, electro-shock, or other therapeutic measures (Figure 10–1—pathway (a)).

With active control, there is a direct feedback path between the logic module and a controller of the physiological input. In the infusion pump example cited earlier, a logic module (in this case a digital computer) converts the measured urine output and central venous pressure to a signal that drives the motor of an infusion pump, thus maintaining a specified fluid balance (Figure 10–1—pathway (b)).

B. ELECTROCARDIOGRAPHY

1. Introduction

The electrical characteristics of the heart and the properties of the electrocardiogram (ECG) have been described in many texts and in the literature.[4-6] The source of the electrocardiogram is the resultant electrical dipole generated by cardiac muscle fibers as a result of the periodic synchronous depolarization and repolarization of their cell membranes. The flow of current generated by this cardiac dipole induces a potential difference between any two points on the body surface. The variations in electrical potential with time, recorded by a set of electrodes placed at specific points on the body surface, is the electrocardiogram. Different combinations of electrode placements or "leads" have been used in electrocardiography. The two sets most commonly used both by cardiologists and computer systems are the twelve-lead system (standard leads) and the three-lead orthogonal system of Frank.[7]

The electrocardiogram is traditionally characterized by a set of amplitude and time dependent parameters for each lead which describes the magnitudes and durations of specific waveform components and the intervals between them. Analysis of an electrocardiogram consists of two basic steps: (1) recognition of characteristic waveforms and calculation of waveform parameters for each lead, and (2) classification of the electrocardiogram into one or more diagnostic categories to which the measured parameter values most nearly correspond. If a prior electrocardiogram is available, a third step in the analysis may be comparison between current and previous waveforms, from which further diagnostic classification may result.

Traditionally, pattern recognition and waveform measurements are performed manually from single or multi-channel strip chart recordings by a cardiologist, who then provides an interpretation of the electrocardiogram based on his knowledge of the field and his past experience. Recently, analysis methods have been developed in which pattern recognition, waveform measurements, and interpretation are performed by automated instruments. Two basic approaches have been used. The earliest methods, pioneered by Pipberger and Caceres, and still the most effective, employ a digital computer.[8-11] More recently, nonprogrammable electronic analyzers have been developed for multiphasic and other screening applications. These devices measure waveform parameters and attempt to differentiate normal from abnormal electrocardiograms, but cannot provide more specific interpretations.

2.   Computer Analysis

a.   Methods.   The three principal steps in computer analysis of electrocardiograms are: (1) analog-to-digital conversion, (2) waveform pattern recognition and measurement, and (3) interpretation. Analog-to-digital conversion is a prerequisite for any type of digital computer analysis. The electrocardiogram waveform, which is a continuous variable or analog voltage, is converted to digital form by sampling the voltage at discrete intervals (typically, every 4 milliseconds) and converting to a digital representation. Conversion may be performed either off-line or on-line. In off-line conversion, the digitized voltages are stored in machine readable form for subsequent batch processing (e.g., on magnetic tape). In on-line conversion, the digitized output is transmitted in real-time to a computer for immediate analysis. Pattern recognition is the computer operation that identifies the presence or absence of characteristic components in the waveform and provides information for measurement of their duration and amplitude. Interpretation of the measurements is the final step in the analysis, in which the diagnostic category of the electrocardiogram is determined. Two approaches to computer electrocardiogram analysis have been used with some success. The first approach is, in essence, a simulation of the mental processes of the cardiologist. Pertinent characteristics and measurements of the electrocardiogram in each diagnostic category are first specified, usually by a group of experienced cardiologists. These specifications are translated into a set of logical decision rules which are then used as the basis for a computer program. Because of the complexity of the decision rules, they are usually formulated as a set of truth tables or decision tables. Programs developed by Caceres, Smith, Pordy, Dreifus, Warner, and Bonner use this basic approach.[11-22]

An alternate approach used by Pipberger employs statistical techniques to correlate an unknown electrocardiogram with a set of known standard electrocardiogram patterns stored in the computer.[10,11] The standard patterns that most closely match the unknown electrocardiogram are selected as the diagnoses. Probabilities can be assigned to the selected diagnoses based on the precision of the match to each standard pattern.

Other analytical methods that have been tested include Fourier analysis, adaptive matched filters, Bayes theorem calculations, and other mathematical techniques, but none as yet have proved as successful as the two approaches previously described.[23]

b. Developmental electrocardiogram analysis systems. Research and development in computer analysis of electrocardiograms are being conducted at many medical centers around the world. The status of ECG analysis systems at five of these centers as of summer 1971 is described in the following paragraphs. (Subsequent system modifications have not been included in this report except where otherwise noted.

(1) Mayo Clinic, Rochester, Minnesota (Smith). This system uses an IBM 1800 computer located in the Mayo Clinic. The operation employs a staff of over 40 people including technicians, clerks, cardiologists, and programmers. Terminals are in the Mayo Clinic and several other hospitals in the area. Nine ECG booths are in operation at the Clinic. ECGs are monitored at a central station by one technician. Technicians in booths at the Mayo Clinic have no monitoring equipment but are in contact with the central technician via intercom. Digital patient identification data is sent from each booth by push button pads. Remote facilities use Marquette ECG carts with touchtone pads. Data from remote carts are multiplexed with an FM carrier, six leads at a time, and transmitted via special phone lines to a Marquette receiver at Mayo. The receiver demodulates the signal and sends it to the computer. Within the Mayo Clinic, the ECG booths are hard-wired to the computer. Abnormal results are screened by a cardiologist. Chart copy ECGs are photographs of cathode ray tube (CRT) plots, including vector traces and standard and Frank leads. Microfilms of CRT plots are stored in aperture cards, of which Mayo has accumulated 500,000 over 3 years. Raw data is stored in analog form on FM tape and in two forms on digital tape: raw data plus ECG parameters, and ECG parameters alone. Programs include waveform analysis with age and sex as parameters, and arrhythmia analysis. Both standard and Frank leads are taken, but only Frank leads are used for analysis.

Mayo Clinic and IBM released the initial version of this program in 1967.[13,19] Since that time, Smith and others who have worked with the original program have made considerable improvements in its diagnostic capability, and a new version of this program may be available in 1973.

Several computer and instrument manufacturers provide this program as part of their basic electrocardiogram analysis system. They include Digital Equipment, Hewlett-Packard, and Marquette.

(2) Mt. Sinai Hospital, New York (Pordy). The ECG programs written by this group with IBM are all proprietary, under the control of Cro-Med Bionics.[17,18,20] Their system uses either an IBM 1800 computer located in Mt. Sinai Hospital or a remote time-shared IBM 360/50. ECG terminals are located in Mt. Sinai Hospital and in about 25 other facilities across the country. ECG terminals are carts manufactured by Cro-Med Bionics, similar to Marquette carts. Each cart has a 3-channel strip chart recorder for monitoring by a technician and digital switches for inputting patient data including identification number, age, sex, clinical diagnosis code, and drug code. Data is multiplexed with an FM carrier and transmitted over voice grade phone lines to Mt. Sinai. A Cro-Med Bionics receiver demodulates, digitizes, and stores the data on IBM compatible digital tape for subsequent batch processing. On-line processing for "stat" requests is under development. A 3-channel strip chart recording is made centrally as well as on the cart. Data may be analyzed on the IBM 1800 computer or sent to the IBM 360/50 processor via a high-speed data channel. ECG interpretations from the IBM 360/50 are printed on labels at Mt. Sinai via a high speed data channel. All printed results are screened by a cardiologist. Final ECG diagnoses are transmitted back to a teletype in the originating facility. ECG parameters are stored on digital tape. Programs include waveform analysis, arrhythmia, and serial comparison. Both Frank and standard lead groups are recorded and used for computer interpretation because they feel that left ventricular hypertrophy and anteroseptal areas are not well covered by Frank leads alone.

(3) Hahnemann Medical Center, Philadelphia (Dreifus). This system uses an IBM 1800 computer located at the medical center. Terminals are Marquette carts located currently in Hahnemann Hospital but in the near future will be placed in other facilities as part of a Pennsylvania regional medical care program. Total operating staff consists of five persons including two programmers. Programs were designed for low-volume operation. Abnormal ECGs are screened by cardiologists. Chart copy ECGs are 3M copier photographs of an oscilloscope trace of vector, Frank, and standard leads. Microfilms of electrocardiogram traces are stored in aperture cards. Raw data is stored on digital tape in selected cases, while ECG parameters are stored for all patients. Interpretations are printed on labels. Programs include waveform analysis and arrhythmia. Frank leads and a V1 lead are used in analysis. A serial comparison program is under development.

(4) Veterans Administration Hospital (VA), Washington (Pipberger). This system uses a CDC 3200 computer located in the Washington, D.C., VA Hospital. It is currently processing about 30 ECGs per day. Remote

hospitals record the ECG data on FM tape units installed on Marquette carts. Tapes are then mailed to the computer center, where they are read by another tape unit connected to a Marquette receiver. Output of the receiver is transmitted on-line to the computer. ECG data from within the Washington VA Hospital is not prerecorded on FM tape but is sent from cart to receiver via phone lines and from receiver into the computer. Thus, while most ECGs are batch processed, the system maintains the capability for on-line analysis. Abnormal ECGs are screened by a cardiologist. Chart copy ECGs are produced by the strip chart recorders on the carts. Raw data, parameters, and interpretation are stored for varying periods of time on digital tape. A series of standard ECGs referred to as the "Well-diagnosed File" is stored permanently. Interpretations are sent by teletype to distant facilities. Programs include waveform analysis (by statistical techniques including discriminant function and cluster analyses) and arrhythmia.[10,11] Program parameters are age and drug intake, but the population includes primarily males over age 18. Only Frank leads are used for analysis.

Programs are in public domain and are available without cost. Digital Equipment, Hewlett-Packard, and Varian provide versions of this program for their ECG analysis systems.

(5) Latter Day Saints' Hospital, Salt Lake City (Warner). A multifunction medical information system has been developed in the Latter Day Saints' Hospital, of which ECG analysis forms one component.[14,15] The system uses a CDC 3300 for on-line functions and has a CDC 3200 for backup and testing. On-line functions include multiphasic, ICU-CCU monitoring, cardiac catheterization laboratory, and various physiological research projects. Multiphasic tests include on-line ECG, pulmonary function analysis, blood pressure, ankle jerk, and lab data. Patients are identified to the system from the multiphasic clinic through a card reader that reads a keypunched identification card. ECG signals are hard wired to an analog-to-digital converter in the computer. Remote facilities use Marquette carts with touch-tone buttons for identification. Several other hospitals in Salt Lake City are connected to this system. Since the multiphasic system is only used on patients admitted to the hospital, the total number of ECG analyses per day is less than 50. Abnormal results are screened by a cardiologist. Chart copy ECGs are 3-channel strip charts. Diagnoses are printed on labels attached to the charts. Forty-two ECG parameters are stored on digital tape.

Programs include waveform and arrhythmia analysis. A serial comparison program has been developed. The programs use Frank leads only. A virtual "V4" lead is created from the vectorcardiogram.

Programs are in the public domain but are written primarily in CDC assembly language. A private company called Medlab has converted these programs to Fortran for the CDC 1700 and is selling the system as a medical information system package. ECG analysis is available as a separate module.

The specifications of the five systems reviewed here and the IBM ECG program are summarized in Table 1.

Another ECG analysis system, which is still in an experimental stage, is one developed by von der Groeben, et al., at Stanford University.[24,25] It is mentioned here because its approach represents a departure from the other systems described. In this system, ECGs are recorded in a modified Frank lead configuration. The ECG waveform is considered to have a much greater bandwidth of interest than the traditional 0.05—100 Hz. Since voice grade telephone lines do not have sufficient bandwidth to transmit 3 simultaneous signals from the orthogonal lead set without loss of fidelity, ECGs are recorded at the bedside on a special digital tape recorder. Analog-to-digital conversion occurs on the 3 leads simultaneously at a rate of 1,000 samples per second, yielding an effective bandwidth for the digitized waveform of 500 Hz. Later the digital tape is converted to industry-compatible format for batch processing on a PDP-8, which performs pattern recognition functions and measures waveform parameters. Diagnostic classification of the waveforms is performed on an IBM 360 computer using a statistical analysis approach. Methods used include the multivariate normal analysis and cluster analysis applied to the instantaneous ECG vector.

c. **Commercial electrocardiogram analysis systems.**   Two types of electrocardiogram analysis systems are commercially available to users who lack programming and engineering resources of their own. These are "turnkey" systems and service bureaus. In addition, several computer vendors offer electrocardiogram analysis programs as program products to users of their computers.

(1) Turn-key systems.   A number of instrument and computer manufacturers now provide electrocardiogram analysis packages in the form of turn-key systems. (A "turn-key" system is one the user buys, turns it on, and begins operation.) A turn-key ECG system consists of one or more ECG input terminals (carts), transmitters and telephone interfaces (for telecommunication from remote locations), data receivers, a digital computer, and one or more printers (for reports). The user may purchase or lease the system as a complete package from the vendor. No programming, engineering, or even personnel training is required on the part of the user; the vendor provides these services, in most cases, as part of the basic contract.

The advantage of this approach is that the user does not have to provide

Table 1.

		MAYO SMITH	MT. SINAI PORDY	HAHNEMANN DREIFUS	VA PIPBERGER	LDS WARNER	IBM BONNER
Facility: **Responsible:**							
Leads:	Type	S+F*	S+F	S+F	F	F	S(+F)
X-mission:	Cart	Marquette	Cro-Med	Marquette	Marquette	Marquette	———
	Method	FM via phone	FM via phone	FM via phone	FM via phone	FM via phone	Dig tape
	# Channels	6; 3F continuous, 3S at a time	3	3	3	3	3
	Bandwidth	Special lines needed	Voice grade	Voice grade	Voice grade	Voice grade	———
	Xmit time	10 sec	10 sec-S 20 sec-F	10.8 sec-S 10.8 sec-F	30 sec	30 sec	25 sec
ADC:	Samp rate	250/sec/ch (variable)	250/sec/ch	250 or 333/sec/ch	500/sec/ch	200/sec/ch	250/sec/ch
	# Channels	6	3	3	3	3	3
Digital I/P:	Method	Push buttons	Digital switches	Touch tone or phone card	Touch tone	Touch tone	Dig tape
	Parameters	ID#, age, sex ht, wt	ID#, age, sex, ht, wt, date, drugs, clinical diagnoses	ID#, age, sex	ID#, age, race, wt, date, drugs	ID#, age	ID#, age, sex, race, ht, wt, date, clinical diagnoses, drugs
Computer:	Type	IBM 1800	IBM 1800 or 360	IBM 1800	CDC 3200	CDC 3300	IBM 360/370
	Batch or on-line	On-line	Batch	On-line	Batch	On-line	Batch
	Core	64K	100K	32K	32K	32K	70K/95K
Analysis:	Method	Decision logic	Decision logic	Decision logic	Statistical	Decision logic	Decision logic
	Leads	F	S+F	F+V1	F	F+"V4"	S
	Parameters	Age, sex, drugs	Age, sex,	Age, sex	Age, drugs	Age	———

	CRT: S+F+ vector; FM tape: 1 yr. Dig tape: raw data, parameters	parameters	S+F Dig tape: raw data, parameters	Dig tape: raw data, parameters	Dig tape: parameters	Dig tape: parameters
# Bytes/record	Parameters: 4000 bytes	S-2200 bytes F-900 bytes	Parameters: 400 bytes raw data: 10 Kbytes	Raw data: 15,000 words	Parameters: 42 words	——
Output: ECG trace	Photo of display	3 ch strip	Photo of display	3 ch strip	3 ch strip	Printout
Parameters and diagnosis	Printout label	Printout label	Printout label	Printout	Printout label	——
Backup: Method	FM tape		Strip chart	FM tape, dig tape	Strip chart	——
General: Patients/day	300		70	30	45	——
Typical cost/ECG:	$9.65	$4.50	$2.50	——	$2.00	$350 mo.
Waveform Anal:	Yes	Yes	Yes	Yes	Yes	Yes
Arrhythmia:	Yes	Yes	Yes	Yes	Yes	Yes
Comparison:	No	Yes	No	No	Yes	No
Prgm. Lang.:	Fortran, Assembler	Fortran, Assembler	Fortran, Assembler	Fortran	Assembler	PL/1, Assembler
Chart copy:	Photo of microfilm, label	Central tracing, label	Photo of microfilm, label	Cart tracing, teletype printout	Cart tracing, label	——

* S = Standard lead set (12)
F = Frank (orthogonal) lead set (3)

the technical resources to develop a system of his own. The vendor installs the equipment, tests it, trains the operators, provides maintenance and repair services and, as program bugs and engineering problems are resolved, provides system modifications and updates, usually at no cost to the user. The more conscientious vendors maintain ongoing programs to improve the hardware, operating system, and analysis programs. As these improvements become available, they are offered to the user at costs dependent on the nature of the modifications. Another advantage is that most systems are capable of handling a large volume of ECGs with little or no increment in cost attributable to the analysis system; it takes about as much equipment and software to process one ECG per day as it does to process 100. Thus, the unit cost (cost per ECG) usually decreases considerably with increasing volume.

The main disadvantage of the turn-key system is that the unsophisticated user is at the mercy of the vendor with regard to service, system reliability, and requests for system modifications. The user should obtain some guarantees from the vendor with regard to system reliability (e.g., in terms of average mean time to failure) and on the availability and promptness of repairs when the inevitable failure occurs. If more than one vendor is involved (e.g., ECG terminal and computer manufacturers), coordination of their repair efforts may be difficult. Provision must be made for backup of the automated system when it fails. The ideal backup (and also the most expensive) is a completely redundant computer system. Other possibilities include saving the electrocardiograms, where possible, on magnetic tape for subsequent batch processsing when the system is repaired, transmitting the ECGs to a service bureau for analysis or simply reverting to manual interpretation by a cardiologist.

Another disadvantage concerns the ability of the user to obtain system modifications that are unique to his facility's requirements. These changes may include modifications to the hardware, operating system, or analysis program. For example, the cardiologists in a facility may be unhappy with the criteria used by the particular cardiologists the vendor consulted in the development of his analysis program and may wish to have them changed. Such individual tailoring of the programs is inevitably expensive because the changes are unique to a facility and the costs incurred by the vendor cannot be shared among the other users. Furthermore, there is often a considerable delay between the initiation of a modification request and its implementation since the vendor must free appropriate personnel from other projects to work on the user's request. On the other hand, if the user maintains his own engineering and programming staff who can perform system maintenance and modifications, the purchase of a turn-key system may well be the most economical route to automated electrocardiogram analysis since initial developmental, engineering, and programming costs are avoided. Clearly, each facility contemplating the purchase of this type of system should carefully evaluate the unit cost (per ECG), projected unit cost as volume increases, cost for system modifications, system reliability, availability of repair service, and most important, acceptance by physicians of the computer's interpretations.

Companies now selling or leasing turn-key systems include: Digital Equipment, Hewlett-Packard, Marquette, Medlab, and Varian. Analysis programs provided by some of these systems include the Smith program (1967 version), Pipberger program, United States Public Health Service (USPHS) ECAN–D, and Warner program (see Table 2).

Table 2.

Company	Ecan-D	Pipberger	Smith	Warner
Digital equipment	X	X	X	
Hewlett-Packard	X	X	X	
Marquette	X		X	
Medlab				X
Varian		X		

The cost of these systems varies with the workload and the options requested. General equipment configurations such as the number of ECG terminals, data receivers, and printers are tailored to the individual facility. Unit costs may be as low as $1 per ECG for a workload of several hundred ECGs per day. More typical costs range from $3 to $5 per ECG for work-load below 100 ECGs per day.

(2) Service bureaus. With the development of standardized analysis programs such as ECAN-D, a number of companies were formed to provide computer analysis of electrocardiograms as a service to health care facilities. These service bureaus contract with individual facilities to provide ECG interpretations at a fixed minimum monthly cost or at a specified cost per ECG analyzed. The unit cost usually decreases with increasing volume. The only system hardware located in the medical facility is the ECG terminal and, optionally, a printer for reporting interpretations. These devices may either be purchased by the facility or leased from the service bureau. Depending upon the requirements of the facility, electrocardio-grams may be recorded on magnetic tape and mailed to the service bureau for analysis or transmitted directly to the bureau over leased or dial-up telephone lines. Results may be printed at the bureau and mailed to the

facility or printed at the medical facility on a teletype or printer connected via phone lines to the service bureau's computer.

Most of the early service bureaus used the original USPH program. They were not very successful because there was considerable disagreement among cardiologists over the accuracy of the diagnoses. Recently, service bureaus have either improved upon the basic USPHS program or written their own.

Typical of service bureaus are Telemed and Cro-Med Bionics. Each serves a number of hospitals throughout the country. Although the exact numbers are proprietary, Telemed claims to have several hundred installations and is processing about 2,000 ECGs per day. Each medical facility is connected to the central Telemed computer (an XDS Sigma-5) in Chicago via leased WATS (Wide Area Telecommunication Service) lines. After the analysis is performed, results are printed on teletypes in the remote facilities.

As with turn-key systems, the principal advantage of the service bureau approach is that the user does not need any computer or engineering expertise to have the benefits of automated electrocardiagram analysis. The service bureau will usually handle as much of the installation, maintenance, training, and system support as the user wishes to contract. Unlike turn-key systems, it is not necessary for the user to make the considerable capital investment required to lease or purchase a complete system. He is paying, basically, for the service alone. A further advantage of service bureaus is that they are usually devoted to a single purpose, namely, providing accurate and timely electrocardiogram analyses. Updating and improving their systems is (or should be) a continuous process. Since they receive many more ECGs than a single facility can generate, they may have access to a greater library of data on which to base improved analysis techniques. Some services have consultant cardiologists who screen abnormal electrocardiograms and verify the computer interpretation prior to its transmission back to the medical facility. This is of considerable advantage to physicians in remote areas who may want the consultation of a cardiologist.

The main disadvantage of service bureaus is that it is next to impossible for an individual facility to obtain a unique modification in the operating system or analysis program. If a bureau feels that a requested modification is of no general use or may be unacceptable to the majority of its users, it may flatly refuse the request. The user has no recourse but to live with the current system or go to another bureau. Similarly, the bureau may make an "improvement" in its program (such as modification of a diagnostic criteria) that a particular user may not agree with. Again, the user has little recourse. Obviously, the reason for this method of operation is that the service bureau cannot afford to tailor its programs to each facility. It would require an enormous effort to keep track of the many versions and version modifications that would result. Since the programs are proprietary, it is rarely possible for a user to obtain a copy to modify and run on his own computer system. In general, the service bureau approach is probably the most inflexible for an individual facility to use in a dynamically changing field; but in certain cases, it may provide the least expensive alternative for automated ECG analysis. Therefore, a medical facility considering the use of a service bureau for electrocardiogram analysis should be sure that its physicians accept or, at least, can live with the diagnostic criteria programmed by the bureau. The facility should be prepared to modify its operations to comply with the requirements of the service bureau, rather than the other way around. They should also try to evaluate the commitment of the bureau to keep its programs up-to-date with new developments in the field.

(3) Analysis programs.   It is possible to obtain computer programs for electrocardiogram analysis independent of the associated hardware. This may be a useful approach to automated electrocardiogram analysis for facilities that have their own computers, programmers, and engineering staff. Some of these programs were developed in the public domain and are free. Others were developed by computer companies and are sold as program products. Information concerning the nature and availability of these programs is given in Table 3. In addition, three of the programs, ECAN-D, Smith, and Pipberger, can be purchased as program products from Digital Equipment Corporation for PDP-15 and PDP-11/45 computers.

(4) Hardware analysis.   Two types of electronic analyzers for the rapid screening of electrocardiograms are represented by the Chuo Electronics Cardiolyzer and the Humetrics Electrocardioanalyzer.

(a) Cardiolyzer.   The cardiolyzer is actually a turn-key mini-computer system which appears to the ECG technician as a rather complicated electrocardiograph. All computer operations are essentially transparent to the user. Twelve standard leads are recorded; measurements proceed automatically and results are displayed and printed in the form of the standard three-digit Minnesota code.

(b) Electrocardioanalyzer.   This device can be used only to distinguish normal from abnormal electrocardiograms. Developed specifically for mass screening applications, the instrument measures 20 parameters of the ECG using 5 leads. Criteria for abnormality are based on amplitude and time parameters of the various competent waveforms of the ECG. Analysis results are displayed immediately on a set of lamps on the front panel. No recordings of the ECG are required.

Table 3.

Program	Computer	Address	Cost
Dreifus	IBM 1800	Dr. Leonard Dreifus Hahnemann Medical College 230 N. Broad Street Philadelphia, Pa. 19102	Free
ECAN-D	CDC 160-A IBM 360/370 PDP-8 PDP-9 XDS SIGMA 2 XDS SIGMA 5	Health Care Technology Division Health Services and Mental Health Administration 5600 Fishers Lane Rockville, Md. 20852	Free
IBM	IBM 360/370	IBM Data Processing Division 1133 Westchester Avenue White Plains, New York 10604	$350/mo.
Pipberger	CDC 3200	Dr. Hubert Pipberger Veterans Administration Hospital 50 Irving Street, N.W. Washington, D.C. 20422	Free
Smith	IBM 1800	Dr. Ralph Smith Mayo Clinic 200 First Street, S.W. Rochester, Minn. 55901	Free
Warner	CDC 3300	Dr. Homer Warner Latter Day Saints Hospital 325 - 8th Avenue Salt Lake City, Utah 84103	Free

C. ELECTROENCEPHALOGRAPHY

1. Introduction

a. Origin of electrical activity in the brain.   Although the electrical activity of the human brain was first recorded over 40 years ago, the origin of this activity is still obscure.[26] A brain wave or electroencephalogram (EEG) is usually recorded as the potential difference between pairs of electrodes inserted in the scalp.[27] The voltages measured are usually in the 10–30 microvolt range—approximately 100 times less in amplitude than the electrocardiogram. The signals are sensed via needle or disk electrodes and usually recorded on paper using high gain amplifiers. The EEG is characterized by rhythmical variations in potential which may contain periodic and nonperiodic components, each of which may vary in amplitude and frequency in a nonstationary manner. EEGs are believed to be generated by electrical activity in the dendritic layer of the cerebral cortex and in other regions of the brain. Animal experiments have shown good correlation between potentials recorded with gross wire electrodes inserted into certain brain structures and potentials from surface electrodes over the structures. Numerous models have been proposed to explain the characteristics of discharging neurons and neural networks, but most features of the EEG that are clinically useful have been deduced from experiment and observation. There is obviously a great deal of information encoded in the EEG, and numerous techniques have been developed to extract this information.

b. Development of analytic methods.   The analysis of the EEG constitutes a formidable problem in pattern recognition. Progress in EEG analysis has come slowly because of the nonstationary characteristics of the waveform and the difficulty in extracting physiologically significant information from the signal. However, with the development of computer analysis techniques, the attempts have been increasingly successful.

The traditional EEG consists of simultaneous recordings of the variation over time of the potential differences between multiple pairs of scalp electrodes. Routinely, a diagnostic EEG requires the application of approximately 21 electrodes, providing signals on up to 16 channels of a strip chart recorder from frontal, central, parietal, temporal, and occipital regions of the brain. Analysis, without the help of automated techniques, consists of visual pattern recognition of waveform characteristics of various lead pairs, including the identification of intrinsic rhythms (alpha, beta, etc.) and of abnormal rhythms or discrete events (spikes, asymmetries, etc.), and manual measurement of waveform parameters. This is a tedious process, and it requires considerable training to develop proficiency in reading EEGs.

The recognition of periodic components in standard EEG recordings led directly to the application of frequency domain techniques to EEG analysis. Early methods involved frequency analysis with analog instruments, using multiple narrow band electronic filters to obtain spectral density distributions.[28] Averaging of evoked responses, auto- and cross-correlation analysis, and other statistical techniques were also applied to the EEG. Complex toposcopic displays on an oscilloscope were used to demonstrate phase relations between different pairs of leads.[29] The basic goal of all these analysis attempts has been to develop signal transformations and property filters for the EEG to facilitate the recognition of patterned activity and to decode the information contained in the signal.

2. Methods of Computer Analysis

Digital computers have provided the electroencephalographer with a powerful tool for the analysis of EEGs.[30-33] Mathematical techniques that could not be applied or were applied laboriously because of the length and complexity of the calculations involved are now being used effectively. As the capacity, speed, and capabilities of computers have increased, new analytical techniques have been developed and applied to EEG analysis.[34,35] Elaborate analog hardware that was formerly used in EEG systems for relatively simple analyses have been progressively replaced by the digital computer, which often can perform the same analyses more rapidly and accurately. Of the many analytical methods programmed for the computer, signal averaging, frequency analysis, and time series analysis will be described below.

a. Average evoked response.   The evoked response is an EEG phe-nomenon that has received intensive study.[36] Almost any physiological stimulus, such as a flash of light or sudden noise, will evoke a definite, repeatable response in the EEG, consisting of a short latent period followed by a specific transient change in potential. In the alert, unanesthetized brain, these response signals are usually masked by the background "noise" of the ongoing EEG. A method for extracting the response signal from the background activity is to increase the signal-to-noise ratio by the averaging of multiple stimulus-response cycles. Signal averaging is easy to do digitally. The averaging cycle must always begin at a fixed time relative to the onset of the stimulus. The computer digitizes the EEG waveform at fixed inter-vals (usually on the order of milliseconds) and stores the data in its memory as a numerical array. The average response is obtained by averag-ing this array point-by-point with the previously computed average response array. The average response may be displayed by converting the computed array to an analog signal and using it to drive an oscilloscope or pen recorder. Although the normal EEG is "nonstationary" in a statistical sense, it may be considered to be "quasistationary" over the relatively short durations of evoked response experiments. Consequently, the background activity will tend to be averaged out, while the evoked response signal will remain. The signal-to-noise ratio improves approximately with the square root of the number of cycles.

Although signal averaging can be performed on any general purpose computer having an analog-to-digital converter, a number of nonprogram-mable special purpose laboratory computers have been developed to per-form this type of analysis. Two of these are the Mnemetron Computer of

Average Transients and the Nuclear-Chicago Data Retrieval Computer. These instruments can also compute time and interval histograms.

b. Spectral analysis. The EEG contains essentially a continuous spectrum of frequencies from under 1 Hz to over 50 Hz. Spectral analysis techniques may be used to analyze the EEG waveforms either in the presence or absence of an external stimulus. It is basically a process that transforms the time domain EEG into its frequency domain representation, in which signal amplitude or power density is expressed as a function of frequency. Early analog devices performed this transformation by means of sets of narrow bandpass electronic filters whose summed passbands covered the desired spectrum.[28] Recently, digital computers have been programmed to operate as ideal signal filters.[37,38] The output of these simulated filters can be either printed or plotted directly as an autospectrogram on a digital plotter.

The autospectrogram can also be calculated from the time domain EEG by Fourier transform methods. A new computer analysis technique, the Fast Fourier Transform (FFT), has improved the efficiency of this approach. The FFT has been programmed for a PDP-12 computer connected to a digital plotter.[39] EEG analysis results are plotted in perspective as simulated 3-dimensional spectrograms, with frequency and amplitude as the x- and y-axes, respectively, and time as the z-axis. These plots provide a graphic display of the variation of the spectrogram with time.

An adaptation of spectral analysis is the cross-spectrogram. This technique relates the activity in two EEG traces. Cross-spectrograms display relative amplitude and phase relations of activity common to the two traces as a function of frequency.

Many of the computer programs that perform these analyses are available from the University of California Los Angeles Health Sciences Computing Facility as part of their BMD series of biomedical computer programs.[40]

c. Time series analysis. Time series analysis involves the use of auto- and cross-correlation functions to extract periodic signals from noise. The mathematical techniques employed are described in detail elsewhere.[41,42] The autocorrelation function contains all the frequencies present in the original EEG and is the Fourier transform of its power spectrum. It has been used on single EEG traces to detect changes in frequency distribution during task performances. Cross-correlation of pairs of simultaneous EEG records have shown relationships between electrical activity in different regions of the brain. Changes in phase patterns have also been correlated with task performance. These techniques, however, appear to be less useful to electroencephalographers than spectral analysis since it is more difficult in practice to extract the same information.

3. Commercial EEG Systems

Most diagnostic evaluations of brain wave activity are based on visual observation of EEG tracings recorded by a standard electroencephalograph. This instrument usually contains a lead selector (for up to 24 leads), up to 16 high gain dc amplifiers, and a strip chart recorder with up to 16 recording channels. Manufacturers of standard electroencephalographs include Beckman, Grass Instrument, Offner Electronics, Spacelabs, and many others.

Recently, a screening electroencephalograph has been developed by Humetrics Corporation. This device, called the Electroencephaloscan, provides automatic rapid scanning of brain waves. It can distinguish normal electrical activity from abnormal but cannot provide diagnoses. If an abnormality is detected, the location of the abnormality is indicated by a display lamp on the front panel. The instrument does not contain a chart recorder but provides auxiliary outputs from the amplifiers for further analysis or display. Although the standard EEG is taken with 21 disk electrodes, only the portion of the information judged useful for screening is analyzed. Screening criteria include abnormal activity in the 3–7 Hz range and in left and right hemispheres for central-occipital and occipital-temporal lead configurations. The instrument is designed to be used in automated multiphasic health testing centers, emergency rooms, and outpatient clinics. An average of four minutes is required for each patient encounter.

D. INTENSIVE CARE AND CORONARY CARE MONITORING

1. Introduction

The purpose of a critical care facility, such as an intensive care unit (ICU) or coronary care unit (CCU), is to provide the most intensive medical and nursing care possible to the critically ill patient.[43–47] Patients in cardiovascular shock or patients recovering from myocardial infarction or open heart surgery are candidates for the ICU or CCU. Effective treatment of these patients requires continuous monitoring of physiological variables that reflect the condition of the patient and communication of any change in their status to medical personnel that staff the unit. This has led to the development of specialized patient monitoring systems for the critical care facility. Vallbona has listed a number of requirements for a physiological monitoring system.[48] These are summarized in Table 4. The types of monitoring systems available can be divided into two broad classes: instrument monitors and computer monitors.

Table 4.   Clinical Requirements for a Physiological Monitoring System

1. Electrodes and sensors easily applied and maintained.
2. High reliability of all monitoring system components.
3. Efficient repair and maintenance service.
4. Accuracy of all measurements.
5. Capability of monitoring a wide variety of physiological signals.
6. Analytic capability for complex calculations and decision logic.
7. Graphic display capabilities for sensor data, derived values, and manually entered data.
8. Capability of generating summary reports which merge monitored with manual data.

In instrument monitoring systems (Figure 10-2), sensors are connected from the patient to signal conditioning modules, where the signals are amplified, filtered, or otherwise transformed to be displayed, usually on an oscilloscope or strip chart recorder. Many monitoring systems provide alarms for the monitored signals, which are triggered whenever the signal exceeds a preset range. More advanced logical circuitry can perform basic pattern recognition functions with the signal, such as the detection of specific events, and can record their incidence or set alarms. An example of this feature is the detection of premature ventricular contractions in the ECG by cardiac monitoring systems.

In most computer monitoring systems (Figure 10-2), signals from patient sensors are conditioned and then transmitted in analog form to a computer. After the signals are digitized, the computer may (1) display the raw data, or some transform of it, in either digital or graphical form; (2) apply a set of decision rules to one or more patient variables and present a conclusion or suggestion for action; or (3) take a specific action directly affecting the patient, such as controlling the rate of infusion of a particular drug.

In a more advanced monitoring system developed recently by General Electric, patient sensors are connected to signal conditioning modules, which are themselves preprogrammed microcomputers capable of performing complex calculations and decision logic. The parameters derived from the input signal are in digital form and are output in this format for display and for further processing by a central computer. This type of signal preprocessing reduces the computational load on the central computer, since analog-to-digital conversion and other signal extraction algorithms that usually require considerable processing time, are now performed by satellite microcomputers.

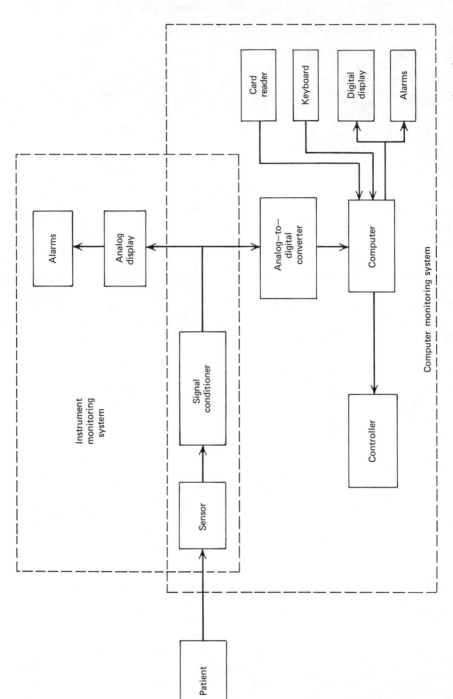

Figure 10–2. Two types of patient monitors. Instrument monitoring system (upper box). Computer monitoring system (lower box).

2. Instrument Monitoring

A coronary care unit (CCU) monitoring system typically includes instrumentation to monitor ECG, heart rate, systolic and diastolic pressures, central venous pressure, and temperature.[43,46] Sensors, electrodes, and monitors are located at the bedside in each room of the unit. ECG monitors usually require three disk or needle electrodes attached to the patient. Heart rate is determined automatically from the ECG. Intra-arterial and intra-venous pressure transducers measure arterial and central venous pressures through intra-vascular catheters. A thermistor probe measures body temperature. At the bedside, the ECG waveform is displayed on an oscilloscope; heart rate, pressures, and temperature are displayed on meters. Calibration controls, upper- and lower-alarm threshold settings, and alarm indicators are usually provided on these instruments. In most CCUs, bedside monitoring units are connected to a central monitor to permit remote interrogation of the status of any monitored variable of any patient in the CCU. The ECGs of several patients are usually displayed simultaneously on a multitrace oscilloscope at the central station. One or more strip chart recorders can provide permanent tracings of any ECG selected. Some systems also provide automatic ECG recording for any patient in the event an alarm condition occurs.

Most medical instrument manufacturers offer CCU monitoring systems that provide some or all of these functions, with innumerable variations. Since many different systems will satisfy the operational requirements of CCU clinicians to approximately the same degree, the primary selection criteria for a monitoring system will be cost, reliability, training and maintenance requirements, and available repair facilities.

Intensive care unit (ICU) systems usually monitor pulmonary function in addition to cardiac function. Monitored variables may include respiratory rate, tidal volume, partial pressures of carbon dioxide and oxygen, and many other measures of pulmonary function. If a patient is attached to a respirator, volume and flow values are frequently measured by a pneumotachograph placed in the airway. A pneumotachograph is a precisely calibrated tube, open at both ends, from which flow rate is computed as a function of the change in air pressure within the tube. Volume measurements are obtained by integration of the flow curve. Carbon dioxide and oxygen levels may be measured by chemical electrodes inserted in the airway.

3. Computer Monitoring

The addition of a computer to a physiological monitoring system extends its capabilities in several areas. It provides automated data collection and

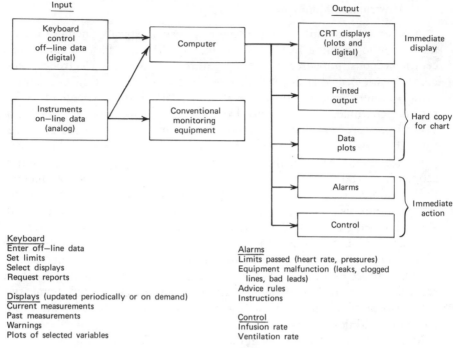

Figure 10-3. Functions of a computer monitoring system.

analysis, the use of complex decision algorithms based on multiple variables, rapid retrieval of monitored and computed data, and organization of data into clinically useful displays and reports; and it can provide automatic control of physiological inputs directly affecting the patient (see Figure 10-3). If the computer monitoring system is operated as part of a medical information system, monitored data can be stored in a permanent patient file and integrated with data collected from other sources (see Chapters Three and Four).

a.   Data collection.   In a computer monitoring system, data can be collected in two ways: (1) directly from monitoring instruments and (2) by manual entry from a data input terminal. In the first case, physiological signals are detected by patient sensors and are transmitted to signal conditioning modules. These instruments condition the signals by filtering, amplifying, and compensating for dc offsets in order to bring the analog voltages within the input range of the analog-to-digital converter (ADC). The ADC samples the continuous signals periodically at discrete points and converts the instantaneous values of voltage to their digital representations. The resulting digital data points are then input to the computer for storage and analysis. This process is represented in Figure 10-4. (In the General

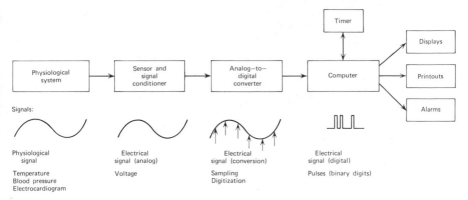

Figure 10-4. Conversion of a physiological signal to its digital representation.

Electric system described above, the signal conditioner is itself a microcomputer which performs its own analog-to-digital conversion and transfers the results to the main computer in digital form.) Physiological signals may be monitored by the computer either continuously or intermittently. Measurements and analyses may be performed either on demand or automatically at periodic preset intervals. Periodic calibration of sensors is easily performed under computer control. Clearly, automated data collection saves personnel time and reduces the possibility of human error in reading the instruments.

Manual data entry is required for the input of any information or physiological measurement that is not directly available to the computer in the form of on-line analog or digital signals. Thus, many clinical laboratory results, physical findings, and patient data (such as age, sex, height, weight, etc.) must be input manually. Some monitoring systems permit the entry of medication schedules, medications administered, vital signs, fluid intake and output, and nurses' notes. A variety of data input devices may be used for manual data entry. These include keyboards, punch and mark-sense card, and visual display terminals with or without light-pens.

b. Analysis. A digital computer can be programmed to perform complex calculations to derive clinically significant physiological parameters from raw data, either on demand or automatically. Examples of derived parameters include cardiac output, stroke volume, lung compliance, tidal volume, alveolar ventilation, respiratory quotient, etc. Other examples of measured and derived variables are shown in Figure 10-5.

c. Display. A digital computer is able to generate a virtually limitless variety of displays ranging from simple printouts of test results to simulated three dimensional plots of multivariate signals. Most computer monitoring

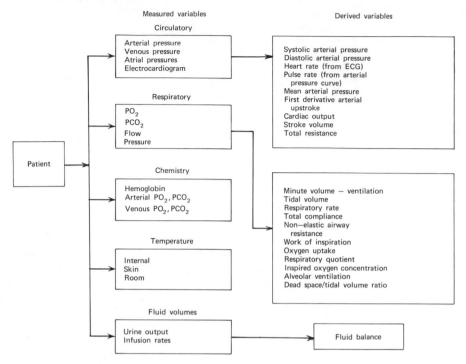

Figure 10–5. Physiological variables measured and derived by a computer monitoring system.

systems provide periodic status reports of monitored variables for each patient. These printed reports show the values of each measured or computed parameter over the period of the report and may be retained in the chart. Daily summary reports summarize the status of the patient over the previous 24-hour period. Cathode ray tubes (CRT) can be used to display the raw data digitally or plotted as a function of time in the form of trend curves or bar graphs. Trend plots show the variation of one or more parameters over periods of time ranging from hours to days. Two-dimensional plots can display the relationship between pairs of variables. Examples of these are vector cardiograms and respiratory flow-volume loops. Hard copy of these displays may be obtained with a digital plotter or printer, or by photographing the CRT. Two-dimensional plots of discrete measurements can be used to demonstrate the correlation between pairs of variables. Time and interval histograms are also available in some systems.

d.   Decision logic.   Most instrument monitors are only capable of making simple logical decisions based on the behavior of a single variable. For example, if heart rate falls outside a certain range, an alarm is triggered. The addition of a computer to the monitoring system permits more complex decisions to be made, involving current values and trends of one or more monitored variables or derived parameters. For example, it is possible to program the computer to distinguish between instrument failure and patient distress, thereby reducing the incidence of false patient alarms. A computer system can distinguish between premature ventricular contractions and movement artifacts and notify the medical staff of the specific problem.

e. **Automatic control.**   A computer monitoring system can be used to control certain physiological inputs to a patient, either environmental (e.g., temperature) or as part of a therapeutic process (e.g., rate of drug infusion). In this mode of operation, the monitoring system functions as a closed-loop feedback control system. The system configuration is represented in Figure 10-6. The inputs to the system are the physiological variables measured or derived from sensor and manual data. The outputs are control signals that drive the appropriate effectors. The effectors are electrical or electromechanical devices which control the input to the patient (from the environment or therapeutic process); to close the loop, these variables in turn control the monitored physiological variables. In operation, when a condition arises in which the value of a measured variable falls outside its allowed range, the system functions through the effector and its controlled variables to bring the measured variable back within range. Examples of monitored and controlled physiological variables are given in Table 5.

f. **Developmental systems.**   There are over 20 projects in various medical centers around the country investigating the use of computers in ICUs and CCUs. Although the emphasis of these projects and the variables chosen for study varies with the local clinical research interests, in general, the systems developed conform to the principles described above. Most of these systems are well described in the literature and will not be reviewed here.[49-62] While most of these computer monitoring projects are still in the research stage, many of them are producing clinically useful information for direct patient care. Although the final medical decisions are still made by the clinical staff, the role of the computer in performing physiological measurements and suggesting courses of action is rapidly expanding.

g. **Commercial systems.**   A few manufacturers of instrument monitoring systems have also developed computer based monitoring systems. Most of these systems have similar data entry and retrieval capabilities, providing automated monitoring of ECGs, pressures and temperatures, manual data entry of laboratory test results and other medical and nursing information, and various types of displays and printed reports. Commercial developers of computer monitoring systems include Becton-Dickenson, General Electric, Gould, Hewlett-Packard, Medlab, Mennen-Greatbatch, and Roche.

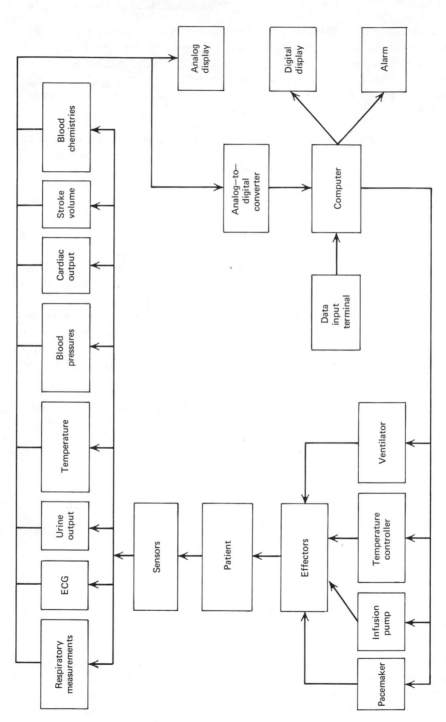

Figure 10-6. Schematic representation of closed-loop computer monitoring system.

Table 5.[49-53]

Treatment	Controlled variables	Effector	Measured variables
Ventilatory support	Tidal volume Inspiratory plateau Ventilator rate Oxygen concentration	Ventilator	Respiration rate Inspiratory and expiratory pressures Dead space volume Partial pressure oxygen Partial pressure carbon dioxide Blood pH
Blood transfusion	Infusion rate	Infusion pump	Pulmonary artery pressure Central venous pressure Plasma volume Red cell mass Cardiac index Stroke volume Urine output Weight
Pacemaker control	Impulse intensity Atrial and ventricular rate	Bifocal pacemaker	ECG Cardiac index Stroke volume Pulmonary artery pressure Central venous pressure Arterial pressure Blood pH Blood lactate

REFERENCES

1. Lion, K. S. "Transducers." In Nastuk, W. L.: *Physical Techniques in Biological Research, Vol. V.* New York: Academic Press, 1964.

2. Spach, M. S.; Barr, R. C.; Honstad, J. W.; and Long, E. C. "Skin-electrode Impedence and its Effect on Recording Cardiac Potentials." *Circulation* 34 (1966): 649–656.

3. Geddes, L. A., and Baker, L. E. *Principles of Applied Biomedical Instrumentation.* New York: John Wiley, 1968.

4. Rushmer, R. F. *Cardiovascular Dynamics.* Philadelphia: W. B. Saunders, 1961.

5. Grant, R. P. *Clinical Electrocardiography.* New York: Blakiston-McGraw, 1957.

6. Dower, G. E. "Polarcardiography." In Manning, G. W., and Ahuja, S. P. *Electrical Activity of the Heart.* Illinois: Charles Thomas, 1969.

7. Frank E. "An Accurate, Clinically Practical System for Spatial Vectorcardiography." *Circulation* 13 (1956): 737.

8. Caceres, C. A., and Dreifus, L. *Clinical Electrocardiography and Computers.* New York: Academic Press, 1970.

9. Steinberg, C. A.; Abraham, S.; and Caceres, C. A. "Pattern Recognition in the Clinical Electrocardiogram." *IRE Trans. on Biomed. Elect.* 9 (1962): 23–30.

10. Pipberger, H. V. "Computer Analysis of the Electrocardiogram." In Stacy, R. W. and Waxman, B. D. *Computers in Biomedical Research, Vol. I.* New York: Academic Press, 1965.

11. Stallmann, F. W., and Pipberger, H. V. "Automatic Recognition of Electrocardiographic Waves by Digital Computer." *Circulation Research* 9 (1961): 1138.

12. Wartak, J. "Computer-aided Recognition of Electrocardiograms." *Acta Cardiologica* 22 (1967): 350.

13. Smith, R. E., and Hyde, C. M. "A Computer System for Electrocardiographic Analysis." *Proc. Third Annual Rocky Mountain Bio-engineering Symposium.* May, 1966.

14. Pryor, T. A.; Lindsay, A. E.; and England, R. W. "Computer Analysis of Serial Electrocardiograms." *Comp. and Biomed. Res.* 5 (1972): 709–714.

15. Pryor, T. A.; Russell, R.; Budkin, A.; and Price, W. G. "Electrocardiographic Interpretation by Computer." *Comp. and Biomed. Res.* 2 (1969): 537–548.

16. Bonner, R. E.; Crevasse, L.; Merrer, M. I.; and Greenfield, J. C. "A New Computer Program for Analysis of Scalar Electrocardiograms." *Comp. and Biomed. Res.* 5 (1972): 629–653.

17. Bonner, R. E., and Schwetman, H. D. "Computer Diagnosis of Electrocardiograms. III. A Computer Program for Arrhythmia diagnosis." *Comp. and Biomed. Res.* 1 (1968): 387–407.

18. Bonner, R. E., and Schwetman, H. D. "Computer Diagnosis of Electrocardiograms. II. A Computer Program for EKG Measurements." *Comp. and Biomed. Res.* 1 (1968): 366.

19. Smith, R. E., and Hyde, C. M. "Computer Analysis of the Electrocardiogram in Clinical Practice." In Manning, G. W. and Ahuja, S. P. *Electrical Activity of the Heart.* Illinois: Charles Thomas, (1969).

20. Pordy, L., et al. "Computer Diagnosis of Electrocardiograms. IV. A Computer Program for Contour Analysis with Clinical Results of Rhythm and Contour Interpretation." *Comp. and Biomed. Res.* 1 (1968) : 408.

21. Macfarlane, P. W. "ECG Waveform Identification by Digital Computer." *Cardiovascular Research* 5 (1971) : 141.

22. Wartak, J. *Computers in Electrocardiography.* Illinois: Charles Thomas, 1970.

23. Stark, L.; Dickson, J. F.; Whipple, G. H.; and Horibe, H. "Remote Real-time diagnosis of Clinical Electrocardiograms by Digital Computer." *Ann. N.Y. Acad. Sci.* 128 (1966) : 851.

24. Von der Groeben, J. *Progress Report to PHS Grant HE 10202. Stanford University, 1970.*

25. Von der Groeben, J. "Decision Rules in Electrocardiography and Vectorcardiography." *Circulation* 36 (1967) : 136–147.

26. Walter, D. O., and Brazier, M. A. B. "Advances in EEG Analysis." *Electroenceph. Clin. Neurophysiol.* Suppl. 27, 1969.

27. Walter, W. G. "Intrinsic Rhythms of the Brain." In *Handbook of Physiology. Section 1. Neurophysiology. Vol. I.* Baltimore: Waverly Press, 1965.

28. Krendl, E. "The Analysis of Electroencephalograms by the Use of a Cross-spectrum Analysis." *IRE Trans. Biomed. Elect.* 6 (1959) : 149–156.

29. Walter W. G., and Shipton, H. W. "A New Toposcopic Display System." *Electroenceph. Clin. Neurophysiol.* 3 (1951) : 281–292.

30. Brazier, M. A. B. "The Application of Computers to Electroencephalography." In Stacy, R. W. and Waxman, B. D. *Computers in Biomedical Research, Vol. I.* New York: Academic Press, 1965.

31. Adey, W. R. "Computer Analysis in Neurophysiology." In Stacy, R. W. and Waxman, B. D. *Computers in Biomedical Research, Vol. I.* New York: Academic Press, 1965.

32. Brazier, M. A. B. "Computer Techniques in EEG Analysis." *Electroenceph. Clin. Neurophysiol. Suppl.* 20 (1961) : 1–98.

33. Kaiser, E., and Petersen, I. "Automatic Analysis in EEG." *Acta Neurol. Scand. Suppl.* 22 (1966) : 1–38.

34. Hamming, R. W. *Numerical Methods for Scientists and Engineers.* New York: McGraw-Hill, 1962.

35. Ralston, A. and Wilf, H. S. *Mathematical Methods for Digital Computers. Vols. 1 and 2.* New York: John Wiley, 1960.

36. Donchin, E. "A Multivariate Approach to the Analysis of Average Evoked Potentials." *IEEE. Trans. Biomed. Engr.* 13 (1966) : 131–139.

37. Walter, D. O. "Spectral Analysis for Electroencephalograms: Mathematical Determination of Neurophysiological Relationships from Records of Limited Duration." *Exp. Neurol.* 8 (1963) : 155–181.

38. Burch, N. R. "Period Analysis of the Electroencephalogram on a General-purpose Digital Computer." *Ann. N.Y. Acad. Sci.* 115 (964) : 827–843.

39. Stockard, J. J.; Schauble, J. F.; Billinger, T. W.; and Bickford, R. G. "Intraoperative EEG Updated: New Techniques and Future Applications." *Proc. of the San Diego Biomedical Symposium* 11 (1972) : 277–286.

40. Dixon, W. J. *BMD: Biomedical Computer Programs.* Los Angeles: University of California Press, 1970.

41. Lee, Y. W. *Statistical Theory of Communication.* New York: John Wiley, 1960.

42. Barlow, J. S. "Autocorrelation and Crosscorrelation Analysis in Electroencephalography." *IRE Trans. Biomed. Elect.* 6 (1959) : 179–183.

43. *Guidelines for Coronary Care Units.* Public Health Service Publication No. 1824. July, 1968.

44. *Proceedings of the National Conference on Coronary Care Units.* Public Health Service Publication No. 1764, March, 1968.

45. Lown, B. "Intensive Heart Care." *Scientific Amer.* 219 (1968) : 19–27.

46. Lown, B.; and Selzer, A. "The Coronary Care Units." *Amer. J. Cardiol.* 22 (1968) : 597–602.

47. Farrier, R. M., et al. "Patient Monitoring in the Hospital." *Ann. N.Y. Acad. Sci.* 118 (1964) : 387–438.

48. Vallbona, C.; Spencer, W. A.; Geddes, L. A.; and Canzoneri, J. "The Clinician's Requirements for Physiological Monitoring Systems." *Biomedical Sciences Instrumentation* 4 (1968) : 3–6.

49. Jensen, R. E.; Shubin, H.; Meagher, P. F.; and Weil, M. H. "On-line Computer Monitoring of the Seriously Ill Patient." *Med. and Biol. Engr.* 4 (1966) : 265–272.

50. Weil, M. H.; Shubin, H.; and Rand, W. "Experience With a Digital Computer for Study and Improved Management of the Critically Ill." *JAMA* 198 (1966) : 1011–1016.

51. Shubin, H., and Weil, M. H. "Efficient Monitoring with a Digital Computer of Cardiovascular Function in Seriously Ill Patients." *Ann. Int. Med.* 65 (1966) : 453–460.

52. Shubin, H.; Weil, M. H.; and Rockwell, M. A. "Automated Measurement of Cardiac Output in Patients by Use of a Digital Computer." *Med. Biol. Engr.* 5 (1967) : 353–360.

53. Shubin, H.; Weil, M. H.; and Rockwell, M. A. "Automated Measurement of Arterial Pressure in Patients by Use of a Digital Computer." *Med. Biol. Engr.* 5 (1967) : 361–369.

54. Sheppard, L. C.; Kouchoukos, N. T.; Kurtls, M. A.; and Kirklin, J. W. "Automated Treatment of Critically Ill Patients Following Operation." *Ann. Surg.* 168 (1968) : 596.

55. Osborn, J. J., et al. "Measurement and Monitoring of Acutely Ill Patients by Digital Computer." *Surgery* 64 (1968) : 1057–1070.

56. Morgan, A. P. et al. "Peter Bent Brigham Hospital—Hewlett–Packard Intensive Care System." *Proc. Sixth Annual AAMI Meeting, March, 1971.*

57. Warner, H. R.; Gardner, R. M.; and Toronto, A. F. "Computer-Based Monitoring of Cardiovascular Functions in Postoperative Patients." *Circulation* 37 (1968) : 68–74.

58. Pryor, T. A., and Warner, H. R. "Time-sharing in Biomedical Research. *Datamation* 4 (1966) : 54.

59. McDonald, L. K.; Gardner, R. M.; Pryor, T. A.; and Day, W. C. "An Exploratory Study of the Costs and Cost Implications in the Operation of a MEDLAB Time-sharing Computer System—a Physiological Measurement Facility. *Comp. and Biomed. Res.* 3 (1971) : 586–603.

60. Warner, H. R. "Experiences with Computer Based Monitoring." *Anesth. Analg.* 47 (1968) : 453–462.

61. Cox, J. R.; Nolle, F. M.; and Fozzard, H. A. "Aztec: A Preprocessing Program for Real-time ECG Rhythm Analysis." *IEEE Trans. Biomed. Engr.* 15 (1968) : 128–129.

62. Hockberg, H. M., et al. "Automatic Electrocardiographic Monitoring in the Coronary Care Unit." *Angiology* 20 (1969) : 200–206.

CHAPTER ELEVEN

Automated Multiphasic Health Testing

by Morris F. Collen

A. DEFINITIONS AND OBJECTIVES

Automated Multiphasic Health Testing (AMHT) is becoming generally accepted in the U.S. It has developed as a result of the increasing demand by the public for low-cost periodic health examinations and the increasing availability of automated equipment and computerized data processing.

The advent of automation and computers into the field of medicine permits speed, efficiency, and quality control in multiphasic screening techniques so that not only more tests but also more accurate and quantitative measurements can be performed at a lower cost. It graduates the screening for the detection of a few diseases into a diagnostic survey for a broad range of diseases, and it permits acquiring and processing large quantities of data for patients "on-line"—before the patient leaves the lab.

More than 20 years ago, multiphasic screening programs began to operate in Massachusetts, Georgia, and California. It was soon found that they were very effective for early disease detection and that they were very efficient in providing many screening tests rapidly to large numbers of people and at great savings in money and manpower.

The first and largest computerized (automated) multitest laboratories have been operating in San Francisco and Oakland, California, since 1964.[1,2] In 1972, there were more than 200 automated multiphasic patient screening programs operational in the United States, Europe, Japan, and New Zealand.[3,4]

The term "screening" for a disease refers to the performance of a test with sufficient likelihood of detecting a disease, if present, in order to separate out persons who probably have the disease from those who probably do not. Multiphasic screening is the term applied to the combining of multiple tests to screen for a number of diseases. Automated multiphasic screening is the expanded concept of using automated and semi-automated electronic and mechanical equipment to perform multiple tests, and to determine automatically whether there is sufficient likelihood of the presence of a number of diseases, again to separate persons who are likely to have these diseases from those who very likely do not. As screening became more comprehensive, precise, and quantitative, Automated Multiphasic Health Testing (AMHT) has become the preferred term.[5,6]

In the past, screening for disease detection (for example, case finding for new or known untreated cases of tuberculosis, cancer, diabetes, etc.) was the primary use for multiphasic patient screening. Then AMHT programs were expanded to provide periodic health examinations.[7] In such instances, the first multiphasic evaluation of the patient usually fulfills the objective of screening for previous unknown disease. When the patient returns for subsequent periodic evaluations, the primary use of multiphasic testing then becomes patient surveillance and disease monitoring.

The periodic assessment of the health of a population by an AMHT program is usually for the purposes of:

(1) health surveillance, or periodic health surveys for the early detection of abnormalities to institute prompt preventive treatment of correctable conditions; and

(2) patient surveillance or periodic re-examination of patients for disease monitoring and preventive maintenance to postpone disability and death from incorrectable disease, and instruction of the patient in understanding and managing his specific disease.

More recently, Garfield[8,9] (see Chapter Two) has begun to use automated multiphasic health testing as a new entry mode to the delivery of medical care to direct and refer the sick and the well for appropriate services. Based upon the findings of the AMHT service, individuals are referred within an organized medical care delivery system to additional new services, either (1) to health care services for health educaton and counseling for the well, or (2) to the preventive maintenance services for the management and monitoring of early asymptomatic and chronic disease. This leaves the conventional sick care services for those who require physicians for diagnosis, treatment, or rehabilitation.

An AMHT laboratory can operate most effectively when associated with a medical center comprising inpatient and outpatient services so as to function as an automated multipurpose laboratory and provide screening and diagnostic services to both hospital and office patients.[10,11] It can be used for admission and preoperative examinations for the hospital patients and for ambulatory patients to provide periodic health examinations, health evaluations for special purposes (industrial, insurance, etc.), early sickness consultations, and diagnostic surveys. The AMHT laboratory can also be used as a new entry mode to the medical center by using its health testing capabilities to identify the needs of patients requesting physician services and refer them to health care services, preventive maintenance, or sick care services as appropriate.[8,9]

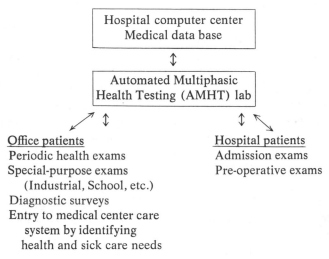

B. DESCRIPTION OF AN AMHT PROGRAM

At each of the two Kaiser-Permanente Automated Multiphasic Health Testing (AMHT) laboratories, "mulitphasic health checkups" are being provided to more than 2,000 patients each month.

Traditionally in the periodic health evaluation, the physician conducts a routine historical review and physical examination; he then arranges for the patient to receive a series of routine laboratory, electrocardiographic, and roentgenographic examinations; subsequently, the patient returns for report, diagnosis, treatment, and follow-up procedures.

In the multiphasic checkup, the patient receiving his periodic health examination first obtains a battery of tests and procedures conducted by paramedical personnel in an AMHT; the doctor then reviews the multiphasic laboratory report, conducts a physical examination, and proceeds in a traditional manner to diagnose, treat, and arrange follow-up procedures. This method of applying multiple screening techniques to periodic health examinations has been used by this program since 1951.[12]

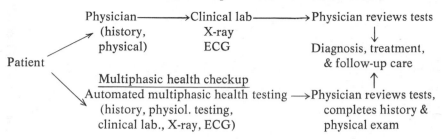

Traditional periodic health examination

Physician ————→ Clinical lab ————→ Physician reviews tests
(history,   X-ray   ↓
physical)   ECG   Diagnosis, treatment,
Patient   & follow-up care

Multiphasic health checkup   ↑
Automated multiphasic health testing —→ Physician reviews tests,
(history, physiol. testing,   completes history &
clinical lab., X-ray, ECG)   physical exam

When a person makes an appointment for a multiphasic health examination, he is sent printed instructions that will explain to him how to prepare for the examination. The patient begins his multiphasic examination by registering at the reception desk. One patient registers at the reception desk approximately every three minutes. It requires two to three hours for each patient to complete all phases in the AMHT. Appointment cards are prepared for 180 patients each day. Due to cancellations and patients failing to keep appointments, the total number of patients examined each working day averages around 150. Appointments for women are alternated for those under and over age 47 to accommodate the mammography schedule. Prior to each appointment, the patient is mailed an appointment reminder, a past medical history questionnaire, and a general information sheet describing briefly each examination phase. At the time of registration, the patient views a four-minute presentation of 40 color slides projected on a screen to inform and prepare him further for the examination.

When the patient arrives, the receptionist identifies the patient, selects the applicable deck of prepunched cards, and verifies the data on the identification card. She places the deck of prepunched cards into a card holder attached to a clipboard, in which is also placed an interval history form. She instructs the patient to answer this questionnaire whenever he has a few minutes to spare between tests. The patient is then directed into a dressing cubicle, undresses to the waist, and puts on a disposable paper gown.

When the patient arrives at the electrocardiography station, he is directed to lie on a table to which have been attached German silver troughs, used as extremity electrodes to speed the procedure. The forearms and calves of the patient are placed in these troughs after the contacting skin has been sponged with alcohol solution. Chest electrodes are applied, and the electrocardiogram is recorded using a multi-channel polygraph. Since it requires 5–6 minutes to complete the electrocardiogram, two tables are connected to the electrocardiograph by a switching device, so that while one patient is being prepared, the tracing is being recorded on the second patient. In this manner, two patients can readily be tested within six minutes to maintain the required three-minute patient flow module. After the

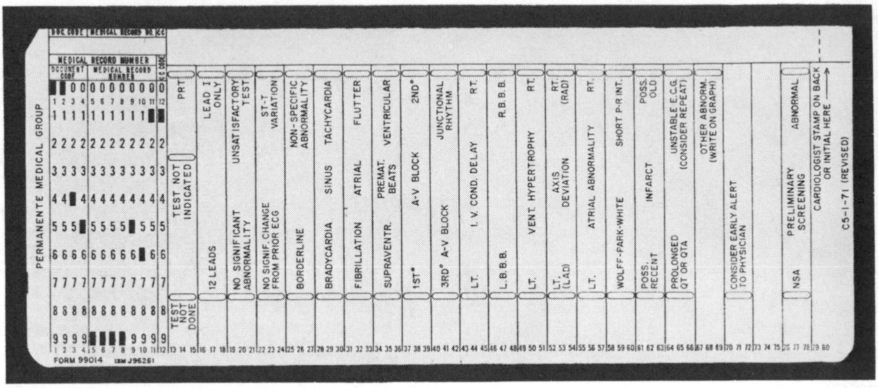

Figure 11–1a

cardiogram is recorded, the electrodes are removed from the patient, and he is instructed to proceed to the next station.

The polygraph paper tracing is cut to a length of 8–9 inches and sent, with the electrocardiogram report mark-sense card (Figure 11–1a), to the cardiologist, who selects the appropriate interpretation by marking it with a special high carbon mark-sense pencil. The cards are returned to the computer center the next day, and the marks on the cards are sensed by a reproducing machine that punches a hole corresponding to each mark, thus converting the marked cards into machine-readable cards.

Recently, many AMHT programs are using computer processing to measure parameters of the ECG waveform and provide automated interpretation. Electrode configurations from specially designed data acquisition carts are used depending on whether the 12-lead "standard" set or the 3-lead "vector" or "Frank" set is required by the analysis program. The cart collects and conditions the signals, produces ECG tracings on a multi-channel recorder, and then converts the signals to a form suitable for further data processing. Sequence numbers identifying the patient are also entered from the cart. ECG signals from the cart may then be transmitted directly to the computer for analysis in real-time or may be recorded on a storage device for subsequent off-line analysis.

The usual method for direct transmission is to transform the ECG into a frequency modulated (FM) signal, which can be carried by a voice grade telephone line using a modulator-demodulator (modem) instrument mounted on the cart. On the receiving end of the line, a data receiver with a similar modem demodulates the signal and provides an interface to the computer. Computer programs analyze the waveform, measure its parameters, check for arrhythmias, and provide ECG interpretations. Results are stored in the patient's computer data file for the printing of the multiphasic summary report.

As an alternative to real-time data transmission, ECG's may also be recorded on analog or digital tape for subsequent off-line analysis. Analog FM tape units may be mounted either on the cart or on the data receiver. Many ECG's may be stored on one reel of tape and played back into the computer interface at a later time. Digital tape units may also be interfaced with the data receiver. With this mode of storage, the ECG waveform is first digitized, then recorded on tape. If the format of the recorded data is logically and physically compatible with the requirements of the computer system, the tape may be remounted on a computer tape drive and read directly. (See Chapter Ten.)

Blood pressure is measured by a trained nurse's aide using automated equipment which produces direct punched card output. A cuff is wrapped around the patient's upper arm and is inflated to a high pressure; then it is allowed to deflate at a standard rate of three millimeters of mercury per second.

Several types of automated blood pressure instruments are available, each using a different principle of detection. (1) Acoustic blood pressure devices attempt to duplicate by automated methods the operation of the traditional manual method. Inflation and deflation of the arm cuff are controlled by an electrical pump and valves. Electrical pulses produced by Korotkoff sounds in a microphone placed over the brachial artery trigger pressure readings at systolic and diastolic points. (2) Pulse wave detection devices are based on the detection of a pulse wave generated by the pumping action of the heart and transmitted through the blood stream to the brachial artery. The pulse wave detector is a cuff placed on the upper arm which contains three inflatable balloons instead of the single one found in the standard cuff. One balloon serves as the systolic detector, while the other two serve as diastolic detectors. Vascular pulsations in the arm are transmitted from each balloon through rubber tubing to detector modules in the instrument. Each pulsation produces a minute puff of air in the detector which is registered by a thermistor. (3) Ultrasonic detector devices detect vascular pulsations directly by recording the change in Doppler shift of the echo of an incident ultrasonic beam, due to movement of the arterial walls. The ultrasonic transducer is mounted on a standard cuff. As cuff pressure is decreased, the onset of pulsations marks the systolic point; the reduction in pulsation amplitude below a threshold marks the diastolic point.

The patients are then weighed and their height measured; the readings are recorded by manual keypunching into the anthropometry test card. Triceps and subscapular skinfolds are measured with calipers, and the readings similarly are keypunched into the card.

At the next station, patients receive a 70 mm posterior-anterior chest x-ray, which is subsequently read by the radiologist who records his inter-

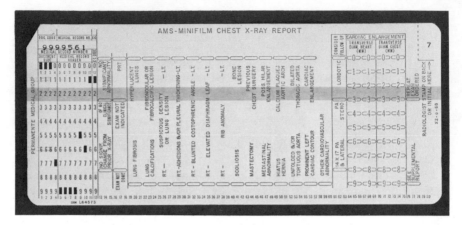

Figure 11–1b

pretation on the mark-sense card shown in Figure 11–1b. The cards are then returned to the computer room for data processing.

All women over age 47 receive an x-ray examination of the breast for detection of possible cancer. Cephalocaudad views of both breasts are taken on one film, with the patient in the sitting position, and then lateral-tangential views of each breast are taken on separate films, with the patient lying in the supine oblique position. Since it requires approximately 10–12 minutes for mammography, only every other woman is scheduled for this procedure, alternating appointments according to age. Further, by utilizing two mammography stations, the time requirements for patient flow can be met.

Mammograms are subsequently read by the radiologist, who records his interpretations on the mark-sense card shown in Figure 11–1c.

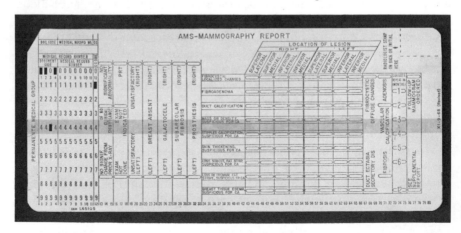

Figure 11–1c

The patient then returns to the dressing booth. Visual acuity and ocular tension are measured and are manually recorded on mark-sense cards. The Achilles reflex one-half relaxation time is measured as a test for thyroid deficiency, and its value is keypunched into a card.

The patient's ventilatory function is measured with a spirometer, which records the one- and two-second forced expiratory vital capacities, total vital capacity, and the peak flow measurements directly into a punched card. The test is repeated three times, and the computer program selects the best of the three tests. Several types of spirometers which compute the parameters from two basic types of me·surements—volume and flow rate— are available. In volume detector spirc eters, air is blown into an expandable enclosure such as a bellows or cyl.nder with water seal or piston. As the flow of air expands the volume of the enclosure, the change in volume is converted to linear motion through a mechanical linkage. Suitable transducers and timing circuits record volumetric and flow parameters. The operation of flow detection spirometers is similar to those with volumetric detection, but they depend on direct measurement of flow rate and integrate flow overtime to derive volumetric parameters. Flow rate is determined either by a pressure transducer or a thermistor. The pressure drop within an array of capillary tubes, which is a function of air velocity, is measured by a pressure transducer. In the second case, the slight change in temperature produced by the air moving past a platinum wire heated to a constant temperature is recorded by a thermistor and is proportional to flow rate.

Hearing acuity is then tested with an automated audiometer and the graphed readings are transferred by the technician to a mark-sense card. A group of six patients are simultaneously tested, each being seated in an acoustically tiled cubicle. High-fidelity earphones are placed on the patient's head, and he is advised that he will hear different sounds. When he hears the sound, he is to press down on the finger switch and hold it down until the sound is gone. When he no longer hears the sound, he takes his finger off the switch until the sound returns. He will hear these sounds first in the left ear and then in the right ear. Each ear is tested for six different frequencies [from 500–6,000 cycles per second]. When the test is completed, the technician averages out the excursions for each frequency and marks the corresponding bubble on the hearing test card.

At the next station, a self-administered medical questionnaire form (which the patient receives at station one and which is completed during any waiting periods between stations) is now audited by a nurse. The patient is given another "inventory-by-systems" medical questionnaire, to which he answers "yes" or "no" by sorting a set of cards prepunched for computer input.

The acquisition of a medical history from a patient is the most difficult part of an AMHT examination. Self-administered medical histories may be acquired by checklists, sort cards, or by interactive terminals.

History questionnaire checklists usually require keypunching for off-line batched data processing but have the advantage of simplicity and economy. Questions on checklists can also be formatted so that answers may be entered on machine readable forms; marks indicating "yes" or "no" and multiple-choice answers to questions are placed in designated areas which then can be read by an optical scanner or mark-sense reader. This eliminates the need for keypunching, and such machine readable forms can be read directly into the computer at a high rate of speed. However, the manual marking of patient identifying numbers introduces a significant error rate. A mark-sense paper and pencil questionnaire has the advantage of very low cost. It is simpler than card sorting and has the flexibility of including multiple-choice questions. Second-level lists of questionnaires can be programmed for automatic printout based upon the responses of the previous questionnaire.

Portable punch cards also permit direct machine readable source documents by using prescored punched cards and, instead of marking "yes" or "no," the patient is instructed to punch out the appropriate prescored hole, which then results in a direct machine-readable card. For example, the patient is requested to punch on the scored, partially prepunched cards shown in Figures 11–2a and b his family history and occupation. Use of these "portable-punch" cards eliminates coding and keypunching of these patient responses.

Card sorting is used by giving each patient a letter box containing a deck of prepunched cards. Each card has a single dichotomous medical question

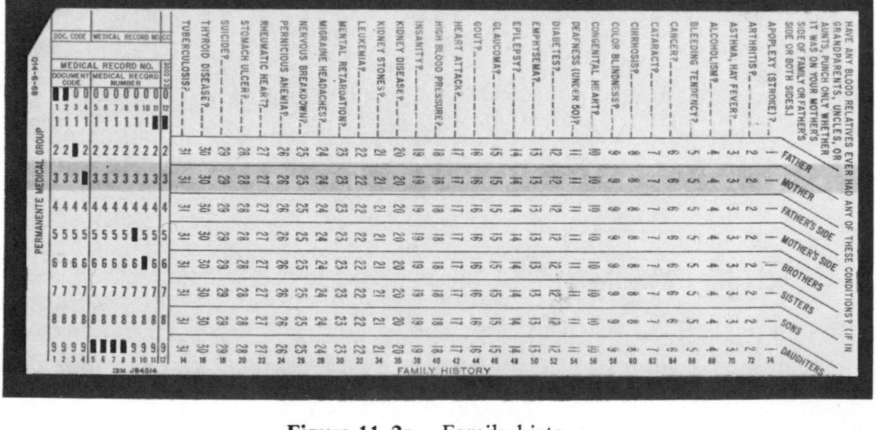

Figure 11–2a. Family history.

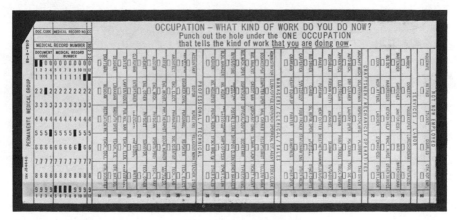

Figure 11–2b. Occupation.

and a prepunched question number printed on it (Figure 11–2c). The patient responds to each question by taking the card from the top section of the divided box and dropping the card into the middle section if his answer to the question is "yes" or "true" or into the bottom section if the answer is "no" or "false." This procedure automatically sorts "yes" responses for direct input to the computer by processing the prepunched "yes" cards through a card reader.[13]

Interactive terminals generally are preferred for automated medical histories since they permit branching questions and explanation to patients who do not understand a question. Such terminals either use questions stored on a film strip or on a random access slide carousel and displayed on a screen or questions stored in a computer and displayed on a cathode ray

483

IN THE PAST <u>YEAR</u>, HAVE YOU HAD BAD PAIN
OR PRESSURE OR TIGHT FEELING IN THE CHEST THAT
FORCED YOU TO <u>STOP</u> WALKING?

(If YES, place card in middle section of box;
if NO, place in bottom section.)

Figure 11–2c

tube terminal. The patient reads the questions which appear on the display and responds by use of a keyboard or by pressing numbered buttons located at the side or bottom of the display. There usually are four possible responses: "yes," "no," "don't know," and "don't understand." The patient answers the questions by pressing one of four numbered keys or buttons corresponding to the four responses. A "yes" response to a general question is followed by a series of specific qualifying questions. A "no" response to a general question results in the skipping of the secondary questions and the presentation of the next general question. When the answers to certain questions are not known or the question is not understood, these questions are clarified.

Either two hours after a standard test meal or one hour after drinking a 75 Gm. glucose solution, the patient is sent to the clinical laboratory where samples are collected for blood and urine analysis. Twelve blood chemistry determinations are simultaneously performed by an automated chemical analyzer; and the values for alkaline phosphatase, total bilirubin, calcium, cholesterol, creatinine, glucose, lactic dehydrogenase, potassium, sodium, transaminase (SGOT), urea nitrogen, and uric acid are punched directly into cards.[14] Blood hemoglobin, red and white cell counts, and red cell indices are automatically measured and punched into cards. A serological (VDRL) test for syphilis is performed. A freshly voided urine specimen, collected midstream, is analyzed for pH, glucose, protein, and blood by paper strip enzyme tests; these results are mark-sensed onto a card. In women, the specimen is cultured for six hours with triphenyltetrazolium chloride for detection of bacteriuria.

A variety of automated chemical analyzers are now available, and they involve the following steps in a typical analysis: (1) volume measurements of sample and reagents; (2) measured volume transfers; (3) mixing; (4) incubation for a measured time at a controlled temperature; (5) precipitation by filtration or centrifugation; (6) extraction or washing of a precipitate, or extraction of an aqueous solution with an organic solvent; (7) light absorbency or other physical measurement; and (8) data recording. Moving and transfer of samples and reagents is accomplished by: (1) a continuous flow analysis system using peristaltic pumps which force fluids in a continuous stream, separating samples by air bubbles; (2) piston pump syringes, pneumatically or mechanically operated, which eject fluids into discrete containers; or (3) using centrifugal force to move fluids into cuvettes located in the edge of a rotor.

At the last AMHT station, the patient returns the medical questionnaires and the packet of cards on which, whenever possible, his test results were directly recorded by punching or mark-sensing to permit their immediate introduction into the data processing system. While the patient is waiting at the last station, the on-line punched cards are read into the computer.[15]

C. DATA PROCESSING REQUIREMENTS FOR AMHT

The computer processing requirements for an AMHT involve: (1) maintaining an appointment schedule for its patients; (2) maintaining a continuing data file for each patient, preferably integrated with all other data for that patient for all inpatient and outpatient services received from the hospital facilities; (3) processing all on-line test data before the patient leaves the AMHT laboratory and providing "advice rules"; (4) processing all off-line test results and providing a summary printout for the physician; and (5) processing follow-up diagnostic data as received from the physician who completes the physical examination procedures.

Appointment cards are prepared for 180 patients each day, and they designate the time of appointment and schedule requirements to allow for 55% women and 45% men; one-half of women are over age 47 and are equally spaced for mammography; approximately one-third may accept a nurse practitioner physical examination on-line if they wish; etc. Cancellation of appointments is handled by a card of a distinctive color. A few days before the patient's appointment time, a keypunch operator prepares an identification "header" card for each patient based upon the information contained in the appointment card and containing the patient's medical record number (a seven digit unique number plus an eighth check-digit), his name, sex, birthdate, appointment date, and physician's name. From these cards, a list is prepared for mailing to the patient of an appointment reminder, a past medical history form, and a general information brochure. From the identification header card, a packet of data acquisition cards is prepared with the patient's medical record number punched into the first field. These cards are used to punch or mark-sense test results from each AMHT station.[15]

In most multiphasic systems, a computer establishes a data file for each patient; as each test result is obtained, it is stored in the file. At the end of the exam, the results are formatted and printed on a standard report. Included in the report are ranges of normal values which may depend on a patient's age, race, sex, height, and weight. Abnormal test results are flagged or otherwise displayed.

In the usual multiphasic system, when a patient leaves the facility, the results are written on digital magnetic tape for permanent storage. Unless test results have been stored in a data base from which they can be later retrieved, it is impossible to integrate the results of previous examinations into one report. In addition, the capability of generating reports containing comparisons of test results of the current examination to prior examinations requires patient record linkage—that is, the collection of all data for a particular person into one file. To simplify this operation, a number is usually assigned to a patient at the beginning of the examination, and each piece of data is tagged with this number. At some installations, patients are arbitrarily assigned sequential accession numbers. In programs such as Kaiser-Permanente, each patient is already identified to the health care facility by a unique number which is assigned for the lifetime of the patient. This number must then be associated with each datum collected for the patient. In facilities in which data is punched or mark-sensed or entered on forms, the number may be prepunched into the cards or written on forms. In facilities with on-line data acquisition, the patient either carries a machine-readable card with his identification number or the technician must enter his number at a data input terminal. In on-line facilities, verification of the number may be performed by the computer against the patient's file number.

A check-digit is often added to the medical record number to attempt to eliminate common transcription errors in instances where the user cannot confirm identification on-line at the time of entry. An important application for check-digits is in the use of optically scanned forms in which the error rate of manually transcribing medical record numbers is relatively high.

The file organization of the data base within which all patient information is stored is based upon an integrated, continuous, variable-length, variable-format record.[16] (See Chapter Four.) Our data base currently contains more than one-third million AMHT patients' records. All records are individually retrievable by each patient's medical record number on a direct access basis. Each individual's record within the computer direct access storage facility is kept and moved together as a continuous string of data— that is, it is never split, fractionated, or otherwise separated for overflow or other reasons. By storing the multiphasic data in the central integrated patient file, physicians in the medical center can retrieve this data along with relevant data from other clinical services. For example, a physician in the emergency room in the San Francisco Kaiser Hospital has direct access to multiphasic data in addition to clinical lab data, prescription drugs, outpatient diagnoses, etc. (See Chapter Six.)

A majority of the test result data generated in the AMHT laboratory has been recorded on prepunched or mark-sensed cards to permit its immediate introduction into the data processing system. As an on-line procedure, while the patient waits at the last station, the computer processes the information from: (1) the punched cards from anthropometry, chemistry, and hematology; (2) the prepunched sorted cards from the medical questionnaire box; (3) the reproduced mark-sensed cards from blood pressure, vision, respirometry, hearing, and urine tests; and (4) the portable punched cards from the questionnaire station. These cards are read into a data communicating system and transmitted via telephone line to the central computer. The computer processor goes through its automated multiphasic screening programs containing various test normal limits and decision rules and prints out a report constituting "advice" as to any additional procedures advisable for the patient to receive in order to assist in achieving a more specific diagnosis. These "advice" rules have been previously established by the physicians and instruct the receptionist to arrange certain additional tests and appointments for the patient before his physical examination visit with the physician.

For example, if the urine analysis shows proteinuria, the computer prints out instructions to the receptionist to ask the patient to return to the laboratory with a first morning specimen for re-test. If the serum glucose is elevated and the patient is not under treatment for diabetes, the advice rule will suggest a standard glucose tolerance test. If a serious abnormality is detected, the computer printout advises the receptionist to ask the nurse to take the patient to see a physician in the emergency room, and then prints out a "Stat" report of all abnormal test data. If the abnormality is not serious, it will advise a preliminary report to the patient's physician, who may consider an early appointment, or it may advise referral to a specialty clinic. These advice rules are programmed from Boolean strings or decision tables. More complex advice rules for nurse practitioners' referrals to preventive maintenance clinics are described by Soghikian in the following chapter.

As an off-line procedure, the computer collates and stores in the patient file the remaining information, which arrives a few days later (mark-sensed cards containing the physician interpretation of the electrocardiogram and x-rays, the remaining laboratory test reports, and the keypunched medical questionnaire form). When all the information has been received and is stored, the computer produces a printed summary of all test reports and questions answered "yes" and the advice rules previously recommended. (See Figure 11–3 and also Chapter Six, Figures 6–2a-d.) If the patient has had prior multiphasic examinations, it is essential that current test results be compared to prior examinations, and the summary printout should reflect this.

When all the "off-line" patient data has been received, the computer compares the patient's tests and symptoms to the "consider" rules program; and if the patient has a combination of test values and symptoms that are identical to one belonging to a specific category, the computer prints out a statement suggesting that the physician "consider" this diagnostic category.

```
                    PERMANENTE MEDICAL GROUP - OAKLAND
           DUPLICATE REPORT - MULTIPHASIC HEALTH CHECKUP (MHC) - 5/20/69

TEST,PATIENT                                    DR. SMITH
M.R. NO. 2258590    BIRTHDATE:  7-1918   FEMALE  LOC. S.F.        J1

LAST MHC  6/16/68.  RANGES ARE LOW-HI VALUES FOR PATIENT MHC EXAMS, 1967-1966

           (TEST)              (NORMAL)  (THIS EXAM)   (1968)      (1967-1966)
        HEIGHT  IN.:                       63.8        64.0       63.5 - 63.9
        WEIGHT  LB.:                       133.5      132.0      131.5 -133.5
        TRICEPS SKINFOLD MM.:   UNDER- 43.0   23.0      18.0      19.0 - 20.0

        CIRCULATORY:
  **    B.P.SUPINE(GODART): 90-159/ 50- 89   164/100   154/104  135-144/ 86- 98

        HEMATOLOGY:                 (BLOOD GROUP=   O)
           WBC                    3500-12000      7700      6600      5500 - 7700

        BLOOD CHEMISTRY
           CALCIUM MG%:          8.0- 10.5      9.9       9.5       9.0 - 10.8

        URINE:
  **     GLUCOSE:                  NEG          MED       NEG       NEG -  NEG

        ECG:          NO SIGNIFICANT CHANGE FROM PRIOR ELECTROCARDIOGRAM
              1968:   NO SIGNIFICANT CHANGE FROM PRIOR ELECTROCARDIOGRAM
              1967:   NSA
  ** HEARING:         CLINICALLY IMPAIRED HEARING IN LEFT EAR
              1968:   CLINICALLY IMPAIRED HEARING IN LEFT EAR
              1967:   CLINICALLY IMPAIRED HEARING IN LEFT EAR

        PATIENT RECEIVED FOLLOWING (ADVICE RULE) DIRECTIONS:
           700-REQUEST PT.RET. AMS LAB FOR 2-HR SERUM SUGAR
           801-NOTICE SENT TO PHYSICIAN: CONSIDER EARLY APPTMT.

        PATIENT ANSWERED YES TO THESE QUESTIONS ON THE MHC 1969 FORM:
           HAD BAD REACTION OR SENSITIVITY TO SULFA DRUGS
           IN PAST 6 MONTHS BAD HEADACHES NOT HELPED BY ASPIRIN, EMPIRIN, ETC
  *        IN PAST YEAR SPELLS OF WEAKNESS OR PARALYSIS OF ARMS OR LEGS
  *        IN PAST YEAR BLURRING OF EYESIGHT LASTING OVER A FEW MINUTES

        TND = TEST NOT DONE   PRT = PAT. REFUSED TEST   TNI = TEST NOT INDICATED
        BND = BLOOD NOT DRAWN  UNSAT = TEST UNSATISFACTORY  - = DATA NOT AVAILABLE
        NSA = NO SIGNIFICANT ABNORMALITY
        * = PATIENT ANSWERED YES ON THIS MHC AND NO ON LAST MHC
        ** = CONSIDER POSSIBLE ABNORMAL         ¬ = NOTE
```

Figure 11-3

Since disease screening approaches disease diagnosis as it becomes more comprehensive, precise, and quantitative, automated aid-in-diagnosis can be used in AMHT. The method employed in this program is based on Neyman's use of likelihood ratios. [1,17] In order to use this method, it is necessary to know only the proportions of individuals with any specific disease who have any combination of a group of selected symptoms and the proportions of individuals without that same disease who have the same combination of symptoms. All symptoms either are dichotomous or are converted to the dichotomous state. On the basis of a patient's response to questions and tests directed towards eliciting the presence or absence of these selected symptoms, the individual is placed into one of two categories: either he warrants further testing since he is likely to have the disease, or he is not likely to have the disease and further testing is not warranted. The degree of likelihood of the patient being categorized as likely to have the disease may be set at any level by the physician and will vary according to the disease under consideration.

When the physician reviews the summary report at the time of the patient's follow-up office visit, he completes his physical examination and records the final clinical diagnoses on a form such as is shown in Figure 11–4. This form is optically scannable, and marked data are automatically punched into machine-readable cards or directly entered into the patient's computer medical record. Printed data recorded at the bottom of the form is key entered as English words.

When a patient is categorized on the diagnosis form as having "no significant abnormality," these patients' data are used to generate test normal limits for this program.[18,19] Traditionally, normal values are based upon measurements of relatively small numbers of people whose state of health has not been extensively evaluated, who were not tested under standardized conditions, and often are unadjusted for age, sex, and environmental factors. AMHT permits the generation of more accurate test normal limits by selecting a healthy group of people and using their measurements to establish the range of normal values for people of comparable age, sex, and race.

For example, the following table compares values of blood uric acid by age and sex for all white males regardless of diagnosis to white males who had no significant abnormality:

Age	All multiphasics			No significant abnormality		
	Number	Mean	Std. dev.	Number	Mean	Std. dev.
30–39	2685	5.58*	1.34	875	5.47*	1.23
40–49	3714	5.61*	1.31	1074	5.52*	1.19
50–59	3448	5.65*	1.36	804	5.52*	1.26
60–69	1925	5.66*	1.39	289	5.39*	1.25

*$P<.001$ comparisons of mean values

D. RESULTS OF EXAMINATIONS

Our experience with AMHT examinations using computer systems has shown that:

(1) It is very acceptable to patients. The patients' time is saved since two to three times as many tests can be provided per hour.

(2) It is an effective method of providing health checkups and shows consistent yield rates; about two-thirds of all adults examined are reported

PERMANENTE MULTIPHASIC EXAMINATION RECORD
PHYSICAL EXAMINATION & DIAGNOSIS

FORM CODE

M E D - C A L   R E C O R D   #

DATE:

NAME:

BIRTHDATE:

MR #

SNAP OFF TOP (ORIGINAL) SHEET FOR COMPUTER ROOM.

KEEP BOTTOM (CARBON COPY) IN CHART.

PLACE A MARK WITH A BLACK PENCIL IN THE SPACE ::::: AFTER YOUR PHYSICAL FINDING OR UNDER YOUR DIAGNOSIS. MAKE EACH MARK BLACK & HEAVY. ERASE COMPLETELY ANY MARK YOU WISH TO CHANGE. DO NOT USE INK OR BALL POINT PEN. UNDERLINE DIAGNOSIS THRU :O: IF "OLD" (PRIOR TO ONE YEAR AGO); THRU :N: IF "NEW" (NOW PRESENT OR ACTIVE IN PAST 12 MONTHS).

Physical Examination (left section)

	NEG	ABNORMAL RT.	LT.
EYES			
E.N.T.			
MOUTH			
NECK			
THYROID ENLARGED			
THYROID NODULE(S)			
CERV. NODES			
HEART			
ENLARGED			
ARRHYTHMIA			
A2	INCR.	DECR.	SPLIT
P2	INCR.		SPLIT
	EXTRA SYSTOLE	OTHER	

	NEG	ABNORMAL RT.	LT.
ABDOMEN			
MASS.			
TENDER			
ING. HERNIA			
OTHER HERNIA			
LIVER			
SPLEEN			
KIDNEY			
RECTUM			
HEMOR-RHOIDS			
MASS			
PROSTATE			

Diagnosis section

GEN'L & GYN.
- NO SIGNIFICANT ABNORMALITY :O:
- NO DIAG. TO ADD TO PRINT OUT :O:
- INFLUENZA :O: :N:
- SYPHILIS :O: :N:
- DRUG TOXICITY OR SENSITIVITY :O: :N:
- PENICILLIN REACTION :O: :N:
- HORSE SERUM REACTION :O: :N:
- CHEMICAL SENS. OR TOXICITY :O: :N:
- FOOD ALLERGY OR POISONING :O: :N:
- DIABETES MELLITUS :O: :N:
- RENAL GLYCOSURIA :O: :N:
- HYPOGLYCEMIA :O: :N:

HEAD & NECK
- UPPER RESPIR. :O: :N:
- EYE PTOSIS :O: :N:
- EXOPHTHALMOS :O: :N:
- CATARACT :O: :N:
- OPTIC NEURITIS OR ATROPHY :O: :N:
- EYE CA OR TUMOR :O: :N:
- OTITIS :O: :N:
- MENIERE'S SYND. :O: :N:
- VERTIGO :O: :N:
- TINNITUS :O: :N:
- DEAFNESS :O: :N:
- NASAL CA OR BENIGN TUMOR :O: :N:

CHEST
- HEART CONGENITAL :O: :N:
- HEART RHEUMATIC :O: :N:
- MITRAL VALVE DISEASE :O: :N:
- AORTIC VALVE DISEASE :O: :N:
- FUNCTIONAL MURMUR :O: :N:
- EXTRASYSTOLES :O: :N:
- PAROXYSMAL TACHYCARDIA :O: :N:
- ATRIAL FIBRILLATION :O: :N:
- ISCHEMIC HT. DISEASE :O: :N:
- ANGINA PECTORIS :O: :N:
- MYOCARDIAL INFARCTION :O: :N:
- HYPERTENSION, PRIMARY :O: :N:

ABD. & G.U.
- CARDIOSPASM :O: :N:
- ESOPHAGEAL HIATUS HERNIA :O: :N:
- STOMACH CANCER :O: :N:
- GASTRITIS :O: :N:
- GASTRIC ULCER :O: :N:
- DUODENAL ULCER :O: :N:
- COLON CANCER :O: :N:
- COLON POLYPS OR BENIGN TUMOR :O: :N:
- DIVERTICULOSIS :O: :N:
- DIVERTICULITIS :O: :N:
- ULCERATIVE COLITIS :O: :N:
- IRRITABLE BOWEL :O: :N:

EXT. & SKIN
- OSTEOARTHRITIS :O: :N:
- RHEUMATOID ARTHRITIS :O: :N:
- RHEUMATOID SPONDYLITIS :O: :N:
- GOUT :O: :N:
- OSTEOPOROSIS :O: :N:
- PAGET'S DIS. :O: :N:
- CERVICAL SPRAIN :O: :N:
- KYPHOSIS OR SCOLIOSIS :O: :N:
- HERNIATED DISC :O: :N:
- LOW BACK PAIN :O: :N:
- PILONIDAL CYST :O: :N:
- BURSITIS OR TENDONITIS :O: :N:

C.N.S.
- PSYCHOPHYSIOL REAC. SKIN :O: :N:
- PSY-PHYS-REAC. LOCOMOTOR :O: :N:
- PSY-PHYS-REAC. CARDIOVASCUL. :O: :N:
- PSY-PHYS-REAC. RESPIRATORY :O: :N:
- PSY-PHYS-REAC. GASTROINTEST. :O: :N:
- PSY-PHYS-REAC. G.U. OR GYN. :O: :N:
- ANXIETY STATE :O: :N:
- DEPRESSION :O: :N:
- HYSTERIA :O: :N:
- OBSESSIONAL :O: :N:
- PASSIVE-AGGRESSIVE :O: :N:
- PHOBIA :O: :N:

DO NOT WRITE OR MARK IN THIS AREA.

APEX.	OBESITY	NASAL POLYP(S)	LEG CRAMPS, NOCTURNAL	CHRONIC FATIGUE
SYST. M. 2 INTRSP.	WEIGHT LOSS	RHINITIS OR SINUSITIS	PERIPHERAL ARTERIOSCLER.	INSOMNIA
4 INTRSP.	HEMOGLOBINOPATHY	HAY FEVER	PERIPHERAL VASCULAR DIS.	CHRONIC ALCOHOLISM
APEX.	MACROCYTIC ANEMIA	ORAL CA OR BENIGN TUMOR	RAYNAUD'S DIS. OR SYNDROME	DRUG ADDICT., HABITUATION
DIAST. M. 2 INTRSP.	HYPOCHROMIC MICRO. ANEMIA	LIP CANCER	THROMBO-PHLEBITIS	SCHIZOPHRENIA
4 INTRSP.	NORMOCYTIC ANEMIA	LEUKOPLAKIA	VARICOSE VEINS	HEADACHE
	POLYCYTHEMIA	GLOSSITIS OR STOMATITIS	SKIN CANCER	MIGRAINE
CHEST TREMOR	LEUKEMIA	TONSILLITIS OR PHARYNGITIS	SKIN BENIGN TUMOR OR NEVUS	CEREBROVASC. INSUFFICIENCY
DIM BR. S. PED. PULSES	HODKINS OR LYMPHOMA	LARYNX TUMOR OR POLYP	KERATOSES	CEREBRAL HEM. OR THROMBOSIS
RALES VAR. VEINS	CAUTERUS OR CERVIX	LARYNGITIS	LIPOMA(S) OR XANTHOMA(S)	PARKINSONISM
ANTERIOR WHEEZES EDEMA (PED.)	DYSMENORRHEA	THYROID NODULE(S)	DERMATITIS, CHRONIC	EPILEPSY
RHONCHI CLUBBING	MENO-METRO-RRHAGIA	THYROID ENLARGED	PRURITUS	SYNCOPE
RALES SPINE	PREMENSTRUAL TENSION	THYROID CANCER	PSORIASIS	PERIPHERAL NEURITIS
POSTERIOR WHEEZES SKIN	MENOPAUSAL SYNDROME	THYROIDITIS	ACNE VULGARIS	HERPES ZOSTER
RHONCHI NERV. SYST.	PREGNANCY	HYPERTHYROID	FURUNCULOSIS OR CELLULITIS	SCIATIC NEURITIS
AXIL. NODES CRANIAL NN.	INFERTILITY	HYPOTHYROID	URTICARIA OR DERMATOGRAPH.	POLIO
SPINAL NN.				LATE EFFECTS

CONSTIPATION
RECTUM CANCER
LIVER CIRRHOSIS
GALLSTONES
GLOMERULONEPHRITIS
PYELONEPHRITIS
URINARY INFECTION
URINARY CALCULUS
BLADDER CANCER OR BENIGN TUMOR
PROSTATE CANCER
BENIGN HYPERTROPHY
PROSTATITIS
SPERMATOCELE
HYDROCELE
TESTIS ABSENT OR ATROPHIC
IMPOTENCE

HYPERTENSION, SECONDARY
HYPERTENSIVE HEART DISEASE
AORTIC ANEURYSM
BRONCHIAL ASTHMA
BRONCHITIS, ACUTE
BRONCHITIS, CHRONIC
BRONCHIECTASIS
LUNG CANCER
PULMONARY TUBERCULOSIS
PULMONARY FIBROSIS
EMPHYSEMA
CHEST MYALGIA, TIETZE SYND.
FUNNEL CHEST
BREAST CANCER
FIBROCYSTIC DISEASE
GYNECOMASTIA

PRINT HERE ALL "NEW" DIAGNOSES NOT LISTED ABOVE; SEE EXAMPLE BOTTOM LINE. DO NOT ABBREVIATE; YOU MAY CONTINUE ON NEXT LINE.

1
2
3
4
5
6

SICKLE CELL ANEMIA   M.D.

ENLARGED PROSTATE NODULE(S)
GENITALIA
TESTES
ING. NODES
EXTREMIT.
JOINTS

BREASTS

REMARKS:

TREATMENT:

ADDIT. STUDIES:

REFER TO:

RETURN: SIGNED:

WRITE ANY ADDITIONAL REMARKS ON REGULAR PROGRESS SHEETS

COPYRIGHT 1966   PI-I-66

IBM H9728

Figure 11-4

by their physicians as having some clinically important abnormality. (See also Chapter Twelve.)

(3) Productivity of physicians is improved; when automated multiphasic testing is performed prior to the physician's physical examination, the great majority of patients can then be taken care of by a single brief physician's office visit.

(4) It provides not only more information on more patients but more information on each patient, thereby producing greater individualization of patient care. Instead of using broad population norms, the computer permits application of specific norms to each individual patient, based upon age, sex, height, time of day, and hours since last food ingestion, thereby improving quality of testing. Since the boundaries between health care/ preventive care/sick care are essentially controlled by programmable limits for normal/borderline/diseased, this capability is essential to decrease the numbers of false positives and false negatives.[20]

(5) It permits on-line quality control, thereby decreasing error rates for instrumental variations and minimizing insertion of data into wrong records.

(6) It allows for programmed decision rules and diagnostic algorithms to "advise" as to secondary testing, possible diagnoses to be considered, and follow-up scheduling. Such utilization of an on-line computer permits determination automatically if there is sufficient likelihood of the presence of a number of diseases, enabling the separation of persons who are likely to have these diseases from those who very likely do not. It may thereby be used as a new entry mode to a medical care delivery system.

(7) Computer data processing with a continuing patient record file provides a comprehensive profile of the patient's current and prior status to the physician in a timely manner. It allows efficient handling of large volumes of medical information on great numbers of patients over long periods of time.

(8) It furnishes printout reports of increased utility to physicians, which show "flagged" abnormalities, individualized patient normal values, comparisons to prior test results, and abstracts of high priority information.

(9) Computer processing permits efficient on-line communication of data to and from the medical data base and the local multiphasic laboratory, the hospital, and the follow-up outpatient services.

(10). A cost analysis[21] of the AMHT showed the total costs per patient examination was $21.32. This included $4.50 for computer center and data processing, of which $2.00 was for research analysis[20] and $2.50 was the data processing cost per examination for data acquisition and storage, on-line advice rules, and a summary report printout. This unit cost was based upon a volume of 100 patients processed daily in two AMHT facilities, or a total of 4,000 patients monthly. Current experience indicates that, with 150 patients daily in two AMHT facilities (6,000 patients monthly), it still costs about $2.50 for data processing per patient because the amount of data stored for each examination has greatly increased.

In addition to determining the cost for the entire multiphasic examination, it is useful to determine the cost to identify a patient with a positive test. This requires a cost center to identify all costs associated with providing the test and knowledge of the frequency with which clinical abnormalities are detected.[22] For example, if the unit cost to complete an electrocardiogram including its interpretation is $2.00 and the average prevalence of abnormalities in adults is 20%, then it cost $10.00 to detect a positive case. Since the prevalence of abnormal ECGs is about 5% in young adults (cost/positive = $40.00) and 33% in those over age 60 (cost/positive = $6.00), this type of evaluation aids in determining the cost effectiveness of each test.

Cost-benefit studies are also being conducted, and preliminary data from a controlled long-term study shows that middle-aged males after seven years of such health surveillance show significantly less disability and mortality and greater net earnings.[23]

REFERENCES

1. Collen, M. F.; Rubin, L.; Neyman, J.; Dantzig, G.; Baer, R.; and Siegelaub, A. B. Automated Multiphasic Screening and Diagnosis." *A.P.H.A.* 54 (1964) : 741.
2. Collen, M. F. "The Multitest Laboratory in Health Care of the Future." 41 (1967) : 119.
3. Schoen, A. V. *Automated Multiphasic Health Testing Program Directory.* 2d ed. Burbank: Bioscience Pub., Inc., 1972.
4. Ryan, G. A., and Monroe, K. E. *Computer Assisted Medical Practice—The AMA's Role.* Chicago: American Medical Association. 1971.
5. *Provisional Guidelines for Automated Multiphasic Health Testing & Services.* Vols. 1 & 2. U.S. Govt. Print. Off. July 1970.
6. *Statement in Multiphasic Health Testing.* Chicago: American Medical Association, 1972.
7. Collen, M. F. "Periodic Health Examinations Using an Automated Multitest Laboratory." *J.A.M.A.* 195 (1966) : 830.
8. Garfield, S. R. "The Delivery of Medical Care." *Sci. Amer.* 222 (1970) : 15–23.
9. Collen, M. F. "Multiphasic Testing as a Triage to Medical Care." *Controversy in Internal Medicine II* Saunders, 1972.
10. Collen, M. F. "Guidelines for Multiphasic Health Checkup." *Arch. Int. Med.* 127 (1971) : 99–100.
11. Collen, M. F. "Implementation of a AMHT System." *Hospitals* 45 (1971) : 49–58.
12. Collen, M. F. "Automated Multiphasic Screening." *Presymptomatic Detection*

and Early Diagnosis Edited by C. Sharp and H. Keen. London: Pitman Med. Pub. Co., Ltd., 1968.

13. Collen, M. F.; Cutler, J. L.; Siegelaub, A. B.; and Cella, R. L. "Reliability of a Self-Admiinstered Medical Questionnaire." *Arch. Int. Med.* 123(1969).

14. Friedman, G.; Goldberg, M.; Ahuja, J.; Siegelaub, A.; Bassis, M.; and Collen, M. "Biochemical Screening Tests, Effect of Panel Size on Medical Care." *Arch. Int. Med.* 129(1972):91–97.

15. Collen, M. F.; Rubin, L.; and Davis, L. S. "Computers in Multiphasic Screening." *Comp. in Biomed. Res.* 1965.

16. Davis, L. S.; Collen, M. F.; Rubin, L.; and Van Brunt, E. E. "Computer-Stored Medical Record." *Comp. and Biomed. Res.* 1(1968):452–469.

17. Rubin, L.; Collen, M. F.; and Goldman, G. E. "Frequency Decision Theoretical Approach to Automated Medical Diagnosis." *Proc. Fifth Berkeley Symposium on Mathematical Statistics and Probability.* U. Calif. Press, 4(1966):867–886.

18. Collen, M. F.; Siegelaub, A.; Cutler, J. L.; and Goldberg, R. "Aspects of Normal Values in Medicine." *Ann. N.Y. Acad. Sci.* 1612(1969):572.

19. Cutler, J. L.; Collen, M. F.; Siegelaub, A. B.; and Feldman, R. "Determination of Normal Values for Blood Chemistry Tests." *Pathologist* (Oct.) 1969.

20. Collen, M. F. "Computer Analyses in Preventive Health Research." *Meth. Info. Med.* 6(1967):8–14.

21. Collen, M. F.; Kidd, P. H.; Feldman, R.; and Cutler, J. L. "Cost Analysis of a Multiphasic Screening Program." *New. Eng. J. Med.* 280(1969):1043–1045.

22. Collen, M. F.; Feldman, R.; Siegelaub, A.; Crawford, D. "Dollar Cost Per Positive Test for Automated Multiphasic Screening." *New Eng. J. Med.* 283(1970):459–463.

23. Collen, M. F.; Dales, L. G.; Friedman, G. D.; Flagle, C. D.; Feldman, R.; and Siegelaub, A. B. "Multiphasic Evaluation Study: 4. Preliminary Cost Benefit Analyses for Middle-Aged Men." *Prev. Med.* 2(1973):236–246.

CHAPTER TWELVE

Preventive Health Maintenance Clinics

by Krikor Soghikian

A. INTRODUCTION

The practice of medicine has been traditionally restricted to the treatment of acutely sick individuals. Preventive health maintenance is a relatively recent and innovative concept in the field of medical care. Currently, preventive health maintenance services are available almost exclusively in the areas of maternal and child health. More and more, however, emphasis is being placed on providing such services to the "early sick," those with asymptomatic, or minimally symptomatic, chronic disease.[1] Disorders such as diabetes, hypertension, and hyperlipidemia are now being discovered frequently in their early phases through a variety of screening programs. It is postulated that appropriate treatment and surveillance of patients with such disorders will lead to a reduction of morbidity and mortality, and this has been convincingly demonstrated in the case of hypertension.[2]

The magnitude of the task of monitoring everyone suffering from chronic disease must not be underestimated; hypertension alone is said to affect 15–20 million people in the U.S.[3] The health facilities presently existing in this country have to be systematically restructured in order to cope with the implied challenge. Such reorganization should take into consideration the special needs of preventive health maintenance and develop appropriate modes of service. More specifically, it should explore the potential of optimal utilization of paramedical and non-medical personnel and the adaptation of systems techniques and electronic data processing to the health care field. Senator Javits of New York has advocated the use of paraprofessionals in the provision of medical care and suggested that "their areas of expertise and responsibility could be substantially increased if we consider the many additional tasks they could undertake if they were able to have also the 'expertise' of computers."[4]

B. PREVENTIVE HEALTH MAINTENANCE CLINICS

1. Introduction

During the past two years, the concept of preventive health maintenance has been actualized as part of a new medical care delivery system at the Kaiser-Permanente Medical Center in Oakland.[5] Ten preventive maintenance clinics have been established for the management of patients with the following common chronic conditions: arthritis, backache, diabetes, gastrointestinal diseases, hyperlipidemia, hypertension, psychosomatic problems ("concerned well"), overweight, smoking, and urinary tract disorders. These conditions have been selected because of their prevalence in the Kaiser-Permanente population (see Table 1), their rate of utilization of medical resources (see Table 2), and the potential of their management through systematic protocols.

The basic design is similar for all clinics and follows a pattern of serial patient care events illustrated by Figures 12–1a through 12–1c (Arthritis Clinic flow chart).

Clinic operations are handled, under physician supervision, by specially trained paramedical personnel who provide patient care in each subsystem according to prescribed protocols. These protocols are presently used manually but are gradually being converted to a computerized mode.

2. Description of Clinics

The Arthritis Clinic provides diagnostic, therapeutic, and monitoring services to patients with arthritis, musculoskeletal disorders, osteoporosis, and hyperuricemia. The criteria for referral to the clinic include the presence of joint, neck, or back symptoms, the finding of significant musculoskeletal abnormalities on physical examination, and the presence of elevated levels of serum uric acid, predefined by age and sex.

The objective of the Back Care Clinic is to instruct patients suffering from chronic or recurrent back symptoms regarding good posture, proper back care, and supportive exercises. Patient eligibility is based on the diagnosis of low backache of any etiology, except when associated with systemic disease such as malignancy, or the finding of a significant postural abnormality.

The Concerned Well Clinic deals with patients who have emotional or

Table 1. Most Frequent Diagnoses among 31,843 Consecutive Multiphasic Patients

	Male and female			
			Percent	
Rank	Diagnosis	New	Old	Total
1	No significant abnormality	—	—	34.97
2	Obesity	4.31	13.04	17.35
3	Hypertension, primary	2.08	5.47	7.55
4	Anxiety state	2.25	5.06	7.31
5	Osteoarthritis	0.76	3.02	3.78
6	Diabetes mellitus	0.93	2.40	3.33
7	Varicose veins	0.79	2.33	3.02
8	Psycho-phys-reaction, G. I.	0.87	2.15	3.02
9	Deafness	0.72	2.01	2.73
10	Chronic dermatitis*	0.56	1.03	1.59
11	Hay fever	0.38	1.14	1.52
12	Depression	0.50	1.00	1.50
13	Ischemic heart disease	0.21	1.21	1.42
14	Duodenal ulcer	0.15	1.27	1.42
15	Low back pain	0.49	0.91	1.40
16	Migraine headache	0.21	0.13	1.34
17	Rhinitis or sinusitis	0.44	0.87	1.31
18	Hypochromic mycrocytic anemia	0.53	0.69	1.22
19	Emphysema	0.32	0.84	1.16
20	Renal glycosuria	0.65	0.50	1.15
21	Hypothyroidism	0.26	0.79	1.05
22	Kyphosis or scoliosis	0.25	0.78	1.03
23	Bronchial asthma	0.21	0.78	0.99
24	Bronchitis, chronic	0.25	0.73	0.98
25	Irritable bowel	0.27	0.71	0.98
26	Hiatus hernia	0.22	0.74	0.96
	Male only			
	Benign prostatic hypertrophy	1.09	1.88	2.97
	Testes, absent or atrophic	0.29	1.00	1.29
	Female only			
	Fibrocystic disease	1.02	2.27	3.29
	Menopausal syndrome	0.75	1.18	1.93

* Condition not otherwise specified.

psychosomatic problems, are high-utilizers of the medical care system, and are not under psychiatric care. The decision to characterize a patient's problem as emotional or psychosomatic is based on the absence of significant physical or chemical abnormalities and a positive response by the patient to selected medical history questions, or the clinical judgment of the provider of care.

The Diabetes Clinic aims to provide knowledge and emotional support

Table 2. Primary Reason for Scheduled Medical Clinic Visits. Kaiser-Permanente Medical Center, Oakland. April 1968.

	Number of visits with single diagnosis (7,114)	Number of visits with 2 or more diagnoses (417)	Total number of visits (7,531)
Multiphasic health testing follow-up	1,255	42	1,297
General check-up	945	60	1,005
Hypertension	781	225	1,006
Obesity	500	213	713
Arteriosclerotic heart disease (ASHD)	476	104	580
Diabetes mellitus	382	118	500
Diseases of gastrointestinal system	449	27	476
Diseases of locomotor system	334	8	342
Psychoses and neuroses	267	36	303
Diseases of cardiovascular system (exclusive of hypertension and ASHD)	212	19	213
Diseases of respiratory system	128	13	141
Neoplastic diseases	123	7	130
Diseases of genitourinary tract	109	15	124
Endocrine diseases	82	13	95
Diseases of blood and reticuloendothelial system	73	13	86
Infectious diseases	82	4	86
Diseases of nervous system	65	4	69
Metabolic diseases (exclusive of diabetes)	47	14	61
Diseases of connective tissue	14	33	47
Allergic diseases (exclusive of asthma)	26	4	30
Miscellaneous	393	0	393
Unclassified	371	14	385

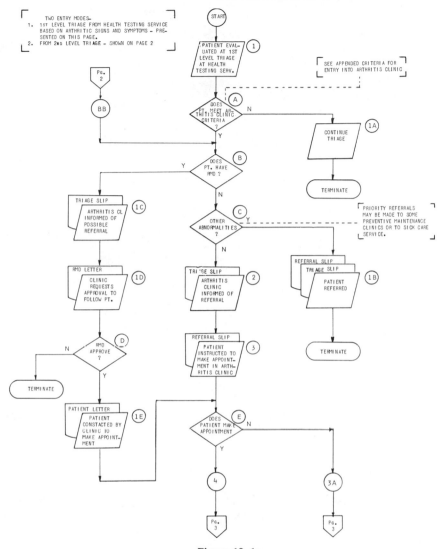

Figure 12–1a

to the diabetic patient and to assist the physician in caring for his patient. To be eligible for the Clinic, the patient's diagnosis of diabetes mellitus must be confirmed by generally accepted criteria, and his disease must be significant enough to require regular follow-up and treatment by diet, oral medication, and/or insulin.

The Hyperlipidemia Clinic is designed for the identification and modification of risk factors predisposing to cardiovascular and cerebrovascular

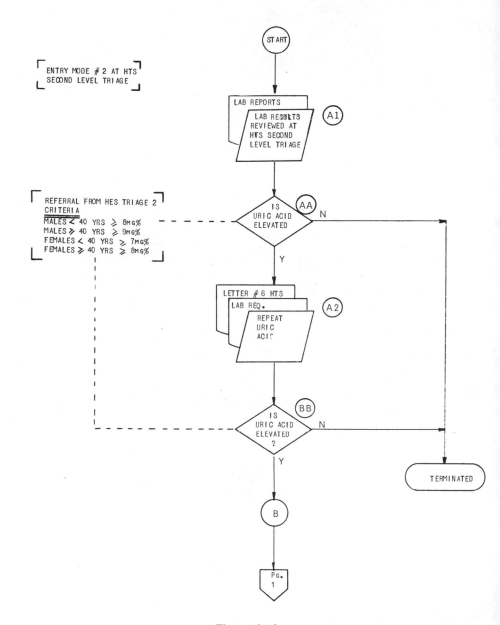

Figure 12–1b

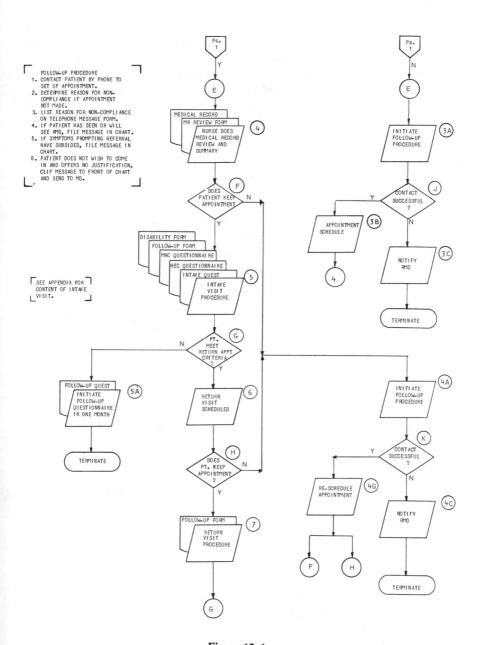

Figure 12–1c

disease, with special emphasis on the risk factor of hyperlipoproteinemia. The qualifying laboratory datum is the lipid panel, which includes serum lipoprotein electrophoresis, and cholesterol and triglyceride determinations, with values adjusted for patient age.

The Hypertension Clinic assists the referring physician in the confirmation of diagnosis, establishment of etiology, and grading of severity of hypertension, and assumes long-term management of patients with recently discovered or already established hypertension through a standard protocol. The patient eligibility criterion is the diastolic blood pressure level, which is modified according to age and sex.

The Special Kidney Clinic goal is the evaluation of patients with specified urinary abnormalities and the treatment and/or follow-up of patients with bacteriuria in accordance with predetermined rules.

The Stop Smoking Clinic uses a health education group approach to quitting the smoking habit and provides a continuing source of support for the new nonsmoking habit. Any smoker who is genuinely interested in smoking cessation is a potential candidate for the Clinic.

The Weight Control Clinic uses a group approach coupled with individual nutritional counseling and is staffed by former Weight Control Clinic members trained as group leaders. Patients must be at least 20% above ideal weight for their age and sex to qualify for the Clinic.

3.   Clinic Design

Each clinic operation is based on a sequence of five strategically linked subsystems, which permits rational matching of observed patient needs to normative modes of care.

The clinic design incorporates the following subsystems:

a.   Identification of clinic candidates according to specified eligibility criteria.   The criteria are based on historical, physical, and laboratory findings and lead to specific referral "advice rules." Positive historical information is focused for significance by means of second level questionnaires, while abnormal physical measurements and test results are rechecked for validation.

b.   Confirmation of diagnosis and eligibility.   Each clinic has its own diagnostic criteria and eligibility requirements. Some of these are included in the advice rules rules described above, while others are applied as part of the clinic's procedures. For example, three elevated blood pressure levels on separate occasions are necessary for eligibility to the Hypertension Clinic.

c. Intake into clinic and baseline data collection. When a patient is found eligible for a particular clinic, he is interviewed by a specially trained nurse who reviews the history, checks the appropriate physical parameters, and orders necessary x-ray and laboratory studies according to a standard protocol. The baseline information is entered on coded forms for computer input.

d. Management of specific conditions and their complications. The clinic nurse and physician consultant discuss the intake data and initiate a management protocol suited to each patient's individual problem. The protocol prescribes tests, treatment, and follow-up based on information obtained at each subsequent visit until the problem has been brought under satisfactory control. An example would be the sequential use of diet and/or drugs to normalize a patient's serum lipid level, or to reduce it by a predefined acceptable decrement.

e. Programmed surveillance and maintenance. This entails periodic observation of a patient who has a borderline problem or whose condition is considered to be satisfactorily stabilized but still in need of regular monitoring to detect any deviations from the steady state requiring medical intervention. The extent of surveillance depends on certain specified patient and disease variables, such as age, sex, duration and severity of condition, complications, etc. A young woman with labile hypertension may have to be surveyed annually, while an older diabetic on insulin therapy may have to be maintained by means of monthly or quarterly visits.

C. REVIEW OF COMPUTERIZED AMBULATORY PATIENT MANAGEMENT SYSTEMS

The development of computerized protocols for the management of ambulatory patients with chronic disease is still in its infancy. Probably the largest effort in this direction is the one undertaken by the Ambulatory Care Project (ACP), a collaborative venture by the Lincoln Laboratory of the Massachusetts Institute of Technology and the Beth Israel Hospital in Boston. In a preliminary study, they found that, of 225 ambulatory residents of an old age home, 77% had chronic disease which required physician visits more than once a year and were therefore potential candidates for protocol management. "Four selected protocols (cardiovascular disease, diabetes, peripheral vascular disease, chronic lung disease) resulted in a potential of saving 74% of all doctor-patient visits; nine protocols could save 61%. The same four protocols could provide total chronic disease management for 41% of the population; the nine could totally serve 61%."

The ACP chronic disease management protocol assumes that the patient's chronic disease is already diagnosed and usually under treatment. It consists of a set of information gathering procedures which include "an automated historical questionnaire, instructions for laboratory testing, and specified physical examination." The information is to be collected by an "aide," whose level of training is not yet defined. The data are then processed according to specific rules which determine whether the patient can be sent home or should be referred to the physician.

The protocol questionnaire is based on "attributes," which can be viewed as miniature programs. Each attribute has a unique name, a documentation section, a set of several questions directed towards a single symptom, a list of management actions, a question presentation sequence, and a narrative summary printing program.[7] Material pertaining to the questionnaire is stored in a computer file, activated by entered data, and manipulated by driver programs. No computer memory base of previous visit data is available; decisions are based solely on information supplied from the current visit. Two protocols based on this scheme have been developed to date, one for the on-going care of diabetes and its complications,[8] and the other for hypertension and its complications.[9] No feedback is as yet available to evaluate their operational use. The problem of the protocol management of patients with multiple chronic disease has also been examined.[10]

A computerized protocol for the management of the outpatient diabetic has been developed at the University of Kansas Medical Center.[11] The protocol relies on 19 input variables at a single visit. There is no past history file for automatic updating of information, but part of the patient questionnaire is geared to determine changes from previous visits. The management program consists of five modules: diet, treatment decision, insulin dosage, insulin dose distribution, insulin reaction, and printout. A comparison of the output of this program with the advice of a consulting physician for 40 patient visits has revealed a correlation coefficient for changes in insulin dose of 0.98 $(P<0.001)$.

At the Pritzker School of Medicine of the University of Chicago, a computer program has been devised for the diagnosis and management of kidney stone disease.[12] Data are obtained by physicians in a specialized diagnostic unit according to listings of pertinent findings that must be documented or included. The program maintains a data file for generating diagnostic reports and subsidiary working reports including laboratory and clinical findings. "An interpretative program can be focused upon laboratory and clinical data obtained between any two dates so that iterative reports can be generated during the course of treatment." Diagnostic reports generated from initial data pertaining to 200 patients who have entered the program are being compared to conclusions derived from the same data by physicians. Presently, work is proceeding on the design of a computerized management protocol for hypertension.

As part of the Cooperative Cancer Chemotherapy Program of Hawaii, a central computerized treatment file which contains baseline laboratory data, drug administration, and toxicity records has been established.[13] One of its functions is "to follow-up systematically and automatically, through the central office, all registered cases through physicians and member units, in order to pinpoint recurrences and metastases early enough to ensure safe and consistent chemotherapy."

At the University of Birmingham in England, computer analysis of symptom patterns is used as a method of monitoring patients who have been treated with radio-iodine.[14] Patients are sent a postal questionnaire 9 months prior to their periodic screening for hypothyroidism every 21 months. If their responses are "abnormal," they are asked to come in for a serum protein bound iodine determination (PBI). If the latter suggests hypothyroidism, the patient is referred to the outpatient clinic for full medical assessment. It is believed that, without this system, the PBI "would have to be performed more frequently, with the need for additional hospital visits by the patient, and with an increase in the cost of the system."

A time-oriented record-keeping system has been devised at Stanford University Hospital, California, which encourages data-based management decisions and decreases chart review time by the physician.[15] Information is entered into the computer through a typewriter terminal and stored on random-access disk packs. Output data provide assistance in the management of individual patients, as well as in teaching and research. Similarly, a manual charting system of organized, sequential data adaptable for computer use has been devised for use by nurse practitioners at the Yale-New Haven Hospital.[16] Feinstein and Koss have reviewed the prerequisites for appropriate classification of information to program computer advice rules for patient management.[17] They have developed the procedures necessary for therapeutic decisions for cancer of the lung. A Clinical Decision Support System has been developed by IBM to be implemented by the user institution.[18] It will assist in acquiring patient data, present these data in summary form, and suggest appropriate decisions as an iterative process.

Risk factor analysis has been used to develop a data reference set as a preventive medical tool for cancer of the breast.[19] The data set includes four categories of advice rules: selective testing, medical surveillance, health education and counseling, and uniform management of abnormalities detected.

The test selection function of the computer has been analyzed in terms of cost vs. benefit in the sequential diagnosis of congenital heart disease and primary bone tumors. The information structure used for each disease consisted of a probability based on signs and symptoms according to Bayes' rules and the costs of tests and misdiagnoses. In terms of diagnostic performance, there was no difference between sequential and complete modes of diagnosis. But the former program used only 6.7 tests vs. 31 for the latter.[20]

D. ADVANTAGES OF COMPUTERIZED PROTOCOLS

The basic capabilities of the digital computer are based on its speed in carrying out the following functions:

(1) storage and retrieval of large amounts of data,
(2) correlation of these data,
(3) performance of lengthy and complicated calculations, and
(4) arrival at decisions based on predetermined rules.

These capabilities can be used to enhance the effectiveness and efficiency of preventive health maintenance programs by:

1. Assisting in Decision-Making

a. Calculations.   Certain decisions are contingent on calculations which can be done faster and more accurately by the computer. For example, eligibility of a patient for the Weight Control Clinic is based on his weight being 20% or more above the median weight for his age and sex. In the Special Kidney Clinic, repeat of abnormal quantitative tests are called for until there is a variation of 10% or less between any two tests.

b. Correlations.   Many decisions are based on the review and collation of previous data, a time-consuming process which can be facilitated by the computer. For example, the evaluation of an abnormally low serum potassium in a hypertensive patient requires the integration of information about symptoms, previous potassium levels, drugs the patient is receiving, renal function, etc. The choice of treatment for a patient with bacteriuria depends on the results of previous urine cultures, bacterial sensitivities to drugs, past history of allergic reaction, previous type and duration of therapy, etc.

2. Monitoring Adherence to Protocol

a. Verification.   A protocol usually requires the performance of many tests and procedures, especially in the confirmation and evaluation of abnormal conditions. For example, the finding of proteinuria in a diabetic patient calls for a number of tests such as repeat urinalysis, 24-hour urine protein, protein electrophoresis, serum glucose, cholesterol, etc., to be performed in a particular sequence. Likewise, the confirmation of hypertension requires obtaining several blood pressure measurements, the value of which determines one of several specific sequences of additional procedures. The computer can easily verify that such tests and procedures are complete and in the appropriate sequence, a function which, if carried out manually, could be time consuming and open to human error.

b.   Reminders.   In the surveillance phase of any chronic disease, certain routine tests have to be performed at periodic intervals. For example, after the successful therapy of bacteriuria, repeat urine cultures are required every three months and renal function tests are required annually, but this schedule is subject to change should bacteriuria reappear. The follow-up of hyperuricemia calls for serum uric acid determinations every six months, and Arthritis Clinic visits annually, but a gout attack alters this planned pattern. The computer is an excellent tool, under these conditions, for reminding the provider of care as to the choice of action and its timing according to a scheduled protocol, or in relation to interval events.

3.   Facilitating Evaluation

The availability of easily retrievable computer stored information permits a continuing analysis of data, evaluation of results, and implementation of rational changes in the areas of:

a.   Quality of care.   One measure of such is the trend in patient management outcomes. For example, the periodic analysis of blood pressure or serum cholesterol values provides an index of the success of treatment in the Hypertension or the Hyperlipidemia Clinics. Another measure is patient acceptance of the management program. Clinic utilization patterns of preventive maintenance referrals in keeping appointments, continuing programmed care, etc., reflect favorable or unfavorable patient reaction to the services offered.

b.   Efficiency of care.   Collection of data pertaining to the operational aspects of preventive maintenance programs promotes the review and updating of methods and procedures. For example, analysis of the data may lead to better definition of functional needs of each program and more optimal deployment of personnel.

4.   Serving as Data Base for Health Care and Health Services Research

The accumulation of valid structured data over time for large population groups provides the capability needed for research in such aspects of health as the natural history of chronic diseases, the outcomes of various modes of treatment, the role of paramedical personnel, the operation of health care systems, etc.

As a consequence of computerization, the following improvements can be expected in the management of preventive maintenance programs:

(1) More time available for individual patient care.

(2) Less physician time needed for consultation.

(3) Ability of paramedical personnel of varying skills to function more effectively.

(4) Readily available data for pinpointing system deficiencies and allowing ongoing operational changes to improve effectiveness and efficiency.

E. DEVELOPMENT OF COMPUTERIZED PATIENT MANAGEMENT PROTOCOLS

1. Requirements

In the diagnosis and management of any disease process, the physician pursues a rational sequence of action. Through physical examination and patient history, he gathers preliminary data which suggest a tentative diagnosis. Through various investigative procedures, he confirms his original diagnosis. He proceeds with further data collection to establish a baseline patient profile to refer to in evaluating future progress. Using the data obtained, he prescribes the most appropriate mode of treatment. He then monitors the patient's response until maximum improvement has been realized. In the case of chronic disease, he continues surveillance of the patient to insure that his status remains stable and to intervene as changes occur.

The physician decides on a patient management program based "on his experience, on his book knowledge, on his mental endowment, and on the occasion."[21] Physician reasoning and clinical judgment have been aptly discussed by Ledley and Lusted[22] and Feinstein.[23] Weed's problem-oriented medical record[24] reflects documentation of the physician's decision making process. The development of an automated program entails systematic analysis of this process and its translation into clear, logical, sequential computer usable rules.

It is obvious that each preventive maintenance clinic requires a distinct protocol. But each protocol can be patterned after a generic model which includes the previously described five subsystems: identification, confirmation, intake, management, and surveillance/maintenance. Each of these can be described as a module of independent decision rules unique for each clinic. These decision rules may involve many submodules, or series of events, which are activated by the type of data entered.

The protocol sequence calls for the routine functions within one module to be completed before progressing to the next module. Smooth operation of the protocol, therefore, depends on the completeness and validity of the data necessary for the decision processing within each module. The system design has to include appropriate safeguards to check for completeness and validity of all data prior to their entry into the computer. This can be facilitated by the use of an interactive terminal, through which the data can be monitored as they are entered. Such a terminal is necessary if the computer is to be used for on-line assistance in decision-making, with the assurance of both quality of data entry and immediacy of response. The latter also requires the presence of a readily accessible information base which contains appropriate patient data and medical decision rules, and a retrieval program which can generate clinically useful reports.

In summary, the requirements for computerizing a patient management protocol are as follows:

(1) Protocol organization into independent decision rule modules.
(2) Quality control of data collection and entry.
(3) Supportive systems of data storage and retrieval.

Methods for fulfilling the first two requirements for the preventive maintenance clinics are described below. The third requirement is discussed elsewhere in this book (Chapter Four).

2. Data Collection

Data is collected during each patient visit to the preventive maintenance clinics, with respect to patient identification, tests, measurements, physical findings, reported symptoms, diagnoses, and orders for diet and medications. A system of structured forms to simplify the organization, communication, and storage of clinical information has been designed for this purpose and is illustrated by the flow chart in Figure 12–2.

Each preventive maintenance clinic has an individually designed form for recording data. These forms allow the recording of several patient visits on the same page so that symptoms and findings of earlier visits can be easily compared with those of the current entry (see Figure 12–3). Some patient care data collected by several clinics, such as physical examination data, are recorded on common forms; these forms are designed to "stand alone" as well as in combination with the regular visit form (see Figure 12–4). A structured telephone message form is also in use because treatment orders

SYSTEM OF STRUCTURED FORMS

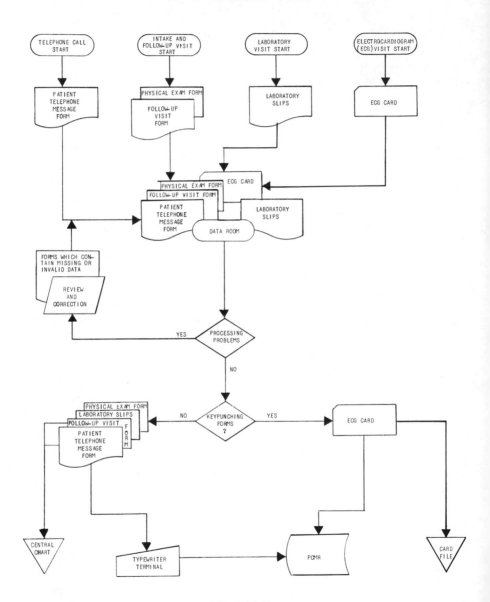

Figure 12–2

are occasionally given over the telephone, and this event would constitute a separate and distinct computer-defined visit (see Figure 12–5). Laboratory results are returned from the laboratory on standard report slips; these slips are used as source documents and therefore do not require that data be transcribed onto intermediate forms for processing.

Code numbers for each item on each form allow the data to be entered into the computer by means of a typewriter terminal. Many of the entries consist of English words belonging to a controlled dictionary of terms. This dictionary is referenced by the nurse, as necessary, in completing the forms and subsequently checked for validity by the computer. Currently this dictionary includes 95 symptoms, 300 physical findings, 180 diagnoses, and 80 drug names.

Coded notation is used to describe the progression of symptoms and diagnoses. For example, N = new occurrence, C = continuing, essentially unchanged since last visit, I = improved since last visit. A grading system is used to describe the severity of certain physical findings, while other findings are indicated only as present or absent.

Experience with the forms has demonstrated that this scheme is versatile and sufficiently flexible to allow for the frequent changes which become necessary as nurses and physicians refine procedure and information documentation.

3. Data Entry

After each patient contact, the appropriate completed form is sent to the data processing room located adjacent to the clinic area. The recorded data are entered from the form into an individualized Patient Computer Medical Record (PCMR) through a specially designed function called GAMMA.

GAMMA is a modular, flexible program for computer entry of patient data. It permits on-line typewriter keyboard entry of medical data by a data input operator and enables this operator to interact in real-time mode with the individual patient's computer medical record. The use of GAMMA removes the necessity that documents be machine readable, leading to increased flexibility of form design, wider scope, and higher density of data content. 90–95% of data recorded can be entered without English word input, and a trained operator can enter data from several hundred visits per working day. This rate, together with the lower cost of form revision and procurement, results in a very efficient system of data management.

GAMMA is driven by a single table which serves the needs of every preventive maintenance clinic. The table defines all current items pertaining to patient care in the clinics and can be easily updated as new items are added; it also describes each item, location, and format in the PCMR, a

KAISER PERMANENTE HEALTH CENTER
DIABETES CLINIC
FOLLOW-UP VISITS

	Visit 1	Visit 2	Visit 3	Visit 4
DATE OF VISIT				
TIME OF VISIT				
NURSE CODE				
APPT OR NON-APPT (CIRCLE ONE)	APP NON 2	APP NON 2	APP NON 2	APP NON 2
REFERRING M.D.				
PT UNDER CARE OF (SMD, RMD)				
130-131 HEIGHT (INCHES) / WEIGHT (LBS)				
202-203 BLOOD PRESSURE (SYS/DIAS)				
145 VISUAL ACUITY, RIGHT				
46 VISUAL ACUITY, LEFT				
CLINIC TESTS				
160 CLINITEST (GLUCOSE) (NEG - 4 +)				
161 URISTIX (PROTEIN) (NEG - 4 +)				
162 URISTIX (GLUCOSE) (NEG LIGHT MEDIUM DARK)				
163 KETOSTIX (ACETONE) (NEG SMALL MODERATE LARGE)				
LABORATORY				

	24 HR. URINE GLUCOSE (GMS/24 HRS)
	F.B.S. (mg%)
	2 HR. PC B.S. (mg%)
	RANDOM B.S. (mg%)
	HOME TESTING
108	METHOD (CLINITEST - TES-TAPE / CLINISTIX - DIASTIX)
109	RELIABILITY OF TESTING (ADEQUATE / INCOMPLETE / NONE)
110	FASTING MODE (NEG - 4+)
111	FASTING HIGHEST VALUE (NEG - 4+)
112	FASTING FREQUENCY OF HIGHEST VALUE (FREQUENT / OCCASIONAL / SELDOM)
114	PC MODE (NEG - 4+)
115	PC HIGHEST VALUE (NEG - 4+)
116	PC FREQUENCY OF HIGHEST (FREQUENT / OCCASIONAL / SELDOM)

	RETINA	NEGATIVE	NOT DONE	NEGATIVE	NOT DONE	NEGATIVE	NOT DONE	NEGATIVE	NOT DONE
530-531	RETINA								
542-543	RETINA EXUDATE (✓)	R / L		R / L		R / L		R / L	
544-545	RETINA HEMORRHAGE (✓)	R / L		R / L		R / L		R / L	
540-541	RETINA MICROANEURYSM (✓)	R / L		R / L		R / L		R / L	
547-548		R / L		R / L		R / L		R / L	

Figure 12-3

DIABETES CLINIC FOLLOW-UP VISITS

DATE OF VISIT

EXTREMITIES

	NEGATIVE	NOT DONE	NEGATIVE	NOT DONE	NEGATIVE	NOT DONE	NEGATIVE	NOT DONE	
EXTREMITIES (✓)	R	L	R	L	R	L	R	L	718-719
FOOT CALLUS (✓)	R	L	R	L	R	L	R	L	596-597
LEG SWELLING (1+ – 4+) (✓)	R	L	R	L	R	L	R	L	602-603
TINEA PEDIS (✓)	R	L	R	L	R	L	R	L	604-605
TOENAIL ABNORMALITY, NFS (✓)	R	L	R	L	R	L	R	L	610-611
SOFT TISSUE INFECTION, NFS (✓)	R	L	R	L	R	L	R	L	600-601
DORSALIS PEDIS PULSE DECR { MILD / MODERATE / ABSENT }	R	L	R	L	R	L	R	L	584-585
POSTERIOR TIBIAL PULSE DECR { MILD / MODERATE / ABSENT }	R	L	R	L	R	L	R	L	582-583
	R	L	R	L	R	L	R	L	615-616

NEUROLOGIC

	NEGATIVE	NOT DONE	NEGATIVE	NOT DONE	NEGATIVE	NOT DONE	NEGATIVE	NOT DONE	
ANKLE VIBRATION SENSE DECR (MILD / MODERATE / ABSENT) (✓)	R	L	R	L	R	L	R	L	612-613

REPORTED SYMPTOMS SINCE LAST VISIT

	MORNING	AFTERNOON	MORNING	AFTERNOON	MORNING	AFTERNOON	
	NONE		NONE		NONE		59
							60-61
							62
							64-65
							66-67
							68-69
							70-71

TIME PROGRESSION CODES:

N – NEW DIAGNOSIS, FINDING OR EVENT
R – RECURRENCE
C – CONTINUING—ESSENTIALLY UNCHANGED
I – IMPROVED
W – WORSENING OR EXACERBATION
O – OLD—NO LONGER ACTIVE OR PRESENT
D – DELETE - CONDITION NO LONGER VALID
P – PROVISIONAL

	MORNING	AFTERNOON	MORNING	AFTERNOON	MORNING	AFTERNOON	
NUMBER OF HYPOGLYCEMIC EPISODES							79

AND TIME OF OCCURRENCE

EVENING	NIGHT	EVENING	NIGHT	EVENING	NIGHT	EVENING	NIGHT		
								230-231	
									232-233

DIAGNOSES

TIME PROGRESSION CODES
SAME AS FOR SYMPTOMS

NOTES

315

DIABETES CLINIC FOLLOW-UP VISITS

		NONE	CONTINUING AS RX	NONE	CONTINUING AS RX	NONE	CONTINUING AS RX	NONE	CONTINUING AS RX
	DATE OF VISIT								
	MEDICATIONS PRESCRIBED (✓)								
300	DRUG NAME								
302	STRENGTH								
366-367	DOSAGE (UNITS)								
303	SIG CODE								
290	RX ACTION (CONTINUE CHANGE ADD DISCONTINUE)								
308	REASON FOR ACTION								
309-310	RX AMOUNT # REFILLS								
311	DRUG NAME								
313	STRENGTH								
368-369	DOSAGE (UNITS)								
314	SIG CODE								
291	RX ACTION (CONTINUE CHANGE ADD DISCONTINUE)								
319	REASON FOR ACTION								
320-321	RX AMOUNT # REFILLS								
322	DRUG NAME								
324	STRENGTH								
370-371	DOSAGE (UNITS)								
325	SIG CODE								

Code	Field	Visit 1	Visit 2	Visit 3	Visit 4
292	RX ACTION (CONTINUE, ADD, CHANGE, DISCONTINUE)				
330	REASON FOR ACTION				
331-332	RX AMOUNT | # REFILLS				
	PHARMACY				
·30-431	DIET PRESCRIBED (✓)	NONE CONTINUING AS RX	NONE CONTINUING AS RX	NONE CONTINUING AS RX	NONE CONTINUING AS RX
	CALORIES/DAY	EXCHANGE NO FREE SUGAR	EXCHANGE NO FREE SUGAR	EXCHANGE NO FREE SUGAR	EXCHANGE NO FREE SUGAR
427	FEEDINGS/DAY				
470	HOME TESTING PRESCRIBED (✓)	NONE CONTINUING AS RX	NONE CONTINUING AS RX	NONE CONTINUING AS RX	NONE CONTINUING AS RX
	METHOD (CLINITEST, CLINISTIX, TESTAPE, DIASTIX)				
471	NUMBER OF TIMES				
487-488	TIME OF DAY (✓)	FASTING PC	FASTING PC	FASTING PC	FASTING PC
489	ACETONE TESTING FREQUENCY				
	FOLLOW-UP				
520-521	RETURN TO DIABETES CLINIC RN	WEEKS MONTHS	WEEKS MONTHS	WEEKS MONTHS	WEEKS MONTHS
	PT TO SEE REGULAR MD	WEEKS MONTHS	WEEKS MONTHS	WEEKS MONTHS	WEEKS MONTHS
	VIA (RET, MHC, N RET, MCDS)				
	PT LAST SAW REGULAR MD	WEEKS MONTHS	WEEKS MONTHS	WEEKS MONTHS	WEEKS MONTHS
501	REFERRAL				
502	REFERRAL				
503	REFERRAL				

PHYSICIANS NOTES

DIABETES CLINIC FOLLOW-UP VISITS

NOTES: PATIENT'S REGULAR M.D.	NOTES: CLINIC PHYSICIAN CONSULTANT	R.N.
VISIT DATE		
		INITIALS
SIGNED DATE	SIGNED DATE	DATE
VISIT DATE		
		INITIALS

SIGNED   DATE   SIGNED   DATE

VISIT DATE

SIGNED   DATE   SIGNED   DATE   INITIALS

SIGNED   DATE   SIGNED   DATE

VISIT DATE

SIGNED   DATE   SIGNED   DATE   INITIALS

KAISER PERMANENTE HEALTH CENTER

HYPERTENSION - HYPERLIPIDEMIA CLINIC
PHYSICAL EXAMINATION RECORD

DATE OF VISIT	TIME OF VISIT	TYPE OF VISIT	NURSE CODE	CLINIC CODE

DISABILITY

PATIENT'S GENERAL CONDITION
TODAY IS ASSOCIATED WITH THE
FOLLOWING LIMITATION IN HIS
USUAL ACTIVITIES:

- NONE
- MILD
- MODERATE
- SEVERE
- COMPLETE

SYSTEMS

NO / SIG ABN — NOT EXAM

- SKIN
- EYES
- NECK
- HEART
- LUNGS AND THORAX
- ABDOMEN
- EXTREMITIES
- NEUROLOGICAL

SKIN

R / L XANTHOMA

EYES

R / L RETINA EXUDATE
R / L RETINA HEMORRHAGE
R / L RETINA MICROANEURYSM
RETINOPATHY HYPERTENSIVE
  K - W CLASSIFICATION (1 - 4)
RETINOPATHY ARTERIOSCLEROTIC
  A - S CLASSIFICATION (1 - 4)
R / L CORNEA ARCUS
R / L LIPEMIA RETINALIS

NECK

R / L CAROTID BRUIT (1 - 4 +)
       CAROTID PULSE
R / L   DECR - MILD
R / L   DECR MODERATE
R / L   ABSENT
       THYROID ENLARGED

HEART

R / L VENTRICULAR HYPERTROPHY (0 - 4)
R / L VENTRICULAR HEAVE
       2ND SOUND INCREASED
         AORTIC
         PULMONIC
       3RD SOUND PRESENT
       4TH SOUND PRESENT
       MURMUR 1
         SYSTOLIC (GRADE 1 - 6)
         DIASTOLIC (GRADE 1 - 6)
       LOCATION:
         APEX
R / L   2ND INTERSPACE
R / L   4TH INTERSPACE
       RADIATION:
         AXILLA
         NECK
         STERNAL BORDER LEFT
       MURMUR 2
         SYSTOLIC (GRADE 1 - 6)
         DIASTOLIC (GRADE 1 - 6)
       LOCATION:
         APEX
R / L   2ND INTERSPACE
R / L   4TH INTERSPACE
       RADIATION:
         AXILLA
         NECK
         STERNAL BORDER LEFT

LUNGS AND THORAX

R / L RALES
R / L RHONCHI
R / L WHEEZES

ABDOMEN

R / L AORTA WIDENED
R / L AORTA BRUIT
R / L RENAL ARTERY BRUIT
       LIVER ENLARGED (CM)
R / L KIDNEY ENLARGED

EXTREMITIES

DOSALIS PEDIS PULSE
R / L DECR MILD
R / L DECR MODERATE
R / L ABSENT
POSTERIOR TIBIAL PULSE
R / L DECR MILD
R / L DECR MODERATE
R / L ABSENT
FEMORAL PULSE
R / L DECR MILD
R / L DECR MODERATE
R / L ABSENT
POPLITEAL PULSE
R / L DECR MILD
R / L DECR MODERATE
R / L ABSENT
R / L PEDAL EDEMA

NEUROLOGICAL

R / L CRANIAL NERVE NEUROPATHY
R / L MOTOR ABNORMALITY NFS
R / L REFLEX   "   NFS
R / L SENSORY   "   NFS
R / L BABINSKI PRESENT
       APHASIA

RN'S NOTES:

G18-11-72

Figure 12–4.

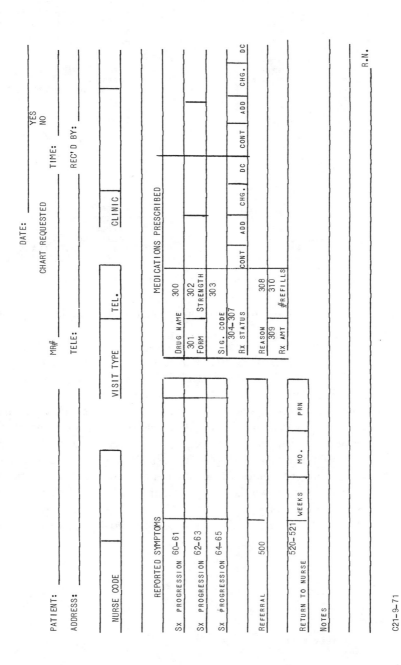

Figure 12–5. Kaiser Permanente Health Center.

```
L(4) *07FC* -901-                                  PHYSICAL EXAMINATICN PROC
     L(5) *0781* -921-                             GENERAL AND PSYCHOLOGICAL
     L(5) *0782* -921-                             SKIN
     L(5) *0783* -921-                             HEAD
     L(5) *0784* -921-                             EYE
     L(5) *0785* -921-                             ENT
     L(5) *0786* -921-                             NECK
     L(5) *0787* -921-                             HEART
     L(5) *0788* -921-                             LUNGS ANC THORAX
     L(5) *078A* -921-                             ABDOMEN
     L(5) *078B* -921-                             BACK
     L(5) *078C* -921-                             GENITALIA
     L(5) *078D* -921-                             RECTUM
     L(5) *078E* -921-                             EXTREMITIES
     L(5) *078F* -921-                             NEURCLCGICAL
     L(5) *07FB* -921-                             PELVIS
          THE FOLLOWING L(6) ITEMS MAY APPLY
          TO ALL L(5) PHYSICAL FINDINGS
          L(6) *0816* -921-                        LOCATION
          L(6) *0813* -921-                        SEVERITY
          L(6) *081A* -920-                        PROGRESSION
          L(6) *08B2* -901-                        ANATOMIC SIZE
          L(6) *09E7* -921-                        PATHOLOGY
          L(6) *0B02* -921-                        RADIATION
          L(6) *0884* -920-                        KEITH-WAGENER CLASS
          L(6) *0AFE* -920-                        SCHEIE A-S CLASSIFICATION
```

Figure 12–6.   Data structure for physical examination procedure.

branching tree-structured patient computer record of variable length and variable format (see Chapter Four).

Each major item category is defined by a specific number called Cataloged Item Identifier of Data (CIID). Figure 12–6 shows the data structure of the "Physical Examination Procedure" item; this item is stored in part 1 of the PCMR, at level (4); its CIID is *07FC* and its format is -901-, which denotes a string of characters (English text). The physical examination procedure is divided into 15 major categories corresponding to the anatomic regions of the body; each region is entered at level (5) of the PCMR and has its own CIID. All physical signs pertaining to a region are considered as different values of a single item and entered in format -921- (encoded English words). For example, all abdominal findings share the same "Px-Abdomen" CIID *078A* (see Figure 12–7). Detailed characterization of physical findings is accomplished by means of "modi-

```
078A
078A     PX - ABDOMEN          *******************************
078A     AORTA BRUIT
078A     AORTA WIDENED
078A     KIDNEY ENLARGED
078A     LIVER ENLARGED
078A     MASS
078A     NEGATIVE
078A     NOT EXAMINED
078A     RENAL ARTERY BRUIT
078A     TENDERNESS
```

Figure 12–7.   Physical examination of abdomen.

```
081A      PROGRESSION              *********************************
081A   CONTINUING
081A   IMPROVED
081A   NEW
081A   OLD
081A   RECURRENT
081A   WORSENING
0813
0813      SEVERITY                *********************************
0813   ABSENT
0813   DECREASED MILD
0813   DECREASED MODERATE
0813   MILD
0813   MODERATE
0813   NEGATIVE
0813   SEVERE
0813   TRACE
0813   0
0813   1
0813   1+
0813   2
0813   2+
0813   3
0813   3+
0813   4
0813   4+
0813   5
0813   6
```

Figure 12-8.   Progression and severity modifiers.

fiers"; each modifier has its specific CIID and is entered at level (6) as an encoded English word. In Figure 12–8 are listed the "Progression" and "Severity" modifier values under CIID's *081A* and *0813*. The same modifiers can be used to characterize other items, such as symptoms or diagnoses.

Another example, Figure 12–9, shows the data structures for "Drug administered" and "Drug prescribed," with PCMR parts and levels, CIID's, and format codes; Figure 12–10 shows the values under "Drug Form," CIID *0537*.

```
L(4) *06E8* -901-                      DRUG ADMINISTERED
    L(5) *0536* -921- MULTIPLE         DRUG NAME
        L(6) *0537* -920-              FORM
        L(6) *053A* -901-              DRUG STRENGTH (UNITS)
        L(6) *06CF* -600-              TOTAL DOSAGE
            L(7) *053B* -901-          UNITS

L(4) *06E9* -901-                      DRUG PRESCRIBED
    L(5) *0536* -921- MULTIPLE         DRUG NAME
        L(6) *0537* -920-              FORM
        L(6) *053A* -901-              DRUG STRENGTH (UNITS)
        L(6) *06CF* -600-              TOTAL DOSAGE
            L(7) *053B* -901-          UNITS
        L(6) *0538* -901-              SIG CODE
        L(6) *088A* -920-              PRESCRIPTION STATUS
            L(7) *088B* -921-          REASON
        L(6) *053C* -600-              ORIGINAL PRESCRIPTION AMT
        L(6) *088C* -600-              NUMBER OF REFILLS
        L(6) *088D* -921-              PLANNED TREATMENT DUR
```

Figure 12–9.   Data structures for drugs administered and drugs prescribed.

```
0537     DRUG FORM              ********************************
0537   CAPSULE
0537   CREAM
0537   INJECTABLE
0537   LIQUID
0537   POWDER
0537   TABLET
```

Figure 12–10.   Values for drug form.

GAMMA makes use of four system parameters:

(1) Location of source of form: The source is one of the Kaiser-Permanente medical facilities in northern California.

(2) Form number: Each form is associated with a department and an account number, which is provided automatically for verification purposes by the computer whenever the form number is entered. The preventive maintenance clinics are within a department called Health Center, which has a specific account number.

(3) Year of data processing.

(4) Operator's name: Each operator has to enter a security password, which the computer recognizes.

Each Kaiser-Permanente member has a unique eight-digit Medical Record Number (MR#) which is entered as a primary identifier on every form used to record patient visit information. When the MR# is entered, the computer references the appropriate record and returns secondary identifier characteristics (name, sex, and birthdate), which can be checked against the patient identification data on the form being entered.

In the computer data set, all possible items of information are identified by "blip numbers." Whenever a blip number is entered, the computer retrieves the item(s) associated with that number and echoes back the data they represent for verification. Some blip numbers require additional information, or a modifier, such as a date, time, number, code, numeric limits, or actual English text. Codes consist of 1–4 alphanumeric characters. Each form using the codes has a group of codes defined specifically for it, and every code entered is checked against this list for errors, e.g., a code modifier used for one form may not be valid for another or, if it is, may mean something entirely different. English text is entered as written on the form immediately after the blip number and is verified when echoed back.

When the operator terminates the computer entry of data from a particular form, the computer types out the blip numbers entered, together with a short description of the blip and its modifier, if any, to allow for checking corrections of entry. Most errors are immediately apparent, and the corrected blip numbers and modifiers can be reentered. If error messages still appear, the form is set aside for review. Even if no error messages are received, an optional editing phase is provided for erasing wrong data and entering correct data.

4.   Decision Rule Modules

Decision rule modules are sets of precise, detailed, and sequentially organized procedures. They can be described in narrative form or be presented as flow charts or decision tables. The latter have the advantage of easy understanding when used manually by a medical person, and of easy programming when adopted for computer use.

Flow charts have been used to document the protocols of the preventive maintenance clinics; they are now being converted into series of decision tables (examples of which will be presented to illustrate the previously discussed clinic design subsystems): identification, confirmation, intake, management, and surveillance/maintenance. The Special Kidney Clinic protocol combines the features of a flow chart and a decision table (see Management Subsystem).

Each decision table has a header which describes the set of procedures. It consists of four basic sections: a double horizontal line divides the table into conditions and actions, and a double vertical line divides it into the stat and the entry. The stat portion gives the names or descriptions of conditions and actions, while the entry portion presents the condition value(s), and the corresponding action or advice rule. Most decision tables constructed are of the mixed entry type, where both conditions and actions may have either single or multiple values.

a.   Identification subsystem.   The identification of candidates for the preventive health maintenance clinics is now computerized as part of automated multiphasic testing, and advice rules are issued for patient referral to the clinics. Figure 12–11 shows the decision table of eligibility for the Arthritis Clinic, based on serum uric acid levels, according to age and sex. Figures 12–12a and 12–12b show the eligibility rules for the Weight Control Clinic, based on weight, height, and sex.

At present, there is no facility for a physician in his office to communicate with the computer regarding eligibility of a patient for a particular clinic. The advice rules are available to him for possible referral on a manual basis.

b.   Confirmation subsystem.   When a patient with elevated diastolic blood pressure is referred to the Hypertension Clinic, a series of procedures are triggered to confirm the diagnosis of hypertension. Confirmation is obtained by two elevated diastolic blood pressure levels measured one week

		1	2	3	4
Sex	Male	Y	Y	N	N
Age	≥40	N	Y	N	Y
Serum uric acid (in mg%) — Current test	≥7.0	—	—	Y	—
	≥8.0	Y	—	—	Y
	≥9.0	—	Y	—	—
	Specimen hemolyzed	N	N	N	N
Previous test	Unknown or <7.0	—	—	Y	—
	Unknown or <8.0	Y	—	—	Y
	Unknown or <9.0	—	Y	—	—
1. Order repeat uric acid		x	x	x	x
2. Consider referral to Arthritis Clinic if uric acid level	≥7.0			x	
	≥8.0	x			x
	≥9.0		x		
Else skip					

Figure 12–11. Multiphasic health testing advice rules for uric acid.

		1					
Sex	Male	Y	Y	Y	N	N	N
	Unknown	N	—	N	N	—	N
Height (in inches)	<55	—	—	—	Y	—	N
	<59	Y	—	N	—	—	—
Weight* (in pounds)	≥139	—	—	—	Y	—	—
	≥150	Y	—	—	—	—	—
	≥193	—	—	—	—	Y	N
	≥253	—	Y	N	—	—	—
	≥20% Median	—	—	Y	—	—	Y
1. Consider referral to weight control clinic		x	x	x	x	x	x
Else skip							

* Refer to Figure 12–12b.

Figure 12–12a. Multiphasic health testing advice rules for weight.

apart. Module A1 defines hypertension severity groups based on age, sex, and blood pressure level. The use of such groups facilitates the definition of advice rules generated by the two blood pressure measurement procedures (Modules A2 and A3). Knowledge of prior treatment of hypertension with antihypertensive medications and/or birth control pills are factors which affect the advice rules. When only one of the two repeat blood pressure

	Men					Women			
Height*	Median	−10%	Weight** +10%	+20%	Height	Median	−10%	Weight +10%	+20%
59	125	112	138	150	55	116	104	128	139
60	133	120	146	160	56	113	102	124	136
61	138	124	152	166	57	117	105	129	140
62	141	127	155	169	58	118	106	130	142
63	145	130	160	174	59	122	110	134	146
64	150	135	165	180	60	123	111	135	148
65	156	140	172	187	61	127	114	140	152
66	160	144	176	192	62	129	116	142	155
67	164	148	180	197	63	133	120	146	160
68	168	151	185	202	64	136	122	150	163
69	173	156	190	208	65	138	124	152	166
70	176	158	194	211	66	141	127	155	169
71	181	163	199	217	67	144	130	158	173
72	186	167	205	223	68	147	132	162	176
73	189	170	208	227	69	151	136	166	181
74	194	175	213	233	70	153	138	168	184
75	198	178	218	238	71	161	145	177	193
76	206	185	227	247					
77	211	190	231	253					

* In inches
** In pounds

Figure 12–12b. Median weight by height of 111,000 multiphasic health testing patients, 1964–1968.

Module A1. Blood Pressure Group

	1	2	3	4	5	6	7	8	9	10	11	12	13	14	15
Sex	—	—	—	F	F	F	F	F	F	M	M	M	M	M	M
Age	<20	<20	<20	20–39	20–39	20–39	≥40	≥40	≥40	20–59	20–59	20–59	≥60	≥60	≥60
Blood Pressure (BP)**	<85	85–119	≥120	<90	90–124	≥125	<95	95–129	≥130	<90	90–124	≥125	<95	95–129	≥130
BP Group 0	X			X			X			X			X		
BP Group I		X			X			X			X			X	
BP Group II			X			X			X			X			X

* For ease of tabulation, patients have been classified in three severity groups based on sex, age, and blood pressure level:
  Group 0 = Normal diastolic BP.
  Group I = Mild to moderate diastolic BP elevation.
  Group II = Severe diastolic BP elevation.
** BP—Casual sitting diastolic blood pressure.

Module A2. First Blood Pressure (1st BP)

	1	2	3	4	5
Known hypertensive?	N	N	N	Y	—
BP Group (MHC* or RMD** referral)	0	0	1-2	—	—
BP Group (1st BP)	0	1	0-1		2
Terminated from clinic	X				
Return for 2nd BP in one week		X	X		
Do orientation to clinic		X	X		
Return for intake in 2-4 weeks				X	
Order intake laboratory tests (initial)***				X	
Continue same medications if under treatment				X	
Consult with RMD or SMD****					X

* MHC=Multiphasic health testing
** RMD=Regular physician
*** Refer to Figure 12–12.
**** SMD=Clinic supervising physician

Module A3. Second Blood Pressure (2nd BP)

	1	2	3	4	5	6	7	8	9	10	11
On birth control (BC) pills?	—	Y	Y	Y	Y	Y	Y	N	N	N	—
Hypertensive prior to starting BC pills?*	—	N	N	N	Y	Y	Y	—	—	—	—
BP Group (1st BP)	0	0	1-2	1-2	0	1-2	1-2	0	1-2	1-2	—
BP Group (2nd BP)	0	1	0	1	1	0	1	1	0	1	2
Return for observation (obs.) in	12 mo.	6 mo.	6 mo.								
Refer to Family Planning Clinic-stop BC pills		X	X	X							
Go to Module A4 (portometer** availability)					X	X		X	X		
Return for intake in 2–4 weeks				X			X			X	
Order intake laboratory tests (initial)***				X			X			X	
Consult with RMD or SMD											X

* It will be assumed that patient was not hypertensive if she did not know.
** The portometer is a portable device for home blood pressure measurement.
*** Refer to Figure 12–12.

Module A4. Portometer Availability

	1	2	3	4
Portometer available?	Y	N	N	N
Type of visit		2nd BP	2nd 6 mo. obs.	12 mo. obs.
Refer for observation (obs.) in	—	6 mo.	12 mo.	12 mo.

Module A5.   Portometry

	1	2	3	4	5
BP Group (portometry) *	0	0	0	1	2
Type of visit	2nd BP	2nd 6 mo. obs.	12 mo. obs.		
Return for observation (obs.) in 12 months	X				
Terminated from clinic		X	X		
Return for intake in 2–4 weeks				X	
Order intake laboratory tests (initial)				X	
Consult with RMD or SMD					X

* Diastolic BP level based on combined means of portometer readings on two successive days.
** Refer to Figure 12–13.

measurements reveal elevated levels, suggesting a labile response rather than sustained hypertension, a portable blood pressure (portometry) procedure is suggested, when available, or an alternative strategy (Modules A4 and A5).

c.   Intake subsystem.   Once the diagnosis of hypertension is confirmed, certain tests are indicated to establish its etiology (Figures 12–13 and 12–14). These tests are ordered in the confirmation modules and reviewed in the intake Modules B1, B2, and B3. The results of this review, together with the determination of cardiovascular complications in Module B4, lead to decisions regarding further observation, institution of treatment protocols, or consultation with the supervising physician of the Hypertension Clinic.

d.   Management subsystem.   As mentioned earlier, the Special Kidney Clinic modules are displayed graphically in a combined flow chart-decision table form. Figure 12–15 is an illustration page from the "MCDS Bypass Loop" module for the "initial treatment" of a patient who has been confirmed to have significant bacteriuria and placed on therapy.[25] On the fifth day of therapy, the patient had been advised to collect a urine specimen and submit it for culture. The nurse receives the result of the culture, searches in the protocol for instruction by looking vertically down the Test/Entry column, and finds the appropriate descriptor, which reads: "fifth day on Rx culture (patient collected)." She then reads horizontally,

1. IVP: intravenous pyelogram.
2. VMA: 24-hour urinary vanillyl mandelic acid.
3. ECG: 12-lead electrocardiogram.
4. Chest x-ray: 14 x 17 film (posterior-anterior projection).
5. Ccr: creatinine clearance adjusted for height and weight.
6. HGB: hemoglobin.
7. WBC: white blood cell count.
8. Urine micro: microscopic analysis of clear voided midstream (CVMS) urine specimen for cellular elements.
9. Urine protein.
10. K: serum potassium.
11. Ca: serum calcium.
12. Uric acid: in serum.
13. Cholesterol: in serum.
14. SGOT: serum glutamic oxaloacetic transaminase.
15. 1° or 2° pc BS: one- or two-hour postprandial blood glucose.

Remarks:
1. Do not order any test listed above which has been done in the past year.
2. Do not order IVP if patient's age is <20 or >50.
3. Do not order IVP, and/or VMA, if patient has had it before, or patient presently on BC pills.
4. Do not order 2° pc BS if patient has already had 1° pc BS in past year.
5. Do not order IVP, or chest x-ray, if patient is presently pregnant.

Figure 12–13. Intake laboratory tests (initial).

1. Ccr.
2. HGB.
3. WBC.
4. K.
5. Ca.
6. Uric acid.
7. SGOT.
8. Urine micro.
9. Urine protein.
10. SGPT = serum glutamic pyruvic transaminase.
11. 2° GTT = two-hour glucose tolerance test.
12. Lipid panel.
13. Urine culture.
14. 24-hour urine protein.

Figure 12–14. Intake laboratory tests (repeat or additional).

Module B1. Intake Lab Test Review I

	1	2	3	4	5	6	7	8	9	10	11	12	13	14	15	16
Intake laboratory tests (initial)*	any	IVP	VMA	ECG	Chest x-ray	Cer	HGB	WBC	urine micro	urine protein	K+	Ca	uric acid	SGOT	Chol	pc BS [2°** (1°)]
Test result available?	N	Y	Y	Y	Y	Y	Y	Y	Y	Y	Y	Y	Y	Y	Y	Y
Test result normal?	—	N	N	N	N	N	N	N	N	N	N	N	N	N	N	N
Find out reason and proceed accordingly.	X															
Go to Module B3 (Intake laboratory test summary)		X	X	X	X											
Order repeat test						X	X	X	X	X	X	X	X			
Order additional test(s)														SGPT	Lipid panel 2°	GTT 2°

* Refer to Figure 12–13.

Module B2. Intake Lab Test Review II

	1	2	3	4
Intake laboratory tests (repeat or additional)*	any	urine microscopic	urine microscopic	any (other than urine micro)
Test result available?	N	Y	Y	Y
Test result normal?	—	N	Y	N
Urine protein normal?	—	—	N	—
Find out reason and proceed accordingly	X			
Order additional test(s)		urine culture	24° urine protein	
Go to Module B3 (intake laboratory test summary)				X

* Refer to Figure 12–14.

Module B3. Intake Lab Test Summary

	1	2	3	4	5	6	7	8
	uric acid	lipid panel	creatinine clearance	chest x-ray	chest x-ray	ECG	ECG	else
Abnormal intake laboratory test								
Cardiac enlargement and/or LVH?†	—	—	—	Y	N	Y	N	—
Use hyperuricemia protocol	X							
Use hyperlipidemia protocol		X						
Go to Module B4 (CV complications)			X	X		X		
Consult with SMD*					X		X	X

* SMD = Clinic Supervising Physician
† LVH = Left ventricular hypertrophy

Module B4. Cardiovascular (CV) Complications

	1	2	3	4
BP Group (Intake)	0	0	1	2
CV complications*	N	Y	—	—
Return for observation in 6 months	X			
Eligible for treatment			X	
Consult with SMD**		X		X

* CV complications—one or more of following:
  1. Cardiac enlargement by x-ray
  2. Left ventricular hypertrophy by ECG (LVH)
  3. Creatinine clearance impairment
  4. Hypertensive retinopathy (KW III or IV)

** SMD = Clinic Supervising Physician

AR #	TEST / ENTRY	VARIABLE	VALUES AND ADVICE RULES
M1.14-M1.16 M1.20-M1.22 M3.5-M3.7 M1.2-M1.4	TREATMENT FORM	RX STARTED	
M3.1	FIFTH DAY ON RX CULTURE (PATIENT COLLECTED)	COL. COUNT	
M3.3	REPEAT CULTURE (CATH.)	COL. COUNT	
	LAST CULTURE $\geq 10^4$	ORGANISM	
	REINFECTION (AR# M3.5 OR M3.6 OR M3.7)	# OF TIMES (IF ANY)	
	ORGANISM	GROUP # **	
	DRUG PROTOCOL	NEXT DRUG IN GROUP	
	NEXT DRUG BY ORGANISM GROUP PROTOCOL	SENSITIVITY	
	NEXT DRUG BY ORGANISM GROUP PROTOCOL	ALLERGY	

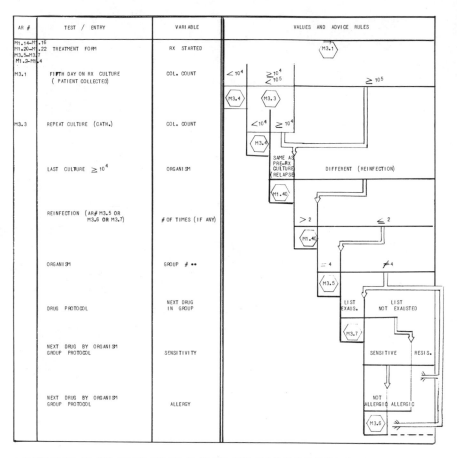

* REFERRAL CRITERIA FOR ENTRY INTO THIS LOOP WILL BE MET WHEN INTAKE AR # M1.14, M1.15, M1.16, M1.20, M1.21, M1.22, M1.2, M1.3, AND M1.4 ARE GENERATED.

** GROUP #	ORGANISM	DRUG TO BE CONSIDERED
1.	E. COLI PROTEUS MIRABILIS	SULFISOXAZOLE, PENICILLIN G (OR AMPICILLIN), FURADANTIN, MACRODANTIN TETRACYCLINE, KEFLEX, NALIDIXIC ACID
2.	AEROBACTER KLEBSIELLA	SULFISOXAZOLE, FURADANTIN, MACRODANTIN, TETRACYCLINE, KEFLEX, NALIDIXIC ACID
3.	ENTEROCOCCUS	AMPICILLIN, KEFLEX
4.	ALL OTHERS	CONSULT M.D.

Figure 12–15

M3. Rules

(MCDS by-pass two weeks treatment loop)

M3.1 _____ (drug name) started _____
(date). Repeat culture (CVMS patient collected) on fifth day on treatment (sensitivity studies if colony count $\geqslant 10^5$).
(CVMS = Clear voided midstream specimen)

M3.2 Colony count between 10^4–10^5. Further confirmation required. Repeat culture (CVMS aide collected). (Sensitivity studies if colony count $\geqslant 10^5$).

M3.3 Colony count between 10^4–10^5. Further confirmation required. Do catheterized repeat culture (sensitivity studies if colony count $\geqslant 10^4$).

M3.4 Colony count suppressed to $< 10^4$ on fifth day of treatment. Repeat culture (CVMS patient collected) one week after treatment completed (sensitivity studies if colony count $\geqslant 10^5$).

M3.5–
M3.7 Reinfection (new organism appearing less than 3 months after treatment, or any organism appearing thereafter).
Start a new two-week course of treatment.
M3.5 Consult MD re choice of drug group (4 org.___ _____).
M3.6 Consult MD re choice of drug (all drugs in group protocol have failed to eradicate bacteriuria).
M3.7 With _____ (drug name).

M3.8 Colony count remains or confirmed to be $< 10^4$ one week after treatment completed. Repeat culture (CVMS patient collected) one month after treatment completed (sensitivity studies if colony count $\geqslant 10^5$).

M3.9 Colony count remains or confirmed to be $< 10^4$ one month after treatment completed. Do urinalysis and culture (CVMS patient collected) three months after completion of treatment (sensitivity studies if colony count $\geqslant 10^5$).

M3.10 Intake 24 hour protein was abnormal. Do repeat 24 hour urine protein at time of next visit.

M3.11 Proteinuria found. Not present on last urinalysis entry. Repeat urinalysis for protein (CVMS aide collected).

M3.12 Proteinuria found on intake has cleared following treatment. Await further instructions.

M3.13 Hematuria found. Not present on last urinalysis entry. Do urine sediment examination (CVMS aide collected).

Figure 12–16. Special Kidney Clinic advice rules.

Module C. Observation Visits

	1	2	3	4	5	6	7	8	9	10	11	12	13	14	15
BP Group (1st Reading*)	0	0	0	0	0	0	0	0	1	1	1	1	1	2	—
BP Group (2nd Reading*)	0	0	0	0	1	1	1	1	0	0	0	0	1	—	2
Type of Visit (Code**)	10	11	12	13	10	11	13	13	10	11	12	13	—	—	—
Return for observation in	12 mo.	12 mo.			6 mo.	6 mo.			6 mo.	6 mo.					
Terminated from clinic			X	X											
Go to Module A4 (Portometer availability)							X	X			X	X			
Return for intake in 2–4 weeks													X		
Order intake lab tests													X		
Consult with SMD														X	X

* During each observation visit two BP readings are obtained 30 minutes apart.

** For ease of tabulation, codes are used for type of visit:
  10 = 1st 6 month observation visit
  11 = 6 months off birth control (BC) pills observation visit
  12 = 2nd 6 month observation visit
  13 = 12 month observation visit

noting in the next column to the right that the variable which will decide future action is the colony count. Moving further to the right, in the column of Values and Advice Rules, she matches the culture report to one of three possible values listed. She then notes, in the hexagonal box below the value, a code number which refers to the advice rule she has to follow; this is listed in the first column under AR# and briefly described in the Test Entry Column—e.g., M3.3 advises "repeat culture (cath.)." The detailed texts of all advice rules are available in numerical order in a user's manual, such as shown in Figure 12–16—e.g., M3.3 reads "Colony count between 10^4–10^5. Further confirmation required. Do catheterized repeat culture (sensitivity studies if colony count $\geqslant 10^4$)." Once the nurse becomes familiar with the protocol, she can bypass referring to the manual with the aid of the abbreviated descriptor in the Test/Entry column.

e. Surveillance/maintenance subsystem. Module C describes the surveillance protocol of patients who have been processed through the Hypertension Clinic identification, confirmation, and/or intake subsystems and have been found to be eligible for periodic observation but not for further diagnostic and/or therapeutic intervention. As the module indicates, data obtained during observation visits may direct patients to termination from the Hypertension Clinic, continued surveillance, or diagnosis and treatment.

F. SUMMARY AND CONCLUSION

This presentation has reviewed current efforts in the development of computerized protocols for the management of ambulatory patients with common chronic conditions. The needs for such protocols and the requirements for their development have been illustrated by examples of implementation in an operational setting. As Schwarz has so succinctly stated: "One may hope that the computer, well-equipped to store large volumes of information, and ingeniously programmed to assist in decision making, will help free the physician to concentrate on the tasks that are uniquely human, such as the application of bedside skills, the management of emotional aspects of disease, and the exercise of good judgment in the nonquantifiable areas of clinical care."[26]

REFERENCES

1. Garfield, S. R. "A New Medical Care Delivery System." *Scientific American* 222(4) (1970):15.
2. Veterans Administration Cooperative Study Group on Antihypertensive Agents: Effects of treatment on morbidity in hypertension.

(a) "Results in Patients with Diastolic Blood Pressures Averaging 115 through 129 mm. Hg." *JAMA* 202(1967):1028.

(b) "Results in Patients with Diastolic Blood Pressures Averaging 95 through 114 mm. Hg." *JAMA* 213(1970):1143.

3. "Report of Inter-Society Commission for Heart Disease Resources. Guidelines for the Detection, Diagnosis and Management of Hypertensive Populations." *Circulation* 44(1971):A-263.

4. Javits, J. K. "Computers and Paraprofessionals." Editorial, *Med. Res. Engineering* 10(1971):4.

5. Collen, F. B.; Madero, B.; Soghikian, K.; and Garfield, S. R. "Kaiser-Permanente Experiment in Ambulatory Care." *Am. J. Nursing* 71(1971):1371.

6. Goldberg, G. A.; Grady, M.; and Budd, M. A. "Applicability of Protocol Management of Chronic Disease to an Aged Population." *Project Report ACP-7 Lincoln Laboratory—Beth Israel Hospital, July, 1970.*

7. Black, W. L., and McCraith, D. L. "Specification of the ACP Driver Software." *Project Report ACP-22. Lincoln Laboratory—Beth Israel Hospital, March, 1971.*

8. Black, W. L.; Pallotta, J. A.; and Stark, W. V. "Protocol for the On-going Care of Diabetes and Its Complications." *Project Report ACP-17, Lincoln Laboratory—Beth Israel Hospital, January, 1971.*

9. Weiner, B. M., and Sherman, H. "Protocol for the On-going Care of Hypertension and Its Complications." *Project Report ACP-18, Lincoln Laboratory—Beth Israel Hospital, January, 1971.*

10. Black, W. L. Protocol Management of Patients with Multiple Chronic Disease: the "Merge" Problem." *Project Report ACP-21, Lincoln Laboratory—Beth Israel Hospital, April, 1971.*

11. Bolinger, R. E.; Price, S.; and Kyner, J. L. "Computerized Management of the Outpatient Diabetic." *JAMA* 216(1971):1779.

12. Coe, J. L. Personal communication.

13. Mi, M. P. Personal communication.

14. Barker, D. J. P., and Bishop, J. M. "Computer Analysis of Symptom Patterns as a Method of Screening Patients at Special Risk of Hypothyroidism." *Brit. J. Prev. Soc. Med.* 24(1970): 193.

15. Fries, J. F. "Time-oriented Patient Records and a Computer Databank." *JAMA* 222(1972):1536.

16. Schulman, J., and Wood, C. "Flow Sheets for Charts of Ambulatory Patients." *JAMA* 217(1971):933.

17. Feinstein, A. R., and Koss, N. "Computer-aided Prognosis. I. Organization and Coding of Data." *Arch. Int. Med.* 127(1971):438.

18. Goertzel, G. "Clinical Decision Support System." *Ann. N.Y. Acad. Sci.* 161 (1969):689.

19. Miller, D. G. "Preventive Medicine by Risk Factor Analysis." *JAMA* 22(1972: 312.

20. Gorry, G. A., and Barnett, G. O. "Sequential Diagnosis by Computer." *JAMA* 205(1968):849.

21. Nash, F. A. "Diagnostic Reasoning and the Logoscope." *Lancet* 2(1960):1442.

22. Ledley, R. S., and Lusted, L. B. "Reasoning Foundations of Medical Diagnosis." *Science* 130 (1959) : 9.

23. Feinstein, A. R. *Clinical Judgment.* Baltimore: Williams and Williams Co., 1967.

24. Weed, L. L. *Medical Records, Medical Education and Patient Care.* Cleveland: The Press of Case Western University, 1969.

25. Resnick, B., and Sadan, B. "The Integrated Multimodular Protocol. A Guide to Extended Paramedical Management of Medical Disorders." (To be published.)

26. Schwartz, W. B. "Medicine and the Computer. The Promise and Problems of Change." *N. Eng. J. Med.* 283 (1970) : 1257.

CHAPTER THIRTEEN

Evaluation of a Hospital Computer System

by Robert H. Richart

A. INTRODUCTION AND BACKGROUND

"The knowledge whereof the world is now possessed, especially that of nature, extendeth not to magnitude and certainty of works" (Bacon, 1920, *Novum Organum*, Trans: T. Fowler, 1889). Bacon posited three and one-half centuries ago that dependence on views of authorities or fanciful guesses constitutes anti-science. His method insisted on dismissing prejudices and preconceptions of all kinds and on the close and methodical observation of phenomena as the path to knowledge and scientific insight.

In subsequent centuries, scientists such as Newton, Leibnitz, Descartes, Gauss, Planck, and Einstein have postulated constructs for systematically transforming "methodologic observation" to increase predictive accuracy about behavior of natural systems. Without question, theoretical formulations have evolved to explain and permit prediction of behavior of a wide range of natural phenomena.

The behavioral sciences have had a shorter history and often pursued knowledge against Bacon's admonition to avoid views of authorities or fanciful guesses. To a large degree, behavioral scientists acted as though physical scientists had created theoretical systems and analytic methods that simply needed adaptation from the physical world to the behavioral domain.

Behavioral scientists have approached the theoretical problems of social systems with great adaptational vigor. Many have assumed that method and concept are interchangeable and have proceeded to use method, however incongruent with observable fact, to rationalize individual and system behaviors. The health system is a prime example of such action.

Medicine has a method called diagnosis. The medical diagnostic method is recognizably a repetitious classification of systems of disease. Repetition of terms is the conceptual operation of the method, as though saying the same thing enough times in enough different ways constitutes phenomenal validity. Practically, the issue of validity of this method is seldom discussed since things cannot validate themselves in science. Method reliability is frequently mentioned—i.e., reproducibility of measures, irrespective of validity. Even on measures of reliability, agreement between medical judges is usually low on nosologic categories applied to supposedly similar problems, and sometimes individual judges have difficulty agreeing with themselves.

In spite of these methodologic inconsistencies, use of diagnosis as a significant parameter in the operation of health care delivery systems is frequent. Behavioral scientists working in the health field have often unquestioningly accepted the views of medical authorities about factors that make a difference in rationalizing models of care delivery systems. As a consequence, few rational models exist late in the twentieth century that offer promise for evolving change that would enhance comprehensive health care opportunities to the public at large. Most of those in existence operate by force of conviction and not by result of substantive evaluation.

Behavioral scientists who have entered the health care arena find themselves, for the most part, statistical testers of unsubstantiated medical opinions about what the health system ought to be and how it ought to work. One might be tempted to claim that behaviorists are in their present condition because they lack power. This is doubtful. The better explanation is that their condition consummates in the lack of conceptual effort and theoretical position that would offer real alternatives to random medical empirics—i.e., clinical intuition.

Postulation of theory and integrated conceptual effort in rationalizing models for understanding operating phenomena in health care settings and evolving systems of prediction—i.e., controlled evolution—is seen as a starting place. Theory and concepts rationally consistent with and measurable in health care settings would constitute a baseline from which to proceed with measurement-theory testing-systems modification-remeasurement sequences—i.e., successive approximation—on which scientific enterprise depends.

Scientific models for systems evaluation which conceptualize the computer must be developed and information technology should be the means only and never the end of the health system. An obvious developmental option is that the health care delivery system and its communication supports can be improved by modification and reorganization of manual structures and procedures. This proposes providing a baseline operation whereby optimality is first achieved in manual system mode. Then, in some future successive approximation, priority options for the introduction of computer-oriented communication applications are determined. Without this approach, the worth of the computer as a communication device in health institutions may never be determined.

Some scientists in the health field have proposed criteria for estimating the worth of technology applied to information systems. Flagle (1970), for example, offered criteria of completeness, timeliness, reliability, operability, and cost as bases for estimating an information system's worth. These are important criteria. Other criteria need to be added, such as relevance to patient care of file content, relevance of modes of care organization for improving availability of relevant information to patient care decision-making, and documentation having measurable utility to patients and staff. In effect, information criteria which more clearly implicate patients and staff as they care for patients must be devised and tested.

Patient care is the core function of the health care system, whether or not computers are involved. As Mumford (1971) warns, "Those who are unable to accept William James' perception that the human person has always been the 'starting point of new effects' and that the most solid-seeming structures and institutions must collapse as soon as the formative ideas that have brought them into existence begin to dissolve, are the real prophets of doom." Keeping sight of patients as the "starting point" and a constant objective of outcome would go far in forestalling potential dissolution of basic concepts.

The conceptual model for health system evaluation which follows adopts people and their health care as the starting point. The evaluation methods devised relate system and process measures and manpower investments to patient care delivery performance. System and human performance is integrated by communication and logistics, both of which are instrumental.

The remainder of this chapter presents sections on: Theory; Methods of Procedure, which contain rationale for study of staff time and effort, process, system utility, and cost analysis; example results from application of methods (excluding cost analysis); and conclusions. Cost analysis was not possible for comparative systems, manual vs. automated, at the time of publication.

B. PRESENTATION OF THEORY

1. Evaluation of any medical data function is principally concerned with the adequacy of a systems integrative function—communication. Criteria of adequacy (meanings) derive from the essential focus of work in the med-

ical system—patients. Evaluation design must be such that measures represent the medical care operations. These operations are series of steps in an activity; activities comprising process and cofunctioning processes constitute the care system. In effect, evaluation data need to reflect operating effects in terms of work steps within a functional activity, effects of activity interaction on process, and effects of process interaction within the system of providing care. All defined effects constitute some translation of impact on patients. Communication is one form of interaction.

Impact on hospital staff of systems effects is a primary focus of systems evaluation at all levels. When any step, activity, or process fails to facilitate patient-directed behavior, unsafe conditions are created for patients in the system. The vulnerable patient, due to his illness, is in danger when conditions in the system distract the staff, and these distractions compete for the staff's time, particularly when staff is drawn into sectors distant from patients. Communication systems as work process facilitators or distractors are a major evaluation concern.

The above statements, it should be understood, are the culmination of more than four years' effort commencing in January 1969. These years of effort started simply. An evaluation was designed to provide baseline data on the manual management of medical data in a hospital in preparation for introduction of a prototype Hospital Computer System (HCS). The initial design called for creation of a comparative data base in a "study" hospital, Kaiser Foundation Hospital-San Francisco (KFH-SF), where the automated system was to be installed and a comparable data base in a "control" hospital, Kaiser Foundation Hospital-Oakland (KFH-Oak), where manual communication procedures would be retained until completion of the research and development program.

Data for the study and control hospitals were to be compared before and after installation of the automated information system in the study hospital. Tests of new data system efficiency, effectiveness, and cost were to be made against the old system for the study hospital. Control tests were to assure that measurable changes were indeed attributable to introduction of a different medical information management system and not to other prevalent external factors. These evaluation efforts were continued annually in 1970, 1971, and 1972.

Theory and design of evaluation have evolved substantially during the medical data system research and development program. Evaluation focus, concepts, and functional objectives have modified and changed. In order for the reader to understand the systems evaluation design, procedures, and results presented later, the underlying theoretical position of the author and the essential aspects of the evolutionary process will be discussed first.

From its inception, the evaluation design was based on tenets from human social ecology (Barker, 1954, 1962), operationism (Bridgman, 1929), and subjective probability (Kyburg and Smokler, 1964) of which Keynes (1921) was an economist proponent.

The "operationism" of Bridgman and "subjectivism" of Keynes aid in specifying substance of methods for operational measures. These theoretical positions, however, provide little basis for specifying the influence, impact, and constraint exerted on human behavior by special purpose, goal-oriented structures (e.g., hospitals, churches, and office buildings).

Theoretical attention to structural considerations and their influence on behavior has been pursued by Barker (1954, 1962), a psychological ecologist, and his colleagues. This theoretical position was recently employed by Williams and Vineberg (1969) in a patient behavior study at the Texas Institute for Rehabilitation and Research. (See Chapter Twenty.)

The conceptual synthesis attempted from these theories, which are diverse in time and discipline, accommodates one major tenet from each of the above positions. The three tenets are:

(1) operationalism—which states that empirical meaning derives from defining behavior in terms of observable operations and expressing empirical significance in terms of "operations" that lend themselves to measurement resulting in accurate prediction.

(2) subjective probability—which assumes that human behavior is predicated on belief and that human belief systems are probabilistic and, thereby, predictive in consequence. A comment is needed to clarify what is meant here by belief. "In the subjectivistic view, probability represents the *degree of belief* that a given person has in a given statement on the basis of given evidence," (Kyburg and Smokler, p.7).

(3) behavior settings—defined as activity areas in which behavioral options are naturally limited by goal-oriented, environmental management functions which are recognized and believed in by participants. This theoretical tenet specifies, in short, that behavior is directed by local, human interpretation of environmental purposes. Structures evolve which support and perpetuate those purposes and degree of individual involvement is determined by "depth of penetration" into those structures. Barker defined "depth of penetration" as knowing what to do, where to do it, and how to do it, and the degree to which the individual contributes to maintenance of the behavioral system.

Given these tenets, the major problem is how to "operationalize belief" as pertains to behavior settings, i.e., how to express belief (imperfect knowledge) in system-related, operational terms (empirical meaning) that result in the prediction of behaviors consonant with expressed systems goals (empirical significance). This synthesis must be consistent with hospital operation and satisfy "rules of patient admissibility" to behavior settings constituting the institutional system of care.

An explanation of the term "patient admissibility" is in order. In this framework, it is through the definition of admissibility that commitment is specified and importance among various commitments is assigned. The empirical test for organization commitment is whether or not resources are assigned. The test of "relative strength" among commitments is determined by differential amounts of resource expenditure to specific commitments, e.g., development and maintenance of communication networks.

The more inclusive our definition of admissible patient "conditions," the more comprehensive our system. The more particular our definition, the more specialized our system. Restricted definitions of admissibility within a common organizational context become functional boundaries for subsystems with focal care goals. For example, an acute general hospital could broadly define admissibility as applying to "any person who, in the judgment of a physician, needs health care requiring application of skills and special equipment that is resident in a special structure wherein human response to such application has to be closely monitored by workers with specific skills." This relatively comprehensive definition admits persons with urgent and nonurgent health conditions, conditions requiring surgical and/or medical intervention, those in need of highly specialized diagnostic procedures, and so on. When special conditions of admissibility, such as degree of urgency, mode of treatment, application of special equipment, etc., are assembled in specific combinations, specification of functional subsystems (specialty units) commences. Within the limits of definition (integrity) of the overall system, functional specification of subsystems provides a ready base for establishing internal operational coherence and evaluation parameters for measures of operation.

Operations are evaluated both in terms of their subsystem efficiency and their contribution to the efficiency of the total hospital care system. Unless schema for evaluation encompass all levels of operational contingency, we will continue to measure highly interactional operations and treat the results as though they derive from system behaviors occurring as separate, autonomous, and functionally unrelated processes. This approach makes knowledge of the integrated whole unattainable.

Having included the element that particular organizations do and should limit their functional commitment through definition of admissibility, additional refinement of the goal of this evaluation model is necessary. Not only is it essential to "operationalize belief" (differentiate investment) commensurate with the particular health service rendering behavior settings, it is imperative that the translation be consistent with express commitments of the total hospital system that have measurable strength. Failure to satisfy this condition is to conduct another study of hospital qua hospital—i.e., define hospital events as though one hospital is like another hospital.

Much, but not all the above, first written in the fall of 1969, has survived subsequent empirical testing. The tenets or concepts discussed have survived, however, with some modification. Before discussing these theoretical modifications, a basic change in perspective will be described.

In the beginning, it was the belief of the author that it was possible to evaluate a medical data system as such. Indeed, there was some conviction that communication constituted a system in itself. This conviction no longer persists. In fact, within the context of a health care delivery system where some aspect of patienthood is invariably the operational criterion, the very title of this chapter is a misnomer. The operation of a Hospital Computer System is not a system, but rather it is a functionally integrative force interfacing care producing subsystems. The notion of communication (information) systems seems an extension of the advent computer, wherein the interacting components of a complex tool come to transcend their own operational usefulness within the context of a human, goal-specific system, taking independent "life" purpose of its own. In that context, operational objectives become those work actions which maintain and continue the computer. Priorities derive not from support and facilitation of staff effort to make sick people well but rather from what resources are necessary to get and to keep an electronic device working. The danger confronting the human goal-oriented system (hospital) is that resources amassed to address human vulnerability may well be dissipated trying to keep a servo-device in operation. It is a prime function of evaluation to address this danger.

As stated earlier, our evaluation theory for a hospital computer system has undergone conceptual modification during the period of study. Initially, resource investments were rationalized by the two factors, Patient Care (PC) and Communication (C). These factors were conceptually arrayed in terms of their interactive presence and absence. Diagram 1 illustrates this construct. This theoretical construction yields four general categories for comparative analysis:

Diagram 1.   Contingent relationships between Patient Care
and Communication.

Patient care

		Yes	No
Communication	Yes	Patient Care– Communication	NonPatient Care– Communication
	No	Patient Care– NonCommunication	NonPatient Care– NonCommunication

(1) Patient Care-Communication (PC-C);
(2) Non-Patient Care-Communication (NPC-C);
(3) Patient Care-Non-Communication (PC-NC);
(4) Non-Patient Care-Non-Communication (NPC-NC).

These conceptual activity sets are detailed in Section E, Methods of Procedure.

Sequential testing of this construct has demonstrated its reproducibility and predictive potential in categorical terms. In accord with the original focus that the principal study target was Patient Care-Communication, test variations (adjusted) from year to year were minimal and nonsignificant for both study and control hospitals.

However, as process variables emerged of empirical operational consequence, certain definitive shortcomings in the model became apparent. First, the process variables that evolved as effectors of performance will be cited. These are:

(1) organization of hospital patient units by medical specialty;
(2) relative patient mobility day-to-day during hospitalization;
(3) day of patient stay in the hospital within specific specialty care units;
(4) transfer of patients within and between patient care units; and
(5) admission, transfer, and discharge per unit over time.

The medical specialty to which a patient is admitted constrains content of care activities and selection of care processes by kind and frequency. Interaction between patient mobility and day-of-stay affects the kinds and volume of work ordered by doctors and executed by nurses within the patient unit. Admission/transfer/discharge all interact to affect work flow, general operating conditions, (e.g., utilization of manpower, etc.), and errors of omission and commission in both patient care and communication.

Review of these effects, which were initially described from the viewpoint of communication, strongly suggested that the more primal concern was disruptions in the care process. Continuance of disruption in caring for actions, at least inferentially, was traceable to absence of criteria for performance monitoring and creation of corrective feedback from day-to-day to those directly implicated in ordering and executing care. Where the model conceptualization did measure the effects of variations in communication, it did not readily indicate the effects a specific change in communication technique could exert at various interfacing stages of care processes —e.g., if a doctor's written order was not carried out, where did the failure occur?

In addition, the model did not specify time lost by nurses from care delivery activities when ancillary services failed to provide support (distraction effect). Whether the failures were due to inadequate communication between subsystems or to inadequate work design was indiscernable. Neither did the model initially differentiate effective expenditure of time in execution of communication and patient care, nor did it estimate differential application of time by various skill levels to varying severity of patient problems. These elements are covered in the revised theory.

The issue is substantially more than whether one operational communication mode is better than others. The substantive systems issue is whether a new or modified communication mode can be integrated into a working system by means of a sequence of operating tests and adjustments, wherein each step yields results confirming that operational targets are closer. The mortar for this evolutionary process is provided by successive approximations of operational consequence which estimate effects of adjustment in target locales and related interactional effects in both proximal and distal subsystems. Achievement of enlarged systems evaluation capability required revision in the theoretical construct and commensurate change in the basic design. Revision was made that permitted comparison with earlier data sets—i.e., Patient Care–Communication, etc.

C. CONCEPTUAL STRUCTURE FOR PERFORMANCE MONITORING

Periodic evaluation of environment specific behavior by workers on behalf of patients is the basis for description of the operating system and the means for monitoring its effects. Monitoring the behavior of workers within specific care delivery settings is the source of essential information about benefits to patients gained from different plans of organization, modes of resource application, and means for achieving integrated care operations. The following pages describe an evaluation structure and a four-criterion model of system analysis for performance in and of a health care delivery system.

It is assumed that the quality of the patient care process is a complex outcome of the application of resources. Consequently, the organization of patient care delivery has to clearly indicate what resources are to be applied to meet identifiable patient need states. Resources and patients' states must be expressed as phenomenally reproducible, consensually valid (believed in) measures. The broad definition of quality, then, is a monitorable system of priorities for assigning resources commensurate with varying patient states wherein changes of predictable "life" consequence are produced. The monitor must evolve in the direction of values and beliefs (operationalized) of participants in the care system. Before defining rules for assigning resources to patients, let us first consider a general concept for functional categorization of essential resource areas and relationships.

Hospital functions as patient-centered events are conceptualized in the present theory as products of two interactive dimensions. The first dimension is *Patient Maintenance*; this factor covers the health care system's general responsibility for life support, and in some ways these supports are like those of a hotel. The services consistent with patienthood are those features which differentiate a health care delivery system from a catering institution. These latter features are aggregated under the second dimension, *Medical Care Delivery*. This term covers the particular resources the hospital care delivery system applies to resolve human problems of health— i.e., illness and infirmity.

Diagram 2.   Contingent relationships between Patient Maintenance and Medical Care Delivery.

		Patient maintenance	
		Yes	No
Medical care delivery	Yes	Operational set— treating e.g., medication	Operational set— testing e.g., lab., x-ray
	No	Operational set— catering e.g., housekeeping, dietary	Operational set— managing* e.g., business, logistics & communication

* Coordination of logistics and communication activities is within the managing operation and integrate other operational sets.

Specific operations are defined in Diagram 2 by corresponding presence and/or absence of these fundamental dimensions. In their contingent relationship, these two principal dimensions effect conceptual sets of operations. This matrix circumscribes operations that constitute a basic structure where planned assignment (actual or simulated) of resources to patient states commences. The model is the basis for priority determination in resource assignment, e.g., specific manpower skills, and the core of a performance monitor.

The operational areas in the priority system are thus:

(*A*) Patient maintenance—medical care delivery = *treating* operations;

(*B*) Nonpatient maintenance—medical care delivery = *testing* operations;

(*C*) Patient maintenance—nonmedical care delivery = *catering* operations;

(*D*) Nonpatient maintenance—nonmedical care delivery = *management* operations.

The priority ordering of resource investment in terms of these operational sets is conditioned by:

(1) relative condition of individual patients;
(2) distribution of conditions of patients aggregated within geographic specialty areas;
(3) coordinated assignment of resources across geographic areas with regard to both resources used for operations within patient care units and those provided for external supports, e.g., laboratory, x-ray, etc.

For example, when individual patients enter as emergencies, the resource priority sequence is often *B* (testing), *A* (treating), *C* (catering), and *D* (managing). Following determination of condition and patient assignment (based on *B*) to appropriate medical specialty area, if hospitalization is the decision, the sequence may change to *A, B, C, D* (where *B* becomes a therapy monitor). As the patient's condition stabilizes medically and recovery commences, the sequence can become *A, C, B, D,* etc.

It should be noted that *A, B,* and *C* components can fail for lack of integration. Substantially, this would indicate breakdown of logistics (transport supply) and/or dissemination of information (communication), which would mean *D* operations become high priority until transitional problems are solved. Failures within *A, B,* and *C* operations constitute internal management problems to be resolved by parochial staffs. Failures between these operations constitute problems of integration between subsystems which are the responsibility of administration.

Given the above structure, the base for analyzing effects of organization and application of resources on behalf of patients is the integral patient care unit. These units are classifiable by measuring interactions in terms of:

(1) structural isolation;
(2) staff complement;
(3) medical specialization;
(4) size (bed capacity).

Structural isolation (integrative limits) is a function of the architecture of the environment. This factor influences patient care delivery, more or less, depending on the adequacy of function of integrative linkages—e.g., transport, communications, etc.

Staff complement refers to staff assignments to a unit. Staff complement influences care delivery by its relative stability (effecting depth of penetration—responsibility commitment). Such factors as turnover, absenteeism, and relative permanence of staff, as well as worker experience and competency, affect responsibility for patient care delivery.

Medical specialization (e.g., orthopedics service) of a unit affects the content and volume of work. This characteristic directly influences magnitude of demand for the supportive services of laboratory, pharmacy, x-ray, etc. Involvement of patient unit staff in care implementation is also affected, competitively, by relative workability of integrative supports—i.e., communication and logistics.

Unit size is a determinant which exerts influence across operational boundaries. For example, one floor is assigned for admission of patients within a given medical specialty. The number of beds on that floor is sometimes insufficient to maintain the number of patients admitted. To overcome the insufficiency of beds, surplus admissions are regularly made to beds assigned to a different medical specialty on another floor (in another area) ; conditions for resource organization and application are thus changed. If operational adjustment is not made to account for the in-fact expansion in unit size (and a different definition of admissibility), the expansion part of the unit is more isolated and probably staff complement stability is jeopardized. In effect, the ability to safely care for patients is jeopardized.

D. EFFECTIVENESS MONITORING

The four general factors cited above are viewed as minimum requirements for selectively monitoring care delivery performance. Each factor exerts its influence on the four basic operations delineated by Patient Maintenance and Medical Care Delivery. A complete monitoring plan must include all essential relationships. However, this chapter focuses on monitoring unit staff complement as a starting point in controlling factors effecting levels of staff performance.

Staff complement data is of three kinds, these are:

(1) data related to direct patient care administration,
    Treating (operation A),
    Catering (operation C);
(2) data related to interfacing with other subsystems,
    Testing (operation B),
    Managing (operation D);
(3) data related to unit staff complement characteristics,
    (a) complement turnover and absenteeism,
    (b) proportion of temporary personnel in the complement,
    (c) distribution of skills and experience in the complement.

The monitoring system under discussion was commenced for purposes of evaluating the effects of converting from manual to automated communication modes on nursing manpower. The data base was used to test the effects of reorganizing nursing activity within patient care units at Kaiser Foundation Hospital–Oakland (the control facility) on nursing time available for direct patient care—i.e., Patient Care-Non-Communication and time shifts between communication categories. Substantially, the modification shifted nursing allocation from a team plan to a plan of Total Patient Care. Total Patient Care makes the care of aggregates of sick patients the prime and total responsibility of professional nurses. It was out of this organizational experiment in nursing, data system analyses, and ecological theory that the performance monitor evolved.

E. PERFORMANCE CRITERIA

This section is devoted to exposition of analytic performance criteria. The four criteria are:

I   Time availability;
II   Time effectiveness;
III Skilled time expended by differential patient need;
IV   Reduction in occurrence of adverse care landmarks.

1.   Performance Criterion I—Time Availability

Patient care units must operate to apply staff resources (time and effort) in Patient care-Non-Communication at some measurably optimum level. The optimum level is determined by examining the ability of different organization modes (systems of applying resources) to produce manpower increases in the Patient Care-Non-Communication monitor category. Optimality of mode is constrained by its relative costs. (The relationship between mode of delivery and the medical data system is an explicit concern.)

To exemplify, during transition in reorganization of nursing manpower (KFH-Oak) 1969–1971, there was sharp reduction in workers. This *did not* effect reduction in actual time spent by nurses administering care to individual patients. In fact, increases in unit nursing time per patient were experienced, as shown in Table 1.

Although there was a cumulative manpower decrease of 27.5% in nursing hours worked per patient per day, actual nursing time spent per patient increased 29.3%. The change from a team nursing mode to assigning blocks of patients to nurses increased nursing time with/for patients while decreas-

Table 1. Nursing Time Hours and Proportions per Patient per Day 1969–1971, Medicine Ward, KFH-Oak.

	Apr. '71	Apr. '70	Apr. '69
Nursing Hrs/Patient/Day	4.20	5.00	5.80
Proportion Patient Care- Non-Communication (PC-NC) (Combined RN & LVN)	0.50	0.36	0.28
Proportional decrease over base 1969	0.28	0.14	—
Time Spent (hrs.)/patient day (PC-NC)	2.10	1.80	1.62
Proportional increase (PC-NC) over base 1969	0.29	0.11	—

ing manhours worked. In terms of Criterion I, Total Patient Care is the optimum of the two resource application modes in making more nursing time available for direct patient care. The sample results also demonstrate that utilization of time differs as design structures support prime work.

2.   Performance Criterion II—Time Effectiveness

Once organizational modes are empirically selected on the basis of prime time availability, a performance criterion of work time effectiveness can be approached. Establishment of this criterion was started with the four major Patient Care and Communication categories. Here it is necessary to recapitulate the methodologic sequence in organizing data for analysis of nursing time and effort, following which work effectiveness determination will be outlined.

Time and effort of specific worker categories (Head Nurse, Staff Nurse, etc.) within patient care units such as Intensive Care, Medicine, Surgery, etc., is organized by making event frequency and time assignments (derived from work sampling observations) into each of the four major activity categories. This assignment routine distributes location, specific staff time, and effort data for each nursing work group. The first order analytical question is, "What proportion of time (by worker group) is spent in Patient Care-Non-Communication?" Patient Care-Non-Communication (PC-NC) is designated as the analytic target cell for evaluating relative function level of each patient care unit and of the hospital as a whole. In effect, PC-NC behavior represents execution of primary work by personnel group with responsibility for delivery and maintenance of patient care.

The target cell for the Hospital Computer System (HCS) is time spent in Patient Care-Communication (PC-C) within patient care units. HCS comparisons to manual communication will center mostly on the patterns of time spent, particularly PC-C and PC-NC relationships. This is to say, HCS would be more effective if its introduction does not drain time from PC-NC activities in the old and from A (treating) and B (testing) operations in the new theory. The more desirable effect on primary patient care personnel, if a time drain does occur, would be from Non-Patient Care-Communication (NPC-C) and Non-Patient Care-Non-Communication (NPC-NC) activities to PC-C or from C (catering) and D (management) to A (treating) and B (testing) operations.

After the determination of proportions of time spent within the four major Patient Care and Communication categories, a second-level determination is performed. The second-level analysis isolates effective time expenditures for Patient Care and Communication for each nursing category within patient care units.

Proportion of effective communication time (P_{Ect}) is operationally defined as the proportion of communication out of total communication time (P_{ct}) expended minus the proportion of time spent conversing (P_{convt}) with other patient care unit staff members. Encapsulated staff conversation does not: (1) produce reusable documents; (2) produce feedback opportunities; nor (3) link patient units with other operating subsystems. Time spent in conversation is partialled out of total communication time, leaving communication work time spent for relevant functional activity sets. The analytic expression of this relationship is:

$$P_{Ect} = P_{ct} - (P_{convt})\big/(P_{ct})$$

This expression applies to both Patient Care and Non-Patient Care-Communication.

Proportion of effective patient care time $(P_{Epc/nct})$ is operationally defined as the proportion of patient care of total PC/NC time expended $(P_{Pe/nct})$ minus the proportion of time spent walking during delivery of care (P_{Pcwt}). Walking by staff members, although a necessary activity, is integrative rather than work productive. Organization of primary work should be such as to minimize the time drain of walking to care for patients. The relationship of walking to delivery patient care is expressed in the formulation:

$$P_{Epc/nct} = P_{Pc/nct} - (P_{Pcwt})\big/(P_{Pc/nct})$$

This expression applies to Patient Care-Non-Communication only.

Proportion of effective time administering Non-Patient Care-Non-Communication activities $(P_{Enp/nct})$ is operationally expressed as the proportion of Non-Patient Care-Non-Communication time expenditure $(P_{Np/nct})$ minus associated walking time $(P_{Npc/wt})$ plus time in *No Action* (P_{Nat}). These relationships are expressed by:

$$P_{Enp/nct} = P_{Np/nct} - (P_{Npc/wt} + P_{Nat})\big/(P_{Np/nct}).$$

Walking is integrative in that it links work across distance. No action is integrative in that time to think and rest is necessary.

The total proportion of effective time spent (P_{Et}) by a worker in a patient care unit is the summation of the above formulations. The expression for P_{Et} (proportion effective time) of a worker is:

$$P_{Et} = [P_{Pc/ct} - (P_{Pc/convt})/(P_{Pc/ct})] + [P_{Npc/ct} - (P_{Npc/convt})/(P_{Npc/ct})]$$
$$+ [P_{Pc/nct} - (P_{pcwt}) (P_{Pc/nct})] + [P_{Npc/nct}$$
$$- (P_{Npcwt} + P_{Nat})/(P_{Npc/nct})]$$

The above expressions are used in generating the effectiveness coefficients presented in Results, Section 4. These comparisons are example applications of Performance Criterion II (Time Effectiveness).

3. Performance Criterion III—Skilled Time Expended for Differential Patient Need

As stated previously, the organization of patient care delivery has to indicate clearly what resources are to be applied to meet which identifiable patient needs. Once nurse time availability and effectiveness are determined which circumscribe nursing resources, application of kinds of nursing effort is defined in terms of relative "skill" levels of nursing groups involved in delivery of care. The skill criterion used presently is based on job title— e.g., Registered Nurse (RN), Licensed Vocational Nurse (LVN), Aide/ Orderly, and Ward Clerk. Admittedly, this credential-based criterion is a gross discriminator of skill. However, it is the one, at the moment, that is relatively reproducible within and between hospitals.

The issue of reproducibility extends to differential classification of patient states as well. Here again, at least in part, it is necessary to adopt a criterion that is believed in and understood by staffs within extant care delivery systems. The estimating criterion of variable patient state having most general consensual validity between patient care professionals and institutions studied is *Relative Patient Mobility*. Variations in Relative Patient Mobility are phenomenally defined as: (1) Ambulatory; (2) Semi-ambulatory (with bathroom privileges only); and (3) Bedfast. These classifications are generally used with similar meaning across medical specialties and between study hospitals. A casual survey suggests that these terms have broad-based belief among doctors and nurses.

Worker skill and patient state are linked in the monitor by means of a time-based, system process variable. This variable is *Day of Patient Stay* in the hospital. In effect, staff response to patient state varies as some function of when in the patient's hospitalization (Day of Stay) that response is required. This is reasonable and expected since physiologic crisis, stabilization, and recovery follow a time continuum which Day of Stay represents.

The preceding is a generalization of staff response to patient state that gains specificity through such modifiers as medical specialization, relative staff certainty about cause of patient infirmity, patient's monitored physiological reaction to therapy, and the like. Simply stated, staff response and application of resources occur proportionally to progressive changes in patient state (from Bedfast to Ambulatory) in regularly diminishing behavioral amounts (reduced allocation of resources) as Day of Stay increases. Controlling for specialization, relative staff certainty, and patient reaction to treatment makes possible accurate prediction of the kind and number of patient care events, event timing and probable duration of hospitalization.

Performance Criterion III, skilled time expended for differential patient need, is that time available for effective work as distributed among classes of workers, whereby the "most" skilled spend the highest proportion of their time with the least mobile patients, particularly regarding uncertain patient states requiring close surveillance. Further, the relationship between high skill and low patient mobility is maintained until relative staff certainty occurs about physiological stability through results from repeated testing operations. When this occurs, principal responsibility for care passes to work groups with intermediate care skills and/or care support skills. These skill requirements are designated when communication occurs that patients are reclassified Semi-Ambulatory and Ambulatory. Commensurate with such reclassification are reductions in patient care messages from doctors in the form of orders. Although the number of care messages from doctors reduces, the number of orders requiring execution by nurses does not necessarily diminish since review of continuing orders and their discontinuance is sporadic at best. This problem needs solution for patient safety and comfort and to conserve manpower.

4.   Performance Criterion IV—Adverse Effects of Care

Once nursing staff *time availability, time effectiveness*, and relevant skills are dedicated to patients' states, operations are set for performance monitoring. Monitoring criteria are comprised of adverse care effects (critical incidents). For example, fecal impactions, bladder infections, intravenous solutions running dry, unordered drugs administered or ordered drugs not administered, doctors' orders not carried out, laboratory tests not reported out, etc. are such adverse patient care effects. The set of effects pertinent to patient groups with special needs has to be empirically determined. The relative sets fitting special patient groups will constitute an operational expression of quality of outcome of performance in delivering patient care.

Tests of this criterion have not as yet begun. The problem is that patient care outcomes, both positive and negative, are not uniformly recorded as part of care documentation. Rarely if ever do recordings link to care steps, activities, or processes in a systems related way—i.e., providing feedback related to the need for change in essential care operations.

It was decided that mastery of this problem and eventual test of the criterion depend on design of a patient care oriented master file (patient chart). This data system would require documentation of work and anomalies of care as the work is occurring. Who is involved in what, where, when and consequences are some of the elements of such documentation.

Once data about adverse effects is being produced in real-time by staff in the care system linking steps, activities, and processes, evaluation monitoring against criteria and feedback procedures may commence. These procedures provide necessary information for making timely adjustment in care to prevent resultant adverse effects.

Such a system for documentation and work monitoring has been designed. This system is presently undergoing tests in the field. Results from this systems research and development effort will be reported in the future.

5. System Utility

As stated earlier, relevant measures of operation and their relative utility must be predicated on beliefs (values) held by those persons responsible for the work of the system. Measuring staff beliefs about operations they perform and interact with provides the human element whereby the four factors cited above can be interpreted in the sense of identifying specific areas and processes where staff views will have to be altered if improvement in existing operations is to be made or new operations (HES) introduced. In effect, operation specific beliefs must be known if estimates of relative system utility (acceptance) are to be made.

Generally, the question is, "What do users perceive as important areas of information system function and what problems do they experience as they employ that system in their work?" Particularly related to a baseline hospital computer system evaluation, "What information problems confront doctors and nurses as they deliver patient care using manual methods of information management that might be solved, at least in part, through introduction of automated methods?" Further, in creating a data base for evaluating comparative staff reaction to different modes of managing information, "Is it possible to identify variable reactions had by different staff groups working within the larger health care system?" It was the immediate purpose of the System Utility Study to answer these questions.

In addition, it was the aim of the evaluation program to develop means for assessing readiness of hospital staff to accommodate programmatic change. The use of task-oriented discussion group techniques were employed as an initial step in this development. Subsequent sections (Methods and Results) describe and explore this attempt.

E. METHODS OF PROCEDURE

The immediate purpose in evaluation in preparing for the introduction of a Hospital Computer System (HCS) is to gauge the various effects on patient care operations of the manual system to be replaced (baseline). The specific goal is to measure the quality and quantity of information in its immediate form and design changes founded on baseline measures that facilitate the communication of medical data by increasing message legibility, increasing speed of message dissemination, improving control over information flow, increasing capability for handling quantities of information, reducing information loss, reducing duplication and increasing information accuracy and relevance, and decreasing communication costs.

HCS baseline studies were made to establish effects of a manual information system on medical personnel working in various hospital patient care areas. Areas of prime interest were units housing hospitalized patients and subsidiary areas where medical support functions—e.g., laboratory, x-ray, etc.—were carried out.

There are additional intermediate and long-term goals as well as immediate goals. These goals, broadly stated, are: improve effectiveness of health care delivery, improve utilization of resources, and improve the information base for planning health services and for improving education and training programs.

Facilitation of intermediate and long-range goals depends largely on an ability to identify the cursors of change and adequately explain how these determinants (e.g., utilization behavior) fit together to effect service behavior. Behavior refers to performance of a total hospital operating plan, performance of a hospital subsystem, performance of functional units within subsystems, and the performance of workers within units. Furthermore, the effects of interactions of people and processes between units and levels of activity, as well as those within functional subsystems, constitute a major emphasis of an effort to evolve a schema for predicting future resource requirements in delivering care.

Essentially the ability to forecast probable workload and its commensurate resources depends on acquisition of data which accurately represents the verity of operations. *Workload must be carefully defined in terms of effective, economic institutional response to relevant differences in human health needs. Failure to pursue creation of predictively adequate operating definitions threatens the very existence of any voluntary system for delivering health care.*

Terms of relationships needing specification are:

(1) identification of patient groups of measurably differing need;

(2) patient objectives that can be realistically achieved through short-range care programs (the duration of short range depends on definition of patient group);

(3) operational requirements (application of resources) for achieving care objectives on behalf of each patient group identified.

Methods for attaining greater specification of these relationships must, in all instances, be empirically meaningful and significant. In this context, it is the prime role of evaluation (operational monitoring) to develop data that quantifies workload in terms of *functional categories* of *need-related response*. This baseline is seen as an essential first step in the evaluation of operational prescriptions which best represent care requirements of different patient groups and for estimating the worth of communication techniques and instruments.

In the face of the human properties influencing the demand for and utilization of health services, we are forced to employ conceptualizations, methods, and measures which, at least, imply the growing impact of subjective, human concerns. The strategy is to develop an evaluation model of predictive consequence without succumbing to the temptation of measuring events for tradition's sake—that is, taking measures simply because others have reported doing so. It is crucial that relative purpose be operationally defined and measures established consistent with definition.

Evaluation methods were designed, mainly, to measure performance in three general areas. The areas are: *staff time and effort* within patient units, *process* which relates units to support functions, and the internal *operation of support functions.*

Methods were constructed to yield data at four levels: (1) systems; (2) work groups; (3) patients; and (4) interactions. As described in Section B of this chapter, conceptual criteria were based in Patient Care and Communication activity. Contingent interaction between these criteria produce four analytic categories:

(1) Patient Care-Communication (HCS study target);

(2) Non-Patient Care-Communication;

(3) Patient Care-Non-Communication (Hospital operation target);

(4) Non-Patient Care-Non-Communication.

1. Time and Effort

Patient care and communication categories were empirically defined to cover the activities of doctors and nursing personnel working within hospital care units. These definitions specified who did what, for whom, where, when, how, and how long it took. These basic descriptions of behavior, bounded in time and space, were observable to anyone who might look. Principally units of behavior were specified as workers varied their Patient Care and Communication activities in relationship to persons, objects, and places within the patient care unit. (See Figure 13-1.)

Time and Effort data were gathered by assigning specific observers to designated units where they observed the work actions of specific personnel groups over an exact segment of time. Staff doctors, residents, interns, nursing supervisors, head and staff nurses, licensed vocational nurses, aides/orderlies, and ward clerks were followed within their work areas. Observers followed one staff member per time segment so long as the worker remained within the work area. No effort was made to detail staff activity taking place outside the patient area. Observations were made daily over five weekdays (Monday through Friday) from 8:00 AM until 9:00 PM.

These observations were recorded on a multi-purpose form called the "Observers Recording-Coding-and-Key Punching Work Sheet." The data items and related codes were designed to allow observers to code their observations directly without necessarily first recording the raw data itself. Displayed for observers on the reverse side of each coding sheet is a shortened form of observation content items and codes. When forms are in a three-ring binder, the "offside" of the coding sheets showing items and codes is visible for ready reference during observation (See Figure 13-2).

When an observed action concerned patient care, the observer gathered data about the patient receiving the care. Only demographic and specific condition-connected items regarding the patient were recorded. The data items included: location of observation code, time segment code, worker code, major activity code, major activity action code, subordinate activity code, primary diagnosis class at time of admission and subsequent changes therein, speed of action, age code, sex code, type admission code, condition at admission code, relative patient mobility code, discharge to code, day of surgery/day of discharge code, other specialty service code, and survey code.

A second form is used on which to record variable data about patients. Patient data—e.g., location, day of stay, relative mobility, etc.—are updated each observation day. When coded in the Time and Effort form, variable patient data corresponds to the day of observation. (See Figure 13-3.)

MILITARY TIME	SPECIFIC SITE	WORKER	CARE CODE	SPEED OF ACTN	MAJOR ACTIVITY	SUB ACTIVITY	AGE	SEX	PATIENT'S MEDICAL RECORD NUMBER	DAY OF STAY	REL MOB	SEQUENCE NUMBER
8 9 10 11	17 18	20 21	24	28	31 32	34 35	38 39	42	45 46 47 48 49 50 51	55 56 57	60	65 66
8 9 10 11	17 18	20 21	24	28	31 32	34 35	38 39	42	45 46 47 48 49 50 51	55 56 57	60	65 66
8 9 10 11	17 18	20 21	24	28	31 32	34 35	38 39	42	45 46 47 48 49 50 51	55 56 57	60	65 66
8 9 10 11	17 18	20 21	24	28	31 32	34 35	38 39	42	45 46 47 48 49 50 51	55 56 57	60	65 66
8 9 10 11	17 18	20 21	24	28	31 32	34 35	38 39	42	45 46 47 48 49 50 51	55 56 57	60	65 66

OBSERVER'S WORKSHEET   H4A-3-72 (REVISED)

Figure 13–1. Observer's work sheet and coding displays.

13-14 LOCATION OF OBSERVATION CODE
(SEE CODING MANUAL FOR SPECIAL INSTRUCTIONS)

```
01-        04-        07-        10-        13-        16-
02-        05-        08-        11-        14-        17-
03-        06-        09-        12-        15-        18-
```

20-21 WORKER CODE

```
01- STAFF DR.
02- RESIDENT
03- INTERN
04- OTHER DR.
08- UNIT MGR
09- RN-SUPER
10- RN HEAD
11- RN STAFF
12- RN OTHER (REGISTRY)
14- LVN
16- AIDE
17- WARD CLERK
18-
19-
20-
```

24 MAJOR ACTIVITY
ACTION CODE
41

```
1- PATIENT CARE
2- NON-PATIENT CARE
```

28 SPEED OF ACTION
CODE

```
01- NURSING STATION
02- CORRIDOR
03- WD CLK'S DESK
04- DR'S OFFICE
05- PNT'S ROOM
06- WORK AREA (PNT'S)
07- MEDICATION CABINET/CHART
```

17-18 SPECIFIC SITE OF OBSERVATION

```
08- UTILITY AREAS (DIET KIT, LIN CLOSET)
09- PROCEDURE ROOM (EXAM ROOM)
10- PEDI PLAYROOM
11- CRT-STATION
12- UNIT MAGR OFFICE
13- TYPEWRITER TM STA.
14-
15-
```

34-35 SUBORDINATE ACTIVITY OBSERVED CODE (MAJOR ACTIVITY CODES 01,02,03,07,09,13,14,15)
READING FROM/WRITING IN OR ON/SEARCHING FOR/TYPW, TERM, CRT-INPUT/CRT-READ/CRT-PRINTOUT

```
66- PATIENT'S CHART
67- DOCTOR'S ORDERS
68- DOCTOR'S PROGRESS NOTES
69- NURSES NOTES
70- T P R RECORDS
71- MEDICATION RECORD
72- RAND FILE
73- LABORATORY REQUEST
74- X-RAY REQUEST
75- OTHER EXAM REQUEST
     (EKG/EEG/ETC.)
76- DIET REQUEST
77- OTHER REPORTS/DOCUMENTS
78- SUPPLY REQUISITION
79- INPATIENT PRESCRIPTIONS
80- LABORATORY REPORTS
81- X-RAY REPORTS
82- OTHER EXAMINATION REPORTS
     (EKG/EEG/ETC.)
83- WARD NARCOTIC RECORDS
84- OTHER THING
85- ASSIGNMENT SHEET
86- CRT-PRINTOUT
87- MESSAGES
88- ADMISSIONS
89- TRANSFERS
90- DISCHARGES
91- DX
92- SIGNS & SYMPTOMS
93- PT. DIRECTORY
94- FLOOR CENSUS
95-
96-
97-
98-
99-
00- UNKNOWN
```

ADMINISTERING (MAJOR ACTIVITY CODES 8 & 10)

```
01- PHYSICAL EXAMINATION
02- MEDICAL HISTORY
03- CHANGING DRESSING
04- COLLECTING SPECIMEN
05- START/CHANGE/CHECK I.V.
06- CATHETERIZING
07- PREPARING MEDICATIONS
08- CLEAN-UP
09- GIVING MEDICATIONS
10- GIVING GEN NURSING CARE
11- TAKING TPRS/VITAL SIGNS
12- SERVING/CLEARING TRAYS
13- COUNTING NARCOTICS
14- PUTTING AWAY SUPPLIES
15- PUTTING REPORTS IN CHART
16- EKG EXAMINATION
17- PHYSIO RX (BEDSIDE)
18- COLLECTING DIET REQUESTS
19- PATIENT
20- OTHER ACTIVITY
21- TRANSFUSE BLOOD & PLASMA
22- BED BATHS
23- FEEDING PATIENTS
24- PROCEDURE SET-UP (BEDSIDE)
25- ADMINISTERING ADMISSION
26- ADMINISTERING DISCHARGE
27- PATIENT TRANSPORT
28- INV/STOCK MAINTENANCE
29- CHART HANDLING
30- MD EXAM/TREATMENT
31- PT. TRANS IN SAME WD.
32- PT. TRANS TO DIFF WD.
33- PT. TRANS TO DIFF SER.
34- ADJUST. PT. APPL.
35-
36-
37-
38-
39-
40-
41-
42-
43-
44-
45-
```

38-39 AGE CODE

IF ACTION BEING OBSERVED WAS NOT CODED AS
"PATIENT CARE" IN CC 24, THEN MARK "00" IN
CC 38-39 "AGE CODE" AND STOP THIS EVENT.
HOWEVER, IF CC 24 WAS CODED TO INDICATE
"PATIENT CARE" — THEN CONTINUE CODING ALL
ITEMS AS INDICATED.

RECORD PATIENT'S AGE AS THAT OF HIS NEXT
BIRTHDAY. (IF AN INFANT IS IN THE NURSERY,
CODE THE AGE "01". WHEN INFANT IS BETWEEN
ONE AND TWO, HIS AGE IS CODED "02", ETC.)

1- STAT
2- ROUTINE

42 SEX	55-56-57 DAY OF STAY
1- MALE	001- DAY OF ADMISSION
2- FEMALE	002- NNN-EACH SUB DAY OF STAY

60 RELATIVE MOBILITY
1- AMBULATORY
2- LIMITED AMBULATORY
3- COMPLETE BED REST

65-66 SEQUENCE NO.
CODE SEQUENCE OF EVENT W/ IN EACH TIME SEGMENT

00- UNKNOWN
SEARCHING FOR/TELEPHONING/CONVERSING/WALKING
(MAJOR ACTIVITY CODES 3, 4, 5, & 6)

31-32 MAJOR ACTIVITY CODE

01- READING FROM
02- WRITING IN/OR
03- SEARCHING FOR
04- TELEPHONING
05- CONVERSING
06- WALKING
07- TYPEWRITER TM INQ.
08- COMM'L. PT'S.
09- TYPEWRITER TM PRTOUT
10- ADMINISTERING
11-
12- NO ACTION
13- CRT-INPUT
14- CRT-READ
15- CRT-PRINTOUT
16-
17-
18-

01- STAFF DOCTOR
02- RESIDENT
03- INTERN
04- OTHER M.D
05- STUDENT NURSE
06- NURSE INSTRUCTOR
07- UNIT MANAGER
08- RN- SUPERVISOR
09- RN- HEAD
10- RN- STAFF
11- RN- OTHER (REGISTRY)
12- LVN
13- AIDE
14- WARD CLERK
15- OTHER PERSON
16- OTHER PLACE

17- PATIENT
18- PATIENT'S ROOM
19- VISITOR
20- NURSING STATION
21- MED. CAB/CART.
22- NARCOMIC LOCKER
23- DIET KITCHEN
24- LINEN CLOSET
25- WARD CLERK'S DESK
26- DOCTOR'S OFFICE
27- TREATMENT ROOM
28- DUMBWAITER
29- WORK AREA-PNT CHT/MED
30- UTILITY AREA-LOUNGE TOILET, ETC.
31- ADMISSION OFFICE
32- BLOOD BANK

33- BUSINESS OFFICE
34- CLINIC (ANY)
35- DELIVERY/LABOR ROOM
36- DIETARY DEPARTMENT
37- "DOCTOR BLUE"
38- EKG DEPARTMENT
39- EMERGENCY ROOM
40- REPORTING
41- LAB TECH-ON WARD
42- LABORATORY
43- PNEUMATIC TUBE
44- MEDICAL RECORDS
45- NURSERY
46- NURSING OFFICE
47- O.R. TECH-ON-WARD
48- OPERATING ROOM
49- PBX

50- PHARMACY
51- RECOVERY ROOM
52- SUPPLY CLK-ON-WARD
53- SUPPLY ROOM
54- X-RAY TECH-ON-WARD
55- X-RAY DEPARTMENT
56- OTHER
57- CRT-STATION
58- CONS. N.PER.CHT.AUTO.
59- CONS. MD CHART AUTO.
60- CONS. OTHER CHT.AUTO.
61- CONS. N.PER.CHT. MAN.
62- CONS. MD CHART MAN.
63- CONS. OTHER CHT MAN.
64- REGISTRATION (CLERK)
65- TYPEWRITER TM STATION
00- UNKNOWN

● Collen - Hospital

Figure 13-2. Backside of Form (Figure 13-1) showing items and codes.

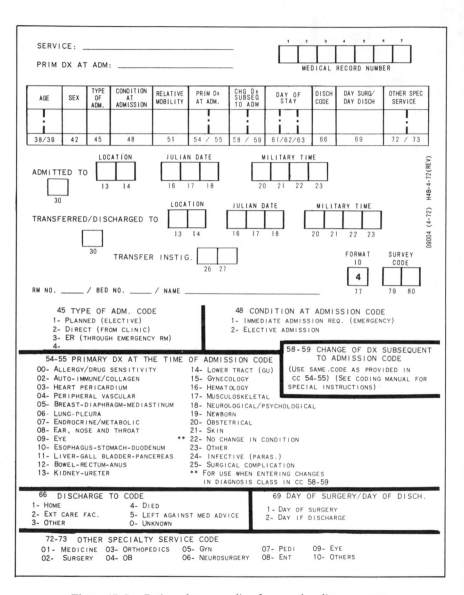

Figure 13–3. Patient data recording form and coding structure.

2. Process

Evaluation methods relate operational events linking care units to medical support functions—e.g., clinical laboratory, pharmacy, etc. These methods delineate information-process sequences that commence in a nursing unit with a doctor's order. The order is then acted upon by nursing personnel, and a message is sent to a supporting service. The service response to the message is work which results in feedback of information and/or material —e.g., laboratory result, provision of supplies, drugs from the pharmacy, etc.—to the initiating care unit. Patient Process Information is a general title ascribed to certain information contained within an overall care process. This process can be defined as a sequence of operations that starts with the admission of a patient and extends through time until the patient is discharged. Admission and discharge are time boundaries that contain various work mixes and communication loops varying in phase and duration.

These admission/discharge bounded work process sequences were detailed in terms of persons and places at each process step, time required, work and information errors observed by kinds of work ordered. The source of Process Data was the patient chart. Care events were time sequenced in two ways on data sheets according to their chronological occurrence during patients' hospitalization. The first time sequence (across rows on the form) detail each unit process loop starting with a doctor's order and ending with information feedback (See Process Data Form—work sheet). These short time-loops (hours or a few days duration) are single acts to be done in immediate time.

The second time sequence is the listing of all recorded care events as they occurred during hospitalization. Reading down the left margin of the form reveals work in sequence covering the duration of the patient's stay.

The data collected from individual patient charts is amplified from records maintained in the service areas supporting care units. These records are used to verify the completeness of patient charts. The verification step helps to insure that all patient care services ordered, written and verbal, are accounted for. Data sources were: Clinical Laboratory, Admission Office, Emergency Room, Operating Room, Pharmacy, and X-ray Department.

Within patient care processes, it is possible to identify three major types of events which are themselves connected together by elapsed time that occurs between the process events. Elapsed time is the integrative event. The three process events with elapsed time when taken together constitute our *Patient Process Information.*

The first process event is the natural outcome of the doctor's order and itself includes all subevents that are characterized by the passage of time. This event is a complete time-loop. The time-loop starts with a doctor writing an order in a patient's chart and ends when a result is attained from a procedure. Each major loop is comprised of subloops which are identified by a succession of steps taken by various staff groups working in different places. For example, a nurse transcribes the order to a card file, writes a laboratory requisition, and sends it to the laboratory. These subevents are time bounded. The subloop is completed when passed on to others for the next step (subloop). Subloops are tied together by various kinds of transport and message transmitting mechanics.

The second event of interest involves intermediate transport of patients for service purposes—for example, the arrival of a patient in the operating room for surgery, his entry into the postoperative recovery room after surgery, and his arrival back in his room from the recovery room. Events of this type are serial in nature and result from a doctor's order. This second distinction in patient care process is necessary to account for those instances when communiques cause patients to move as well as causing information to flow.

The third event is concerned with the termination of a loop. For our purposes, termination depends on results being available to a doctor in the patient's chart for decision-making or the actual administration of a treatment to a patient. Completed laboratory and x-ray reports and treatment administration, when directly traceable to a specific doctor's order, are posted to the chart, whereby linkage events are documented or implied; thus the terminates are operationally defined.

The forms (Figures 13-4 and 13-5) used to record Patient Process Information consist of a face sheet that provides space for the following information: date, name of abstractor, patient medical record number, patient category (includes age, sex, patient condition on admission, point of entry), admitting date, admitting diagnosis, service admitted to, attending physician's specialty, discharge date, discharge diagnosis, and service from which discharged.

Continuation sheets provide space for the following details: doctor's orders, day of stay, accession number (orders numbered serially), other events, stat or routine, time order written, time paper work done, time of first work, time in service, time completed, and time results are available.

A third area of evaluation relates directly to subloop processes within the operational domain of support services. The clinical laboratory in the Kaiser Foundation Hospital in San Francisco (KFH-SF) will be used to illustrate the evaluation procedures followed. This facility is of interest in that it developed its internal communication network through a series of stages—i.e., from paper and pencil only, then to unit record equipment, followed by a computer log-in and result reporting system. This communi-

MDS PROCESS DATA FORM
COVER SHEET

DATE_____ ABSTRACTOR_____

(1-7) MEDICAL RECORD NUMBER [ ][ ][ ][ ][ ][ ][ ]

(80) STUDY # [ ]

} TO BE USED ON ALL CARDS
IN THIS SET

ADMISSION DATA

(8-9) POINT OF ENTRY [ ][ ]   (10-11) DAY OF STAY [O][/]   (12-13) ACCESSION # [ ][ ]

(26-29) SERVICE ADMIT TO   ADMIT DAY:(41-43) [ ][ ][ ]   (44-47) ADMIT TIME: [ ][ ][ ][ ]
[ ][ ][ ][ ]

AGE	SEX	ADMIT DX	ADMIT CODE
70 71	72	73 74	75

DISCHARGE DATA (TO BE FILLED IN WHEN ABSTRACTION IS COMPLETED)

(8-9) LOCATION [ ][ ]   (10-11) DAY OF STAY [ ][ ]   (12-13) ACCESSION # [ ][ ]
A/E

INITIATION OF ORDER: (14-16) DAY [ ][ ][ ]   (17-21) TIME [ ][ ][ ][ ][ ]

(26-29) SERVICE DISCHARGE FROM [ ][ ][ ][ ]   DISCHARGE DAY (62-64) [ ][ ][ ]

(65-68) DISCHARGE TIME
[ ][ ][ ][ ]

AGE	SEX	ADMIT DX	ADMIT CODE	DISCH DX	DISCH CODE
70 71	72	73 74	75	76 77	78

2A-3-71(REVISED)

Figure 13–4

cation system, at present, is independent of the visual display hospital computer under development in KFH-SF.

In 1969, evaluation methodology was developed to follow doctors' orders into the laboratory without measuring internal work processes. Principal interests were in establishing baseline data on communication inputs and outputs relating to laboratory function in order to measure the effect of a punch card-oriented system on the laboratory's ability to manage information. The card-oriented system was to become backup for the next information systems iteration which used the computer.

The laboratory evaluation monitor, designed in 1969 and used 1970–71, tracked work volume by medical specialty unit into and out of the laboratory. Communication error determinations were made. Cumulative work times and delays were determined according to work sequence flow charts of laboratory operations. Initial evaluation compared measures of manual operations (1969) to unit record operations (1970) in terms of the parameters specified above.

Following determination of the relative worth of the unit record data

H2B-3-71 (REVISED)

MDS PROCESS DATA FORM - STANDARD PAGE

PAGE _____ OF PAGES _____

(1-7) MR #

(80) STUDY #

(TO BE USED ON ALL CARDS IN THIS SET)

(HEAD ALL CARDS IN THIS GROUP)   DITTO PREVIOUS:

(8-9) LOCATION #   (10-11) DAY OF STAY   (12-13) ACCESSION #

INITIATION TIME: (14-16) DAY

N/E

(17-21) TIME   (22-24) M.D. #   (25) PRIM./CONSULT

ORDER EVENTS	#TESTS DRUGS	NEW/CONT SINGLE/MULT	S/R/OTHER	PAPERWORK TIME		FIRST WORK		TIME INTO SERVICE		TIME OUT OF SERVICE		TIME AVAILABLE		ERROR	REMARKS
				DAY	TIME	DAY	TIME	DAY	TIME	DAY	TIME	DAY	TIME		
26 27 28 29	30	31 32	33	34 35 36 37	38 39 40	41 42 43 44	45 46 47	48 49 50 51	52 53 54	55 56 57 58	59 60 61	62 63 64 65	66 67 68	69	

ORDER EVENTS 26 27 28 29	#TESTS DRUGS 30	NEW/ CONT 31	SINGLE/ MULT 32	S/R/ OTHER 33	PAPERWORK TIME DAY 34 35 36 37	TIME 38 39 40	FIRST WORK DAY 41 42 43 44	TIME 45 46 47	TIME INTO SERVICE DAY 48 49 50 51	TIME 52 53 54	TIME OUT OF SERVICE DAY 55 56 57 58	TIME 59 60 61	TIME AVAILABLE DAY 62 63 64 65	TIME 66 67 68	ERROR 69	REMARKS

Figure 13-5

system, a new work sequence flow was designed for the next modular change; the computer supported information system. The 1969, 1970, and 1971, experience is reported in the results section of this chapter. The computer supported system (result input-computer reporting) was tested in 1972.

Comparisons of manual baseline, unit record system, and computer supported result reporting system tests are described in the next section.

3. System Utility

The immediate objective of the study of system utility was to assess the contemporary reaction of doctors and nurses to the manual medical information system at KFH-SF and then to determine from this reaction what major problem areas existed in the view of staff and what were some of the specific process details that caused difficulty. Once the automated system is operating, similar reactions will be sought and comparison made to the staff reactions generated by the manual system.

In the longer view, it is an objective of the study to develop a reliable measure of group readiness for system change. Herein it is assumed that work groups responding to conditions with "inordinate" amounts of positiveness (euphoric) are not ready to exert the emotional energy required to solve problems or make changes. On the other hand, when group reactions are disproportionately negative and untempered (frustrated), energy investment in change is not apt to be forthcoming due to a "What's the use?" attitude. When staff groups manifest mixed reaction to complex and often trying conditions of work, wherein both positivism and negativism are realistically tempered, it is sensible to assume the greatest readiness to invest the energy change requires.

The system utility study used two related techniques. These were: (a) discussion groups and (b) questionnaire responses. The first was a series of group discussions involving staff members that were recorded for later analysis. The second made use of a self-administered questionnaire.

4. Rationale for the Two Techniques

The group discussion method was used in the present study to provide the opportunity to obtain from the present users their own reactions to the on-going methods of exchanging data. Ideas come out in a verbal open-ended discussion that may not surface otherwise. The topics and issues concerning the data system noted by users in these discussion groups provided a base for summarizing the issues. Based on the staff-generated issues, a questionnaire that touched on topics important to the users was devised. By completing a questionnaire, a large segment of the hospital staff then had an opportunity to respond to the same issues that were raised in the discussion groups. This method of identifying issues and problems the staff see in the present data system was preferred to one where nonusers develop an evaluation questionnaire. Using a questionnaire developed on ideas from users provides a means for surveying the hospital staff in an economical manner. The resultant data lends itself to efficient data analysis techniques.

a. Discussion groups.   Discussion groups were organized to include physicians and nurses. Open discussion was invited by a moderator for the participants to discuss the current system in terms of its assets and liabilities. An example of an introductory question posed to discussion participants is as follows: "How does the present data system serve your needs in patient care?" Thus, the sessions were loosely structured on purpose to allow participants to bring up issues in the present data system relative to patient care. The interest was on how the processes in the medical care departments relate to or interact with the ancillary services in the hospital through present manual means of data exchange.

(1) Participants. Eight groups consisting of approximately eight participants each were selected from the hospital physician and nursing staffs. There were four sessions for each of these professional groups. Participants were chosen at random from available staff. Specific invitations to attend were issued by department chiefs.

Those users included were chiefs of services, staff physicians, resident physicians, interns, supervising nurses, head nurses, staff nurses, and licensed vocational nurses "approved" to dispense medications.

(2) Discussion session procedures. Prior to beginning the group discussions, a memo was sent to the hospital staff noting that such sessions were scheduled and participants' cooperation was requested.

Group discussion sessions were specifically scheduled, and certain persons were invited to attend. An informal format was established by the moderator, who usually referred to the memo and made some statements similar to the following:

"The attempt here is to get baseline data concerning the operation of the present medical data system for comparison following the time that the automated data system is installed. The discussion topics are left open to you because we don't want to tell you any more than necessary to stimulate a discussion on what the assets and liabilities of the system are or on what bothers you or what you see that works well in the hospital data system." Each session was tape recorded.

b. Questionnaire. Based on the topics and issues brought up in group discussion on the data exchange process in the hospital setting, questions were prepared and a questionnaire was developed. An accompanying response display from which responses could be selected was provided. This particular response display provided the opportunity for the respondent to evaluate each question in terms of two dimensions.

(1) Criteria for views of system utility. The criteria for assessing utility—i.e., ability of the data system to solve common needs of the staff— was established in two dimensions: user responses regarding *frequency of occurrence* of events which create problems, and responses regarding *degree of difficulty* created by the occurrence of such system problems. A response was recorded by their choosing a number from 1 to 10 from the response display on the questionnaire, which is shown below.

Order of difficulty	Frequency		
	Often	Sometimes	Seldom
Much difficulty	(1)	(2)	(3)
Some difficulty	(4)	(5)	(6)
Little difficulty	(7)	(8)	(9)
	(10) no opinion		

(2) Participants. Responses to the survey questionnaires were requested from the physician and nursing staffs in the hospital. The persons included were chiefs of services, staff physicians, resident physicians, interns, nursing staff supervisors, head nurses, staff nurses, and licensed vocational nurses.

(3) Questionnaire procedures. Questionnaire completion was carried out by having a member of the evaluation team attend a weekly meeting of the various departments and, after giving uniform instructions, asking the staff to respond to the questions. The questionnaires were picked up as respondents completed them.

(4) Variables associated with views of system utility. Variables used for studying associations with the utility criteria include certain characteristics of the staff who use the data system as follows:

Age: Age of staff members.

Experience: Experience the staff has had with the data system represented in terms of length of service with Kaiser Foundation Hospital.

Extent of use: Extent of use refers to the volume of data handled by a person in a particular staff assignment. The staff members who process the greatest amount of data are those in the medical department of the hospital.

This group consists of less than half of the staff, yet they process in the neighborhood of three-fourths of the data flow. Comparisons will, therefore, be made of this staff group as compared with all other staff as a group. Thus, service assignment is a tool for assessing *extent of use* of the data system.

Remoteness: Remoteness of staff member from the data system may be represented by his position in the hospital and by the extent of day-to-day involvement in patient care. Chiefs of services have less involvement than do the nurses who work in patient care units a greater portion of the time. The latter staff members deal with large numbers of orders and other activities that are carried out regarding the care of patients and, hence, are less remote from the data system as a whole.

c. Preparation of data for analysis.

(1) *Discussion group data.* The group discussion sessions with physicians and nurses were tape recorded. A systematic review of these tape recordings was made. Each statement was noted in sequence, and the following data was identified about each. Each speaker was identified from notes taken by an evaluation team member who acted as a secretary during the sessions, and the department the speaker represented was noted. The subject of the statement was noted as it referred to the several service departments (admissions, laboratory, staffing, pharmacy, x-ray, dietary, or other). The analysis was carried out by evaluation team members. The length of time spent on each statement was recorded. Space was reserved to make comments. It was found from a review of the tapes that the great majority of comments were relative to liabilities or problems in the system, but notation was made of statements about assets of the present data system as those comments occurred.

From the summary worksheet of the taped discussion sessions, certain analyses were made. The number of statements and length of time spent on each, as they relate to the several activities in the various service departments, was determined. A ratio of statements concerning assets and liabilities was determined.

Commentary which cites unique judgments and reactions of physicians and nurses participating in the discussions was noted.

(2) *Questionnaire data.* Coding of the questionnaire was as follows: Each completed questionnaire was numbered, and the demographic data was coded for card punching.

(3) *Data analysis.* The data was studied for:

(1) Characteristics of respondents as to:
    (a) Do younger staff members respond differently than older staff members?

(b) Do staff with shorter length of service respond differently than those with longer service at KFH–SF?

(c) Do staff members who make greater use of the data system respond differently than those who use it less?

(d) Do staff members who are more remote from the data system respond differently than those who are closer?

(2) Utility of the system:

(a) With which communication functions do staff have the most difficulty?

Results addressed to these questions are at the end of the next section.

5. Impact Cost Analysis

Impact costs are all expenses conceptually affected by the computer—i.e., increased, decreased, or shifted from one major activity to another (a major activity being Patient Care-Communication or Non-Communication and Non-Patient Care-Communication or Non-Communication). Conversely, Nonimpact costs are expenses assumed not to be affected by the computer.

Included in payroll expenses are salaries, wages, payroll taxes, and benefits for those employee categories surveyed, excluding all physicians.

Interns, residents, and staff physicians reflect salaries, payroll taxes, and employee benefits only.

Other expenses are all nonpayroll direct operating expenses assumed to be impact costs.

Direct operating expenses consist of three types of expenses: (1) all payroll costs for employee categories not surveyed; (2) student nurses services; and (3) nonpayroll expenses assumed to be nonimpact.

Allocated location expenses include the following expenses and departments which are allocated to the cost centers:

Property expenses
Personnel
Plant operation & maintenance
Housekeeping
Linen and laundry
Dietary

Nursing supervision
Central supply
General patient services and
    administration
Location expenses allocated to
    interns and residents

Property expenses consist of all location property costs (depreciation, property taxes, building maintenance, etc.), reduced by rental revenue, plus a proportionate share of financing costs, interest, insurance, and facility replacement provision.

General patient services and administration is comprised of the following hospital departments: medical records, gift shop, social service, volunteer's services, local administration, claims, communications, motor service, and storeroom.

Allocated regional expenses include the proportionate share of the community service program, professional and public liability, Permanente Services, Inc. charges, and regional administration.

6. Allocation to Locations

All expenses are taken directly from the general ledger with the following exceptions:

(1) Regional property expenses (financing costs, interest, and insurance) are allocated based on gross property values;

(2) Facility replacement provision is calculated on the capital asset balances of the preceding month;

(3) Regional expense allocations are based on total direct operating expenses.

7. Allocation to Departments

The method of allocating location expenses to the departments is essentially the same as used for Medicare. Two major changes are (1) facility replacement provision has been added, and (2) pharmacy and admitting are not allocated to the nursing departments since they will be terminal areas for the hospital computer system.

The bases for allocation are:

Property expenses:	square feet and value of equipment
Personnel:	hours worked by departments
Plant operation and maintenance:	square feet
Housekeeping:	hours worked in cost centers
Linen and laundry:	poundage
Dietary:	meals served
Nursing supervision:	hours worked in cost centers
Central supply:	hours spent on services provided
General patient services and administration:	total expenses

Intern, resident, and staff physician costs are based on total hours worked in a department times average hourly rates for each physician category. The hourly rates include payroll taxes and benefits.

Location expenses for interns and residents are further allocated to the nursing departments based on total expenses.

Regional expense allocations are based on total expenses.

8. Allocation of Floor Nursing to Subdepartments

Payroll expenses are charged on an actual basis.

Intern, resident, and staff physician costs for each subdepartment are based on total hours worked in the subdepartment times the average hourly rate for each physician category.

Other expenses and direct operating expenses are allocated based on total payroll expenses for the subdepartments, except for those costs which can be identified with a specific subdepartment.

Location expense allocations are charged to the subdepartments on the following bases, which were used due to a lack of statistics for the subdepartments. When statistics are available, the allocations below will be on the same bases as:

Property expenses:	patient days
Personnel:	hours worked—KFH employees only
Plant operation and maintenance:	patient days
Housekeeping:	patient days
Linen and laundry:	patient days
Dietary:	patient days
Nursing supervision:	hours worked—all personnel (including registry personnel)
Central supply:	
General patient services and administration:	patient days patient days
Interns and residents:	hours worked

Regional expense allocations are charged to the subdepartments as follows:

Community service program:	hours worked—KFH employees only
Professional and public liability:	patient days
Permanente Services, Inc. charges:	hours worked—all personnel
Regional administration:	hours worked—all personnel

9. Allocation within Departments by Major Activity

Payroll expenses, interns, residents, and staff physicians are allocated to the four major activities based on the percentage of time spent in each activity during the survey. All other expenses are prorated on payroll expenses for the major activities as indicated in Schedule I.

There are no results presented on comparative impact cost analysis, as mentioned earlier. Comparisons will be made once computer supported communication procedures are operational. This was targeted for mid to late 1973.

F. RESULTS FROM TYPICAL EVALUATIONS

1. Exploration 1969

The initial thrust of our Hospital Computer System (HSC) was to explore the hospital Patient Care and Communication system for criteria of measurement that reproducibly explained expenditure of care resources, principally manpower used to communicate. Criteria were necessary, within conceptual restraints, at three levels of performance: (1) individual activity; (2) process, linking activities, and subsystems; and (3) integrated systems—e.g., laboratory study. Analyses revealed several such criteria for further investigation.

Analyses of time and effort data showed that effort was expended in Patient Care-Communication activities by care worker categories—i.e., staff MD's, residents, interns, head nurses, staff nurses, licensed vocational nurses, and aides in direct proportion to the work group status. Investment in Patient Care-Non-Communication activities (direct patient care) was inversely related to staff status in the patient care unit—i.e., aides and vocational nurses highest, followed by staff nurses, head nurses, and doctors.

In short, those with high status in the patient care unit communicate much about patient care in writing and conversationally; those with low status communicate relatively less about patients but are more active in its delivery. This result strengthens interest in the question about correspondence between patient care needs and staff skills required to satisfy those needs.

The analysis certainly confirmed that Patient Care-Communication was an expensive activity in the hospital system. The expense of these activities has been broadly discussed in the literature. However, the larger question emerging was whether or not the manual system (which produced communication expenditures of 25–35% of physician and nurse staff time in patient care units) was not satisfying hierarchical requirements—i.e., status, rather than functional requirements suggested by patient needs.

Early review of processes which linked patient care units with service functions, e.g., laboratory, pharmacy, x-ray, admitting, etc., shed some light on this question. Review of early process data relating to admission of elective surgeries, admissions through the emergency room, and patient care unit interaction with the laboratory produced insights of systems consequence, which required attention prior to implementing a hospital computerized admission and laboratory communication system.

Elective admissions were decided between surgeon and patient in the outpatient clinic, and date and time were agreed. The surgeon's nurse

Schedule I. Areas of Impact Cost Arranged by Categories of Patient Care and Communication

	Communication		Non-Communication	
	Non-Patient Care	Patient Care	Non-Patient Care	Patient Care
Other expenses				
Office supplies	X	X	X	X
Other materials and supplies	X	X	X	X
Equipment rentals*			X	X
Equipment repairs				X
Non-capital equipment			X	X
Other expenses			X	X
Direct operating expenses				
Payroll expenses for employee categories not surveyed	X	X	X	X
Drugs and pharmaceuticals			X	
Dressings and other medical supplies			X	
Instruments			X	
Vaccines and IV solutions			X	
Housekeeping supplies			X	X
Loss of patients' property				X
Dues, subscriptions and periodicals	X	X		X
Disposable linen			X	
Disposable medical and surgical supplies			X	
Auto mileage				X
Student nurses services**	X	X	X	X

Allocated location expenses

Property expenses	X	X	X
Personnel			X
Plant operation and maintenance			X
Housekeeping		X	X
Linen and laundry		X	
Dietary		X	
Nursing supervision			X
Central supply		X	
General patient services and administration	X	X	X
Interns and residents†	X	X	X

Allocated regional expenses are all prorated between Non-Patient Care Communication and Non-Communications.

* If the equipment can be identified with a specific patient, the cost was allocated to Patient Care; if not, the expense was assigned to Non-Patient Care.
** Allocation based on LVN percentages only.
† Allocation based on interns' and residents' percentages.

would confirm agreement with the operating room secretary, who scheduled the procedure. This routine was done 1–6 weeks in advance of surgery. The scheduling routine covered about 40% of all hospital admissions. The routine called for the elective patient to be admitted the afternoon before the day of the scheduled procedure. Presurgical admission occurred Sunday through Thursday of each week.

Findings indicated that 25–40% of these admissions were unknown to the admitting department the day they arrived. These patients were also unknown to the patient units to which they were admitted. Early in the week, fitting patient problems to appropriate medical specialty beds was relatively simple. As the week wore on and the hospital filled, patients were placed in any open bed with increasing frequency, and demand mounted on doctors to discharge patients early.

During these times, it was apparent that doctors and nurses were spending their time in patient communication deciding on how and where to realign unit censuses so that incoming patients could be admitted. This problem achieved crisis proportions about Wednesday of each week.

As the bed problem intensified in the hospital, management of patients in the Emergency Room (ER) became increasingly difficult. Patients needing admission from the ER occupied observation beds, often to the extent that the ER looked and operated much like a ward set aside for overflow of medical cases (emergency surgicals were more quickly admitted). Given a patient care population in bed for observation, monitoring and initial treatment tended dramatically to increase the ER's requests for laboratory work (emergencies amounted to half or more of STAT work in the hospital).

The elective admissions, known and unknown, also produced laboratory requests that had to be done immediately on patient arrival, or surgical procedures were delayed. Delivery of these results was difficult, when known, because of the frequent movement of patients by transfer once admitted (35–100 adult patients transferred each 24 hours). This patient movement made it difficult to get the results of laboratory testing done, back to patient charts (10–15% of orders transmitted to the laboratory and done had no result in patient charts).

The movement of patients from the view of care units made it difficult to keep track of what doctors' orders had been processed. In the case of the laboratory (highest work volume support area in the hospital, 15 of every 100 orders were omitted (never done).

Transcription of doctors' orders and preparation of transmittal messages —e.g., laboratory requisition—were and are traditional duties of nurses. Principally, decisions relating to patient transfer within the hospital are made by nurses. These two performance areas interact to effect performance in other subsystems when they occur as parochial nursing activities, and no feedback is transmitted to others needing to know.

The doctor had substantial difficulty physically locating his patient. Once his patient was located, he had difficulty knowing which of his orders had been executed, which ones were in progress, and which were lost. The admitting department had problems keeping track of which patients were where, which rooms and beds were available, and which had been prepared by housekeeping for occupancy. Aside from issues of patient location, the laboratory (and other diagnostic services) suffered to know about work needing to be done on patients that were unknown to admitting and what to do with laboratory results for those patients whose charts were not locatable. It is notable that, as these unknowns flourished, the amount of time spent in all departments by all work groups on the telephone increased to where each patient care unit devoted the equivalent of one nurse to telephone duty during the day shift [about 14 workers/day during the week for patient care units in KFH-SF and support units such as laboratory required multiple people (4–6 per day) to respond to the telephone demand].

This crisis-oriented response-demand mechanism may very well be helped by computer-oriented telecommunication. It was thought at this point in the evaluation, however, that better advantage would be taken of any methods improvement using computer technology if first the system of care delivery (alignment of resources with patient needs) could be initially better integrated between care performing subsystems.

It was decided to investigate and evaluate some options for improving subsystem alignment—i.e., interfacing. First, a nursing system option was investigated. Second, the laboratory study mentioned above was conducted. Third, a method was developed for integrating admitting, nursing, housekeeping, and emergency room in managing the patient census. This method aimed at increasing shared information (collected once) needed for collaborative decision making. These investigations, simply stated, studied options for modifying patient care subsystems effecting increased expenditure of nursing time and effort in direct patient care and increased ability to keep track of work ordered, and integrating communication among diverse departmental functions in collaborative decision making. Conduct of these studies required method refinement. Some refinements were stated earlier. Where necessary, additional refinements will be noted in presenting results of the three devlopmental studies which investigated various dimensions of operation effecting or effected by communication mode and technique.

2. Nursing Reorganization Study

The measured effects of shifting from team nursing to Total Patient Care (TPC—staff nurse centered) in KFH-Oakland on nursing time availability (Performance Criterion I) was reported in Section E. The results presented here illustrate application of Performance Criterion II (time effectiveness) and III (expenditure of effective time by different skill groups against estimated patient need).

The Medicine and Surgery units in KFH-Oakland are organized for Total Patient Care (TPC). The Orthopedic and Gynecology units remained team nursing operations. KFH-San Francisco as HCS study facility did not modify its basic nursing organization structure (which is modified team nursing) and is not discussed here.

Tables 1 through 4 distribute proportions of time and effort in Medicine (Table 1), Surgery (Table 2), Orthopedics (Table 3) and Gynecology (Table 4) by three nursing worker groups in KFH-Oakland, April 1971. Each table presents three time proportions—i.e., P_{Int}^* = integrative time; P_{Work}^* = work time; and P_{Tot} = total time by activity category. [E.g., P_{Int} for Patient Care-Non-Communication (PC-NC) is time walking. P_{Work} is the remainder of time spent in (PC-NC).] These proportions are derived for each major activity category—i.e., Patient Care-Communication; Non-Patient Care-Communication; Patient Care-Non-Communication; and Non-Patient Care-Non-Communication. Categorical proportions pertain to each primary care worker groups—i.e., Staff RN, LVN, and Aide-Orderly.

Tabular presentations exclude total effectiveness coefficients (P_{Et} described above) since the meaning of this summative index figure is still under analytic investigation. Consequently, only categorical coefficients are compared and discussed at this time. The Patient Care-Non-Communication (hospital system manpower target) coefficients are the principal focus for comparative discussions.

Examination of Patient Care-Non-Communication proportions shows generally that Staff RN's and LVN's spend significantly more effective time in direct patient care in the Total Patient Care (TPC) units (Medicine and Surgery), Tables 1 and 2, than do their counterparts in the Team Nursing units (Orthopedics and Gynecology), Tables 3 and 4. Also, the proportions of walking time required to deliver patient care substantially reduce in relationship to proportions of effective work time for RN's and LVN's in TPC units compared to Team Nursing units.

The ratios of work to walking for RN's are about 1 (walking units) : 3 (work units) for TPC units and less than 1:2 for Team Nursing units. Ratios for LVN's show the same but less uniform tendency. TPC LVN ratios approach 2:9. Team ratios are from less than 1:4 down to 2:3.

Table 1. Proportions of Work and Integrative (P_{int}) Time Spent by Primary Nursing Groups in Major Activity Categories Medicine (Total Patient Care) Kaiser Foundation Hospital Oakland, April 1971

Work groups	Staff nurse			Lic. vocational nurse			Aide		
proportions									
Activity categories	P_{int}	P_{work}	P_{tot}	P_{int}	P_{work}	P_{tot}	P_{int}	P_{work}	P_{tot}
Pt. Care/Comm.	.18	.28	.46	.16	.15	.31	.10	.03	.13
Non-Pt. Care/Comm.	.03	.00	.03	.02	.00	.02	.10	.04	.14
Pt. Care/Non-Comm.	.12	.36	.43	.10	.45	.55	.13	.23	.36
Non-Pt. Care/Non-Comm.	.02	.01	.03	.11	.01	.12	.29	.08	.37

Table 2. Proportions of Work and Integrative (P_{int}) Time Spent by Primary Nursing Groups in Major Activity Categories Surgery (Total Patient Care) Kaiser Foundation Hospital Oakland, April 1971

Work groups	Staff nurse			Lic. vocational nurse			Aide		
proportions									
Activity categories	P_{int}	P_{work}	P_{tot}	P_{int}	P_{work}	P_{tot}	P_{int}	P_{work}	P_{tot}
Pt. Care/Comm.	.11	.17	.28	.09	.18	.27	.08	.10	.18
Non-Pt. Care/Comm.	.02	.02	.04	.02	.01	.03	.04	.02	.06
Pt. Care/Non-Comm.	.14	.47	.61	.10	.43	.53	.17	.25	.42
Non-Pt. Care/Non-Comm.	.04	.03	.07	.16	.01	.17	.29	.05	.34

Table 3. Proportions of Work and Integrative (P_{int}) Time Spent by Primary Nursing Groups in Major Activity Categories Orthopedics (Team Nursing) Kaiser Foundation Hospital Oakland, April 1971

Work groups	Staff nurse			Lic. vocational nurse			Aide		
Activity categories proportions	P_{int}	P_{work}	P_{tot}	P_{int}	P_{work}	P_{tot}	P_{int}	P_{work}	P_{tot}
Pt. Care/Comm.	.12	.39	.51	.26	.21	.47	.13	.22	.35
Non-Pt. Care/Comm.	.07	.04	.11	.06	.03	.09	.04	.00	.04
Pt. Care/Non-Comm.	.14	.22	.36	.08	.31	.39	.19	.23	.42
Non-Pt. Care/Non-Comm.	.01	.01	.02	.02	.03	.05	.03	.16	.19

Table 4. Proportions of Work and Integrative (P_{int}) Time Spent by Primary Nursing Groups in Major Activity Categories Gynecology (Team Nursing) Kaiser Foundation Hospital Oakland, April 1971

Work groups	Staff nurse			Lic. vocational nurse			Aide		
Activity categories proportions	P_{int}	P_{work}	P_{tot}	P_{int}	P_{work}	P_{tot}	P_{int}	P_{work}	P_{tot}
Pt. Care/Comm.	.09	.22	.31	.10	.25	.35	.11	.14	.25
Non-Pt. Care/Comm.	.05	.04	.09	.05	.01	.06	.06	.00	.06
Pt. Care/Non-Comm.	.16	.30	.46	.18	.27	.45	.19	.27	.46
Non-Pt. Care/Non-Comm.	.10	.04	.14	.05	.09	.14	.16	.07	.23

Ratios for Aides are slightly better for TPC units but relatively high walking, low work (TPC 3:5, Team 5:6).

It is noteworthy that, as TPC units developed, the number of aides were reduced. Professional nurses replaced aides at a ratio of 3 professionals for 5 aides. In effect, the few aides remaining lost function which had previously been mostly execution of patient care. These activities were now the primary responsibility of professional nurses.

When the TPC units (Medicine and Surgery KFH-OAK) were compared before and after change from Team Nursing organization, certain marked differences were notable in Patient Care and Communication categories between baseline (1970, Team Nursing) and TPC operation (1971). Tables 5 (Medicine) and 6 (Surgery) array these comparisons of activity categories in effectiveness coefficients for Registered Nurses, Licensed Vocational Nurses, and Aides.

As indicated in both Medicine and Surgery tables, reorganization to TPC increased work effectiveness coefficients (P_{Work}) in Patient Care-Non-Communication for the three primary nursing care worker categories. The most significant increases were for Registered (RN) and Licensed Vocational Nurses (LVN). In work group comparisons, the work coefficients (P_{Work}) for Patient Care-Communication showed varied change. RNs decreased for both experimental units. LVNs decreased in medicine but increased in surgery. Aides demonstrated minimum involvement in either unit.

Nursing reorganization clearly effected the change target, Patient Care-Non-Communication. The variability of change in Patient Care-Communication raised the question, Did information exchange suffer after institution of TPC? Since both experimental units were major users of the clinical laboratory, a preliminary test was run of information processing errors produced in working laboratory orders by these units before and after nursing reorganization. The types of errors used for test purposes were: (1) order written but work not done (consistently the most frequent error committed); and (2) order mistranscribed by the nurse (effecting the wrong work to be performed). In this case, 1969 data were used for comparison since the medicine experimental unit was in transition during 1970 (see Table 7).

In both experimental units, production of relatively common errors attributable to nursing performance decreased significantly following the experiment change. Although time spent in Patient Care-Communication went down for RNs after the change, their Patient Care-Communication effectiveness (by limited test) inferentially improved significantly. This is illustrative of the point made earlier that improvement in the manual work system prior to introduction of information technology (computer) may

Table 5. Comparative Proportions of Time Effectiveness in Patient Care and Communication Categories for Primary Nursing Work Groups in the Medicine Unit, KFH-Oakland, 1970–1971

	Registered nurse			Licensed vocational nurse			Aide		
	P_{int}	P_{work}	P_{tot}	P_{int}	P_{work}	P_{tot}	P_{int}	P_{work}	P_{tot}
1. Pt. Care/Comm.									
1970	.11	.38	.49	.20	.36	.56	.07	.08	.15
1971	.18	.28	.46	.16	.15	.31	.10	.03	.13
2. Non-Pt. Care/Comm.									
1970	.02	.03	.05	.01	.02	.03	.02	.04	.06
1971	.03	.00	.03	.01	.01	.02	.10	.04	.14
3. Pt. Care/Non-Comm.									
1970	.10	.26	.36	.12	.26	.38	.12	.19	.31
1971	.12	.36	.48	.10	.45	.55	.13	.23	.36
4. Non-Pt. Care/Non-Comm.									
1970	.04	.06	.10	.03	.00	.03	.36	.12	.48
1971	.04	.02	.06	.11	.01	.12	.29	.08	.37

Table 6. Comparative Proportions of Time Effectiveness in Patient Care and Communication Categories for Primary Nursing Work Groups in the Surgery Unit, KFH-Oakland, 1970–1071

	Registered nurse			Licensed vocational nurse			Aide		
	P_{int}	P_{work}	P_{tot}	P_{int}	P_{work}	P_{tot}	P_{int}	P_{work}	P_{tot}
1. Pt. Care/Comm.									
1970	.30	.26	.56	.09	.10	.19	.06	.11	.17
1971	.11	.17	.28	.09	.18	.27	.08	.10	.18
2. Non-Pt. Care/Comm.									
1970	.05	.00	.05	.14	.02	.16	.10	.02	.12
1971	.02	.02	.04	.02	.01	.03	.04	.02	.06
3. Pt. Care/Non-Comm.									
1970	.09	.22	.31	.08	.28	.36	.10	.22	.32
1971	.14	.47	.61	.10	.43	.53	.17	.25	.42
4. Non-Pt. Care/Non-Comm.									
1970	.03	.05	.08	.29	.00	.29	.39	.00	.39
1971	.04	.03	.07	.16	.01	.17	.29	.05	.34

well provide a superior base for comparison and thereby yield more realistic estimates of what technology can be expected to contribute to the delivery of patient care.

The Team Nursing unit operation was compared to the Total Patient Operation in terms of relative cost effectiveness for the experimental nursing units. Cost effectiveness was defined in terms of the cost of effective time spent in Patient Care-Non-Communication (Change Target) vs. the cost of nondirect care effort (balance of activity) which was target ineffective. These comparative cost fractions were related to the number of hours worked by RNs, LVNs and Aides and the number of patient days of care rendered in the experimental units April 1970 and 1971. Table 8 shows the comparisons.

Both units show that nursing hours per patient day in direct patient care increased substantially with decrease in time spent in other activities (non-care). Similarly, nursing costs ("N" hour costs expended for work) went up while cost for other activity went down. For Medicine, there was an increase in total "N" hour costs 1970 to 1971 of $1.53 per patient day. For Surgery, there was a decrease of $1.74. No attempt was made to correct these cost estimates for inflationary trends. However, were this adjustment made for the years in question, the inference drawn from these data is that the change was preliminarily, at least, a cost effective one if the target of optimizing primary nursing personnel for Patient Care-Non-Communication is accepted.

Table 8 illustrates impact (targeted) cost-analysis technique used in evaluating system performance and effects of system modification. (See Method section E. S. on Impact Cost Analysis).

Conversion to the new evaluation model, Patient Maintenance and Medical Care Delivery, from Patient Care and Communication prompted an exploration inquiry into the issue of differential expenditure of skill group time and effort between Team Nursing and Total Patient (Performance Criterion III) Care Units. For purpose of illustration, primary nursing groups in the Medicine Unit KFH-Oakland 1969 (Team Unit) are compared to similar groups in the same Medicine Unit 1970 (Total Patient Care Unit).

Table 9 proportions time spent by RNs, LVNs, and Aides Treating, Catering, Communicating, Walking, and Administering in comparative Medicine Units.

The clear skill differences shown in the table are that the aide in the TPC unit becomes significantly less involved in the treating function than is the Team aide. Also, the TPC LVN is more implicated in treating than the Team LVN. Further, the TPC LVN is less implicated in catering and more in communicating than her Team counterpart. Proportion of time

Table 7. Error Rates, Laboratory Orders Written but Work Not Done (Error 1) and Laboratory Orders Mistranscribed (Error 2) in Medicine and Surgery Units KFH-Oakland 1969 (Baseline) and 1971 (Total Patient Care).

	Medicine			Surgery		
	Error 1 E's/100	Error 2 E's/100	# Lab orders	Error 1 E's/100	Error 2 E's/100	# Lab orders
1969	7.0	1.7	1106	8.2	2.2	837
1971	1.4	0.1	1200	2.0	0.3	916

Table 8. Comparison of Patient Day, Primary Nursing Costs (Wages Paid to RN's, LVN's and Aides) for Patient Care Delivered (PC-NC) and Non-Care Related Activity in Medical and Surgical Units in KFH-Oakland April 1970 and April 1971

Units	Pt. Days	"N"* Hrs.	"N" Hrs/ Pt. Day	P_{Epc-nc}	"N" Hrs/ Pt. Day	"N" Hrs Non-Care	Avg. $/ "N" Hr.	"N" $/ Pt. Day Care	"N" $/ Pt. Day Non-Care	"N" $/ Pt. Day Total
Medicine										
1970	1612	5387	3.34	.25	0.84	2.50	4.08	3.43	10.20	13.63
1971	1320	4564	3.46	.38	1.31	2.15	4.38	5.74	9.42	15.16
Surgery										
1970	1454	7959	5.47	.24	1.31	4.16	3.76	4.93	15.64	20.57
1971	1305	5748	4.40	.45	1.98	2.42	4.28	8.47	10.36	18.83

* "N" = Hours worked by primary care providers, RN, LVN, Aide

** P_{Epc-nc} = Effectiveness proportion Patient Care-Non-Communication—i.e., walking time extracted.

Table 9. Proportional Distribution of Time Spent, in Treating, Catering, Communication, Walking, and Administering Activities by Primary Nursing Groups in the Medicine, KFH-Oakland, April 1969–1970.

	April 1969			April 1970		
	RN	LVN	Aide	RN	LVN	Aide
Treating	.15	.08	.21	.15	.14	.04
Catering	.10	.26	.26	.13	.16	.30
Communicating	.49	.15	.27	.51	.34	.28
Walking	.17	.29	.16	.14	.25	.28
Administering	.09	.22	.10	.07	.11	.10
	1.00	1.00	1.00	1.00	1.00	1.00

spent communicating generally is the same for RNs and Aides in the units compared.

The important point is that the nursing reorganization experiment (TPC) effected the expenditure of primary staff effort away from nonskilled treating toward skilled treating. However, time spent communicating remained the significant domain of the RN. It is posited that the TPC LVN changed because her work in the new unit was redefined closer to that of the RN. Nonetheless, communication remained a large, significant time requirement in the care of patients on which the computer and information technology can produce an impact.

3. Clinical Laboratory System

This section illustrates evolutionary evaluation of an information system in the medical support (testing) area. The laboratory information system started as a manual (paper and pencil) system (1969), first developed a machine oriented backup (unit record) system (1970 and 1971), then commenced implementing a computer-terminal oriented result reporting system (testing began 1971). The Clinical Laboratory at Kaiser Foundation Hospital in San Francisco (KFH-SF) is a facility providing inpatient and outpatient services to local medical centers and special testing services to other medical centers in the Northern Region of Kaiser/Permanente.

The baseline laboratory study in 1969 was of a manual information processing system (I). Followup studies in 1970 and 1971 were on a unit-record oriented information processing system (II), which was designed and implemented as the functional backup system for the automated laboratory request log-in and result reporting system (IIA). The followup study in April-May 1972 commenced evaluating system IIA in relation to System II.

Table 10. Total Number of Tests* by Type Processed in the Clinical Laboratory KFH-SF Second Quarter, 1969, 1970, 1971, and 1972

	1969	1970	1971	1972	% Increase/decrease 69–70	69–71	69–72
Bacteriol.	12,539	17,290	28,477	20,252	+37.9	+127.1	+61.5
Chemistry	42,854	59,290	65,653	73,197	+38.3	+53.2	+70.8
Hematology	50,128	52,412	72,058	66,800	+5.3	+43.7	+33.2
Imm./Serol.	20,046	19,541	22,852	19,971	−2.5	+13.9	−0.0
Parasitol.	1,445	1,478	1,013	670	+2.2	−29.8	−50.6
Spinal Fl.	1,172	333	174	125	−71.5	−85.1	−89.3
Urine	31,600	47,628	23,860	23,856	+50.7	−24.4	−24.5
Spec. Proc.	1,566	194	1,652	2,895	−87.6	+5.4	+84.8
	161,350	198,166	215,739	207,766	+22.8	+33.7	+28.8

* The number of tests were abstracted from the report titled *The Permanente Medical Group Statistics for 1969, 1970, 1971, 1972.*

Table 10 compares general volumes of laboratory testing by test categories, e.g., bacteriology, chemistry, etc.—April 1970, 1971, and 1972 to April 1969 HCS study baseline for both hospital and ambulatory patients.

Table 10 shows the general volumetric growth of KFH-SF laboratory operation over the study years. General cumulative growth over three years was 28.8%. The major areas of growth were in chemistry (70.8% cumulative), bacteriology (61.5%), hematology (33.2%) and special procedures (84.8%). Volumetric declines are observed in spinal fluids (89.3%), parasitology (50.6%), and urinalysis (24.5%). Increases experienced tend to be in higher cost testing functions and decreases in lower cost functions when adjusted by relative volume.

It should be noted that the proportion of the total test volume represented by the hospital services has increased annually through the study years. In 1969, hospital laboratory tests were approximately 33% of the total test volume, 37% in 1970, 40% in 1971, and 44% in 1972. This means not only that the volume of laboratory testing has increased sharply but that growth is proportionately more in the direction of hospital originated tests.

The laboratory work volume generated by the hospital shows the growth pattern was still increasing in 1972. The baseline hospital volume was about 53,000 tests in 1969, increasing to 73,000 in 1970, to 86,000 in 1971, and to 91,000 in 1972. This is a cumulative increase of 74.5%. This indicates the growing significance of the laboratory HCS for the medical operation of the hospital. As has been determined during the years of study, transmission and work errors increase and work completion rates decrease as the volume of tests ordered per day increase when information is managed in manual (paper and pencil) mode. Large and growing paper volumes in laboratories clearly threaten accuracy and utility (timing) of test results (the prime produce of the laboratory) if not managed by relatively high-volume systems which are machine supported.

The subsequent pages describe analysis and discuss the three system iterations. Delays are presented in work flow sequence. Error and completion rates are reported. Relative manpower allocations are tabled for comparison. Finally, operational findings from a special laboratory system field test are presented and discussed.

Manual baseline, unit record, and semi-automated laboratory systems were detailed in operational flow charts. These flow sequences include communication and processing steps. Process delays are indicated by place and kind in the flow sequence and communication mode—e.g., paper and pencil—with which it is associated.

Systems I (Manual baseline) and II (Unit Record) flow were reviewed in terms of delays produced by procedural steps. Summation of these delays provides a gross estimate of the occurrence of nonroutine delay and total non work time affecting turn around time for results of routine tests. The base sequence is bounded by doctor's laboratory test order and test result in chart.

Table 11 shows cumulative delay by type for the manual system 1969 (I) compared to unit record system 1970 (II) and modified unit record 1971 (IIA) for laboratory test sequences order to chart. The times summated were delay estimates based on third quartile measures—i.e., turn around time for three-fourths of the work done by the laboratory. Redesign of the laboratory HCS effected redistribution of delay and reduction in its effect on turn-around time. System II eliminated delay accruing from lack of clerical control. It reduced substantially delays resulting from transport inadequacy and inadequate control over presences of essential work mate-

Table 11. Laboratory Process Sequence Delays in Minutes, Chart to Chart, for Inpatient Testing Comparing Manual to Unit Record Information Systems, 1969 to 1971.

	Type of delay				
	(1)	(2)	(3)	(4)	Total
System I (1969)	75	600	125	55	855
System II (1970)	435	90	15	0	535
System IIA (1971)	315	90	15	0	420

(1) Delay (expected idle time) between completion of one process step and commencement of the next step in sequence.
(2) Delay when work request is conveyed without essential work materials.
(3) Delays accruing from methods of transport.
(4) Delays accruing from lack of clerical control.

rials—e.g., test specimens. The system revision did increase idle time expected between process steps. The net effect was delay reduction of 320 minutes or 37.4% between 1969 and 1970.

By 1971, an additional reduction of 115 minutes had been accomplished in idle time between process steps, bringing the cumulated delay reduction to 435 minutes or 50.9%.

Comparison of the new log-in routine in System II which established an input routine from patient care units with arrival time specifications greatly reduced delay created by random dumbwaiter rides and reception of requests in the laboratory before they could be processed. This procedural change is elaborated in the context of the System III revision.

4. Laboratory Process Loops

The steps subsequent to the doctors' orders in System II remain the same as in Laboratory System I up to entry of the requisition into the laboratory except that the thirteen $8\frac{1}{2}"\times 5"$ test requisition slips used previously were consolidated into three $8\frac{1}{2}"\times 11"$ five-part requisition forms.

Once in the laboratory, requisition processing changed from manual paper and pencil to unit record card oriented methods. Routine daily work was commenced each morning under System I by manually sorting laboratory slips. In System II, the daily routine started by pre-logging the morning's work. This includes assignment of laboratory accession numbers to requisitions and preparations of punch cards containing necessary patient and work information. The cards are then used to make work assignments. Several process control steps exist in System II that were not possible in System I. For example, the technician drawing a specimen can now match patient's medical record (M.R.) number and laboratory accession numbers before drawing specimens, thus reducing the error incidence of wrong tests and duplication on patients. Color coding of specimens is also used in the monitor in conjunction with matching M.R. and accession numbers.

Where specimens are taken and subsequently accompany requisitions to the laboratory, the accession number is assigned and matched to the patient's M.R. number. (The specimens are not color coded). The logging-in process then continues as above with preparation of patient identifier and work cards.

Routine specimens and cards are then batched by laboratory department in their respective work queues. Tests are performed and results recorded on test cards by technicians. The test cards then go to laboratory clerks where results are transcribed to the requisition. If the results are partial, a copy is pulled from the requisition set and sent to the nursing unit. The first copy is retained in the laboratory until all results are complete. Provision of partial results is a capability of Laboratory System II that did not exist under System I.

Dissemination of results under System II changed substantially. Where dissemination was previously loosely managed, it is now managed by programmed delivery via a messenger. Some new problems were observed—e.g., charts not available due to patient transfers. However, many problems associated with using delivery by dumbwaiter and ward clerk insertion of results in charts have been resolved.

The modifications described for System II were studied in terms of processing and communication errors it produced by medical service compared to System I. Table 12 arrays error production rates. Error types are calculated per 1000 tests for 1969 (I), 1970 (II), and 1971 (III).

In general, error production was reduced by about 63% from 1969 to 1971. The new system effectively reduced work omissions, frequency of unrecorded orders, lost results, and uncontrolled duplication. In the units of greatest impact, which are the high laboratory request services, Medicine shows an error reduction of 65%, Surgery 64%, and Gynecology 58%. The low-volume services produced a more mixed picture.

When system error definition was expanded to include misidentification of patients, errors in patient location—e.g., incorrect room number—and doctor not indicated or misidentified, similar reductions in error rates were notable, as seen in Table 13.

Communication error rates for patient location and doctor identification are not shown for 1969 and 1970. These data were first collected in 1971. The differences in these specific areas are attributable to a census procedure and doctor identification chart, and are maintained by the laboratory. This is an important interim step until the day there is stable, hospital-wide census management system.

Next, relative ability of the various system interactions were measured for completeness of test result reporting. Table 14 shows reporting completeness rates (completion per 1000 tests). The terminal event is a usable result in the patient's chart.

The 1972 row in Table 14 indicated both unit record and computer operation. These results were compiled from measures of the Unit Record System (II) and a field test of the automated log-in/result report system (III).

The field test study was conducted over two 24-hour laboratory operating cycles (May 30–31, 1972). All requests for laboratory, inpatient and outpatient, were logged into the system and all results from tests run were entered and reported. Results completed during the study days, tests ordered earlier, and results from work done for other facilities were entered but excluded from analysis. Also excluded were bacteriology requests and

Table 12. Process Errors by Medical Service per 1000 Laboratory Tests, Clinical Laboratory KFH-SF, April 1969, 1970, and 1971

Specialty service		Types of error*																
		(1)			(2)			(3)			(4)			(5)			Total	
	69	70	71	69	70	71	69	70	71	69	70	71	69	70	71	69	70	71
Med. 69	72			30			13			8			18			141		
70		44			22			6			14			2			88	
71			30			10			4			1			1			49
Surg. 69	24			11			4			9			10			58		
70		13			16			2			7			2			40	
71			8			8			2			3			0			21
Gyn. 69	6			9			3			0			6			24		
70		14			4			0			0			0			18	
71			6			4			0			0			0			10
Pedi. 69	1			2			2			0			1			6		
70		4			1			7			0			3			15	
71			1			0			2			0			0			3
OB 69	3			1			1			0			0			5		
70		4			3			3			0			2			12	
71			2			1			1			0			0			4
Ortho. 69	0			1			1			0			0			2		
70		4			0			0			0			0			4	
71			1			0			0			0			0			1
Tot. 69	106			54			24			17			35			236		
Tot. 70		83			46			18			21			9			177	
Tot. 71			48			23			9			7			1			88

* The major type of errors are: (1) record of laboratory order in chart, but work done and result in chart; (2) no record of laboratory order in chart, but work done and result in chart; (3) record of order in chart, work done, no result in chart; (4) no record of order in chart, work done, no result in chart; and (5) duplicate work ordered.

Table 13. Communication, Work Omission, and Identification Errors per 1000 Laboratory Tests, KFH-San Francisco Clinical Laboratory April 1969, 1970, 1971, and 1972

	Commun. errors/1000 lab test	Test not done omission errors per 1000 tests	Pt. misiden. errors/1000 tests	Other identification errors	
				Pt. mislocate/ 1000 test	MD not or mis- iden/1000 test
1969	236	106	90	X	X
1970	177	83	60	X	X
1971	88	48	5	300	300
1972	49	29	1	100	220

Table 14. Laboratory Test Result Reporting Rates (Completions per 1000) by Manual, Unit Record and Computer Modes for the Clinical Laboratory System KFH-San Francisco, April 1969, 1970, 1971, and 1972

	I Manual (baseline) results reported/ 1000 tests	II Unit record results reported/ 1000 tests	III Computer results reported/ 1000 tests
1969	800	X	X
1970	X	900	X
1971	X	960	X
1972	X	990	990

results which were not entered into the system and results from laboratory procedures not completed within a 24-hour work cycle.

The laboratory tests aggregated for analysis were same-day hematology, chemistry, and urinalyses for inpatients and outpatients. The first study day was used to identify and work-out obvious mechanical problems in operating the log-in/result reporting procedures for all lab activities. The second day was the test day. Note that no special preparation was made to prime lab staff for test operation, all regular work was done, and reports were generated in existing unit record mode (System II) with care to protect the integrity of the operating, patient care, and reporting system.

All accession numbered inpatient and outpatient laboratory requests for a day (850 + 200 multiphasic requisitions) were logged in. No requests were omitted nor tests lost. For routine work that could be done the same day (70–75% of all lab testing), more than 99% was completed and reported within four hours of the specimen's arrival in the laboratory. Nine omissions out of 900 possible inpatient result report statements were counted. Fifteen omissions were counted in 1000 possible outpatient report result statements.

In all instances of test reports, the result values were in perfect agreement with results recorded by the technician on the unit record test card. Same-day results were available to doctors in the hospital 1.5–3.5 hours earlier than with the manual reporting system. As indicated in Table 14, completion was approximately equivalent to that of the Unit Record System. In addition, the 30 man-hours needed per day to transcribe results was eliminated. Finally, the variable errors produced when results are manually transcribed from test card to report sheet were totally eliminated.

Substantially, System III field test indicated that the computerized laboratory was viable. It lost no tests at log-in (quality control point), and its omissions were clearly those that would be overcome by modification in work procedures and computer programs.

The last item to be covered in this section is the effects of laboratory systems change on laboratory manpower and space. Table 15 displays full-time equivalents (FTES) by personnel category working in the laboratory during study months. FTES for 1970, 1971, and 1972 are compared to the Baseline 1969.

Table 15. KFH-SF Clinical Laboratory Fulltime Equivalents (FTES) by Worker Category for April 1969, 1970, 1971, and 1972

	Baseline 4/69 # FTES	System II 4/70 # FTES	System II 4/71 # FTES	System II 4/72 # FTES
Doctors (incl. residents)	3.6	3.6	4.2	4.2
Lab supervisors	3.0	3.0	4.0	7.0
Technologists, etc.	48.0	50.0	50.0	46.0
Secretaries	3.0	3.0	1.0	1.0
Recept., clerks, etc.	13.5	26.2	28.0	24.1
	71.1	85.8	87.2	82.3

There was a general increase in manpower of 15.8% from 1969 to 1972. The increase peaked during 1971 (22.6%). It should be remembered that 1971 was also the peak laboratory production period of the years studied— i.e., 1971 had a test production increase of 47% over 1969, and 1972 was 42%. However, as a ratio relationship, production/manpower, 1972 was the greater gain—a ratio of 2.66 while 1971 was 2.08.

Space allocation has remained unchanged during the years of study. The laboratory operated in approximately 10,000 square feet of space. Internal configurations have varied slightly from year to year.

The general conclusion from this special study is that an evolutionary approach to introduction of information technology yields progressive benefits. Mainly these benefits are marked reductions in result reporting delays and errors. Completeness of laboratory information increased. These effects are achieved with reduction in laboratory result producing manpower—i.e., more work (results) is produced in fewer manhours worked. Certainly this stepwise approach permits people to learn and reorient to a different way of working with advanced information tools.

5. Intradepartmental Coordination Study

In 1970, after nursing in KFH-Oakland had successfully converted one unit from Team Nursing to Total Patient Care (TPC), a work group of evaluation and nursing members was commenced to discuss and plan what supports were necessary in order to maintain gains from TPC. Discussions quickly surfaced the fact that, although nursing (and nurses) had changed its mode of operating, support service such as admitting, housekeeping, and dietary continued to do the same things. This meant that support activity was out of synchronization with the delivery of patient care. For example, service and supply was basically stationary, and whatever staff mobility was necessary in procurement was generated by nursing. Nurses fetched and carried even though other staff was hired to do so. In effect, although nurses spent more time in direct patient care, they continued to spend a major fraction of that time walking places to procure things needed to deliver care. This behavior was traceable directly to communication deficiencies between patient care units and support functions.

A year of discussion went on about effective means for mobilizing available resources and design of an effective communication system so that nurses were less often needlessly drawn away from patients. The nursing work group clearly believed it knew what was needed from whom, and most time was spent on how to approach various problems with support functions.

After many false starts, the group decided to define programmatically one area of operation for remediation. The area chosen was management of patient census. The group decided to work on improving communication about Admission/Transfers/Discharges so that control could be exercised over nurse staffing within care units. At the time this decision was made, the number of admissions, transfers, and discharges per day in KHF-Oakland were comparable to those described earlier for KFH-San Francisco (50 admissions, 50 discharges, and 80 transfers).

Discussion went on for a time about which departments were most implicated in census management and who should be invited to join the work group. The first department to be represented at a work group meeting was admitting. Immediately dialogue was commenced concerning the assignment of beds. Nursing does so traditionally. However, the admitting supervisor suggested this function be transferred to admitting since admitting was the department that had the most information related to admissions. Admitting was in a position to provide advanced notice about elective admissions and to coordinate transfers from emergency, coronary care, etc., to any ward; it also was a coordination point through which information could flow to and from the operating room, medical records, housekeeping, and outpatient clinics.

Group agreement was reached that an admitting representative should make daily rounds, decide with head nurses where patients might be assigned, then on the basis of those exchanges assign admissions. This effort was made for a short time by the admitting supervisor. She reported back to the work group that the effort was not working since she had difficulty making connection with head nurses at mutually convenient times with any regularity.

Once again the group addressed itself to means. This time, however, the identity of necessary participants at rounds was also discussed. The outcome of this exchange was that at least housekeeping should be invited to join with admitting and nursing since lack of room-readiness was most often the reason admissions were delayed once discharges occurred. Also, the possibility was discussed of nursing, admitting, and housekeeping making collaborative hospital rounds.

The housekeeping supervisor joined the group. The possibility of making daily rounds to determine patient condition and bed status was discussed. He concurred in the decision to make rounds twice daily (morning and afternoon) on a trial basis to see what could be learned.

Following a trial period of two weeks, the group reviewed its efforts. Several things were changed. First, the group decided to reduce the number of people making rounds and rotate those going to spread the experience. There was always to be representation from nursing, admitting, housekeeping, and unit management. They would begin to standardize the content of information sought, providing a base for engendering unit level participation. Rounds would be timed to suit the work of the care units and provide head nurses time to determine patient need and room status before they arrived.

A new rounds schedule was derived and a standard information sheet designed. The census information sheet specified patient condition—e.g., relative mobility, day of stay, isolation, etc., special equipment needs, anticipated admission, transfers, and discharges (including special devices needed at admission or discharge—was an ambulance required for discharge, etc., were patients being isolated unnecessarily or staying too long in isolation; when were beds emptied, time of day, and how long did it take to prepare them for the next admission?) .

Using this experience as a working data base, an analysis sheet was prepared for doing "Needs to Know" determinations (base for communication networking) which specified who needs to know what, when is it needed, and who communicates by what means (note that all communication is in manual mode).

From "Needs to Know" analysis came:

(1) Admission schedules to patient care units;

(2) Discharge schedules to maids in housekeeping;

(3) Special equipment and supply lists for admissions, transfers, and discharges;

(4) Special accommodation lists—e.g., review isolations and review schedules so determinations can be made of when special patient needs for service and supply cease commensurate with patient improvement;

(5) Determination of social considerations effecting patient comfort—e.g., placement by sex, age, smoking/nonsmoking, TV watching, preference for visitors, etc., and;

(6) Determination of family arrangements and transport when discharged.

Experience with "Needs to Know" analysis made clear another analytic level, "Needs to Participate." The departments represented were able to make considerable impact on management of admissions and transfers. Their effort at improving discharge planning and implementation was minimal.

They succeeded in reducing the elapsed time required for admitting 20–30 surgeries from 7 hours to 4 hours. Before the program, it was common to feed patients (6–10) in the lobby in front of admitting and in the staff dining room. By the time the program was a month old, all patients were having dinner in bed in their rooms. Review of isolation procedures, reasons for transfer, and bed assignment control by admitting reduced transfers by 25%. Advanced notice of discharges to housekeeping improved bed readiness by two hours, and a special private telephone number for maids to call admitting directly when they finished a bed (room) shortened the admitting delay even more.

Discharges present a different picture. About half of the discharges occurring each day are unknown to admitting, nursing, and housekeeping until the afternoon of that day. Admitting/nursing/housekeeping need to know discharges anticipated by members of the medical staff at least the day before discharge. This realization resulted in "Needs to Participate" determination. A presentation was prepared and made to Medical Center and Medical Administration of the status of the work group's effort and its awareness that further progress was minimized without involvement of the medical staff and other medical center departments. As a consequence of this exchange, progress reports were made by the work group to medical staff and other department heads. Following these work group presentations, administration established a task force to interface with the work group in planning more effectively for discharge.

During the course of this study in interdepartmental collaboration, a telecommunication terminal for managing patient census was installed and tested in the study facility (KFH-San Francisco). Many of the manual paper and pencil techniques and procedures worked out by the Census Management Work Group, KFH-Oakland, were adaptable on the terminal installed at KFH-San Francisco.

Initial testing of the terminal's effect on census maintenance in KFH-San Francisco was striking. It was clearly not an acceptable operating device when first evaluated (1972). It did, however, present a real-time opportunity to monitor its function in relation to current manual methods of census management. This monitoring effort clearly indicated where and what training efforts were needed to incorporate the terminal behaviorally— that is, to substitute it for other devices in use. Monitoring of the terminal also indicated significant problems across the interface between admitting and patient care units. For example, the best, most current information about patient census is maintained on each patient care unit independent of admitting. The units inform admitting of census changes when convenient for them, which is frequently hours and sometimes the day after the change occurs. Inaccurate information in admitting, due to uncontrolled input from care units, causes doctors, support functions, and visitors to be misinformed about patient location.

Combination of the human system development in KFH-Oakland and one technologic development in KFH-San Francisco strongly suggest a new, shared approach developing and evaluating telecommunication devices in health care delivery systems. The role perceived in this context, of computers in communication, is beyond high-speed information processing. The computer's new role is that of a primary evolutionary instrument permitting short delay determination of operational consequences of communication procedure designs in the delivery of care. Quickly acquired data can be used in accelerating data based systems modification.

6. Results of Preliminary System Utility Study

a. **Discussion groups.**   There were four discussion groups where 41 physicians participated; of these, 27 were staff physicians and 14 were residents. In this group, there was one female resident; the rest were males. There were also four discussion groups of nurses; all were females except one. Participants included a cross section of hospital departments with physicians and nurses from the following specialty areas:

Obstetrics	Medicine
Gynecology	Surgery
Nursery	Orthopedics
Pediatrics	Otolaryngology
Ophthalmology	Urology
Emergency room	Pathology
Radiology	Nursing service (Director's office)

A member from each of the specialty areas was not necessarily present at each discussion group. Consequently, specialty areas actually represented at the meetings are shown in the tables presented. The analysis of tape recording contents revealed that, almost exclusively, group discussions centered on problems associated with the utility of the information system. Tables 16 and 17 have been constructed to show, in summary fashion, the number of comments and the proportion of time spent by participants discussing the problems of information system utility.

For physicians, problems associated with the staffing of nurses was seen as the most troublesome. The laboratory subsystem was viewed as a close

Table 16. Staff Physician Response During Group Discussions, Organized by Proportion of Time Spent Discussing Information Problems

Subject	Number of comments[1]	Proportion total time	Proportion of time spent commenting by specialty department participants				
			Ob/ Gyn	Surg.	Med.	Ped.	Other med. spec.[2]
X-ray	9	.048	.000	.003	.003	.003	.039
Lab	43	.191	.032	.024	.073	.029	.033
Pharmacy	5	.036	.028	.000	.000	.000	.008
Admitting	24	.113	.040	.007	.018	.000	.048
Staffing	56	.223	.000	.000	.007	.007	.030
Dietary	7	.044	.052	.040	.083	.016	.032
Other*	63	.345	.043	.048	.063	.019	.172
Total	207	1.000	.195	.122	.247	.074	.362

* Problems contained in "Other" were unrelated to information commerce.
[1] A comment is a group exchange of varying duration on a specific subject.
[2] Opthalmology, Orthopedics, Otolaryngology, Urology.

Rank by number of comments			Rank by time spent	
Staffing	56		Staffing	.223
Laboratory	43		Laboratory	.191
Admitting	24		Admitting	.113
X-ray	9		X-ray	.048
Dietary	7		Dietary	.044
Pharmacy	5		Pharmacy	.036
Other*	63			

Table 17. Nurse Response During Group Discussion by Proportion of Time Spent Discussing Information Problems

Subject	No. of comments[1]	Proportion total time	Proportion of time spent commenting by specialty department participants						
			Ob/Gyn	Surg.	Med.	Ped.	Other[2] med. spec.	Other[3]	Nsry. & del. rm.
X-Ray	28	.050	.001	.016	.003	.017	.013	.000	.000
Laboratory	101	.262	.023	.148	.038	.010	.032	.002	.009
Pharmacy	59	.139	.018	.076	.026	.001	.016	.000	.002
Admitting	72	.180	.020	.115	.020	.005	.019	.001	.000
Staff	49	.096	.018	.045	.015	.000	.013	.000	.005
Dietary	24	.073	.002	.051	.000	.000	.012	.008	.000
Other*	72	.190	.012	.063	.063	.010	.028	.002	.012
Total	405	1.000	.094	.514	.166	.043	.133	.013	.028

* Problems contained in "Other" were unrelated to information commerce.
[1] A comment is a group exchange of varying duration on a specific subject.
[2] Opthalmology, Orthopedics, Otolaryngology, Urology.
[3] Emergency Room, Pathology, Radiology, Nursing Service (Director's Office).

Rank by number of comments:
Laboratory	101
Admitting	72
Pharmacy	59
Staffing	49
X-Ray	28
Dietary	24

Rank by proportion of time spent:
Laboratory	.262
Admitting	.180
Pharmacy	.139
Staffing	.096
Dietary	.073
X-Ray	.050

second. Physicians were also concerned with the problems of the admitting subsystem. Less concern was shown regarding the problems of the x-ray, dietary, and pharmacy subsystems. This was true for both the number of comments made and for the time spent discussing these issues.

The nurses focused primarily on the laboratory subsystem as the most problem-laden. The admitting and pharmacy subsystems were each seen by the nurses as containing problems of much the same magnitude. The nurses did not see staffing problems in the same light as did the physicians. However, physicians and nurses agreed that the dietary and x-ray subsystems presented the fewest problems.

b. Questionnaire responses.   The questionnaire was completed by 131 physicians and 68 nurses for a total of 199 completed questionnaires. Two physicians turned in incomplete questionnaires which are not included in the study report. The breakdown was as follows:

Chief of Service	14		Supervisor RN	4
Staff doctor	83		Head RN	9
Resident	22		Staff RN	46
Intern	12		LVN	9
	131			68

(1) Characteristics of respondents.

(a) Age of staff. Table 18 shows that, for all questions in the questionnaire, younger physicians saw a significantly greater number of problems than did older physicians. It may also be noted in this table that the younger physicians had fewer "no opinion" responses than did older ones. (Note the median age of 37 was used to divide physicians).

Younger and older physicians' responses on both dimensions, frequency of occurrence and degree of difficulty were significantly different, as can be observed from Table 18.

Table 19 indicates that, for nurses on all questions, there was not a significant response difference attributable to age. When examining nurses' views in terms of frequency of occurrence and degree of difficulty, there was significant age difference. The older nurses reacted to more information system problems.

(b) Length of staff service. Physician responses (Table 20) indicate that there is a significant difference between those with shorter and those with longer lengths of service with the organization. The difference holds for both problem frequency and degree of difficulty induced by the problems. Physicians of shorter tenure reported more and severer problems.

Nurses showed no general difference when compared by length of service (Table 21). However, nurses of longer service did react significantly to the degree of difficulty information problems create in the hospital.

Table 18. Physician Response to All Questions by Age Groups and for Frequency of Occurrence and Degree of Difficulty Such Problems Were Seen Creating

Total Responses	System Utility Response Matrix Response Options										
Age	1	2	3	4	5	6	7	8	9	10	Total
Younger 36 and less	559	409	150	174	450	218	106	165	556	975	3762
$N=66$	15	11	4	4	12	6	3	4	15	26	100%
Older 37 and more	278	296	289	213	511	269	51	149	522	1127	3705
$N=65$	8	8	8	6	14	7	1	4	14	30	100%
Total response	837	705	439	387	961	487	157	314	1078	2102	7467

$$X^2=36.54 \ (p<.0001) \ df=1^*$$

Frequency of Occurrence of Such Problems									
Age	1	2	3	4	5	6	7	8	9	Total
Younger 36 and less	559	174	106	409	450	165	150	218	556	2787
$N=66$	20	6	4	15	16	6	5	8	20	100%
Older 37 and more	278	213	51	296	511	149	289	269	522	2578
$N=65$	11	8	2	11	20	6	11	11	20	100%
Total response	837	387	157	705	961	314	439	487	1078	5365

$$X^2=59.06 \ (p<.0001) \ df=1^*$$

Degree of Difficulty Such Problems Created									
Age	1	2	3	4	5	6	7	8	9	Total
Younger 36 and less	559	409	150	174	450	218	106	165	556	2787
$N=66$	20	15	5	6	16	8	4	6	20	100%
Older 37 and more	278	296	289	213	511	269	51	149	522	2578
$N=65$	11	11	11	8	20	11	2	6	20	100%
Total response	837	705	439	387	961	487	157	314	1078	5365

$$X^2=17.91 \ (p<.0001) \ df=1^*$$

* Throughout this section, p is estimated from *A Nomogram for Chi Square*, J. Am. Stat. Assoc., March, 1965, p. 345.

Table 19. Nurse Response to All Questions by Age Groups and for Frequency of Occurrence and Degree of Difficulty Such Problems Were Seen Creating

Total Responses   Systems Utility Response Matrix Response Options

Age	1	2	3	4	5	6	7	8	9	10	Total
Younger 29 and less	280	253	73	83	303	116	28	86	352	307	1881
$N=33$	15	13	4	5	16	6	1	5	19	16	100%
Older 30 and more	331	225	160	109	226	113	35	99	291	376	1995
$N=35$	17	13	8	5	11	6	2	5	14	19	100%
Total response	611	508	233	192	529	229	63	185	643	683	3876

$$X^2 = 2.43 \quad df = 1^*$$
N.S.

Frequency of Occurrence of Such Problems

Age	1	2	3	4	5	6	7	8	9	Total
Younger 29 and less	280	83	28	253	303	86	73	116	352	1574
$N=33$	18	5	2	16	19	6	5	7	22	100%
Older 30 and more	331	109	35	255	226	99	160	113	291	1619
$N=35$	20	7	2	16	14	6	10	7	18	100%
Total response	611	192	63	508	529	185	233	229	643	3193

$$X^2 = 5.26 \ (p < .025) \quad df = 1^*$$

Degree of Difficulty Such Problems Created

Age	1	2	3	4	5	6	7	8	9	Total
Younger 29 and less	280	253	73	83	303	116	28	86	352	1574
$N=33$	18	16	5	5	19	7	2	6	22	100%
Older 30 and more	331	255	160	109	226	113	35	99	291	1619
$N=35$	20	16	10	7	14	7	2	6	18	100%
Total response	611	508	233	192	529	229	63	185	643	3193

$$X^2 = 12.57 \ (p < .0005) \quad df = 1^*$$

Table 20. Physician Response to All Questions by Length of Service for Frequency of Occurrence and Degree of Difficulty

Total Responses	System Utility Response Matrix Response Options										
Length of service	1	2	3	4	5	6	7	8	9	10	Total
Shorter 3 years or less	509	386	160	163	436	214	102	138	523	960	3591
$N=63$	14	11	4	4	12	6	3	4	15	27	100%
Longer 4 years or more	328	319	279	224	525	273	55	176	555	1142	3876
$N=68$	8	8	7	6	14	7	2	5	14	29	100%
Total Response	837	705	439	387	961	487	157	314	1078	2102	7467

$X^2=22.65$ $(p < .0001)$ $df=1*$

Frequency of Occurrence of Such Problems										
Length of service	1	2	3	4	5	6	7	8	9	Total
Shorter 3 years or less	509	163	102	386	436	138	160	214	523	2631
$N=63$	19	6	4	15	17	5	6	8	20	100%
Longer 4 years or more	328	224	55	319	525	176	279	273	555	2734
$N=68$	12	8	2	12	19	7	10	10	20	100%
Total Response	837	387	157	705	961	314	439	487	1078	5365

$X^2=37.96$ $(p < .0001)$ $df=1*$

Degree of Difficulty Such Problems Created										
Length of service	1	2	3	4	5	6	7	8	9	Total
Shorter 3 years or less	509	386	160	163	436	214	102	138	523	2631
$N=63$	19	15	6	6	17	8	4	5	20	100%
Longer 4 years or more	328	319	279	224	525	273	55	176	555	2734
$N=68$	12	12	10	8	19	10	2	7	20	100%
Total Response	837	705	439	387	961	487	157	314	1078	5365

$X^2=16.65$ $(p < .0001)$ $df=1*$

Table 21. Nurse Response to All Questions by Length of Service for Frequency of Occurrence and Degree of Difficulty

Total Responses	System Utility Response Matrix Response Options										
Length of service	1	2	3	4	5	6	7	8	9	10	Total
Shorter 2 years or less	254	219	65	105	264	102	30	83	336	252	1710
N=30	15	13	4	6	15	6	2	5	19	15	100%
Longer 3 years or more	357	289	168	87	265	127	33	102	307	431	2166
N=38	16	13	8	4	12	6	2	5	14	20	100%
Total Response	611	508	233	192	529	229	63	185	643	683	3876

$$X^2 = 1.02 \quad df = 1*$$
N.S.

Frequency of Occurrence of Such Problems										
Length of service	1	2	3	4	5	6	7	8	9	Total
Shorter 2 years or less	254	105	30	219	264	83	65	102	336	1458
N=30	17	7	2	15	18	6	5	7	23	100%
Longer 3 years or more	357	87	33	289	265	102	168	127	307	1735
N=38	20	5	2	17	15	6	10	7	18	100%
Total Response	611	192	63	508	529	185	233	229	643	3193

$$X^2 = 2.90 \quad df = 1*$$
N.S.

Degree of Difficulty Such Problems Created										
Length of service	1	2	3	4	5	6	7	8	9	Total
Shorter 2 years or less	254	219	65	105	264	102	30	83	336	1458
N=30	17	15	5	7	18	7	2	6	23	100%
Longer 3 years or more	357	289	168	87	265	127	33	102	307	1735
N=38	20	17	10	5	15	7	2	6	18	100%
Total Response	611	508	233	192	529	229	63	185	643	3193

$$X^2 = 19.99 \ (p < .0001) \quad df = 1*$$

Table 22. Comparison of Responses by Medical Staff and All Other Staff Including Responses Concerning the Ancillary Services in the Hospital

All	Systems Utility Response Matrix Response Options										
Questions (57)	1	2	3	4	5	6	7	8	9	10	Total
Responses of medical staff	461	445	212	213	468	228	57	103	416	533	3135
$N=55$	15	14	7	7	15	7	2	3	13	17	100%
Responses of all other staff	991	767	458	372	1020	490	164	397	1306	2243	8208
$N=144$	12	9	6	5	12	06	2	5	16	27	100%
Total all responses	1452	1212	670	585	1488	718	221	500	1721	2776	11343

$X^2=21.078$ $(p < .0001)$ $df=1^*$

Admission Questions (9)	1	2	3	4	5	6	7	8	9	10	Total
Responses of medical staff	82	66	32	37	78	36	19	20	72	53	495
$N=55$	17	13	6	7	16	7	4	4	15	11	100%
Responses of all other staff	159	114	69	56	152	78	39	69	230	330	1296
$N=144$	12	9	5	4	12	6	3	5	18	26	100%
Total all responses	241	180	101	93	230	114	58	89	302	383	1791

$X^2=49.91$ $(p < .0001)$ $df=1^*$

Laboratory Questions (20)	1	2	3	4	5	6	7	8	9	10	Total
Responses of medical staff	217	214	80	80	165	71	16	26	98	133	1100
$N=55$	20	20	7	7	15	6	2	02	9	12	100%
Responses of all other staff	408	363	209	148	394	181	64	131	366	616	2880
$N=144$	14	13	7	5	14	6	2	5	13	21	100%
Total all responses	625	577	289	228	559	252	80	157	464	749	3980

$X^2=94.27$ $(p < .0001)$ $df=1^*$

Table 22 (continued)

Staffing Questions (7)	Systems Utility Response Matrix Response Options										
	1	2	3	4	5	6	7	8	9	10	Total
Responses of medical staff	58	66	27	21	82	31	6	16	45	33	385
$N=55$	15	17	7	5	21	8	2	4	12	9	100%
Responses of all other staff	130	105	69	49	167	83	12	57	159	177	1008
$N=144$	13	10	7	5	17	8	1	6	16	17	100%
Total all responses	188	171	96	70	249	114	18	73	204	210	1393

$X^2=25.00$ ($p < .0001$) $df=1^*$

Pharmacy Questions (8)	1	2	3	4	5	6	7	8	9	10	Total
Responses of medical staff	13	19	27	21	37	31	5	18	100	169	444
$N=55$	3	4	6	5	8	7	1	4	24	38	100%
Responses of all other staff	40	51	45	25	84	52	27	45	276	511	1152
$N=144$	3	4	4	2	7	5	3	4	24	44	100%
Total all responses	53	70	72	46	121	83	32	63	376	680	1596

$X^2=9.37$ ($p < .013$) $df=1^*$

X-Ray Questions (9)	1	2	3	4	5	6	7	8	9	10	Total
Responses of medical staff	70	69	37	33	69	48	5	11	73	80	495
$N=55$	14	14	7	7	14	10	1	2	15	16	100%
Responses of all other staff	144	96	53	67	156	77	17	62	222	402	1296
$N=144$	11	8	4	5	12	6	1	5	17	31	100%
Total all responses	214	165	90	100	225	125	22	73	295	482	1791

$X^2=52.97$ ($p < .0001$) $df=1^*$

Table 22   (continued)

Dietary	Systems Utility Response Matrix Response Options										
Questions (4)	1	2	3	4	5	6	7	8	9	10	Total
Responses of medical staff	21	11	9	21	37	11	6	12	27	65	220
$N=55$	10	5	4	10	17	5	3	5	12	29	100%
Responses of all other staff	110	38	13	27	67	19	9	33	53	207	576
$N=144$	19	6	2	5	12	3	2	6	9	36	100%
Total all responses	131	49	22	48	104	30	15	45	80	272	796

$$X^2=0.4 \text{ N.S.}$$

(c) Extent of use of information system. The reaction of staff on Medicine is compared to combined staffs from other services. This division was based on the determination that Medicine is the source of greatest use of the information system. (More than 50% of all intramural messages originate from Medicine.)

The data in Table 22 shows that there is a significant difference in responses to problems with the manual information system between staff in Medicine and other hospital staff members. The staff in Medicine saw the greatest number of problems with the information system. This represents responses of both physicians and nurses.

(d) Remoteness of staff to information system. Another facet of staff's judgment about utility is determined by the relative distance of their primary work assignment from the phenomena being studied. In effect, it is speculated that persons spending most of their time and having prime responsibility in settings where study events take place have different reactions about s ̦stems problems than persons whose primary work assignment is elsewhere.

It is asserted that workers assigned in (proximal to) the system under investigation are more urgently familiar with day-to-day information processes and requirements and will, therefore, respond more strongly to questions about relevant operating problems. The assertion is made that persons closest to, more immersed in, and reliant on information outcomes (results) will express the strongest views concerning the relative influence given problems will exert.

The above assertions were preliminarily tested by examining the proportional responses of work groups, more and less remote, in terms of strong response (Cell 1, Most Difficulty and Most Frequently—see Section E.4.b.)

and no response (Cell 10, No Opinion). Table 23 arrays the former, and Table 24 arrays the latter.

As seen in Table 23, nurses generally respond to problems in all areas more strongly than do doctors. Direct responsibility for execution of routine operations rests with the nurse. She is therefore more proximate to system problems, while the doctor with less direct responsibility for execution is more remote.

This relationship holds generally between subcategories within the nurse group and subcategories within the doctor group. Considering Head Nurses, Staff Nurses, and LVNs as least remote, they report stronger concern than any other group, with one exception. Residents and interns report greater concern than other groups about laboratory problems. Since this group has major concern with the results from this area, such an outcome is consistent

Table 23. Proportional Response of Staff Groups to Questionnaire Items by Problem Areas in Terms of Most Difficulty and Most Frequently*

		Most difficulty and most frequently					
		Adm	Lab	Staff	Pharm	X-ray	Diet
1	Chiefs	.10	.07	.10	.01	.03	.02
2	Staff	.13	.13	.10	.01	.12	.07
3	Res. & Int.	.11	.29	.14	.003	.10	.10
4	All drs	.12	.16	.11	.01	.11	.07
5	Supervisor nurses	.17	.09	.11	—	.03	.25
6	Head nurses	.15	.19	.17	.06	.17	.31
7	Staff & LVN	.16	.15	.19	.08	.15	.36
8	All nurses	.16	.43	.18	.07	.15	.35

* Proportions represent Cell 1 responses only (Most Difficulty and Most Frequently) from the response display. (See Section B.4.b)

Table 24. Proportional Response of Staff Groups to Questionnaire Items by Problem Areas in Terms of No Opinion*

		No Opinions					
		Adm	Lab	Staff	Pharm	X-ray	Diet
1	Chiefs	.30	.37	.17	.70	.40	.54
2	Staff	.21	.23	.18	.55	.31	.43
3	Res. & int.	.19	.10	.09	.48	.23	.40
4	All drs	.21	.21	.16	.55	.30	.44
5	Supervisor nurses	.06	.09	.04	.16	.19	.19
6	Head nurses	.14	.08	.11	.21	.12	.14
7	Staff & LVN	.24	.16	.15	.22	.22	.16
8	All nurses	.22	.15	.14	.21	.21	.16

* Proportions represent Cell 10 only (No Opinion) from the response display.

with the assertion. Similarly, it is not surprising that chiefs of service generally report fewer strong responses to problems since they are farthest removed from actual execution of routines.

Results shown in Table 24 are also consistent with the assertion that remote work groups will yield no response to problem-oriented questions. Generally, the proportions in Table 24 are inverse to those in Table 23. For example, in comparing chiefs of service to staff RNs and LVNs in Table 24, chiefs of service respond with significantly higher proportions of "No Opinion" for all problem categories than staff RNs and LVNs. In Table 23, exactly the reverse is so. Staff RNs and LVNs respond with significantly higher proportions of strong reaction in all areas than do the chiefs of service. Comparisons within and between other categories of doctors and nurses show similar tendencies.

(2) Relative response by ancillary service. Table 25 provides a different view of utility by depicting relative doctor and nurse responses to ancillary service functions as relative problem generators. Doctors and nurses alike report that laboratory procedures created most difficult and frequent problems. The similarity of view between the groups is largely contributed by resident and intern reaction to laboratory problems. If responses by chiefs of service and staff doctors were considered alone, this emphasis would be greatly reduced for the doctor group.

The strength of group response to problems in one other service area can be broadly explained in terms of the part played by the service in the

Table 25. Comparison of Physician and Nurse Responses Regarding Relative Utility of Ancillary Services

Physicians—Most Frequent and Difficult Problems			Nurses—Most Frequent and Difficult Problems		
	Number	Percent		Number	Percent
Laboratory	422	51	Laboratory	203	33
Admitting	143	17	Dietary	95	16
Staffing	101	12	Staffing	87	14
X-ray	124	15	Admitting	98	16
Dietary	36	4	X-ray	90	15
Pharmacy	11	1	Pharmacy	38	6
Total	837	100%	Total	611	100%
Total responses	=7467		Total responses	=3876	
Responses viewed as being most frequent and creating the most difficulty (Cell 1)	= 837		Responses viewed as being most frequent and creating the most difficulty (Cell 1)	= 611	
Percentage total	11		Percentage total	16	

work of the group and the relative frequency of contact between group function and the service. Nurses are intimately involved in feeding many patients; and they have frequent, intense discourse with dietary. This is not so for doctors. Nurses report relatively high order problems with dietary whereas doctors generally report low order problems.

Other service areas generate comparable reaction to problems by both groups, except for pharmacy. Pharmacy apparently is reacted to as an area of high utility.

(3) Comparison to HCS. The present evaluation of utility of the manual information system for hospital staff groups provides a base for comparison of similarly extracted staff reaction following the installation of HCS.

In addition to the results reported, results from refined analyses of the utility data will be available. For example, the comparisons reported in Table 22, Medical Staff against other staff, are being refined to determine which specific subgroups are contributing to the observed differences. Is the source of difference doctors or nurses generally, subgroups of each specifically, or are all groups in the medical service equal contributors? This and other questions are under study.

Additional data are being developed to evaluate staff reaction to the system at a different level. Measures of group-related absenteeism and turnover are being taken and examined. A subsequent report of this effort will be made. Rates of absenteeism and turnover under the manual system will be compared to rates under HCS.

(4) Staff readings to change. This dimension, mentioned above, is receiving current attention with respect to development of adequate procedures of measurement. This effort will be reported on as progress is made.

G. CONCLUSIONS

The studies presented in the preceding section point out the types and range of concerns which exploratory and definitive systems evaluation has in preparation of assessment required by a system change of the magnitude of a Hospital Computer System (HCS). Reconstruction of an information system influences operation of nurses in patient care units wherein Patient Care-Non-Communication can be adversely effected by computer terminal introduction while Patient Care-Communication is made more efficient. Reconstruction of the clinical laboratory information system similarly can produce adverse effects on laboratory operation and patient units alike. Introduction of terminals as interfaces between patient care units and support areas threaten to exaggerate existing difficulties in cooperation between subsystems, the problem to which the patient census management work group experiment addressed itself.

These baseline efforts have a common theme. The theme is that communication technology (data processing) is not an end but a means. To be effective in a human system sense, means must facilitate behavior that achieves goals valued by active participants in the system as well as more formally stated system objectives. Those performing needed research and development in creating new HCS prototypes—policymakers, designers, and evaluators alike—must not confuse the means they are struggling to invent with the ends they are obliged to honor.

The staff of patient units function at the core of an operation obligated to maximize their effort to care for the sick. Any instrumental means must abet that effort. In a sense, the clinical laboratory serves as an instrumental means for identifying patient problems and monitoring the effects of treatment. The principal function of communication is to provide conveyance for instrumental information like that produced in the means-ends relationship of laboratory to patient problem solution.

In small part, the problems the laboratory has in receiving work orders from patient units, locating patients so that specimens can be drawn, and performing its own work speedily and accurately to assure timely reception of results illustrate the more general need to bring about a strong spirit of cooperation between participants remote from one another who share a common stake in patients' welfare. The Patient Census Management work group study was started to determine methods of approach that effectively interfaced these operationally remote participants so stronger ties of cooperation emerged. Through this effort, it was thought, insight could be gained about what support people would need to assist in adjusting their existing patterns of work behavior if computer terminal communication devices were to be given fair operational trials.

Evaluation of staff in the evolution of the Patient Census Management group in KFH-Oakland and preliminary evaluation of staff during test trials of various terminal operations in KFH-San Francisco in 1972 suggested similar conclusions about the future.

Both enterprises, one person-oriented, the other computer-oriented, suggest that people do not change long-standing behavior even when they perceive common problems. Innovation is probably not possible until perceived ends, not means, are internalized by essential partners in complex operations. It is often said that it is relatively easy to get persons to agree about ends (objectives), but collaboration breaks down over means. The evaluation experience, both with the work group and trial tests of terminal operation, are pursuasive that difficulties in interfacing human effort, either by manual or computer means, arise from basic disagreement about operational ends and effects among people at parochially diverse but related stations.

The relative success at cooperation by nursing, admitting, and housekeeping in the work group is attributable to adoption and internalization of statements of common ends, visible through their dedication to collaboration in mutual hospital rounds. Once this action had taken hold, they were willing to evolve the means—e.g., communication network, informational content, forms, etc. Evolution of structure and content became a continuous, common learning experience which reinforced their shared sense of goal.

The disadvantage of manual communication methods in the evolutionary training process is the long time that is required by manual monitoring means to determine if what you are doing differently advanced you to your goal any better than what you *were* doing. This disadvantage, as was clear during terminal tests, is overcome when computer devices are used to monitor human reaction to work generally and specifically to assist in attempts to adapt behavior and modify environment. Presence of the computer shortens the period for evaluating operations to days from the weeks and sometimes months necessary in the manual mode.

The implications of the above statement for system improvement and evolution are great. Effort can be made to permit people to experiment with means if they can emotionally agree to functional ends. The process of experimenting (the computer provides control) can be short-term tests of relational changes in agreed-to operations where effects of change can have high human utility with minimum operational trauma and at low cost. It provides a foundation, virtually, for guiding training as you go. From the view of system science, a meaningful study could be done each week. Each study yields knowledge about interactional complexity and information, needed by collaborative performers who must know which turn in the road to take next.

REFERENCES

1. Barker, R. and Wright, H. *Midwest and Its Children.* New York: Henry Holt, 1954.
2. Barker, R. "The Ecology of Motivation" *Symposium of Psychological Ecology, U. of Missouri, 1962.*
3. Flagle, C. D. "Evaluation Techniques for Medical Information Systems." *Proceedings of a Conference on Medical Information Systems, National Center for Health Services Research and Development, Rockville, Maryland, 1970.*
4. Keynes, M. "Subjective Probability." *Royal Acad. Econ.* 31 (1921) : 60–69.
5. Kyburg, H. E., Jr., and Smokler, H. E. *Studies in Subjective Probability,* N.Y.: John Wiley, 1964.
6. Mumford, L., *The Pentagon of Power,* N.Y.: Harcourt, 1970.
7. Williams, E. P., and Vineberg, S. E. "The Interface of Environment and Behavior." *Ecological Research in Complex Organizations. Symposium, Annual Meeting Amer. Psychol. Assoc., 1969.*

CHAPTER FOURTEEN

Operations Research with Hospital Computer Systems

by Charles D. Flagle

A. DEFINITIONS AND OBJECTIVES

Operations Research (OR) is concerned with the rational allocation of resources to meet objectives. Historically, it has been applied to complex, organized human activities in which some critical resources are scarce, where new technology requires forecasts of performance of future systems, and where objectives are fairly clearcut. Historically, also, its applications have been in competitive situations in which a winning strategy, military or commercial, is sought and a variety of alternative strategies are available. The exercises in operations research have had the nature of playing out, on paper or in small field trials, the various alternative strategies in order to forecast the consequences of each. In the military and in industry, operations research has been the necessary concomitant of new technology, whose contribution to operations has to be forecast in order to plan rationally and to avoid costly errors.

In the health services, applications of operations research have had some of the character of their predecessors in the military and in industry. The attribute of allocation of scarce resources has certainly been present, for many of the OR studies have had their origins in the shortage of physicians and nurses or the congestion of clinics. The objectives have most often been to find ways to do more with the limited resources available—to care for more patients with the given set of human and physical resources. Increasingly, the same objective is posed in the hope that some new technology may aid in this expansion of human capacities. Such technology, or products of technology, such as prepackaged disposable supplies, automated laboratory equipment, and computers all have the potential to increase human producitvity on the scene of medical care. The immediate problem to be analyzed is how they can be made to do so; and the long-term question is whether, if we relax the constraint of personnel shortage, some technologically aided system is preferable to a more labor intensive one? What is the optimum mix of manpower and technology needed to render good health care to the population? What is the best organization form and network of services? These are the questions asked by some hospital directors, health planners, and administrators.

The objective of operations research teams (or systems analysts or industrial engineers) is to help answer those questions by observation and analysis and by design, trial, and evaluation of new alternatives. The immediate roles of the computer in the operations research process are twofold: first, it is a means of providing operational data; second, it is a computational tool to aid in projecting outcomes of alternative possible operations. There is the greater role of the computer as an integral part of the cybernetic process of communication and control of resource allocations. The following account of operations research studies in hospitals and the emerging comprehensive health care systems illustrates in many cases the need for more sensitive and timely processes of observation and analysis of operations in order to rationalize the allocation of medical care resources from an economic point of view and a human one as well.

At the outset of this chapter, it should be noted that our topic is in a very dynamic state at the time of writing. A review of some of the hospital centers in which developments are underway to install computers as an integral part of the management process reveals a great preoccupation with making new technology work in a pragmatic way. It is too early for evaluation, too early for exploring various alternatives for achieving some specified operational goal, too early to attempt to exploit the data-providing potential of computer based information systems for research aims.

All the examples cited here of operations research with hospital computers should be read with an awareness that they are seen at a point in time. One cannot say for sure where any one example may lead; but the efforts, taken together, reveal the growth of hospitals and health services as vastly more information-rich systems. This has both good and bad points. No one needs an increased flow of uncoordinated data. Therefore, much of the operations research being built upon the appearance of computers in hospitals has the character of exploring alternatives for use of increased data flow for decision processes.

B. COMPUTERS IN RESEARCH ON HOSPITAL OPERATIONS

The development of operations research activities in hospitals predates, for the most part, the use of computers in the same hospitals for administrative purposes. While there may have been university computing systems available to the early operations researchers in the health field, these were often different machines than those ultimately adopted by hospitals.

A few hospitals were interested and often made their first investment in equipment suitable for business operations in the late 1950's or early 1960's. Motivations for their use were the direct substitution for routine payroll, purchasing, and billing operations, with programming in languages more suitable for business operations than for research. It was possible to have two different computer systems under the same roof, with research and business separated in their own computer centers.

Nevertheless, routine reporting for business purposes quickly produced some opportunities for extending operations research studies already underway. The collection of inpatient drug orders for charge purposes, for example, made possible a calculation of cumulative dosages given to patients as well as aggregate consumption of drugs as an aid in inventory control. This came at a time when several investigators were making comparative studies of drug administration systems on hospital wards. It revealed the potential contribution to the medication process by hospital administration and the potential of coordinating the processes of medical care, business operations, and research in a single, computer-based information system. It is of interest to trace the evolution of operations research studies in hospitals and to see the convergence with developments of computers in hospitals. The following examples are drawn from studies of patient care in inpatient and outpatient settings and from studies of ancillary and support services.

1. Research in Outpatient Services and Evolution of Computer Simulation Models

An early focus of research attention was on the operation of hospital outpatient clinics, especially in the large urban medical complexes. These clinics had become notoriously overcrowded; it was often expected that a clinic visit would cost the patient one full day of work. A close examination of some clinic operations revealed a basically adequate facility and staff, but congestion and delay were related to block appointment systems and to erratic patterns of patient arrivals and physician availability.

A first approach to such problems was an analysis of models of patient flow through the system in terms of queuing or waiting-line theory. Bailey[1] was able to show that long waiting lines of patients were not necessary to protect the physician from idle periods and that only a few waiting patients could reduce the probability of an empty queue to very low levels. However, queuing theory required some simplifying assumptions about the statistical patterns of patient arrivals and service times. The real clinic was somewhat more complicated, and the next step in modeling—a test of validity of theory—was to build a simulation model of the clinic. Such a model could accept any arbitrary distribution of arrival and service times.

One of the earliest studies of patient flow in an outpatient clinic was reported by Gabrielson, et al.[2] in an effort to reduce delays and congestion in the Pediatric Outpatient Clinic in the Johns Hopkins Hospital. The basic data for the study were time histories of the sequence of events experienced by children and their escorts passing through the various services in a pediatric clinic. From these histories it became possible to extract distributions of service times, delay times, and numbers of people waiting for service. An analysis of the data led to some speculations about improved organization of services. Based on ideas of queuing theory, a combining of some administration functions and a providing of parallel channels of flow could be expected to reduce probabilities of delays and bottlenecks. However, the theory rested on some simplified assumptions about the randomness of arrival and service times. In reality, the arrival patterns were in part random, in part scheduled and periodic. To test the hypotheses about improved patient flow, two simulation models of the clinic administration services were constructed, one with the existing configuration of services, the other with a rearrangement for parallel flow. The same arrival pattern was imposed on each configuration. The results indicated large queues of patients forming in the simulation of the actual clinic in just those services where they did, in fact, form. These bottlenecks disappeared in the simulation. Several administrative functions were revised, and the general principal of parallel flow has prevailed since then.

Perhaps more important in the long run than the specific improvements in clinic operation was acceptance of the idea of a flexible simulation model of the clinic as an administrative tool. By fortunate coincidence, the redesign of the pediatric outpatient service described above for a new building occurred at a time when a computer became available to the medical director of the newly formed Comprehensive Child Care Clinic at Johns Hopkins. By the additional fortunate coincidence of interests in exploiting computer technology, the earlier simulation model was expanded greatly, including medical as well as administrative services. In the simulation model in its present form, the controllable variables include patient arrival and scheduling processes, number of physicians and their assignment schedules, fraction of missed appointments, and distribution of service times. The output variables reflect the nature of patient flow and physician activities; the numbers of patients waiting, the length of time required for service, and the fraction of consultation time a patient is not available.

From an operations research point of view, the most striking difference between the present clinic and its predecessor is the availability of information about clinic operations. The computer-based information system now makes available, as a matter of course, those data that required special study forms and efforts in the past. The continuity of gathering operational data makes possible the identification of trends and recurrent utilization of various services. There is now a combination of data on major trends in clinic utilization and knowledge of the effect of these trends on clinic operating characteristics. The combination, founded on the computer based systems, renders operations research a more powerful tool to aid in the management of outpatient services.

2. Research in Nurse Staffing

One of the most difficult problems of hospital administration has been that of staffing and supplying nursing units. The inherent problem of staffing lies in the need for continuous coverage around the clock; this is exacerbated by many other characteristics: a chronic shortage of nursing personnel in many hospitals, a widely varying pattern of patient needs from day to day, and an increasing number of services supplied by other departments at the patients' bedsides.

Initial operations research studies focused on observation of the patient care process. Some of these examined the activities of staff and the distribution of responsibilities. Other studies were patient-centered, attempting to relate observed services performed around the clock to the apparent physical and psychological needs and dependencies of patients. This work has been reported by Connor,[3] Wolfe, and Young.[4, 5] The most striking find was the extreme variability of the aggregate set of patient demands imposed upon a hospital unit nursing staff. It was not uncommon in the medical and surgical units of a teaching hospital to find total time of direct patient care three to four times as great on some days as it had been on that day the week before. The determining factor was found to be the number of intensive care patients. This number is randomly variable and leads to several alternative administration procedures for matching nursing resources to patient needs. All of these call for a short-term prediction of patient need and an ability to assign staff or to place patients to achieve a matching. Ideas of progressive care from intensive to self care units, controlled variable staffing, and controlled admissions all have the rudimentary characteristic of a cybernetic system, with observation of patient characteristics forming the basis for decisions about staffing or patient placement. The mechanisms for predicting patient needs have involved minimal computations of a simple nature, which can be tolerated in a development situation. Mills, Fetter, and Carlisle[6] have developed a computer-based system for classifying patients according to their need for basic resources of the institution.

In retrospect, the work on nurse staffing, which began in the late 1950's and early 1960's, appears to have been on the right track but has not been adequate to bring about striking improvements. All the administrative schemes based on nurses' assessments or classification of patients have the potential of bringing together a compatible number of nurses and patients; however, serious problems remain. Part of the wide and random variation in patient needs lies in the fact that the patients are being treated by a number of physicians, each writing orders independently for each patient. The fact that the skill and number of nurses present is inherently compatible with the needs of a set of patients does not ensure that a rational process of allocation of time will follow or that all physicians' orders will be carried out.

The important role of physicians' orders in determining the pattern of nursing activities has been developed by Simborg[7] in an acute hospital setting and Spencer[8] in a rehabilitation center. In both cases, their efforts to transform a set of physicians' orders for a group of patients into a schedule of activities for nurses has required or justified a computer to handle the multitude of details and to carry out the computations and tests of feasibility of working schedules and assignment of tasks to personnel of various skill levels. Each has performed some operational analysis in ward settings before and after introduction of computer-based workload planning. Each reports about 30% increase in the number of physicians' orders correctly carried out with the guidance of printouts of hourly patients.

These promising ideas in nurse staffing are in the developmental stages. It is evident that increasingly complex algorithms will eventually be required to make optimal use of costly nursing resources in hospitals. The number of variables involved in decisions about staffing is large, the number of options in scheduling activities and allocating tasks is extremely large, and the environment in which decisions must be made is constantly changing. The development of staffing procedures calls for the continued collaborative efforts of physicians, nurses, computer systems analysts, and operations researchers.

3. Management and Logistics Procedures

As noted earlier, the initial application of computers in hospitals were for traditional management purposes. This spurred some efforts toward operational analysis of those functions, particularly in inventory control. An important contemporary development of this kind is to be found in the Federal Health Programs Service of the U. S. Public Health Service.

The development of computer based management systems in the U. S. Public Health Service hospitals has been the responsibility of its Health Services Research Unit, located in the Baltimore USPHS Hospital. It is interesting to see the directions taken in development of a hospital computer when this development is carried out under the aegis of research rather than administration. A review of the many projects underway reveals several striking features. First, the bulk of computer uses are related to medical care processes, particularly in ambulatory care. Second, the demands of installation of the computer system have absorbed the energy of the research group so that existing projects are strongly directed toward system development rather than research. An example of the work of this group, applied to a major administrative logistical problem, is the inventory control system described below.[13]

This inventory and supply system was developed to meet the increasing need of dynamic and flexible information by the Supply Officers in the U. S. Public Health Service Hospitals. This system can and will be changed very easily as future requirements change. The system does not, however, require any changes in the procedure, operational guidelines, and policy set forth by "Headquarters."

Objectives of the system are:

(1) To provide all the information on expendable supplies and capital equipment that is needed by administrative personnel in FHPS Headquarters Offices and each hospital, by each Supply Department within the system, and by the individual sections within each hospital that are associated with the system.

(2) To supply the Finance Departments (or section) in each of the USPHS Hospitals with issue information in the month of issue to satisfy the requirements of the HEW "Umbrella" accounting system.

(3) To update the present system by using more sophisticated data processing equipment, increasing speed, and increasing versatility.

(4) To integrate the present expendable supply information system to the FHPS Management Information System. An Item Set-up Form is required to establish an inventory item in the system. This form contains all necessary data associated with this item that is referred to for all future transactions and reports. This information, once established, will be stored in the computer and changed only when data on that item changes.

The issuing procedure is not changed. That is, the issues by the Supply Department (or section) to each hospital department is carried out by an issue book. *Note:* if the hospital department has more than one CAN number, each CAN number could be considered a separate department. Each issue book contains a list of stocked items and their consumer levels. The department enters the order for supplies in the issue book and returns it to the Supply Department. The Supply Department will forward the issue book to the storeroom where the request will be filled and the amount will also be entered in the book.

The original copies of all departmental issue books which contain the quantity issued in a month become the basis of the "demand analysis report." This report is used then to review quantity replenished.

The system produces purchase orders and a transaction register automatically, as well as many other management reports.

All input forms used in this system will be typed or printed with the Optical Character Reader (OCR) font for scanning purposes. Some of the output reports are used not only as "reports" but as turnaround input forms. These are demand analysis, receiving reports, and inventory adjustment reports.

The main features of the system are:

(1) Trivial capital investment in new equipment; requires only that an OCR font ball be purchased with any existing IBM selectric typewriter (10 characters per inch).

(2) Simple installation, or conversion.

(3) Completeness. The system handles transactions beginning with the vendor of the item to the item's ultimate destination.

(4) Facilitation of the procurement process and reduction of the clerical effort involved in preparation of purchase orders.

(5) Production of compatible financial records of transactions made by the Supply Department.

(6) Resolution of problems inherent with differences in packaging of items received from vendors and then later issued to departments in different packaging units.

(7) Provision of separate and generous length description fields for fully describing the item to both the users of the item and to the supplier of the item with packaging differences handled by the system.

(8) Provision of total, accurate, and rapid accounting of supplies and cost reports for the departments.

(9) Management by exception—reports of unusual conditions in the system with adequate data present for the manager to utilize his resources most effectively.

(10) Use of "grocery list" approach in listing items to users. This greatly minimizes problems in filling orders from stock.

(11) Identification of items by general ledger account and expense class for use with the financial system.

(12) Use of "turnaround documents" in critical areas of issuing, purchasing, and receiving of materials. This eliminates 90% of manual data entry for these transactions and their error.

(13 Comprehensive audit trail of transactions by multiple routes such as department, items, and vendor of all transactions.

(14) Use of "State of Art" techniques to calculate reorder points and economical order quantities. This greatly reduces out-of-stock conditions while permitting inventory levels to be kept at a minimum.

(15) Economical order quantity formula taking into account up to three levels of quantity discounts.

(16) Handling of items with a limited shelf life.

(17) Multipurpose use of forms to minimize the number of forms in the system and make training of operating personnel easier and faster.

(18) Flexibility to adapt to changes.

(19) Multiple places on different forms which can be added to change some of the more frequently changing data elements, such as packaging and prices of items.

(20) Simple adjustment procedures to correct errors.

(21) Closed-loop system that provides for strict control of data in the system.

(22) Simple physical inventory-taking "turnaround" documents to provide for fast, accurate data collection.

(23) Timely and accurate preparation of summary reports on performance of the system.

(24) Low cost of operation.

(25) Maintenance of a 13-period history of usage of an item for usage forecasting purposes, as well as providing a foundation for calculating reorder point and EOQ quantities. Normally a period will be one month.

(26) Generation and support of a voucher register used by the Supply and Finance Departments.

The system was designed to facilitate the hospital supply department in carrying out its functions of providing other hospital departments with needed supplies and in placing and monitoring orders to outside vendors.

The system makes extensive use of a computer to automate various data processing tasks. An extensive data base is established, including information on each item normally stocked in central supply, all vendors supplying the hospital on a regular basis, and the items normally ordered by each hospital department.

This data base enables the hospital to use the methods of inventory theory to establish optimal reordering policies for items in the system. Included in the information stored for each item is a demand history for the previous thirteen months, the current price, any quantity discounts available, the shelf life, the vendor, and any constraints on the quantity of the item that can be ordered.

The system is designed to calculate an EOQ (Economic Order Quantity) for each item to be reordered. This suggested quantity is reviewed by the Supply Chief and he may accept the EOQ or alter it, as he sees fit.

After the system is in operation for some time, various inventory policies will be compared and evaluated using the demand history for each item. It will be possible to compare the costs of the actual reordering policy used for each item with the costs of any other proposed reordering policy. This can be readily done using the established data base and the ability of the computer to carry out large numbers of calculations quickly. It will be possible for the computer "dynamically" to choose the best of several possible reordering policies for each item and use that policy to calculate the suggested EOQ for the item.

4.   Evolution of Research in Clinical Laboratories

The automation of some clinical laboratory procedures, notably blood chemistries, has brought an increase in demands for laboratory services. The role of computers in reporting laboratory results is described in Chapter Seventeen. The work of Barnett and White[9] offers an example of operational research performed simultaneously with the introduction of new technology. They seek to assess the impact of the computer-based reporting system on laboratory activities. The typical problems of hospital operations are quickly revealed; volume of activity is subject to sharp, short-term fluctuation using part-time, unskilled workers with little upward mobility and high turnover and a large reserve of personnel to cover peaks in the workload and deficits in staffing due to vacancies and absenteeism. These problems are exacerbated by a rising trend in demands—about 200% in the past decade.

A review of the results of work studies shows the primary impact of the computer to be one of increasing productive capacity without increasing staff. In part, this comes about by accommodation or stabilization of the peak load phenomenon, in part by replacement of some clerical functions. Studies of the speed and accuracy of reporting laboratory results show some improvement, though the quantitative measures comparing manual and computerized procedures do not reflect the strong subjective preference of staff for the new procedures.

In another set of studies dealing with the impact of computer based reporting of laboratory results, Rappaport[10] has demonstrated the economy of scale phenomenon associated with high cost–high productivity technology He reports a halving of reporting costs, but only when volume of reporting reaches 1500 tests per day.

The kind of analysis reported by Barnett and by Rappaport falls in the categories of work study and cost analysis. Another interest of operations research in the laboratory area is the decision process or inferences drawn from test results. There are numerous studies of computer-aided diagnosis carried out for the most part on research samples of screening or diagnostic data. As the volume of laboratory testing increases, the pressure also increases to base abnormal findings on patterns of test results rather than on limits of single tests. The question is, when will this kind of analysis emerge from research or pilot applications to routine use using hospital computers for analysis and reporting. We are beginning to see such applications in the field of nuclear medicine, where small general purpose computers can be interfaced to a scintillation camera. Wagner and Natarajan[11] have reported the routine use of the computer for image processing by scanning the distribution of a radioactive tracer in studies of the thyroid, lungs, cardiovascular and renal systems. In the case of thyroid disease, in addition to image processing, there is a computer program for calculating and printing out the probabilities of abnormalities. The creation and refinement of such programs is a role of operations research. The routine use of the computer builds rapidly the data base for continuous research in disease processes in screening and diagnosis.

C. OPERATIONS RESEARCH IN HEALTH SYSTEMS PLANNING

Much of the work just described deals with day-to-day operations of hospitals. The concern is for scheduling and allocating existing resources to whatever set of tasks emerges from the particular mix of patients' needs and physicians' orders created each day. The contribution of the hospital computer to these functions lies in its potential for routine collection and reporting of data that would otherwise necessitate a special research effort. Routine collection of significant data over time reveals trends in utilization of resources and facilitates projections and time series analysis. These are useful for planning purposes for they reveal those services which may become over- or under-loaded at some time in the future. As a planning mechanism, the simple consolidation of utilization experience is inadequate in one major respect. It does not provide a rational basis for extrapolating trends into the future, for it relates only to the past experience of the installation, not to the human population from which demand for the institution services originate. Adequate planning can occur only if the institution knows the population it serves and the alternative medical resources available to that population.

One sees an increasing number of hospitals involved in one form or another of comprehensive health services. These take the form of service to a defined population, often covered by contract, with an organized ambulatory care service and provision for extended care beyond the acute hospital. The creation of such a system opens the door to a new set of applications of computers for service and research. Whereas operating units have been the focal point for data collection and analysis in the institutional setting, the patient or subscriber becomes that focal point in the comprehensive care system.

From an administrative point of view, the capability of planning is greatly expanded. If the population to be served is known, demand for services may be predicted on the basis of fairly stable age-sex utilization rates of physicians and hospital services. Furthermore, projections of the age-sex distribution of the population permit forecasts of future demands. Fetter[12] has developed a model of the principal service elements of a hospital. By simulation processes, he can input a forecast pattern of patient demand on the system in terms of arrival rates and lengths of stay in each component. In this way, capacity requirements for clinics and wards can be projected.

D. CONCLUSIONS

The use of hospital computers for operations research is just emerging as this chapter is written. We see a few examples of operational and planning studies built upon routine use of computers in medical and administrative routines. This will undoubtedly increase as the ingenuity and energy of innovators can be turned from the problems of making new systems work to the interesting problems of exploiting the new technology for better management and clinical systems.

REFERENCES

1. Bailey, N. T. J., and Welch, J. D. "Appointment Systems in Hospital Outpatient Departments." *Lancet* 1 (1952) : 1105–1108.
2. Gabrielson, I. W., et al. "Analysis of Congestion in an Outpatient Clinic." *Final Report, USPHS Grant No. W-36.* Baltimore, The Johns Hopkins University, School of Hygiene and Public Health, Department of Public Health Administration (Operations Research), 1960.

3. Connor, R. J., et al. "Effective Use of Nursing Resources; A Research Report." *Hospitals* 35 (1961) : 30–39.

4. Young, J. P., and Wolfe, H. "Staffing the Nursing Unit. Part I. Controlled Variable Staffing." *Nursing Research* 14 (1965) : 236–243.

5. Young, J. P., and Wolfe, H. "Staffing the Nursing Unit. Part II. The Multiple Assignment Technique." *Nursing Research* 14 (1965) : 299–303.

6. Mills, R. E.; Fetter, R. B.; and Carlisle, J. H. "Autogrp-Automated Grouping System." *Administrative Sciences Technical Report No. 52*. New Haven, Yale University, December, 1971.

7. Simborg, D. "Impact of Computerized Information Systems on Hospital Nurse Staffing." *Proceedings of the Invitational Conference on Research on Nurse Staffing in Hospitals, 1972*. Washington, D.C., Division of Nursing, Bureau of Health Manpower Education, National Institutes of Health, 1972.

8. Spencer, W., et al. "Daily Treatment Planning with an On-line Shared Computer System." *Meth. of Infor. in Med.* 8 (1959) : 200–205.

9. White, W. D., and Barnett, G. O. "An Evaluation of the Impact of a Computer Based Information System on the Chemistry Laboratory." *Boston, Massachusetts General Hospital* (mimeographed).

10. Rappaport, A. E., and Gennaro, W. D. "The Economics of Computer Coupled Automation in the Clinical Chemistry Laboratory of the Youngstown Hospital Association." *Comp. in Biomed. Res.*, Vol. 4. Edited by R. Stacy, and B. Waxman. In press.

11. Wagner, H. N., Jr., and Natarajan, T. K. "The Computer in Nuclear Medicine." *Progress Report under USPHS Grant GM 10548*. Division of Nuclear Medicine, The Johns Hopkins Medical Institutions, Baltimore, Maryland (mimeographed).

12. Fetter, R. B. "Planning Models for Health Care Systems." *Administrative Sciences Technical Report No. 52*. New Haven, Yale University (mimeographed).

13. Health Services Research Group. "Computer Application in Health Services Delivery." Federal Health Program Service, H.E.W., April, 1973.

CHAPTER FIFTEEN

Medical Education with Hospital Computer Systems

by Donald A. B. Lindberg

A. THE PROBLEM

The impact of hospital computer systems upon medical education is as inevitable as that of refined gasoline upon the internal combustion engine. Indeed, it is amazing that medical education has for so long run on "bottled gas." This is not to suggest that the mere advent of computing devices in the hospital has in itself at once laid bare for thinkers and learners the facts of medical care for their analysis and consumption. Yet this will happen.

B. DISCLAIMERS

Not included in this present essay are considerations of the pure research uses of computers in medicine.[1] Statistical analyses of experimental data, development of new mathematical techniques for medicine, closed-loop control of physiological manipulations, and computer language development are all of great importance but are more closely linked to university computing centers than hospital computing centers.

The largest experiments in computer-aided instruction are occurring outside of medicine. The alternative examples of a large central machine vs. a distributed network have recently been reviewed.[2] Good technical manuals and programming strategies have been presented for a specific teaching computer.[3] These will not be mentioned further in this chapter.[4]

We will not consider explicitly the contribution made to the learning environment by pure management information systems in hospitals. Let us rather consider those situations in which medical education is formal— that is, in which the individual is consciously trying to learn or teach.

In many areas of medical computing—especially hospital computing—it is possible to consider what theoretically might be accomplished and then to review the real world to check off those potential accomplishments which have been realized. It was obvious ten years ago that clinical laboratories and radiology departments would evolve automated processing systems. The current contributions of coronary care and other intensive care units to reduced patient mortality now make it perfectly plain that such systems will be further refined and widely adapted, regardless of whether the calculations are performed upon general purpose central processors or within dedicated circuitry. Similarly, there can be little doubt that the simple economics of increasing labor costs will make computer-based patient record systems a necessity. Today the problem is in evolving suitable mechanisms for allocating the costs to users for central computer record keeping and, regrettably, to collecting for those costs in advance. The chapters of this book give the reader a chance to examine such a list of accomplishments.

With respect to medical education, the picture is not so clear. It would do the reader a disservice to pretend that hospital computer applications in this field are divided into recitational, tutorial, simulation, and patient management. This or any other current inclusive analysis would ignore the fundamental reorganization which is occurring in the 1970's in medical education. There are good reasons to believe that computers will play a significant role in the educational system which emerges, but it is by no means clear now just what the system itself will look like.

C. THE NEW MEDICAL EDUCATIONAL SYSTEM

The teaching of interns and residents has always been hospital-based. The teaching of medical students is increasingly spreading out of the universities and into the clinics and hospitals. Almost every medical school has increased the number of its hospital affiliations and is leaning more heavily upon the old ones. Many medical schools do not own their own teaching hospitals, and at least one state has forbidden its new state medical schools ever to own a hospital. Part of this trend is explained by a greater willingness on the part of schools to accept broad social responsibility for indigent care. For example, all medical schools in New York City take responsibility for and send their medical students to at least one municipal hospital. Part of this trend is due to the rising financial burden of operating teaching hospitals, a burden which medical schools and universities are no longer able to shoulder.

Along with these changes, one must remember the previous pedagogical changes of the 1950's and 1960's within the medical school itself. Notable events included the virtual death of the lecture system, commitment to enormously increased free and elective time blocks for students, construction of student carrells and "multidisciplinary labs" in order to break the large classes up into ever smaller peer groups, a vast enthusiasm for audio-tutorial and other self instructional schemes, and general abandonment of numerical grading and compulsory quizzing. To these may be added greatly increased enrollments under vigorous federal prodding,[5] shortening of curricula under pain of diminished federal support,[6] substantial attempts to enroll numbers of necessarily unhomogeneous underprivileged students, the happy decimation of the ranks of the medically indigent patient, the burgeoning and then rapid decline of faculty research support, and changes in the basic interests and concerns of the individual medical student himself.

The house officer and resident have been involved in many of the events already noted. They have themselves, however, been subject to change. During the past ten years new medical specialties have arisen, including Family Practice and Nuclear Medicine and five subsidiary boards.[7]

The American Board of Internal Medicine, largest of the specialty certifying groups, has seen fit to eliminate the bedside examination from its schema for certification of clinical competence and has initiated, along with the National Board of Medical Examiners, a project to develop a computer-based examination for certifying clinical competence in internal medicine.[8] There is good reason to believe that other specialty groups would like to follow suit because of the difficulty in examining the increasing numbers of candidates and also because of difficulties in the reproducibility of bedside examinations.

The practicing physician has always been a vital part of the medical educational system. Increasingly his attention is being focused on formal continuing education, with the Family Practice Board, for example, having established explicit requirements.

Outside of the physicians group, even greater changes have occurred. Numerous new paramedical or allied health professional groups have arisen since the advent of the first computers in hospitals twelve years ago. Such new groups are receiving training which is hospital-based rather than university-based.

The following problems arise out of the changes referred to above:

(1) more education of all sorts is occurring in hospitals;

(2) more of this is occurring in community and municipal hospitals;

(3) these activities are increasingly clinically oriented;

(4) more responsibility for learning is being placed upon the individual student (of whatever kind), and the students themselves are more heterogeneous in training, educational levels, and social background;

(5) with an increasing number of Assistant Deans, it is difficult to know which students are where, why, and what they're learning;

(6) consequent to all these difficulties, there is a renaissance of interest in the final certification and performance testing of the various students by non-medical school organizations.

Much more could be said by an historian or sociologist about the changes in our times and their reasons. All of these considerations point directly to the need for nonhuman systems which can keep track of one's progress in learning, afford one a means of self-appraisal of his medical performance, and fetch up the records and facts of patient care so that all students may learn independently (as inevitably they must). Above all, they point to the need for schemes with which each student's medical thinking can keep pace with the new knowledge and new ways of thinking which time brings to us.

D.   POTENTIAL COMPUTER CONTRIBUTIONS

The full application of computing systems in hospitals is still incomplete. Thus, it may be well to consider rather broadly how potentially they might contribute to learning and teaching. For each of eight kinds of contribution, we may consider first the nature of the potential function and then what would be required for the function to be performed. Insofar as many of the "requirements" cannot be satisfied in a single institution or region, the function often can be seen in the real world only in a fragmentary form. The following points, then, describe a desired potential, a pie-in-the sky objective for computers in medicine. Under the subsequent heading there will be examples of some current applications. As will be apparent, much of what exists today has yet to reach the objectives here proposed.

1. *The computer might tell us what's happening to our patient.*

The implication here is that an automated system could well be of assistance in bringing together the facts which are developed about an individual patient in the course of his past care, present illness, current work-up, etc. This concept is a familiar one; the computer (via printed summary, cathode ray tube inquiry, or some other scheme) performs the same function as the traditional chart. The benefits added by computation are still expected to consist of: more rapid reporting, better integration of materials, increased

DOOLEY PATRICK J	0215112	1136
DOOLEY PHILLIP	1377523	0655
DOOLEY ROBERT E	7570091	0935
DOOLEY ROGER W	1598686	0967
DOOLEY SEAN E	1106546	0327
DOOLEY THERESE LOUISE	0908908	1045
DOOLEY TOM J	0272523	1037
DOOLEY WILLIAM F	1608541	1151
DOOLEY WINIFRED Y	0974323	0332

Figure 15–1a. On-line inquiry into integrated file of patient care data at the University of Missouri.

legibility, and improved accuracy and reliability of the data items themselves.[9] Figures 15–1a and 15–1b are examples of one such application.

2. *The computer might tell us what kind of decision space exists for our patient.*

The function I have in mind here is not, What should one do next in patient management? Rather, it is, What are my choices? What must be considered? Recognition of the decision space is (almost by definition) the most important of all considerations from the patient's point of view, and the least written about from the computational point of view.

```
                     U.M.M.C. INTEGRATED FILE INQUIRY              06/28/72
        ▇▇▇▇▇▇ROBERT W              11-66-75-1      AGE  45          SEX M
  REC'D     REP'D        T  E  S  T  S                  RESULTS
10/19/70 10/20/70   SERUM UREA NITROGEN               13.00  MG %
10/19/70 10/20/70   SERUM ELECTROLYTES
                      NA                              143.00  MEQ/L
                      K                                 4.10  MEQ/L
                      CL                              110.00  MEQ/L
                      HCO-3                             28.00  MEQ/L
 *NO MORE PATIENT DATA* TYPE NEW PATIENT #;'END' IF THRU;'??' MORE INFO¢!
```

```
                     U.M.M.C. INTEGRATED FILE INQUIRY              06/28/72
        ▇▇▇▇▇▇MARTHA G             75-23-33-5      AGE  23          SEX F
  REC'D     REP'D        T  E  S  T  S                  RESULTS
06/29/71 06/29/71   SERUM AMYLASE                     39.00  SOMOGYI UNITS
06/29/71 06/29/71   SERUM UREA NITROGEN               11.50  MG %
06/29/71 06/29/71   SERUM GLUCOSE                    144.00  MG %
06/29/71 06/29/71   SERUM ELECTROLYTES
                      NA                              141.00  MEQ/L
                      K                                 4.40  MEQ/L
                      CL                              107.00  MEQ/L
                      HCO-3                             27.00  MEQ/L
PROCEED-HIT ENTER; ELSE TYPE NEW PATIENT #;'END' IF THRU;'??' MORE INFO¢!

06/24/71 06/24/71   SERUM UREA NITROGEN               10.00  MG %
06/24/71 06/24/71   FASTING SERUM GLUCOSE             91.00  MG %
!
```

Figure 15–1b. On-line inquiry into integrated file of patient care data at the University of Missouri.

Proper resolution of the question requires primarily that the logic for medical decision-making in previous circumstances has been made explicit. The computing system would have to reflect to the student (M.D. or otherwise) the decisions which derive from the differential diagnosis, those which derive from appropriate recognition of confidence intervals bounding laboratory and physical measurements, and (perhaps most important of all) the availability of help. If the "leukemia cells" in peripheral blood without anemia might be spurious, where does one get a collateral opinion? If the system knows that all those unsuccessful hip pinnings can now be re-done with a new orthopedic procedure, to whom should the patient go?

Figures 15–2a and 15–2b deal with the question, "Granted the patient has a cancer, what are the therapeutic options?" Figure 15–3 deals with the question, "In a patient with an abdominal problem, anemia, and the possibility of hemorrhage, what diseases might be considered."[24,28]

3. *The computer might tell us what's happening to similar patients.*

The implication here is simple. The medical profession, like the individual student, has always learned by observation of actual practices and

1. Tumor Location

2. Distant Metastasis

3. Contiguous Spread

4. Involves 1 kidney & contralateral kidney abn/abs?

5. Involves 1 ureter & contra-lateral ureter abn/abs?

6. Involves both ureters in pelvis?

7. Involves non-removable vital organ?

8. Attachment to pelvic wall prevents resection?

9. Perforation

10. Obstruction

Figure 15–2a. Questions which are asked by the CAMEO Therapeutic Logic System; answers serve as input to the medical logic portion.

I. PRIMARY PROCEDURE (CONVENTIONAL OR EN BLOC)

   A. R. HEMI-COLECTOMY
   B. R. HEMI-AND PARTIAL L. COLECTOMY
   C. L. HEMI-COLECTOMY
   D. L. HEMI- AND PARTIAL R. COLECTOMY
   E. ANTERIOR SIGMOID RESECTION
   F. ABDOMINAL PERINEAL RESECTION
   G. SEGMENTAL (SLEEVE, WEDGE) RESECTION
   H. INTERNAL INTESTINAL BYPASS
      A. ILEO-TRANSVERSE
      B. ILEO-SIGMOID
   I. PELVIC EXENTERATION
   J. DELAYED COLECTOMY
   K. NOTHING

II. ANASTOMOSIS:
   A. DIRECT
      1. END TO END
      2. END TO SIDE
      3. SIDE TO SIDE

   B. NONE
      1. PROXIMAL COLOSTOMY
         A. TEMPORARY
            1. DIVERTING
            2. DECOMPRESSING
         B. PERMANENT-END
      2. DISTAL MUCOUS FISTULA
      3. CLOSE DISTAL RECTAL STUMP

III. OTHER CONSIDERATIONS:
   A. DRAIN
   B. DELAY PRIMARY SKIN CLOSURE
   C. CLOSE PERFORATION

Figure 15–2b. A list of the management options for carcinoma of the colon; these are the output of CAMEO.

```
  — ABDØMEN                                                — STUDENT INPUT
  — ABDØMIN...
  — ANEMIA
  — HEMØRRHAG...
  — /EQU
   USING GIVEN LETTERS, FØRM EQUATIØN.  FØR EXAMPLE:
   A*B*(C+D)                        * = AND, + = ØR
   A ABDØMEN                         191
   B ABDØMIN...                      514
   C ANEMIA                          376
   D HEMØRRHAG...                    646
   TYPE:  EQUATIØN, ØR '?', ØR '/REDØ'.

  — (A+B)*C*D
   EQUATIØN BEING PRØCESSED AS:  (A+B)*C*D
   (ABDØMEN ØR ABDØMIN...) AND ANEMIA AND HEMØRRHAG...
   27 RECØRDS SATISFIED THIS EQUATIØN.
   TYPE:  '/REDØ', ØR '/TITLES', ØR '/BEG', ØR '/SØRT', ØR '?'

  — /SØRT,FØ
   FØ    SØRT IS PRØCEEDING
   LIST ØF TITLES      DATE: 07/10/72   TIME: 15.52.39    SØRT: FRQØCC
   A   06   -     .   DUØDENUM, ULCER
   B   03   -     .   HEMØSIDERØSIS, PULMØNARY, IDIØPATHIC
   C   05   -     .   ERYTHRØBLASTØSIS FETALIS
   D   06   -     .   ABDØMEN, PØSTØPERATIVE DEHISCENCE
   E   07   -     .   GLØMERULØNEPHRITIS, ACUTE
   F   07   -     .   PLACENTA, ABRUPTIØ
   G   00   -     .   LUPUS ERYTHEMATØSUS, SYSTEMIC
   H   05   -     .   SPLEEN, INJURY
   I   06   -     .   MECKEL DIVERTICULUM
   J   06   -     .   HYPERTENSIØN, PØRTAL
   FIRST PAGE.  TYPE:  CTL-XØFF, /EXP,A, ØR ANY CØMMAND.

  — /EXP,F
   EXPANDED TEXT ØF 4150
   TT          PLACENTA, ABRUPTIØ
   AT          PLACENTA, PREMATURE SEPARATIØN; ABLATIØ PLACENTAE.
   ET          MARGINAL, VENØUS SINUSES RUPTURED BY TRAUMA, CØITUS,
   .           SEVERE CØUGHING; IN LABØR, SUDDEN EMPTYING ØF LARGE
   .           HYDRAMNIØS; VERY SHØRT CØRD; MANUAL MANIPULATIØN
   .           DURING VERSIØN; TØXEMIA ØF PREGNANCY; TRAUMA; UNKNØWN.
   SM          VAGINAL HEMØRRHAGE; SUDDEN, SEVERE, CØNTINUØUS ABDØMINAL
   .           PAIN FØLLØWED BY DULL ACHE; VIGØRØUS FETAL MØVEMENTS.
   SG          INCIDENCE ABØUT 1 PERCENT; ØNSET USUALLY AFTER 28 WEEKS
   .           GESTATIØN; PALLØR, CØLD SWEATY EXTREMITIES; RAPID,
   TYPE:  CTL-XØFF, 'B', '/RET', ØR '?'.

   EXPANDED TEXT ØF 4150
   SG          THREADY PULSE; IRREGULAR ØR INAUDIBLE HEART SØUNDS;
   .           LØW SYSTØLIC BLØØD PRESSURE; SHØCK DISPRØPØRTIØNATE
   .           TØ VØLUME ØF BLØØD LØST; DISTENDED ABDØMEN; FIRM,
   .           PAINFUL, ENLARGED, FREQUENTLY BØARD-LIKE UTERUS.
   CM          CØUVELAIRE UTERUS; PØSTPARTUM UTERINE ATØNY; ACUTE
   .           RENAL FAILURE; FETAL DEATH.
   LB          URINE PØSSIBLY CØNTAINING ALBUMIN, CASTS; FIBRINØGENØPENI/
   .           ; ANEMIA.
   PA          PURPLISH RED DISCØLØRATIØN ØF UTERUS; MULTIPLE HEMØRRHAGE!
   .           AT SITE ØF PLACENTAL DETACHMENT; INTRAMURAL HEMØRRHAGES
   TYPE:  CTL-XØFF, 'B', '/RET', ØR '?'.

   EXPANDED TEXT ØF 4150
   PA          SURRØUNDING SMALLER VEINS, SEPARATING BUNDLES ØF MUSCLE;
   .           EDEMA; HEMATØMATA ØN MATERNAL SURFACE ØF PLACENTA;
   .           ENGØRGEMENT ØF BRØAD LIGAMENTS.
   AU          EASTMAN 618
   .           DANFØRTH 640-7
   THIS IS THE END ØF THE EXPANDED TEXT.  ENTER 'B' ØR '/RET'.
```

Figure 15–3. CONSIDER inquiry by medical student.

the records of them. Operative procedure A is preferred to B because patients generally live longer, or generally do not require additional surgery, or recover faster. Antibiotic A is preferred because generally such microbes are now resistant to Antibiotic B. Our institution is seeing more patients with Diagnosis X than in the past.

While such statements in theory can be confirmed or denied by any accredited hospital (when an accrediting body insists), a computer file greatly facilitates such a process. The major missing link for meaningful answers, however, is a regional or national system of medical record linkage. How else even to know that a former patient has died?

Figures 15–4 to 15–7 present examples of such applications, operating on an institutional, not a national basis.[24-27]

4. *The computer might tell us what's been written about such patients.*

The issue of computer-assisted literature citation services is well described elsewhere. Currently, the tendency is for individual health care practitioners to inquire in person or via computer terminals to regional or national central files.[10] A recent National Academy of Sciences study places the entire national library problem in a planning perspective.[11]

Figure 15–8 is an example of a system which makes didactic audio recorded information concerning electro-cardiography available to medical practitioners in a timely fashion.

Figure 15–9 is an example of a system which makes information concerning drug interactions accessible through a digital computer system.

5. *The computer might tell us, as individuals, what kinds of patients we have seen.*

Would it be helpful for a student to know that he's seen a proper spectrum of cases? Would it be an aid to learning for a practitioner periodically to review his experience?[12] Certainly yes; that's why we all keep lists.

To accomplish this via a computing system needs only that the information of a medical "encounter" enter the system. This includes patient and doctor identification, date, diagnosis, and procedure. This is essentially the same information needed for Medicare/Medicaid reporting. Figure 15–10 presents an example of such a tracking and alerting system.

6. *The computer system might tell us where we might see more of the kinds of patients we need to see in order to complete training and the elements of information or skill required for our training.*

Teachers of medicine are beginning to accept the beliefs of educationalists that one should make explicit statements of goals and objectives for a teaching segment, that the achievements ought to be measurable by some independent gauge, and that this structure should be known to the student as well as the teacher. These dicta become increasingly difficult to follow as the students' course work becomes more clinical.

```
DATA CONCERNING TEST 1713, SERUM CALCIUM     , FROM 01-01-68 THRU 05-31-71 RECORDED IN THE CHEMISTRY SUMMARIES TAPE FILE. PAGE  1

      AGE SPECIFICATIONS- 30 THRU 50     SEX SPECIFICATIONS- FEMALE     RESULT SPECIFICATIONS- FIELD 1, 0011.00 AND HIGHER
```

PATIENT NUMBER	MD SEX RACE	BIRTH DATE	CORRECTED FC RESULT	TEST CODE	REPORTED DATE	DESCRIPTIVE	1ST	2ND	3RD	4TH	5TH	6TH	7TH
415615	XX F C	03-13-19		1713	01-02-68		0011.00						
423198	XX F C	11-03-25		1713	01-15-68		0011.30						
419269	XX F C	05-23-32		1713	01-16-68		0011.50						
751237	2N F C	04-22-21		1713	01-18-68		0011.10						
100757	E6 F ?	10-11-18		1713	01-22-68		0011.50						
096147	E6 F ?	12-05-37		1713	01-24-68		0011.00						
100829	M4 F C	05-14-23		1713	01-24-68		0011.10						
093108	01 F C	08-16-26		1713	01-25-68		0011.00						
098273	M5 F C	06-25-23		1713	02-14-68		0011.30						
091210	M4 F ?	04-01-26		1713	02-15-68		0011.10						
098273	M5 F C	06-25-23		1713	02-15-68		0011.00						
426222	XX F C	07-24-24		1713	02-21-68		0011.20						
417920	XX F C	06-14-24		1713	03-19-68		0011.60						
425848	XX F C	07-14-22		1713	03-20-68		0011.10						
420610	XX F C	10-07-35		1713	03-20-68		0011.10						
422631	XX F C	07-18-25		1713	03-20-68		0011.30						
135105	E6 F C	03-01-22		1713	10-27-70		0013.00						
135105	E6 F C	03-01-22		1713	10-28-70		0013.00						
135105	E6 F C	03-01-22		1713	10-29-70		0012.90						
135105	E6 F C	03-01-22		1713	10-31-70		0012.50						
135105	E6 F C	03-01-22		1713	11-02-70		0013.50						
096167	06 F C	08-31-23		1713	11-24-70		0011.80						
096167	06 F C	08-31-23		1713	11-24-70		0012.00						
096167	06 F C	04-31-23		1713	11-24-70		0012.00						
083967	E5 F C	07-31-36		1713	02-10-71		0011.00						
090456	MC F C	08-26-36		1713	02-18-71		0011.10						
106332	M6 F C	02-15-22		1713	03-27-71		0011.70						

```
NUMBER OF RECORDS THAT MET TEST SPECIFICATIONS          37719

NUMBER OF TESTS THAT MET DATE SPECIFICATIONS            23079

NUMBER OF TESTS THAT MET AGE SPECIFICATIONS             10095

NUMBER OF TESTS THAT MET RESULT SPECIFICATIONS          02511

NUMBER OF TESTS THAT MET SEX SPECIFICATIONS             19432

NUMBER OF RECORDS THAT MET ALL SPECIFICATIONS           00212
```

Figure 15-4. Batch inquiry into clinical chemistry files.

PREGNANT PATIENTS AND PATIENTS WITH TOXEMIAS OF PREGNANCY WHO ALSO

HAVE A DIAGNOSIS OF ONE OR MORE OF THE FOLLOWING DISORDERS POSSIBLY

INDICATIVE OF CHRONIC RENAL DISEASE—ACIDOSIS NOT DUE TO DIABETES,

HYPERPHOSPHATEMIA, HYPOCALCEMIA, HYPERKALEMIA, OR HYPONATREMIA.

```
000402  002051  003187  006690  007626  009273  011930  012956  015023  015236  018858  021671
022294  024573  027997  031139  031522  036011  039997  045660  047310  049456  049988  057536
057760  063612  064484  064918  065627  065565  068049  068122  075078  079827  083260  084295
086610  069021  092307  113265  117731  119226  122639  123990  125130  128111  129994  132139
133749  133593  134253  135821  136661  138174
```

NUMBER OF PATIENTS FOR THIS COUNT - 00060

```
* * * * * * * * * * * * * * * * * *
```

ALL PREGNANT PATIENTS WITH KIDNEY DISEASE DUE TO INFECTION, EXCLUDING

URINARY TRACT INFECTION AND CYSTITIS

```
000163  000603  000686  000674  000804  000620  001266  001264  001390  001402  001431  001466  001467
001512  001523  001807  002116  002283  002314  002850  003016  003125  003187  003757  003798  003945
004537  004354  004525  004789  004849  004912  005021  005111  005301  005669  005805  006356  006381
006732  006733  006807  006817  006932  006949  007147  007285  007607  007626  007815  007956  008597
008654  009104  009146  009273  009496  009550  009553  009674  009987  010054  010596  011137  011217
011359  011390  011450  011568  011675  011860  011930  011978  012363  012386  012441  012734  012917
012955  013074  013843  013989  014392  014408  014825  014918  015221  015428  015609  016125  016180
016182  017100  017544  017000  017975  018057  018380  018423  018550  018648  018880  019182  019439
019908  020105  020322  020400  020492  020876  021431  021557  021671  021729  021986  022097  022294
022955  023061  023559  023982  024124  024134  024310  024593  025388  025429  025571  025851  026714
026867  026589  027486  027553  027813  027836  027640  027884  027997  028125  028529  028556  028722
029260  029586  029838  029980  030748  031070  031139  031243  031344  032125  031466  031522
032510  033058  033131  033476  033553  033592  033982  034022  034346  034352  034442  034522  034529
034942  035686  035203  035460  035515  036046  036671  036952  037516  037619  038173  038471
038472  038796  039197  039465  039819  040246  040046  040546  040025  040766  041264  042175
042764  047560  043911  043989  044101  044435  044480  044861  045252  045540  045682
045809  046662  047240  047537  047898  048731  049053  049261  049660  049988  050665  050799
050394  051304  051730  052428  053084  053182  055344  055632  055837  057766  058034  058458
058462  059307  059369  059483  059528  059773  060851  061222  061368  062072  062117  062138  062599
062897  063414  063956  064130  064743  064964  065080  065050  065488  067377  067903  068594  070005
070065  070614  071183  073101  073170  073759  074500  074899  075319  075864  075958  076471  076969
085231  079331  080720  080858  081467  081623  082393  083740  084016  084760  084951  085223
085224  084549  087848  088646  088872  089870  090054  090902  091905  092925  093976
093981  095013  095713  095792  096242  096646  096475  097701  097918  098098  098461  099092
000102  100824  101264  101331  101993  102525  103247  103444  104064  104298  104319  104612  104726
105172  105239  106213  106233  106324  106415  107400  107645  107782  108197  108561  109639
110554  111239  111262  111432  111883  112706  112709  116196  116366  116499  116973  117088  117384
119226  121459  121606  122595  122619  122839  123791  125940  127101  128761  128972  129094
132869  133068  133735  139394  141053  141364  142799  145126  145508  128111  146273  148161  153319
153631  154468
```

NUMBER OF PATIENTS FOR THIS COUNT - 00380

```
* * * * * * * * * * * * * * * *
```

Figure 15-5. TP500 inquiry to coded diagnosis file.

161163-1   SEX F, RACE N, F/C-5F, OP DATE 06-28-72, AGE 15-YEARS,   OR SUITE A   , ATTENDING-REDDIN,
SURGEON-KOBBERMAN, ASSISTANTS-MEDEAKIS M/4, ANESTHETIST-SHOULTS M/3, MCCORD, CIRC NURSE-LEONARD, SCRUB NURSE-HAMILTON, OGDEN,
OPERATIONS-EXCISION OF CONDYLOMATA, PERINEUM, CAUTERIZATION, CONDYLOMATA, LABIA MAJORA, CAUTERIZATION, CONDYLOMATA, VAGINA, OP
START 1123, OP FINISH 1140, ELAPSED TIME 0017, AN START 1105, AN FINISH 1145, ELAPSED TIME 0040, ELECTIVE OPERATION, ANES
TECH-INHALATION, MASK, SPONGE COUNT NOT DONE, , D5LR   -0300, PRE OP DX-CONDYLOMATA OF PERINEUM, LABIA & VAGINA, POST OP
DX-CONDYLOMATA OF PERINEUM, LABIA & VAGINA

161255-7   SEX M, RACE C, F/C-5E, OP DATE 06-28-72, AGE 48-YEARS,   OR SUITE G   , ATTENDING-SCHERR,
SURGEON-BUCKINGHAM, ASSISTANTS-CRAIG   , ANESTHETIST-EGGERS, MCCOY, CIRC NURSE-NEPPL,
SCRUB NURSE-SNELL, OPERATIONS-FASCIOTOMY, RT. ARM, RELEASE OF TRANSVERSE CARPAL LIGAMENT, DRAINAGE OF PALMAR SPACES, OP START 0200,
OP FINISH 0300, ELAPSED TIME 0100, AN START 0130, **EMERGENCY OPERATION** , ANES TECH-LOCAL, AXILL.BL., SPONGE COUNT NOT
DONE, DRAINS-PENROSE SM., D5LR   -0500, BLOOD LOSS-0225, PRE OP DX-QUESTIONABLE PAINT STRIPPER TOXICITY, POST OP DX-QUESTIONABLE
PAINT STRIPPER TOXICITY

161269-7   SEX M, RACE C, F/C-1A, OP DATE 06-28-72, AGE 10-YEARS,   OR SUITE G   , ATTENDING-SCHERR,
SURGEON-KLEIN, ANESTHETIST-JONES, LUCAS M/3, CIRC NURSE-SHIREMAN, DILLON, SCRUB NURSE-MADDOX, OPERATIONS-DEBRIDEMENT, LT. THIGH
WOUND, IRRIGATION, LT. THIGH WOUND, CLOSURE OF DEBRIDED AREA, CLOSED REDUCTION OF FRACTURE OF LT. FEMUR, INSERTION OF STEINMANN PIN
IN TIBIA, LT.., OP START 1325, OP FINISH 1410, ELAPSED TIME 0045, AN START 1240, AN FINISH 1415, ELAPSED TIME 0135, ELECTIVE
OPERATION, ANES TECH-INHALATION, ET, SPONGE COUNT NOT DONE, DRUGS-ANTIBIUTICS DRAINS- RUBBER,PENROSE , ISOLYTE-P -0350, BLOOD
LO5S-0100, PRE OP DX-FRACTURE OF LT. FEMUR, POST OP DX-FRACTURE OF LT. FEMUR

161293-0   SEX F, RACE C, F/C-5E, OP DATE 06-28-72, AGE 58-YEARS,   OR SUITE E   , ATTENDING-DEWEESE,
SURGEON-NICHOLS, ASSISTANTS-SINCLAIR, HORN M/3, ANESTHETIST-GRAZIS, LOWRY, CIRC NURSE-RATHKE, NEPPL, SCRUB NURSE-MILLER M/3,
OPERATIONS-VAGOTOMY, PYLOROPLASTY, GASTROSTOMY WITH #22 FR FOLEY, OP START 2206, OP FINISH 0025, ELAPSED TIME 0219, AN START 2150,
AN FINISH 0035, ELAPSED TIME 3245, **EMERGENCY OPERATION** , ANES TECH-INHALATION, ET, SPONGE COUNT CORRECT, SN,
DRAINS-GASTROSTOM, WHOLE BLOOD-2500, BLOOD LOSS-2100, PRE OP DX-G.I. BLEEDING, POST OP DX-GASTRIC ULCER

161297-2   SEX F, RACE C, F/C-5E, OP DATE 06-28-72, AGE 15-YEARS,   LR SUITE C   , ATTENDING-GRIFFIN,
SURGEON-DORIAN, ASSISTANTS-WILLIAMS, ANESTHETIST-GRAZIS, RATHKE, SCRUB NURSE-OGDEN, OPERATIONS-CORNUAL RESECTION OVIDUCT, OP START
2035, OP FINISH 2110, ELAPSED TIME 0041, AN START 2030, AN FINISH 2120, ELAPSED TIME 0050, **EMERGENCY OPERATION** , ANES
TECH-INHALATION, ET, SPONGE COUNT CORRECT, DR., WHOLE BLOOD-1000, D5LR-ALBUM-1530, BLOOD LOSS-2000, PRE OP DX-RUPTURED
INTERSTITIAL ECTOPIC PREGNANCY, POST OP DX-RUPTURED INTERSTITIAL ECTOPIC PREGNANCY

161300-6   SEX M, RACE C, F/C-11, OP DATE 06-28-72, AGE 18-YEARS,   OR SUITE D   , ATTENDING-ROBINSON,
SURGEON-ROBINSON, ASSISTANTS-TUCKER, ANESTHETIST-GRAZIS, VANDER BEEK, CIRC NURSE-RATHKE, SCRUB NURSE-OGDEN, OPERATIONS-SKIN GRAFT
TO NECK LACERATION, REPAIR FACIAL FRACTURES, OP START 2340, OP FINISH 0625, ELAPSED TIME 0645, AN START 2300, AN FINISH 0630,
ELAPSED TIME 0730, **EMERGENCY OPERATION** , ANES TECH-INHALATION, ET, TRACH , SPONGE COUNT NOT DONE,
DRUGS-ANTIBIOTICS , WHOLE BLOOD-2000, D5LR-D5W -1500, BLOOD LOSS-2000, PRE OP DX-CAR ACCIDENT WITH MULTIPLE TRAUMATA TO NECK AND
FACE, POST OP DX-CAR ACCIDENT WITH MULTIPLE TRAUMATA TO NECK AND FACE

END OF O.R. LOG
TOTAL = 022

Figure 15-6.   Example of computer generated surgical operating room log.

SUR0001

SELECT PATIENTS WITH PACEMAKERS

O.R. REPORT ON PATIENT NUMBER 0617229
DATE OF OPERATION: 66C713
OPERATIONS -- 1ST: REMOVAL OF PACEMAKER
PRE-OP - 1ST: COMPLETE AV BLOCK
POST-OP - 1ST: COMPLETE AV BLOCK

O.R. REPORT ON PATIENT NUMBER 0180378
DATE OF OPERATION: 661117
OPERATIONS -- 1ST: REPLACEMENT OF G.E. PACEMAKER GENERATOR
2ND: IRRIGATION OF INCISION WITH 2M UNITS PENICILLIN
PRE-OP - 1ST: COMPLETE A-V BLOCK
POST-OP - 1ST: 444   X36: COMPLETE A-V BLOCK

O.R. REPORT OF PATIENT NUMBER 0180378
DATE OF OPERATION: 661117
OPERATIONS -- 1ST: REPAIR MALFUNCTIONING CARDIAC PACEMAKER
PRE-OP - 1ST: MALFUNCTIONING CARDIAC PACEMAKER
POST-OP - 1ST: MALFUNCTIONING CARDIAC PACEMAKER

O.R. REPORT OF PATIENT NUMBER 0752121
DATE OF OPERATION: 661120
OPERATIONS -- 1ST: REPLACEMENT OF PACEMAKER GENERATOR #676017 (OLD) #701002
   GENERATOR (NEW)
PRE-OP - 1ST: PACEMAKER GENERATION DISFUNCTION
POST-OP - 1ST: PACEMAKER GENERATION DISFUNCTION

O.R. REPORT ON PATIENT NUMBER 0676985
DATE OF OPERATION: 671129
OPERATIONS -- 1ST: RE-EXPLORATION OF STERNAL REGION
2ND: PLACEMENT OF TEMPORARY PACEMAKER ELECTRODE
PRE-OP - 1ST: POST AORTIC VALVE REPLACEMENT-BLEEDING
POST-OP - 1ST: POST AORTIC VALVE REPLACEMENT-BLEEDING

O.R. REPORT ON PATIENT NUMBER 0712693
DATE OF OPERATION: 680320
OPERATIONS -- 1ST: CARDICTOMY
2ND: WITH REPLACEMENT OF S.E. VALVE WITH STARR-EDWARDS AORTIC VALVE MODEL #1200
   SERIAL #14A-48037
3RD: MEDTRONIC PACEMAKER LEADS INSERTED
PRE-OP - 1ST: CONGESTIVE HEART FAILURE
2ND: SECONDARY TO AORTIC INSUFFICIENCY, SEVERE
POST-OP - 1ST: CONGESTIVE HEART FAILURE
2ND: SECONDARY TO AORTIC INSUFFICIENCY, SEVERE

O.R. REPORT ON PATIENT NUMBER 0954951
DATE OF OPERATION: 690522
OPERATIONS -- 1ST: FRENCH FLAP CLOSURE OF LATERAL & MEDIAL ULCER OVER PACEMAKER
PRE-OP - 1ST: ULCERATION WITH EXPOSURE OF PACEMAKER, RT ANTERIOR CHEST-LATERAL
   & MEDIAL
POST-OP - 1ST: ULCERATION WITH EXPOSURE OF PACEMAKER, RT ANTERIOR CHEST-LATERAL
   & MEDIAL

O.R. REPORT ON PATIENT NUMBER 1031317
DATE OF OPERATION: 7CC8C6
OPERATIONS -- 1ST: PACEMAKER REPLACEMENT-MEDTRONIC CHARDACK PULSE GENERATOR
   MODEL NO. 5842 SERIAL NO. 0R04175

2ND: (OLD PACEMAKER - 5841 - 6R2212)
PRE-OP - 1ST: MALFUNCTIONING PACEMAKER
POST-OP - 1ST: MALFUNCTIONING PACEMAKER

Figure 15–7. Sample search of contents of surgical operating room file.

443

MO.RMP-EKG PROJECT-UNIVERSITY OF MO. COLUMBIA
COMPUTER PROCESSED ELECTROCARDIOGRAM
WCMH POTOSI

PT 0000107 TAPE1234 DATE 12-10-69 2:48 PM JULIAN 339 S.S.N. 107100107
71 YR MALE 5 FT 6 IN 160 LBS MEDS NONE   BP NORMAL

	I	II	III	AVR	AVL	AVF	V1	V2	V3	V4	V5	V6	
PA	.	.09	.10	-.06		.11	.07	.	.04	.	.03	.03	PA
PD	.	.12	.7	.08		.13	.05	.	.06	.	.05	.06	PD
Q/SA	-.04	-.10	.	.		.	.	.	.	.	.	.	Q/SA
Q/SD	.04	.02	.	.		.	.	.	.	.	.	.	Q/SD
RA	.49	.70	.31	.08		.47	.20	.63	1.41	1.58	1.09	.63	RA
RD	.04	.03	.05	.01		.04	.04	.04	.05	.06	.04	.04	RD
SA	-.05	-.14	.	-.53		.	-.53	-.81	-1.04	-.80	-.41	-.17	SA
SD	.03	.03	.	.03		.	.06	.04	.05	.06	.03	.03	SD
RPA	.	.	.	.15		.	.	.	.	.	.	.	RPA
RPD	.	.	.	.03		.	.	.	.	.	.	.	RPD
STD	-.03	.05	.	-.02	-.02	.	.12	-.03	.02	.09	-.07	-.02	STD
STM	.	.04	.	-.02	.01	.	.14	.04	.08	.12	.01	.01	STM
STE	.02	.05	.01	-.03	.03	.	.15	.07	.17	.18	.04	.01	STE
TA	.16	.	-.5	-.12		.	.33	.47	.69	.57	.19	.15	TA
TPA	-.06	.	.	.		.	.	.	.	.	-.09	.	TPA

	I	II	III	AVR	AVL	AVF	V1	V2	V3	V4	V5	V6	
PR	.	.17	.16	.14		.18	.15	.	.13	.	.10	.11	PR
QRS	.11	.08	.05	.07		.04	.10	.08	.10	.12	.07	.07	QRS
QT	.46	.	.43	.40		.	.42	.40	.40	.43	.51	.38	QT
RATE	56	66	69	71		66	70	58	69	71	70	70	RATE

	I	II	III	AVR	AVL	AVF	V1	V2	V3	V4	V5	V6	
CODE	3	2	3	4	U	2	3	2	2	4	3		CODE
CAL	96	96	96	96		96	96	96	96	96	96	96	CAL

AXIS IS   P   QRS   T   Q   R   S   STD   ST-T QRS-T
DEGREES   96   37   247   48 250 111

PROLONGED QT INTERVAL   . CONSIDER ELECTROLYTE IMBALANCE,
                                   . DRUG EFFECTS
                                   .
8611 ABNORMAL P AXIS   . ABNORMAL ATRIAL FOCUS
                                   . OR NODAL RHYTHM
                                   .
I LEAD NOT MEASURED   .
                                   .
                                   .
                                   . BORDERLINE ECG
                                   .
MSDL APPROVED VERSION   . --------------- M.D.
   D 41-42-22-11   . UDIO M.C. TEL NO. 314-449-XXXX

Figure 15–8. Report of computer interpreted electrocardiogram with audio consultation.

A familiar example, however, is seen in the usual conduct of classes in physical diagnosis. In this case, the teacher has traditionally been able to give printed lists of physical signs which the student should arrange to observe in some patient somewhere and has usually been able to limit objectives to the hope that the student presented with an unknown patient could observe and recognize some appropriate subset of the signs. After

```
A*B*C*D
EQUATIØN:  A*B*C*D
CØUMADIN AND DIANABØL AND INTERACTIØN AND HUMAN
1 RECØRDS SATISFIED THIS EQUATIØN.
TYPE:  '/REDØ', ØR '/TITLES', ØR '/BEG


/T
LIST ØF TITLES        DATE: 07/12/72   TIME: 16.42.17    SØRT: RECNØ
A      -       .    ANABØLIC STERØIDS PØTENTIATE ANTICØAGULANT EFFECT
LAST PAGE.  TYPE:  B, /EXP,A, ØR ANY CØMMAND.


/EXP,A
EXPANDED TEXT ØF 1026
TI          ANABØLIC STERØIDS PØTENTIATE ANTICØAGULANT EFFECT
AT          METHANDRØSTENØLØNE, DIANABØL; NØRETHANDRØLØNE, NILEVAR;
•           NANDRØLØNE DECANØATE, DECA-DURABØLIN; NANDRØLØNE
•           PHENPRØPIØNATE, DURABØLIN
•           WARFARIN, CØUMADIN SØDIUM, PANWARFIN; WARFARIN PØTASSIUM,
•           ATHRØMBIN-K; BISHYDRØXYCØUMARIN, DICUMARØL.
CI          ANABØLIC STERØIDS SUCH AS METHANDRØSTENØLØNE AND
•           NØRETHANDRØLØNE PØTENTIATE THE HYPØPRØTHRØMBINEMIC EFFECT ØF
•           CØUMARIN ANTICØAGULANTS, ALSØ INDANDIØNES.
•           THESE STERØIDS DØ NØT AFFECT THE DISTRIBUTIØN ØR RATE ØF
CI          METABØLISM ØF ANTICØAGULANTS.
•           THE USE ØF METHANDRØSTENØLØNE AND NØRETHANDRØLØNE SHØULD BE
•           AVØIDED IN PATIENTS RECEIVING ANTICØAGULANTS FØR IT MAY
•           PRECIPITATE HEMØRRHAGIC CØMPLICATIØNS; IF URGENTLY REQUIRED,
•           LØWER CØUMARIN DØSAGE AND CLØSELY FØLLØW PRØTHRØMBIN TIMES.
•           MAY ACT SYNERGISTICALLY WITH THE CØUMARINS 10 DEPRESS
•           HEPATIC SYNTHESIS ØF VITAMIN K DEPENDENT CLØTTING FACTØRS ØR
•           MAY INCREASE THE AFFINITY ØF THE RECEPTØR SITE IN THE LIVER
•           FØR THE ANTICØAGULANT.
EX          10 PATIENTS WITH CORØNARY HEART DISEASE WERE WELL STABILIZED
EX          ØN MAINTENANCE THERAPY WITH WARFARIN (7) ØR PHENYLINDIØNE
•           (3).   THEY WERE GIVEN METHANDRØSTENØLØNE 10 MG DAILY FØR 14
•           DAYS.   AN INCREASED SENSITIVITY TØ WARFARIN BECAME EVIDENT
•           IN ALL CASES DURING METHANDRØSTENØLØNE THERAPY.
•           THE DØSAGE ØF WARFARIN REQUIRED TØ MAINTAIN THE PP VALUES
•           WITHIN THERAPEUTIC RANGE WERE SIGNIFICANTLY REDUCED.  AFTER
•           STØPPING METHANDRØSTENELØNE THE ANTICØAGULANT REQUIREMENTS
•           RØSE WITHIN A WEEK TØ THE SAME LEVEL AS BEFØRE THE ANABØLIC
•           STERØID.  (PYØRALA AND KEKKI)
•           THE RESPØNSE TØ A SINGLE DØSE ØF 20 MG ØF WARFARIN IN
EX          HEALTHY SUBJECTS (8) WAS FØUND TØ BE INCREASED WHEN THEY
•           TØØK METHANDRØSTENØLØNE 10 MG DAILY FØR 10 DAYS (PYØRALA AND
•           KEKKI).
•           SIMILAR RESULTS WERE REPØRTED IN 7 MALE VØLUNTEERS TAKING 10
•           MG ØF NØRETHANDRØLØNE DAILY FØR 2 WEEKS.  ØN THE 10TH DAY,
•           DICUMARØL WAS ADMINISTERED (100 ØR 150 MG).  THERE WAS NØ
•           CHANGE IN THE HALF-LIFE ØF DICUMAPØL ØR THE ACTIVITY ØF THE
•           VITAMIN K-DEPENDENT CLØTTING FACTØRS (THRØMBØTEST).
•           (SØLØMØN AND SCHRØGIE).
•           AN ADDITIØNAL STUDY WITH 2 PATIENTS ØN METHANDRØSTENØLØNE
EX          GIVEN WARFARIN SHØWED A MARKED PØTENTIATIØN ØF ANTICØAGULANT
•           EFFECT EVEN WHEN VITAMIN K1 WAS ADMINISTERED (DRESDALE AND
•           HAYES).
RF          "DECREASED ANTICØAGULANT TØLERANCE DURING METHANDRØSTERØNE
•           THERAPY", K. PYØKALA AND M. KEKKI, SCANDINAV. J. CLIN. LAB.
•           INVEST. 15:367-374, 1963.
•           "THE ANTICØAGULANT RESPØNSE TØ BISHYDRØXYCØUMARIN II.  THE
•           EFFECT ØF D-THYRØXINE, CØLFIBRATE AND NØRETHANDRØLØNE", H.
•           M. SØLØMØN AND J. J. SCHRØGIE, METABØLISM 16:1029-1033,
•           1967.
RF          "PØTENTIAL DANGERS IN THE CØMBINED USE ØF METHANDRØSTENØLØNE
•           AND SØDIUM WARFARIN," F. C. DPESDALF AND J. C. HAYES, J.
•           MED. SØC. NEW JERSEY 64: 609-612, 1967.
CL          INTERACTIØN, HUMAN
THIS IS THE END ØF THE EXPANDED TEXT.  ENTER 'B' ØR '/RET'.
```

Figure 15–9.   Terminal inquiry to CONSIDER system concerning drug interaction.

```
                                               SEND TO:  M660

                     UNIVERSITY OF MISSOURI

                        MEDICAL CENTER

                     BIRTH DEFECTS CENTER

              RELEVANT CENSUS INFORMATION              06/23/1972
```
11-19-65-6 , BRIAN T   WAS ADMITTED TO ROOM # E714-2 PEDIATRICS
10-70-14-2   , DAMON   WAS ADMITTED TO ROOM # 609-2 UROLOGY
06-26-50-5   , CHERYL ANN   WAS MOVED FROM ROOM # E719-4 TO E719-5 NEURO-SURGERY

Figure 15–10. Sample listing of patients now present in the hospital who are part of multiple handicap study.

reading a text, the only remaining question is logistic: Where to find the patient with Sign X or physical finding Y? As the hospital and its network of affiliated facilities have increased, the informal list of patients in the chief resident's pocket becomes less and less adequate. How simple to keep such a list for one or more hospitals in a computer! How simple to have the machine keep track of one's progress through the list and to set up the appropriate schedule for teaching visits!

The technical requirements for such a system would be trivial. The real difficulty would be in establishing the explicit lists of what findings (outside of this single course) one needs to observe, in adding this information to the patient's entry in the current hospital census, and in dealing with the sociology of the hospital service so that the teaching visits become pleasant and desirable.

7. *Test competence and ability.*

The computer might permit us periodically to test and certify our own knowledge and competence, and to certify these.

Ohio State University Medical School is in the midst of a very ambitious experiment in which a computer-aided instruction system is utilized to provide tutorial self-evaluation exercises for students and instructional management reports for faculty. The course material eventually to be included spans the entire basic science medical curriculum.[13] An example of a management report is given in Figure 15–11.

In addition, computer-aided instructional materials have been prepared under Regional Medical Program support. These are accessed via telephone lines and remote terminals by nonmedical students.[14] Samples of the titles of such offerings are presented in Figure 15–12.

One should note, in addition, the existence of the ADIS catalogue of computer assisted instruction courses.[15] Generally these are used only sparingly by hospitals (as opposed to medical schools). Generally the user is

```
                             'PILOT '
                       PILOT MEDICAL SCHOOL
                   WEEKLY STUDENT PROGRESS REPORT

DATE OF REPORT  05/08/72                    STUDENT NUMBER      403
FACULTY ADVISOR    DR. GARY WISE            STUDENT NAME
TOTAL TIME ON TES TO DATE:  51:09



COMPLETED MODULES AS OF REPORT DATE (IN ORDER OF DATE COMPLETED)
     CODE   DATE COMPLETED   MODULE NAME                TIME ON TES

** MODULES   A-7  COMPLETED **
      Q        3/20/72       BIOSTAT.-PREVENTIVE MED.       0:59
      P        3/20/72       PATHOLOGY                      3:39
      R        4/20/72       MICROBIOLOGY                   3:21
      S        4/22/72       DRUG MECHANISMS                3:54
      T        5/05/72       HEMATOLOGY                     7:16



SUBMODULE PROGRESS DURING REPORT PERIOD
     CODE   DATE COMPLETED   SUBMODULE NAME             TIME ON TES

      TC       5/01/72       MYELOID ELEMENTS               1:13
      TD       5/02/72       LYMPHORETICULAR DISEASES       1:06
      TE       5/03/72       FUNCTIONAL DIS-IMMUNE ORG      0:33
      TF       5/05/72       IMMUNOHEMATOLOGY               1:08



STUDY PRESCRIPTIONS FOR REPORT PERIOD (IN ORDER ACCORDING TO DATE RECEIVED)
     DATE      TIME    CODE   PRESCRIPTION

05/01/72    21:51    TC    RX WEAKNESS IN NEUTROPENIA
05/01/72    22:09    TC    RX WEAKNESS IN ACUTE AND CHROMIC LEUKEMIAS


CURRENT TES LOCATION     UA
DATE OF LAST USAGE       05/05/72
```

Figure 15–11. Computer report to faculty member concerning the performance of a medical student.

expected to be a medical student, but there are exceptions to both these generalizations.

Learning is a lonely and solitary process, and the book is a comfortable and efficient guide to knowledge and understanding. Yet there have always been teachers. Indeed, they've increased in number faster than books. This is because one needs to ask and to be asked questions in order to be certain he has learned, to ascertain his understanding in new environs, to integrate new knowledge into old ideas, and to stretch his grasp till he reaches its limit.

Regrettably, a list of questions is not as efficacious as a conversation with

Closed Drainage Systems for the Thoracic Cavity
Nursing Care of the Patient with Coronary
    Heart Disease
Nutritional Anatomy for Medical Dietetics
Anesthetic Agents and Adjunct Drugs for Nurses
Food Nutrient File
Gross Anatomy Self-Evaluation Exercise
Juvenile Diabetes
Orthopedic Lesions
Reading the Patient's Medical Record
Medical Technology (Various Units)
Musculoskeletal System Self-Evaluation
Neuro-Anatomy Self-Evaluation
Physiological Chemistry of Nutrition
Examination of the Fundus
Optometry
Oral Cancer Recognition
Short Topics for Patient Usage
Patient Management of Diabetes
Risk Factors in Coronary Heart Disease
Statistics for Quality Control
Clinical Organ Scanning
Review Topics for Medical Personnel
Service Mode Topics
Review of Antibiotic Therapy
Review of Tracheal Suctioning
Serum Electrolytes, Acid Base Disorders
Library Information Request Service
Cardiac Arrythmias
Stroke Rehabilitation
Medical Terminology
Physiology and Disorders of Body Temperature
    Regulation
Anticoagulant Medication
Measurement and Recording of Urinary Output
Venipuncture
Ventricular Arrhythmias
Neuromuscular Morphology

Figure 15–12.   Sample titles of Ohio State CAI system.

questions; and so far, the computing systems have not been good question-askers let alone good conversationalists. Computers do, however, have the potential for as much branching in their dialogue as one has wit to program. Their use as aids in formal learning is slowly increasing, although the "experiments" are costly and practically limited to medical schools.[16-20]

The most important approach to the problem has been to let the computer play the patient rather than the teacher. In this situation, the burden for question-asking is shifted to the student, with the computer-patient containing the "answers." Figure 15–13 exhibits a portion of such a computer dialogue.

Recently the Lister Hill Center for Biomedical Communications has initiated a small federally subsidized subnetwork with which these and other medical computer programs may be accessed by distant institutions.

While use of computers for instruction of students and residents is moving rather slowly, a major impetus for use of computers to certify specialists has occurred. CBX, the Computer Based Exam joint project of the American Board of Internal Medicine and the National Board of Medical Examiners, has already created a series of prototype exams which are aimed ultimately at measuring and certifying (along with traditional examinations) the clinical competence of internist candidates.[8] Were the project to end successfully, it would stimulate a great interest in the use of hospital computer terminals as a means of gauging one's ability, of preparing for examinations, and of judging what is required by his specialty on a national instead of a local scale.

The proposed examination is a computer simulation of a patient with whom the examinee interacts via remote terminal, obtaining a history and doing a simulated physical and laboratory examination. There is now preliminary evidence that the use of free English text for these processes better separates criterion test groups than the use of numbered procedure lists.

The computer terminal interaction exhibited in Figure 15–13 was part of such an experimental testing procedure.

8. *The computer might assist in medical discovery.*

This function is really the essence of research in the sense that it is concerned with the production of new knowledge. Yet it bears mentioning in connection with teaching because of the extent to which modern medical education is attempting to be scientific and also because of the rapidity with which new observations enter the daily public news media. So far as I know, there is yet no example of computers directly assisting in the discovery of any major new medical relationship, however much we believe that they ought to. The classical counterexample was the discovery of the association of thalidomide with phocomelia through noncomputer means[21] in spite of the fact that considerable fetal life data had been collected in machine-readable form prospectively.

— What brings you in today, Mr. Bond?
I'm not feeling so great. For about a
month now I've been feeling so tired and
run down. I figured it was time I saw
another doc about it.

— How long has this been going on?
I began noticing this about one month
ago.

— Do you usually have a fever?
I feel a little feverish now. Not too
much, but a little, you know? I don't
remember when it started...

— How old are you now?
I had a birthday last month and that
made me 44 years old.

— Have you had any other serious illness in the past?
Nothing serious...
I occasionally get a carbuncle on the
back of my neck, but other than that
I don't have any other complaints...

— Have you had a carbuncle recently?
I have carbuncles on the back of my neck
and they occur about every couple of
months, but I put some hot soaks on them
and they go away by themselves.

— p

** physical exam **

— skin
            skin--
a painless red-blue lesion is noted on
the palm of the right hand. this lesion
is 2 mm in diameter

• • •

(— INTERVIEWER)

Figure 15–13. Example of part of CBX testing session using CASE computer program.

A favorable outcome of computer analysis resulted from the coronary care units and myocardial infarction units pooling their experience for computer-assisted analysis. The joint experience of a number of hospitals made statistically certain what had always remained questionable for a single hospital—namely that morbidity was reduced by intensive care units and that antiarrthymia drugs ought, in fact, routinely to be employed in the treatment of a patient with an acute myocardial infarction.

A comparable overview of pooled hospital records has been required for the testing of over 300,000 potential chemotherapeutic drugs in the cancer program. There are also the observations of undesirable side effects in other drugs such as chloramphenicol and MER/29. Development of such important information is wholly dependent upon reliable clinical observation and good record-keeping. The consequences immediately influence clinical practice—i.e., that which is to be learned. Therefore, it seems desirable and likely that all health profession students have contact and experience at least with the (terminal) data gathering end of such systems.

E. A PREDICTION

Even in the next decade, reason and economics suggest that hospitals in general will not become the custodians of in-house hospital computing systems which will do a great spectrum of jobs appropriate to teaching and learning. Their computing systems will remain oriented about and cost-justified by patient record-keeping, accounting, and institutional management matters. The record-keeping functions of hospitals, however, will be most important since this is how patient care information will become susceptible to computer analysis.[31] In most cases, such data are qualitatively better in the sense of more accurate and more reliable when they have been acquired through computer editing and quality control programs.[9, 32]

The records of the patient care given by individual hospitals must indeed be linked, integrated, and made available as a regional and/or national data base, but this responsibility will fall upon the government. Creation of such data bases will, of course, be costly. However, they will be essential for rational management of current and future health insurance programs.

Use of the patient care data base systems for teaching and learning at individual hospitals will be the responsibility of the hospital and/or the affiliated medical school. As such data bases are created, it is expected that the federal government may do a better job of studying, writing about, condensing, and reporting on their data than in the past. Even so, the most reasonable manner for hospitals or individuals to study a large computer data base is via a computer, not by reading descriptions.

Costs and history suggest that subsets of the data bases will be created, in the fashion of the national Census Tapes, and distributed as needed for inquiry processing at the local level. "Local" in this case would likely mean distributed to hospitals large enough to have appropriate computers, to non-profit health service agencies like Regional Medical Programs, or (as in the case of the Census Tapes) to for-profit service bureaus who could handle searches on a fee-for-service basis.

How will hospital people heavily involved in the education of so many kinds of health care professionals get access to relevant computer assistance? As indicated above, insofar as the computer system needs regional or national patient care data bases, their access must inevitably be through federally provided tape files. Large hospitals will search their own tapes containing the subset of information they deem appropriate. Small hospitals will search the same or different subset tapes via computer terminal connections to nonprofit or fee-for-service computer centers.

Much of the teaching and learning will derive from a study of computerized actual patient records in this manner. The record need not have been stored totally within the computer. Computerization of signal parts will make it possible, much more effectively, to select those paper records which are required for detailed study.

Even so, other computer services which are relevant for medical education will be needed. Those involving diagnostic decision-making, prompting, and testing will almost certainly be best obtained by dial-up computer terminals that access to whichever remote computer is capable of providing the service required. Doubtless there will be new federal and commercial telephone data networks to facilitate these accesses. The important thing to note is the likelihood that the educational requirement of any given hospital will cause it to be in touch with many computer centers for many different purposes. It will be a consumer of computer services rather than primarily a proprietor of a computer center. Its own computer (if it has one) will be dedicated to data gathering, storing of data for its local use, and management functions. Specialized teaching functions will likely be served by centers dedicated to the provision and maintenance of educational subsystems.

REFERENCES

1. Stacy, R. W., and Waxman, B. eds. *Computers and Biomedical Research.* Vol. 1, 2, 3. New York: Academic Press, 1965.
2. Hammond, A. L. "Computer Assisted Instruction: Two Major Demonstrations." *Science 176* (4039) (1972):1110–1112.
3. Dwyer, C. A. "Teaching Strategies and Tactics for Computer-Assisted Instruc-

tion." *CAI Laboratory Report No. R35. College of Education,* Pennsylvania State University, June, 1970.

4. Mitzel, H. E.; Hall, K. A.; Suydam, M. N.; Jansson, L. C.; and Igo, R. V. "A Commonwealth Consortium to Develop, Implement and Evaluate a Pilot Program of Computer-Assisted Instruction for Urban High Schools: Final Report." *CAI Laboratory Report No. R47.* College of Education, Pennsylvania State University. July, 1971.

5. Kennedy, E. M. "Health Care in the Seventies." *J. Med. Educ.* 47 (1972) : 15–22.

6. Swanson, A. G. "The Three Year Medical School Curriculum." (Editorial) *J. Med. Educ.* 47 (1972) : 67.

7. *Directory of Med. Specialists. 1972–1973.* 15th edition. Chicago, American Board of Med. Specialists.

8. Hubbard, J. P. "Measuring Medical Education: The Tests and Test Procedures of the National Board of Medical Examiners." Philadelphia: Lea & Febiger, 1971.

9. Lindberg, D. A. B.; Schroeder, J. J., Jr.; Rowland, L. R.; and Saathoff, J. "Experience with a Computer Laboratory System." *Multiple Laboratory Screening.* New York: Academic Press, 1969.

10. *National Library of Medicine News* 27 (1972).

11. "Libraries and Information Technology: A National System Challenge." *Report of the Information Systems Panel, Computer Science and Engineering Board, National Academy of Sciences.* Washington, D.C.: October, 1971.

12. Bjorn, J. C., and Cross, H. D. "Problem Oriented Practice." Chicago: Modern Hospital Press (McGraw-Hill), 1970.

13. Griesen, J. V.; Beran, R. L.; Folk, R. L.; and Prior, J. A. "A Pilot Program of Independent Study in Medical Education." *Presented at the 5th Rochester Conference on Self-Instruction in Medical Education.* Rochester, New York. April 1–3, 1971.

14. Griesen, J. V. "Description of CAI Course Data Base." Personal Communication. June 28, 1972.

15. "Information Index, Computer Assisted Instruction in the Health Sciences; Health Sciences Interest Group of Association for the Development of Instructional Systems." c/o Christopher R. Brigham, Dept. of Community Medicine, College of Medicine and Dentistry of N.J., Rutgers Medical School, New Brunswick, N.J.

16. Kamp, M. "Evaluating the Operation of Inter-active Free-response Computer Programs." *J. of Biomed. Systems* 2 (1971) : 31–44.

17. Harless, W. G.; Drennon, G. G.; Marxer, J. J.; Root, J. A.; and Miller, G. E. "CASE: A Computer Aided Simulation of the Clinical Encounter." *J. of Med. Educ.* 46 (1971) : 443–448.

18. Dickinson, C. J. "A Digital Computer Model to Teach and Study Gas Transport and Exchange between Lungs, Blood, and Tissues ('MacPuf')." *Proceedings of the Physiological Society* pp. 7P–9P, March, 1971.

19. Dickinson, C. J.; Ingram, D.; and Shephard, P. "A Digital Computer Model for Teaching the Principles of Systemic Haemodynamics ('MacMan')." *Proc. Physiol. Soc.* pp. 9P–10P, March, 1971.

20. Dickinson, C. J., and Shephard, P. "A Digital Computer Model of the Systemic Circulation and Kidney for Studying Renal and Circulatory Interactions In-

volving Electrolytes and Body Fluid Compartments ('MacPee')." *Proc. Physiol. Soc.* pp. 11P–12P, March, 1971.

21. Mellin, G. W., and Katzenstein, M. "The Saga of Thalidomide: Neuropathy to Embryopathy, with Case Reports of Congenital Anomalies." *New Eng. J. of Med.* 267 (1962) : 1184–1193; 1238–1244.

22. Watson, F. R. "Will the Art of Medicine be Destroyed by the Automation of Medical Logic?" *Missouri Med.* 68 (1971) : 936–940.

23. Watson, F. R., and Glass, R. L. "Cameo—Cancer Management and Education Optimization." *Missouri Med.* 67 (1970) : 875–877.

24. Lindberg, D. A. B. *The Computer and Medical Care.* Illinois: Thomas, 1968.

25. Lindberg, D. A. B.; Reese, G. R.; and Buck, C. R., Jr. "Computer Generated Hospital Diagnosis File." *Missouri Med.* 61 (1964) : 851–852, 858.

26. Buck, C. R., Jr.; Reese, G. R.; and Lindberg, D. A. B. "A General Technique for Computer Processing of Coded Patient Diagnoses." *Missouri Med.* 63 (1966) : 276–279.

27. Addison, C. H.: Blackwell, P. W.; Smith, W. E., Jr.; Shields, R. W.; and Sweeney, J. W. "GIPSY: General Information Processing System." *Information Science Series.* Monograph No. 3, University of Oklahoma, Norman, Oklahoma, 1969.

28. Lindberg, D. A. B.; Rowland, L. R.; Buck, C. R., Jr.; Morse, W. F.; and Morse, S. S. "CONSIDER: A Computer Program for Medical Instruction." *Proc. 9th IBM Medical Symposium.* White Plains, N.Y., 1968.

29. Lindberg, D. A. B., and Amlinger, P. R. "Automated Analysis of the Electrocardiogram " *Missouri Med.* 65 (1968) : 742–745.

30. Garten, S.; Rowland, L. R.; Morse, S.; Stewart, W. B.; and Lindberg, D. A. B. "Drug Information Data Base Organization and Access." *Proceedings of the Fifth Hawaii International Conference on System Sciences, Supplement: Computers in Biomedicine. Western Periodicals* (1972) 220–222.

31. Lindberg, D. A. B. "A Statewide Medical Information System." *Comp. and Biomed. Res.* 3 (1970) : 453–463.

32. Brecher, G., and Loken, H. F. "The Laboratory Computer—Is it Worth its Price?" *Amer. J. Clin. Path.* 55 (1971) : 527–540.

Section II

CURRENT STATUS OF HOSPITAL COMPUTER SYSTEMS

CHAPTER SIXTEEN

King's College Hospital Computer System (London)

by John Anderson

A. INTRODUCTION

This chapter will discuss the general situation of medical computing in the National Health Service in the United Kingdom and the part that medical information and communication plays in this service. At present, much of the information used to manage the system is generated by administrative action and measures service activities related to the patient but not the real aspects of patient needs nor how the Health Service meets these needs. There are also massive and costly medical record cemeteries where unique data lies buried for as long as its upkeep can be afforded. Such data cemeteries are a monument in memory of the concept that the Health Service management should be based on real health data. Unfortunately, the data is not used because each medical record is unstructured except to its originator and unanalyzable by any automatic system.

Medical records, too, are influenced by the theories of medicine held at any one time and by the existing system into which the records fit. At present, there are changing views about medical records that reflect the different attitudes of doctors towards the present medical care situation.

Having discussed this, the chapter will go on to the objectives of an ideal computer project. It will delineate the objectives and the various elements explored thus far in the King's College Hospital Computer Project and the present implementation, including the problems that have arisen.

1. National Health Service

Health care is now becoming a major issue and rightly so, as it faces difficult problems with the increasing range of services that can be offered to patients in primary care as well as in modern hospital specialist care. Medical research has extended the horizons greatly in the investigative facilities for different diseases and in therapy, not only in the physical but also in the psychological domain. Moreover, in the United Kingdom the general practitioner has maintained his status as the doctor rendering primary care to the patient and has acted as a regulator for access to hospitals and other services. Inevitably, he has dealt not only with a welter of minor recoverable illnesses but also with psychological and social problems. Thus the workload in different parts of the Health Service is different, and the medical record created should reflect this.

These changes have thrown great stress on the systems for management and organization. In the post-World War II era the tide of optimism was for curative medicine, and the need for preventive medicine and other types of care was barely recognized. However, renewed interest in the management of the Health Service has led us to take different attitudes towards patient care and to rethink our concepts of disease. For example, should diseases be regarded as "things" or occurrences that "happen" to people, or are they manifestations of abnormal relationships between individuals and their social and physical environment. In other words, should illness be viewed as something that can be "fixed" by the doctor, that can be cured; or should the medical profession declare that it can help people identify their individual and general health problems and enable them to either resolve or contain them? Thus the Health Care Service could be judged on its capacity to investigate and treat abnormal pathology, or, alternatively, on its accomplishments in helping patients and their families understand and manage their problems. Moreover, in the modern era attention must be given to the fact that society has to decide who is going to receive care. Should it go to all who can pay for it, to all who need it, or only to those who seek it? Thus new and basic problems are arising which require new solutions.

The Health Service has found it difficult to deal with its complex problems and their management, preferring to view the oscillations in the system as medical, financial, or administrative problems rather than as constraints in a system where little real data is available about patients and their illnesses in a codified way, which would give a real understanding of how things are and how they work in a rigorous detailed manner.

For example, we have recently had the problem of making available transplantation facilities and arranging that those who are about to die can give their organs to others who urgently need them. The battle on the international scene has largely resolved itself into one of personalities rather than looking in detail at the individual patient and his illness and the problems of the relatives of would-be donors. The system which would enable this kind of work to be carried out has been approved without any comparative costing and without establishing the relationship between transplantation and all other health care activities.

A similar problem has arisen in relation to general practitioner care in screening populations to detect early disease. In the United Kingdom multiphasic screening has not been popular because it has been largely thought to unearth diseases for which there are no treatments. Here again the problem seems to be attitudinal rather than realistic, for there are treatments available for many common diseases such as hypertension and diabetes which do prolong life and which, while they may not be curative, are certainly effective in decreasing symptoms and minimizing long term complications.

The present version of the National Health Service has three monolithic areas of medical activity: the hospitals, general practice, and local health authorities, all handed down from the past by a series of historical accidents. As a result, there is a structure with the lowest organizational exchange point: the Department of Health. Few cross-links are forged and little integration in any real sense is proposed even when the Area Health Authorities arrive in 1974. All this is the result of a welter of enquiries, committees, white, green, and other papers, which will fail to integrate the system because of the rigidity of its institutional set. At present, the Service is far too occupied with its peculiar organizational structure and antecedents, its internal power struggles (both lay and professional), its level of status, its costs, and its tendency to solve its management problems in terms of political factors and emotional stress. At present, the emphasis is on "cost benefit" and the deployment of the fashionable policies of the industrialist.

There are other solutions based on different strategy involving a set of objectives, the study of real resources and real restraints, which will enable us to create new model systems and test them against real data to arrive at a more optimal dynamic system, recognizing both patients and all those who offer care. While the Service was founded on a post-war tide of a desperate need for curative care, with preventive care left to the local authorities, other regulative systems are now necessary to meet changes both in society and medicine to defend the health of all.

The basic need of the Health Service is information about the health status of the people it serves based on adequate medical records, whether this is done in general practice, hospitals, or in the local health authority. This is no new cry. Parry was after it a century ago, and recently the Tunbridge Committee struggled to induce a semblance of order into medical records. It is this need that necessitates the development of computer information systems in health services. From an adequate system of lifetime patient health records not only would the patient benefit through the possibility of better medical management, but the Health Service would know how the system works, how environment affects not only people but their decisions. Why is so little done about medical information in spite of numerous opinions about it?

A patient-oriented system with complete patient medical records for life is the essential for a health care information system. Not only can it endeavour to maintain the patient in an optimal state of health, but the means can be qualified in terms that will yield new data with which to manage the system in a realistic fashion at the appropriate time. At every stage, the investigation and treatment of illness can be seen as transforming that patient's data set and producing a new one, either better or worse or the same as before, based on recognized and agreed-upon medical criteria.

At present, if one were able to study the information flow with special spectacles that viewed only data and its movement, the vision would show why the patient feels he is lost in a conflict-ridden system and with the usual comment "he is as well as can be expected."

Revens, in his studies over many years, established the principle that the length of an inpatient's stay is directly related to the staff turnover rate at all levels. Where the information system was poor because of inadequate communication, the patient was kept in bed until doctors and nurses were able to get adequate information.

The problem of complex regulatory systems is not usually with the individual component, as information generally flows well in a restricted area, but with its boundaries, communications, and constraints, which are ill defined and not understood. Health care is a vast, interactive control system for regulating not only the health of individual patients but its own performance. The urgent need is for studies about real medical information so that a new system can be modeled and studied before change overtakes us and wafts the health service into a new format not designed to meet changing needs.

2.   Medical Concepts about Illness

In addition to changes in the concepts at the basis of the Health Service management, there have been sweeping changes in our knowledge of the theoretical concepts of the disease process. It is proposed to review briefly changing concepts about illness and its management covering the Hippocratic system of prognosis, the concept of the natural history of disease, diagnostic classification of disease, homeostasis, and control systems in health. This deals with the framework within which the health professional views disease, and the information system must now directly reflect these ideas.

Hippocrates separated medicine from religion by deducing from basic data about the history of the patient and some physical signs a prognosis or medical prediction of the future of that patient. This was the first great use of medical information. It was not until the 17th century that Thomas Sydenham, the "English Hippocrates," developed his ideas of the natural history of disease based on medical records. He attempted to unravel the part endemic disease played in relation to epidemics of other fevers. Following the classification of plants by Linnaeus (1735), the idea of the classification of disease into diagnostic categories developed, mainly in France, but later elsewhere in Europe. At first, classification systems were based on symptoms alone and were unsatisfactory. As medical knowledge grew, pathological lesions and detailed changes in signs and other data were included. Further observations of the natural history of disease in the 20th century have seen amplifications relating to the patient's emotional state and social background as well as physical status.

Two other major developments in the present century have still to leave their impression on the concept of disease and its features. The first concept is that based on the work of Claude Bernard and culminating in the formulation by Walter Cannon of the idea of the steady state, especially of the internal system with "agencies acting or about to act to maintain stability." This has been amplified by the development of the idea of negative feedback in control systems. The other field deals with the development of statistical techniques to interpret data, beginning in the medical field with Pierre Alexander Louis and amplified by Karl Pearson, Seeley-Gossett, and Robert Aylmer Fisher. Thus statistical techniques of handling medical data became familiar, although many doctors still find this type of manipulation of medical data rather difficult.

3. Present Medical Records

Having covered some of the past history and influences on medical records, it is important to review present attitudes briefly. Alas, one has to record that many of the strictures in medical education about students keeping good medical records are based on the idea that the medical-legal purpose dominates all and without this the doctor is liable to find himself in trouble with the law. Yet the use of medical information is still the basis of good medical practice. In present-day circumstances, where one person can no longer assume total responsibility for patient care throughout his practicing life, medical records are essential for communication between the professional and patients. They are also necessary for communication, not only between doctors and nursing staff at the bedside of the patient but also between the doctor and the various investigative and therapeutic services which he has at his disposal. Thus, from the educational point of view, a great deal of information can be obtained from adequate medical data and medical records.

New ways of solving the medical information problem are a challenge to all departments of medicine interested in clinical research. The quality and type of data recorded in the existing handwritten medical record leaves a lot to be desired. Most doctors, trying to write a thesis in their ardent young days, come up against the problem of nonsystematic records and find essential information is not recorded. Indeed, the defects of present medical records reflect the attention paid to records during the training of the students in basic sciences. Here, as experimental records in basic sciences are not realistic and designed to provide new information, the assumption is made by the students that records of observations do not matter as long as the result matches that expected by the teacher. The student often feels that this is all records are intended to show. Thus, bad habits of recording original observations are infiltrated at an early stage, and this type of situation is prolonged into the clinical recording period. Here the stresses and strains on the student making his medical record are much greater, for he is dealing with people with emotional and attitudinal problems as well as learning to make new types of observations. Thus, the tendency is for him to prolong bad habits long after they ought to exist. This is perhaps one of the serious defects of our training in medical record systems. There is a lack of uniformity in recording systems even within a single hospital or medical school. It seems as if none of the senior doctors wish to agree on what they want to record. Should it follow the doctor's pattern of logic, or just record data in a systematic way and ignore the process? Should it be classification or decision oriented?

Even the Medical Defence Societies (organized for physician legal protection) find great difficulties in persuading some doctors to have any records at all, never mind having a systematized, organized record wherein data can be filed and found whenever it is needed. Medical records, too, are falling into disrepute as they tend to get lost in the existing hospital filing systems, especially as there is only one unique medical record. Thus, there are problems associated not only with input and retrieval of the unique medical record but with the content of the record. However, in the modern health team system of taking care of patients, such accurate communication documents are essential.

A practice that has become recently popular at the Case Institute of Technology and Western Reserve University in Cleveland, Ohio, deals with the ordering of diagnoses and the labeling of subsequent investigations and treatments to connect them with the strategy of the working hypothesis. Working diagnoses have been revived by Weed in his problem oriented record. This has had a marked effect in interesting many in the power and usefulness of clinical records to guide and rationalize patient management. In many places, both in hospitals and general practice, physicians are trying to implement these concepts and are rediscovering the usefulness of the medical record.

The problem oriented record, however, has its difficulties in defining the problem that is being explored. Is it the patient's problem as he sees it, or as the doctor sees it? Or should it be just a series of working diagnoses in the physical, psychological, and social domains?

This challenge is pressing. Whatever else is being achieved, Weed is certainly forcing many to revise their concepts about the many facetted meaning of the term diagnosis and the use of a problem approach to the medical record.

B. AIMS OF A MEDICAL INFORMATION SYSTEM

1. Aims

There are certain basic assumptions made about any medical information system. The first assumption is that the data derived from the patient by the variety of procedures ordered by the doctor is useful not only for the management of the patient's illness at the time it is occurring, but will be useful for dealing with the optimal treatment of similar cases and for allocating and managing resources in the health care service mobilized to treat that illness. For all illness there will be that part which is individual to the particular patient and another component which appears in similar illnesses in different people and about which generalizations can be made in relation to the course of the illness, its investigation, and its treatment. To some extent this will be coloured by the attitude of the physician, who views disease either as something to be cured or something which he encourages the patient to accept and acknowledge, working with him to improve or stabilize the condition. This too will have a bearing on the nature of the record. Usually the basic convention is that the information will be recorded but not the process by which it is obtained.

If the basic data derived from the patient is to have an impact on the medical management of the patient, there must be a means of deriving and transforming information so that it will be appropriate to the time when it will be used. Decisions concerning the management of that particular patient's illness and the mobilization of resources to meet the demand must be considered. In biological systems information derived from part of the system is used as feedback to regulate the ongoing activities of the organism over different time cycles. The same is likely to occur in a human information system.

There will be different time cycles of information feedback that will be used by health care personnel at appropriate times. The time scale for the use of such information appears to be such that each cycle is six to ten times longer than the preceding cycle generating the feedback. For example, a doctor's reflex response time for initial information is likely to be one or two seconds. The next response time is likely to be about two minutes, as he thinks over the information and ponders a decision, especially if the problem can be easily solved. The next time cycle is within two to three hours, when an investigation is underway and the cycle is approaching completion. The next cycle is that of review after one or two days, followed by a subsequent review in two or three weeks. A final integrative review will take place after three months or more. Of course, each cycle refers only to linked processes in a system. In illness each perturbation of the optimum healthy state has its own cyclical feedback processes. These cycle times have yet to be validated in reality. It does seem that a biological model may be very useful in developing suitable time cycles for data collection and decisions, including those about investigation and treatment. It is important to get these right, otherwise, as in biological feedback systems, the system may either develop spasticity or become totally paralyzed due to information arriving rapidly or slowly in the latent period.

If there is to be information feedback in a medical records system, it should preferably be entered into the system at the time it is obtained by the observer. This is necessary to avoid errors of transcription, which become appreciable if there are many transfers of data, for errors arise at each stage in a transfer process. The information entered into the data base then has to be transformed in different ways so as to be useful as feedback in the various time cycles when it will be required. Thus, for any such information system to work not only must there be input but there must also be rules for labelling each entry and arranging the storage of information so that it can be retrieved in a variety of ways when it is required.

It will be noticed that the information feedback is not in the form of decisions but is feedback as advice and information that enable the medical decision maker, who is trained to develop judgements, to function at his optimum. In other words, it should provide some of the data to assist in decision making. In medical activities the doctor and nurse are the key persons whose judgements and decisions affect the whole health care system. They must have the best possible information at the time when they need it to make the optimally effective decisions. Naturally, the type of information required in different situations will vary for different doctors and nurses. For example, the information required for general practitioners to improve general practice decisions will be different from that needed for specialist decisions in a hospital.

If the gathering and storage of information by means of handwritten patient medical records is not adequate for organizing and transforming such information, then other systems must be modelled, developed, and tested. Such feedback must be generated from the archives of records with minimal effort on the part of the doctor or nurse using the system. Only with the advent of new automated tools will this state be possible.

Properly programmed computer information systems can process such information and at the same time check for errors at every stage. But because of the complex nature of medicine it will be difficult to achieve an ideal system quickly. Parts of such an overall system can be developed according to different models, and testing is underway in some areas. Unless there is an overall design and model, however, there will be difficulties in overall integration that can preclude further development.

This offers a different philosophy about medical records in that it endeavours to create a dynamic information system, adapted to change, which would use medical information transformed as feedback to various individuals operating in the health service to guide their decisions. These people would not only be doctors and nurses, but administrators and, if necessary at certain levels, patients as well. Inevitably, the appropriate information should filter back to the politicians essentially controlling the service. While control systems concepts in relation to man's internal system have been fairly well developed, those relating to his external environment have been little explored. The application of control systems ideas to the interpretation and management of a patient's illness is one further step out into the unknown.

A control system model of disease was postulated, which would account not only for symptomatic disease, with physical signs and complications, but also for presymptomatic illness. Here the perturbations brought about by the assaults of pathological processes, whether they be infective, environmental, or of other cause, bring about responses in the essential control systems that the patient influences. This will cause alterations to be made either in the physical or biochemical environment of the patient or give rise by feedback mechanisms to changes in his mental and emotional state which are described by the patient as symptoms.

The progress of the abnormalities in the control system indicates how the patient and his environment are changing. The changes observed record the correction in whole or in part of the abnormality with or without thera- peutic activity on the part of the doctor. This view of patient care is a dynamic rather than a static concept, which has as its attributes a flexible diagnostic content and adaptable therapy. This model sees disease as taking place over a period of time by interactions within and without the patient, not only in the physical but also in his social and emotional domains.

The development of control systems theory in industry has not been possible without a new man-machine interface, the computer. To record the different types of change in the ill-human system, it is necessary to docu- ment more and new medical information to ensure reliability and validity of the medical record. To do this, computer systems are essential.

It will be necessary not only to apply the statistical techniques of the past to interpret such data, but to go on to develop new and different analytical methods. For example, the concept of confidence limits is only meaningful if one can analyze repeated samples of patients and has little meaning in the case of a single patient. Many of the existing algorithms we have for analyzing medical data give rather poor results; for example, Bayes' method and discriminant analysis do not solve all the existing diagnostic problems. Many young graduates have already proved once more the work of the 18th century physicians, especially those in France, that a different diagnostic problem cannot always be solved from symptoms alone. It is interesting to see medical history repeating itself with a more expensive tool.

Medical record systems cannot ignore the problem of definition of con- cepts and terms in medicine. It is important to have a complete medical dictionary to give backup information about definitions of terms in the medical record, including diagnosis and other procedures. This type of dic- tionary should contain not only information about meaning and syntax, but also lists of synonyms and related phrases. There should be provisions for phonetic description, as speech might well become an important method of input to a computer system during the next decade. Synonyms, phrases, and words related to the terms given need to be defined carefully to allow for flex- ible analysis as the medical record develops. Such basic sets of information can interact with the information entered into the system so that each set would be useful to support and extend the other. Thus, a dynamic kind of dictionary and vocabulary would be developed which would have a real place in medicine, not only in the medical record but also in training and teaching. This is a new dimension for medical dictionaries and vocabu- laries, but it is an important one. It is the basis on which information and communication rests. It is important to develop not only the definition of terms but to indicate the limits and logical relations. This means that doctors are going to have to accept and use logical operators (Boolean logic) in order to improve the efficiency of the medical record system. Computer systems cannot ignore the importance of semantics in communication and information analysis.

2. Data Entries and Summaries of Information

A medical record must have some structure if it is to be useful in all areas. Indeed, modern medical teaching concentrates on a very general structure when obtaining information from the patient about the present history of illness, past history, and information related to occupation and social circumstances. It then moves on to data collected by means of the observations of a doctor, a physical examination, and bedside tests.

This is the essential information needed to describe the illness. Preferably it should include not only the symptoms and their amplifications, but also the order of their presentation over a period of time, culminating in the total condition at the time the illness was determined. Hypotheses, usually called *working* or *provisional* diagnoses, or *problems* in the Weed context, are recorded. These usually deal with the generalizable part of an illness common to groups of patients. These diagnoses or problems lead to further investigation and, if necessary, to treatment.

The diagnosis or problems also have implications in recording the management of the patient. In the Weed system each problem is followed through as it is explored. It may disappear or be merged in another problem, but it has to be followed. This gives some logic to patient management. In the present heuristic system of patient management, transformations of the original data set of symptoms and signs should be followed and decisions about investigation and treatment should include the evidence on which they are based. If the patient's condition is improving, then the symptoms and signs discovered in the initial history and physical examination ought to improve. In the Weed system, all further investigation and treatment will be linked to the problem under consideration. There is thus a necessity to transcribe data from the initial state to the patient management area. Manipulation of data within the medical record will become necessary as various segments of the record are developed by different types of personnel, and some data will be moved when it is used as data for the decision-making process.

In the past, the patient management area has been too individually oriented to allow any deeper kind of structure. One of the important things Weed has done is to draw attention to the difficulties that arise because of lack of structure and to offer his problem oriented approach as a solution. There is also a need to allow for the entry of new segments of data into the area, such as data dealing with patient education about his illness. There must be other models of the system, as there is considerable opposition to his proposals.

Other types of data manipulation will be required for different types of summary; for administrative purposes; and for communication with the general practioner, other departments in the hospital, and doctors in outpatient follow-ups. New ways have to be explored for automatically assisting these summary procedures by labelling on data entry, labelling by the system, and editing by doctors and nurses.

In reviewing the existing records, it has to be stressed that as more information becomes available, many different types of summary will have to be created to enable the user to review the medical record usefully. These must save time and also direct the information to meet the needs of the individual doctors and nurses who consult that particular summary of data. Thus, there is a need in medicine not always to review the total information base that has been recorded, but to rely on summaries.

Summary information is, of course, only derived from the information entered into the system. Particular summaries that have been specifically designed, therefore, require specific information. For example, the summary that is required for the patient's general practitioner after his discharge from hospital will have a different orientation than that required for the doctor who is going to review the same person in the outpatient part of the follow-up process. Both summaries, however, will be derived from the total information available on that patient in the system. In order to do this the original information must be properly labeled and the machine must be programmed to organize it into the particular summary that is required. Similar summary information at a different level has to be recorded about repeated episodes of illness both in general practice and in the hospital. Thus, it is becoming plain that different types of summary provide feedback to different types of doctors in different ways. These summaries, however, are derived from the initial data base by labeling in ways that allow the system to derive the particular summary. Editing the machine summary will have to be a medical activity, for only doctors can assess the importance of the information in the system. In this way some feedback is created by doctors for those who will consult and use the system later.

3.   Nursing Record

The medical record must include the nursing record, which records not only vital signs and nursing information about a patient but the execution by junior nurses of the appropriate decisions made by senior nurses. A great deal of treatment and much of the basic requirements for investigation are carried out by nursing staff. Without information and process control systems of their own, they cannot contribute optimally to patient care. Thus, nursing decisions and their results are an important part of the medical record. The necessity to preserve a great deal of nursing information created about an individual patient has not yet been established. It is possible that a summary of information could be used in the medical record.

In some hospitals it is thought by those responsible for medico-legal affairs that the nursing record is useful, and it is usually kept in the medical record. The decisions about nursing records and their preservation in the future are not essential considerations at present. Different types of experiments need to be conducted to determine the usefulness of these records at later dates. Usually the tradition in medicine is that most of the nursing decisions have to be recorded, although the detailed information about how these decisions were carried out and executed does not.

4. Medical Management Cycles

It is worthwhile to explore management cycles more fully for they can become complex. We have already emphasized the importance of management and decision cycles for the individual doctor who will be making decisions within a time scale of a minute or more. He will expect to operate on information from requests to the investigative and therapeutic departments of the hospital within a time scale of a few hours. In the request/report investigation cycle the doctor wants to know if the patient or a specimen of his blood or urine has reached the investigative department and if what is provided at the laboratory matches up to the particular investigation ordered. It is important to recognize that here, as well as on the ward, logical checks have to be applied to ensure that the correct patient specimen is present. As the investigation proceeds it is necessary to apply process control checks to ensure that the result and the specimen are both known. Quality control of the measurements obtained is necessary before the data can be permanently recorded in the patient's record or before it is fed back to the physician. This information feedback allows the physician to monitor his decisions about the patient care. A facility should be available to tell him of errors that occur so that he will not be waiting for a result which will never come, and he should be able to interrogate the system to determine whether at any stage an error has occurred. Then if the specimen is not acceptable or there is an error in the experimental procedure, he can obtain further specimens and thus, without delay, obtain the result.

It is anticipated that such cycles can be completed between three and

six hours with an effiicient system. At present such cycles may take anywhere from two to three or as many as seven days. The present request/
report cycles are slow because of poor communications systems and
difficulties in transporting and matching specimen and request. This tends
to prolong investigative cycles. Indeed, it slows down all medical and
nursing investigation and care. Naturally, this is frustrating to both the
medical and nursing staff and make them feel that management cycles
are difficult. Sometimes they feel that the effort they have put in is hardly
worthwhile. It also makes them unobservant as to the duration of a patient's
stay and unresponsive to the cost of providing hotel facilities. There is a
tendency to blame these on the system rather than to try and make the
system work more efficiently. Unless computer systems can contribute
markedly to the area of improved investigation and communications they
are not going to be accepted.

Longer cycles are related to major changes in management and planning
during the patient's illness cycles and these are related to the review of
medical decisions by senior doctors. Usually there are three to four review
cycles occurring during the patient's average stay in hospital (eight to
ten days). Initially some overall episode management plan has been provided either by the patient's junior doctor or by a computer system to
deal with the patient's particular illness. The computer held plans can be
modified by the doctor and nurse to offer different types of plan for different days of a patient's illness as investigation and treatment proceed.
Initially these types of plan have only been developed for a few common
conditions, but as experience progresses they can be established for many
different types of illness. Inevitably, this means that some formalization of
the management of a patient's care has to occur. This raises difficult
psychological problems for doctors who feel that part of their responsibility
is taken away. However, only by experimentation with different ways of
managing patient care can we find the optimum strategies of doing this.
Undoubtedly, the traditional plan of investigation and treatment relates
only to personal experience and decision. Exploring different types of
strategies is impossible in this mode of action.

Once general and specific plans have been developed for the management of a particular patient's illness, it is possible to delegate the tasks
of ordering and supervising these plans to specially trained personnel. A
record planning officer, who has special training not only in nursing but
in the use of a computer system and developing and using patient plans
for investigation and treatment, can enter data into a computer system
and help to co-ordinate the procedures. This would certainly save medical
time once the appropriate decisions had been made.

Later information cycles feed back information from the computer data base not about individual patients, but about groups of patients with similar conditions. There are a variety of ways and methods to feed back information for clinical management. Progress of individual patients can be compared to a group of previous patients to see if the specific result is optimal or if the individual patient management can indeed be compared with an optimal model. The model can not only be evaluated for the effectiveness of medical management, but also for the expenditure of both human and financial resources that are committed by such decisions. In this way medical information can feed back to the administrative and managerial level of the service to produce changes in planning patient care as well as in hospital management.

Management data for longer cycles tends to be oriented not towards the individual patient but towards dealing with and exploring disease entities, usually classified according to causes of death. It will have to change when we consider the living patient. As yet there is little information about the usefulness of such management cycles in the Health Service, for detailed information of the kind proposed has not been available.

5.   Privacy and Confidentiality

Relevant to all this is the constraint of privacy and confidentiality. There are social and emotional constraints in dealing with medical information which mean that it is necessary to restrict access to such information. At present, the rules relating to privacy and confidentiality of medical information are accepted by all medical and other staff who work in hospitals either passively or formally so that they will not disclose information about patients to another person. On the medical side, if medical information identifying the individual patients leaves the hospital or general practice, it is only passed through another doctor and often only after the patient agrees in writing to allow it. In addition to these constraints is the difficulty in accessing and retrieving the ordinary written medical record which makes the system fairly secure. Often the impossibility of decoding the written entry is an additional safety measure.

In the computer system, because of identification checks on the user, the information is undoubtedly more secure. But any system is only as safe as the people who operate it. The system will certainly contain more data about patients in a readable format, but this would be more difficult to get. It is certain that very few people need access to the total patient data base, and here restrictions are great. As systems develop, it is important to keep this issue under review.

A great deal has been written about record linkage and also about sending summaries of information on all patients to central computers for information to be derived. Already the system of centralizing records is being reviewed as it allows a greater inroad into privacy if the system is broken. Issues are already being raised by doctors about the central reviewing of hospital information about patients which allows diagnoses, especially psychiatric diagnoses, to be associated with individual patients. The demand is rising for data banks to be kept locally and to be restricted to local individuals. The dangers of large central stores of data about individual patients are becoming obvious. What is needed to be held centrally is disease- and diagnosis-oriented records. The necessary summaries and digests can be prepared from local data banks and only the summary tables transferred. Why do people keep on insisting they have more summay information than they require? It only tends to obscure the real decision-making process.

C.   CHANGES IN TECHNOLOGY AND MANAGEMENT

An important aspect of the management of all long term projects is not only to get the objectives stated, agreed to, and implemented, but to consider that these need to be reviewed and brought up to date repeatedly as projects progress. The objectives must take into account that there will be, during a long project, changes in technology, especially in such a rapidly progressing field as computer technology. Not to anticipate that changes will take place in software design, in the power of the hardware available, and in communication networks is to deny such a project the improvements that will accrue from such advances. Unless a long term project predicts such changes and modifies its objectives to accomplish them, it will lose momentum and may create more problems than it solves.

If this is the case, managing such a project is not a field for the tyro, and even *futures experts* will find it difficult. It is of interest to look at the projection of Murray Laver in 1964 in relation to Post Office requirements for communication and computing power in 1974. He predicted a great increase in computing power and of computer methods which has nearly been reached. He also anticipated that voice methods of entry into a computer system would have arrived by the early '70s. The technology to do voice entry exists, but the pressure to speed up data entry into computers to the limits he envisaged is not likely to arrive until the late '70s, or perhaps even later. Let us hope that the health care services can apply as much pressure as the entertainments industry. Nevertheless, it is obvious that there have been marked increases in computing power in the last five to six years, and also in the sophistication of the hardware systems that are available.

On the other hand, our initial feasibility studies revealed that the problems in medicine, especially those in relation to the medical record, were complex and difficult, although not beyond the range of the possible. The major difficulty lay in isolating the information flow and disentangling the communications systems from all the other procedures used by the many individuals who back up health care systems. It was also realized that although the system appeared simple to the various individuals who took part in it, it was much more complex because of the allowance they had to make for exceptions and adjustments to different situations. Information systems do not easily undertake the adjustments which seem simple to human beings. Indeed, it was seen that systems analysis of information areas in medicine would raise problems, but in fact operational research, process control, and other techniques—not information science—were required to improve the situation.

Another danger existed in that the rising tide of optimism about the use of computers in the Health Service in the late 1960s and early 1970s created its own difficulties. There was a general feeling that everything could be achieved with a great expenditure of resources and not much thinking. Utopia was just round the corner.

Nothing could be further from the truth. It was felt with the advent of real-time computing in the airline seating business that medical computing would be much easier, certainly not as complex as it is. What was forgotten was that attending to the average sick patient is as complex a task as running an entire aeroplane, including engineering and control aspects as well as seating requirements. In a hospital patient management information system or health care system, we are considering the equivalent of moving a fleet of aircraft round the world every day, seven days a week. Such problems have never been tackled, much less solved. Thus, the Health Service was entering an area where expectations and delivery of reality were going to be very far apart.

Many users of the Health Service thought that their own special area existed in isolation from others. Many felt that this was an opportunity to make hay and raise personal status. Medical and nursing personnel have tended to have their individuality sharpened by the existing system. The problems associated with excessive individualism tend to make co-operative teamwork difficult, especially in areas dealing with information from a whole variety of sources. It was also not realized that the kinds of personnel attracted to the Health Service would have had little experience in systems design in an area where profit was no longer a guiding force. Business experience tends to highlight a range of systems which have attributes that are not necessarily transferable to the health area. It was also different from the business field in that the targets were less manageable in the sense that profitability was no longer the motive and finance did not appear, on the surface at least, to be a very large constraint. Motivation and urgency, therefore, did not receive a high priority. The time taken to deal with the complexity was also overlooked. It was anticipated that like all minor research projects medical computing could be solved within a few years.

With the kind of systems analysts that were attracted, it was not surprising that they tended to overlook the complexity of the problems. It was more comfortable for them to dig themselves into small areas and design limited systems, ignoring the cross-links and communications that are so essential in medicine. This specialization is comforting in that it allows the system designed to produce something within a reasonable space of time and to get it working, often at the expense of the expansion of the system. For example, it is fairly easy to produce results from an automated chemical laboratory system by changing the output devices and producing numerical values as results. What is much more difficult is to create the essential communications between the person who issues the order, the laboratory, and the network which brings the results to the bedside. These problems were much more difficult and tended to get overlooked at an early stage when small systems were developed. The fact that they tended to ignore boundaries and constraints and create their own limits made it difficult to incorporate them into larger systems.

Medical records, too, were of little interest to most people in medicine unless they were trying to resolve a clinical research problem. In this case, only limited numbers of records were thought to be useful. No attempt was made to understand the whole range of medical records in an institution or, in fact, the differences in recording procedures between general practice, hospitals, and local health authorities. Thus, there were major problems in system design that could be anticipated, but were not necessarily conveyed to the systems analysts who arrived. General expectations, in hospitals especially, tend to be rather high as the quality of personnel is both highly motivated and able. It was not realized that, initially, such systems would attract average systems engineers and analysts, and that they could not be expected to produce high technological results from their previous training and experience. The fact that they needed a period of time to adjust to the procedures in the Health Service usually went ignored, and little or no training was offered.

On the software side, difficult decisions had to be made. There was the problem of relating the type of operating system with the various hardware that was bought or given to support the research. There were decisions to be made also about the computer languages that would be used in the project. Should specialist languages be used? How many constraints in the languages implemented by the manufacturer would influence the direction and depth that the problem could take? There were difficult decisions if only one language was to be chosen. In the mathematical field Fortran undoubtedly reigns supreme, but Cobol was more acceptable for the problems that arose in the medical records area. It is better to use several languages and choose the one that is most suited to the application. There were, in the past, other software problems associated with the operating system, especially if the operating system was going to be modified to allow real-time working to take place on what was basicallly a batch-processing machine. Thus, there were software problems very near to the machine, as well as those in the applications area.

A much larger software problem arose in relation to file structures and the data base. In the medical area, inevitably, there is much manipulation of the information stored. The complexity and speciality of the data base problems tended to be overlooked. It was just assumed that medicine required some special file structures, but nothing that was really elaborate. Indeed, to make the information in the files available without a great deal of duplication, it is probably wise to adopt a data base concept. Inevitably, there is a price to pay for embarking on such a system. It is difficult initially to see the end, although the software implications of such a decision are fairly clear.

The effective operation of a data base requires the formation of a new and highly skilled section in the technical area to design and control its use. Its decisions about the data base affect the data circulating throughout the whole enterprise. A great deal has been written in recent years about the data base administration, whose function is to cope with such tasks as arbitration of the ownership of data, optimization of the performance of the data base system, and the documentation of all data. Also, whatever data base system is adopted initially would have to be open to improvement and modification as the computer system itself grew and changed. Thus, there will be continuing problems in relation to such developments. However, the implementation of data base concepts will benefit users and speed the development of new applications. It does separate applications programs more clearly from the data base, and programmers can concentrate on the logic of the appplication and not be so deeply concerned with the details of data manipulation and file design. Nevertheless, data bases still have many problems and there is no ideal solution available.

Hardware too has its difficulties. In the initial feasibility studies and the feasibility proposal, the problems were such that it was difficult to fit the proposed system into any existing hardware. Eventually a decision was reached. The hardware at King's College Hospital was a compromise solution which seemed best suited to answer some of the problems raised about investigating the medical record.

The machine itself has proved to be rather more flexible than was at first anticipated, and the hardware peripherals chosen early on for their real-time capability have given excellent service. Indeed, one of the major problems for management was that the initial system was developed rapidly and appeared to be more effective than it really was. In relation to the development problem, appearances on occasions can be deceiving. For the proper evaluation it is the details that matter and how the problem is solved. This is not often understood by those managing projects. They often prefer to bask in the opinion of others equally ill-informed. Inevitably, as the hardware becomes older then the downtime of the central processor and peripherals can be expected to increase. In this situation, unless adequate software backup is available and used, there will be problems. Such problems were anticipated in the first study, but there was no real response. In fact, in the first two years of the life of the project, the reliability of both the software and hardware was more than adequate to reassure the users. With increasing age, however, many hardware faults became apparent. When a system goes down in a hospital for three days or more, there are real problems. Even standard backup cannot deal with catastrophes of this kind over such a long period of time.

If there are to be many peripherals and many different laboratories, investigative, and therapeutic areas linked with other data processors, then it will be necessary to establish an adequate communications system. There were two possibilities and a whole range of compromises available initially. The preferred choice in the late 1960s tended to be large computers, on the assumption that the bigger the better. But, of course, a price had to be paid in designing a bigger, more comprehensive and safer operating system where the requirements on such a system grew disproportionate to the size of the computer. Inevitably, the main computer dealing with patient records has to be of considerable size. However, there is no real requirement that all systems need to be hung on one central main frame, and there are arguments for considering links with other small computers which will take over process control, quality control, and communications inside laboratories.

There are problems if a number of small computers are located within an institution. They must be able to communicate, not only with each other, but with the main central record processor. These communication links give rise to problems of compatibility between computers, transfer of software, and maintenance. The necessary hardware and software interfaces between such computer systems require a great deal of work and study with a specialist team. Such problems, although they have not been resolved initially, must be continually thought about. Resolution will be achieved in the light of study and experience gained.

D. KING'S COLLEGE HOSPITAL COMPUTER PROJECT

1. King's College Hospital Group: Medical and Dental Schools

King's College Hospital Group and the Medical and Dental Schools at present form one of the twelve London teaching hospitals, situated some six miles south of the river Thames. It serves a district of approximately 300,000 people covering hospital care in all its aspects and has a major interest in health care in this district. It has about 1,800 beds, and these provide inpatient services ranging from the care of the newborn after hospital delivery of the mother to geriatric care.

The Medical School takes 100 medical and 60 dental students annually and undertakes clinical training in both these subjects. Basic science training is given at King's College, Strand near the river Thames, or in the preclinical basic science department in the Universities of Oxford, Cambridge, and elsewhere. Thus, students arrive at the medical school having had basic scientific training, and this has to be born in mind in planning the clinical part of their training. Here medical records provide one of the bases for evaluating their progress through clinical training.

There are five hospitals in the King's College Group; they are in separate buildings usually one or two miles apart. Most were giving local district care before becoming part of the teaching group. One of them is a specialist pediatric hospital; the other gives special geriatric care. Within the general hospital group there are specialist units, which offer both routine medical care and promote research in their own special area of medical practice.

Each year the hospital admits some 40,000 inpatients. About 390,000 out-patients a year, being referred by their general practitioners, use its services. It also has a very active Accident and Emergency Department, which deals with well over 300,000 casualty attendances each year. It is perhaps the most service-oriented of the London teaching hospitals. Some 80% of its patients live within two or three miles of the hospital. It has good relationships with more than 200 general practitioners, whose patients it serves. Because of its optimal size for teaching and patient care and its important influence in the local community, the hospital forms a natural center of health care. As it offers a broad spectrum of medical care, its patient medical records reflect the real situation of medical need.

The hospital is managed by a Board of Governors with lay and professional members, the chairman being a layman appointed by the Ministry of Health. The Board is directly responsible to, and gets its budget allocation from, the Ministry of Health and Social Security, in the same way as all the other 26 teaching hospitals in Great Britain at present. The Board of Governors receives advice from the Medical Committee consisting of over 130 medical consultant staff, and they assist the board in formulating medical policy. Most of the teaching staff are part-time consultants in the National Health Service and mix public and private practice on a part-time sessional basis. The academic staff are full time and organized into departments, such as the Departments of Medicine and Surgery. These departments have clinical as well as academic responsibilities and carry out research as well as teaching.

As the project deals with medical information about health care, it is wise to have some idea of the part medical information plays in the existing system. There are unique handwritten records at present, created on every patient by a variety of doctors, of variable format and length, with standard investigation pro-forma and results. The medical record library has some 500,000 records and covers a large area. There are associated x-ray film libraries as well as other record libraries associated with investigative departments. In the hospital group records department, there are about 200 full and part-time staff under the charge of the records officer. There are many other people involved in medical records, such as medical receptionists, clerks, porters to carry them to and fro, as well as medical and nursing personnel. A study of the retrieval of medical records and their availability reveals that some 20% are not available when required. This can be a minor problem with inpatients but a crisis in an emergency or in the outpatient department. Some 3–5% of our records are permanently lost to the system, not only because of filing and retrieval problems but also because of unauthorized removal by staff without a trace card being completed. An estimate of the annual cost of creating and maintaining patient medical information by this system is about 8% of the Group hospital budget, some £600,000. Thus, medical information is not a cheap commodity, and the costs are not only financial but a considerable expenditure of careful, devoted human effort, which is without price.

Because of the expansion in medical records due to changes both in the theory and practice of medicine and the need for reliable, real data about health care, the system of creating, organizing, analyzing, and transferring information needs a new look.

2.   Feasibility Studies

Many of the difficulties in medical records were experienced between 1960 and 1965 in trying to implement a small card-based information system in a special clinic. The project did not fail, but took at least twice to three times as long as anticipated to obtain the necessary data. In the end it did not meet the requirements of users and so was disbanded. Because it was a card-based system which required batch runs, there were difficulties due to computer bureau problems and also in relation to the time spent by doctors and nurses in encoding and checking data. This project had a very difficult time with cards in that some 30–40% of the cards, after initial punching, were found to have errors. To diminish the number of errors in the cards dealing with the patient records some six to eight computer runs and a great deal more card punching were required. This thoroughly disillusioned the doctors using the system. In the end, because of the continuing problems, it was felt that the return for the effort was not worthwhile. The data obtained from this project has been subsequently published and thus it yielded results.

However, such a system did teach the important lesson that the ease of entry of data into the system was important and without it medical computer systems were unlikely to grow and develop. Data entry also had to take place at times appropriate to the users, who were in the main engaged in their clinical activities. It did indicate the necessity for structure in the record. Given that such data could be structured, then computerization of medical records was possible. It became apparent that it would not be possible to do this within the existing system by batch-processing methods. It was a requirement that the computer record should replace the paper record. In this initial experiment, both records were run side by side and hence the amount of work done was doubled.

Following this project, thorough studies were undertaken to determine the type of information stored in the medical record, its recording time requirements, and also the overall general structure of the hospital medical records. It was recognised that specialist departments would want their own special parts of the medical record. The overall general structure should be comprehensive and include all possible permutations. Studies, therefore, were done on 200 medical records and 100 surgical records, which revealed that they were of variable format and length, ranging from a few hundred words to several thousand. The average medical record contained about 850 words, usually four characters in length. The average surgical record was less than half of this. It suggested that the average medical record of a patient's stay had in it about 3,500 characters and numbers. The bulk of the medical record, especially the clinical part comprising the medical history, physical examination, working diagnoses, initial investigations and treatment, was created during the first three days of a patient's stay. The remainder of the medical record largely included investigative and therapeutic data. On occasion some data about the information on which decisions were made was recorded. Decisions tended to be disguised as opinions.

In most of the records it was apparent that little was known about the procedures and times of investigation or treatment. Often it could be very difficult to decide whether investigations or treatment had been carried out. It appeared that every patient had during his stay at least six investigations of varying type, nursing, drug treatment and physiotherapy. Here again the scatter of numbers of investigations was great and the figures derived were only useful as guidelines. It was not possible to get precise information from such a study because of the variability of the records. This was not necessarily related to differing clinical conditions. It was noted on several occasions, where groups of three or four patients had the same condition, that the length of the medical record could vary by a factor of 2 or 3. The information content of the record did not always accurately reflect its length.

It was evident that the basic initial information in all records could be described under such segments as the present medical history with subcomponents such as the past medical history, family, social and occupational histories of that particular patient, and physical examination. Usually included as part of the physical examination were bedside tests, such as tests for protein and blood in urine. This data was usually recorded on different paper than that of the history and physical examination.

Next followed the classification of the generalizable parts of that patient illness. The individual part of the diagnostic statement was covered by components of the medical history. Usually, the clinical diagnoses were described as "provisional" or "working" diagnoses, or occasionally as clinical impressions. What was the purpose of such a classification? Hopefully it was designed to lead to further diagnostic refinement by means of investigation. It also gave a clue as to possible treatment, which could be tailored to individual requirements by the physician. Usually more than one working diagnosis was stated. The obvious plan was to refine and make precise the diagnostic description by including structural and functional data leading to the etiology of the illness. Thus, tests were planned to elucidate the various working diagnoses in terms of etiology and to differentiate between these. Information was also required for therapeutic action, which usually took place at the same time as investigation was proceeding. Thus, the process of investigation tended to obscure the course of the illness and little attempt was made to correlate times of investigations with the progress of the patient.

It was apparent, therefore, that the existing medical record had not developed a suitable way for investigating strategies of patient management. Indeed, it seemed to be necessary to explore further the various details of patient management so that one could determine whether the signs and symptoms elicited in the history and physical examination had improved, were static, or were getting worse during this period. Medical decisions could only be inferred from actions. Thus, more definition of the various areas involved in the patient's management record was required.

It was noted that nowhere in the existing medical record was there a segment which dealt with patient education. Thus, it was difficult to determine what the patient had been told about his disease by doctors and nurses, and there was no clue as to what he understood about this. Procedures of recording discharge details were vague and the record did not always contain evidence whether the patient had in fact left hospital or had died.

Various summaries were created about the patient, these being an immediate general practitioner letter and summary some three to five months later. A further summary could be made for use in the outpatients clinic when the patient was reviewed. Sometimes the general practitioner and outpatient summary were, in fact, the same, although the objectives of each should be different. The fundamental assumption, accepted in general, appeared to be that a new total look at the patient's medical history and physical examination was required on each hospital admission.

The basic recording process was that the history data and physical examination were entered in detail by junior staff. Both house physicians and house surgeons had this as one of their main duties. This information was occasionally repeatedly recorded by registrars and other senior personnel, but more often they amended the data when appropriate. It was apparent that medical recording was far from a uniform procedure, and its extent of detail tended to depend on pressure of work and clinical interest. Outpatient records tended to be made by more senior staff, and usually the record of their findings was available. No matter what the previous record, junior staff usually went through the whole medical record routine as part of their education if the patient was admitted to hospital.

Reiteration of information appeared to be useful in that it tended to uncover new or confirm previous information. It often led to the discovery of new facts. It became apparent, too, that much information that may be absent from the medical history was already known by the general practitioner, who was not very informative in his letter of referral of the patient. Often such information only became known if it was included in the doctor's letter to the consultant. Part of the difficulties in medical records appears to arise from the system of communication between the general practitioner and the hospital. There were also variable results because of a lack of uniformity in recording occupation, social class, family information, and psychological history.

The physical examination of the patient followed the medical history and provided new information. It was very variable and the depth of signs investigated depended on the view taken by the doctor of the patient's illness. If he thought it was serious, then the principal system involved was investigated in great depth. Otherwise, he might only enter "no abnormality detected" or "NAD." To some extent, this policy depended on the policy of senior colleagues about medical records and what they expected to be recorded. In general, there appeared to be no agreement on the basic physical data to be recorded, i.e. pulse rate, blood pressure. No basic agreed-to physical examination was performed on all patients in the hospital, regardless of medical or surgical specialities. Thus, errors of both omission and commission were possibilities.

However, if we are to have computer records then more structure must be given to the record to prevent errors. Naturally, the type of record young doctors create reflects not only the type of training they have been given during their undergraduate days, but also the importance senior medical management attaches to these important procedures. The manipulation of this type of information within the medical record is usually not viewed at all, although it tends to be updated by senior colleagues in general. Often the procedures expected of a particular unit or firm were learned from the preceding holder of the post rather than by consultation with senior personnel or through established printed rules.

Bedside tests were included as part of the physical examination. This usually included the investigation of urine and other body fluids. A record was made of body temperature, pulse rate, and respiratory rate by the nursing staff. These were usually recorded, but in a small percentage of patients they were not traceable to any existing record. It was possible for the data to be in the nursing record and not in the medical record. Sometimes the records of these investigations were kept on the temperature chart, at other times in various places in the nursing notes. Sometimes they were kept as special records or as part of the general record.

There appeared to have been few checks that such data was either normal or abnormal after it had been obtained. Often abnormalities were, in fact, recorded without any appropriate action being taken by medical staff. In some records urine tests were carried out and reviewed once a week with other ordered tests. In others, there appeared to be no system for review even if abnormalities appeared.

Diagnostic statements and working diagnoses (sometimes called clinical impressions) were recorded in a variety of ways. Often the differential diagnosis was expressed as a series of diagnostic statements. Rarely were the diagnoses listed in order of importance to the individual who was investigating the various diagnoses. Only rarely was the individual part of diagnosis given expression. Usually it was tacitly implied from the remainder of the patient's record. As there were usually no ordering of diagnoses it was difficult to establish logical investigation and treatment plans. Usually, house staff listed the investigations they thought were relevant and ticked them off as they sent the necessary request forms with the specimens. Such brief notes were often difficult to decode and virtually understandable only to the individual who made the record. The main aim of the list of orders appeared to be to check that request forms had been sent and the necessary administrative procedures put in action.

It was seen that the links between diagnostic statements and patient management were not implicit in most of the medical and surgical records consulted. Treatment was rarely entered into the written part of the medical record but separate treatment sheets were attended to carefully and often reviewed, as judged both by medical cancellation and amendments. The treatment sheets were placed in the patient's record at the end of the episode of illness. Usually, entries in medical records tailed off sharply after this, unless the patient was acutely ill or something drew the attention of the medical staff to a change in his clinical condition. In the medical part, more than 20% of the records consulted gave no clue as to when the patient was discharged or to his state on discharge. Usually, this was only obtained by cross-reference to the nursing record. There were rules in some of the firms whose records were consulted that entries about acute patients should be made by medical staff at least once a day and for patients who were not acutely ill, at least twice a week. Often these rules were not enforced. There was no evidence that those who were carrying out the medical recording procedures thought them to be very important. It was felt generally that the segment of the medical record dealing with patient management required much more thought and action than the preceding segments. Although not recorded, the standard of care was high, but there were no records to prove it.

Nursing records, such as temperature, fluid balance, and other charts in the record were often the only real guide to the management of the seriously ill patient. There were obviously very well established nursing routines for certain disorders. The process of carrying out the orders was usually not stated, although the orders were held on record. In general, the nursing records went to great detail and also said much more about the patient's general clinical state than the medical records. The Kardex system of the nursing record was referred to by doctors as well as nurses. It appeared to be the only quick reference means of ascertaining the patient's condition. It became evident that nursing records were an integral part of the medical record. It was evident that if optimal use of investigative and therapeutic services was to be achieved, a better system needed to be established. This would involve both doctors and nurses.

Some sub-systems were excellent in certain specialities. For example, surgical operation records were excellent in detail and always available, having been written by the surgeon himself. It was noticeable that rarely was the duration of any operation specified, although often the procedures were given in great detail. Certain basic anaesthetic records were kept and they appeared to have both a basic system and room for special records by different consultants. Social and other relevant records were also kept in the main clinical record. The Department of Social Work was, in fact, used in much the same way at other investigative departments. Psychiatric records were not included in the general medical record and were specially stored in the Department of Psychiatry. Usually, however, a clinical abstract of the psychiatric record was included in the main record so that the doctor could get some information about how a patient's psychiatric state was progressing.

Further work on the input arrangements for the relevant segments of the medical work was done. The transformation of data that might be required from each segment of the record was considered along with the various forms of output that would flow from this information. Thus, by detailed consideration of all the segments of the medical record and the manipulation of that information for various information feedback cycles, it was possible to generate basic concepts for a data base. The complexity of the medical record problem was then apparent to computer staff. There was a much more comprehensive approach to the medical record problem as a result.

It was obvious that all the decisions made in the initial phase were totally relevant to the future medical record. From this followed the idea that it would be wise to experiment with such a record in a test-bed area while development continued. This meant that the problems that would arise during implementation would be restricted. It would also provide a center for training others in the recording techniques if it was successful. An attempt was made to make the initial implementation both comprehensive and in-depth.

Further investigations were made of the main investigative and therapeutic departments, such as Chemical Pathology, Haematology, Microbiology, Radiology, and the Pharmacy. The data input and output of each of these departments was observed, and the number of information transfers every fifteen minutes, whether in or out, was recorded. The work load of most of these departments was between 300 and 500 investigations a day. However, most of the input and output arrived during a space of about two to two-and-a-half hours in the morning and two hours in the afternoon. Peak input and output rates arise in the middle of the morning between 10 and 11 o'clock, and the value peaked in the afternoon at two-thirds of the morning peak at about 3 P.M. Thus, it became apparent that the input and output from laboratories had a high rate of data transfer at certain times, and very little during the rest of the day. The study was continued for a week, and it was apparent that the day-to-day fluctuations were not major. At the weekend the number of investigations dropped considerably, and there was no real pressure on data input and output. There were, however, individuals rendering emergency service during this period, who were different from those concerned during the week and who would need some training to use a new system.

Another problem in the investigative laboratories of the pathological services was that the load appeared to be increasing by about 25% per year. It was apparent that this rate of increase would continue unless there was a change in system. Thus, it became important in planning for information recording to allow for future expansion in such areas. Any information system had to be capable of absorbing an increasing work load which is reflected in an increased data load. It became obvious that the investigative and therapeutic information systems were largely geared to peak day work loads. To some extent these work loads reflected clinical demand, but were also created by the pattern of work of the departments in response to that demand. Looked at in system terms, it appeared to be a costly system to operate and to have serious leak problems. It inevitably meant that all the equipment had to be geared to peak load.

In spite of the laboratories now becoming automated they are labour intensive still. It appeared from questioning laboratory personnel that extended shift work was not acceptable to them. Thus, the only way of improving the performance in laboratories appeared to be by more automation and also by an improvement in the information system in which they operated. It was also apparent that a great deal of communication, because of the slow nature of the paper response, was done by telephoning laboratories. Usually, a telephone in each laboratory was manned fairly permanently during the working day.

Further studies were made on the availability of the existing clinical record. It was realized that such a record at present in written form was unique and that it was not always available where and when required. A study of the accessibility of individual patient medical records for both inpatients and outpatients was made over a period of several months by the Department of Medicine. It was found that about 20% of the records were not available when they were needed at any one time, either by a consultant or other doctors. This may mean that the record was not available on the ward when a doctor wanted to consult it because the patient had been referred to Radiology or other investigative or therapeutic departments and the notes had accompanied the patient. Sometimes the notes did not arrive back with the patient and were being returned by another route. This meant that they were neither available in the department to which the patient had been sent nor on the ward, but were in the process of transit. It became apparent that some 3–5% of the records were lost for more than seven days and a small percentage were lost forever in the system due to misfiling and other reasons.

There was a huge problem of filing medical records and maintaining a Master Index. Records were filed by number and when records were removed from the main records store, a trace card was placed in its place. There is no doubt that a large number of records, between some 20 and 30%, were continually out of the medical records department, being in different departments or wards of the hospital. Some were, of course, removed for other purposes. Indeed, it was useful to have these 20% of records missing from the record department, for there was not space to house them if they were all returned. Difficulties of retrieving an individual record by hand were great.

With 1,800 unique inpatient records circulating in the hospital at any one time and 1,000 or more outpatient records also in circulation, including casualty records, difficulties were far from trivial. Many individuals had tried to improve the system without much success, but it did reach a fairly high stable level of service. It appeared to be very difficult to improve its efficiency. Indeed, it was only by the devoted labour of several hundred records staff that the existing system worked at all. It was interesting that no matter what the perturbations, accompanied by the annoyance of the medical and nursing staff, it was very difficult to change the system in any degree.

Communications between the general practitioner and the hospital were made by means of letters. The general practitioner usually sent a letter to the hospital, and the hospital replied on discharge of the patient by sending both a brief discharge summary fairly immediately and later a clinical summary. A study of discharge letters usually revealed that the diagnosis and treatment of the patient were on the letter and these were sent out promptly within two days. However, a copy of such a letter was not always available in the hospital patient medical record, although it had most likely been sent.

There was, however, a much bigger problem with clinical summaries, which usually went off weeks and sometimes months later. There was a ten day cycle after the patient had left hospital for all the investigative and other results generated about the patient to be consolidated in the record before it was presented to the doctors for summary. This tended to allow a period to elapse after the departure of the patient when, in fact, the record was not available for summary purposes. This meant that medical staff tended to forget about patients and their summaries, only to be reminded about these by secretarial and other staff at a later date.

There was some inertia in the system, and the motivation to dictate summaries and get them out promptly to the general practitioners was variable and usually on the low side. A perennial cycle in relation to summaries had been taking place for a decade in the Department of Medicine. A check was kept on the number of summaries sent out per month and how late they were after the discharge of the patient. There appeared to be a period of four to six months during which the backlog of summaries would gradually increase from a mean dispatch time of one month to a time of four to six months. When the duration of the cycle reached this length it was necessary to review the whole procedure to increase the motivation and pressure on people to do something about the summaries and speed up the whole system again. In general, the system slowly became inefficient over another three month period and the whole cycle would be repeated. It was apparent that the communication cycles between the general practitioner and the hospital were only kept going by the eternal vigilance of senior personnel. It was apparent, too, that junior doctors did not view the system as really useful to the general practitioner.

In relation to the creation of summaries and the dictation of these, there was a tendency to overlook the secretarial component. There was no doubt that secretaries were mostly overloaded with work and the motivation of temporary secretaries was not always high. Also, secretaries tended to have problems in relation to the medical records, as they often felt that the communications that took place between doctors about patients were not of value. One of the medical secretaries described the process she was involved in as "dilatory hospital doctors reluctantly dictating irrelevant information to other doctors who wanted different information urgently." Thus, the system from this aspect had major problems associated with it.

There were obviously problems in transforming the original data for the summary because of omissions, and also problems in educating doctors to see that such data was used when it was provided. The system in general seemed to contain many errors. A detailed study of the differences between the records of different doctors was not investigated at that time, but the investigation took place later. It seemed important to use a new medical record procedure to try to eliminate as much error in the system as possible, which was revealed as very "lossy" in its present shape, especially in regard to medical data. In general the "lossy" nature of the system was recognised by doctors and this was remedied to some extent by including a large amount of redundant information.

It was essential to try and speed up reliable communication, not only in the hospital but with the general practitioner as well. There was also a great deal of redundancy in relation to investigations and often an investigation was repeated several times to ensure that at least one test arrived back at the bedside within a reasonable length of time. Little monitoring of investigations took place, the main objective appeared to be to get these done as soon as possible. Little information useful to medical and administrative management was derived from the medical records. Because of the nature of the medical record, it would have been very difficult to get this. However, some information on the record was obtained by means of small and costly abstracts about diagnosis and disposal designed to provide hospital information on inpatients for statistical purposes. This required special effort on the part of the medical records clerks. Usually the diagnostic descriptions were difficult for them to formulate. The usefulness of such information was viewed with great suspicion by the medical staff. There was little belief amongst medical staff that medical information was the real data base on which hospital decisions should be reached. Thus, there not only appeared to be a systems problem, but a great deal of re-education and re-orientation to be done in relation to the users of medical records.

A brief investigation was made into fundamental cycles of information and the times at which these would be relevant. It was seen that there was a need for the doctor to reach decisions within a minute or so of obtaining information at the patient's bedside. He may also need in this time scale to interrogate various segments of the record to check that certain things had been done or to obtain some idea of the information that had been input when the patient was admitted so that he could compare this with the patient's present state. Nursing information was reviewed in the same time cycles and decisions made about its relevance and importance to the patient.

Investigative cycles usually took two to three days on average. There were some delays before requests went off with samples. Often a request made late one evening would not be implemented and the blood sample taken until the next day. Usually the laboratory worked on the sample that day, and the investigative result was available by the evening of the second day. Communication through the records personnel, to get the investigation back in the patient's medical record and available for the doctor at the bedside, took a further day. It was, of course, possible for the doctor to short-circuit this investigative cycle by telephoning to the department. It was realized initially that the doctor had no means of knowing whether his specimen and the request reached the laboratory and was accepted. He was not informed whether the specimen was lost or was not appropriate to the investigation he was requesting. He was not informed if the specimen was lost during the process of doing the investigation and would not become aware of this until no result became available. Thus, short of learning that the computed result had arrived back at the bedside, the doctor had no means of knowing whether his order had any chance of completion.

The cycles in relation to therapy were on a closer time scale. Drugs ordered urgently were given within a few minutes and routine treatment within a few hours. Further cycles of review took place once or twice a week when senior doctors reviewed the work of junior personnel. During these cycles a reassessment of the existing patient data in the medical record was made, along with a check on the working diagnoses and on patient management and care so far. Advice and decisions about future management were also given. Usually, decisions about discharge were taken at such meetings. A nursing representative was present during such ward rounds, and decisions about management which affected the nursing staff were made at this time.

A brief survey was also conducted into general medical outpatients and into special clinics such as the diabetic and hypertensive clinics. It was felt that medical records implementation in outpatients would be extremely difficult due to the high work load and busy nature of the outpatients in a district hospital such as King's. Here any breakdown in the system, where there were some 40 or 50 patients being attended to in an afternoon by a small group of doctors, would be extremely serious.

The systems required in outpatients appear to be similar to those used in inpatients. It was felt that some new techniques needed to be developed for outpatients, however. The need here was for speed and accuracy to meet appointment times. From his clinical data entry the doctor should be able to indicate the summary data required for the general practitioner's letter in reply to the letter of referral. It was also noted that the information in the referral letter should be entered in the data system. This problem was rather more complex than it appeared at first sight. Casualty work involved health survey work as well as reviewing the local acute sick and serious emergencies from trauma, etc. The medical record did not have any record of health survey work done. This was an area in clinical recording that had yet to be developed in the United Kingdom, but which had been well explored elsewhere in the world.

A further investigation was made into the typing ability of students in the medical school. It was found that most students could not type more than six words a minute and there were 10 to 20% spelling errors in any fairly long medical statement typed by such students. A grant was obtained from the Abbeydale Trust and students were given tuition for touch typing courses. At the end of the course most students could type about 10 to

20 words a minute. However, the main problem of the correct spelling of medical terminology still remained. Thus, it became apparent that if we were to use typing as a means for junior doctors to enter data, it would be a slow process. There would have to be data vetting checks of spelling and format to ensure that such errors were corrected before entry into the computer record. Thus, some kind of dictionary look-up procedure would have to be available if such an entry of free text was permitted. If free text was the main method of data entry, there were also obviously going to be problems in format, of data vetting, and analysis of such data.

In general, it was found that medical students did not have an aversion to typing provided their seniors attached some importance to it. It was very interesting that for two and a half years after the initial typing classes, the medical records in the medical unit were some of the best medical records we had ever had. They were both legible and much more logical. It appeared that once the record could be read, there was much more pressure on a doctor to make it a logical and comprehensive document. It is sad to relate that no further funding from the Medical School could be obtained for such an activity, and the typing course had to be closed when the grant ran out.

The results of these and other studies indicated that it would be preferable for the computer system to suggest messages for doctors to manipulate rather than have doctors responsible for entering free texts which the computer system would have to analyze later. Nevertheless, both facilities are necessary. There was also a need, felt by the users, that they should be able to manipulate and use a variety of input devices. Doctors and nurses recognized that, if data had to be transferred from them to record clerks before entering the system, there would be problems, not only of errors creeping in in the transfer of data, but of verification by the person who had originated the data. It was therefore felt that whatever devices for data entry were chosen, they should be used by the personnel who originated the information, namely the doctor and the nurse. At this time visual display units were becoming available in the United States and British computer companies were interested in such devices. It was felt that these were much more suitable than teletypewriters for entering information into the medical record, although far from ideal. They had the facility of allowing information in the system to be interrogated and displayed on the television screen. This would allow the doctor and nurse to enter information in seconds and retrieve information from the system within short periods of time. Thus, the computer system would be real-time and would involve multi-programming.

This inevitably meant that the complexity of the system from the technical point of view was going to be great. There would be problems that were medical in relation to data structure and also those that were technical in relation to data input and output. It was felt at this time not only should the medical record project take cognizance of the individual episode of illness that occurred in hospital, but that the record project should be much more comprehensive and consider the patient medical record for life, of which the hospital episode would only be one part.

It was calculated that each patient would have one or two visits to a general practitioner each year of his 70 years of life, making perhaps some hundred to 140 visits in all. Each of the records of the visits would have messages that would have 100 to 200 words in them. Each patient would perhaps have two or three admissions to hospital during his lifetime and these would comprise 1000–2000 words in length. If health survey information and other information about the patient was to be included it could well be that the total medical record for life would comprise some 20,000–30,000 messages of perhaps 10–20 characters in length. Since this type of record would have to be held on all patients, the recording and retrieval problem would be a formidable one. Inevitably, there would be a demand for summaries about the patient's health state at different levels, and these would have to be structured in some fixed format. Both a philosophy and standards of implementation would have to be developed for the overall patient medical record. A means of evaluating the usefulness of such a record was an essential requirement.

With these factors in mind a feasibility proposal was done with International Computers Limited of Great Britain and was submitted in 1967 and 1968 to the Department of Health. The project was successful in obtaining approval, and authority was given to implement the project in 1968.

3. Hardware and Software

The computer that was given to us was an International Computer Limited (ICL) 1905E. The central processing unit had 48K store of 24 bit words. The central processing unit was able to write to four exchangeable disk systems and each recording head had six disks in the form of a cartridge with 200 tracks on each surface. The exchangeable disk control units could each handle 8 units, and there were two visual display control units which were capable of handling 64 visual display units (VDU's). There were also six magnetic tapes in decks of two, and the tape was 7-track ½″ magnetic tape. There were eight visual display units, six of which were to go in the test bed area; two were used for both teaching and systems development. There were also punchcard readers and paper tape readers. There were two line printers which printed at 300 lines per minute. The hardware, after trials, was accepted in six weeks. Its reliability was about 98% during the first two years of the project.

Initially, International Computers Limited (ICL) supplied the operating system, and further real-time software was written by the project programmers, who found it necessary to do a great deal of fairly low-level programming work because of our special medical requirements. The systems software was carefully developed and rigorously tested for reliability. Over the initial two years there were only two software faults which caused major breakdowns, and this is an indication of program reliability. We feel that the policy of making reliable software has paid off with our users, who have come to regard the system as reliable as well as useful. It is often forgotten that software reliability is just as important as the hardware, if not more so. As the system developed, it was important to keep the basic software in mind because there were limitations as to what could be undertaken.

The truth of this came home when a new type of visual display unit, not produced in the United States but in the United Kingdom, was introduced into the system. It was decided, when the changeover in objectives was made to a communications system, to order 40 new visual display units which had entirely different characteristics. This meant a major applications software rewrite was necessary when the new hardware came. It also posed problems for users. The display system screen generated far more characters (2,000) and therefore threw out of alignment the displays which had been written for a smaller screen with considerably fewer characters. It was inevitable that such a system would go through many cycles of reiteration with improvements and alterations ongoing all the time.

4.   Personnel

It was decided at the implementation of the project that there should be two part-time directors of the project—the Senior Hospital Administrator and the Professor of Medicine—a Project Leader and one secretary. There were also to be two full-time doctors engaged on the project and 15 systems analysts, half of whom should be senior analysts. On the programming side there was to be a programming manager, seven senior programmers and eight programmers; two of whom would be trainees. The operations staff was to consist of an operations manager, nine computer operators, and three data preparation staff. It was expected that the staff would take a year or more to recruit and this proved to be the case. There were problems in relation to the balance and number of staff. Although staff make-up had been agreed to by the Ministry of Health when the project began, there had always been reservations about the classification of staff who engage in high technology. It was evident that we needed some of our programming staff to be systems programmers, but such a term was not acceptable to the Department of Health. There was also a need to create staff who could deal with a data base system. It was realized that in comparison to the number of systems analysts, the number of programmers was small. Indeed, the whole staffing of the project was modelled on that of computers in industry. The same type of staffing arrangement did not necessarily apply to the Health Service.

5. Project Objectives

The objectives of the project were stated initially in 1969 and formalized in 1970 with the system going live. They were accepted by various committees in the hospital dealing with the computer project. The central objective was to establish a patient medical record for life. It was seen that this objective would take seven or more years to implement.

Initially, a patient medical record for life would have in it various types of summary data related to the patient. It should contain necessary basic information for medical and nursing staff from the physical, psychological, and social domains. In addition, summary data of the patient's last four admissions to hospital and the last four visits to general practice would also be recorded. The current list of diagnoses and treatment given would be available. There would also be available on a slightly longer timescale, various summaries of the patient's episodes of illness. The record would follow the episodes of illness that befell the patient, whether they took place in general practice or in the hospital. It was anticipated that a part of the medical record would have to be allocated for the entry of medical survey data. Immunisation and other data held by the local authority would be part of the physical data held about that patient at the beginning of the medical record. This type of data could be added to or amended, but not deleted.

The next objective was to deal with the medical record of an episode of illness in a hospital. The type of medical record held in a hospital would differ in structure, detail, and depth from that held in general practice, as the information needs of hospital doctors and general practitioners were different. It was necessary, however, to concentrate on the episode in hospital rather than the episode in general practice early in the development of the project. The experiment was to be done in a test bed area of 40 beds in the professional unit, and a further development was to be in a surgical eye ward in the hospital.

The approach to the basic patient medical record for life was to be through the episode of hospital illness, first implemented on a test bed area and then gradually expanded to cover the hospital. It was recognized that computer-held records would have to take in the records of many special departments. There would be a need to meet these specialist requirements as the medical record developed from the test bed area to spread hospital-wide. It was decided to experiment with the usual clinical format of the record. It was felt that as this was being developed in a general medical ward, its problems would be comprehensively explored. As it expanded elsewhere, there would be a need for certain special modules to be developed, but the overall format would remain.

The record began with the information in the present medical record, which included the history of the present illness, the relevant past history (which would in future be part of the total medical record for life), and the social, occupational, and psychological histories as appropriate to that patient's illness. It was recognized that in future much of the last part of the data would eventually be available as part of the fixed data given in the initial part of the medical record for life. It was decided to try experiments with different ways of recording the history once it was shown that a record comparable to the existing record could be created and maintained. It was hoped to explore both the form and extent of history and physical examination recorded by a proactive and retroactive problem-solving method. It was thought that this would allow some insights into different ways of medical thinking. If the recording procedure mirrored the thinking process it may make recording easier.

Physical examination was to be recorded and bedside tests were recognized as part of the physical examination. Here different ways of speeding up the entry of this type of data were to be explored, including the use of questionnaires filled in by the doctor. This type of approach would be useful if the system went down, so that input could still take place. It was decided to allow doctors to label messages with a number relative to their importance. It was hoped that this would allow automatic summaries to be prepared by the machine.

This would follow a segment dealing with diagnoses, which would include working diagnoses at several conceptual levels and the generalizable part of the diagnoses. The first was asymptomatic diagnoses, the next that associated with a symptom or sign. This was followed by further descriptions indicating structural and functional system change and etiology. It was decided to do experiments into the problem oriented record later when computer recording procedures had been accepted. That would include operational plans about investigation and treatment, comment about changes in the symptoms and signs already found on admission as to whether they were progressing, improving or stationary—and also comment about the relevant prognosis. The segment of the medical record known as patient management would be the most difficult and complex, for new and old information would be used. It was envisaged that there would be routing plans of orders for investigations and treatment for common disorders. This should improve the facility for recording and also improve the logical strategy of patient investigation and treatment.

Thus, the emphasis was to be on decision directed records initially, which would record both the data on which decisions were based and the decision. It was felt that it was not worth recording the process of thinking or the process which was gone through to derive either the information or the decision. However, it was thought to be desirable that the computer system should follow medical logic if possible. The system was not, however, seen to be reaching decisions. It was merely presenting data and, if necessary, associated information to the doctor so that he could reach the necessary judgements that were required of him professionally.

Following the statement of some 50 detailed objectives dealing with various parts of the medical record and the medical data base, the objectives went on to describe the necessity of having a medical vocabulary and some list of procedures which could be standardized. The medical vocabulary was not only to contain the name of a term and its correct spelling, but also if possible to have a definition of the term. It should also show where the term was to be used in the medical record, whether it was in medical history or physical examination, and also the various logical connections of that particular term. It was also felt that such a vocabulary ought to have phonetic spelling incorporated in it as speech might be used as an input device at a later date. It was felt that if we had a display system for creating messages, it would be necessary to back this up with a medical vocabulary so that the two would run in harness, each improving the other.

When it came to ordering the objectives for system design and for programming, it was seen that the major effort initially should be in two areas. The first was to expand the operating system so as to create a real-time system in which multi-programming could be effective. The second was to arrange special programs to drive the visual display units and to allow many types of display to be manipulated on to the screen as a major input method to the system. In relation to the display system it was arranged so that the displays should be handled indirectly by programs so that it would be possible to change displays without greatly changing the programs that manipulated these displays when messages were formed.

E. IMPLEMENTATION OF THE SYSTEM

1. Medical Record

The problem of input was seen as urgent. It was necessary in the first year to create some 4,000 displays to cover the various segments of the medical record. There were great problems both in relation to medical manpower and also to the design of such a system. Little published work existed about display systems. The rules were created from the experience gained by analysis of the existing medical record. The work was parcelled out in systems and both the doctors on the project and part-time doctors were given some systems and encouraged to develop displays according to a rather crude set of rules. It was not possible, because of the time constraints, to check all displays and there was inevitably some unevenness in the logic of the displays created during this period. It was felt, however, that the majority of displays would be adequate and that the ones that were in error would easily be corrected as they were used during the first six to nine months of development in the test bed area.

It was also thought that there should be backup for the existing system by means of patient questionnaires. Already the Medical Unit had considerable experience with patient questionnaires in trying to improve the medical record. It was felt that an extension of the questionnaire principle could well provide a great deal more information off-line which could lessen the recording load for the doctor. Unfortunately, a management decision by a committee prevented the use of questionnaires in the system. It is likely that the decision was made without full knowledge of the problems of input by junior doctors.

The problem of output presenting information to the user was seen in relation to the type of messages in the file system. It was arranged so that the system labelled messages in relation to the segment of the medical record, with the name of the user and the time of the message. The users were also asked to label their message with a number from between 0 and 8 in relation to the importance of that message to both diagnosis and to the effective management of that patient. This was one of the means of indicating that a message which had been formed and put on the screen had been checked for errors and was acceptable to the system. It was hoped that by using such number systems appropriate summaries could be generated automatically from the original data in the medical record.

Initially, a decision was made that the real-time system should go live within one year in order to get experience in medical records in the test bed area. The philosophy of the project was that it was better to create versions of the medical record and recognize mistakes than to try to anticipate these in vacuo and try to avoid them. It was recognized that there were great problems in systems design as the systems analysts had no experience in the medical area. It was also certain that the project doctors would have had no experience in computing. As a result, there was a great mis-match between the two in relation to terminology and other concepts.

It was not realized at this time that management was also inexperienced and would be the source of additional problems. At the start, the team was small and six or eight people were responsible for the major developments in the first year. During this period the manufacturer provided two systems analysts and, intermittently, one or two programmers. It became obvious that it was not always useful to divide the team into system engineers, programmers, and computer operations staff. Often programmers and system engineers had to co-operate to solve many of the difficult problems. The problem of archives, data base, and specialized file structures was looked at and investigated cursorily. Shortcuts naturally had to be taken to get the system alive. It was decided that the problem of archives and file structure should be more thoroughly investigated at a later date. It was important to get into action, to check both input and output modes of information transfer.

At this time it was not envisaged that transformation of information would be great, because the necessary displays for patient management had not been implemented. It was proposed that the project would link with one laboratory, namely the Hematology laboratory, and that requests would be transferred to that laboratory and the result reported by a visual display unit from that laboratory. Further development of a communication system between the test bed area and the laboratories was to be undertaken with a view to verifying that the computer-held medical record was a viable entity and met in terms of reliability and efficiency the requirements for it to replace the existing medical record. It would be an improvement on the existing record if it was both organized and legible. Information in it should be just as valid as the existing handwritten record and also reliable.

About this time the administrative director had made a visit to the United States and returned in late 1970 with a different set of objectives. It was suggested that the medical record, although it was the basic project on which the funds had been granted, was not necessarily as important as the need to establish a communications system in the hospital. Thus, there were difficulties early in the project relating to the different objectives which were held. At the time, this was not thought to be important; it was felt it could be solved. Only one set of objectives was seen by the medical staff and by the computer project committee.

We will now deal with the type of entry made into the medical record by the display system. The logic of the display system is that in taking the medical history, the doctor identifies the main symptoms concerned in the order in which the patient experienced them as well as minor symptoms. The computer system will then allow symptoms to be identified and offer the user various choices for analyzing a symptom, indicating its severity and associated factors that link it to a diagnostic set. To do this the system takes the doctor through an engine-like analytical process. It is possible for the doctor, while forming his message, to get out of this analytical loop whenever he wishes. He can have the message he has created presented to him on the screen at any time by using a function key. After verification he can enter it into the system.

The message is composed of the elements of the user's choices by typing a number relevant to that choice as he descends the "tree structure" of symptom descriptors. Symptoms can be accessed by the physical system with which they are associated, or by an alphabetical list, or by typing in the first few letters of a symptom. This will then enable further choices to be made. Initially, only the tree structure was implemented. It was also necessary to allow the user free text entry facilities at any time. Only single choices were allowed at the upper levels of the tree, but as the message built up, the doctor and nurse could involve multiple choices of information presented at lower levels of the tree. For example, choosing a symptom, a message could be built up not only describing the original symptom, but its duration, severity, the frequency of attack, factors alleviating or aggravating the symptom, and information associated with that symptom. Thus, any symptom had descriptors of varying kinds associated with it.

Once a doctor felt he had completed the message, no matter where he was, he could see it displayed on a screen by using a function code. After checking the accuracy, he could either amend, reject, or verify it by giving it a number in order of its importance. It was entered into the medical record as a correct observation. There was an error checking procedure involved immediately after message formation. There is no doubt that the decision about giving a rating factor to messages did create many problems for the doctors and was a very unusual system for them to accept.

Let us give an example of a series of displays. A patient may complain of headaches. This could be entered by consulting the Nervous System list of symptoms and selecting the symptoms listed HEADACHE. If the headache was situated over both frontal sinuses and was throbbing in nature the next display situation would encourage a choice to be made of OVER BOTH FRONTAL SINUSES. The character of headache is then entered and the choice is THROBBING. Its frequency is INTERMITTENT. The doctor chooses not to specify the frequency of attack and goes on into ALLEVI-ATED BY ASPIRIN. After choosing GETTING WORSE GRADUALLY, he then decides he has recorded his full message about the symptoms which, when he has it displayed, reads:

SYMPTOMS   NERVOUS SYSTEM.
HEADACHE BOTH FRONTAL SINUSES.
THROBBING AND INTERMITTENT.
ALLEVIATED BY ASPIRIN.
GETTING WORSE GRADUALLY.

Thus, the system tends to follow medical logic and adapt itself to a doctor's recording needs. He controls the message by his choices. Inevitably, it takes a doctor a little while to adapt this type of analysis to his interview with the patient. There is a tendency for the doctor, when entering messages in this way, to allow the system to encourage him to go to a greater depth than he would in the handwritten system. However, the great advantage of using displays and messages was that these messages were subject to analysis and other checks before entry into the system. They could be retrieved at any time. Thus, there was a dividend for the junior doctor, but it was small. The major assets were for his seniors.

It was also possible to collect data about symptoms from patient questionnaires and have the positive information entered into the medical history segment off-line. Here the positive replies to the questions could be decoded by the system and presented as text. It was anticipated that questionnaires could be given to patients by general practitioners before they came to hospital. The patient would then complete his questionnaire and send it to the hospital in advance of his arrival. The hospital information system would then collect this data and enter it into the computer system and have it printed out for the doctor before he saw the patient. This seemed to be a way of providing not only another method of entering data, but also backup for when the main system was down. These records could be entered at a later suitable time. It was recognized that instead of having patients answering questions on paper, it was also acceptable for patients to sort punched cards carrying statements about symptoms. They could encode documents by drawing lines which indicated their choices and thus provide similar information. It was felt that it would be useful to encourage patients to spend some time in working with a system where it was possible for them to feel they could help the doctor.

Thus, it was anticipated that historical information could reach the data base by a variety of methods and doctors could assess and use this. It could always be verified by patient confrontation. It was anticipated that senior doctors would check and amend the patient's history by using the same display system whenever they found this was necessary. There would not be several histories in the system, but one history amended by different doctors who felt that such alterations were required. It was recognized initially that the system was entirely dependent on peripheral equipment, the visual display units. It was hoped that later other types of peripheral equipment would come along and be incorporated into the system. However, it was likely that such equipment would always require system changes. Perhaps front-ending of the central processor would be possible at a later date.

It was decided that output from the system would be in two ways:

(a) The doctor could interrogate the existing medical record by a page turning procedure which would take him back through the existing medical record. In this way, he would see the most recent data very quickly and more remote data later.

(b) The second output was a print-out of the patient's medical record every 24 hours to provide backup for the display unit. This would be changed at the end of the day and a new record substituted. It was also arranged that copies of this record would be available not only on the ward in the existing patient's folder, but also for the consultant, who would then be in a position to review the patient's clinical progress elsewhere and not be entirely dependent on coming to the ward.

The possibility of using secretaries to enter much of this data was investigated. The method was rejected because of the problems of errors arising in data transfer and the necessity in a medical environment for those who originate the data to at least verify that it is correct in the system. It also meant that visual display units would have to be manned 24 hours a day, seven days a week, and the cost of providing this was likely to be greater than the system could tolerate. As a general principal, it was preferred that data collected from the patient or original observations about specimens that he provided should be entered directly into the system by those who originated such information. It was preferable that such information should not be punched on cards or go through other manual operations before entry into the system, otherwise errors would increase.

It was arranged that at any time, in any segment of the medical record, the user had the right to free text entry and could override the computer display system. Thus it was possible for him to bypass all the questionnaires, branching tree logic lists, etc. if he wished. It was hoped that by allowing him entry of free text, it would be possible for us to find out from free text entries the system's weaknesses. It was proposed to review free text entries periodically and to amend the display system and tree logic by the incorporation of such information. It was noted, however, that initially all doctors had to enter free text under various segmental areas of the medical record. There were no restrictions on its use.

It was realized that there would be criticism of the output initially, in that the print-out would tend to be atypical and not look like the written record format. It certainly was condensed, and lack of grammar and style would make reading different and perhaps difficult. It was recognized that the display system would tend to put a brake on individual medical styles of recording and tend to make things more uniform. There would also be problems of lack of syntax. The difficulties had to be faced, but it would hopefully be improved later by having a syntax editor associated with such output.

It was hoped that some logical deductions could be developed from information entered to help the doctor. Symptoms could be coded by the system itself from decision tables which would indicate to which systems a symptom belonged. If more than two or three symptoms belonged to the same system, then the computer would be able to indicate to the doctor the systems involved. Physical signs could also be coded by system and thus a weighting would be given to diagnoses which were linked with certain systems. This was intended to be a primitive aid for the junior doctor. It was also hoped that it would provide help of an educational nature.

The real-time system went live in early 1970. It was thought there would be difficulties due to problems in display design as the logic was not uniform. Difficulties in user education were anticipated as few personnel could be spared for this purpose. In general, it was accepted that one learns better and quicker by making mistakes and improving on these, than trying to solve the whole problem theoretically before implementation.

The pilot scheme was implemented in a test bed area of 40 medical beds in the wards of the Department of Medicine, which had been involved in the project from the beginning. As well as a display system for data entry by doctors, a display system to enter nursing orders into the computer system was also developed. Doctors and nurses around the patient's bedside would be able to use the computer system together. The system got off to an interesting start and by June/July 1970, some 600 messages a week were being entered into the system, about 400 of these being about patients by doctors and some 100 messages by the nursing staff about the same patients. In the early months of the project there were problems in educating the users to use the display system. It took about three months for the message rate to rise much above 200 messages a week. Following this the project progressed rapidly and by mid-1971 there were some 1,500 or more messages a week.

The computer unit, knowing the need to learn from experience, set up several monitoring systems. Not only was the number of messages logged by doctor and by time, but an attempt was made to measure the time devoted by junior doctors to data input, the difficulties of data input, and the amount of free text entered into the system. The effectiveness of the display system in the various segments of the medical record was observed. These monitoring systems were intended to give some guide to the effectiveness and reliability of the system.

Most computer people and others were surprised in October 1970 when Opit and Woodruffe, who had previously worked in the project and left, published two journalistic papers; the first describing the display system, and the second being critical of the whole venture. They reported the work of others in a form which could have easily been misunderstood as being their own. While on the project the main tasks allocated to each of them did not result in a contribution which has produced an effective benefit. One worked on progress notes, or patient management, and the other on the drug system. In any event, one development could not be implemented and the other was taken down after two days as it failed to meet user requirements.

Although they were critical of the progress of the project as judged by the message entry rate per week, even the data here was only roughly correct as they had to obtain it from others. Judged by their stated criteria, the message rate of 1,500 messages a week or more in 1971 would have indicated success. It did illustrate that a medical record akin to the conventional type could be created and held by computer methods.

What was most difficult to tolerate was the inability of others to have their views stated in our "free" press. Replies to these papers and their allegations were not published by either the medical journal or the "free" press which had commented on them. While we are free from government restrictions about publication, it would seem that the tyranny of the editor can be just as severe as that of the censor. In general, it was apparent that computers aroused deep emotion and they had to be knocked. The main problem is that premature publication of insufficiently considered results casts doubt on any claim investigations have of scientific probity.

Looking at the papers in retrospect, there was one point which the authors commented on that was valid. They had not apparently been made aware by management that there were objectives. This problem has unfortunately continued and been a major source of difficulty ever since.

Unfortunately, the authors' contribution was ignored in the tide of anger at the turn of events. In reality, it was not possible to access the impact of such a far-reaching project or the success of the implementation. A reassessment of its objectives should have been made at this time. However, data from monitoring the project was used to guide the development of the project records.

The nursing system has been described by Smith (1970) and also by Knight (1972), and is referred to later. It will be seen from what has already been said that there was a major achievement in software development, both in the basic real-time multi-programming system and with the many applications programs that were written to manipulate the displays and collect other types of information, including patient registration. During this period too, the hardware behaved extremely well and the reliability of the equipment adequately met the users' need. It was not possible at this time to have the computer system up for more than two shifts a day. This meant that the doctors had a difficult time in entering the data of patients who arrived late at night when the system was down. There were problems in catching up on much information. Towards the end of the study, this became one of the major complaints of the doctors in the test bed area.

By 1971 it was apparent that the clinical, nursing, and medical record could be held in the computer system. By means of simulation of laboratory requests being entered and reports generated, it was possible to demonstrate that a computer medical record could be created which was every bit as comprehensive as the old medical record, and was considerably more legible. However, it had the important disadvantage, because of lack of effort devoted to the development of other ideas about the input of data, that it took considerably longer to create than the written record. From the studies done at about this time, it was apparent that most doctors spent about 30% or more of time creating the computer medical record than the handwritten record. However, the computer system usually did produce a more detailed clinical record than the handwritten system.

It was hoped to go on and develop different ideas about the entry of the medical record but, by this time, the interest of one of the directors of the project had changed. What became apparent was that in spite of active user participation to develop and expand the medical record system, there was a complete resistance on the part of computer management. The idea of a "communication system" was popular and accepted by most of the medical staff at King's. It was felt that the orientation of the project should change towards a communications system, which the administrative director had found to be very popular and successful in the United States. Unfortunately, to institute a change of this kind there must be a total development of new objectives which need to be stated, not only to the medical and nursing users, but also to computer personnel. It became apparent subsequently that no such objectives were forthcoming. Changes were made to the whole system by management on rather vague grounds such as "improving patient care." The development of a communications system proceeded without giving it any size, shape, boundaries, or content.

About this time, user committees were created with computer personnel on them to explore the communications between the different investigative departments such as Hematology, Microbiology, Chemical Pathology, Radiology, Morbid Anatomy, Pharmacy, and the wards. It was hoped that a great communications system could be created which would eventually link with the medical record project. As there was lack of management definition of what was to be done, individuals who were allocated to these different projects became confused, and overall integration became obscure. Certainly there was no correlation between the general aim of creating a communications system and the likely software and hardware that had to be available to implement such a system. After about a year and a half of study, it was apparent to most systems analysts that the project was, in fact, impossible given the hardware that existed, including a further order for more visual display units. The software development would have been huge. It would not be possible to implement a widespread communications system on the same machine which was also going to do the nursing records hospital-wide, even if there were no medical records. Because of the impossibility of the tasks, gradually computer personnel did their best to avoid being involved.

Management had, by this time, virtually stopped all effort on the medical record side of the project. It was evident that from 1971 to mid-1972, there had been no change whatsoever in the whole medical record project, in spite of urgent demands. The users in the Department of Medicine had, by this time, spent two or three man-years trying to improve the system. The frustration of the users was very recognizable. Junior doctors are not inclined to let their views go unknown. About this time there were hardware difficulties and, at times, the computer system was down for three days. The chaos that ensued when the computer system on a ward was not available for long periods could not be tolerated. The doctors, by this time, had certainly demonstrated that the computer medical record was viable, that it could be done. It was felt that it was not necessay to tolerate total indifference on the part of the management towards their problems. They felt that the project was no longer medical record-oriented. They suggested that the project be postponed until attention could be devoted to the needs of the medical record.

The management did not appreciate this criticism as a problem, and no attention was diverted from the communications system to other areas until the end of 1972, when it became obvious that there was a total loss of morale and effort in the computer centre. All prospective users were becoming aware that problems were not being solved. Then occurred an inward turning of viewpoint as computer people tried to learn to do medicine and doctors were trying to instruct computer people how to do computing. By this time it had become obvious that an investigation had to be instituted into the causes of the problems in the project. The investigators took some nine months or more to reach a conclusion.

At this time, it was suggested that the Professor of Medicine, who had resigned from the project over a year earlier due to his disagreement with the management of the project, be asked to take it over. He was to investigate it for a period of three months with a view to restating the objectives and putting it back on a course to fulfill the original objectives. By now it was apparent that the design of a communications system, given the software and hardware resources that were available and the extent of the commitment, was a total failure. However, this failure did not apply to the medical record, which was still an advanced project and could be improved and revived as and when resources became available within the limits of the existing hardware.

2. Nursing System

The nursing record has always been viewed as an essential part of the medical record system and the relationships between the two are important for the team working at the patient's bedside. The nursing system deals with nursing orders given by the sister or nurse in charge of the ward. A planned program of nursing care is decided about patients in advance by the head nurse, and these orders are given to the computer system through the display system. The nursing staff also implements medical management and treatment plans. The head nurse or deputy not only creates the necessary planning of orders but also amends daily orders for patients in relation to changes in their clinical state.

These orders are organized by the computer system either into a patient-oriented nursing system or into a job-oriented nursing activity. This means that nurses can be deployed to nurse groups of patients especially at times when we have ample nursing staff or, in times of nursing shortage, a job-oriented system can be adopted and priority tasks given. This has proved to be useful, as we have a nursing crisis in our hospital and are short of nurses on many occasions. The nursing tasks are delineated by interrogating the system or by consulting a 24-hour printout, which shows both systems of nursing tasks. Once a task has been done, it can be notified to the system as having been carried out; more frequently, marks are made on the computer printout to indicate that these tasks have been completed.

The drug orders are still given to the nurses through the drug charts and are one of the few charts left on the ward. All other information goes through the computer system. At present, temperature, pulse, and respiratory rates are also chartered as well as entered into the computer system. At present, the nursing system is restricted to the test area of 40 beds but is planned to go across the whole hospital of 700 beds as one of the essential key systems.

The following example indicates how the nursing order system works. The head nurse or her deputy, after logging in and having selected the nursing area from the initial display in the system, then identifies the patient and checks that this is the patient about whom orders are to be given. She enters into nursing display 2:

e.g., **NURSING CARE 2**   One choice
  1. NURSING CARE
  2. VITAL SIGNS IN NURSING
  3. PATIENT REGISTRATION
  4. EDUCATION
  5. FACILITIES FOR INTERROGATION

and then, selecting say, "Nursing Care," presses Key No. 1. The following display is shown:

e.g., **NURSING CARE 3**   One choice
  1. BATHING
  2. MOBILITY
  3. CARE OF PRESSURE AREAS
  4. FEEDING
  5. ORAL HYGIENE
  6. LAVATORY
  7. DRESSINGS
  8. SPECIAL TREATMENT
  9. INVESTIGATION
  10. END OF NURSING PROCEDURES

This is a single choice; the nurse makes Choice 7, which indicates "Dressings." The nurse then goes on to choose more about dressings, where she has several choices which are descriptions of the dressing she wanted to do.

e.g., **NURSING CARE 4**   Several choices
  1. CLEAN WOUND WITH
  2. PACK WOUND WITH

3. IRRIGATE WOUND WITH
4. SAVALON 1/20
5. NORMAL SALINE
6. METHYLATED SPIRIT
7. HALF-STRENGTH EUSOL
8. EUSOL
9. HYDROGEN PEROXIDE DILUTED 1:4
10. DISTILLED WATER
11. CHLORHEXIDINE 1 IN 5,000

Choices taken here would be 2 and 7. The next display in dressing amplifies the existing displays.

NURSING CARE   Several choices
   Dressings 2
1. APPLY DRY DRESSING
2. APPLY TULLE GRAS
3. APPLY NONADHERENT DRESSING
4. APPLY ALUMINUM PASTE
5. APPLY CHIRON BAG TO COLOSTOMY
6. APPLY NOBECUTANE
7. APPLY AMINOCRINE CREAM LOTION

Here the nurse chooses 1 and goes on to a further display.

NURSING CARE
   Dressings 3
1. DAILY
2. TWICE DAILY
3. THREE TIMES DAILY
4. FOUR TIMES DAILY
5. WHEN NECESSARY
6. AFTER BATH

The nurse here chooses 6. The following message should then come up on the screen:

NURSING CARE
   NURSING PROCEDURES. DRESSINGS.
   PACK WOUND WITH HALF-STRENGTH EUSOL.
   APPLY DRY DRESSING AFTER BATH.

The nurse gives it a rating factor if correct of 1 to 8. Otherwise, she uses a function code. In this way, the nurse forms messages which are the nursing orders. The computer system will then format either the patient-oriented or job-oriented specifications for the ward patients and print these from the nursing order data base. The nursing order system, having been a limited segment of the medical record project, has been successful and very popular with the nursing staff. It allows some of the time spent in handing over patients with the appropriate orders to be spent with patients. It has proved to be both effective and efficient.

Work is now going forward to try and derive nursing load information from the type of nursing orders given about that patient and develop modifying factors dependent on the diagnosis of that patient and degree of disability. It is hoped that by using the data already in the system it will be possible to form some idea of the nursing load on a particular ward on any day and so allow for better scheduling of nurses.

3. Patient Scheduling

As all hospital inpatients are admitted by the system either by the routine admission clerk using a visual display unit in the Admissions Department during working hours or by the ward secretary, nurse, or doctor during the rest of the day, it is possible to get statistical data derived from the data recorded on admission. There is a bed census program for inpatients which now updates the bed state every day; it is planned to update bed state four times a day. This will enable the bed bureau, which initially deals with admissions and is responsible for emergency admissions, to find beds more easily when they are required.

4. Master Index

The inpatient record data is used to update information about patients on the master file. All patients who have been admitted previously have their basic information checked again on re-admission. The system also produces every week a directory with correct names and addresses of inpatients who have been admitted, which facilitates searching for the ordinary records of individual patients. The errors in the existing master file are slowly being eliminated by this new data, which improves the accuracy of what is recorded. In a few years, little will remain on the master file that was there originally, and it will have been updated completely.

5. Emergency Admissions

An emergency admission scheme was also investigated and a scheme for updating appointments on waiting lists for consultant physicians and surgeons was also tried. Unfortunately, the systems work was badly done and the importance of having a rapid response in updating the bed state and informing the clinicians who wanted to admit emergencies was not realized. Thus, the system was specified to be updated every 48 hours. It was therefore possible for clinicians to know that beds were empty when in fact the system was not responding. Also, little study was made of the typed data required for emergency admissions. Errors tended to creep in and become cumulative. Because of errors, the data entry forms were repeatedly rejected by the system and clinicians, and secretaries then failed to have them corrected. After the system had been live for two days, because of the accumulating problems it was taken off. From it the systems analysts learned a great deal and now are much more careful to look at the system as a whole rather than accepting what the user may think he wants. They now are coming back to him with what they think his requirements are. Generally users have difficulty in specifying a system. What they feel they ought to say does not always reflect their true needs.

6. Identification and Registration of Patients

Patient identification is by hospital number, name, age, and the unique National Health Service number when the patient remembers it. Some redundancy is introduced into the identification to ensure that all data does check out. Thus, the patient's address, the doctor who attends him, his religion, marital status, etc., all describe him more fully. Not only does identification have to be correct for the patient, but also for those who enter the information into the system. Doctors, nurses, and other personnel were identified to the system in the past by typing in codes which enable the computer to decide what they will be allowed to do as well as identifying them. If the system expands to 40 visual display units in the near future, identification of users will be by a special magnetic card which the machine will read. This will not only contain the user's identity but also have information on it regarding the user's needs, file access requirements, interrogation facilities, etc.

At present, students are identified in the system by special code. When arrangements are made for them to have print-outs of the patient's record, the patient's name, address, and other identification will not be printed out, but the student's name will be substituted for that of the patient. This will ensure confidentiality and privacy, as the students are not always as careful as others of how they dispose of their medical record. However, they are expected to come under the same rules of privacy and confidentiality as everyone else, and this is stressed.

Patient data on registration, as well as including hospital and National Health Service number, includes data about the patient's name; current address and telephone number; religion; marital state; general practitioner's name, address, and telephone number; date of birth; next of kin's name, address, and telephone number; social class according to the official classification; whether a waiting-list, emergency or private patient on admission; and the source of admission, whether from general practitioner, outpatient, etc. This larger subset of information about the patient is very useful for identification when a problem arises and would certainly be very helpful in an area where the patient is no longer present to ensure that identification is correct.

Different areas of data are flagged by the computer system so that the system can generate information about admission policy, inform the different clergymen of the number and location of patients of their faith, and provide essential data for communication with general practitioners. It is possible also to code the area where the patient lives for epidemiological purposes. Thus, transformations of this small amount of data about a patient may be used in many different ways. Junior doctors can refer to it when they need to telephone the local general practitioner or contact relatives. The data is also used to generate information required by the Ministry of Health about inpatient admission. Also produced are directories of inpatients' names and addresses; these are used in the records room to identify all the inpatients they have on file. This is checked against the total master file kept about all patients who have ever had records in the system, which is updated with the same information.

7. Service Units

a. **Clinical laboratories (hematology, clinical biochemistry, microbiology).**   This project was planned initially to link one laboratory, namely hematology, with the ward test bed area. The experiment was to examine the usefulness of the visual display unit in the laboratory for interrogating patient data and also for teaching. Initially, the laboratory was to use a batch processing system for generating and checking its results before releasing these to the wards, outpatient department, and general practitioner. This was to be used initially to deal with blood examinations, red and white cell counts, and blood film, then with clotting, serology, and later with the blood bank.

While the other investigative systems have been developed and implemented, the blood bank system has been delayed because of its special problems of reliability and also the necessity to have adequate information facilities about blood groups whenever they are required. The blood bank cannot stop for main-frame failures when information is wanted urgently. Thus, it was decided that, while the system was to be developed, it was not to be recommended until adequate facilities were available.

Initially the laboratory system deals with the identification of specimen and patient data, the analysis of the specimen, and the result and quality checks of the system control. It was hoped that the system would be reporting data to the test bed terminals by the real-time system as soon as it was available. The automated requesting of tests would be implemented quickly. However, while the system was able to respond to these demands, the resistance of laboratories to communicating with the wards by the computer system has been great, and they demand the traditional paper forms.

They have not viewed the need to get results urgently to the patient's bedside a necessity. Indeed, investigative departments are very happy to continue with the rather slow existing paper system. They feel that the introduction of a communication system will decrease their autonomy; they will not be able to get the control requests, and they will be overworked in consequence. There seems to have been a problem in changing the attitudes in laboratories to the communication of data with the wards and also in convincing them how they might use the computer system more effectively than the existing system. The clinicians view the obtaining of laboratory results as an urgent problem, but their colleagues are reluctant to change. Similar problems have been encountered in designing and implementing a batch processing system for the laboratory data in microbiology, showing that its general procedures are not different from hematology. In clinical biochemistry, it was possible for the laboratory to obtain research funds for a small local computer to process the automated laboratory results and print out cumulative result forms for the ward. The system had its initial teething problems due to both hardware and software faults. Aspirations on the software side were far beyond the initial specification, and there was inadequate planning of resources. The computer hardware, however, is quite different from that of ICL, so there are going to be problems in interfacing the small computer with ICL equipment. Eventually it is hoped to develop the necessary communications link apart from paper tape, as used at present. It may be that a front-end processor would not only solve this data link problem but also enable users to have a variety of different peripheral terminals linked to the main ICL machine.

The main pathological laboratory system has been successful in dealing with the automated analyses and is moving over to become a total reporting system. It is becoming much more important to unify the systems effort and see what common kinds of programs such departments can use. While this type of development has been useful both to the laboratory and to the hospital, it has highlighted the importance of peripheral computers. Somehow these have to be made to work with the main central system, but they offer certain advantages depending on the type of programming system adopted.

Laboratory doctors and technicians are now changing their attitudes to the application of data processing techniques. With increasing work load and the need for process and quality control of investigative results, computer techniques are becoming essential as staff are in scarce supply. Now they are certain that the future without such techniques will be extremely difficult.

F. MANAGEMENT OF THE PROJECT

Projects involving a multi-team approach to problems using advanced technology, such as computer science, have difficult managerial problems. There are several known tendencies in projects such as ours, being run by a series of committees, which lead to confusion and wrong decisions. In such projects the committees of lay and professional people put great stress on the technical, as well as the administrative, abilities of the manager. Data has to be presented to them not in lay terms, but reflecting the technical, administrative and strategic problems about which a decision is required. Our institution, like many others, tends to have conversation-style minutes, and rarely are data or decisions in recorded precise terms. This method tends to obscure what has been achieved and only creates further problems when decisions are being interpreted and implemented.

Experimental projects always run on limited resources, especially of people, and these have to be used and managed well. Not only does effort then reap its reward in terms of results, but by co-ordination the whole project moves forward at an optimum rate. To the present, the persons in day to day control have either been an administrator with some computer knowledge, covering another management services post as well, or a computer expert with some experience in management, and problems with management were increasing rather than resolving. A solution has been to involve a medical manager with computer expertise.

The attitudes of medical and administrative staff in the hospital are important and have to be fostered and changed. Most senior personnel have become adjusted to the status quo, and change—in the form of advanced technology—is not always a welcome idea. Often in such projects, many senior medical staff do not wish to have the trauma associated with data processing techniques which change hospital and general practice routines. Moreover, some very senior medical staff feel very strongly that any experiment in computerized medical recording is either axiomatically useless or possibly a future danger to their clinical freedom. On the other hand, while junior medical and nursing staff, laboratory technicians, and clerical officers are usually favourable, their day to day contact with the system, which is bound to have its problems, demands that they receive some education about the part they play in the project.

However, it has to be stated that administrators supervising projects, while they may recognize the need, feel that the recipients of the research money ought to do their own dirty work. Very often too—and the present project is no exception—the work load to junior staff, significantly heavy before the introduction of data processing techniques, usually increases, and staff are left to decide where their duty lies. The need for specialty staffing in such projects is usually not foreseen or even accepted. For example, in medical recording doctors and nurses are asked to discard a recording device to which they are entirely used for one quite foreign and time consuming. They usually have no guarantee that the computer will support them in a way as reassuring as a file of notes or investigation forms. Rarely, too, is the system initially able to give them further support commensurate with the measured workload.

Projects must anticipate user difficulties and be able to contain them by illustrating how the objectives of the project will lead to a better and more rewarding system. Lack of recognition of difficulties is not only at the implementation level and with users, but extends throughout the whole project. Management objectives in such projects appear to be the only way of letting users, designers, and implementers see the problems of co-ordination which are crucial to most large projects.

The committees ultimately responsible for guiding projects also need a firm grip on objectives. It is their job to insist that objectives are continually updated or evaluated. If they cease to be relevant, new objectives must be agreed to, established, and communicated to the whole project. In the end, committees have to acknowledge that projects are run by people and their interests and motivations have to be fostered.

The present project has had difficulties because objectives have been changed without the committees' realizing and without conveying new objectives. These difficulties also confuse those who were left to implement the project, for the direction of progress becomes obscured. Also systems tend to be developed in small areas without acknowledging intercommunication boundaries or the necessary dependence on a firm agreed core of medical data. The communication project, which has now been superseded, floundered in problems of definition and interrelationship, as no firm objectives were ever stated.

It is important too, to draw computer people into the social area of the hospital. Unfortunately, in the present project, computer staff are several hundred yards from the main buildings on the other side of a busy highway. Communication between the users, computer centre staff, and administrators tended to be difficult. Recently a survey of computer staff revealed that more than half of the staff had not been in a hospital ward recently, and the majority had never had the workings of a ward explained to them. Few had visited the medical records department or had any concept of the size and shape of the problem. In addition, computer staff themselves found it difficult to fully understand the changing social contexts in which they are working.

Hardware changes and equipment developments are full of problems, and such change is not always well managed. Equipment has to be ordered, engineering work put in hand to receive it, and software designed to make it work. Co-ordination of effort here is essential. In the present project a new type of visual display unit was ordered and installed without the management and committees realizing that this implied a complete revision of the existing applications program. Because the implications of equipment changes were not discussed with computer staff or users, further unnecessary problems arose. Far too often in our society decisions are made by management without reference to others and without realization that they are outside their area of competence.

There is no doubt that management techniques are well known. The difficulty appears to be that most managers tend to be swayed by day to day problems. They never seem to establish systems which would contain the routine forward progress. If they would do so, they would be free to deal with the exceptions and the management of people. In most computer projects there are recurrent crises because the problems being investigated are difficult. There is no excuse for the absence of a systematic approach.

The last area of discussion is that in computer technology not only are there problems of injut and output, but that data base problems and file structure problems are always present. At the beginning of the project the ideas about data base problems and archives were very elementary. However, work was begun on the medical side to define a structure for the record and to deal with the terms in it so that its manipulation could be defined. Unfortunately, development ceased in this area. The difficulties encountered in the medical recording project did not even suggest that this might be a hidden reef. The failure of the communications system once more indicated the need for a firm core of agreed upon medical data. Without fairly rigorous definition here, and of necessity clarification by experiment, the manipulations and transformation of data become merely day dreams.

H. EVALUATION AND REVIEW

During this period an Evaluation Team was created under a part-time director. He had an operation research officer, a systems analyst, and a part-time doctor to help with evaluations of the different projects. Unfortunately, the current emphasis was on cost benefit. The arguments were of doubtful validity and many become lost in the sea of matching cost of benefit in a patient care environment. As the objectives tended to change it was difficult for the evaluators to evaluate implied objectives. They, like many others, had their doubts about a vague and amorphous approach to management or, as they saw it, to administration.

The Evaluation Team, nevertheless, had a very beneficial action. Those engaged in projects had their interests sharpened when they realized that there was a means of closing the loop and assessing the progress. The Team also found it necessary to explore existing problems so as to throw light on the changes that would be brought about by data processing techniques. They have provided an essential ferment in the whole process.

I. FUTURE

At present it is proposed, once the success of the new nursing recording system is demonstrated in the next year, to adopt this system hospital-wide. This will add a new dimension to equipment problems and push forward the importance of deciding about monolithic systems, or whether it would be better contained, with better backup and security, if we had a number of small computers dealing with the existing central computer. The arguments to define the optimal strategy are still continuing.

The medical record project may move forward to explore proactive and retroactive methods of data entry to the system. An extensive system of established routines for investigation and treatment of various common disorders will be explored. Hopefully, management will move forward and computer techniques will be used more extensively to generate the data that is required to keep the project on course. While gale force winds of change and occasional disappointment will assail us, the forward progress will put heart into both the designers and users of the system.

REFERENCES

Anderson, J. *Information Processing of Medical Records*. Edited by J. Anderson and J. M. Forsythe. N. Holland (1970): 3–13.

Anderson, J. *Information Processing of Medical Records*. Edited by J. Anderson and J. M. Forsythe. N. Holland (1970): 22–27.

Anderson, J. *IRIA Colloque Informatique Medicale* 3 (1973): 87–97.

Chalke, R. *Med. Lab. Tech.* 29 (1972): 297–302.

Crocker, N. J. *Data Processing* (July 1970): 342–343.

Gray, C. H., and Walter, M. *Brit. J. Hosp. Med.* (Nov 1971): 25–30.

Fisher, R. A. *Statistical Methods for Research Workers.* Edinburgh (1925).

Knight, J. *IRIA Colloque Informatique Medicale* 1 (1972) : 349–359.

Knight, J., and Streeter, J. *Nursing Times* 66 (1971) : 233–235.

Laver, M. Paper to Committee on the Application of Computers to the Construction Industry. *HMSO* (1966).

Louis, P. C. A. *Researches on Phthisis.* Sydenham Soc., London (1844).

Opit, L. J., and Woodruffe, F. J. *Brit. Med. J.* 4 (1970) : 76–79.

Opit, L. J., and Woodruffe, F. J. *Brit. Med. J.* 4 (1970) : 80–82.

Pearson, K. *Phil. Mag. Series* V (1900) : 157–162.

Smith, B. *Nursing Times* 64 (1970) : 1426–1429.

Revans, R. W. *The Hospital as an Organism: A Study in Communication and Morale.* Pergamon Press, Oxford (1969).

Weed, L. *Medical Record, Medical Education and Patient Care, the Problem Oriented Record as a Basic Tool.* Case Western Reserve University Press, Cleveland, Ohio (1969).

CHAPTER SEVENTEEN

Massachusetts General Hospital Computer System (Boston)

by G. Octo Barnett

A. MEDICAL CARE ENVIRONMENT

Massachusetts General Hospital (MGH) is a privately endowed, short-term general medical and surgical hospital. It is a community hospital, a referral hospital, and one of the principal teaching hospitals of Harvard Medical School. The capacity is 1,077 beds; and in 1970, the average census was 919. All services are represented except obstetrics. The accommodations include ward, semi-private, and private, with one-third of the beds being on the teaching services. There are approximately 6,000 individuals on the MGH payroll and the total yearly expenditure is approximately $70 million (research expenditures would add another $30 million). About 40% of the patients have some type of private insurance coverage, about 30% have Medicare, and about 30% are covered by state welfare funds. The average length of stay during 1970 was 12 days, and the five most common discharge diagnoses were:

Chronic ischemic heart disease
Acute myocardial infarction
Cholelithiasis
Inguinal hernia
Displacement of intravertebral disk

There is an associated ambulatory care practice which includes private physician offices, numerous specialty clinics, and a full-salaried small group practice. During 1970, there were 180,666 visits to the outpatient department (excluding visits to the private physician offices). There is an increasingly active emergency room (75,558 visits in 1970) and a "walk-in," no-appointment clinic (approximately 14,000 visits in 1971).

Associated with Harvard Medical School is a comprehensive prepaid health care system known as the Harvard Community Health Plan (HCHP). At present the HCHP has 30,000 members enrolled, with the great majority of care being given in one central ambulatory care facility.

B. DEFINITIONS AND OBJECTIVES

Our primary objectives are: (1) to develop the computer technology appropriate for interactive, real-time collection of information and simultaneous, multi-user data base management; (2) to apply this technology to areas of potentially high impact on patient care; and (3) to develop, implement, and support computer-based information systems that are closely integrated into daily hospital activities and funded from the hospital operational budget.

C. GENERAL SYSTEM CONCEPTS

There are two different approaches to the development of a medical information system: the "total systems" approach and the "modular" approach. The total systems approach gives priority to the identification of all information processing tasks, subjecting them to a systematic and detailed study, charting a comprehensive map of the total data flow, and then developing a "universal" computer system which records everything from the complexity of a doctor's progress note to the trivia of the housekeeping department. This approach presupposes the availability of a very large computer facility, a great number of different input-output devices at various sites in the hospital, and an extraordinarily powerful data management programming system that can support simultaneously, and without conflict, many specialized and diverse application programs. In reality, a "total" hospital information system has never been approximated even in planning, much less in implementation. However, the tactical approach of attempting a comprehensive systematic, multi-faceted development has been very attractive to many computer projects, particularly those initiated or dominated by large industrial firms.

Our approach shares many of the long-term objectives but is much less ambitious in scope and has very different short-term priorities, objectives, and operating procedures. In the modular approach, the primary emphasis is given to the identification of the functional information processing units (or "modules") of medical activity (e.g., the chemistry laboratory, x-ray, etc.). The identification is not done as a unilateral exercise by an outside "system group" but by an "in-house" full-time hospital group through a prolonged interaction with the operational management of the hospital. The problem areas are chosen primarily on the basis of recognized and urgent problems in the day-to-day carrying-out of patient care. In contrast to the somewhat abstract nature of a total systems approach, the modular approach emphasizes a close articulation into the real and concrete medical information needs of operating departments or units of the hospital. The priorities of such an approach are: explicit definition and agreement on objectives and procedures in a limited context of hospital operation; smooth "phasing-in" of the computer system with the regular working routines of the operational units; and finally, a continuing evolution of the computer system with the linkage of an increasing number of "modular" systems into a "total" system in a way that does not overrule or stultify the continued usefulness of each of the modules at a "lower" operational level.

There are a number of advantages which the modular approach has over the total systems approach. These advantages, which have been discussed in detail elsewhere,[1] include technical feasibility, achieving organizational agreement, minimizing the problems of change and phasing-in, lower start-up costs, greater reliability, more rapid achievement of a useful system, greater flexibility for change and growth, and greater potential for transferability.

Among the potential weaknesses of the modular approach are: (1) it may lead to an inefficient use of computer hardware; (2) it may result in closed-end small systems that cannot easily evolve or be integrated into a larger system; and (3) it may make more difficult the creation of a "total" patient medical record. The potential weaknesses have also been discussed in detail elsewhere,[1] with the thrust of the defense being that these limitations can be avoided (or if not avoided, minimized) by the proper choice of computer hardware and software.

About six years ago, the engineers of this laboratory (led by Neil Pappalardo, and Curtis Marble) began the development of a programming system to meet the somewhat unique specifications for a modular medical information system. This language, MUMPS (MGH Utility Multiprogramming System), has played a key role in the computer developments of our laboratory[2-4] and has made it possible to have relatively easy transferability of the approach and the applications to a number of other hospitals and to industrial software support companies.[5]

The characteristics of the language which are particularly important are: (1) the language is interpretative, thus facilitating the rapid development of new applications; (2) the language has powerful string-manipulating commands facilitating the data management of the nonnumerical data which make up the largest part of medical information; (3) the file structure is a sparsely filled tree-structured array where space is allocated only as needed, allowing efficient use of disk storage space; (4) the method of storing data in this hierarchical array allows both relative independence of access by the different modules (and thus relative independence of development of the modules) and yet easy exchange of data (thus facilitating the development of an integrated medical record); and (5) the language is implemented on a dedicated time-sharing system in a very efficient form so that a relatively large number of users can be supported in simultaneous use.

D. PROJECT ORGANIZATION AND MANAGEMENT

The research, development, and maintenance of the operational systems are done by the Laboratory of Computer Science (LCS). The LCS is a unit of the Department of Medicine of MGH and Harvard Medical School, located at the MGH. There are 41 full-time professionals and 7 support staff in the LCS, including 3 physicians and 13 members with advanced degrees in computer science, electrical engineering, pharmacy, operations research, nursing, education, and mathematics. There are 3 physicians who are research fellows receiving training in computer science applications for a period of 2 to 3 years. In addition, there are usually several MIT and Harvard Medical School students carrying out research electives or thesis work in the laboratory.

Most of the work of the laboratory is carried out by loosely structured project teams made up of individuals representing a number of different disciplines. There is also a central core support staff which operates and maintains the computer systems, develops the special electronic interface equipment needed, and supports the on-going systems programming development.

The major support is a research and development grant from the National Center for Health Care Research and Development (HS-00240). All of the operational projects are supported from MGH operational funds (about one-third of the budget of the laboratory). There are three smaller projects supported by contracts from the Bureau of Radiation Health, from the National Library of Medicine, and from the National Board of Medical Examiners.

E. SUBSYSTEMS

1. Patient Medical Record

A number of modules have been developed and implemented in daily operation throughout the hospital. A much larger number are in various states of development. In terms of the patient medical record, these modules are designed to support the information processing activities of the individual hospital units; as part of this support, the computer system generates reports which are included in the medical record. We do not anticipate any sudden transition from a manual paper record to a computer-based system, but a gradual phasing-over with more and more of the data being collected directly by and through the computer-based system and an increasing amount of the information retrieval being done by direct inquiry of the computer system. There will almost certainly be some type of paper record, if only for certain archival functions, for a number of years. The major impact of the computer system in the next decade will be that more and more of this paper will be generated by the functioning of the computer-based medical information system.

An integrated patient medical record in a computer-based system is achievable in *any* system, however limited, using *any* file structure, however fragmented and primitive. Indeed, integration of medical information does not require that all information, whatever the source, reside on the same physical storage device, or even on the same computer. The critical aspect of an "integrated medical record system" concerns the ease and timeliness with which the user can access any or all parts of the information, independent of the type of information and independent of the source of collection. The providing of such access, in a variety of forms and across a variety of dimensions, requires a powerful data management system. It is our conviction that the MUMPS language has few rivals (indeed, no rivals on systems of comparable cost) in providing such data management.

2.   Administration Functions

In the MGH, these functions are supported by an IBM (360/40) computer administered by the Comptroller's office. Our MUMPS based information system communicates with the IBM system through a direct computer linkage (the MUMPS computer functioning as though it were a terminal to the IBM system) so that changes in bed occupancy information can be immediately transmitted from the IBM system to the MUMPS system. This permits the patient census data base to be maintained automatically in an accurate and timely fashion on the MUMPS system. The billing information which is generated by the various modules on the MUMPS system (e.g., the Chemistry laboratory charges) are stored on magnetic tape; this tape is carried to the IBM computer center each day to allow daily up-dating of patient bills.

3.   Service Units

There are three modules now functioning (clinical laboratory, medication order processing, and pulmonary function interpretation) and four additional modules being developed (hematology, pathology, x-ray scheduling, x-ray film folder inventory control, and x-ray reporting). These modules are all written in MUMPS but are implemented on several different but functionally identical computer systems. Where necessary or desirable, data bases are automatically exchanged from one computer system to another through a moderate-spread communication channel (100 characters/second) under application program control. This is useful in those situations where medical record activities are concurrently operating on different computer systems.

a. **Clinical laboratory report system (chemistry and bacteriology).** The computer-based laboratory information system (illustrated in Figure 17–1) implemented at the Massachusetts General Hospital is one of the largest in the U.S. and differs from the more usual, dedicated small laboratory system in three respects: (1) It is a file-oriented system, the purpose of which is to support the information processing involved in receiving specimens, preparing worksheets, and preparing laboratory test reports (rather than being primarily concerned with on-line data collection). In addition, the data base is used in answering test result inquiries and in providing accounting and statistical reports for management. (2) It is an on-line system supporting a variety of remote terminal devices and allowing multiple users to perform multiple functions simultaneously. The emphasis on on-line interactive use permits rapid time response and facilitates quality control with immediate detection and direct feedback of errors as they occur.

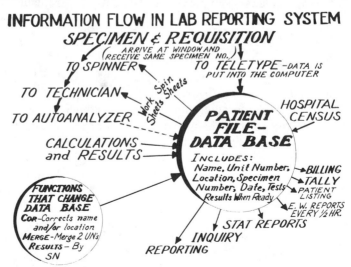

Figure 17–1. A simplified diagram of the information flow in the Chemistry Laboratory.

Sharing of multiple functions permits the system to reflect current information in its data base at all times. (3) The system has been developed in a modular fashion. Functions have been designed, introduced, and put into operation as separate phases of the evolving project.

The first module in the system was the internal laboratory processing in the chemistry laboratory, which involved the logging in of specimens and production of spin-sheets and worksheets. The second phase was a set of programs for entry of results and for the production of cumulative patient reports. The third phase involved the introduction of various procedures for calculation and conversion of raw results to reportable units. In the fourth phase, the system was extended to include the information processing concerned with the bacteriology laboratory. The fifth phase tied the MUMPS based laboratory test computer system to the hospital's IBM administrative computer system to allow direct computer transmission of census information. The sixth phase consisted of development of techniques for automated data acquisition from instrumentation.

Chemistry test requisitions arrive in the laboratory and are logged into the computer by clinical lab personnel. The computer automatically produces spin-sheets which list the work benches that require portions of each specimen and the tests requested. Technicians from the different work areas request their own work sheets which list specimen number and patient identification for each batch and item. At the same time, a file is created so that data can be entered in the order specified on the work sheet. In the majority of cases, raw data are entered and the computer automatically calculates the final results. The data from certain of the automated instrumentation are entered directly into the computer system using analog-to-digital-conversion, operating under a MUMPS application program control.

Reports are printed in the chemistry laboratory on medium speed printers twice each day. (Figure 17–2 is an illustration of a typical report.) A change in a patient's data triggers a report at the next printing. Reporting is cumulative over the course of a week; each report supercedes the last, and on Saturday a summary report is printed for inclusion in the permanent medical record. A terminal is located in the emergency ward for immediate and direct reporting of "STAT" requests from that area.

Each night a "garbage" program deletes old data from the files, verifies the integrity and quality of the disk files, and produces relevant lists (tally statistics, pending tests, terminal usage). Data are deleted from the on-line files and stored on magnetic tape only after a result has been printed on a summary report and included on a hard copy summary list for the clinical laboratory record.

The cost of the computer system to process the chemistry laboratory

EXAMPLE OF CHEM LAB REPORT:

12/25 SUMMRY MGH   SMITH, JOHN   WH11   812-34-67

COLLECTION DATE   12/19   12/20   12/21   12/22   12/23   12/24   12/25

**** ELECTROLYTES

	12/19	12/20	12/21	12/22	12/23	12/24	12/25
SODIUM [135-145 MEQ/L]	131*	138	139	133*	131*	140	131*
POTASSIUM [3.5-5.0 MEQ/L]	4.3	3.5	4.1	4.8	4.9	4.8	5.7*
CHLORIDE [100-106 MEQ/L]	92*	91*	99*	99*	98*	101	103
CARBON DIOXIDE [24-30 MEQ/L]	31*	33*	28	22*	21*	23*	18*
OSMOLALITY [285-295 MOSM/L]	280*			279*			
CALCIUM [8.5-10.5 MG%]			8.7	7.9*	9.2		
MAGNESIUM [1.5-2.5 MEQ/L]			1.8				

**** BLOOD/SERUM METABOLITES

	12/19	12/20	12/21	12/22	12/23	12/24	12/25
BUN [8-25 MG%]	32*	19	14	17	14	17	22
CREATININE [0.7-1.5 MG%]	1.6*	1.8*		1.8*			
BLOOD SUGAR [70-100 MG%]			135*				
TOTAL PROTEIN		5.4*		5.9*			

EXAMPLE OF BACTI LAB REPORT:

12/25 SUMMRY MGH   SMITH, JOHN   WH11   812-34-67

            --- URINE

12/24   CLEAN VOIDED URINE
        CULTURE..POSITIVE

            --- BLOOD

12/12   BLOOD
FINAL REPORT:
        MODERATE ENTEROCOCCI..MD NOTIFIED
            PEN R   METH R   ERYTH S   CEPH R
            TETRA R   CHLOR S   AMP R

12/16   BLOOD
FINAL REPORT: NO GROWTH

12/24   BLOOD NEG TO DATE

Figure 17–2. A typical summary report of the Chemistry and Bacteriology Laboratory results. The organization of the data is both by day and by class of test.

information and report results is approximately 9¢ per test. There is considerable evidence to suggest that this cost is not an additional cost but that the total chemistry laboratory activity, considered on a per-test basis, is less expensive due to a decrease in personnel requirements as a result of the computer system.

The handling and flow of information in the bacteriology laboratory is similar. Specimens are logged in, accession sheets produced, work cards created, results entered, reports printed, and the files checked nightly. Antibiotic sensitivity results are measured and input by an automatic zone size reader. A significant advantage for the bacteriology laboratory is the ability to perform statistical analyses on organisms isolated and sensitivity patterns in relation to the cumulative experiences of the different care units.

This system operates 24 hours a day, 7 days a week. Excellent reliability (less than 0.2% down time) of this operation has been achieved by having a fully redundant hardware configuration. In the event of a system malfunction on the clinical laboratory service machine, an equivalent machine can be quickly put into operation in its place. Images of the system and information on the disk are dumped onto magnetic tape four times a day. When it is necessary to change machines, an image of the system can be reloaded from the most recent set of dump tapes in the rare situation where the information on the disk is irrecoverable.

Current efforts focus on the evaluation of this laboratory system and the integration of the laboratory data into the computer-based medical record. The system is also used to determine utilization patterns and to combine this information with an educational program to modulate what many feel to be excessive laboratory utilization.

Test volume is increasing at a rate of 10–15% a year; last year about 1 million determinations were made in the chemistry laboratory, and some 200,000 specimens were cultured in the bacteriology laboratory. The increase in test volume causes a disproportionately larger increase in the problems of routing and collating information within the clinical laboratory. It is the impression of the laboratory administration that the MUMPS computer-based information system has greatly facilitated this information processing. Similarly, the physicians, who are being presented with an ever-increasing volume of data about each patient, believe that the timely summarization and reporting of this laboratory information facilitates patient care.

b. Medication order processing. One of the central objectives of this project is the development of computer systems that will facilitate the information processing involved with medication ordering, preparation, and recording. The first module in this area forms a part of an intravenous additive system operating on two floors of the pediatric service. Using a direct "hot-line" telephone, the nurse on the clinical unit who is transcribing the doctor's orders calls all orders for the intravenous additives to the pharmacy. The pharmacist enters the order into the computer via a cathode ray tube in an interactive mode.

The computer has a formulary data base (maintained by the pharmacy) consisting of: (1) intravenous drugs, with maximum and minimum daily dose per kilogram, incompatibilities, and stability; and (2) intravenous fluids. Using this data base, the computer does compatibility and stability checks and does checks according to patient weight. If the order falls outside the acceptable ranges, the computer advises the pharmacist to obtain a doctor's override before processing the order. After the order is verified by the pharmacist, labels (Figure 17–3) are automatically produced for enough admixtures to last until 10:00 a.m. the next day.

The pharmacist has access to the following information at any time: (1) all information in the formulary, or all information about any one drug or fluid; (2) active orders on one or all patients; (3) total orders written since admission on one or all patients. This information may be displayed on the cathode ray tube or printed on the teletype. The pharmacist may modify or discontinue any order if indicated by the doctor.

Each morning an active order list (Figure 17–3) is produced for the morning rounds on the clinical unit. The computer also provides a pharmacy log sheet containing a listing of admixtures required for the next 24 hours. A system summary is produced each morning containing a list of overridden orders entered during the previous 24 hours, including the reason for requiring the override and the name of the doctor overriding.

Literature on drug safety strongly supports a pharmacy-based intravenous additive service. Using a computer to assist in providing the service has saved the pharmacist time by doing routine checks, by calculating divided doses and duration time, by providing complete, legible labels for all admixtures sent to the clinical unit, and by compiling routine work lists.

c. **Pulmonary function interpretation.** This is a relatively straightforward application of numerical computation and algorithmic manipulation wherein the user enters a set of raw data on an individual patient and the computer program carries out a number of well-specified data processing steps to produce a report concerning the pulmonary function of the patient. The input data are demographic (e.g., age, sex), directly measured variables (e.g., vital capacity) and raw data from various instrumentation. The output report gives the derived values for various pulmonary function parameters (taking into consideration the predicted normal values) and includes a relatively simple statement of the type and severity of the ob-

```
                ORDER 2
JOHNSON,DAVID   155-23-42 BUR 5
PENICILLIN G POTASS  10 MU
  IN DEXT 5% IN WATER  200ML
  GIVE 50 ML/DOSE
    ON 10/28 : 2P-8P
       10/29 : 2A-8A
DO NOT USE AFTER 2PM 10/29


        This label is attached to the
        bottle, which is sent to the
        unit after admixture.
```

```
        ACTIVE ORDER LIST FOR BURNHAM 5  11:15 AM 10/28/71

                        ACTIVE ORDER LIST
  166-21-38                   REBECCA SMITH              25 KG.
                    ORDER                         TOTAL AMOUNT
  #1 ERYTHROMYCIN  500 MG/DOSE                     (2 GM/DAY)
     IN 50 ML OF DEXT 5% IN WATER
     GIVE EVERY SIX HOURS                         (200 ML/DAY)
               START TIME   2:00 PM  10/27/71



                        ACTIVE ORDER LIST
  155-23-42                   DAVID JOHNSON             45 KG.
                    ORDER                         TOTAL AMOUNT
  2 PENICILLIN G POTASS 2.50 ML/DOSE               (10 MU/DAY)
    IN 50 ML OF DEXT 5% IN WATER
    GIVE EVERY 6 HOURS                            (200 ML/DAY)
               START TIME   2:00 PM TODAY



                        ACTIVE ORDER LIST
  153-27-46                   ROBERT MURPHY             30 KG.
                    ORDER                         TOTAL AMOUNT
  1 VIT B COMPLEX WITH C   2 ML                    (2.40 ML/DAY)
    IN 500 ML OF ISOLYTE M
    GIVE AT 25 ML/HR                              (600 ML/DAY)
               START TIME   12:00 N TODAY
```

Figure 17–3. An example of a computer-generated label for an intravenous admixture, and a computer-generated list of all currently active intravenous orders.

served abnormality. The contribution of the computer program is to reduce clerical errors in routine computation and transcription, to standardize rules of interpretation, and to decrease the amount of time required by both the technical and professional staff of the pulmonary function laboratory in carrying out and reporting pulmonary function studies. This computer program is believed to be cost-justified by the pulmonary function laboratory and is being provided as a routine service with the computer costs fully reimbursed.

d.   Modules under development for service units.   The modules under development in the service units (e.g., in hematology) will have many similarities to the operational modules in terms of mode of interaction, file structure, and types of output. The major exception is in the x-ray functions where there are several unique characteristics. In the x-ray film folder inventory control system, there will be a large on-line file containing only a small amount of information about previous x-ray examinations on a very large number of patients. In the x-ray reporting activity, the narrative information relating to description of the findings and the interpretation will be entered by the radiologist using an interactive cathode ray tube. This interaction consists of displaying a structured list to the radiologist from which he selects appropriate items using a light-pen. The computer then selects subsequent frames for display as a function of previous choices by the radiologist. The narrative report is produced by the computer as a compilation of concepts and terms selected over the series of frames and various items selected.

4.   Clinical Units

a.   Nurses' station system.   Over the past eight years we have tried several different techniques of capturing information through a terminal located on the care unit.[6] All of these have been unsuccessful, primarily because the interface of the physician or nurse with the computer system did not favorably compare with the ease of use, availability, and reliability of the classical method of recording information or orders through written communication in the doctor's order book. The use of a terminal on the care unit for inquiry or for reporting is relatively straightforward, the only limiting factor being cost justification—i.e., demonstrating that more timely retrieval of information through a terminal at the nurses' station justifies the cost differential of remote terminal operation compared with manual distribution of reports.

The direct collection of information on the care unit is very different and is a much more demanding challenge. The "cultural shock" to many physicians and nurses that has resulted from attempting to introduce on-line, real-time computer interaction has led to the damnation and rejection of every experimental system that has yet been conceived. The only systems that have survived are those which have finessed the whole input issue by allowing the physician to write the information in the routine fashion and then use clerical personnel to enter the information into the computer system. The inherent weakness in this strategy is that the computer interaction is not with the individual who is generating the order, but with a clerical staff member who has no decision-making power. This almost completely eliminates the power and usefulness of an on-line computer system in checking the completeness and acceptability of an order, in giving back pertinent current information about the particular patient (e.g., the current active orders), in identifying and resolving scheduling conflicts, or in checking an order against the data in the computer record (e.g., checking for drug-drug interactions or drug-laboratory test value interactions, or known allergic reactions to the drug). If this information is not given back immediately to the physician at the time of the initial creation of the order, then it is virtually useless. This is particularly true if there is a significant time delay between the writing of the order and the entry into the computer system. If this occurs, the responsible physician will usually have left the care unit and clarification of the code will be very difficult and time-consuming.

The strategy we are developing is to make available two parallel order-capturing routines wherein the physician can either enter the order directly using the CRT or else use a "hot-line" telephone to a central information unit for the verbal communication of the order to a trained terminal operator. In the latter situation, the operator would enter the order in the computer system using an interactive terminal and efficient coding. Hopefully, it would be possible to enter the order as rapidly as it was dictated so that there would be an immediate CRT display of the order to the physician. This approach provides a method of capturing the order without requiring the physician to use the terminal and yet takes advantage of the computer system's ability to audit the order and give back pertinent information at the time the order is created.

There are very critical aspects of this plan, and the feasibility has not yet been demonstrated. The major issue is the acceptability of the computer-based ordering system to the physician user. A very sophisticated computer program is required since response time is critical when dealing with the capture of the order in real time. The development of an information central unit is a novel activity and undoubtedly will present problems of cost/justification and personnel management. If successful, the scaling-up of such a system from the two medical floors (where the initial implementation will take place) to the entire hospital will present major technological challenges.

b. Outpatient clinics. The most important module now operational in a clinical outpatient unit is a computer-based ambulatory medical system developed for the Harvard Community Health Plan (HCHP).[7] This system has been functioning for three years and is the primary medical record for over 30,000 members with over 100,000 visits annually. The same information system also serves the administrative data processing needs of the HCHP in regard to membership enrollment, and providing the aggregate statistics required for insurance rate-setting, utilization review, and planning for resource allocation.

The computer-based medical record consists of an on-line computer medical record and computer-generated reports in a traditional medical record binder. Each time a patient uses the resources of the plan for any health care reason (either a scheduled visit, a "walk-in", or a telephone encounter), the health provider (either physician or nurse) completes a self-encoding checklist form (Figure 17–4 is an abbreviation of a typical "encounter form") providing information concerning (a) the problems or diagnoses of importance; (b) the laboratory tests requested; (c) the active medications and other therapy prescribed; and (d) disposition and referrals. The laboratory test result information is entered through a terminal located in the clinical laboratory; the information on the encounter report is entered by a medical record room staff through interactive terminals at the HCHP. The care provider may also write a limited amount of free-text information for each item selected on the encounter form and this text is also entered into the computer. Since the encounter form is uniquely structured for the particular needs of each specialty, most of the problems encountered in this ambulatory practice (particularly for return visits) can be relatively well-described without requiring a dictated note. In those situations where a dictated report is required, the dictated note is placed in the paper medical record but not in the computer system and is therefore not available in the on-line record.

After the information has been entered, the computer system generates a report for that visit (equivalent to a progress note). In addition, the computer merges the information into the patient's file and produces an up-dated summary (Figure 17–5) of the patient's medical status including all active problems, the latest test results, and the active medication orders.

This status report is included in the patient's medical record and is also maintained in the on-line file where it is instantaneously available for display on cathode-ray-tubes located in the various provider units at the HCHP. The availability of this on-line report should make a significant difference in the care of the walk-in patient and the advice and care given over the telephone since, for the first time, the care provider has immediate access to a relatively complete summary of the current medical status of the patient.

Generation of statistical reports for management of the plan requires no additional data collection or input. These reports may be regular member-ship or utilization statistics, or may be special studies such as the produc-tion of a list of women whom the physicians wished to contact because they

Figure 1

7

INTERNAL MEDICINE ENCOUNTER*

1. DATE: __9/23/71__   2. M.D. _B. Walters_
3. VISIT: a. Long _____   b. Short __✓__

VITAL SIGNS
10. Ht. (in.) _____   12. Pulse/Min. _____
11. Wt. (lbs.) _____   13. BP _____

20. DIAGNOSES (Circle P if presumtive, D to delete)
DIAGNOSIS   MODIFIER   30. MEDICATIONS (To delete, circle D)

GENERAL   RX
____ A102 P - D Well Adult _____   ____ D118 D Aldomet _____
                                               ____ I180 D Allopurinol _____
METABOLIC   ____ B113 D Ampicillin _____
____ A150 P - D Obesity _____   ____ H166 D Anusol Suppos. _____
____ N011 P - D Gout _____   ____ E111 D.A.S.A. _____
____ B120 P - D Diabetes mellitus _____   ____ G131 D Benylin Expect _____
                                               ____ E161 D Cafergot _____
PSYCHIATRIC   ____ F121 D Chlorothiazide _____
____ P110 P - D Anxiety RXN _____   ____ A111 D Chlor-trimeton _____
____ P100 P - D Alcoholism _____   ____ E112 D Codeine _____
____ P120 P - D Depression _____   ____ H143 D Combid _____
                                               ____ H141 D Compazine _____
HEENT   ____ E153 D Daprisal _____
____ O190 P - D Migraine headache _____   ____ E113 D Darvon _____
____ E260 P - D Sinusitis _____   ____ I123 D.D.B.I. _____
____ E120 P - D Otitis externa _____   ____ D111 D Digoxin _____
____ E252 P - D Allergic rhinitis _____   ____ F171 D Dilantin _____
____ E410 P - D Pharyngitis _____   ✓ H151 D Donnatal _T tal QID_
____ G270 P - D URI _____   ____ E122 D Elavil _____
                                               ____ E134 D Equagesic _____
PULMONARY
____ G121 P - D Acute bronchitis _____   40. DISPOSITION
____ G122 P - D Chronic bronchitis _____ Future appointment:
____ G100 P - D Asthma _____   ____ a. days _2_ (b) weeks ____ c. months __
____ G140 P - D Emphysema _____   ____ d. Return PRN
                                               ____ e. Patient to call M.D.
CARDIOVASCULAR   ____ f. M.D. to call patient
____ J110 P - D Hypertension _____   ____ g. Patient to call nurse
____ I230 P - D HCVD _____   ____ h. Nurse to call patient
____ I270 P - D Myocardial infarction _____ ____ i. Other _____
____ O134 P - D Cerebrovascular disease _____
____ I100 P - D Angina pectoris _____   41. REFERRALS
____ J140 P - D Varicose veins _____
                                               _____
GASTROINTESTINAL   ____ days ____ weeks ____ months
____ K210 P - D Gastritis _____
____ K170 P - D Duodenal ulcer _____
____ K131 P - D Spastic colitis _____   _____
____ K150 P - D Diarrhea _____   ____ days ____ weeks ____ months
✓ K199 P - D Abdominal pain _____
____ V170 P - D Post Cholecystectomy _____   *N.B.: Encounter Forms are two-sided.
____ V100 P - D Post Appendectomy _____   This example represents a con-
____ K230 P - D Hemorrhoids _____   densation of the Internal
                                                      Medical Encounter.
GENITO-URINARY
____ L101 P - D Urinary tract infection _____
____ L222 P - D Prostatitis _____

Figure 17–4. A self-encoding checklist ("encounter form") for the collection of pertinent information about a patient for an ambulatory practice in internal medicine.

Figure 3

9

```
                    PATIENT STATUS REPORT                        PAGE 1

    BARTON, WILMA SAMPLE
    HCHP PT 00-00-00

    MARRIED FEMALE DOB: 04/13/40
    77 MASS AVE, CAMBRIDGE, MA
    TEL:   864-6900


    DIAGNOSES AND PROBLEMS

        ABDOMINAL PAIN [K991]                    B. WALTERS, M.D. (09/23/71)

        CHRONIC DEPRESSION [P120]                S. FRENCH, R.N.  (03/15/71)

        MONILIASIS [M191]                        F. WELLER, M.D. (10/20/70)

        PENICILLIN ALLERGY [A113]
          SKIN RASH                              B. WALTERS, M.D. (07/06/70)

        ASTHMA [G100]
          MODERATE, NEEDS REASSURANCE            B. WALTERS, M.D. (07/06/70)


    TEST RESULTS

        09/23/71    HCT                    41

        10/20/70    VAGINAL CULTURE        CANDIDA ALBICANS

        07/06/70    WBC                    7900
                    DIFF                   NORMAL
                    KUB                    NO ABNORMALITY
                    URINALYSIS             NEG
                    GLUCOSE (IPC)          100
                    VDRL                   NEG
                    PAP SMEAR              NEG
                    CHEST PA & LAT.        NORMAL


    MEDICATIONS/THERAPY

        09/23/71    DONNATAL               1 TAB QID

        03/15/71    GROUP PSYCHOTHERAPY WEEKLY

        10/20/70    MYCOSTATIN             AS DIRECTED

        07/06/70    ORTHONOVUM             AS DIRECTED
                    TEDRAL                 1 TAB QID
                    AMINOPHYLLINE SUPP     PRN
```

Figure 17–5. A computer-generated summary of a patient's present medical status. It includes the currently active problems, the latest test results, and the active medication orders.

were taking a particular type of sequential birth-control pill which had been removed from the market by the FDA.

The important and somewhat unique feature of this medical record system is that it supports primary patient care and also supplies necessary management and administrative statistics and insurance reimbursement data. Of equal importance is that this record system is to some extent a general purpose data management system. The format and content of the input and of the output can vary within wide limits. Thus, this same record system is being used for specialty clinics at the MGH such as the cancer registry (tumor clinic) and the anticoagulation clinic. In addition, other hospitals are developing record systems using this system as the central management activity but specifying their own input and output formats.

c. Physician consultants. One of the characteristic features of most large hospitals is the increasing challenge of managing the actuely ill patient. This management can be an extraordinarily complex activity, in part because the physician must make decisions based on the analysis and integration of a large number of separate items of information. This computer program gives management guidelines for the care of patients in acute respiratory failure.[8] These guidelines are based on a model resulting from experience collected over the past decade in the respiratory care unit of the Massachusetts General Hospital.

Data on the patient's status are collected through a conversational interaction between the physician and the computer. The user enters the information by replying to a series of questions with either a "Y" (yes), an "N" (no), or with the appropriate numeric value. For patients requiring mechanical ventilation, he enters the type of ventilator and artificial airway being used, the length of time each has been used and where appropriate, the settings of the ventilator. The program is designed to handle five types of ventilators as well as nine possible kinds of airways. While the program requires an answer to most questions, those dealing with pulmonary mechanics (such as vital capacity and inspiratory force) are optional and can be skipped if no measurement has been made. Additional information is entered concerning arterial blood gases, the patient's state of consciousness, and certain laboratory test values.

The computer then prepares and prints out a summary of the patient's current respiratory profile in tabular form; this includes both the information which has been entered as well as a number of calculated values such as alveolar-arterial O_2 gradient, dead space-tidal volume ratio, and physiologic shunt (Figure 17–6).

The user may also request the computer to print out an interpretation of the information on the patient under consideration (Figure 17–7). Five major areas of assessment comprise the program output:

SUMMARY OF VALUES ON 12/29/7Ø at 8:ØØ PM

NAME   DEMO, GEORGE

SEX   M   WT   88.6Ø KG
AGE   69   TEMP   37.8Ø CENT
HT   172 CM   HCT   6Ø %
VCP   3.5Ø L   SAB   2.5Ø CM %
FRCP   3.48 L

DROWSY
FULL-TIME ON VENTILATOR
BENNETT VOLUME-CYCLE -- BEING CONTROLLED
6 DAYS ON VENTILATORS
PRESTRETCHED NASOTRACH TUBE
ENDOTRACH TUBES FOR 3 DAYS

MODE	EEP	FIO2	PAO2	PACO2	PH	HCO3-
VENT	--	1	45Ø	58	7.37	35
VENT	--	Ø.3Ø	57	6Ø	7.34	34

MODE	EEP	FIO2	AADO2	VD/VT	SAT	VT
VENT	--	1	2Ø3	Ø.63	1ØØ	Ø.6Ø
VENT	--	Ø.3Ø	86	Ø.56	88	Ø.5Ø

QS/QT ON VENT   Ø.Ø9 (AV-DO2 ASSUMED 6 VOL %)

FRC   1ØØ% OF FRCP
VC   9 ML/KGBW
FEV   38% OF VC
IF   25 CM H2O

EFFECTIVE COMPLIANCE   15 ML/CM H2O ON 1ØØ% O 2
EFFECTIVE COMPLIANCE   14 ML/CM H2O ON FIo2 OF Ø.3Ø

VCO2 IS 195 ML/MIN (STPD) ON VENT 1ØØ% O2
VCO2 IS 234 ML/MIN (STPD) ON VENT REC. FIO2

Figure 17–6. A computer-generated summary of the patient's current respiratory profile.

RESPIRATOR VALUES -- FIO2=0.9-1.0

PH OF 7.37 (H+= 43 NM), PACO2 OF 58 TORR AND HCO3 OF 35 MEQ/L
ARE CONSISTENT WITH: CHRONIC RESP. ACIDOSIS
CHRONIC RESP. ACIDOSIS -- CHRONIC HYPERCAPNIA (DURATION>24 HR) HAS
RESULTED IN A COMPENSATED ACIDOSIS (RENAL RETENTION OF HCO3).
NOTE: VE IS 9.10 L/MIN AND VA IS 3.40 L/MIN
FACT THAT VE IS NORMAL (>7 L/MIN) STRONGLY SUGGESTS THAT
CAUSE MAY BE ALVEOLAR HYPOVENT. WITH NORMAL VE BUT HIGH VD/VT IN
DISTURBANCES WITH V/Q IMBALANCE SUCH AS PNEUMONIA, COPD,
PULMONARY EDEMA OR INCREASED INTRA-ABD. PRESSURE.

----TO ACHIEVE DESIRED FIO2 OF 0.37 ON BENNETT VOLUME CYCLE

THE DESIRED 37% O2 CAN BE APPROXIMATED WITH THE % O2
SETTING ON THE RESPIRATOR CONTROLS. THIS IS ONLY AN APPROXIM-
ATION AND SHOULD BE CHECKED WITH AN O2 ANALYZER. THIS ALSO
ASSUMES THAT THE RESPIRATOR IS CONNECTED TO PURE O2.

VD/VT RATIO'S ARE 0.63 AND 0.56 ON RESPIRATOR
THE LOWEST VALUE 0.56 HAS BEEN SELECTED FOR ANALYSIS.

-- COMPARISON OF RESPIRATOR VALUES
AA DO2 ON 100% O2 OF 203 TORR SHOWS MILD ALV GAS EXCHANGE DEFECT.
VD/VT OF 0.56 SHOWS MARKED V/Q ABNORMALITIES.
THE DIFFERENCE IN ABNORMALITY SUGGESTS SEVERE V/C
IMBALANCE AS SEEN IN CHRONIC OBSTRUCTIVE LUNG DISEASE.

          ALVEOLAR VENTILATION ASSESSMENT

MINUTE VOLUME (BTPS)= 7 L/MIN
ALVEOLAR VENTILATION (BTPS)= 3.10 L/MIN
CO2 PRODUCTION (STPD)= 234 ML/MIN

PACO2 SHOULD BE LOWERED TO AT MOST 45 TORR UNLESS THERE IS A
SPECIAL REASON FOR MAINTAINING THIS LEVEL SUCH AS CHRONIC HYPERCAP.
PATIENT'S TIDAL VOLUME IS 5.60 ML/KGBW.
TO LOWER PACO2 (IN ORDER):
-- RAISE VT TO NORMAL RANGE (9-15 ML/KCBW) OR 0.80 TO 1.30 LITER.
-- ADJUST RESP. RATE
-- SINCE YOU HAVE NO DEAD SPACE TO REMOVE YOU WILL HAVE TO USE A HIGHER
   THAN DESIRABLE VT OR RESP. RATE

PACO2 SHOULD BE RECHECKED IF ADJUSTMENTS ARE CARRIED OUT ON
TIDAL VOLUME, RESP. RATE, OR MECH. DEAD SPACE.

          AIRWAY ASSESSMENT

INCREASING AM'T OF AIR REQUIRED FOR SEALING CUFF SUGGESTS THAT
TRACHEOMALACIA IS OCCURRING. REPOSITIONING IS NECESSARY.

          -- ADDITIONAL SUGGESTIONS --

A COURSE OF BRONCHODILATORS SUCH AS AMINOPHYLLINE MAY PROVE USEFUL
GIVEN AMOUNT OF EXPIRATORY AIRWAY OBSTRUCTION PRESENT.

Figure 17–7. A portion of a computer-generated interpretation and
assessment of the respiratory status and recommended therapy.

(1) Oxygenation assessment: the program scans all arterial oxygen tensions and makes a recommendation for the "ideal" oxygen concentration.

(2) Acid-base assessment: it determines if the PCO_2 and pH are within normal limits; if not, it categorizes the acid-base disturbance.

(3) Alveolar ventilation assessment: it considers the tidal volume, respiratory rate, and mechanical dead space and suggests the tidal volume and respiratory rate required for optimal CO_2 elimination consistent with airway stability. (i.e., optimal ventilation pattern).

(4) Weaning assessment: it evaluates the patient's ability to be "weaned" from the ventilator if he is using one, and makes recommendations as to how to carry out this weaning.

(5) Airway care: it recommends appropriate procedures for dealing with the particular airway, and gives recommendations for changes.

Like most of the other modules, this program has gone through numerous revisions, primarily to make the interaction with the physician as comfortable as possible, to increase the variety of the data that can be considered, and to improve and enhance the interpretation provided by the computer. One version of this program has been used extensively for patients in the Respiratory Care Unit and for patients seen on consultation by the respiratory care group at the MGH. It is clear that it is a valuable teaching tool which helps the inexperienced physician to organize an approach to a complicated respiratory situation. We are now trying to document the usefulness of the program for improving patient care. The initial positive reaction of others suggests that the program may have an exciting potential in the community hospital to help guide patient therapy and afford immediate access to the most recent therapeutic developments.

F.   EDUCATION AND RESEARCH

One of the most fundamental characteristics of patient care is that each patient encounter contains elements of abstract problem-solving of an often sophisticated nature. The science of clinical medicine, of "clinical judgment," is the intellectual challenge of correct diagnosis, choice of appropriate therapy, and estimating the likely outcome. The approach of medical school to teaching "clinical judgment" is basically an apprenticeship training wherein the fledgling medical student is expected to acquire the necessary diagnostic skills by a relatively informal association with more experienced clinicians. Over a period of several years, he receives decreasing direct supervision and formal instruction and assumes more and more independence and increasing patient care responsibility. Nowhere in this process is emphasis given to formal instruction in the elements of the decision process. In fact, the success of the educational process is heavily dependent on the individual initiation of the student, the chance assignment to an excellent instructor, and the availability of a good medical care environment with a good mix of patient care opportunities.

In this laboratory, we have undertaken the task of developing and evaluating computer-based techniques to teach clinical judgment and to monitor clinical competency. The particular approach we are emphasizing is using the computer to simulate clinical case material in a similar fashion that the LINK trainer was used to simulate the cockpit of an airplane in teaching pilots to fly. The scenario of a student-computer interaction is that of the computer being the "unknown" (the patient) and the student being the problem-solver (the physician). We are still in the process of experimenting with different types of computer-based educational experiences, and the different computer programs emphasize different clinical skills. Two examples of the types of interaction we have developed include:

(1) A model where the objective is to reach the correct diagnosis after carrying out a dialogue with the computer to collect information in an "optimal" fashion. This dialogue consists of asking for specific items of information by entering numbers chosen from a vocabulary list. The educational objective is to teach the student how to choose a rational strategy for working-up a patient, and how to integrate, classify, and interpret the data he has collected. The decision strategy used by the computer model is a modification of a Bayesian probability process. Figure 17–8 illustrates a typical student-computer interaction and Figure 17–9 illustrates a computer-generated interpretation of one fragment of the interaction.

```
        THIS ABDOMINAL PAIN CASE, WHICH IS PRESENTED TO EVERY STUDENT AS THEIR
INITIAL CASE, IS DESIGNED TO BE A RELATIVELY SIMPLE ONE.  ITS PURPOSE IS TO
ALLOW THE STUDENT AN OPPORTUNITY TO BECOME FAMILIAR WITH THE COMPUTER TERMINAL
AND WITH THIS PROGRAM.  PLEASE BE PATIENT - - OTHER CASES WILL PROVE MORE
CHALLENGING MEDICALLY !  A 45 YEAR OLD WHITE MALE USED CAR  SALESMAN IS
BROUGHT TO THE EW BY HIS ANXIOUS WIFE BECAUSE HE COMPLAINS OF MODERATE EPI-
GASTRIC PAIN WHICH STARTED ABOUT A WEEK AGO AFTER A NIGHT OUT WITH THE BOYS
PLAYING POKER.


ITEM  #3  HOW LONG DO THE PAINS LAST :  THE PAIN SOMETIMES GOES AWAY
ALMOST COMPLETELY, BUT THEN IT COMES BACK BAD AS EVER.


ITEM  #4  WHEN DID YOU FIRST HAVE THIS PAIN?  :  I'VE BEEN HAVING PAINS
LIKE THIS FOR A NUMBER OF YEARS;  IT SEEMED TO START WHEN I WAS IN KOREA.
IT GETS PARTICULARLY BAD WHEN THE NEW MODEL CARS COME OUT IN THE FALL.
```

Figure 17–8. An example of a student-computer interaction in clinical problem-solving. For purposes of illustration that portion of the text which was entered by the student is underlined. This is a program in which the student is attempting to gather information in an optimal sequence in order to make the correct diagnosis and management decisions in the case of acute abdominal pain.

```
(100)     AGE  :  40

(101)     SEX  :  MALE

(102)     LOCATION OF PAIN  :  EPIGASTRIC

(103)     SEVERITY OF PAIN  :  MILD

(104)     WHEN DID THIS PAIN START  :  ABOUT A WEEK OR MORE AGO

*****AT THIS POINT*****

ESTIMATED DISEASE PROB
(3)  PEPTIC ULCER  (GASTRIC/DUODENAL)  0.226
(7)  ACUTE GASTROENTERITIS  (VIRAL OR BACTERIAL)  0.112
(6)  ACUTE GASTRITIS  0.082

++  TEST STUDENT CHOSE

     (3)  HOW LONG DO THE PAINS LAST  :  A FEW MINUTES AT A TIME (INTERMITTENT)

TEST 3 IS

     POTENTIALLY V GOOD  (62) IN CONSIDERATION OF

          (7)  ACUTE GASTROENTERITIS  (VIRAL OR BACTERIAL)

     POTENTIALLY V GOOD  (51) IN CONSIDERATION OF
          (3)  PEPTIC ULCER  (GASTRIC/DUODENAL)
     POSSIBLY GOOD  (29)  IN CONSIDERATION OF
          (6)  ACUTE GASTRITIS

     USELESS  (0)  FOR DISCRIMINATING
          (3)  PEPTIC ULCER  (GASTRIC/DUODENAL) AND
          (7)  ACUTE GASTROENTERITIS (VIRAL OR BACTERIAL)

COMPUTER'S TOP TESTS
(1)  CHARACTER OF PAIN (0)
(4)  WHEN DID YOU FIRST HAVE THIS PAIN? (0)
(18) DOES EATING A MEAL AFFECT YOUR PAIN (0)
(3)  HOW LONG DO THE PAINS LAST (0)

++  POINTS STUDENT LOST = 0

*****AT THIS POINT*****

ESTIMATED DISEASE PROB
(3)  PEPTIC ULCER  (GASTRIC/DUODENAL)  0.235
(7)  ACUTE GASTROENTERITIS  (VIRAL OR BACTERIAL)  0.098
(6)  ACUTE GASTRITIS  0.088
```

Figure 17–9. A computer-generated interpretation of one sequence of
the student's interaction in the clinical problem-solving simulation.

Three Different Segments of Student's Interaction with Cardio-Pulmonary
Resuscitation Program

THE PATIENT IS A 81-YEAR OLD MAN WHO IS 2 DAYS POST IRIDECTOMY.
YOU ARE A STAT CONSULT BECAUSE THE PATIENT DOES NOT LOOK RIGHT.
  WHAT DO YOU DO FIRST?

1. TAKE AN EKG
2. START AN IV
3. CHECK MAJOR VESSELS FOR PULSES, SEE IF PATIENT IS RESPONSIVE
4. GIVE A SHOT OF INTRACARDIAC EPINEPHRINE

>1

  THAT WILL TAKE SEVERAL MINUTES ASSUMING YOU HAVE AN EKG
MACHINE IN THE ROOM AND LONGER IF YOU HAVE TO GET ONE....
THE PATIENT, IF TRULY ARRESTED, WILL BE BEYOND
RESUSCITATION BY THE TIME YOU DOCUMENT THE FACT.

— — — — — — — — — — — — — — — —

  THE BICARB IS RUNNING. NOW IT IS TIME TO TRY SOME SPECIFICS.
LET'S TAKE A LOOK AT THE PATIENT'S RHYTHM.

THE RHYTHM STRIP IS SHOWN ON PAGE 6; IS THIS

1. VENTRICULAR FIBRILLATION
2. VENTRICULAR TACHYCARDIA
3. SLOW IDIOVENTRICULAR RHYTHM
4. ELECTROMECHANICAL DISSOCIATION

>2

  CORRECT. NOTE THAT IT COULD ALSO BE THE SINE WAVE OF
HYPERKALEMIA, A CHOICE YOU WERE NOT OFFERED.

— — — — — — — — — — — — — — — —

  THE FIRST SHOCK TOOK YOU FROM V TACH TO VF SO AN
IMMEDIATE RESHOCK IS REASONABLE, IN FACT...

  A FEW SECONDS OF ASYSTOLE...
THEN GOES TO THE RHYTHM SHOWN ON PAGE 3.
WHAT WOULD YOU LIKE TO DO...

1. DEFIBRILLATE AGAIN
2. GIVE 1 MG EPINEPHRINE IV, MASSAGE, THEN SHOCK
3. START A LICOCAINE DRIP THEN SHOCK

>3

  THAT MAY WORK, THOUGH IN THE SETTING OF FINE
FIBRILLATION MY FIRST CHOICE WOULD HAVE BEEN EPI.
THE XYLOCAINE IS RUNNING AT 4 MG/MIN, SHOCK, AND...

Figure 17–10. An example of a student-computer interaction in a problem of the diagnosis and management of cardio-pulmonary arrest.

(2) A model where the underlying clinical situation changes during the course of the student's interaction. In this model, the information about the signs and symptoms of the simulated patient are not constant, but change as a function of the natural evolution of the disease process as modified by the student's intervention. The simulated patient can have a complete recovery or have a progressive deterioration, dependent of the appropriateness of the various choices of the student. The education objective is to teach the student strategies of management of a variety of disease entities, and help him gain an awareness of the types and manifestations of the possible complications. The underlying computer model may be either a relatively straightforward branching algorithm (using Boolean conditionals) or a more sophisticated analytical model of the disease process. Figure 17–10 illustrates an example of this approach where the student is attempting to manage a case of cardiac arrest. An example of the latter approach is a program involving the management of diabetic ketoacidosis where the clinical and laboratory manifestations of the disease process (e.g., the blood sugar, the serum pH and potassium, etc.) change with time as a function of the choice of treatment given (e.g., the amount, type, and route of insulin, the volume and type of intravenous fluids).

These programs seem to be very well accepted by the students and faculty. The National Library of Medicine has provided contract funds to make this resource available to over twenty different medical schools and hospitals across the United States on a nationwide computer network. These programs seem most useful both as ad-lib supplementary educational resources but may also have a role as specific elements in a planned educational curriculum.

G. HARDWARE AND SOFTWARE

There are four functionally equivalent computer systems on which the various modules are implemented. Since all of these systems operate under MUMPS, it is invisible to the application program which particular system is being used. Three of these systems are Digital Equipment Corporation PDP-9 machines, and the other is the newer version, a PDP-15. Each system has 32K of 18-bit core, 3 million characters of fixed-head disk and 52 million characters on movable head disk packs (the latter can be expanded to 208 million characters on each system). We believe very strongly that duplicate hardware systems are essential to provide the high degree of reliability necessary in a medical information system. We do not believe it is a viable option to depend on a manual backup system: if a computer system is truly effective in making a significant improvement in information processing, then the hospital will come to depend absolutely on continuous operation. If continuous availability cannot be provided, then there will be a "credibility gap," and the computer system will almost certainly be rejected. We use these redundant systems in a hierarchical fashion—i.e., if one computer system is not available, the various modules can be shifted around so that the highest priority activities will continue to operate while the lower priority activities (e.g., programming development) will be temporarily halted.

As discussed previously, all of these systems operate under MUMPS. The MUMPS time-sharing system is designed to support optimally the needs of a multi-user data management activity. This optimization is particularly important in the disk handling routines where the actual physical block allocation on the disk is done in such a manner that access time is minimized (on the fixed-head disk, the average access time to any datum is about 25 milliseconds). Because the user's program is never compiled but kept only in symbolic form, the amount of core required for any application program is much smaller than in the case of a compiled program. Because of this small core requirement, the time-sharing implementation uses partitioning of core, rather than the classical mode of repeated swapping of programs from disk to core. On our 32 K core systems, there are a maximum of 20 simultaneous users with a guaranteed response time of less than 2 seconds, with the average being on the order of 0.5 seconds (dependent in large part on the amount of disk activity).

The MUMPS language is designed to interface with a variety of input-output devices (e.g., A-D converter, light-pen, plotter, Selectric typewriter, audio-visual control devices). For the most part, the programs are device independent with no programming modifications required to change from output on a teletype to a cathode-ray tube to a high-speed printer.

H. IMPACT AND EVALUATION

Given the very fragmented and dispersed nature of this hospital complex and given the course we have undertaken of modular development, it is impossible to make any sweeping generalizations about the impact of the computer systems. The applications in the clinical laboratories are now deeply imbedded in the ongoing activities of the hospital. The laboratories, the clerical administration of the care units, and the physicians are heavily dependent on the continuous functioning of the computer system for data management with the laboratory and for result reporting to the 50 different patient care areas. These subsystems have had major impact in the following areas: .

(1) The cost of data management in the clinical laboratories (both in terms of personnel and space) has been stabilized despite a steadily increasing volume of tests (increasing at the rate of about 15% per year).

(2) The management of the clinical laboratories has been made a more rational and predictable activity since the computer system provides a stable, defined, reliable and coherent set of procedures and support structure. This contribution is important in a situation where there is a relatively high turnover of personnel, where personnel supervision is often difficult, and where it is difficult to monitor the performance of each individual work station.

(3) Many of the potential sources of error in measurement, calculation, and transcription have been eliminated.

(4) The test reports to the physician are legible, organized, and summarized both temporally and by class (e.g., all liver function tests are grouped together). In addition, every abnormal test result is indicated by an asterisk. The availability of the summarized reports and the standardization of the laboratory information processing have had a primary beneficial effect of facilitating the physician's use of the laboratory test information; in addition, there has been a secondary beneficial effect of minimizing the interpersonnel conflicts on the care unit. Because of the more reliable and less ambiguous processing of information, there is a reduction in the tension generated by the lack of information on the current state of processing of a lab test, or by the unavailability of the test result information.

The evaluation of the computer-based laboratory information system is relatively "soft" in terms of quantitative data of cost/effectiveness, primarily because the benefits cannot be easily measured in terms of monetary units. The major limiting factor in terms of any formal evaluation of a computer-based information system is that focusing on the cost/effectiveness of the component or subsystem technical performance measures may be misleading since the major impact may be on performance at the system level, (i.e., the functioning of the entire care unit, provider staff, clerical staff gestalt) and on the less well-defined outcome variables involving patient and result. Flagle[9] has discussed the problems of evaluating technology in these latter two areas, pointing out that in such evaluations we are dealing not just with technology but with man-machine systems and human organizations and that there will be other inputs to the system than the initial technological ones. We would certainly agree with Flagle's analysis and also with his argument that the role of technology may not be as a controllable variable as such, but as a facilitating variable in the sense of augmenting the substance of medical practice.

The difficulty in measuring technological contributions in terms of process measures or of piecemeal beneficial effects is of critical importance when evaluating more sophisticated and extensive activities such as the computer-based ambulatory medical record. A manual, hand-written, unorganized medical record is probably the cheapest (in terms of monetary cost) record system available (other than a record system which was maintained only in the physician's memory). A computer-based system almost certainly will be more expensive unless the cost of the record system includes more intangible elements such as the cost of incomplete or illegible information, the cost of the delay or the failure to locate a record, the cost of the personnel conflicts involved in attempting to locate a record, and the cost of poor communication between different providers. In addition, there are other dimensions of effectiveness which must be considered. For example, we believe the three major questions which must be considered in evaluating the automated medical system at the HCHP to be:[7]

(1) Does the availability of computer-generated patient status reports and statistical summaries promote physician efficiency and quality of care?

(2) Does the availability of a combined administrative/medical data base contribute to more effective resource allocation and planning?

(3) Does content control for completeness and accuracy contribute to the efficiency and quality of care?

To a certain degree, these questions involve a circular argument since the answers to the questions can be obtained only when a computer-based record system has been installed (since the manual system does not permit an adequate characterization of the population served and the care delivered).

It appears that a critical and complete cost/benefit evaluation of a computer-based medical information system is at times a hopeless quest. The major limitations are not so much relevant to the computer technology but to the characteristics of the external environment—e.g., there are virtually no clearly defined specific objectives for health care delivery as an integrated activity, no parameters of success that can be readily measured, and no easy way to separate the contributions of the computer-based systems from the weaknesses and strengths of the other elements of the health care system. There is no doubt that the issue of critical evaluation of the technology is of vital importance and must be addressed. There is equally no doubt that, given the nature of the problem and the state of the art, we often will be forced to be satisfied with fragmentary and compromised efforts. Perhaps the two strongest evaluation techniques now available are pragmatic measures: (1) Will the operational management continue to pay for support of the computer system from non-governmental funds over a prolonged period of time? and (2) Will other institutions successfully copy or modify the programs and implement similar operational systems?

I. SUMMARY

The successful application of computer technology to improving patient care is not a limited short-term task; it is a process that, like other technological applications, will continue to evolve as the needs change and as the technological opportunities and resources change. Likewise, the development of a computer-based "total" information system is not an objective that can be completely achieved; such an information system, if it is of any merit, must be dynamically defined. A rigid and static system, however attractive on initial consideration, will soon be obsolete and unacceptable. The absolutely essential characteristic of any viable computer-based information system which attempts to serve a complex, time-changing set of needs is the ability to meet presently defined objectives in a reliable and cost-effective fashion and yet have the capability to evolve smoothly. These dual criteria are applicable not only to the computer hardware and software; they are also applicable to other characteristics of an information system, including the more intangible aspects such as the caliber of the technical personnel and the leadership, the organizational structure, and the funding mechanisms.

In addition, from another point of view, the success of a computer-based information system cannot be judged as an abstract phenomenon, isolated from the environment. The information system of any large organization is deeply involved with the totality of the organization's existence and with the operation of many of the diverse parts of the organization. For the potential of a computer-based system to be realized, the organization as a whole must be viable and functioning at a reasonable rational level.

In summary, we do not claim to have achieved the objective of implementing a medical information system in any total sense. However, we do believe we have begun, that the philosophy and the technology are sound, and that several viable modules have been successfully developed and are now functioning in reliable and effective operation.

ACKNOWLEDGMENTS

I wish to express my appreciation to Paul Egerman, Barbara B. Farquhar, Jerome H. Grossman, M.D., Edward P. Hoffer, M.D., Fredric E. Jones,

Carl B. Lazarus, James W. Poitras, Don Schmechel, Daniel E. Souder, M.D. and Rita Zielstorff for their contributions to this manuscript. The systems described in this chapter represent a considerable number of man years of effort by a talented group at the Laboratory of Computer Science. The author expresses his appreciation to these individuals not only for their development of these systems but also for the pleasure of working together.

REFERENCES

1. Barnett, G. O. "The Modular Hospital Information System." *Comp. and Biomed. Res. Fourth Volume.* Edited by B. Waxman and R. W. Stacy. Academic Press (in press).
2. Barnett, G. O., and Greenes, R. A. "High Level Programming Languages." *Comp. and Biomed. Res.* 3 (1970) : 488–494.
3. Greenes, R. A.; Pappalardo, A. N.; Marble, C. W.; and Barnett, G. O. "Design and Implementation of a Clinical Data Management System." *Comp. and Biomed. Res.* 2 (1969) : 469–485.
4. *MUMPS Users Manual.* rev. ed. Laboratory of Computer Science, September, 1972.
5. Ruderman, M., and Pappalardo, A. N. "The Hospital Computer Comes of Age." *Computers and Automation* 19 (1970) : 1–6.
6. Gouveia, W. A.; Diamantis, C.; and Barnett, G. O. "Computer Applications in the Hospital Medication System." *Am. J. of Hospital Pharmacy* 26 (1969) : 140–150.
7. Grossman, J. H.; Barnett, G. O.; Koepsell, T. D.; Nesson, R. H.; Dorsey, J. L.; and Phillips, R. R. "An Automated Medical Record System For A Prepaid Group Practice," *J.A.M.A.* 224 (1973) : 1616–1621.
8. Menn, S. J.; Barnett, G. O.; Schmechel, D.; Owens, W. D.; and Pontoppidan, H. "A Computer Program To Assist Acute Respiratory Care." *J.A.M.A.* 223 (1973) : 308–312.
9. Flagle, C. D. "Evaluation and Control of Technology in Health Services." *Proceedings of Conf. on Technology and Health Care Systems in the 1980's.* U.S. Govt. Printing Office. 1973.

CHAPTER EIGHTEEN

Current Status of the Karolinska Hospital Computer System (Stockholm)

by Paul F. L. Hall

A. MEDICAL CARE ENVIRONMENT

The Karolinska Hospital is a 2,000-bed teaching and research hospital and the only hospital entirely run by the state. Each year approximately 40,000 inpatients and 450,000 outpatients are taken care of within the 25 different clinical departments and the 25 different ancillary service units—laboratories, x-ray departments, etc. The departments and service units are organized according to the scheme in Table 1. The permanent staff of the hospital is approximately 5,000, including 400 physicians.

The hospital is responsible for primary care of a population of 90,000 people, but for several clinical consulting specialities the population served may be close to 2 million. The budget per year for the hospital operations is approximately $120 million.

B. DEFINITIONS AND OBJECTIVES

The Swedish Agency for Administrative Development (SAFAD), which is the central authority responsible for the efficient use of government resources, started the Karolinska Hospital computer project (the KS project). The goal of the KS project was determined in 1965 and expressed as a desire to set up a complete hospital information system for patient care, medical education, and clinical research.

It was realized, however, that the creation and introduction of such a system requires many years, and the developmental work was thus primarily geared to the main functions, namely the computer medical record and the computer scheduling/booking functions. One consequence of this concentrated activity was that from the beginning administrative and laboratory or service unit routines were only affected to the extent necessary for the design of the project. The variety of service units and administrative routines were looked upon as subsystems to the above-mentioned main functions.

The following were the basic conditions required in the feasibility study for the development of an information system for use in patient care as well as for short- and long-range planning as resource allocation and clinical research.

(1) A data collection and communication system was required for the acquisition of all necessary data and the distribution of the computer output. Self-administered questionnaires, forms, and checklists should be usable for data acquisition using punch cards, punched paper tape, optical mark readers and online computer terminals for data input. Communication and distribution of computer output should be accompanied by visual display terminals and/or printouts (hard copies).

(2) A data bank, or library for the medico-administrative computer record system was needed for collection, storage, processing, and retrieval of all kinds of data and information. The data bank should be accessible from sophisticated on-line terminals or from satellite computer systems such as laboratories or intensive care units.

(3) A computer booking system with an appointment register and the following functions was also needed: reports on all bookings concerning a particular patient; reports on the total number of inbooked patients any given day and place; reports on available resources, e.g., within an x-ray or an outpatient department.

(4) A reorganization of personnel might be necessary on different levels of the hospital, partly to facilitate the collection of data, to create and support the data bank, to administer and perform the computer system operation, and to facilitate the efficient use of data and information.

C. GENERAL SYSTEM CONCEPTS

The basic idea behind the KS computer project was to develop a patient information system and not only a hospital computer system. A hospital information system can be designed for the specific needs of a specific hospital—e.g., for a large "production-oriented" hospital without the goal of patient care activities outside the hospital. A patient information system has to be designed for all patient care activities including education and

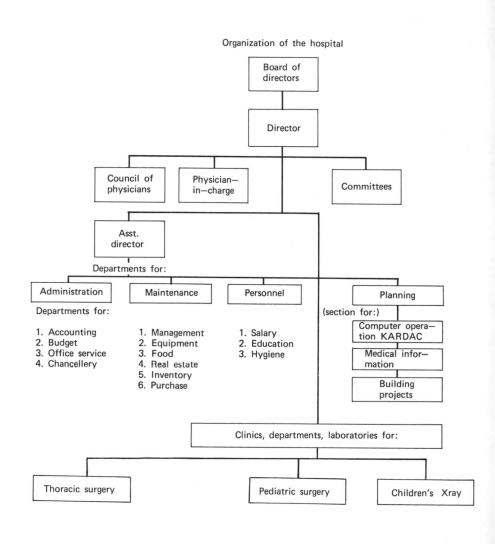

Organization of the hospital

Board of directors

Director

Council of physicians

Physician—in—charge

Committees

Asst. director

Departments for:

Administration

Maintenance

Personnel

Planning

Departments for:

1. Accounting
2. Budget
3. Office service
4. Chancellery

1. Management
2. Equipment
3. Food
4. Real estate
5. Inventory
6. Purchase

1. Salary
2. Education
3. Hygiene

(section for:)

Computer opera— tion KARDAC

Medical infor— mation

Building projects

Clinics, departments, laboratories for:

Thoracic surgery

Pediatric surgery

Children's Xray

Table 1.

Thoracic surgery	Pediatric surgery	Children's x-ray
Otolaryngology	Pediatric medicine	Neuroradiology
Plastic surgery	Pediatric psychiatry	X-ray diagnoses
Dental and jaw diseases	Obstetrics	Thoracic radiology
Orthopedics	Gynecology	Thoracic physiology
Ophthalmology	Neurosurgery	Clinical physiology
General surgery	Neurotraumatology	Clinical bacteriology
Urology	Psychiatry	Radiopathology
Thoracic medicine	Social medicine	Pathology
Dermatology	Experimental psychiatry	Clinical chemistry
Rheumatology	Alcoholic diseases	Clinical neurophysiology
Allergology	Neurology	Radiobiology
Vocational medicine	Neurological rehabilitation	Gynecological radiotherapy
Special cardiology	Physical medicine	General radiotherapy
Endocrinology	Thoracic anesthesia	
Internal medicine	Emergency room	
	Central operation theatres	
	Blood donor center	
	Central anesthesia	
	Intensive care	

A new organization is planned and will be introduced in the near future.

research inside and outside the hospital. As an example, visual display terminals may be the perfect solution to data acquisition inside the hospital but an economical and unpractical technical solution outside, where dictating equipment, optical readers, or even punch cards may be more efficient.

System analyses and system design were thus directed towards the patient's course through the health care delivery system. Due to the rapid development and diversification of medical care in an increasing number of different clinical specialities, it is increasingly difficult to plan the patient's course through a large hospital. The growing specialization gives rise in the patients and in the hospital personnel to a feeling of insecurity discernible in all large hospitals today.

The basic concept was that, as decisions made by physicians are or should be documented in the manual medical record and as over 50% of the operational cost of a hospital are due to procedures which are planned, ordered, and performed by the physicians, the core of the computer system should be the automated medical record system. An important subsystem to the automated medical record system was the patient scheduling and booking system for better planning of the patient's course through the health care delivery system. It was realized that all other systems such as administrative or service units were subsystems to the automated medical record system or data bank.

The requirements of a hospital computer system or medical record system can briefly be presented as follows:

(1) the system should be able to receive and store data and information of both medical and administrative character from hospitals as well as from other sources;

(2) all alphabetic and numeric data should be acceptable by the computer system;

(3) all available input media should be applicable—punched cards, punched paper tape, optical mark readers, remote terminals, etc.;

(4) both coded data and free text should be permitted. Natural language (free text) must be used for qualitative data which is not always easily dealt with by a coding system;

(5) new data and information, new forms, or new documents should be introducible at any time to the computer system without new computer programs;

(6) each computer function should be one program one module, and each program should be combinable with different programs (functions) in an optional way;

(7) all data in the computer record should be in an accessible, retrievable form;

(8) all data should be presented, irrespective of storage format, in an easily understandable form; and the system should be easy to use without knowledge of computer programming;

(9) the system should allow statistical and mathematical analyses.

D. PROJECT, ORGANIZATION, AND MANAGEMENT

The KS project, during the first phase 1965–1970, was directed by a special committee with members from the hospital, the Karolinska Institute, and the Swedish Agency for Administrative Development. During this period, a special clinic—the "Medical Development Clinic" (MDC)— was made available to the project team, and this clinic furnished the basic material necessary for the work. A special agreement was reached during the same period between the Swedish Agency and IBM for cooperation in developing and testing a hospital information system.

Since 1967, various computer applications have been in full operation without parallel manual routines, and these are managed by the ordinary organization of the hospital. One division (KARDAC) of the hospital handles the daily operation of the two computers (IBM 360/40 and IBM 1800); another division (Department of Medical Information) is responsible for further implementation, testing, and development. The total staff including all members totals 50, equally divided between the two divisions.

E. HARDWARE AND SOFTWARE

Within the hospital computer center, the following equipment is located:

1. IBM 360/40

IBM 2040	Processing unit	256 K bytes memory
IBM 1052	Console typewriter	
5 IBM 2402-03	Magnetic tape units	
IBM 2314	Disk storage unit	Up to 233 million bytes
IBM 2540	Card read punch	Reads 100 cards/min, punches 300 cards/min
IBM 2671	Paper tape reader	
IBM 1403	Line printer	1100 lines/min

2.   IBM 1800

IBM 1801	Processor-controller	32 K words of core storage
3 IBM 1810	Disk storage unit	512,000 words each
IBM 1816	Console typewriter	
IBM 1442	Card read punch	Reads 300 cards/min, punches 80 col/sec
IBM 1443	Printer	240 lines/min
IBM 1627	Plotter	

Distributed throughout the various subsystems of the hospital is the following equipment:

3.   Terminal Equipment

12 IBM 2260	Display units
IBM 1826/2	Terminal for digital input-output signals
IBM 1828/2	Terminal for analog input-output signals

15 punch card and 10 paper tape punch machines.

F.   THE COMPUTER MEDICAL RECORD

The development of the automated medical record system started in 1962 at the Seraphimer hospital in Stockholm. The system consists of a number of functions or modules for collecting, storing, processing, and presenting data. These functions have attained such a degree of flexibility that new applications can be introduced without additional or repeated programming. This degree of flexibility is necessary since new computer applications that cannot be anticipated are emerging, and new diagnoses, symptoms, laboratory tests, pharmaceutical drugs, etc., do appear constantly. Within health and sick care, one works with an unlimited and undefined amount of rapidly changing data and information which can be only partly (up to 80%) standardized and codified. The amount of data and information also differs from patient to patient—e.g., a patient with an uncomplicated fracture of the leg may require very little data compared to a patient with a myocardial infarct and in severe shock. It is against this background that the requirements for general and flexible computer systems have developed in the world of medical data processing.

The software program for the automated medical record system is called "J5," where J stands for journal or record and 5 indicates that the first four versions were not fully designed because the need for a flexible, general system was not yet understood.

J5 was originally programmed in Algol-Genius for SAAB D21. In January 1967, a reprogramming of J5 in Cobol for IBM 360 was started at the Karolinska Hospital as an activity for using automatic data processing in health organizations and hospitals. The following summarize the main functions which J5 can perform:

(1) Read, store, decode, and write out coded items associated with medical histories, physical examinations, doctor's notes, nurses' notes, laboratory data, discharge summaries, etc. or any coded information.

(2) Read, store, and write out additional information in natural language (free text) as it was entered, or by key-words.

(3) Retrieve and select a specific medical record or part of a record.

(4) Make simple statistical calculations as well as provide linear pattern recognition.

In addition to the above-mentioned main functions, several minor functions are available. New functions which have been added to the first batch-version of the J5 system include on-line facilities for admission routines, for updating of the medical record system, and for booking procedures. The new data bank is called "J5-T1."

In this computer system, the "medical record library" is stored on magnetic tape (the cheapest suitable storage device); and one reel of tape can store between 4,000 and 15,000 patient records. The computer medical record library allows storage of all data and information about one patient on the same physical spot on the tape. Different records or parts of records from different hospitals' subsystems are merged together and linked to one record. The record linkage is made possible through the use of the individual patient's civic registration number, assigned to him at birth, and/or a reserve number (see below).

The magnetic tape is a slow access device, and the automated record system produces hard copies only once a day. At the beginning, record printouts were produced twice a day, but our experience with the integrated manual and automated record system of today showed that this frequency was not needed. For fast access, it is possible to retrieve by remote terminals only a small portion of the record, mainly including admission and administrative data. No clinic data are presented as yet on on-line terminals because of unsolved problems in security and privacy of patient information.

1.   A Brief Description of System J5

A central function in J5 is the ability to create, maintain, and retrieve a computer library which exists as data and information on magnetic tapes or disks. The main file in which information on patients (or other individuals) is stored and accumulated is identified in the following pages as the Computer Medical Record Library (CMRL). In the library, all data and information which can be expressed as digits or alphabetic characters, so-called alphanumeric information, can be stored.

All medical and administrative data can thus be stored in the computer medical record library, but the total mass of data is split into a number of computer records (CR). There is almost always more than one computer record per patient. The number of alphanumeric characters and the type of data and information varies for different computer records within wide limits—from 10 characters to thousands of characters. The size of the computer record is to a large extent dependent on the individual (the user) who adds data and information to the library (CMRL). The individuals adding to the record library generally give their data and information according to some relationship, medical or administrative, between the sets of information which are registered within one computer record. In addition, it is generally required that data within one computer record shall pertain to one individual patient and be registered in one place at one point of time.

In the computer record library, the computer records are so arranged that all records pertaining to one single patient will follow in direct sequence. The computer records on a single patient are stored per type of information in the data segment, within type of information per date, and within date per clinic and wards. As a rule, this order is changed at the time of presentation of information from the CMRL.

To transport data to and from the library and to make possible processing of the information, e.g., of statistical nature, a number of data processing procedures have been created within J5. These procedures or functions are described in the programming language, which is Algol-Genius for the SAAB D21–22 systems and Cobol Assembler for the IBM 360–370 systems.

The procedures can be linked in a flexible way to chains of data processing applications. Such a chain of procedures can, for example, provide for input, interpretation, storing, and printing of the data. In another application of retrieval in the computer medical record library, statistical processing and display of results, may be required.

The data in the computer medical record is self-interpretative—that is, each term is preceded by a label. At the time of data input, which can be performed from punched cards or tapes or on-line terminals, the label corresponds to symbols preceding each type of term. Examples of symbols are *n, *cln, and *date, which mean name, clinic, and date, respectively. Several symbols are defined and, together with certain other symbols, they make up the J5 language. Also information which originally is not self-interpretative can be accepted. For example, a punched card in which no symbols are punched but where the meaning of the terms depends on their position in the card is interpreted through a dictionary in which the data fields of the card are described in advance and which, therefore, can add the correct symbols to each term.

At the time of printout of information from the computer record library, the codes have to be substituted by free texts for the sake of readability. A separate dictionary exists in which for each code the corresponding free text statement is registered.

When information is read into the computer record library or printed out from it, the system J5 uses a number of auxiliary files:

(1) symbol dictionary, containing the J5 language symbols;

(2) field description dictionary, containing descriptions on input cards, field by field;

(3) text dictionary, containing the free text statements corresponding to the codes; and

(4) register of forms and code orders.

The picture below shows the information flow within J5-T1:

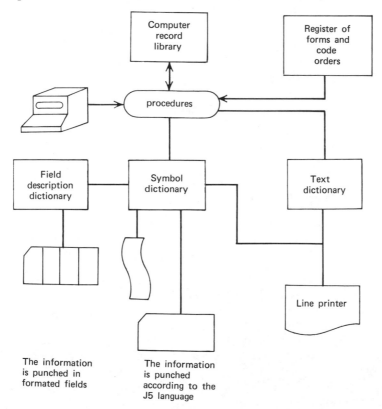

The information punched according to the J5 language in paper tape or on punched cards or added to the system over on line terminals must pass a symbol dictionary in connection with the input. There the symbols are interpreted and converted into the labels, which are stored together with the data in the computer record library.

Cards or magnetic tape with fixed structure information are read in via the field description dictionary in which data from different fields in the card will be augmented with the correct symbols. Then interpretation via the symbol dictionary will take place as described above. At the time of printout of information from the computer record library, the system uses mainly the text dictionary, but also the symbol dictionary will be used in this connection for "reverse" interpretation of certain labels which are to be printed out in free text—e.g., dates.

The retrieval of information from the computer record library can be performed in several ways. The most common form is when somebody has asked for printout of a patient's record (everything which is stored in the library about that patient) or parts thereof. This retrieval is guided by symbols which are included in the J5 language. For instance, when using the symbol *rout, one will get as printout a full record on a patient.

A more advanced method of retrieval exists for the case when someone wants to retrieve data from the records for several patients for whom a set of certain conditions are met—e.g., that the value on a certain laboratory test or the patient's age shall not exceed a certain limit. The conditions according to which the retrieval should take place have to be specified according to rules defined for J5.

Following retrieval, the information can be treated in different ways—e.g., printout of the data can be made or the data can be transformed within a statistical process.

2.   The Computer Record (CR)

Each computer record (CR) can be divided into one fixed and one variable part called header and data segment, respectively.

Header segment	Data segment
Header terms (fixed number)	Data terms (arbitrary number)

The computer record always starts with a number of terms, called header terms and data terms. The header terms are fixed to the extent that they include a fixed number of data fields in a fixed sequence. Data and information to be stored in one of each of these fields are also predetermined. The data in the header segment pertain to patient identification;

reporting hospital clinic, and ward; and date for registration as well as flags or form numbers for what type of data and information exist in the data segment—e.g., data on chemical laboratory tests, report on a surgical operation, discharge summary. The fixed structure of the header facilitates routine data processing of computer records.

The number of header terms is fixed and needs no labelling, since the type of the header terms is determined by their position in the record.

3. Comments on Header Terms

a. Date of birth.   This describes for whom the data and information in the data segment are valid. It expresses year, month, and day—e.g., 03 12 24 if the patient was born on December 24th, 1903.

b. Birth index number.   This is the 3-digit number which follows the birthdate in the complete Swedish civic registration number. If the true birth index number is missing, a negative number is stored instead.

c. Health care unit.   This identifies the hospital or any other health care delivery unit (cottage hospital, private practician, etc.), and this term is a code. A free-text sentence defined in the symbol dictionary and corresponding to the code is written at the time of printout of the medical record.

d. Clinic.   Can be a maximum of 12 alphanumerical characters.

e. Ward.   Can be a maximum of 12 alphanumerical characters. Note that the terms health care unit, clinic, and ward describe the place where the information in the data segment was registered. This may not necessarily be the same clinic or ward where the patient is presently located.

f. Sequence number.   Can be a maximum of 7 digits.

g. Form number.   The term is an integer (maximum 7 digits) which is a code for the form used for the registration of the information in the record.

h. Version.   Version is normally zero except in computer records in which the data segment contains the patient's name, address, telephone number, occupation, etc. The term is a positive integer:

Version	The data segment contains only
1	Name
2	Address
3	Telephone number
4	Postal address
5	Occupation

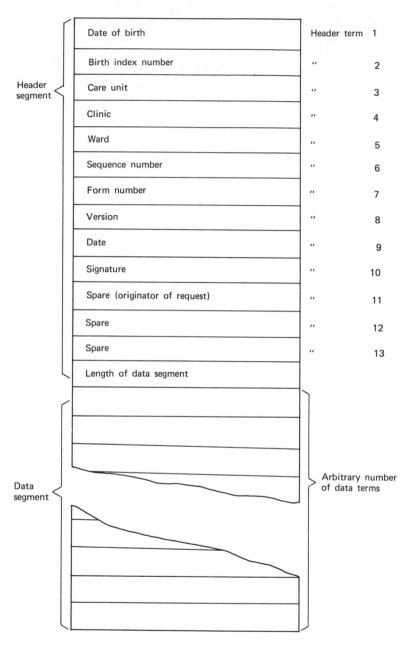

The structure of the computer record, Cobol/360.

i.   Date.   This is the date when the information was registered.

j.   Signature.   Identifies the person responsible for the registration of the information. (Maximum 12 alphanumerical characters.)

k.   Length of data segment.   Expresses the length of the data part in number of words of 4 bytes.

l.   Spare segment.   The spare terms are of importance only for the internal handling of the records in the system and will not be further described here.

4.   Control Symbols for the Header Terms

Symbols are needed in input data to generate labeling of data terms. In the same sense, control symbols preceding the header terms are needed for proper positioning of terms in the header part of the record. These *header symbols* are the following:

Header term	Control symbol
Civic registration number (birth date *and* index number)	*i
Care unit	*cau
Clinic	*cln
Ward	*ward
Patient number	*no
Sex	*mal *fem
Form number	*fno
Date	*date

The data segment, which as a rule contains a much larger number of alphabetic characters than the header, has a variable structure that fully adapts itself to the data and information to be registered. To save space in the computer medical record library and to facilitate retrieval, attempts have been made to create a reasonable standardization of the free text information into fixed sentences and to store in the library only numerical codes corresponding to those sentences. The relation between the storage space needed for a code and the storage space needed for the corresponding free text varies from 1:1 to 1:100.

The data segment can be looked upon as consisting of an arbitrary number of code groups, each containing one or more terms. The total number of terms is thus unlimited. If the sum of the length of the terms exceeds a certain limit, the record will be subdivided into a number of computer records. All these subrecords will have an identical header part. This circumstance will create no problems for the user.

The term is the smallest accessible data unit in the data segment of the computer record. A term consists of a sequence of characters, and/or digits and/or special symbols—alphabetic information. The type of information contained in a term, as well as the length of the term and in some cases a fixed text which is to appear before the term in the print-outs must be defined in the system by the user.

The data segment can be regarded as a sequence of an arbitrary number of terms. The meaning of a term can best be explained by some examples. The most common terms are codes; and least common are measurement values, free-text sentences, numerical identifiers, signatures, etc. All terms that are not coded are preceded by a label which, among other things, describes the type of term. Depending on the label information, the term 1235 can be interpreted as the time 12:35 hours, as a measurement value, or as a numerical identifier. In other words, we discuss here self-interpretative data since each term is described by a label which immediately precedes it (the absence of a label preceding the codes is in itself a type of labeling). New terms can easily be introduced into the J5 system, provided that these terms are initially defined to the system to generate a correct labeling during the subsequent data processing. For most types of terms, the restriction exists that they have to be tied to such data which can be presented by codes to make the content of the term meaningful. A single measurement value represents meaningless information. The free text, however, is an exception from this rule since a free-text sentence in many cases can be meaningful without being tied to any other kind of data.

To clarify the concept of term further, the most commonly used terms will be reviewed and summarized.

A code is a positive integer. Each single code represents the information which the user has decided it to represent. A code may mean an answer to a question in a questionnaire, a name of a laboratory test, etc. At the time of presentation of the information from the library, the codes are generally translated into such corresponding sentences in free text that the user has decided upon.

A code followed by an arbitrary number of terms is identified as a code group, and the initial code is called major code. There is no rule preventing the codes following the major code to consist fully or partly of codes.

The second most common type of term is the label. This type of term is special to the extent that the label is used only to describe the term immediately following it or, in some cases, a number of terms. All existing labels must be defined in the system. In the library, they are stored as negative integers.

For example: A sequence of terms consisting of a code, a label, and an additional term are stored in sequence in the following way:

Code	Label	Additional term
12	−101	1230

This sequence of terms is interpreted according to the following logic:

The term 12 is a positive integer, and thus it is a code. The meaning of this code depends on the form number which is stored in the header segment of the computer record and is specified in the system by the user; it may, for example, be WHITE BLOOD CELLS. The term -101 is negative and is thus interpreted as a label. The meaning of the label is registered in the system (symbol dictionary). In this case, the label indicates that the additional term 1230 is a value that should be tied to the preceding code 12. Taken together, the exemplified sequence of terms thus means: The number of WHITE BLOOD CELLS are 1230.

If in place of the label another negative integer had appeared, e.g., -1112, the content of information in the sequence of terms would have changed. the label -1112 means that the following terms should be regarded as time-tied to preceding code, and the information is then: WHITE BLOOD CELLS at 12:30 hours.

A label describes the following term(s) and links them to the preceding code. The description in general includes the three following characteristics; type; length; storage format (only of interest from a data-processing viewpoint). Besides codes and labels, the following are examples of terms which have been defined in the system:

Term	"External" control symbols to generate labeling
Value	A decimal point somewhere in the value
Alphabetical text	*a (or *aa)
Negative statement	Minus sign preceding the code
Uncertain	*after the code
Not carried out	**after the code
Date	*date
Number	*no
Signature	*sgn
One alphanumerical word	*word
Time	*t
Integer	*int
Decimal number	*dec
Diagnosis ⎫	*di
Surgical operation ⎬ (codes)	*su
Anesthetics ⎭	*an

A term of any of the above-mentioned types will thus be preceded in the library by a label that describes its type, length, and storage format. To make labeling possible in connection with storage of terms, all the terms used (e.g., punched in tapes or cards) have to be preceded by symbols corresponding to the labels, or so-called control symbols. The control symbols will be reviewed in more detail in connection with the J5 language, of which they form a part.

5. Code Groups

A code group is a sequence of one or more terms. The first term of the code group is always a code which is called the major code.
Code group:

CODE	TERM$_1$	TERM$_2$	$\cdots$	TERM$_N$

The structure of the code group is often such that every second term is a label and every second term one of the term types stated above. For example:

CODE	LABEL	TIME	LABEL	VALUE	LABEL	TEXT

Such a structure would be created in connection with storage of information such as the following:
WHITE BLOOD CELLS AT 12:30   120—WRONG COUNT?
punched in the following way (12 is the code for white blood cells):
          12 * t 1230 120. *a WRONG COUNT?
Several of the terms of the code groups (except the major code) can be codes. These codes in the code group must then be preceded by a label, called level label, which states that the codes belong to the code group. Without such a label the codes would be interpreted as superior codes in new code groups. An example of such a code group structure is:

CODE	LEVEL LABEL (descending)	CODE	TERM$_1$	TERM$_2$	...TERM$_N$	LEVEL LABEL (descending)	CODE	LEVEL LABEL (ascending)

Thanks to the level label, all 3 codes above will belong to the same code group. The concept of "level" points to the circumstance that the codes within the code group can be regarded as subordinated to the opening code—i.e., the codes exist on different levels. A code on a certain level is regarded as superior to all codes on a lower level within the same code group. In the level labeling, there exists, consequently, also information on which level the following codes (and possibly other terms) belong to. In the J5 language, the levels are identified by brackets. If, for instance, the codes 10, 50, and 70 should be stored on successively lower levels, the following is punched:

$$10 \ (50 \ (70))$$

As a summary, it can be stated that a code group consists of an arbitrary number of terms preceded by a code.

6. Summary of the J5-T1 System

a. A data processing system for patient information.   In 1966, the Council for Hospital Operational Rationalization (SJURA) in Sweden investigated the demands on a computer oriented medical record or a patient information system. According to the council, such a system should allow:

(1) storage of all alphanumeric data about the patient on a computer oriented medium, e.g., magnetic tape, disks, or drums;

(2) use of all kinds of input media—punched cards, punched paper tape, on-line terminals etc.;

(3) retrieval of every item of all data about the patient;

(4) presentation of all data in noncoded form, which means that the output should be completely verbal and readable by anyone;

(5) processing of all data by statistical or nonstatistical methods;

(6) entry of new data from new applications into the automated system should not require extra programming work unless new functions are needed;

(7) codification of practically all data should be allowed for, but the system should be able to handle free text or narrative information;

(8) access time to the data should depend upon the application.

b. Characteristics of J5-T1.   The J5-T1 system consists of about 40 computer programs and is built on the above-mentioned specifications. J5 is a batch processing system capable of handling all kinds of alphanumeric data and storing it on magnetic tape. The on-line part with disk storage is called T1 and is specially designed for admission and discharge routines and for appointment scheduling functions. The on-line part can present administrative data and a small amount of medical data. All alphanumeric data and information can be added to the medical record system J5 through T1.

The flexibility in the J5 system is maintained by using modularity, general storage format, and parameter control of computer programs. Modularity implies that the system consists of a number of separate modules of computer programs and that every function of the system corresponds to one program.

The programs can be linked in various ways in order to satisfy the demands of various applications. The condition for modularity is a general way of storing data within the system, which means that no intermediate ways of storing data are used. Every program generates an output which can be handled by every other program. An exception is the specialized programs which transfer data to and from the system. That means that data and information are stored in the computer record in variable field length. The on-line part of the system has, however, a fixed field length.

7. J5-T1 in Clinical Practice

Data are collected in special forms, questionnaires, etc., which provide structures and codes for data and information. Forms have been designed for physical examination in, e.g., surgery and internal medicine. Questionnaires have been developed for medical history-taking in allergology, internal medicine, multiphasic testing, etc. New or redesigned forms or questionnaires can be used in the computer system without reprogramming. Data and information can be both alphabetic and numeric and are transferred to the system by paper tape, punch cards, magnetic tape, or on-line terminals. Data, mainly administrative, are partly stored in the on-line part T1, and all data and information are stored in the batch system J5, the medico-administrative record system. The data are printed out in decoded form with additional narrative data which is entirely verbal. The presentation can without reprogramming be changed according to specifications by the user. Simple statistical calculations—frequency analysis, mean values, standard deviation—as well as discriminant analysis can be performed.[1-6]

G. THE PATIENT SCHEDULING/BOOKING SYSTEM

Patient care involves qualified personnel and expensive equipment distributed over several clinical specialities (clinics) and service units (laboratories)—approximately 50 at Karolinska Hospital. In a manual system, it is difficult—or almost impossible—to coordinate all these resources to achieve efficient utilization and an even workload. To plan the patient's course through the health care delivery system is even more difficult.

It is usually the hospital medical staff who spends considerable time scheduling patient activities—laboratory examinations, x-ray investigations, visits to outpatient departments or to special consultants or physicians, admission, discharge, etc. The patient's general well-being could be positively enhanced by reducing the time he spends waiting for and/or traveling to and from the appointments.

With a manual scheduling system, improvements in these areas are extremely difficult to accomplish, especially if a large number of facilities and a high volume of appointments are involved. However, if all of the data required to schedule appointments were centralized and a monitoring agent were able to scan them, such improvements would be feasible.

These features characterize our computerized scheduling system. The computer programs scan the resources available and coordinate the appointments around the patient's course through the health care delivery system.

A summary of the major features of the Computerized Scheduling System:

(1) more effective scheduling of patient's time and course.

(2) reduced number of visits for the patient to the hospital for different laboratory examinations, consultations, etc.

(3) increased "real" nursing and physician time and reduced administrative work.

(4) increased effectivity of communications.

(5) productivity control.

1. General Description

The Patient Scheduling System is a real-time system complemented by batch (off-line) functions and is a part of J5-T1 system. A computer terminal may be physically attached to the computer (local mode) or communicate with the computer via telephone lines (remote mode). This means that terminals can be located at each ward, at each clinic, or at central locations in the hospital—so-called hospital administration centers (HAC).

Scheduling alternatives are provided by the computer programs after they have scanned the disk files according to parameters entered from the terminal. Stored on the disks are various files which contain such data as the type of and the length of each examination, facilities at which each examination can be performed, pre- and post-examination time required, and the current time available for appointments at each facility. These files are created by the user and may be altered at any time as his requirements change. The system can be used to solve scheduling problems other than within a hospital because of the high degree of flexibility.

Parameters which steer or guide the programs in scanning the data are entered via the terminal. These parameters are derived from the specific requirements of each patient. The varied use of these parameters depends on the specific patient's situation: his condition, the urgency of the appointment, the patient's personal schedule.

After obtaining "guidelines" from the terminal, the program scans the disk files to locate the resources, the appointment time, the facility, or the combination of appointments which meet the specifications. The appointments selected are presented on the visual display unit so that the terminal operator may make the final choice or, if appropriate, reject the alternatives. The appointments actually scheduled as a result of this procedure are sent to the terminal printer.

In addition to actual scheduling, the system also includes on-line cancellation functions, display of current appointments per patient and facility, and display of remaining available time per facility. The batch functions include summary lists of appointments per patient, lists of appointments per facility per day, and large-scale file maintenance. In addition, the data stored in the scheduling can be transferred to the computer medical record system, where different statistical procedures are available.

2. Disc Files

The system requires the following disc files:

(1) Time-Available File
(2) Examination File
(3) Facilities File
(4) Facility Selection Code File
(5) Appointment File

It is the user's responsibility to load the first four files with the data which meet his requirements. The fifth, or Appointment File, is the "output" file, which will contain the scheduled appointments.

The Time-Available File contains the time currently available for appointments at each facility. It encompasses a period of three months. (See Figure 18–1.)

The Examination File is loaded with information about each examination. Figure 18–2 shows the categories of data contained on this file. It is organized according to examination codes, which are those codes used as the scheduling parameters.

The Facilities File contains specific information about each facility, such as the name, emergency time for priority cases, and a code to indicate its physical location in respect to other facilities. The file is organized according to facility codes, the same used in the Examination File records.

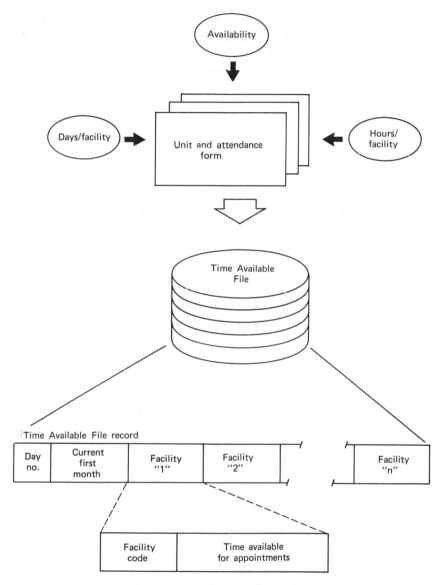

Figure 18–1. Time-Available File.

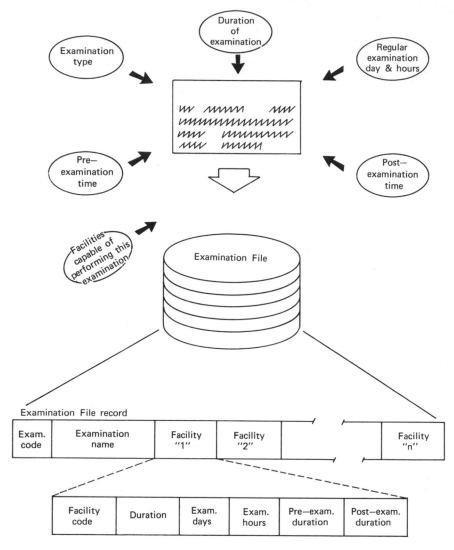

Figure 18–2. Examination File

Contained in the Facility Selection Code File are the preassigned combination codes which represent groups of facilities.

When a patient is referred to the hospital as an inpatient or outpatient, or during the ward round or the visit to an outpatient department, the doctor or the nurse fills in an Examination Request Form (Figure 18–3) specifying the type of laboratory tests, x-rays, consultations, etc., to be performed. This form is sent to the ward secretary, who will schedule appointments for

EXAMINATION REQUEST FORM

KAROLINSKA SJUKHUSET   Ansvarig vårdgrupp nr

UTREDNINGSPLAN   ....

| Läkare *Hall* |
| Sjuksköterska |
| Sekreterare |

22 08 15 5453
Eltinsson Sven D
Vasa Ö Valthornsg.7
VALLHAMN

DATUM FÖR IFYLLNAD	År	Datum 5/10	Datum	Datum	Datum	Datum	Datum	Datum	Datum	Datum	Datum	Datum	Datum	Datum	Datum
KEM LAB, HÄMATOLOGI Hb		X													
Hämatokrit															
MCV/MCHC															
Vita blkr		X													
Diff		X													
Trombocyter															
Retikulocyter															
SR		X													
Blodsocker															
TT															
KEM LAB, URIN Osmolaritet i morgonurin															
Protein och glukos		X													
Sediment															
KEM LAB, FAECES Weber															
Blodgruppering															

KS 800

Figure 18–3a.

EXAMINATION REQUEST FORM

KAROLINSKA SJUKHUSET   Ansvarig vårdgrupp nr

UTREDNINGSPLAN   ....

Läkare **Hall**
Sjuksköterska
Sekreterare

22 08 15 5453
Eltinsson Sven D
Vasa Ö Valthornsg.7
VALLHAMN

DATUM FÖR IFYLLNAD	År	Datum 5/10	Datum	Datum	Datum	Datum	Datum	Datum	Datum	Datum	Datum	Datum	Datum	Datum
ÖPPEN VÅRD Läkarbesök		X												
Nybesök, intyg, förlängt besök etc														
Sjuksköterskebesök														
DAGVÅRD														
SLUTEN VÅRD														
JOURNAL UTAN PATIENT														
FRÅGELISTOR Tidigare sjd		X												
Nuvarande sjd		X												
Socialanamnes														

Anteckningar (stansas inte)

År	Mån	Dag	
....	....	....	
....	....	....	
....	....	....	
....	....	....	
....	....	....	

	AVSLUTAD BEHANDLINGSPERIOD Ingen ytterligare åtgärd (EJ–ÅTG)	☐		SJUKSKRIVEN T O M ÅR MÅN DAG
........l....l.......	Remitterad till (REM)	☐ inremitterande läkare (INLÄK)		........l....l.......
........l....l.......		☐ annan ext läkare (EXTLÄK)		........l....l.......
........l....l.......		☐ annat sjukhus (AN–SJH)		........l....l.......
........l....l.......	Journalkopia, epikris till:			

Figure 18–3b.

EXAMINATION REQUEST FORM

KAROLINSKA SJUKHUSET	Ansvarig vårdgrupp nr	22 08 15 5453

UTREDNINGSPLAN ....

Eltinsson Sven D

Vasa Ö Valthornsg.7

VALLHAMN

Läkare	*Hall*
Sjuksköterska	
Sekreterare	

DATUM FÖR IFYLLNAD	År	Datum 3/10	Datum	Datum	Datum	Datum	Datum	Datum	Datum	Datum	Datum	Datum	Datum	Datum
VÅRDGRUPPS– ÅTGÄRDER Omläggning														
Proktoskopi/Rektoskopi														
Vikt														
Blodtryck														
KONSULTER Kir														
Med														
Öron														
Gyn														
Ögon														
Kurator														
Dietist														
FYS LAB EKG		X												
Arbetsprov														
Spirometri														
FKG														

Figure 18–3c.

EXAMINATION REQUEST FORM

KAROLINSKA SJUKHUSET   Ansvarig vårdgrupp nr   22 08 15 5453

UTREDNINGSPLAN   ....   Eltinsson Sven D

Läkare   *Hall*   Vasa Ö Valthornsg.7

Sjuksköterska   VALLHAMN

Sekreterare

DATUM FÖR IFYLLNAD	År	Datum 5/10	Datum	Datum	Datum	Datum	Datum	Datum	Datum	Datum	Datum	Datum	Datum	Datum
RÖNTGEN Pulm		X												
Cor		X												
Urografi														
Colon														
Galla														
Ventrikel														
Sinus														
PATOL LAB STP														
Cyt/Px ( )														
BAKT LAB Sputumodling														
Urinodling		X												
Gc-kompl bindn														
WR														

Figure 18–3d.

EXAMINATION REQUEST FORM

KAROLINSKA SJUKHUSET   Ansvarig vårdgrupp nr   22 08 15 5453

UTREDNINGSPLAN   ....   Eltinsson Sven D

Läkare _Hall_   Vasa Ö Valthornsg.7

Sjuksköterska   VALLHAMN

Sekreterare

DATUM FÖR IFYLLNAD	År	Datum 5/10	Datum	Datum	Datum	Datum	Datum	Datum	Datum	Datum	Datum	Datum	Datum	Datum	Datum
KEM LAB, BLOD/SERUM Järn, TIBC															
Kreatinin															
Elektrolyter (Na, K, Cl, Bi)		X													
Kalcium															
Fosfor															
Bilirubin															
GOT, GPT															
Alkaliska fosf															
Sura fosf															
Kolesterol /triglyc															
PBJ/T_3															
Glukos															
Serumelektrofores															

Figure 18–3e.

the examinations via the display unit. The secretary may contact the patient before or during the scheduling procedure so that his personal schedule can be considered when the actual appointments are made.

3. Scheduling

Scheduling begins with a request for the scheduling form, which is presented on the display unit. Such a "form" is shown in Figure 18–4. The completion of the scheduling form with the appropriate digits and codes provides the parameters used to steer the scheduling process.

4. Use of Scheduling Parameters

a. Patient identification number (line 1).   This is a unique number which is assigned to a patient when he is registered in the data bank J5-T1. The scheduling system uses it to retrieve the patient's name, address, and clinic from the on-line files. If, at the time of scheduling, this information is not present in the files, the system will register the patient before proceeding. (See the admission routine below.)

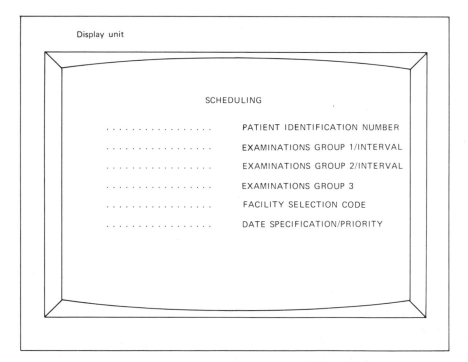

Figure 18–4.   Scheduling form as it appears on the display unit.

The civic registration number is used as the Patient Identification Number. It is a 10-digit number consisting of the birth date in the form YYMMDD, a 3-digit sequence number, and a check digit. However, if this number is not available, a temporary reserve number is assigned. One example of this type of number is a 10-digit combination containing the year the patient was treated at the hospital for the first time (YY), a 2-digit number between 90 and 99 (identifying it as a temporary number), a 5-digit sequence number, and a check digit. (See patient registration below.)

b.   Examinations group 1–3 (lines 2–4).   An examination is expressed by a 4-digit code. A group of examinations is, by definition, the examinations which are to be scheduled on the same day. One to three examinations may be included in each group. Each examination code is separated by a comma. As many as nine examinations for one patient may be entered in one scheduling form. If additional appointments are necessary, any number of additional entries may be made.

c.   Interval codes (lines 2–3).   An Interval Code, included after either or both of the first two examination groups, restricts the ordering of the appointments. Normally, each "group" of examinations will be scheduled on different days and on the earliest possible day for each group. By entering a digit of value from 1–96 as an Interval Code, two groups will be forced apart that number of days. For example, in Figure 18–5, examination 0010 (Group 3) will be scheduled three or more days later than examination 0525 (Group 2), regardless of the first available day found for examination 0010. An Interval Code of "0" or "A" causes the two groups to be scheduled on the *same* day. The difference between these two codes is the arrangement of the examinations on *that* day. The "0" parameter code directs all of the examinations in the first group to be arranged before the second group's examinations, while an "A" code indicates that no special order need be maintained.

d.   Facility selection code (line 5).   Normally the system chooses a facility from the group of all units capable of performing an examination. If this is not desirable, the selection may be limited to a specific facility or facilities. This selection is indicated by entering a code representing a particular facility or combination of facilities. For example, in Figure 18–5, if the Facility Selection Code 1050 represents unit 51, it will be the only facility checked for available time in scheduling examination 0010. Asterisks indicate no special facility considerations for the corresponding examinations.

e.   Date specification (line 6).   The system always seeks the first available day. The day on which the scheduling is being done is not considered

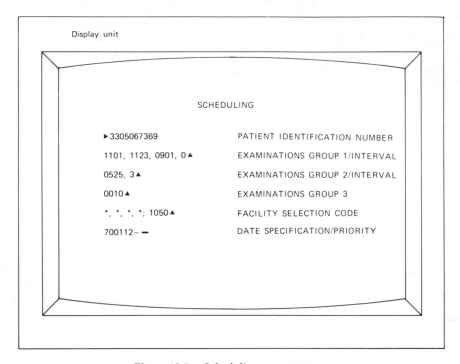

Figure 18-5. Scheduling parameters.

available, but unless a Date Specification parameter is entered, all other days are checked. If "YYMMDD-" is entered, no days before that date will be considered. If "-YYMMDD" is used, no days after that date will be checked. Correspondingly, an entry of "YYMMDD-YYMMDD" specifies a period of unavailable days.

f.   Priority (line 6). Time can be reserved at each facility for emergency cases. By specifying an "F" on line 6 following the Date Specification, the reserved time will be added to the currently available time for each facility, thus assuring that the patient will be scheduled as soon as possible.

5.   Scheduling Logic

After the completed form has been sent from the terminal, the scheduling programs create a table in core for each appointment requested. Each table contains the possible appointment times still available; the three earliest possible days are selected. In the case of interrelated appointments on the same day, the most optimal combination is selected. The most optimal solution is the earliest day on which all examinations can be scheduled and the appointment times on that day which provide the shortest interval between examinations.

Three alternatives for each group of examinations are sent to the display unit. A suitable alternative for each group is chosen by the terminal operator by transmitting a coded "answer" back to the system. The "answer" indicates to the system the alternatives which should be registered in the Appointment File. The remaining alternatives are restored to the Time-Available File. After a list of the newly registered appointments is sent to the terminal printer, the scheduling procedure is complete.

6. Experience with the Scheduling System

While the scheduling system was in use for two years in the Medical Development Clinic, there were definite indications of the effects discussed in the introductory paragraph. The simplified communications is an obvious result. By storing the data for the available resources centrally, the number of contact routes is considerably reduced.

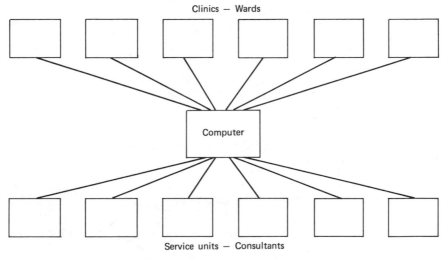

Communication via computer.

The scheduling process has been considerably simplified, resulting in less time spent on actual scheduling tasks. The time gained is conceivably absorbed by the nurses for actual nursing tasks. The overall coordination of the patient's examinations has also resulted in a reduction in a patient's total time at the hospital. This is advantageous to the patient as well as to the hospital staff and facilities. The scheduling/booking system is a very valuable subsystem to the automated medical record and includes "administrative" data about the patient and the resources. The results of the scheduling procedures—laboratory test results, doctor's orders, therapy, diagnoses, etc., the "medical" data—are naturally not stored or handled in the scheduling system but in the automated record system.

H. SUBSYSTEMS

1. Administrative Functions

a. Patient registration and identification.   Since 1966, a specific computer system has been in use for the inpatient admission and discharge routine. Approximately 40,000 admissions have been included per year. The computer system was a batch processing system, but since 1968 the routine has been integrated in the automated medical record system and is now a subroutine to the data bank; the J5-T1 and can be updated on- or off-line (Figures 18–6, 18–7, and 18–8).

In the data bank, a reference or identity register is created for the registration of all admissions for inpatients as well as outpatients. When, for example, a referral note arrives, the secretary in the Hospital Administration Centers (HACs) finds out if the patient is already registered in the data bank. If not, she waits for the registration form to appear on the IBM 2260 terminal. The identity register can also be updated by punch cards or paper tape, and the register is the first part of the automated medical record. The identification of the patient is obtained by an unique Civic

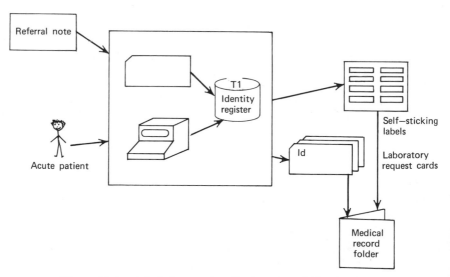

Figure 18–6.   Admission routine. Registration of identity data.

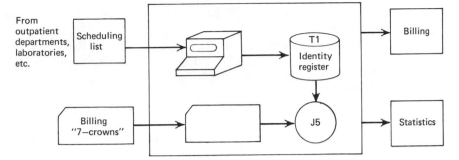

Figure 18–7.   Admission routine. Outpatients.

Registration Number (CRN) or when it is not available by a special Reserve Registration Number (RRN). The CRN is a 10-digit number composed of three parts:

(1) Six digits for birthdate in the order year (two last digits of birthyear), month, day.

(2) A 3-digit regional sequence number given to the individual shortly after birth. Males become odd numbers, females even ones.

(3) One check-digit calculated from the other digits according to the modulus-10 rule.

The digits of the CRN are normally written in sequence or with a space or a hyphen between birthdate and the following digits—i.e., 3610114310 or 361011 4310 or 361011-4310.

The RRN is used when the patient has no CRN—i.e., a newborn baby or a foreigner—or when the patient's CRN for any other reason is not at hand and data about him must be entered into the computer system. The composition of the 10-digit RRN is as follows:

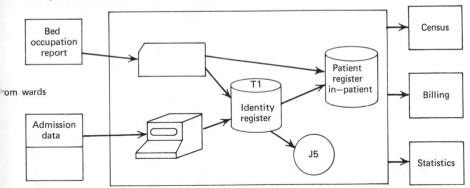

Figure 18–8.   Admission routine. Inpatients.

(1) Two digits for the year when the patient was given the RRN, i.e., 72 for 1972.

(2) One digit which is greater than 1. This separates the RRN from a CRN because the third digit in a CRN, which corresponds to the first digit of the month in the birthdate, can never be greater than 1.

(3) A 6-digit sequence number from 000001 to 999999.

(4) One check-digit calculated in the same way as for the CRN.

It is possible to create a series of 8 million RRNs every year. Each of these numbers will be unique and will not appear again during a period of 100 years. Hitherto it has been necessary to use an RRN for only about 2% of all patients.

Each new patient obtains through this admission routine a number of self-sticking labels upon which are printed by the computer the identity number, name, address, telephone number, etc.[7]

Since 1970, an admission routine for all outpatients has been in operation. The routine uses the J5-system, and approximately 450,000 admissions are taken care of per year. The two systems for inpatients and outpatients are from a technical point of view integrated in one computer system, which takes care of approximately 0.5 million admissions per year (see Table 2).

b. Billing, accounting, and payroll. Two separate billing systems are in operation in the hospital—one for inpatients and one for outpatients. The inpatient billing routine has been in operation since 1966 and is a part of the above-mentioned admission routine for inpatients. Since 1968, this subsystem has been an integrated part of the automated medical record system J5-T1. The outpatient billing routine is identical with J5 and is a part of the above-mentioned admission routine for outpatients.

Non-sophisticated and sophisticated accounting and payroll computer systems are undergoing testing and are in trial operation in the hospital. The payroll system will be implemented for all employees (appr. 10,000). The integration of economic data and medical information have been planned for and pilot tests are being undertaken in, for example, neurophysiology.

2. Service Units

The service units use several different computer systems, mainly the IBM 1800 but also the IBM 360/40 and other smaller computers located within or without the hospital. Only short descriptions will be given in the following chapter about the different computer routines, of which some are today totally independent and specific systems, some are partly integrated in the

Table 2. Status of Administrative Functions

	Onset	No. per year	Status	Comments
Patient registration and identification, admission, discharge, bed census, etc.				
(1) Inpatients	1966	40,000	Op	Specific batch system
(2) In- and outpatients	1968	2,000	Op	J5-T1 integrated with the above-mentioned specific batch system
	•	•		
	•	•		
	•	•		
	•	•		
	•	•		
	1972	100,000		
Billing, accounting, and payroll				
(1) Inpatients	1966	40,000	Op	J5-T1 integrated with the above-mentioned specific batch system
(2) Outpatients	1970	450,000		J5-T1
(3) Payroll	1972	Under test and implementation		
(4) Inventory control	1970	Operational batch system for appr. 5,000 different items.		

Op: An operational system is a computer system without parallel manual system which has been tested and analyzed during an experimental period and then approved by the hospital board.

automated medical record system J5-T1, and some use only the record system.

a. Hematology. All data from service units (coded or not coded) including all hematological tests were presented via J5-T1 in accumulated lists (Figure 18–9) during 1968–70 at the Medical Development Clinic; today, several clinics (e.g., thoracic medicine, internal medicine, general surgery) successfully utilize these routines. Except for accumulated lists for clinical use, the computer system gives all statistics for each test or variable, individually separated—if so desired—per clinical unit, outpatient department, etc., or per ordering physician, or per individual patient over an unlimited period of time.

Laboratory request forms are still on the traditional paper sheet, but several different versions of punch cards with or without optical reading have been tested.

UTSKRIFTSDATUM: 730621

```
--------------------------------------------------------------------------------
KEMLAB                                                                    KEMLAB
                   720921 721025 721201 730614 730620 730621               730621
                   ****** ****** ****** ****** ****** ******
HÆMATOLOGI:
  HB              (G%)    14.4   12.5   13.3   13.7   13.3
  HÆMATOKRIT      (VOL%)  46                                 40
  VITA   (1000/MIKROL)                   6.0            5.2
  TROMBOCYTER
               (1000/MIKROL)                           332.0
DIFFERENTIALRÆKN:
  STAVKÆRNIGA     (%)                     1
  SEGMENTKÆRNIGA  (%)                    52            60
  EOSINOFILA      (%)                    20             1
  BASOFILA        (%)                     3             1
  LYMFOCYTER      (%)                    17            27
  MONOCYTER       (%)                     7            11
ERYTHROCYTBILD
  ANISOCYTOS                            (+)           (+)
  POIKILOCYTOS                                        (+)
BLOD/SERUM:
  SR            (MM/1 TIM)             KOM    13       15
  JÆRN/S          (MG %)   0.047  0.061  0.075  0.088
  TIBC          (MIKROG%)  0.393  0.362  0.357  0.388
  JÆRNMÆTTNAD     (%)      12     17     21     23
  NATRIUM/S     (MEKV/L)               140           142
  KALIUM/S      (MEKV/L)               4.5           3.4
  BIKARBON/S   (MMOL/L)                 24            30
  FOSFOR/S        (MG%)                2.7           2.8
  GOT   MIKROMOL/L/MIN                         7      7
  GPT   MIKROMOL/L/MIN                         4      4
  ALK FOSF (10-40 U/L                         28     24
  BILIRUBIN TOT (MG%)                         0.4    0.3
PROTEINANALYS:
  ALBUMIN  (G/100 ML)                 4.3    4.8    4.2
  HAPTOGLOBIN
        (MG/100 ML)                          128
                                             0.94
  IG A    (MG/100 ML)                        295
  IG M    (MG/100 ML)                        110
BLOD/SERUM:
ELFORESKOMMENTAR:                           U. V. A.
  KREATININ/S    (MG%)                1.2            1.3

                   *********************************************************
KOMMENTARER        DATUM
BLOD/SERUM:
  SR           (MM/1 TIM) 721201   30   NÅGOT SLØJIG
```

Figure 18–9. An example of an accumulated list of hematology data

Laboratory test scheduling is included in the booking/scheduling system J5-T1, and there is no specific system for hematology or chemistry.

b.   Chemistry.   A special computer system—the IBM 1800—has been in use at the hospital since 1968 for laboratory automation and for medical research. Approximately 3,000 chemical tests are processed per day, which is 60% of the total load of the laboratory. Plans have been developed for the interfacing of the IBM 1800 with the IBM 360/40, but the linkage will not be in operation until 1973.

c. Microbiology. A bacteriological computer system was developed during 1966 for acquisition and presentation of accumulated lists of data (Figure 18–10). Approximately 125,000 analyses are processed through the system per year. During 1971–72, this computer sub-system has been integrated with the automated medical record system J5-T1 and is now implemented in all wards and outpatient departments of the hospital.

d. Pathology (autopsy and tissue). The Standard Nomenclature of Pathology (SNOP) for registration of coded data has been used for several years without a computer system. Plans have been developed for an integration of pathology data into the databank J5-T1, but no decisions as to implementation have been made at this time. Specific research projects do use the automated medical record system for statistical analyses.

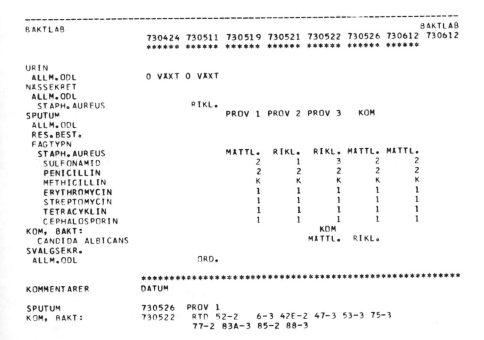

Figure 18–10. Example of accumulated list of bacteriological data.

e.   X-ray.   Interpretations of x-ray pictures in partly coded form and in free text have been stored and presented in the J5-T1 system for, e.g., the medical development clinic, different multiphasic or health screening projects, and medical research. A new x-ray request form has been tested but not yet implemented over the whole hospital.

The appointment scheduling and booking system was introduced in 1971 into the main x-ray department (in total there are five different departments) at the hospital, and it is now under expanded implementation.

f.   Pharmacy.   A request form from wards and outpatient departments to the central pharmacy store has been introduced, and a specific computer system for inventory control and administrative statistics is in daily operation.

In the medical development clinic, a punch card designed as a patient prescription card and as a request card for ward stock of drugs was tested but will not be implemented over the whole hospital without further tests. The punch card was used for data acquisition to the automated medical record system, and registered drugs were presented in accumulated lists (Figure 18–11). This part of J5-T1 is now in use in one ward and for one outpatient department.

g.   Electrocardiogram, electroencephalogram.   Interpretations of electrocardiograms provided by cardiologists are in coded and/or noncoded form added to the automated medical record system J5-T1. This system is in use in a few wards and departments and is a part of the problem and/or source oriented automated medical record in J5-T1.

Interpretations of electroencephalograms and other neurophysiological signals have been stored and processed for all clinical departments and wards since 1968, totaling approximately 6,000 per year. The different forms in use include several hundreds of coded variables and unlimited space for free text. During the last years, "economic" data have been added to the system—e.g., cost per electroencephalogram including personnel cost.

Automated analysis of analog signals is included in several research projects using the IBM 1800 for A-D conversion and processing. Electrocardiograms and electroencephalograms and other signals are analyzed.

h.   Pulmonary function.   Spirometry analyses are done on a routine basis on the IBM 1800.

i.   Automated multiphasic screening.   The automated medical record system J5 has been used for multiphasic screening purposes since 1965–66. Two pilot projects of multiphasic screening were handled—one for government employees and one for a population of the Stockholm county.

The main project for multiphasic screening in 1972 is a health care sys-

UTSKRIFTSDATUM: 730621

TERAPI	700709	700904	701002	710209	710408	710511	711011	TERAPI 720315
	******	******	******	******	******	******	******	******
FARMAKOTERAPI								
20252 DIGITOXIN T. 0.1 MG		1X1	1X1	1X1			1X1	
25251 LASIX T. 40 MG		1X2	1X2	1X2			1X1	
25700 ALDACTONE NOVUM T. 25 MG	2X2	2X2		2X2			1X1	
30400 KALITABS D. 0.57 G		1X3		1X3			1X1	
042510 SOLVEKALK T 0.75 G		1X3						
61602 AP T. 50 MG		ESO						ESO
101901 DECA-DURABOL 25MG/ML					UT FM 10			
111301 MEPROBAMAT T. 0.4 G						1 VB		
111302 MEPROBAN T. 0.4 G				2 TN				
122702 PARAFLEX COMP T.	2VB							
143001 NATRIUMFLORID T 55MG		UT						

TERAPI	730206	TERAPI 730206
	******	
FARMAKOTERAPI		
20252 DIGITOXIN T. 0.1 MG	1X1	
25700 ALDACTONE NOVUM T. 25 MG	1X1	
111301 MEPROBAMAT T. 0.4 G	1VB	

Figure 18–11.   Example of accumulated lists of registered drugs.

tem for the personnel of the Stockholm county, approximately 12,000 individuals per year. The system includes several different questionnaires for actual symptoms and earlier diseases as well as for social and environmental factors. A semi-problem oriented record is used for presentation and storage of data.

3.   Clinical Units

a.   **Nurses' station system.**   Nurses' station terminals have not been planned within the so-called KS-project except for intensive care units and operation theaters at the thoracic clinics, where a special computer system is in operation—see special inpatient services below.

A basic concept in the project was to give nurses and doctors more time for patient care; this is the rationale behind the Hospital Administration Centers' (HAC's) intent to work as the "administrative center" of clinics or a number of wards. Its personnel are mainly secretaries.

Computer-connected terminals and other equipment are available in these centers to attain better allocation of medical resources—doctors, nurses, and expensive equipment—by continuous planning of all stages of diagnostic and therapeutic routines.

Doctors' and nurses' orders are, if needed and desired, handled by these HAC's both for the wards and for the outpatient departments. Currently, two centers are in operation—one for the department of thoracic medicine and one in the main building of the hospital for the departments of internal medicine, general surgery, and endocrinology and for the emergency room.

b.   The appointment scheduling system.   The computer scheduling system was tested without parallel manual operation in the medical development clinic for approximately three years. Currently the system is in daily operation from Monday to Friday—8 hours a day—and gives on-line service (T1) to several clinics and service units. The implementation of the system started in 1971 in the HAC's of thoracic medicine, internal medicine, general surgery, endocrinology, emergency room, and general x-ray. Hundreds of different resources are booked over this system.

Bed scheduling is not, for the moment, included in the booking procedure but may be without any new computer programs.

The total number of terminals in daily use are 12, and the functions except for scheduling are the admission and discharge routine and medical record request from J5-T1.

The scheduling procedure starts with doctors' orders; and upon the request of the medical record technician, the secretary takes care of the computer terminal operation. Scheduling lists are produced through the system—e.g., for laboratory work including lists for blood sampling and for daily routines in the medical record library. If the patient is in the outpatient department, a letter is mailed to him/her about appointments to x-ray departments, laboratories, consultations, and visits to the physician.[8]

c.   Medical information processing.
(1) Automated histories.   Self-administered medical histories have been included in several clinical routines since the project started. The first questionnaire was designed for outpatient care of internal medicine and

for multiphasic screening in 1964 and included approximately 500 questions. Comparisons between the traditional manual record and the computer record obtained by self-administered questionnaires did show limited differences in the number of "bits" of information. A redesigned questionnaire was used during 1968–70 in the medical development clinic. One section of this questionnaire was designed for actual symptoms (120 questions), another for past or earlier diseases and symptoms (80 questions), and a third for special problems (60–120 questions). More specific questionnaires have also been developed—e.g., for allergology (the questionnaire routine saves the patient and the doctor one-quarter of the time of the first visit), for hematology (a questionnaire for patients with suspected coagulation abnormalities), for cardio-pulmonary diseases, for multiphasic screening (different questionnaires for actual symptoms, past history, social, and environmental factors), and for different research projects.[9,10]

All questionnaires include, except for "yes-no" answers, other coded variables, but they also allow unlimited amount of free text. The "positive" findings are keypunched on punch cards, paper tape, or on an on-line terminal and entered into the automated record system as a complement to the traditional conversation—the medical history—between the patient and the doctor. Results of experiments in the use of self-administered questionnaires have been presented by one member of the project team.[11]

The following findings were made:

(a) The amount of positive data ("yes" answers) increased with age but did not vary with sex. The increase with age was due to an increasing number of positive answers to questions about previous disease and present symptoms. This result may indicate different questionnaires for different age groups.

(b) General, high-level questions followed by specific, low-level ones were found to be of limited value, as 1 out of 5 patients gave contradictory answers.

(c) Free text was found to be necessary to the coded questions even if the text can only be analyzed by the human brain (and with great difficulties by a computer). On repeated identical questions—the same questionnaire was used after an interval of one week—initial "no" responses were again answered with "no" in 98%; but a "yes" answer was followed by a "no" answer in 83%. Physicians' evaluation and analysis of positive answers were studied and showed a very great variation.

In another study[12] based upon data from a multiphasic screening project, the "clinical value" of questionnaires and other variables were analyzed.

1,352 diagnoses were made on 943 patients, and only 22% of the patients were without a diagnosis. The following groups of examinations were undertaken:

(a) Self-administered questionnaire for the medical history
(b) Simple blood and urine tests (sedimentation rate, hemoglobin value, and urine tests for albumin and sugar)
(c) 12 different blood tests from the chemical autoanalyzer
(d) Vaginal smear
(e) Urine culture
(f) Chest x-ray
(g) Electrocardiogram
(h) Physical examination
(i) The medical history obtained by the doctor

All diagnoses were made by one doctor, who also decided for each diagnosis which of the above group (s) of examinations were of importance for decision-making. One, two, or three of these groups of examinations could be registered for each diagnosis, and the total number of these registered groups were 1,531 in 1,342 diagnoses. The distribution of these groups of examinations was as follows:

Self-administered questionnaire	592	39%
Simple tests	159	10%
"Automated" tests	103	7%
Vaginal smear	28	2%
Urine culture	42	3%
Chest x-ray	17	1%
Electrocardiogram	60	4%
Physical examination	342	22%
Medical history obtained by the doctor	188	12%
	1,531	100%

In spite of the fact that from the beginning the doctor in charge of the test center was not very impressed by the questionnaire technique, the result became clear: the medical history obtained by questionnaires and by the doctor provided the most important data for decision-making.

The 1,342 diagnoses were made on 732 individuals. In only 225 (32%) patients were actions taken for further analysis, consultations, therapy, etc. The total number of registered groups of examination were 596 in these 225 patients, and the distribution of the groups was as follows:

Self-administered questionnaire	170	28%
Simple tests	108	18%
"Automated" tests	70	12%
Vaginal smear	12	2%
Urine culture	27	5%
Chest x-ray	9	2%
Electrocardiogram	23	4%
Physical examination	121	20%
Medical history obtained by the doctor	56	9%
	596	100%

The clinical value of the medical history and the questionnaire was again documented. The questionnaire only "diagnosed" one out of five individuals (21%), and the questionnaire plus all "laboratory" tests except for physical examination and the medical history obtained by the doctor "diagnosed" three out of four (74%).

(2) Physical examination. Checklists for physical examination have been tested in the departments of internal medicine, surgery, thoracic medicine, gynecology, allergology, etc. These lists, including more than 3,000 variables, have shown their usefulness not only in clinical practice but also for medical education. The checklist routine has been shown to be a very fast method to record a physical examination; it is faster than handwriting or dictating. Today the checklists are in use at the departments of internal medicine, thoracic medicine, endocrinology, etc. and are parts of the problem oriented record.

The checklists are entered into the data bank by the secretaries in the hospital administration centers, using on-line terminals or paper tape punch.

(3) Progress notes. "Daily" notes or progress notes are not included in the computer system except in experiments with the problem oriented record where each problem is updated in a chronological order. Progress notes are written in free text, and very few variables are in a coded form. The notes may be written not only by doctors but also by nurses, physical therapists, social workers, etc. The traditional separation of records into one for the doctor, one for the nurses, one for the social workers, etc. may disappear and be replaced by one problem oriented record. The "total" problem oriented record for data acquisition, storage, and presentation is used only in one ward at thoracic medicine and by a few physicians in internal medicine.

(4) Discharge summaries. Semi-standardized discharge summaries from the department of otolaryngology have been stored in the J5 system since 1968. This project started with the basic idea of keeping the tradi-

tional manual record and storing only a summary of the record in the computer. Our experience with more than 12,000 records is that the automated discharge summary tends to replace the manual record and that additional data, mainly in free text, from follow-up visits in the outpatient department has been added.

(5) Registers for coded diagnoses and operations. A specific computer subsystem for registration of coded diagnoses and operations in inpatients was programmed during 1966. This program gives monthly and yearly statistical reports on inpatients—e.g., number of patients, bed occupancy, number of diagnoses according to the Scandinavian modification of the International Classification of Diseases (ICD), and number of operations according to a specific code for operations developed by the Swedish national board of health. All clinics and wards have used this subsystem since 1966, and the registered number of inpatients is approximately 40,000 per year. Punch cards are used as input media.

In the outpatient departments of dermatology (approximately 1,300 new patients per year), endocrinology (approximately 5,000 per year), thoracic medicine (approximately 3,000 per year), internal medicine (approximately 8,000 per year), and general surgery (approximately 12,000 per year), diagnoses and operations are registered in the "problem list" of the automated medical record system J5-T1. In this system, the coded diagnoses and operations are stored together with an additional short description in free text, as only coded data are of limited value in clinical practice. Punched cards, punched paper tape, and on-line terminals are used as input media.

The inpatient computer subsystem for registration of coded diagnoses and operations will be replaced by the automated medical record system during 1973–74.

d. Special inpatient services

(1) Real-time data system for intensive care, operations, theaters, etc. An advanced real-time data system has been implemented in the thoracic clinic. The system developed by STAN SAAB uses a special computer called Censor 908 and different on-line terminals:

(a) The "grafoskop" (a visual display terminal equipped with a typewriter keyboard) in which data are presented in form of curves, tables, and text;

(b) the "alfaskop" (visual display terminal equipped with a typewriter keyboard) in which data are presented in form of tables and text;

(c) the "intercom 411" (terminal for numeric input), which also is a part of the intercom telephone system; and

(d) special hard-copy printers.

The system has from the beginning been implemented in the surgery theaters and in the intensive care unit where quick access to data is needed, where handling of a high flow of patient data in real-time is desired, where built-in warning systems for critical situations are of importance, and where immediate updating of patient records is of great value. The system is gradually expanded to other applications like data handling of information about patients with pacemakers. The system communicates with the J5 system for long-term storage and statistical analyses via paper tape.

The total number of patients registered and handled by this real-time system is for the moment approximately 900 per year.

(2) Record-keeping in clinical anesthesia. An off-line record system for clinical anesthesia has been developed and implemented in all operation theatres in the hospital except for the above-mentioned in the thoracic clinic. Approximately 12,000 records are handled per year since 1966.[13] The record includes one section for premedication, another for anesthesia and operation, and a third for the immediate post-operative condition. The system uses a special form which has been tested, analyzed, and redesigned several times. The form is used by ward nurses and by anesthesiologists and includes several coded data but also additional space for narrative information. Paper tape punch is used for data acquisition, and the J5 system is used for storage and analyses. The total cost including keypunching and computer time is approximately $1.

The medical goal for the system was to create possibilities for a systematic follow-up of routine activities in clinical anesthesia. The administrative goal was to create a sound basis for rational planning and use of available resources. The two goals have been satisfied as the system has been used for planning of new departments, clinics, theaters, etc. in surgery and in gynecology and has at the same time given valuable results for decision-making about anesthetic agents. Results and experiences from about 70,000 anesthetic records are published in a thesis by B. Hallén during 1973.[17] Among other things, preanesthetic data are analyzed for their importance in risk-grouping and prognosis. One result can be mentioned—the more complicated the patient is, the more narrative data and free text is needed to describe him.

(3) Blood bank system. Special computer routines for different functions and applications in the blood transfusion service organization have been worked out in a joint study between the South Hospital of Stockholm, the Academic Hospital in Uppsala, and the Karolinska hospital. Several routines have been implemented for several years—e.g., scheduling and calling of blood donors, inventory control, and statistical reporting. The system is a batch processing system using punch cards for input.[14]

e.   **The problem oriented medical record.**   During the first period of the computer project, the attempts were to "automate" the source-oriented, traditional medical record. A record, which is bulky and poorly organized for search and evaluation, which presents problems in record filing and availability, and which is difficult to maintain in high quality, may be the goal for computer activities; but it is difficult and almost impossible to handle from a system analytical point of view. The objectives were also described in vague, ill-defined terms like "to facilitate clinical research," "to provide statistical and management information," "to give better patient care." During the first years, source-oriented computer routines were programmed—e.g., for medical histories, for physical examinations, for chemistry, for statistical retrieval. These "mistakes," called J1 to J4, gave us as a result the following rules: A computer system in the clinical level has to be built around the patient and the patient's course through the health care delivery system (not only through a hospital), and the computer system has to be almost independent of the user (not built upon detailed specifications which will be old and obsolete tomorrow).

These two main rules were not properly understood until 1965, and the significance for the whole KS-project was not accepted until 1969–70. The second major step towards a solution of patient information processing was taken during 1968, when it was realized that an automated source-oriented record could be replaced by a problem oriented record. The problem oriented medical record as described in the literature is a method to systematize patient care and improve medical education and follow-up routines. The basic elements of this record are the problem list and the problem oriented progress notes.

The computer-stored problem list (Figure 18–12) is gradually appearing in the old manual records in the hospital and is the first part of the patient's chart. The use of the automated problem list started in the thoracic clinic in 1968 and is now in use in several other clinics. In the future, there will be one list per patient for all clinics in the hospital as different problems are linked together in the J5 library. The problem oriented progress notes, which are independent of the patient's location in the hospital—e.g. in- or out-patient departments—and which can be written by consultants and physiotherapists, are in use for several thousand patients per year. The traditional source-oriented, manual record will thus gradually be replaced by an automated problem oriented record.

The amount of narrative information in the problem oriented progress notes creates a great demand on computer storage. Each problem, however, can be summarized after resolution, after discharge of the patient, or at any time during the patient's stay and transferred to an inactive magnetic tape with an access time of 1–30 days. The inactive file may then be transferred

UTSKRIFTSDATUM: 730621

```
----------------------------------------------------------------------
                          AKTUELLA PROBLEM                    AKTUELLA PROBLEM
KAROLINSKA  SJUKHUSET
MED
LÄKBES
                          PROBLEM  1
720928   JOHNSSON
        2                     250,09 DIABETES SUSP.  ?

                          PROBLEM  2
720928   JOHNSSON
        2                     595,09 CYSTIT  ?

                          PROBLEM  3
720928   JOHNSSON
        1                     244,09 HYPOTHYREOS

                          PROBLEM  4
720928   JOHNSSON
        1                     713,00 ARTHROSIS COXAE

                 --------------------------------------------------------
                          VÅRDADM. UPPGIFTER                  VÅRDADM. UPPGIFTER
MEDV15

720530
        20                L ÄKARBESÖK  EKLUND

HKLAC

720929
        19                INREMITTERAD  FRÅN  DR  JOHNSON

MEDV15

721019
        20                L ÄKARBESÖK  STRANDELL

730601
        20                L ÄKARBESÖK  NORBECK
```

Figure 18–12.   Problem list.

to microfilm for long-term storage. The different levels of access and storage of medical data can today be summarized in the following way:

(1) Traditional medical record libraries including hard copies of computer-stored patient data and information.

(2) Automated medical record library—J5-T1.

(2.1) On-line input: all alphabetic and numeric characters; on-line output: administrative data as patient identification, address, earlier visits to the hospital, scheduling and booking data, etc. No medical data are presented.

On-line data processing is limited to the period from 8:30 AM to 4:30 PM Mondays to Fridays.

(2.2) Off-line input: all alphabetic and numeric characters. Active file input media: paper tape, punch cards, magnetic tape. Active file output media: the whole or part of the medical record and numeric data and codes for statistical use. The hard copies of the computer file are stored in the manual chart or record. A new hard copy may replace the old one or only include new datas.

Off-line data processing is mainly conducted from 4:30 PM and during the night shift.

(2.3) Off-line input and output: same as (2.2). Inactive file access time: 1–30 days.

(3) Microfilm

Levels (2.3) and (3) have not yet been implemented.

Level (2.3) can be divided in one part with numerical and coded data which can be processed by statistical and mathematical methods and in a second part which includes narrative data. The last part may to some extent be transferred to level (3) within a short period of time for permanent storage. Clinical research projects will be handled during the data acquisition period on level (2.2) and stored on level (2.3). Several major projects are handled in this order today.

I. IMPACT AND EVALUATION

The most successful applications of computers in hospitals have been in the area of accounting and administration. In automating these procedures, hospitals have relied on experiences from the industries as there has been no model for a complex medical system. Automation of service units (laboratories) has also been rather successful. The progress in clinical practice and patient care, however, has been slow. Administration and service units are artificial systems (constructed by human beings), which use, to an overwhelming degree, data in numeric and/or coded form. Patient care and the decision-making about diagnosis and therapy is a nonartificial system consisting of data in numeric and coded form and to a large extent narrative data or free text.[11,15,17]

The KS-project around the IBM 360/40 was from the beginning centered on patient care activities. The results have been that clinical practice and clinical research have been facilitated by an automated problem oriented medical record system and that the planning procedures around the patient's course in the health care delivery system has been simplified by the scheduling system. The impact of the experimental phase from 1966–1970 has been noticed in different areas:

1. Personnel organization in the clinics and the outpatient departments is gradually changing towards so-called "care groups"—that is, team care.

Each group is composed of one physician, one nurse, and one secretary. In many clinics or departments, one nurse can serve several physicians at the same time, and one secretary can take care of several physicians and nurses. The basic idea with the "care group" is to have individualized care around the patient, to delegate decision-making to nurses and secretaries, and to leave most of the clerical work and computer operations to the secretary— the medical record technician.

2. The scheduling system and the above-mentioned personnel organization have increased the capacity of the outpatient department. Less square meters are needed in spite of the fact that more physicians and nurses are working in the outpatient department of say, internal medicine.

3. The problem oriented record has shown the importance of the patient for all functions of the hospital. The patient himself starts the health care delivery system and is really the one who is making the first diagnosis and the first decision to seek help and care. The traditional concept of cost per hospital bed, average length of stay, cost per laboratory test, etc. is gradually changing into a new dimension where all factors, needs, and costs are related to the individual patient.

4. All computer activities within the hospital have an important impact on consideration of cost benefit and cost effectiveness analysis. Evaluation of hospital information systems, automated medical record systems, and laboratory systems in economical or medical terms is, however, in its early childhood. Cost effectiveness and cost benefit analysis are naturally of limited help because benefits from health care are difficult to measure. New methods of norms and measurements and ideas have to be developed; and more research in hospital, health, and patient care operations and procedures are needed in the future.

5. The daily routine operations and patient care activities are gradually changing because of the implementation of the computer systems and/or hospital administration centers. Daily routines include several steps such as referral notes to the hospital, definition of problems, description of problems, ordering and planning of tests and procedures, visits to the outpatient departments, medical history-taking with questionnaires, consultations, therapy planning, prescriptions, etc.

The number of clinical research projects is continuously growing. An increasing number of simple statistical calculations—frequency analysis, mean values, standard deviations, etc.—as well as sophisticated retrieval and mathematical problems are included in the daily operations. The analytical problems are mainly handled by a linear discriminant analysis system which is one module or function in the J5 system.[16]

6. The slow progress of automation in clinical practice will gradually change, and the conservative attitude of clinicians will disappear in the

future. In reference to the stethoscope, it was mentioned in the London *Times* in 1834: "that it will ever come into general use notwithstanding its value is extremely doubtful, because beneficial application requires much time and gives a good bit of trouble to both patient and practitioner: because its hue and character are foreign and opposed to all our habits and associations."

The stethoscope has over the last century given us an enormous knowledge about the heart and lungs and become a characteristic symbol of physicians; the computer will during the next century give us more knowledge than ever before about our patients but will never become more than a tool, a fast adding machine, which has been "foreign and opposed to all our habits and associations." Beneficial applications in clinical practice have required much time and have given a good bit of trouble to all involved. The result of automation, however, as the result of using any other tool, depends upon the skill and the experience of the user.

ACKNOWLEDGMENTS

The author wants to express his great gratitude to the Karolinska Hospital, the Swedish Agency for Administrative Development (SAFAD), the agencies called SJURA and SPRI, and to Mr. Torlek Danielsson, Dr. Christian Mellner, Dr. Hans Selander, and the many others without whom this chapter would never have been written.

REFERENCES

1. Hall, P.; Mellner, Ch.; and Danielsson, T. "J5—A Data Processing System for Medical Information." *Method. Inform. Med.,* 6(1967):1–6.
2. Hall, P. "Le traitement automatique de l'information et des documents concernant les malades." *Médicine Hospitalière,* 17(1967)74–76.
3. Hall, P. "The Computer as an Aid to Clinical Practice." *Automatisierung des klinischen Laboratoriums."* F. K. Schattauer Verlag, 1968, pp. 267–275.
4. Hall, P. *"The Application of Computers for Hospital Records."* London. Royal Society of Health, 1968, pp. 47–56.
5. Hall, P.; Danielsson, T.; Mellner, Ch,; and Selander, H. "Automation of Data Flow." *Annuals of the New York Academy of Sciences* 161(1969)730–739.
6. Mamelle, N., and Hall, P. J5: Systéme de gestion des observations médicales de l'hôpital Karolinska." *Rev. Informatique méd.* 2(1971).
7. Selander, H. "Patient Identification." *Proceedings of the IFIP-TC4 working conference on information processing of medical records.* North-Holland Publishing Company, 1970. pp. 71–81.

8. Selander, H. "Patient and Resource Allocation." *Proceedings of the IFIP-TC4 working conference on information processing of medical records.* North-Holland Publishing Company, 1970. pp. 149–159.

9. Mellner, Ch.; Gårdmark, S.; and Parkholm, S. "Medical Questionnaires in Clinical Practice." *Proceedings of the IFIP-TC4 working conference on information processing of medical records.* North-Holland Publishing Company, 1970. pp. 106–115.

10. Simborg, D. W.; Rikli, A. E.; and Hall, P. "Experimentation in Medical History-Taking." *JAMA* 210 (1969) : 1443–1445.

11. Mellner, Ch. "The Self-Administered Medical History." *Acta Chir. Scand.* Suppl. 406 (1970).

12. Hall, P.; Molin, L.; and Jahn, O. *Die Bedeutung der Fragebogeanamnese bei einer automatisierten Patientenuntersuchung.* F. K. Schattauer Verlag, 1971. pp. 183–191.

13. Hallén, B., Eklund, J., Gordh, T., and Hall, P. "Computer Application in Clinical Anaesthesia. A Report on Two Years Experience." Excerpta Medica International Congress Series no. 200, 1968. pp. 618–622.

14. Högman, C. F. "The Use of Computers in the Blood Transfusion Organisation." *Il Pensiero Scientifico* Editore, Roma, 1969. pp. 84–99.

15. Hall, P. "Information Science, the Patient and the Medical Record." *Proceedings of the IFIP-TC4 working conference on information processing of medical records.* North-Holland Publishing Company, 1970. pp. 31–40.

16. Hall, P.; Hallén, B.; and Selander, H. "Linear Discriminatory Analysis: A Patient Classifying Method for Research and Production Control." *Meth. Inform. Med.* 10 (1971) : 96–102.

17. Hallén, B.: "Computerized Anesthetic Record-Keeping." *Acta Anaestheliologica Scand.* Suppl. 52 (1973).

CHAPTER NINETEEN

Medical School of Hannover Hospital Computer System (Hannover)

by Peter L. Reichertz

A. MEDICAL CARE ENVIRONMENT

The Medical System Hannover (MSH) is the integrated computer system of the Hannover Medical School Hospital. It is developed and operated by the Department of Biometrics and Medical Information Science of this medical school. The Medical School of Hannover is an independent college of Medicine and not part of a university. It was founded in 1964, and the first students were admitted in 1965. First a city hospital was used as a teaching facility and construction work for the major buildings started in May 1965. The first inpatients were admitted on July 19, 1971. The number of patients has increased ever since at a steady rate approaching a maximum of 600 toward the end of 1972 (Figure 19–1). As new wards are brought into operation, the capacity of the main building will eventually reach 1,160 beds, which will probably happen toward the end of 1974. The overall projected total capacity of the Medical School Hannover is approximately 2,000 beds with some clinical disciplines (dermatology, pediatrics, gynecology, psychiatry, and rehabilitation) being housed in separate buildings (Figure 19–2). The computer center is housed in the building of the central laboratories. The ground view of the main hospital building is shown in Figure 19–3.

The actual outpatient admittance is approximately 250 per day and is expected to attain 600–800/day.

The Medical School has been projected for 140 students per year. The capacity is presently extended to 200/year plus 60 students of dentistry.

The Medical School Hannover does not follow the traditional concept of

598

DATE: SEPT. 1972

BEGINNING CONSTRUCTION	**MAY 1965**
BEGINNING OF DETAILED EDP PLANNING	**OCTOBER 1969**
INSTALLATION OF COMPUTER	
FIRST PHASE	**AUGUST 1970**
FIRST IN-PATIENT	**JULY 19, 1971**
BED CAPACITY JULY 1971	**100 BEDS**
PRESENT CAPACITY	**539 BEDS**
INCREASE OF IN-PATIENTS	**(UP TO JULY 72, MAX.438):**

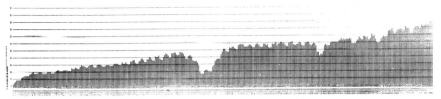

CAPACITY OF MAIN HOSPITAL BUILDING	**1160 BEDS**
PROJECTED TOTAL CAPACITY M.S.H.	**2000 BEDS**
OUTPATIENT ADMISSIONS	**~250/DAY**
PROJECTED CAPACITY	**600–800/DAY**

Figure 19–1. Description of the environment of the Medical School Hannover. The plot in the lower part of the figure (compare Figure 19–26) shows the increasing bed capacity of the hospital. Wards are brought into service sequentially in order to allow for training of personnel and completion of facilities.

German-speaking countries. It has attempted to amalgamate advantageous features of both American and German medical schools.

The Medical School is owned and operated by the State of Lower Saxony; so far, approximately 600 million marks have been spent for its construction. At the moment, the staff includes 134 academic teachers and 493 residents and postgraduate students. The actual number of students is 842. The catchment areas involve Hannover city and surrounding rural areas.

Figure 19–2.   Plan of the campus of the Medical School Hannover. UBF stands for examination, treatment and research.

In a census taken on January 5, 1973, for example, the ratio was 1:8—that is, the city population provides the majority of all admitted patients. Of the service units of a modern large hospital, only orthopedic surgery is missing at this moment (there is a large special hospital for orthopedic surgery within 5 miles).

B.   DEFINITIONS AND OBJECTIVES

1.   Definition

The Medical System Hannover (MSH) attempts an integration of a great variety of hospital functions. It has to carry out both hospital and patient

Figure 19–3   The Radiological Institute with its nuclear reactor in front of the main hospital building. To the right are dormitories for nurses, and to the left, the children's hospital.

management. As an institution of academic learning, various projects of computer-aided instruction, computer-aided testing, procedural training, and scientific analysis as well as special research projects have to be supported. In the framework of this variety of tasks as well as in the hospital alone, the main functions of an integrating computer system are:

(1) Communication
(2) Integration
(3) System flow control (see Figure 19–4)

It is very difficult to define a hospital in general terms. The specific requirements vary greatly. They depend on the underlying social and/or economic structures, patient flow, therapeutic activities, and the overall health care delivery system. Nevertheless, it is possible to conceive basic modules of functions. Their mosaic may form the system meeting the individual needs of a specific hospital.

In this context, the word "system" had been used. In general, a system may be defined as a set of interdependent elements.[45] These elements react with computer systems and are one or more procedures consisting of various manual, semi-computerized, and computerized modules forming (often repetitively) specific tasks or complexes of tasks.[45] The tasks of a hospital computing system lie in the overall areas of information science, which are:

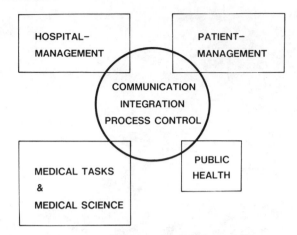

Figure 19–4. Principal functional areas within a hospital. The areas of hospital management, patient management, medical tasks, medical sciences, and "public health" tasks are combined by the functions of communication, integration, and process control. The computer may render specific services in these areas.

(1) Data acquisition
(2) Information validation
(3) Information management
(4) Information evaluation
(5) Information (or system) flow control.[45,46]

A hospital computing system has to cover both administrative and medical areas, which may not be completely separated. Basic functions should be:

(1) Information functions
(2) Process control functions

In detail, services which are expected are:

(1) Data collection
(2) Communication
(3) Documentation
(4) Information integration
(5) Information presentation
(6) Information derivation
(7) Quality control
(8) Optimization of functions
(9) General administrative functions

not necessarily in this order of priority.

The greatest problems of a hospital computer system lie in the medical rather than in the administrative area. Information changes in regard to relevance. However, the user expects decision support in various areas in which the relevance of data may change.

The primary targets of a hospital computing system may vary depending upon whether they are defined by the administration or by the physicians (Figure 19–5). Eventually, both priorities meet.[45,46,48]

PRIMARY TARGETS:

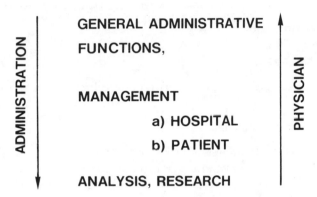

Figure 19–5. The primary objectives of automation as seen by the hospital administration and the physician differ. There are always links of varying importance between the two categories.

2. Objectives

The objectives of the Medical System Hannover are dictated by the complexity of the problem of medical information science and the multiple tasks originating within a large hospital that is at the same time an institution of academic medicine.

Therefore, the objectives of the Medical System Hannover are:

(1) to provide a system for information acquisition, integration, retrieval, and analysis concerning patients and human and material resources of the Medical School Hannover teaching hospital to support patient and hospital management and scientific purposes;

(2) to support teaching activities and academic administration of the Medical School Hannover;

(3) to provide services and systems for scientific data analysis;

(4) to provide the basis for research and teaching in the area of medical information science.

It is evident that this list of objectives contains a variety of multiple tasks not necessarily compatible in their priorities. The system concept tries to cope with these problems.

C. GENERAL SYSTEM CONCEPTS

1. Basic Systems Approach

Integral functions of the main objectives were considered to be:

(1) Communication
(2) Integration
(3) System flow control

In order to perform these functions, two basic vehicles were considered:

(1) Teleprocessing systems
(2) Integrating data banks

Furthermore, it was felt that a time-sharing system would be capable of providing the various facilities in order to permit the simultaneous operation of different computer systems to perform the tasks in the various areas.

2. Hardware

Accordingly, in 1969, IBM 360/67 was chosen. At this time, IBM had not yet generally adopted the concept of virtual storage and virtual machines.

The present hardware configuration is given in Figure 19–6. Not shown in this figure are various dedicated computer systems such as an IBM 1130 in the central laboratory,[32] a KRUPP EPR 2500, a KRUPP EPR 2300 and a PDP8 in nuclear medicine,[12] and laboratory equipment in the basic sciences. On-line communication is developed for the central laboratory system and the central computing facilities.

3. Software

The general software hierarchy is outlined in Figure 19–7.

The central supervisor is a system CP/67 (which in the meantime has become the basis for the IBM virtual machine system VM). This supervisor allows the operation of virtual machines which are independent of each

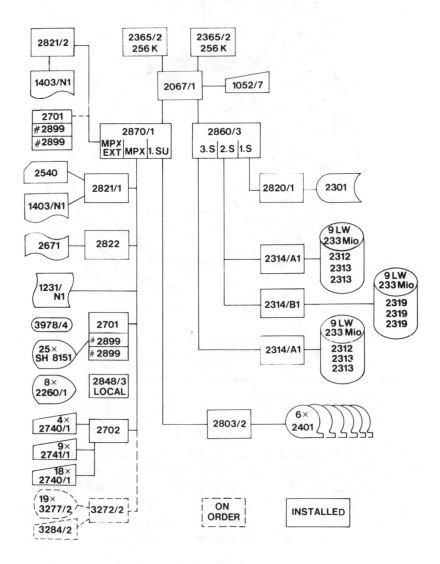

MEDICAL SCHOOL HANNOVER

HARDWARE CONFIGURATION MEDICAL SYSTEM JAN. 73

Figure 19–6. Hardware diagram of the Medical System Hannover (MSH) as of January 1973. The broken lines show those units which are to be installed during 1973.

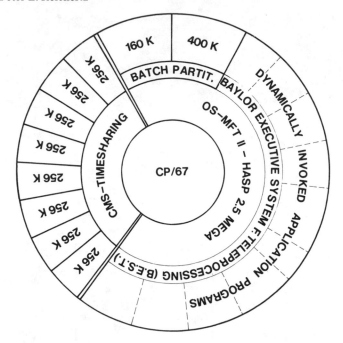

Figure 19–7. Software diagram of the MSH. The IBM 360/67 is controlled by CP-67. Though DOS (Disk Operating System) and starter systems are occasionally run, routinely two types of virtual machines are used: (1) The CMS (Conversational Monitor System) Time-sharing machines for time-sharing services and program preparations of those programs to be sent over to (2) a 2.5 megabyte OS MFT II/HASP virtual machine.

other, are self-sustained in their system, and share real core on a virtual core/paging mechanism. The virtual machines are operated from IBM 2741 consoles, which may be remote. In principle, it is possible to run different multiprogramming operating systems at the same time (such as OS and DOS). In routine operation, the MSH uses only one larger multiprogramming operating system and multiple conversational monitors (Figure 19–8).

The operating system is OS-MFT II with HASP. At the moment, the MSH uses 2.5 megabytes of virtual core for this operating system, allocating 1.8 million to the teleprocessing monitor. This monitor is the Baylor Executive System for Teleprocessing (BEST).[10] This system is relatively terminal-independent and allows the user to communicate with various application systems. For programming application systems under this monitor, a special set of PL/1 macros has been developed.[47] In the background, batch jobs may be processed and may access the same file as the CP system.

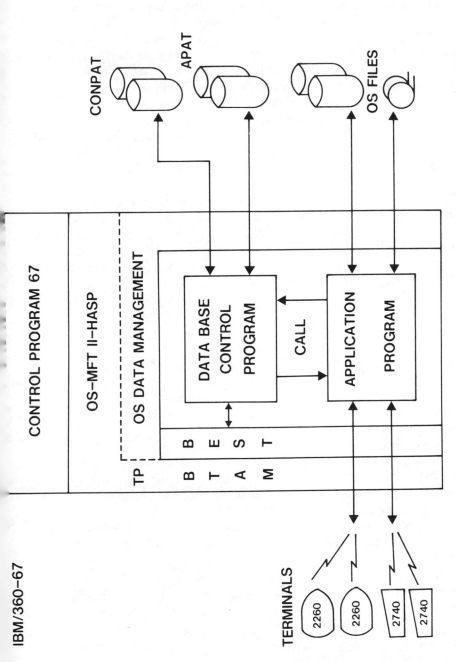

Figure 19-8. Diagram showing the usage of the data base control program (DL/1-IMS) from both batch partitions and the BEST. The TP system allows addressing of various types of terminals (cathode-ray tube, start/stop-operation, BSC operation; typewriter terminals, teletype).[47,58]

To build and maintain the integrating data base, the data base language DL/1 [now IBM IMS (14)] has been selected. This data base system permits the design of a hierarchical data bank with logical definitions of data bases and file structures independently of physical data storage organizations. BEST has been modified in order to interface with this data bank system so that the relevant files may be accessed both from the batch IMS region controller as well as from the teleprocessing system.

The overall logical structure of the MSH data base concept is shown in Figure 19–9.[11,44] The operations of a hospital being oriented toward the patient as an individual, the main access criteria is the patient's identification. As identification number we chose a preponderant patient-defined number sequence which has the structure: DDMMYYNNSX, where DDMMYY stands for day, month, and year of birth and NN is a 2-digit number code based on the first 2 letters of the birth name. This code has been designed to achieve an equal distribution.[53,54] S stands for the sex of the patient; in those cases (approximately 1 per 6000) where two different patients coincide in the first 9 digits of their identification number, X will be incremented in order to differentiate between them.

The data base concept distinguishes between two types of data:

(1) Permanent (summary)
(2) Temporary (detail)

where permanent refers to remaining on random access devices. The access to the data base can also be made using the name of the patient or individual in the data base; generic searches are permitted. From here the correct identification number can be (automatically) retrieved and used for further information.

This concept shows that the attempt is made to use an integrated data base for all types of applications. The same is true for other data bases used in the system. Names for patients and for personnel are kept in the same data base structure. More details about the medical content and format are given below.

The basic philosophy of the input systems to the data bank is shown in Figure 19–10. All communications, be it from batch or on-line devices, including satellite computers, are kept in intermediate files for speed and data security. Later an updating is made. In the meantime, a log is kept where the information is to be found in order to provide transparency for the user.

4. Functional Concepts

a. Hospital. Figure 19-4 (page 602) describes the main functional areas within a hospital. Hospital management provides general administra-

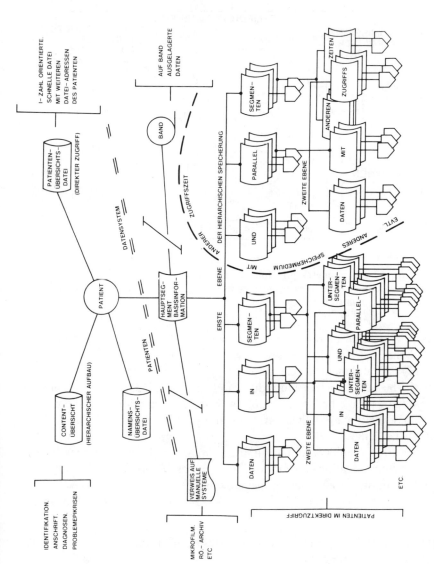

Figure 19-9. General concept of the data base structure.[44] The primary identification is the patient's ID-number.

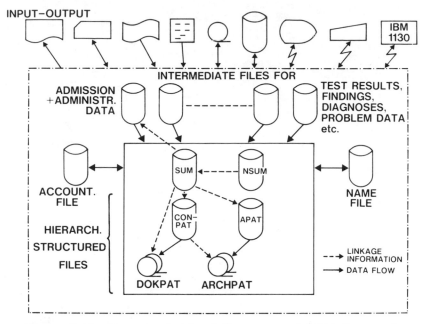

Figure 19–10. General principle of file strategy of MSH. Input and output coming from various devices are stored in intermediate files for reasons of data security and speed.

tion and allocation of rescources and facilities. Patient management deals with the individual patient before, during, and after his stay in the hospital. Medical tasks and medical science are the specific medical activities in dealing with the patient as an individual and in general. Of growing concern is the area of public health, meaning both the introduction of tasks related to regional health care delivery systems and problems of prophylactic (preventive) medicine.

Figure 19–4 emphasizes that all these areas are linked together by the tasks of communication, integration, and process control. In this area, the hospital computer system has its specific charges.

The word "management" in Figure 19–4 has to be understood in a very broad sense:

(1) coping with the increasing quantities of information
(2) optimizing functions
(3) decision-making
(4) justifying of cost by effectiveness

Figure 19–11 attempts to give a few examples of the feasible modules within the functional blocks of Figure 19–4.[46] The figure is to be under-

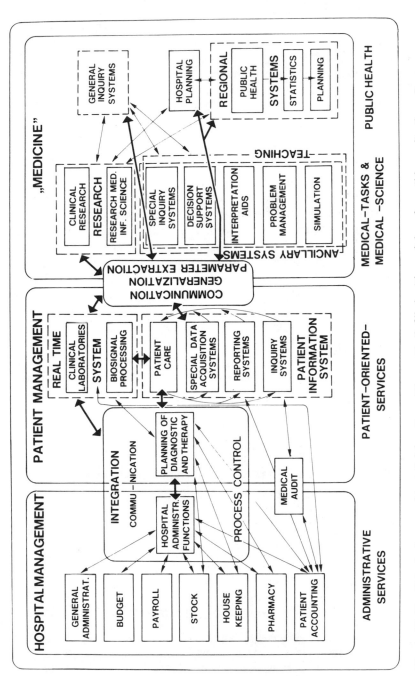

Figure 19–11. Principal areas of hospital functions (Figure 19–4) filled with modules of possible applications. Programs may serve different areas and different applications using the same modules. In the patient-oriented area real time systems can be separated from patient information services due to their differing requirements.

stood in such a way that the section of "medicine" is also directly connected with hospital management. The communication and integration links are shown and are understood as connecting each block with any other one. Ancillary systems, in this context, are not the different services within the hospital but those systems that assist the physician with specific medical tasks. These systems may also serve as a teaching aid both to teach facts and procedures and to learn from specific responses and answers (dynamic model).

b. File utilization strategy.   In designing the different modules, first temporary data sets are used for testing (Figure 19–12). This provides the necessary information in order to design the permanent outlay or to define the segments of the main data base to be made accessible to the application system. During the first part of operation, the system still accesses the temporary files, thus accumulating enough information about performance and reliability. Whenever the permanent structures are developed and information is fed into the main data base, it has to be decided what files have to remain to receive temporary information and what information has to go into the data base. Here also a decision has to be made as to whether or not the information going into the data base has to be kept in intermediate storage in order to provide backup and speed for on-line systems (see Figures 19–10 and 19–12).

It has to be decided whether this philosophy is to be maintained whenever other teleprocessing (TP) systems are chosen with built-in backup

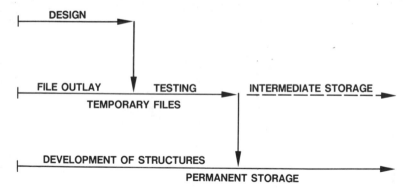

STEPS OF SYSTEM DEVELOPMENT

Figure 19–12. Strategy of system development. During the period of early system development test files will be used, which eventually become temporary files during the first months of actual usage of the application system.

and recovery features. However, the problem will remain that some data are only needed for a short period of time and that not all data should be entered into permanent storage.

D. PROJECT ORGANIZATION AND MANAGEMENT

As already mentioned, the project is identical with the service and research functions of the Division of Medical Information Science of the Department for Biometrics and Medical Information Science. The two directors of the divisions of this department alternate as Department Chairman (Figure 19–13). The function of the department chairman is a reduced administrative one; the basic units of the Hannover Medical School are the divisions. Computer operations are exclusively the charge of the Division for Medical Information Science. This does not apply, as far as

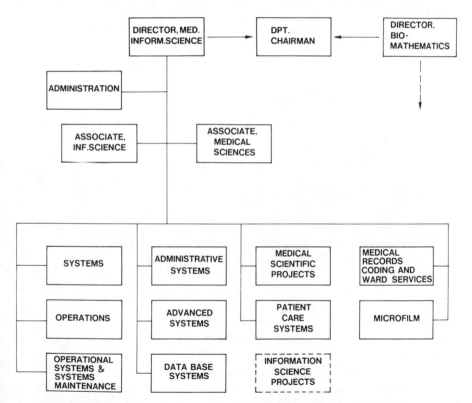

Figure 19–13. Administrative structure of the Division of Medical Information Science and Computer Operations of the Department of Biometrics and Medical Information Science.

operations are concerned, to separate computer activities in other departments such as nuclear medicine and clinical laboratory. However, it is a charge of the division to provide advice and integration.

The different boxes in Figure 19–13 show various functional areas. The medical scientific project and patient care systems consist of various individual projects. Service-oriented units are operations, administrative systems, medical record coding, and microfilm subdivision. All areas, however, participate in scientific development of their own fields of interest. Two associate directors and the chiefs of systems, operations, administrative systems, advanced systems, and medical scientific projects form the immediate staff of the division.

At the moment, 82 people are working on the project, 18 of them being professionals with either M.D. or electrical engineering background. Basic research in information science has been started. A main area of interest in this regard is linguistic analysis and the development of a medical meta language.

E. SUBSYSTEMS

1. Patient Medical Record

The basic concept of the Medical System Hannover is that of a systematized common data base with definition of logical subsets for specific purposes. Figure 19–14 gives an example of such a logical file definition relating to a physical systematized data base. Data may be provided to a specific user as if he would be operating on his own data base, or data may be grouped according to problems defined by the physician. Therefore, one of the principle characteristics of the data base is that data are not grouped according to problems but that problem groupings are part of the data.

The principle of storage is shown in Figure 19–15. It attempts to keep condensed relevant information on-line as long as possible. One of the aids in achieving this goal is the utilization of a problem summary,[9,60] which is called the "problem epicrisis." This problem epicrisis gives a general description of the status of the patient when he was admitted and when he was discharged and an evaluation of the problem at the beginning and the end of the treatment.[17,18] An example of such a problem epicrisis, as tested on a pediatric ward, is shown in Figure 19–16.[17]

This problem epicrisis is stored in the content summary, as shown in Figures 19–9 and 19–10. The logical structure of this content summary is described in Figure 19–17. There may be twin segments for diagnoses and supplements to the coded diagnosis. In general, more than one coding pro-

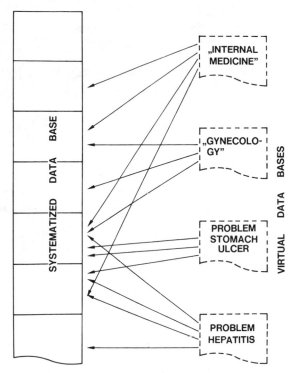

Figure 19–14.   General strategy of data base approach. It is attempted to design a systematized data base with files for the various applications and problems. Segments are made sensitive to related applications.

cedure may be used for the same patient. Various disciplines are given up to three suffixes for each major code category in order to assure retrieval according to the main keys when, especially for scientific purposes, a more detailed coding than provided in the dictionary is wanted. In addition, it may be specified as a clinical suspicion or a verified diagnosis. Furthermore, additional segments may describe diagnoses as having occurred during the hospital stay, being already in existence for a longer time, having occurred after treatment or operations, etc.[43,54] The content summary file CON-PAT[52,54] also contains administrative and personnel data. The segments for risk facts contain information about continuous treatment, allergy, diabetes, and so on.

Figure 19–18 gives the principal outlay of the data bank part for actual patient data.[52,54] Data structures for this data bank are continuously being developed. It is intended to keep these data for one treatment period. Data are then unloaded on tape in specific DL/1 or IMS (14) program structures so that they may be subject to reloading or statistical searches.

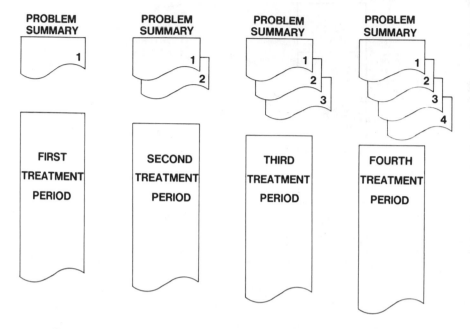

Figure 19–15. Principle of storage.[43] Content and problem summary is kept on-line as long as possible, whereas detailed data are kept on line only during the actual treatment period.

The data base has not yet replaced the manual chart, which is microfilmed and is to be destroyed after the patient's discharge. Though the system provides online information, it does not contain enough data in order to be comprehensive. Its content, however, is rapidly growing after the mastery of the data base software in the first years of system difficulties. The software concept, however, does not distinguish between disciplines, and even the personnel data are kept in the same file structures. At the moment, basic data of about 50,000 patients are on-line, allowing for searches for diagnoses and their combinations as well as their occurrence in the various age groups (see Figure 19–19).

2. Administrative Functions

The Medical System Hannover (MSH) performs various administrative functions. Some of these functions are performed on-line, others are performed in batch processing.

a. Admission.   The admission of all inpatients is done centrally and on line. In case the patient has to be admitted directly to the ward, either the

Medizinische
Hochschule
Hannover
KINDERKLINIK

PROBLEMLISTE
EPIKRISE

GESAMTBEURTEILUNG BEI DER AUFNAHME: (bitte Kästchen ankreuzen)

a) [1] = nicht leidend ☒ = krank [3] = schwer krank [4] = intensivpflege

b) ☒ = gehfähig [2] = sitzend transport. [3] = liegend transport.

GESAMTBEURTEILUNG BEI DER ENTLASSUNG: (bitte Kästchen ankreuzen)

a) [1] = geheilt ☒ = gebessert [3] = unbeeinflußt

[4] = verschlecht. [5] = verstorben [6] = nicht beurteilbar

b) ☒ = gehfähig [2] = sitzend transport. [3] = liegend transport.

PROBLEMLISTE

Probl NR	Zuord- nung	PROBLEMFORMULIERUNG	TYP	DATUM	TYP	DATUM	Zuord- nung	Beurteil- ung
1		Obstruktive, rezidivierende Bronchitis	2	20.3.	2	26.3.		2
2	1	Lungenzyste	1	20.3.	4.	26.3.		6
3	1	Bronchiektasien	1	20.3.	1	26.3.		6
4	1	Sinusitis maxillaris bds.	2	20.3.	2	26.3.		2

Erklärung der Problemtypen: [1] = Verdacht auf [2] = gesichert [3] = Zustand nach [4] = Verdacht nicht bestätigt [5] = therapeutisch inaktiv [6] = untergeordnet

Von der Dokumentationsassistentin einzutragen

Probl. NR	DIAGNOSE SCHLUSSEL	Probl. NR	DIAGNOSE SCHLUSSEL
1	5 0 6 3 5		
3	5 0 7 5 1		
4	2 9 6 5 1		

Stat.Arzt:
Dr. ro

Figure 19–16. Problem list and epicrises as used in tests in the children's hospital. When the patient comes to the hospital, an evaluation of his general status is made (Gesamtbeurteilung bei der Aufnahme). A general description of his status is made when he leaves the hospital (Gesamtbeurteilung bei der Entlassung). In addition, evaluations are to be made in regard to the individual problem (dotted line). The lower part of the figure shows room for diagnostic coding and signature of the physician responsible for the ward.[9,17,18,60]

CONPAT: LOGICAL DATA STRUCTURE

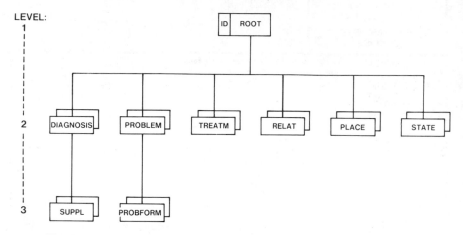

Figure 19–17. Outlay of the Content Summary Data Base.[53,55] Diagnosis segments may contain up to 5 diagnoses belonging to the same code. Additional diagnostic segments may be built if necessary and may contain codes belonging to a different nomenclature.

APAT: LOGICAL DATA STRUCTURE

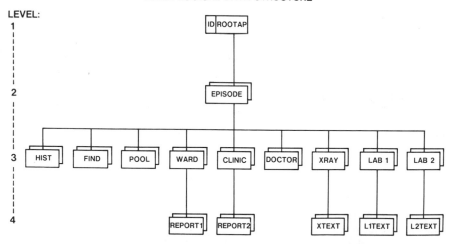

Figure 19–18. Data base for actual patient data.[52,54] Segments show the logical content. "POOL" contains miscellaneous data.

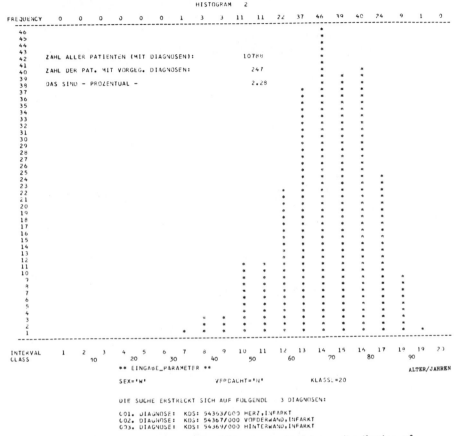

ALTERSVERTEILUNGEN OSTSTADT-PATIENTEN(INFARKT)

Figure 19–19. Data base search. Of interest was the age distribution of all patients with coronary infarction being of female sex. The intervals are by 5 years of age, the height of the column indicates the frequency of this diagnosis in this age group.

ward clerk admits the patient from the terminal on the ward or sends the patient's data to central admission via pneumatic tube to be input into one of the administrative terminals. The "admission dialogue" consists of up to 72 questions about the patient's address, insurance type, employer, secondary carrier, relatives, referring physicians, referring hospital, and so on. The program branches according to the answers, and the average admission dialogue takes 8–10 minutes. Without special effort, 30 patients can be admitted with one terminal/day. During the admission procedure, multiple checkings for formal errors are done; at the end, the data are presented for echo-verification.

From the patient's birthday and his birth name, his identification number is composed and compared against the patient numbers in the data bank. If nine of his ten identification numbers coincide with the number of an already existing patient, a check is performed to determine whether the patient is identical with a previous entry, and a secondary storage area is allocated. In the case of an "identification-number twin," the last digit of the 10–digit identification number is increased by one in order to distinguish between the two different patients. When the patient's admission is completed, an aluminum foil containing the most basic administrative information and, in a binary coded form, the patient's identification number is embossed on a typewriter terminal (Figure 19–20). By means of this aluminum foil, the information can be transcribed on all kind of documents, including optical reader forms (Figure 19–20) in such a way that the binary coded identification number covers the appropriate mark-sense positions. It is therefore possible to identify documents in a machine-readable form without transcribing the 10-digit identification number. All information coming from the patient will be linked to this identification number.

When the aluminum foils are embossed, stickers are printed with the patient's name, ward number, and identification number. These stickers are used for various purposes, including laboratory identification. All information acquired by the admission procedure is printed on appropriate forms and sent to the wards in order to become a part of the patient's chart. Since 80% of all admitted patients belong to obligatory insurance plans, requests for insurance coverage are printed in a standard way and made ready for signature for the physician in the ward.

In the MSH, every inpatient has been registered since the opening of the hospital. Therefore, detailed data in regard to time of admission, quantity and seasonal fluctuations have been obtained (see below).

b. Billing. The main basis for billing is the number of days spent in the hospital. Accordingly, the admission and discharge procedures provide the necessary information to produce the documents. Additional information may be added and will ultimately be retrieved automatically from the files.

For accounting services units (radiology, for instance), on-line programs have been developed that allow one to specify in a free-text approach the procedure that has been performed. Similar to "ODARS,"[14–39] a table look-up is performed to find those entries in the list of procedures that contain the given keyword; and the appropriate entries are made in the patient's records. If desired, a bill with a short description of the procedure can be produced. These programs, however, are not yet used on a routine basis.[41,42]

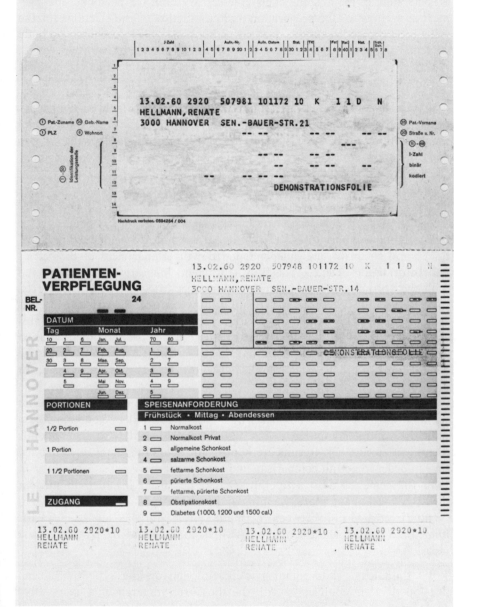

Figure 19–20. Output of the admission dialogue. All information pertinent to the patient including ID-number, admission number, ward, financial status, and previous visits to the hospital will be entered.

c.   Personnel.   The data bases of the MSH contain information about all personnel in the hospital. This is necessary both for personnel management as well as for the preparation and conduction of the elections for the self-governing bodies of the medical school in which teachers, graduate students and residents, students, and technical personnel are represented. A personnel inquiry system contains all relevant data and serves the hospital and departmental management.

d.   Other services.   Other on-line programs are available for budgetary purposes for the hospital as a whole and for the different departmental units. Naturally, all these systems are data-protected. Telephone service administration is done from paper tape punched by the automatic interchange, and appropriate accounting is done.

3.   Service Units

a.   Clinical laboratories.   The clinical laboratories along with hematology and chemistry are independent from the Department of Biometrics and Information Science. The fully automated laboratories are connected with the Infractronics data acquisition system MISDAS and multiplexed into an IBM 1130.[32] Work sheets and quality control are provided by this system. Trend analysis and preparation for final reporting is done in this satellite system. The complete unit is fully tested and operational; routine reporting is expected to be started in 1974, when the links with the central hardware have been established in order to assure transmission of identification and results.

Laboratory examinations are requested on optically read forms. Within the laboratory, a sample number will be assigned; and by communication with the central computer, a link will be established with the patient's identification number. Results are kept in the satellite system for a defined time in order to permit comparison and trend analysis.

In the same fashion, a satellite system has been installed in nuclear medicine.[12] Here automatic scanning and scan analysis are done. There will be no direct data link between the main system and this subsystem in the immediate future. Data communication is intended to be performed via tapes.

b.   Pathology.   For pathology reporting, an on-line system has been developed[62-64] in connection with the thesaurus research of a cooperative study between major European German-speaking institutes for pathology.[51] Cytology and tissue pathology are done completely on-line and without manual backup. The on-line system keeps records of all reports, checks against a previous reporting whenever a new report is entered, and does the necessary bookkeeping for the different laboratories. The reports are dictated in a standardized form and then entered via display terminal by secretaries. During this phase, various checking procedures are invoked, and multiple aids can be used in order to generate the report. Figure 19–21 gives an example of a frame asking for the summary of a consultation requested from the cytology laboratory. All reports may be reviewed on-line, and the hard copy is produced and transmitted to the sender (Figure 19–22). On three terminals, up to 200 reports are generated on three terminals. Autopsy reporting has not yet been started on a routine basis.

Diagnostic findings will be subjected to automated text analysis for retrieval using various methods for free-text analysis. The thesaurus allows classifications according to localization of primary and secondary order, modifiers, and hierarchical classes.[49,50] Research has been initiated with A. W. Pratt and his co-workers.[29,33,34]

c. Radiology. The radiology modules which have been developed together with Lodwick and Templeton[20,39,58] have not yet been used within

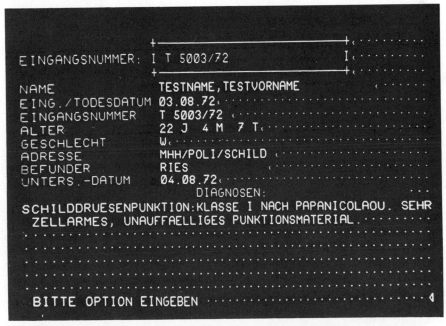

Figure 19–21. A frame of the P.R.S. System (Pathology Reporting System).[62-64] This frame displays the diagnostic description of a cytology examination. The frame shows the patient's name, the date, when the sample was received, the entry-number, his sex, the address of the sender and the date of examination.

624   Peter L. Reichertz

```
PROF.DR.MED. A. GEORGII              3000 HANNOVER,DEN 17. 8.72
PATHOLOGISCHES INSTITUT              KARL WIECHERT ALLEE 9
MEDIZINISCHE HOCHSCHULE              TEL.(0511) 532 2921



MEDIZINISCHE HOCHSCHULE
CHIRURGISCHE POLIKLINIK
SCHILDDRUESENAMBULANZ

3000 H A N N O V E R
------------------------------
KARL-WIECHERT-ALLEE


        +---------------------------------------+
        |         CYTOLOGIE : T 5003/72   W     |
        +---------------------------------------+

NAME: TESTNAME,TESTVORNAME           EINGANGSDATUM:         03.08.72
I-ZAHL: 26.03.50 OC 29               UNTERSUCHUNGSDATUM: 04.08.72
                                     UNTERSUCHER: RIES
                                     VORBEFUND: T 6702/71

UNTERSUCHUNGSMATERIAL:
----------------------
SCHILDDRUESENPUNKTION

CYTOLOGISCHE BESCHREIBUNG:
--------------------------
DAS AUSSTRICHPRAEPARAT ENTHAELT NUR SEHR SPAERLICHES ZELLMATERIAL,
VORWIEGEND ELEMENTE DES PERIPHEREN BLUTES. DIE AEUSSERST SPAERLICHEN
SCHILDDRUESENEPITHELIEN SIND UNAUFFAELLIG.

BEURTEILUNG:
------------
KLASSE I NACH PAPANICOLAOU. SEHR ZELLARMES, UNAUFFAELLIGES
PUNKTIONSMATERIAL.



        DR.RIES                      PROF.DR.MED. A. GEORGII
```

Figure 19-22. Report generated by the P.R.S. (Pathology Reporting System).[62-64] The input is made by secretaries acording to a structured way of reporting and then the reports will be generated and the information stored.

the MSH. They have been adapted to the German language, and installation of visual display units in the department of radiology is planned for the year 1973.

ODARS is a typical example of the strategy to combine syntactical machine operations with semantic human evaluation (Figure 19-23).[37,40] The radiologist or the secretary first specifies the type of examination by giving a keyword which consists of the first four letters of any word within the descriptive term. A table look-up is then performed, and the appropriate

"Odars"

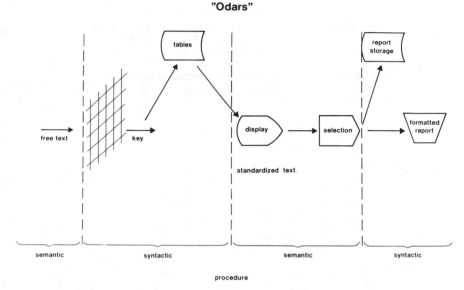

Figure 19–23. Sequence between semantic and syntactic operation as used in ODARS (On-line Diagnostic and Reporting System).[20,37,39] Quasi-free text information is input through the grid of keywords consisting of the first letters of a word in the intended descriptive noun phrase. A table look-up is then performed and the physician makes his choice. The report is stored and sent to the ward.

entry is selected. In the same way, the anatomic site and the diagnosis is specified. In all instances, the keyword leads to an extended display of the possible examinations, anatomic sites, or diagnoses. Any of these entries may be modified by a table of modifiers, or additional information may be added by precoded phrases. After the diagnostic evaluation, a confidence level is given in order to enable the radiologist to specify different weights of his evaluation or differential diagnosis. At the same time, diagnostic aid is available in the areas of solitary lung nodules,[57] gastric ulcers,[61] thyroid disease,[8,35,65] bone tumor,[19] and heart disease.[56] At the moment, a model is developed for acute abdominal symptomatology. The mathematical algorithms used in this module are of probabilistic nature. A typical report generated by this system is shown in Figure 19–24.

d. Pharmacy. The dispensing of drugs in German hospitals differs from the dispensing in U.S. hospitals. Many drug categories are ordered by and dispensed from wards. Therefore, specific preparation of drugs in the pharmacy is not necessary. On the other hand, detailed registration occurs in the ward. In accounting for drugs, much drug treatment is covered by the

```
SAMSTAG        JANUAR 20,1973; ZEIT: 14.23 UHR
*************************** ROENTGENBERICHT ****IZAHL : 20.09.30 5010*
NAME :DOE          PAUL G.    GEB. : 20/09/30 SEX : MAENNL
STATION OD. ABTLG.: A5        KOSTENTRAEGER: S.Z.
    UNTERSUCHUNGSART:THORAX, P.A. UND LATERAL
            TOPOGRAPHIE:LUNGE
                            RECHTS
            TOPOGRAPHIE:OBERER LAPPEN
                DIAGNOSE:CARCINOM BRONCHIOGEN
                            ZUVERLAESSIGKEITSGRAD  6
                DIAGNOSE:PNEUMONIE
                            CHRONISCH
                            ZUVERLAESSIGKEITSGRAD  4
DIE ANGEGEBENEN DIAGNOSEN SIND ALS DIFFERENTIALDIAGNOSE AUFZUFASSEN
ES WIRD TOMOGRAPHIE EMPFOHLEN
    UNTERSUCHUNGSART:GALLENBLASENAUFNAHME (ORALES
                    KONTRASTMITTEL)
            DIAGNOSE:NEGATIVE GALLENBLASENDARSTELLUNG
                    ZUVERLAESSIGKEITSGRAD  9
                            P.L. REICHERTZ
```

Figure 19–24. Radiology report using ODARS.[20,39,58] The report is structured showing type of examination, anatomic site, and diagnostic reading. A confidence level describes the confidence of the reporting physician.

lump sum paid per day by the insurance company. The need for individual accounting of drug administration therefore comes more from medical concerns than from the economic requirements of the hospital. However, expansive or restricted drugs have to be ordered directly from the pharmacy for each patient.

The pharmacy system of the MSH is still under development. It will be implemented in three steps:

(1) The first step is operational. It accounts for the drug movements to and from the wards and serves the purposes of medical audit and administrative accounting and survey.

(2) The second step will account for drug administration to each individual patient, thus establishing his drug profile.

(3) The third step is linked to the first one and will provide the stock inventory of the pharmacy.

At the same time, the drug inquiry system will be implemented, thus providing the physician with information about actions and side effects, contraindication, indication, and incompatibility. At a later period in time, the drug profile and the patient will be matched against these data in order to optimize therapeutic actions and to avoid contraindications and incompatibilities.

e. Physiology. Within the Medical School Hannover there exist two additional divisions which work in the area of biosignal processing. Both groups are research projects funded by the Federal Government.

The group Schneider/Zywietz is in the phase of implementing the routine analysis of electrocardiograms. Programs of Pipberger[31] have been expanded and adapted to a SIGMA II.

Künkel and co-workers are pursuing the problem of automatic analysis of electroencephalograms on a Telefunken Hybrid Computer TR 86.

Both applications are not yet in full routine. ECG reporting, however, is done using the FTSS system [see sections 4.c.(2) and (6)].

f. Automated multiphasic screening. There is no service module in the Hannover Medical School Hospital to perform automated multiphasic screening on a routine basis. Screening procedures are performed by the various clinics, but an overall system has not yet been implemented. The major mandatory insurance plans do not support general screening procedures and only provide support for certain measures which mostly are performed by the general practitioner.

g. Patient dietary. Patient menus are prepared on an automated tray line. A variety of 30 different menu plans may be preprogrammed in such a fashion so that the trays proceed through an "assembly line," where the different ingredients are put on the trays according to light signs in front of the employees. In such a fashion, it is possible to employ both unskilled workers as well as non-German-speaking personnel. Furthermore, the production may be highly automated.

In order to control this "assembly line," a punched card has to be prepared per patient and meal indicating what type of menu and what portion size (three choices, especially in diabetes to specify calories and carbohydrates) are to be dispensed. Also the name and the ward has to be marked for the food transport.

The necessary control cards are produced by the MSH on a daily basis. Updating of this system respective to the change of the diet plan is done either by optically read forms (as partly seen in Figure 19–20) or by on-line modules. The ward clerks or the nurses on the wards can specify the desired change, and appropriate control mechanisms will be invoked.

Figure 19–25 gives an example of such a dialogue. The conversation is carried out from a typewriter terminal, and all user input is circled. Code word of the user and patient identification have been blanked out. (A typewriter printout has been chosen in order to show more than one query/answer sequence.) After the user has given his code-word and has been admitted to the system, he is asked to specify the number (which in this case is 14). Subsequently, all patients on this ward (maximum 18) are dis-

```
$$patstat
..OK
SIE SIND BENUTZER NR:          2
                         **** PATSTAT ****
            INFORMATIONSSYSTEM FUER DIE PATIENTENVERPFLEGUNG.
       BITTE GEBEN SIE IHR KENNWORT FUER DIE BENUTZUNG DES SYSTEMS AN:
          (DAS PROGRAMM HAT EINBLICK IN PATIENTENDATEN,WIDERRECHTLICHE
                               BENUTZUNG IST STRAFBAR)
PROGRAMMIERUNG UND SYSTEMDESIGN: G.ENDERLEIN, E.SCHIEL, R.ENGELBRECHT
  ¢d:      '9
*** SCHLUESSELWORT WIRD GEPRUEFT ***
LIEBER BENUTZER REICHERTZ
BITTE GEBEN SIE DIE STATIONSBEZEICHNUNG EIN:¢14
LISTE DER PATIENTEN DER STATION 14       K P    K P    K P

 1 R          UST        30.01.11  910   0 3    0 3    0 3
 2 HA         'E         07.03.r  9220   0 3    0 3    0 3
 3 ALb                   01.0" 7 0010   13 0   13 0   13 0
 4 NAR1                  08  ɔ.10 9620  13 2   13 2   13 2
 5 FECHI                 :..06.15 1710   3 1    3 1    3 1
          ENDE DER LISTE,BITTE NEUE EINGABE ¢ae,5
          AENDERUNG FUER          ,WILHELM
          ZEITPUNKT
               1   ZUM FRUEHSTUECK
               2   ZUM MITTAG
               3   ZUM ABENDESSEN
          PORTIONSGROESSE
               0   KLEINE PORTION
               1   NORMALE PORTION
               2   GROSSE PORTION
          KOSTFORM  (NACH SCHLUESSEL)
  ¢2,2,11
               IST ALLES RICHTIG ? (JA/NEIN)
STATION: 14
STAND FUER         ,WILHELM        11.06.15 1710
FUER DEN 05.11.72  KOSTFORM   PORTION
FRUEHSTUECK            3         1
MITTAG               11          2
ABEND                11          2¢
```

Figure 19–25. Patients' Dietary System. (The user's answers are circled with pencil.) The system informs the user about confidentiality levels, then the code word is asked (blanked out). The user specifies he wants to see the patients of Ward 14. These patients are displayed (names and ID-numbers partially blanked out). The user indicates a change in the dietary status of patient no. 5 indicating that he wants the following change effected for next noon: (2) a large portion (2) of diet no. 11 (a special diabetic diet). Tne system then redisplays this new status and asks for final confirmation.

played. Their identification numbers and their present dietary status are given. The user now indicates that he wants to change patient number 5. He receives more detailed instructions on how to do so, and the request is redisplayed for echoverification.

4. Clinical Units

a. Nurses' station system.   The nurses now operate the dietary system from the ward. At the moment, there are no nurses' notes entered. (Nurses' notes are not part of the traditional chart in German hospitals). Inquiries can be made from the wards, and patients may be admitted. Research is being done in this area.

b. Patient scheduling and hospital admitting.   Automated scheduling is not yet performed. The automated admission procedure, however, yields valuable planning data and provides statistics about queuing problems, preferences for admitting and discharging, average stay per hospital ward, diagnosis, and age classes as well as catchment areas of patients.

Figure 19–26 gives an overview of the first year of operation. The plot shows the number of admissions per day, the number of discharges per day, and the total number of beds occupied. The lower graph (total number of beds occupied) shows a remarkable dip during the time of Christmas, Easter, Pentecost, and 1st May (general holiday). Furthermore (not seen in this graph), a decrease of beds occupied could be seen this year during the beginning of the general vacation in the state. It is remarkable that after the decrease no compensatory increase is seen. In addition, the hospital shows a gradual increase in capacity. The summary graph shows weekly undulations also. From the upper graph and the presentation of discharges/ week (Figure 19–27), it can already be summarized that there were higher admission frequencies at the beginning of the week and lower ones at the end. In looking at the graphs of the admissions, it becomes quite clear that the peaks at the beginning of the week invariably lead to either overutilization of human and material resources during the first parts of the week or to underutilization at the end.

But also the distribution of admissions/hour/day shows a peak during the first two hours of the day (Figure 19–28) and demonstrates that 80% of all patients have been admitted by 1:30 PM (Figure 19–29).

The average stay of the patients in the hospital is around 13 days, including psychiatric patients. Histograms of the patients' stay (Figure 19–30) show a high peak after 1 day (discharge of emergency patients) and after 1 week, with smaller maxima every seven days.

The histogram of the average stay per patient per ward points out

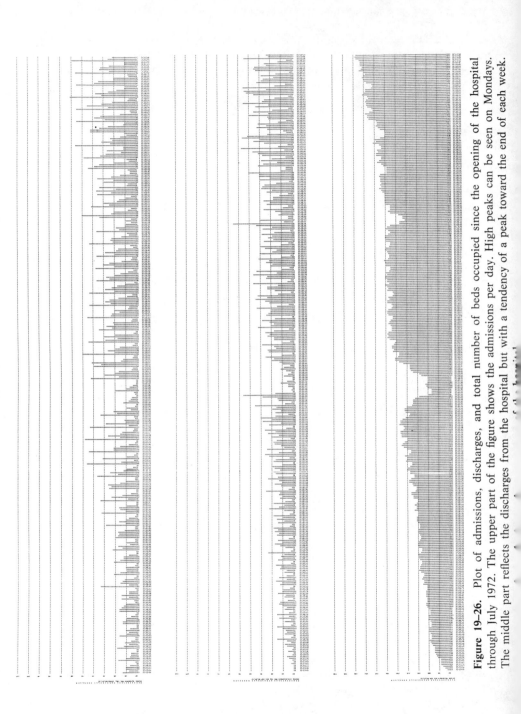

Figure 19–26. Plot of admissions, discharges, and total number of beds occupied since the opening of the hospital through July 1972. The upper part of the figure shows the admissions per day. High peaks can be seen on Mondays. The middle part reflects the discharges from the hospital but with a tendency of a peak toward the end of each week.

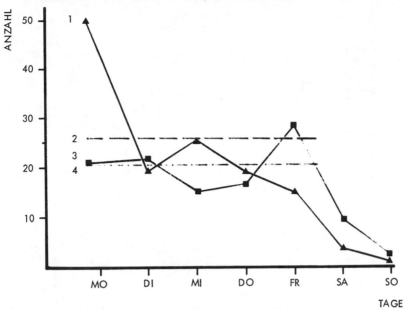

AUFNAHMEN UND ENTLASSUNGEN EINER WOCHE

(17. – 23. Januar 1972)

1 Aufnahmen   3 Entlassungen

2 Mittelwert Aufnahmen   4 Mittelwert Entlassungen

(Die Mittelwerte beziehen sich nur auf MO–FR)

Figure 19–27. Schematic diagram of the week January 17–23, 1972.[5] Number 1 delineates the admissions for each day of that week. Curve No. 2 shows the average. No. 3 indicates the fluctuation of the discharges and curve No. 4 gives the mean values of the discharges.

immediately the areas with a longer-than-average stay of the patient, mostly caused by the different type of service (Figure 19–31). Ward 30, the psychiatric day care center, has a longer stay. The average stay per ward varies from 2.6 days (emergency admission) to 51.6 (ward 30 shown in the histogram, Figure 19–31). The listing of length of stay per diagnosis naturally shows a different picture. The average stay for patients with coronary infarction, for instance, was 23.5 days, with a slight difference between the anterior and posterior walls (i.e., 23.6 days vs. 23.3 days).

c.   Medical information processing.

(1) Automated histories. A research project addresses itself to the automated acquisition and evaluation of patient histories.[22,23] The "Clinical Decision Support System"[26,27] has been adapted both to OS and our tele-

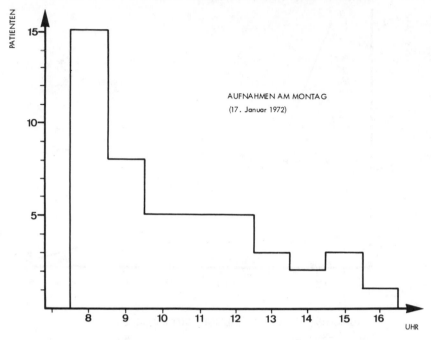

Figure 19–28. Frequency of admissions during the hours of the first day of the week in Figure 19–27.[5] Between 7:30 and 8:30 AM fifteen in-patients have been admitted.

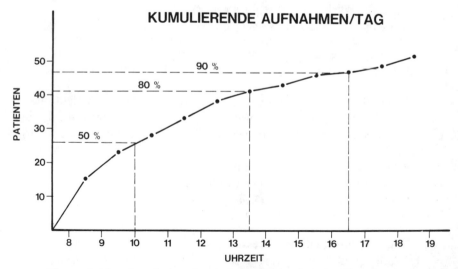

Figure 19–29. Cumulative description of the admissions on the same day as shown in Figure 19–27. 50% of all patients have been admitted by 10 o'clock, 80% by 1:30 PM and 90% by 4 PM.

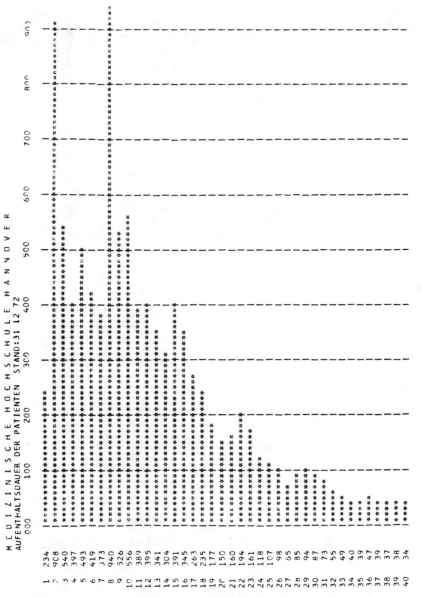

Figure 19-30. Plot of the stay of patients in the hospital.[5] The first row of numbers indicates number of days; the second row represents the number of patients in the hospital on those days. The asterisks give a graphic representation of these facts.

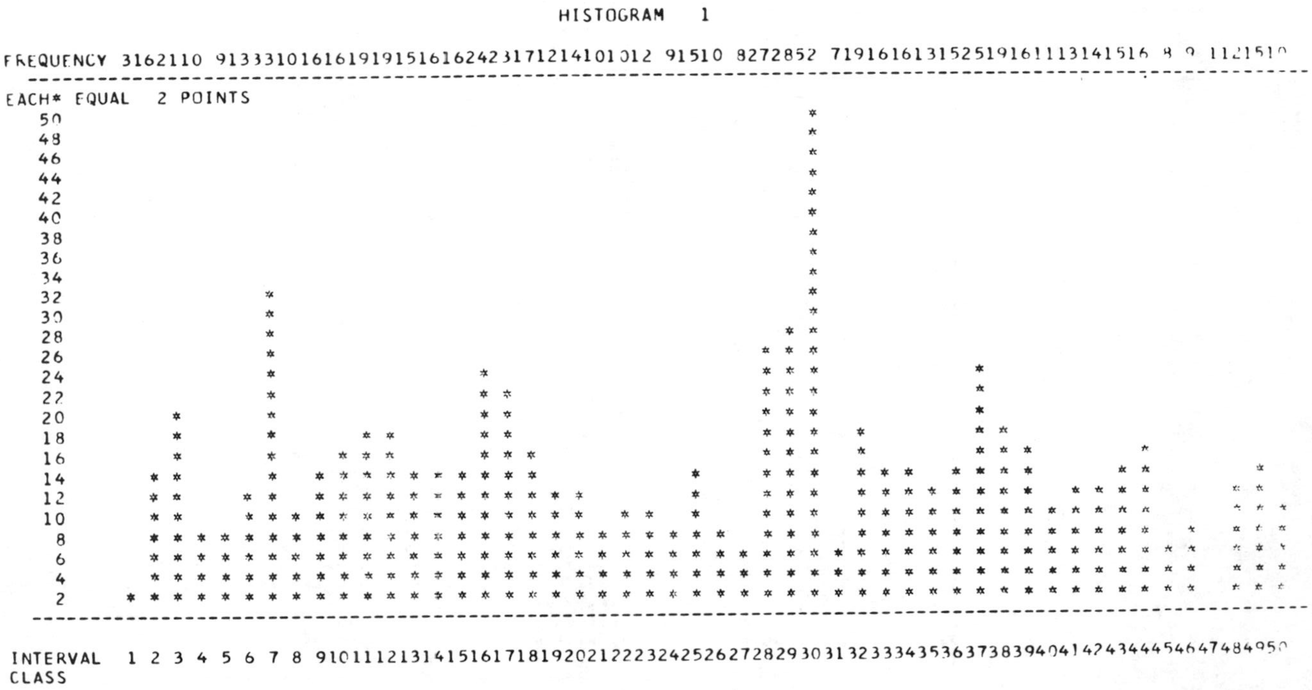

Figure 19–31. Average stay of patient per ward. "Frequency" at the top of the figure indicates the average number of days in the ward indicated by "interval." The high average stay (52 days) for Ward no. 30 is due to the psychiatric patients in this service.

processing system as well as to the IMS data bases. History acquisition can be done both by use of optically read forms produced by the line printer and by interaction with a display. A typical questionnaire is comprised of approximately 400 questions detailing the patient's sociological history, his environment, and his reactions to the procedure. For the printout, the grouping of the answers is done according to the requirements of the discipline. Figure 19–32 gives a sample printout of the systematic review covering head, neck, thorax, and respiratory system.

(2) Physical examinations and FTSS. For some kinds of physical examinations and reporting, the Free Text Synthesis System (FTSS[16]) is used. This system is based on optical-reader forms which may also be used as primary documentation in the patient's chart. Figure 19–33 gives an example for the pediatric department. The optically read form shown in Figure 19–33 is a part of the history of a child describing the thoracic part of the systematic review. The user may specify in a command language how the findings reported on the optically read form should be printed and synthesized either to a description of the physical findings (Figure 19–34) and/or consultation report (for another example, see below).

(3) Problem oriented record. One of the MSH research projects is based on the concept of the problem-oriented record.[9,13,17,18,61] Test applications have been started, especially on pediatric wards. The system allows for specification of problems, critical evaluation of problems, updating, and free-text-adding to reports to be generated from optically read forms with FTSS.[16]

A major part of the system is the generation of discharge summaries (described as problem epicrisis: see Figure 19–16).[17]

d. Special inpatient services. For special inpatient services, so-called "ancillary systems" have been designed and implemented. The term "ancillary system" has been defined as follows:[42,45] Ancillary systems are those systems which support directly the physician's activity in dealing with the patient. In this category fall:

(1) special inquiry systems;

(2) decision support systems;

(3) interpretation aids (discipline oriented, problem oriented)

(4) problem management systems (e.g., fluid balance calculations, flow rates, heart and lung diagnostics, simulation systems, etc.);

(5) aid in specific research projects (data acquisition, grouping, and analysis).

(1) MHBS. A typical ancillary system is the "Mineralhaushaltbilanzierungs System" (MHBS), which is a service system to perform balance

SYSTEMUEBERSICHT
KOPFBEREICH:

KOPFSCHMERZEN FRUEHER (VOR MEHR ALS 6 MONATEN) ,JETZT NICHT MEHR
SCHWINDELGEFUEHL ODER -ANFAELLE
AUGENBESCHWERDEN:
SEHKRAFTVERMINDERUNG AUF EINEM ODER BEIDEN AUGEN, SEHKRAFT
    VERMINDERUNG DURCH BRILLE ODER KONTAKTLINSEN KORRIGIERBAR
BRENNENDES GEFUEHL AN DEN AUGEN
VERMEHRTER TRAENENFLUSS
JUCKEN DER AUGEN
SKOTOME (SCHWARZE PUNKTE VOR DEN AUGEN) INNERHALB DER VERG. 6 MON.
PAT. FINDET SICH IN DER DUNKELHEIT SCHLECHT ZURECHT

OHRENBESCHWERDEN:
SPRACHVERSTAENDNIS IN LEISER UND LAUTER UMGEBUNG OHNE UNTERSCHIED
ABSONDERUNG AUS DEM GEHOERGANG INNERHALB DER VERGANGENEN 3 MONATE

NASENNEBENHOEHLEN BESCHWERDEN
ERKAELTUNGEN ALS HAEUFIGER ALS BEI ANDEREN AUFTRETEND EMPFUNDEN
PAT. HAT HAEUFIG MANDELENTZUENDUNG

VERAENDERUNGEN IM BEREICH DER MUNDHOEHLE
BRENNEN DER ZUNGE INNERHALB DER VERGANGENEN 6 MONATE
ZUSTAND DER ZAEHNE ALS SCHLECHT BEURTEILT
PAT. LEIDET UNTER ZAHNFLEISCHBLUTEN
PARADENTOSE (ZAHNFLEISCHENTZUENDUNG) VON ARZT FESTGESTELLT

HALSBEREICH:

KNOTEN IM BEREICH VON HALS, ACHSELHOEHLE, LEISTENGEGEND
PATIENT HAT STRUMA (VERGROESSERTE SCHILDDRUESE, KROPF)
KLOSSGEFUEHL IM HALS, MANCHMAL

THORAXBEREICH:

.
HERZGERAEUSCHE VOM ARZT FRUEHER FESTGESTELLT
FRUEHERE HERZERKRANKUNGEN:
EKG-FRUEHERE UNTERSUCHUNGSERGEBNISSE

BLAESSE VON PAT. BEOBACHTET

KREISLAUF:

ABSTERBEN DER FINGER UND FUESSE IN DER KAELTE
UEBERWACHUNG DES BLUTDRUCKS WURDE BEI FRUEHEREN GELEGENHEITEN
    ANGERATEN
ERHOEHTER BLUTDRUCK FRUEHER VON ARZT FESTGESTELLT

Figure 19–32. Example of a history taken with CDSS. [22,23,26,27] The
data are obtained in a question-answer sequence other than those shown
on the final printout. The printout may be grouped according to special requirements, or regrouped for other purposes. Here a systematic survey
is given showing head, neck, chest and circulatory system.

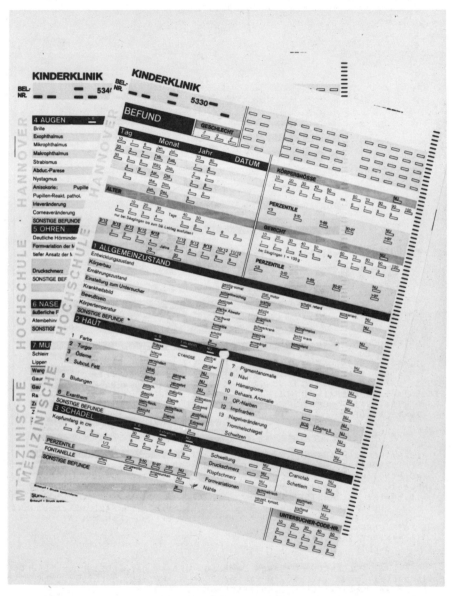

Figure 19–33. Optically read form of the children's hospital to record physical findings.[17] The findings then may be compiled in a summary description as shown in Figure 19–34.

BETRIFFT: C3.11.63 7920 , STATICN 62

UNTERSUCHUNGSBEFUND VOM
       .   20   MAERZ   .   72
    1.**ALLGEMEINZUSTAND**
       CAS MAEDCHEN IST :   8 JAHR(E) *   6 MCNATE ALT*   139 CM
GROSS, LAENGEN-PERZENTILE 90-97 , WIEGT   27 KILOGRAMM, GEWICHTS-
PERZENTILE IM NCRMBEREICH(11-89) * NORMAL ENTWICKELT,
KOERPERTEMPERATUR NCRMAL.
    3.**SCHAEDEL*
       KOPFUMFANG: 52   CM, PERZENTILE NICHT UNTERSUCHT ,
    LYMPHOME:
       FEHLEN
    10.**THORAXORGANE**
       SYMMETRISCHE THORAX-DEFCRMIERUNG BDS., ATEMFREQUENZ WACH ,
22 PRO MIN., RASSELGERAEUSCH OBERFELD RECHTS HINTEN ,LINKS HINTEN
FEINBLASIG
    11.**HERZ UND KREISLAUF**
       BLUTCRUCK AM RE.ARM   125 /   85 MM/HG ZENTRALF HERZFREQUENZ
    WACH,   85 PRO MIN. PALPATICN UHNE PATH. BEFUND , AUSKULTATION
CHNE PATH.BEFUND ,
    14.**WIRBELSAEULE**
       SKOLICSE CER BWS ,

       AN FCLGENCEN ORGANEN WURDEN KEINE PATHCLOGISCHEN BEFUNDE
FESTGESTELLT: HAUT ,AUGEN ,CHREN ,NASE ,MUND-RACHEN ,HALS ,ABDOMEN
,GELENKE ,KNOCHEN ,NEURCLCG.UNTERSUCHUNG .

Figure 19–34. Description of findings as recorded on mark sense forms
(Figure 19–33) used in the children's hospital.[17] To compile this summary a general purpose free text system has been used (FTSS).[16,17]

calculations for intensive care patients, especially for those recovering from neurosurgery.[66,67]

The system provides modules for admission and discharge to and from the ward. It then permits entering of data specifying the loss of fluid, saliva, gastric juice, stool, urine, blood, weight, etc. and compares these values to the intravenous intake. In order to specify the various intravenous fluids, about 100 different preparations are listed and can be reviewed in regard to their components (see Figure 19–35). Upon request, the program calculates a balance for the given observation period as well as for the whole stay.

From the patient's profile, a specific intravenous therapy can be computed. Therefore, the standard preparations are matched against the needs of the patient; the best match is chosen, and additional electrolytes to be added are specified, if necessary.

(2) AKOS. "Allgemeines Kodierungssystem" (AKOS) provides a system for encoding diagnoses allowing for free-text entry of five or more letters of a significant word in a diagnostic term. Upon this entry, a table look-up in the specified code is done and all matches are displayed, naturally eliminating trivial retrievals. The user then may specify the most significant match, and this code is added to the patient's record. It is possible to request all code synonyms be displayed. When retrieved, standard (preferred) descriptions are chosen (see Figures 19–39 and 19–40).

Figure 19–36 gives an example of such a coding process (abbreviated). After the patient has been identified (not shown in Figure 19–36), the user specifies that he wants to code a disease containing the string "GELBS." All possible choices within the chosen code are displayed, and he elects to see the key synonyms connected with choice 2, which indicates jaundice caused by leptospirosis. After reviewing the key synonyms, the user chooses entry 2 to become part of the patient's chart. Now the user may specify additional information about the state of diagnosis (old condition, recurring condition, etc.), connection with medical action, localization, and time (during the hospital stay, before admission). After the additional code has been entered, all information is redisplayed for echoverification before it is stored away.

(3) Diagnostic aid. In the research environment of the medical school, several diagnostic models are used for research purposes. One of the therapeutic decision-support features has already been described under MHBS (see (1) above). Here a profile comparison was done between a negative balance and a possible preparation for intravenous therapy.

In the area of medical diagnosis, the problem becomes more complicated. Other than in systematic description—as, for instance, in zoology and botany—diagnostic classes have to describe transient states of individuals.

```
••••••••••••••••••••••••••••••••••    M M d S    ••••••••••••••••••••••••••••••
••••••••••••••••••••••••••  MED. INFORMATIK - STOFFWECHSELBILANZEN  ••••••••••••

BILANZ NR.:    4

    DUE            JOHN           20.09.30.5010.52IJ    BILANZ VOM 20.01.73   0 -16 UHR
```

	FLUES	GES_N	NA	CL	K	CA	FS	KH	ALK	KHX	MG	HCO3	ACET	LACT	MALAT
EINFUHR: LOESUNG															
EINFUHR: AMIN	250	1	8	2	6	0	0	12	0	0	1	0	8	0	5
EINFUHR: A-10	250	2	8	9	6	0	0	24	12	0	1	0	8	0	5
EINFUHR: LIP1	100	0	0	0	0	0	9	0	0	4	0	0	0	0	0
EINFUHR:															
EINFUHR:															
EINFUHR:															
EINFUHR:															
EINFUHR:															
EINFUHR:															
GESAMTINFUHR:	600	3	16	11	12	0	9	36	12	4	2	0	16	0	10
OXYDATIONSWASSER	300														
AUSFUHR: URIN	200	0	35	39	19	1	0	0	0	0					
AUSFUHR: MAGENS.	50	0	2	4	14	0	0	0	0	0					
AUSFUHR: STUHL	200	0	6	14	0	0	0	0	0	0					
AUSFUHR: SPEICHEL	10	0	0	0	0	0	0	0	0	0					
AUSFUHR: KOND_WAS	70	0	0	0	0	0	0	0	0	0					
AUSFUHR: DRAINAGE	0	0	0	0	0	0	0	0	0	0					
AUSFUHR: SCHWEISS	814	0	47	36	8	0	0	0	0	0					
GESAMTAUSFUHR:	1294	0	90	93	41	1	0	0	0	0	1	0	16	0	
TAGESBILANZ:	-394	3	-74	-82	-29	-1	9	40	12	2					-0.2

```
ZUSAETZLICHE TAGESWERTE:

            KCAL SOLL:  2200      KCAL DIFF:  -1757
            KCAL IST:    443

            BLUTZUFUHR:  250      BLUT DIFF:   150
            BLUTVERLUST: 100

            TEMPERATUR: 38.8      GEW. DIFF:   -0.2
            GEWICHT:    78.2


                                              GEWICHT
                          BLUT  300             -0.8
                          CA     -1

GESAMT - BILANZ:   FLUES  GES_N    NA     CL     K     CA
                   -714     7    -163   -175   -56    -1


BILANZ ERSTELLT VON REICHERTZ
```

Figure 19-35. Printout of the system (MHBS)[66,67] used to calculate input and output of electrolytes, minerals, and calories in an intensive care ward (neurosurgery). In a question/answer dialogue the losses of the patient (urine, stool, condensation water, drainage, etc.) are specified along with the intravenous therapy he has undergone. The system then balances intake against loss, including blood, and gives values.

```
 (GELBSucht

   1 GELBSUCHT,UEBERTRAGBARE
   2 GELBSUCHT,LEPTOSPIROESE
   3 GELBSUCHT,BOESARTIGE IN DER
     GRAVIDITAET
   4 GELBSUCHT
   5 GELBSUCHT,BOESARTIGE
 SUCHWORT:GELBS    DIAGNOSE DURCH CODEZAHL WAEHLEN.    ENDE DER    5 DIAGNOSEN
  BITTE EINGABE:
  (s2)

 UNTER DEM KDS     95/000 GIBT ES FOLGENDE BEZEICHN.
 ICD: 10011 GELBSUCHT,LEPTOSPIROESE
 ICD: 10011 IKTERUS SEPTICO-HAEMORRHAGICUS
 ICD: 10011 IKTERUS,LEPTOSPIROESER
 ICD: 10011 INFEKTION DURCH SPIROCHAETA IKTEROGENES
 ICD: 10011 INFEKTION DURCH LEPTOSPIRA IKTEROHAEMORRHAGIAE
 ICD: 10011 LEPTOSPIROSE,IKTEROHAEMORRHAGISCHE
 ICD: 10011 WEIL-KRANKHEIT
 ENDE DER SCHLUESSELSYNONYMALISTE¢

 (2)

 SOLL FUER DEN PATIENTEN EIN ZUSATZSCHLUESSEL ABGESPEICHERT WERDEN?
 (WENN JA DANN BITTE NACH CODE EINGEBEN,SONST NEIN EINGEBEN.)
   Z U S T A N D       AERZTLICHE  M A S S N A H M E N    L O K A L I S A T I O N
 A1 AELTERER BEFUND    B1 ZUR DIAGNOSTIK  C1 OPERATION    D1 RECHTS
 A2 REZIDIV NACH       B2 ZUR THERAPIE    C2 BESTRAHLUNG  D2 LINKS
 A3 ZUSTAND NACH                          C3 ISOTOPEN     D3 BEIDSEITIG
 A4 BEFUND NACH                           C4 MEDIKAMENTE
                                          C5 SONSTIGES      A U F T R E T E N
                                                          E1 INTERKURRENT
                                                          E2 VOR AUFNAHME

 (A2)

 SIND ALLE ANGABEN RICHTIG?  IZAHL:   20.09.30 5010
 NAME: DOE,     JOHN
 ARZTCODE:   123
 KDS:    95/000          ICD: 10011
 TEXT:
 GELBSUCHT,LEPTOSPIROESE
 DIAGNOSENZUSATZ:
 DIAGNOSENZUSTAND: REZIDIV NACH

 (JA/NEIN)(ja)
```

Figure 19–36. Coding of Diseases. "AKOS" (Allgemeines Kodierungs-system[7]) follows the approach of ODARS[20,39,58] as indicated in Figure 19–23. A string of 5 or more characters of any word in the noun-phrase describing the condition is entered. A table look-up is performed and the result is displayed (in this Fig. "GELBS" has been entered and all entries with "jaundice" are retrieved as shown in the "Klinischer Diagnosenschluessel"[15]).

These states vary in regard to extent and are not static. A disease is a reaction of multiple cybernetic control systems to causes of disturbances inside and/or outside the body. This reaction is dependent upon the internal and external environment as well as upon the multitude of cross-regulations between the various cybernetic systems. Nevertheless, diagnostic classification is a valid shorthand to describe the findings in an individual case and to establish a base for diagnostic and/or therapeutic action. Furthermore, these classifications are necessary for epidemiological research. Due to the dynamics and the variety of diseases, it cannot be expected that general models will lead to a general classification in detail. It might, however, be expected to find modules to deal with well-defined subcategories or, on the other hand, to establish classification within larger categories for further decision and detailed examination.

The physician in a clinical environment does not expect primarily a scientific classification in a diagnostic model, but he does want to have some recommendations resulting from a computer-aided diagnostic process. He is not so much looking for categorical descriptive classes as for action models. The physician often has to take action without completion of the diagnostic process; often the therapeutic action becomes part of the diagnostic evaluation.

The diagnostic process in clinical medicine is a strategy using multiple approaches and reacting to the actual status of the patient. Therefore, by and large, successful diagnostic models will have to be adaptive and dynamic models which show a strategic approach and use more than one mathematical way of proceeding.

Within the MSH, the research is done mostly with two models:

(a) Probabilistic model. The probabilistic model chosen is the Bayescan theorem.[1,21,59] The program vehicle used is the CADS (Computer Aided Diagnostic System) of ODARS (see E.3.c). Defined are models for thyroid disease,[8,35,37,65] bone tumor,[19] gastric ulcer,[61] heart disease,[56] and solitary lung nodules.[57] A model for acute abdominal symptomatology is under development.

Figure 19–37 reflects a dialogue in the part of CADS dealing with heart diseases. Symptom after symptom is described (the program may skip symptoms according to user's answers), and eventually the diagnostic evaluation is displayed and percent ratings are given. Individual symptoms may now be changed in order to investigate their influence upon the final diagnosis. The data of the patient may be stored in order to fit into the probabilistic matrix.

(b) The deterministic model. The deterministic model used in the MSH environment is the neuron-like concept of CDSS (Clinical Decision Support System)[26,27] which has been adapted to OS and the BEST TP environ-

```
ALTER                              GESCHLECHT
   A 3 MONATE ODER WENIGER.           K MAENNLICH
   B 4 MONATE BIS 5 JAHRE             L WEIBLICH
   C UEBER 5 JAHRE BIS 20
   D UEBER 20 BIS 45
 BITTE MIT DEM KODEBUCHSTABEN ANTWORTEN; KEINE INFORMATION : 0, ENDE : Z
¢DK


ZYANOSE                            HERZGROESSE
   A JA                              K NORMAL
   B NEIN                            L GROSS 1 +
                                     M GROSS 2 +
                                     N GROSS 3 +
 BITTE MIT DEM KODEBUCHSTABEN ANTWORTEN; KEINE INFORMATION : 0, ENDE : Z
¢BK


LINKES ATRIUM                      RECHTES ATRIUM
   A NORMAL                          K NORMAL
   B GROSS                           L GROSS
   C RIESIG
 BITTE MIT DEM KODEBUCHSTABEN ANTWORTEN; KEINE INFORMATION : 0, ENDE : Z
¢ak

STIEFEL FORM                       ASZENDIERENDE AORTA
   A JA                              K KLEIN
   B NEIN                            L NORMAL
                                     M GROSS
 BITTE MIT DEM KODEBUCHSTABEN ANTWORTEN; KEINE INFORMATION : 0, ENDE : Z
¢bl




AORTA KLAPPEN STENOSE
   = 67
OFFENER DUCTUS ARTERIOSUS
   = 8
PULMON. KLAPPEN STENOSE
   = 8
VENT. SEPT. DEFEKT
   = 5
ARTERIOSKLEROTISCHE HERZERKRANKUNG
   = 5
AORTEN COARCTATION
   = 2
FALLOT'SCHE TETRALOGIE
   = 2
DIFF. DIAGN. IN GEW. KATEGORIE. FORTS.: <U> & <E>; OPTIONEN : X : LEVEL
DISPLAY; # : ENDE; 0 : ZURUECK ZU RADIATE; A : SPEICHERE DATEN DES PAT.
¢#
```

Figure 19–37. Conversation with the CADS (Computer-aided Diagnostic System, part of ODARS),[20,37] abbreviated checklist of the heart disease model.[56] Two symptoms with a varying number of choices of possible answers are always displayed. Selection is done by entering the appropriate code letter. "No information available" may be indicated.

ment. The system permits both input by terminal and optical-reader forms; as diagnostic model, a decision-support has been developed for the interpretation of blood gas analysis.[24,25] The laboratory values are entered, and then diagnostic recommendations are calculated, including explanations as to possible causes and recommendations for therapy.

Figure 19–38 shows a dialogue (abbreviated) to obtain an interpreta-

```
BLUTGASANALYSEN INTERPRETATION
  BITTE <UMBLAETTER>    (/V)(/v)

  BITTE GEBEN SIE DIE PERSONALDATEN AN:
1  ZUNAME              DOE
2  VORNAME             JOHN,P.
3  STATION             11B
4  ALTER               54

1  PO2                 62.9
2  PH                  7.311
3  PCO2                28.9
4  BE                  -8
5  KOERPERGEW. (KG)    78.5

   BEKOMMT DER PATIENT SAUERSTOFF ODER
1  WIRD ER BEATMET?
      J,N, ZAHLE(EN) OD./V
   1(n)
BITTE WARTEN; INTERNE BERECHNUNGEN

  HYPOXIE UND  METABOLISCHE AZIDOSE, TEILWEISE  RESPIRATORISCH KOM-
  PENSIERT  ODER  METABOLISCH UEBERKOMPENSIERTE  RESPIRATORISCHE
  ALKALOSE.

  ALS  URSACHE DER  HYPOXIE OHNE  GLEICHZEITIGE HYPERKAPNIE  KOMMEN
  INFRAGE:
  VERTEILUNGSSTOERUNGEN UND/ODER  ERHOEHTES INTRAPULMONALES  SHUNT-
  VOLUMEN
  DIFFUSIONSSTOERUNG

  THERAPIEVORSCHLAG: BEHANDLUNG DES GRUNDLEIDENS,
  02-GABE,EVTL. BEATMUNG

  DIE HYPOKAPNIE IST ALS AUSDRUCK DER RESPIRATORISCHEN KOMPENSATION
  EINER METABOLISCHEN AZIDOSE ANZUSEHEN.
  DAS GERINGE  AUSMASS DER AZIDOSE MACHT  KEINE KORREKTURMASSNAHMEN
  NOETIG. DENNOCH  SOLLTEN BEI  DER BEHANDLUNG  FOLGENDE MOEGLICHEN
  URSACHEN EINER AZIDOSE BERUECKSICHTIGT WERDEN:

  AKUTES NIERENVERSAGEN
  DIABETES MELLITUS
  KREISLAUFVERSAGEN
  SELTENE STOFFWECHSELSTOERUNGEN
  RENALE KOMPENSATION EINER METABOLISCHEN ALKALOSE
  IATROGENE UEBERKOMPENSATION EINER METABOLISCHEN ALKALOSE
  GABE VON CARBOANHYDRASEHEMMERN
```

Figure 19–38. Deterministic model to support medical decision-making.[23,26,27] Interpretations of blood gas analysis.[24,25] After the blood gas values have been entered, the system may request further information. Then an interpretation of the values is given (hypoxemia and acidosis). Possible causes are discussed (diffusion disorder and/or augmented intrapulmonary shunt volume). Recommendations for therapeutic actions are made.

tion of a patient's blood gas data. The system gives the interpretation of a hypoxemia and metabolic acidosis, partially compensated by respiration or a metabolically overcompensated respiratory alkalosis. The causes of the hypoxemia are discussed as possibly being diffusion disorders and/or increased intrapulmonary shunt volume. As therapy, administration of oxygen is suggested. Possible causes of the alkalosis are discussed.[24,25]

Other models have been implemented for the differential diagnosis of bone marrow smears.[22,24,30] Here also our own[30] modules have been written and implemented under BEST.

(4) Individual Retrieval System for Diagnosis (IRSD). An individual retrieval system for diagnoses has been developed to cover special areas and research projects. Here diagnoses (or other coded information) are inverted for a smaller subpopulation in order to permit fast categorical retrieval. It is intended to provide inversion of certain information when stored into the main data base.

This system uses the coding mechanisms of AKOS for the specification of the code and for the free text interpretation of the coded information. Figure 19–39 gives an example of a retrieval from a subset with endocrinological diseases. The search string FETTS (first five letters of the diagnosis "Fettsucht," i.e., obesity) has been specified, and all diagnoses containing this search string are displayed. Then a specific diagnosis is selected (in this case, exogenous obesity), and all patients having this diagnosis are displayed (another option allows the names of the patients to be added and the number of diagnoses stored for each patient). When so specified, the precise data of a patient are displayed.

(5) The Patient Information Display System (PIDS) is one of the several inquiry systems to access the general data base. It is designed to give access to the diagnoses and risk facts recorded during previous stays of patients.

Patients' data may be retrieved by giving their names or their identification numbers. Also, only parts of the name may be chosen in order to obtain a "generic" retrieval (Figure 19–40). The physician may then review the basic administrative data of the patient and may obtain information about a chronic medication (in this case, digitalis and antibiotics). Blood group information may be obtained and a message is added to indicate that such information does not render unnecessary matching before transfusion. Former treatment periods in the different hospital complexes are given, and the diagnoses are listed in the reverse chronological order.

Other inquiry systems accessing the same data base are developed for quick references to administration and information.

e. Outpatient clinics. In principle, outpatient clinics are treated in the same way as the main hospital. The general, patient-specific identification

```
(FETTS

  1 FETTSUCHT,KONSTITUTIONELLE        11 FETTSKLEREM
  2 FETTSUCHT,HYPOPHYSAERE            12 LUNGE,FETTSPEICHERUNG
  3 FETTSUCHT,FAMILIAERE
  4 FETTSUCHT,EXOGENE
  5 FETTSUCHT,ENDOKRINE
  6 FETTSUCHT,ENDOGENE
  7 FETTSUCHT,ALIMENTAERE
  8 FETTSUCHT,ADRENALE
  9 FETTSUCHT DURCH HYPOTHYREOSE
 10 FETTSUCHT
SUCHWORT:FETTS-- DIAGNOSE DURCH CODEZAHL WAEHLEN *** ENDE DES SUCHVORGANGS
        BITTE EINGABE
   (4)

FOLGENDE PATIENTEN HABEN EINE DIAGNOSE MIT DER KDS    2461
   1     08.04.27 1020       2    08.10.56 8910      3    22.06.55 9810
   4     22.11.10 2020       5    01.01.54 7720      6    10.01.51 9820
   7     10.04.41 9320       8    25.02.43 0420      9    10.06.44 7710
  10     17.04.48 1120      11    26.03.59 1110     12    11.10.12 8920
  13     14.06.23 5820      14    26.07.97 4520     15    29.10.46 8920
  16     14.07.20 6920      17    14.12.58 6720     18    31.03.46 5820
  19     05.10.25 0720
ENDE DER LISTE
   (3)


22.06.55 9810    ████████      4 DIAGNOSE(N) BEKANNT (IMMICH-KDS):
00420: PUBERTAS TARDA
02461: FETTSUCHT,ALIMENTAERE
11821: BLUTDRUCKSTEIGERUNG
79345: KRYPTORCHISMUS
BITTE ARBEITSMODUS, PATIENTENNR. ODER >REP< EINGEBEN      ¢
```

Figure 19–39. IRSD (Individual Retrieval System for Diagnoses[2]). Retrieval system with inverted files for special purposes. After the selected code has been entered, all patients with the specified diagnosis (exogenous obesity) are displayed, if desired, with full names. A patient now may be selected and all diagnoses in the patient's file are given.

number allows for a comprehensive record linkage. At the moment, outpatients are entered into the main base using off-line procedures. Individual services are performed for several departments (such as reporting and consultation). For these purposes, emergency patient numbers are taken temporarily for identification.

f. Physician consultation. For physician consultations, the FTSS (see p. 635) is used. Specifically, there exist data structures for gynecology,[3,16] and new ones are under development for ear, nose, and throat consultation, traumatology, and dentistry. As already mentioned, ECG reports are generated this way both for internal medicine and for pediatrics.

Figure 19–41 gives an example of a consultation report generated from an optically read form used in gynecology.[3,16]

```
ςn̄,beͿ
NR  --- ZUNAME,VORNAME ---*** I-ZAHL ***

1     BEL-C         A        21.  .49 0410
2     BELA'                  06. ).55 0410
3     BELG          IED      07. 5.16 0410
4     BEL                    03  3.98 0820
5     BEL           ;IA      17  7.42 0410
6     BE'           CO       0) J8.63 0410
7     BE            :        3  03.42 0410
8     B'            ILHELM   2  .01.10 0410
9     B        .. ' ' cF     '  .08.72 0410
BITTE NR DES GEFUND. PAT. EINTIPPEN OD. WEITERBLAETT.
ς4)


IDENTIFIKAT.-DATEN:
PATIENT(IN)            BE_  ` ` `
I - ZAHL               0:  -`.` 320
GEBURTSNAME
GEBURTSDATUM           03.09.98
WOHNORT                D   3000 HANNOVER
STRASSE                `~`~` .  34

** GEFAEHRDUNGSKATASTER **
DAUERB.M. DIGITALIS
DAUERB.M. ANTIBIOTIK.


****** BLUTGRUPPE ****** --KEINE ANGABEN--

ACHTUNG: DIESE ANGABEN ENTBINDEN DEN ARZT NICHT VON
         SEINER SORGFALTSPFLICHT (Z.B. KREUZPROBE)
-->EINGABE 'NO', FALLS KEIN DISPLAY 'FRUEH. BEHANDL.'ς◯

-- ,`,`~`  :    0?  `◡`  820 KLINIK(EN):

--------  FRUEHERE BEHANDLUNGEN IN DER MHH  -------
LETZTE BEHANDLUNG IN:
         MHH - RODERBRUCH 1971
               OSTSTADT   1969
               NORDSTADT  KEINE


***** DIAGNOSEN-LISTE *****        DATUM :   20.11.69  (UNGEFAEHRES DATUM)
ARZT: 231                          KLINIK:   OSTSTADT  31
DIAGNOSE: KDS: 67611/000
CHOLEZYSTITIS
DIAGNOSE:  KDS: 72611/000
NIERENBECKEN,ENTZUENDUNG
DIAGNOSE:  KDS: 54772/000
HERZ,DEKOMPENSATION
ZUSATZ: OB. DIAGNOSELINKS
WEITERE DIAGNOSEN FOLGEN
r◯
```

Figure 19–40. Query into main data base.[52,53,54] Access is possible either by the patient's identification number or by his name.[44] In this case only three characters of the patient's last name have been entered. The system displays all qualifying patients. The fourth patient is selected for further display; his basic data are given. "Risk facts" are listed (continuout treatment with digitalis and antibiotics). A blood group analysis has not been made in this case. The system shows former treatment periods in the Medical School Hospital and associated city hospitals. Finally the diagnoses are listed in reverse chronological order.

SEHR GEEHRTE FRAU KOLLEGIN ,

IHRE PATIENTIN SUCHTE HEUTE AUF IHRE UEBERWEISUNG HIN DIE POLIKLINIK DER FRAUENKLINIK AUF.

WIR MOECHTEN IHNEN UEBER UNSERE UNTERSUCHUNG VOM 17 . APRIL 1972 BERICHTEN :
DIE PATIENTIN KLAGTE UEBER FOLGENDE BESCHWERDEN :
REICHLICH BRAEUNLICH-BLUTIGER AUSFLUSS. BLUTUNGEN OHNE ERKENNBARES ZYKLISCHES GESCHEHEN .
AUS DER ZYKLUSANAMNESE:
DIE BESPRECHUNG DER ZYKLUSANAMNESE MIT DER PATIENTIN ZEIGT, DASS EINE METRORRHAGIE VORLIEGT.
ALS DER GEBURTENANAMNESE:
4 SPONTANE GEBURT(EN). 3 OPERATIVE GEBURT(EN) : VAKUUMEXTRAKTION ,FORCEPS ,MANUALHILFE BEI BECKENENDLAGE . 1 FRUEHABORT(E).
AUS DER OPERATIONSANAMNESE:
ABRASIO BEI ABORT .
ALLGEMEINBEFUND:
ADIPOESE PATIENTIN VON FRAULICHEM HABITUS.

BEFUND DER SPECULUMEINSTELLUNG UND DER TASTUNTERSUCHUNG:
VULVA:
RESTE DES HYMENALSAUMES.
SCHEIDE:

IN DER SCHEIDE WENIG ALTES BLUT .
UTERUS UND ADNEXE:
EIN ENDOPHYTISCH WACHSENDES CARCINOM DER VORDEREN MUTTERMUNDSLIPPE MIT UEBERGANG AUF DIE SCHEIDE . TONNENFOERMIG AUFGETRIEBENES COLLUM UTERI. DAS CORPUS UTERI IST NORMAL GROSS . DIE LINKEN ADNEXE ZART. DIE RECHTEN ADNEXE NARBIG. DAS RECHTE PARAMETRIUM UNAUFFAELLIG. DAS LINKE PARAMETRIUM IM ANSATZ KNOTIG INFILTRIERT. DIE SACROUTERINLIGAMENTE BEIDERSEITS STRAFF. FREIER DOUGLAS'SCHER RAUM.
KOLPOSKOPIE DER PORTIO:
NEOPLASMA . DER KOLPOSKOPISCHE BEFUND ZEIGT EINE MALIGNE VERAENDERUNG AN .

DIE PHASENKONTRASTUNTERSUCHUNG DES SCHEIDENSEKRETES ZEIGTE ATYPISCHE ZELLEN .
UNSERE DIAGNOSE(N) :
CARCINOMA COLLI IIB
(CA. D. ENDOCERVIX: COLLUMKNOTEN)

WIR HABEN MIT DER PATIENTIN DIE AUFNAHME IN UNSERE KLINIK VEREINBART.

MIT KOLLEGIALER HOCHACHTUNG,

DR.

Figure 19–41. Report to referring physician synthesized from entries made in optically read form designed for the recording of physical findings in gynecology.[3,16]

F. EDUCATION AND RESEARCH

The Department for Biometrics and Medical Information Science provides courses for students and faculty members in various programming languages and techniques. Furthermore, there are specific tasks defined for the education of medical students. During a mandatory class of 12 hours in the second clinical year and by additional seminars, the student is familiarized with the most basic principles of medical information science and data processing and introduced to existing systems. These classes are attended after instructions in biomathematics and basic statistical procedures.

Curricula are being developed for graduates with medical, computer science, or engineering background. For specific purposes, there exist teaching and utility programs.

1. SIS

The Sequential Instruction System (SIS) provides a tool for computer-aided instruction.[39] This system asks questions in the multiple-choice fashion and branches to explicatory frames whenever a wrong answer is given. Upon correct answers, frames may be skipped; and upon wrong answers, the student may be referred backwards. At the moment there exist modules with medical content as well as with programming and system concepts.

2. Computer-Aided Testing

For seminars and examinations, a system has been developed that permits the students to answer on optically read forms so that an overall evaluation can be made.[6] The program generates output for the instructor as well as the students. The students may be grouped into four groups with permutated questions, and the questions may have different weights.

Distributions are computed and plotted and indices are calculated, describing difficulty, separation, and selectivity of questions. The student himself receives a printout giving his score compared with the maximum possible score. Furthermore, he will find the correct answer, the answer he has given, the weight of each answer, and the percentage of correct answers for each question within his group as well as the percentage of the correct answers in all groups which contain the same questions in different order.

3. Literature Retrieval

A system for literature storage and retrieval of project literature is available to the researchers. The Personal Information Retrieval System (PIRS) [36] allows searches for character strings by the author, title, or bibliography section of a literature citation, keyword retrieval, and combinations of both. The literature may also be grouped for reference lists in publications. The system is accessible both for on-line application and for batch searches. An abbreviated search is shown in Figure 19–42 (For off-line queries, keyword printout may be obtained also in English).

4. Statistical and Mathematical Systems

An on-line system [11] gives access to the main statistical procedures. Data may be entered from the terminal, and immediate evaluation is possible. The off-line library covers the most well-known packages.

For CMS (Conversational Monitor System) users, a conversational system is also available; it allows for advanced formulation of algorithms and mathematical models (Gille).

G. HARDWARE, SOFTWARE, AND OPERATIONS

The principal hardware and software philosophy has been described under C. Hardware and software have been chosen according to the general system concept.

The detailed configuration is given in Figure 19–6. 512K of real core provides the basis from the time-sharing system which pages on to an IBM 2301 drum with 4 million bytes of storage. The system has three selector channels, one of which services the drum and two of which provide the communication lines between CPU and three 2314 disk units with eight accessible packs each. This external storage of more than 600 million bytes is necessary to support both the variety of operations as well as the on-line data base. CP and OS residence require at least one drive each. Two additional drives are dedicated to the CMS system.

The projected bed capacity of the Medical School Hospital is 2,000 patients. Based on the present average stay of approximately 14 days, this will result in an admission of $1/14 \times 2,000$—that is, 243 patients/day. Polyclinic admissions are now approximately 250/day and will attain 600–800/day. If only inpatients are taken into consideration, the projected admission will result in 50,000 new medical computer records/year, provided that 60% of all admitted patients are new to the system.

```
                  ***  P I R S  ***
    EINGABE DER VERSION, BITTE
    (OPTIONEN :RETRIEVE,UPDATE)
    (retrieve)
    VERSION        RETRIEVE, INPUT DATA SET NO.          5
    SOLL WORTTRENNUNG VERMIEDEN WERDEN (JA/NEIN)?
    (ja)

    SUCH-VERSION ? (1=SEQUENZ,2=SCHLUESSEL,3=CHARACTER-STRING)
    (2)

    WIEDERGABEMODUS (1=MIT SCHLUESSELWORTEN, 2 = OHNE)
    (1)

    ANZAHL DER SUCHBEGRIFFE (BITTE VIERSTELLIG ANGEBEN)
    (0001)

    SOLL ERGEBNIS AUF KARTEN GESTANZT WERDEN? (JA/NEIN)
    (nein)

    BITTE JETZT SUCHBEGRIFFE EINGEBEN
    (0280)

                          LIST OF REFERENCES
    THIS IS A COMPUTER PRINTOUT. DISREGARD FOLLOWING SELECTION COMMENTS WHEN PRIN-
    TING
    TO BE SELECTED
     280
    OPTION     2      REFERENCES SELECTED BY KEYWORDS
    PRINTOUT WITH KEYWORDS
         KEY-WORDS (SCHLUESSELWORTE)
         VOLKSWIRTSCHAFTLICHE ASPEKTE UND DATEN
      1 EHLERS,C.TH.
         MEDIZINISCHE INFORMATIONSSYSTEME UNTER EINSCHLUSS VON AERZTLICHER
         VERSORGUNG UND ADMINISTRATIVEM MANAGEMENT.
         11TH IBM MEDICAL SYMPOSIUM,HEIDELBERG (1972),SEPTEMBER 4.-6.
         KEY-WORDS (SCHLUESSELWORTE)              REFERENCE NO.        830
         VOLKSWIRTSCHAFTLICHE ASPEKTE UND DATEN
         PHARMAZIE-SYSTEM
      2 WOLTERS,H.E.
         GESUNDHEITSWESEN UND GESUNDHEITSINFORMATIONSSYSTEM IN BERLIN
          11TH IBM MEDICAL SYMPOSIUM,HEIDELBERG (1972),SEPTEMBER 4.-6.
         KEY-WORDS (SCHLUESSELWORTE)              REFERENCE NO.        840
         STRUKTURPROBLEME (SOZIO-OEKONOMISCH)
         REGIONALER EINSATZ
         IDENTIFIKATIONSPROBLEME (GENERELL)
         BEFUNDKONDENSATION
         RECORD-LINKAGE PROBLEME
         AUTOMATISIERTE KRANKENHAUSSYSTEME
         VOLKSWIRTSCHAFTLICHE ASPEKTE UND DATEN
```

Figure 19–42. Literature retrieval using PIRS (Personal Information Retrieval System).[36] A search using the key word, socio-economic considerations and data is specified. The result of the (abbreviated) search is displayed with the keywords associated with the references.

This clearly delineates the need for external storage, especially if information has to be kept on-line as long as possible. If 1,000 bytes are needed for patients, the patients of one year would need 50 million bytes. But much of the information is redundant and is reflected in various files for medical and administrative purposes. Reporting systems need their own text files and intermediate structures to cope with the requirements of an operational on-line system. At the moment, the basic information of approximately 50,000 patients is kept on-line.

The multiplexer channel of the system has a selector subunit to service six tapes. At the moment, eight IBM 2260 cathode ray tubes and 25 SIEMENS 8151 are used as teleprocessing devices. The latter operate in BSC mode using full duplex lines with 4800 baud. Twenty-two IBM 2740 typewriters are used as output units, whereas nine 2741 devices serve as consoles for virtual machines under CP/67. Nineteen IBM 3270 terminals are currently being installed. An optical reader and a papertape reader provide means for both manual and automated input.

The on-line system leads to its own requirements. If only five information transactions are assumed per patient each day (an estimate which is much too low) and if one assumes that the central processing unit needs five seconds to provide all operations for these transactions, the resulting CPU time is 167 minutes when the hospital is fully occupied. In these figures, additional processing of information is not reflected nor are administrative programs taken into consideration. On the other hand, one transaction "binds" a terminal for at least ten seconds. This would result in a terminal "binding" for at least five hours if only one transaction has to be made. This time has to be multiplied by the number of transactions/ patient.

These time and hardware considerations will make a second computer necessary both for backup and performance since ultimately all teleprocessing applications have to be separated from development and research.

The present software configuration has "grown" and will be superseded by new developments both in the data base sector and in systems software. However, in order to adapt the programs to other teleprocessing systems, a set of extended macros has been used which facilitates a transition to new teleprocessing (TP) system, such as IMS/TP. This also means that systems may be more easily adapted to other environments with different teleprocessing software.

There is no system back-up at the moment. It is a general philosophy that all application systems have a manual or semi-manual back-up procedure which might cover the immediate need for information and information transactions.

The teleprocessing system is on-line from at least 7:30 AM to 10:00 PM without interruption. Maintenance is done on-line every day and for two hours in the late evening every two weeks. Before transition to this schedule, approximately 3 hours were spent for maintenance/week. The average number of batch jobs processed per week is 1,200, with a meter time of approximately 130 hours/week. The actual CPU time lies around an average of 40 hours/week, of which roughly 80% is used by OS. Detailed statistics are kept for each virtual user and the overall system performance of the TP and the batch system; appropriate CP changes have been made in order to favor OS and the teleprocessing system over the ordinary time-sharing user.

Transitions to new releases always create problems, and whenever done there are disruptions of the teleprocessing system. Many months of good performance are forgotten when the system goes down and the user has to wait for the recovery procedures. The motivation of the user is highly influenced by response time of his terminal and reliability of operations. Operators, on the other hand, often do not understand the needs of a remote user. The frequency of hardware or system trouble ranges from 2–8 week, of which approximately 2–3 may be partially recovered without sudden interruption of the teleprocessing services. In almost all instances, immediate recovery is possible with resumption of operation within 5–8 minutes. More serious hardware failure has been experienced every 6–8 months.

For system breakdown, an emergency admission procedure has been developed to assign an emergency identification number to a patient. Aluminum foils are pre-embossed for this purpose, and a special data base structure provides the necessary linkage whenever the valid data of the patient are obtained.[4,5]

H. IMPACT AND EVALUATION

Since computer operations started together with the Medical School Hospital, it is difficult to assess the impact. Personnel planning for administrative services was already done in regard to the projected functions of electronic data processing. The admissions department, for instance, started on-line operations with the first patient. It is therefore difficult to compare traditional services with improvement due to the computing system. An evaluation therefore has often to be made against hypothetical assumptions. So the admission procedure compared to traditional handling of new patients in a ratio of DM 160,000/100,000 when roughly 350 patients were in the hospital. The break-even point is considered to occur when the total number of beds occupied lies in the neighborhood of 600.

However, in these figures the gain in accuracy and the elimination of error and duplication has not yet been reflected. Better figures will be obtained from the pharmacy system, which started operation within the second quarter of 1973 and where traditional handling has been done for the past three years. The same is true for patient billing, which was started in the fall of 1972.

The evaluation must also be done against the long-term plans (Figure 19–43). In this time schedule, the ongoing work in the area of basic tele-processing and data base software is reflected, as is the development of the different areas and methods as shown in Figure 19–4 and 19–12 and described in C. All this non-project-specific development has to be taken into consideration when specific applications are evaluated. In order to do so, a team of economists and systems analysts are setting up procedures to evaluate cost/effectiveness, which, at the moment, is only done for specific well-defined areas.

The impact on patients, doctors, nurses, and hospital efficiency has not yet been scientifically studied. The different areas have varying exposure to the computer system and, therefore, have varying reactions. Psychologi-cal and human factors have a great influence upon the acceptance or non-acceptance of a system and are examined in a special study group. As a

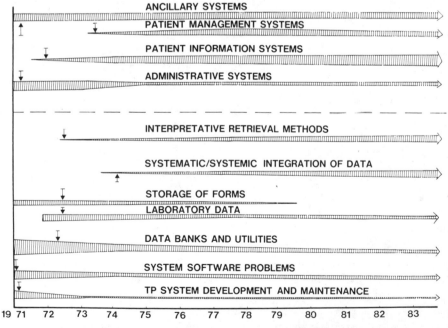

Figure 19–43. Long-term schedule of activities. The upper part shows target systems; the lower part shows principles of methods and basic sys-tems. Arrows show where parts of the system have become operational.

general rule, improvement of quality without immediate benefit is only a very hypothetical incentive for cooperation. Immediate benefits for the provider of the information, however, cannot always be generated. For instance, when the admissions department has to spend more minutes with a patient in order to obtain better and more valid data, this is often negatively reflected in its own time balance consideration without realizing that perhaps much more time would be lost in the periphery in order to obtain necessary information. This indicates the necessity of continuous education and information between both academic and administrative departments and among their units.

It is also difficult to evaluate the scientific yield of administrative and medical data. First, these data will allow for a better scheduling of patients and planning of hospital operations. It is quite interesting that the most common diagnosis during the last 3 years was diabetes mellitus and that cardiovascular diseases ranked second. It is also necessary to link the diagnoses with the average stay in order to anticipate loads and optimization functions. On the other side, research in the area of information science with the objective to obtain more information about diagnoses and diagnostic classification can only be done if accurate data are collected and made available both for patient care-oriented and categorical retrieval. This naturally carries a certain overhead which has to be taken into consideration when comparing immediate costs with immediate benefits.

I. SUMMARY

The overall goal of the Medical System Hannover is to perform research and developmental work in the area of medical information science with specific emphasis on the hospital as an integral part of the health care delivery system and its three main functional areas: hospital management, patient management, and medical tasks and science. The system, furthermore, has to cope with the requirements of basic and applied research in the area of medical science as well as in information analysis and processing of medical data.

The system concept has anticipated the general idea of virtual storage and virtual machines. The basic charges of operations within a hospital have been defined as being communication, integration, and system flow control. For these purposes, various modules have been developed. One of the major tasks is the development of a medical data base.

The overall goal is to store data in a systematized form so that they can be grouped logically together for various applications and inquiries. The concept of virtual operation is applied to the data base so that file structures may be conceived for modules and logically constructed out of the common data base. Problem orientation is a major goal of data collection and retrieval. However, the data storage ultimately will not be problem oriented, but problem grouping will be specific data of a higher hierarchical order to allow changes of problems and redefinitions of clinical approach.

Hospital operations have been established. The impact on the operating hospital is of varying degree and very complex. Parallel to continuous development, methods and ways of evaluating impact on structure and function must be developed and applied.

The experience with on-line systems may be summarized in the positive observation of great impact and efficiency. A negative observation is the high cost, the programming overhead, the dependence upon performance, and the vulnerability whenever services are disrupted.

The more operations are performed on-line, the more terminals will be needed all over the hospital. The question arises, how can information be made accessible on ubiquitous terminals? This general availability, however, does not mean general accessibility. It has to be determined whether terminals of lower hierarchical order, such as a telephone, might fill a broad gap for data collection and, if voice-response is used, even data retrieval.

The satellite concept for data collection and preprocessing in areas with great data intensity (such as nuclear medicine and laboratories or patient monitoring) has to be looked upon with the requirements for overall integration of information. The identification problem arises whenever the information has to be linked to the other patient's information categories within a hospital or even a region.

One of the principles of medical operations is that on-line procedures have to be developed for specific tasks with restricted application in one area or during a restricted time. Satellite concepts do not facilitate general inquiry systems which often are needed in the periphery of diagnostic evaluation of, for instance, laboratory data. It will be difficult to achieve equal information flow from the central processor to satellite stations, whereas the flow from the periphery to the central processor is more easily obtained. The inherent problems of software and system concept have to be solved in order to achieve the desired integration.

The medical problems are of a great magnitude. There are many questions still to be solved in the area of information science. On the other side, still much work has to be done with basic software systems and with problems of hardware and software reliability. Transitions to new systems bring new advantages but often may not avoid unrest and instability. To further the development of applications, some rest on the systems scene would be desirable.[46] However, progress cannot be excluded and will eventually be the prerequisite for further improvement.[45]

Medical Information Science within a hospital spans the range between basic administration, operation optimization, and medical applications and science. These tasks will need special training and curricula for both students with medical background and those with computer science backgrounds. Research and education are of great importance when computer systems in hospitals are to be successful.

REFERENCES

1. Bayes, T. "An Essay Towards Solving a Problem in the Doctrine of Chances." *Phil. Trans.* 43 (1963), 370.

2. Boehme, G., and Reichertz, P. L. IRSD "(Individual Retrieval System for Diagnoses), System Design und Anwendung auf dem Gebiet der Endokrinologie." In: Fuchs, G., Wagner, G.: KrankenhausInformationssysteme, Schattauer Verlag, Stuttgart (1972), 305–310.

3. Boerner, P., and Jacobitz, K. "Werkzeuge fuer Dokumentation und Arztbrief in der Gynaekologischen Poliklinik." IBM-Form GK12-1048-0, (1972).

4. Engelbrecht, R. "Aufnahmeverfahren an der Medizinischen Hochschule Hannover." Der Computer am Arbeitsplatz IBM-Seminar Bad Liebenzell, 2.–4. Feb. 1972, IBM-Form NR.

5. Engelbrecht, R.; Schmeetz, D.; Wolters, E.; Bendt, J.; and Reichertz, P. L. "Automatisierte Patientenerfassung, Analyse einer einjachrigen Erfahrung." Methoden der Informatik in der medizinischen Datenverarbeitung, Fachtagung GI und GMDS, Hannover, 12.–14. Oktober 1972.

6. Engelbrecht, R. "TESTAT," Ein Auswertungsprogramm fuer Multiple-Choice Tests, in Vorbereitung (in preparation).

7. Engelbrecht, R. "Entwicklung eines Computerunterstuetzten Systems zur Ver— und Entschluesselung von Beschreibungen und Texten unter Besonderer. Beruecksichtigung klinischer Diagnosen" (1973) Hannover, Dissertation.

8. Fitzgerald, D. L. T., and Williams, C. M. "Computer Diagnosis of Thyroid Disease." University of Florida Printing Office, Gainesville, Fla. Sept. 1964.

9. Hall, P.; Mellner, Ch.; and Danielson, T. "J5–A Data Processing System for Medical Information." *Meth. Inform. Med.* 6 (1967) : 1–6.

10. Hobbs, W., and McBride, J. "Baylor Executive System for Teleprocessing (BEST)." IBM Contributed Program Library 360D–05.1.018 (1969).

11. Hultsch, E. "Statistikprogrammsystem STAT1," in: MSH User's Guide.

12. Hundeshagen, H. "Clinical Application of Modern Nuclear-Medical Instrumentation in: Pabst, L. Nuclearmedizin, 8. Jahrestagung der Ges. F. Nuclearmedizin Hannover, 16.-19. 9. 1970 (Stuttgart, 1972) :487–497.

13. Hurst, J. W. "How to Implement the Weed System." *Arch. Intern. Med.* 128 (1971) : 456–462.

14. IBM. Information Management System/360, Version 2, General Information Manual. IBM Publication GH20-0765-1 (1971).

15. Immich, H. "Klinischer Diagnosenschluessel (KDS)." F. K. Schattauer Verlag (Stuttgart, 1966).

16. Jacobitz, K., and Boerner, P. "Ein Allgemeines System zur Syntheses Medizinischer Berichte aus Markierungsboegen (FTSS)." *Meth. Inf. Med.* 11(1972): 163–172.

17. Jacobitz, K.; Bogenstaetter, P.; Kroslak, B.; and Reichertz, P. L. Das Problemepikrisenblatt des medizinischer Systems Hannovers. "Methoden der Informatik in der medizinischen Datenverarbeitung," Fachtagung GI und GMDS Hannover, 12.–14. Oktober 1972.

18. Kroslak, B., and Jacobitz, K. "Das Problemorientierte Krankenblatt." In: Fuchs, G., and Wagner, G.: Krankenhausinformationssysteme, Schattauer Verlag, Stuttgart (1972), 51–61.

19. Lodwick, G. S. "Radiographic Diagnosis and Grading of Bone Tumors with Comments on Computer Evaluation." Proceedings of Fifth National Cancer Conf., Philadelphia, September 1964, 369–380, J. B. Lippincott.

20. Lodwick, G. S.; Reichertz, P. L.; Paquet, E.; and Hall, D. L. "ODARS," A Computer Aided System for Diagnosing and Reporting. Part I: Clinical Problems." In: De Haene, R., and Wambersie, A.: Computers in Radiology (Proceedings of the International Meeting on the Use of Computers in Radiology, Brussels, Sept. 1969), Basel 1970:279–282.

21. Lusted, L. B. "Logic of the Diagnostic Process." *Method. Inform. Med.* 4(1965):63–68.

22. Moehr, J.; Odriozola, J.; Ries, P.; and Reichertz, P. L. Einsatz und Erfahrungen mit einem System fuer klinische Entscheidungshilfe (Clinical Decision Support System). In: Fuchs, G., and Wagner, G.: Krankenhausinformationssysteme, Schattauer Verlag, Stuttgart (1972), 347–353.

23. Moehr, J. "Informatik-entscheidungshilfe in der Klinik." *Med. Ass.* 4(1972): 9–12.

24. Moehr, J.; Reichertz, P. L.; Odriozola, J.; Hartmann, W.; and Pape, H. "Zur Verwendung deterministischer Verfahren in interaktiven Systemen," Methoden der Informatik in der medizinischen Datenverarbeitung, Fachtagung GI und GMDS, Hannover, 12.–14. Oktober 1972.

25. Moehr, J.; Hartmann, W.; and Fabel, H. "Computerunterstuetzung fuer klinische Entscheidungen." Deutsche Gesellschaft f. Med. Dokumentation u. Statistik, 17. Jahrestagung, 8.–11. Oktober, Muenchen 1972.

26. Moore, F. J. "Concept of a Clinical Decision Support System." IBM Advanced Systems Development Division, 2651 Strang Boulevard, Yorktown Heights, N.Y. (1966).

27. Moore, F. J. "Development of a Clinical Decision Support System." IBM Advanced Systems Development Division, 2651 Strang Boulevard, Yorktown, Heights, N.Y. (1968).

28. Odriozola, J.; Pape, H.; Moehr, J.; and Dommes, B. "Erfahrungen mit der Anwendung eines deterministischen Verfahrens zur Teilautomatisation der Befundung Zytologischer Praeparate." Methoden der Informatik in der medizinischen Datenverarbeitung, Fachtagung GI und GMDS, HANNOVER, 12.–14. Oktober 1972.

29. Pacak, M., and Pratt, A. W. The Function of Semantics in Automated Language Processing. Symposium on Information and Retrieval.

30. Pape, H.; Odriozola, J.; and Moehr, J. Automatisierte Diagnostik von Knochenmarksausstrichen im online-Verfahren mit einem Netz von Schwellenlogik-

elementen. Deutsche Gesellschaft f. Med. Dokumentation u. Statistik, 17. Jahrestagung, 8.–11. Oktober 1972, Muenchen.

31. Pipberger, Hubert V. "Clinical Applications and Differential Diagnosis. New Computer-Assisted Concepts in Electro- and Vector Cardiography." Conference of the American College of Cardiology, January 10–11, 1969, Washington, D.C.

32. Porth, A. Die Bedeutung von Satellitensystemen in der medizinischen Informationsverarbeitung, Fachtagung GI und GMDS, Hannover, 12.–14, Okt. 1972.

33. Pratt, A. W., and Pacak, M. "System for Identification and Transformation of Terminal Morphemes in Medical English." *Meth. Inform. Med.*, 8 (1969) : 84–90.

34. Pratt, A. W. "Automatic Processing of Pathology Data." Conference de l'Institut de Recherche d'Informatique et d'Automatique (IRIA) (1971) Mars 1–5, St. Lary, France.

35. Reichertz, P.; Winkler, C.; and Kloss, G. "Computer-Diagnostik von Schilddruesenerkrankungen." *Dtsch. Med. Wschr.* 90 (1965) : 2317–2321.

36. Reichertz, P. L. "PIRS" (Personal Information Retrieval System), A Multi-Purpose Computer Program for Storage and Retrieval of Reference Files." *Method. Inform. Med.* 7 (1968) : 165–172.

37. Reichertz, P. L.; Lodwick, Gwilym S.; Lehr, James L. "Medical Records in Radiology." In: Anderson, J., and Forsythe, J. M.: Information Processing of Medical Records; Proceedings of the IFIP TC4 Working Conference on Information Processing of Medical Records, Lyon, April 6–10, 1970; North-Holland Publishing Co. Amsterdam/London 1970, 191–197.

38. Reichertz, P. L.; Courtney, D.; and Birznieks, F. B. "Sequential Instruction System (SIS)." *Meth. Inform. Med.* 9 (1970) : 182–187.

39. Reichertz, P. L.; Lodwick, G. S.; Paquet, E.; and Hall, D. L. " 'Odars', A Computer Aided System for Diagnosing and Reporting. Part II: Technical Problems." In: De Haene, R., and Wambersie, A.: Computers in Radiology (Proceedings of the International Meeting on the use of Computers in Radiology, Brussels, Sept. 1969) Basel (1970) : 283–288.

40. Reichertz, P. L. Auswirkungen der elektronischen Datenverarbeitung auf die Struktur der Medizin 4. Deidesheimer Gespraech, April 25/26, 1970, Deidesheim, BRD, Arzneim.—*Forsch.* 21 (1971) 173–181.

41. Reichertz, P. L. Aufbau eines Informationssystems und Terminal-Dialog-Betriebs in einem Klinikum. In: Graul, E. H. "Computerssysteme in der Medizin (Koeln, 1973) : 93–116.

42. Reichertz, P. L. Allgemeine Grundlagen, technische Moeglichkeiten und Entwicklungstendenzen der elektronischen Informationsverarbeitung in der Medizin Nieders. *Aertzteblatt*, 45, (1972) : 211–217.

43. Reichertz, P. L.; Sauter, K.; Moehr, J.; Kroslak, B.; and Zowe, W. "Konzeptioneller Aufbau eines integrierten Patientenfile." In: Fuchs, G., and Wagner, G.: Krankenhausinformationssysteme Schattauer Verlag, Stuttgart (1972) : 73–87.

44. Reichertz, P. L. "Hospital Information Systems, Concept and Implementation of the Medical System Hannover (MSH). "Man and Computer," Conference Bordeaux/Frankreich, 11./16. 9. 1972.

45. Reichertz, P. L. "Summary-Address: Analysis and Concept." XI. IBM-Medical-Symposium, Heidelberg, September 4./6., 1972. (7.)

46. Reichertz, P. L. The Medical System Hannover (MSH) and Regional Activi-

ties in Germany. Proceedings of MEDIS '72 Osaka International Symposium on Medical Information System (9/29–30/72), Kansai Institute of Information Systems (1972):127–153.

47. Reichertz, P. L.; Wolters, E.; and Engelbrecht, R. "A Teleprocessing Interface Macro System (TIMS)." Methods Inform. Med. (in press).

48. Reichertz, P. L. Aerztliche Informatik 107. Tagung Gesellschaft Deutscher Naturforscher und Aerzte, 8.–12. Oktober 1972, Muenchen.

49. Roettger, P.; Reul, H.; Klein, I.; and Sunkel, H. "Die Vollautomatische Dokumentation und Statistische Auswertung pathologisch-anatomischer Befundberichte." Meth. Inform. Med. 8(1969):19–26.

50. Roettger, P.; Reul, H.; Sunkel, H.; and Klein, I. "Neue Auswertungsmoeglichkeiten pathologisch-anatomischer Befundberichte. Klartextanalyse durch Elektronenrechner." Meth. Inform. Med. 9(1970):35–44.

51. Roettger, P. "Analyse der Textstruktur medizinischer Befundberichte." Methoden der Informatik in der medizinischen Datenverarbeitung, Fachtagung GI und GMDS, Hannover, 12.–14. Oktober 1972.

52. Sauter, K., and Reichertz, P. L. "The Integrated Patient Data Bank of a Hospital Information System." Journees d'Informatique Medicale 1972, Institut de Recherche d'Informatique et d'Automatique, Tome 1(1972):9–27.

53. Sauter, K.; Zowe, W.; Reichertz, P. L.; Hill, D.; and Weingarten, W. "Patienteninformationssystem und integrierte IMS-Patientendatenbank im medizinischen System Hannover (MSH), Erfahrungen und Ergebnisse." Methoden der Informatik in der medizinischen Datenverarbeitung, Fachtagung GI und GMDS, Hannover, 12.–14. Oktober 1972.

54. Sauter, K. "Integrierte Datenbank und Patienteninfomationssystem im medizinischen System Hannover." Habilitationsschrift, Medizinische Hochschule Hannover, Oktober 1972.

55. Steinbuch, K. "Maschinelle Intelligenz und Zeichenerkennung." Naturwiss. 58 (1971):210–217.

56. Templeton, A. W.; Lehr, J. L.; and Simmons, C. "The Computer Evaluation and Diagnosis of Congenital Heart Disease, Using Roentgenographic Findings." Radiology 87(1966):658–682.

57. Templeton, A. W. "Computer Aided Diagnosis in Pulmonary Nodules and Heart Disease." National Conf. on Computer Applications in Radiology, Columbia, Mo., 1967.

58. Templeton, A. W.; Reichertz, P. L.; Paquet, E.; Lodwick, G. S.; Lehr, J. L.; and Scott, F. I. "RADIATE, Up-dated and Re-designed for Multiple Terminals." Radiology 92(1969):30–36.

59. Warner, H. R.; Toronto, A. F.; Veasy, G. L.; and Stephenson, R. "A Mathematical Approach to Medical Diagnosis." J.A.M.A. 61:177 (1961):175–183.

60. Weed, L. L. "Medical Records, Medical Education and Patient Care." Press of Case Western Res. University, 1969.

61. Wilson, W. J. "Computer Aided Diagnosis in Gastric Ulcer." National Conf. on Computer Applications in Radiology, Columbia/Mo., 1967.

62. Wingert, F. "Klartextverarbeitung in der Pathologie." Nieders. Aertzteblatt, 45, (1972):156–159.

63. Wingert, F. Das Pathologie-befundsystem Vortrag:Sitzung des Arbeitskreises Pathologie der GMDS, Graz 18.5.72.

64. Wingert, F. "Das Pathologische Befundsystem." Methoden der Informatik in der medizinischen Datenverarbeitung, Fachtagung GI und GMDS, Hannover, 12.–14. Oktober 1972.

65. Winkler, C.; Reichertz, P. L.; and Kloss, G. "Computer Diagnosis of Thyroid Diseases. Comparison of Incidence Data and Considerations on the Problem of Data Collection." *Amer. J. Med. Sci.* 253, 27–34, 67.

66. Wolters, E., and Luedecke, B. "MHBS (Mineralhaushalt-Bilanzierungssystem) Aufbau eines Dialogsystems fuer den Bedarf der Intensivpflege." In: Fuchs, G., and Wagner, G.: Krankenhausinformationssysteme, Schattauer Verlag, Stuttgart, (1972), 89–93.

67. Wolters, E. Bilanzierungssysteme zur Ueberwachung von Intensivpflegepatienten. Dissertation, Hannover (1973).

CHAPTER TWENTY

Texas Institute for Research and Rehabilitation Hospital Computer System (Houston)

by Carlos Vallbona & William A. Spencer

A. MEDICAL CARE ENVIRONMENT

The Texas Institute for Rehabilitation and Research (TIRR) is a regional, 81-bed, special-purpose hospital in the Texas Medical Center at Houston. It is a private, nonprofit, scientific, educational institution; the professional activities are directed by physicians and scientists from various departments of Baylor College of Medicine with which it is formally affiliated. It delivers comprehensive rehabilitation services to people with a wide variety of physical disabilities. The primary facility is located in the Medical Center. An annex three miles away houses 20 of the more stabilized patients.

The Institute is equipped to provide a wide range of medical services, with both wards and semiprivate rooms, an intensive care unit with patient monitoring facilities, a surgical suite, clinical and cardio-pulmonary laboratories, physical and occupational therapy departments, orthotics, a pharmacy, and x-ray and dental departments. It also provides a complete range of nonmedical services, including psychological, social, and vocational counseling.

TIRR focuses on specific problems that fall into the field of rehabilitation and physical medicine. Sixty percent of the patients have traumatic spinal cord injuries, 30% have respiratory problems (primarily cystic fibrosis), and the remaining 10% have similar functional problems (e.g., paralysis resulting from nontraumatic neurological disease, or congenital defects like spina bifida that result in some form of functional disability).

662

Patients range from infants through the teen-age and young adult group to the adult group. In 1971, the Institute served 552 inpatients who had a total of 673 admissions and 1,283 outpatients for a total of 4,402 visits. The average stay of the inpatients was 30 days.

In addition to the hospital functions, the Institute also is engaged in teaching and research. Affiliated with the Baylor College of Medicine, the Institute houses the Baylor Departments of Rehabilitation and Physical Medicine. Students from the College rotate through the hospital, and doctors on the active medical staff of the Institute have appointments to the faculty of the College. Many of the Institute staff are engaged in research. Their clinical and health services research projects are, for the most part, funded by federal research grants and contracts.

Because of many of these factors, the Institute provides a rather good laboratory in which to experiment with innovative changes to the health care delivery system. Because the Institute and its professionals are research-oriented and because the staff is relatively stable (over half of the existing staff have been with the Institute for over five years), many of the problems in implementing organizational and procedural changes are not as great as would be found elsewhere. The relatively small size reduces the magnitude of the logistics problems, and the complete range of services provides a smaller, more easily understood model of the larger facilities while retaining all of the relationships and communications pathways. Another perhaps more significant difference is the nature of the care planning process. At TIRR, which is a long-stay institution, the patient care plans are relatively stable over a longer period of time. In short-stay institutions, care activities change rapidly during the first few days of the patient's hospital course. The function of care planning, however, is appropriate to both long- and short-stay institutions. The more stable nature of the care planning process at TIRR facilitates the research by reducing the logistics problems involved during the experimentation.

B. DEFINITIONS AND OBJECTIVES

A hospital computing system should: (a) facilitate the integration of goals, orders, directives, and specific events into a coherent whole that makes the most effective and efficient use of available institutional resources, (b) facilitate communication between all staff involved in patient care, (c) communicate the goals for each patient to the departments concerned with the accomplishment of these goals, (d) facilitate the reorganization and display of data for different users, and (e) provide a clear audit trail and improve cost control.

The major objectives of our hospital computer system are to: (a) expedite the flow of information between the patient and the physician and between the physician and the rehabilitation team, (b) enhance efficient hospital management, (c) provide data for the study of cost of rehabilitation, (d) improve the outcome of disability, and (e) facilitate utilization of clinical data for research. A parallel purpose is to evaluate the impact of the computer system on the patient and on the hospital operations.

C. GENERAL SYSTEM CONCEPTS

Regularly operating computer modules use a medium-scale general purpose computer (IBM 360/50) for both batch and teleprocessing. This computer is housed at the Baylor College of Medicine in the Institute of Computer Science and serves as a basic resource for a variety of medical research programs and projects in addition to providing operation support for TIRR teleprocessing and batch activities.

Functions that require frequent acquisition or changes of data have been implemented for teleprocessing. Those functions include timely provision of data reflecting the patient status of a potentially critical nature. Eight cathode ray tube display terminals and five typewriter terminals are located in various service areas of TIRR for easy accessibility by the staff.

Hardware and software performance requirements have been set using two primary considerations: high availability and cybernetic design. If the system was to be accepted and depended upon by the users, it had to be available when needed with as little inconvenience as possible to the user. The end product of this research was to be a cybernetic information system. It had to be functionally valuable, effective, physically transferable, and flexible. Software techniques and standards include: (a) high level languages, (b) multi-programming—background/foreground—virtual memory, (c) table-driven programs, (d) queuing contention problems, (e) access accountability, (f) spooling, and (g) rollout/rollin.

D. EVOLUTION OF THE TIRR HOSPITAL DATA MANAGEMENT SYSTEM

The TIRR Hospital Data Management System has been evolving since 1957 with the following milestones of progress.

1957: Prior to opening the hospital, an analysis was made of potential uses of electronic data processing techniques in hospitals. A data processing system was established and testing began with the opening of TIRR in February 1959 as a rehabilitation and chronic disease hospital.

1959: In 1959, nurses' notes and laboratory and physiological test data were recorded on specially designed source documents.[1] The data were then coded in numerical form, keypunched, and processed on a batch basis with unit record equipment. The software consisted of diagrams of complex patch boards. This system was not practical for entering bedside data because of the need to code all information in numerical form; however, the results of laboratory and physiological tests were effectively stored on punched cards. Measurements made in 1959 are included in the present data files.

1961: The availability of IBM 1401 and 1620 computers at TIRR allowed for processing both numerical and alphabetical data. Source documents in use in 1961 were more flexible than earlier ones. Storage of data on magnetic tape further enhanced data retrieval capabilities. Computer-generated reports of nurses' notes were demonstrated. These reports were prepared at the end of each shift and at the end of the day. The volume of data and numerous errors made during keypunching significantly limited the usefulness of the system.

1964: In one ward of TIRR (General Clinical Research Center for Chronic Illness), an IBM 1050 typewriter/card reader terminal was installed to allow nursing personnel to enter data in response to prepunched query cards. Initially this terminal was connected by telephone line to a remote paper tape punch machine located at Baylor. Data were batch processed on the IBM 1410 computer at the medical school a few hours after collection.[2] The lack of error-detecting capabilities at the time entries were made and the slow speed at which data entries were made on the remote terminal were two basic problems which contributed to the decision to convert to on-line operations.

1965: On-line operations were started in 1965 by means of an IBM 1026 control unit connected to the IBM 1410 computer. A teleprocessing clerk was trained to input data. Entries were made by the clerk via the remote typewriter terminal located at TIRR. With the establishment of conversational mode between the terminal and the computer, error detection and correction by staff personnel became feasible. Limitations in storage caused many entries to be truncated, causing a loss of portions of data. Magnetic tapes and disk with random access retrieval capabilities were used to store data. On-line recording of vital signs, obtained by physiological monitors, was effectively demonstrated using this system.[3] Hardware and software systems limitations (inability to set priorities, interrupt, or protect storage) restricted effective use and development. Each terminal was polled by the computer; once a terminal was in conversation mode, no other terminal could access the computer. Retrieval of data during peak hours was thus inhibited by competition for computer access.

1967: The availability of an IBM 360/50 computer, utilizing the Baylor time-sharing software, made possible the development of an online information system. CRTs and typewriter terminals located in the Institute were connected by telephone lines to the IBM 360/50. With implementation of the on-line system came problems of core limitations and system availability.[4]

1968: In July 1968, a large-core storage unit was installed to relieve the core limitation problem. Two principal types of automated procedures were needed: those that demanded response and action by the processor within several minutes and those that could sustain a somewhat longer delay. This difference in time-dependence guided the selection of algorithms implemented during the following years. System availability considerations led to the early implementation of automated procedures that could sustain the longer delay. Pertinent considerations included the reliability of terminals, communication lines, central hardware and software, and the mean time to restore the system to an operable condition given a failure in any one of these areas.

1970: Development continued from 1968 through 1970 on both types of automated procedures. The use of teleprocessing techniques in solving problems of information management in health care delivery were demonstrated. During this period, decision support became available in laboratory procedures for pulmonary functions and blood gas analysis, and in data retrieval and analysis. Much was learned about on-line digital data collection techniques, file organization and maintenance requirements, and hardware and software performance. Application and system software was upgraded as new demands arose.

1971: During the evolution of the TIRR Hospital Data Management System, many systems were tested and put into operation without emphasis on cost. A prototype system that had features desirable in the final model was developed in a research environment. While this system continued to be improved, efforts turned to the area of transferability. Hardware and software considerations were studied, and a decision was made to test the system on a minicomputer. During 1971, a Four-Phase Systems, Inc. minicomputer was installed to test economical transferability of the systems developed in the research environment.

Current systems information is as follows. Most inputs are through cathode ray tube (CRT) display terminals. Output can be either a visual display on the CRT or a hard copy produced on a high-speed printer located in the Baylor computer facility. Output varies with the application program. The present data base contains approximately 48,000 records, averaging 167 characters in length. This data base is maintained in a partially inverted file and involves approximately 4,000 transactions per week.

Peak loads for data entry and retrieval occur at the beginning of the week. These vary, however, with the number of hospital admissions. An average of 7,000 additions, 1,300 deletions, and 300 modifications are made to the data base each month.

E. DESCRIPTION OF THE BASIC TIRR INFORMATION SYSTEM (TIRRIS)

New application developments, as well as routine operations, are facilitated by TIRRIS, a conversational terminal-oriented data collection and file maintenance system. TIRRIS provides the user with the capability to enter, delete, modify, and display data in the TIRRIS file. Where possible and efficient, the system is driven by disk-resident tables. The tables describe the record format, identify the field, and provide information that permits TIRRIS to query the user for the necessary items and to check his response for errors. Where indicated by tables, the user's responses to queries are checked for validity and reasonableness. Tests may be made for valid numerics, numerics within a preset range, valid codes, or for the omission of essential data entry. Procedures for creating one kind of record are the same as those for creating other records. Thus, once the user is familiar with one TIRRIS data collection procedure, he is equipped to handle entry of any class of data, including system control messages.

Both sequential and branching query techniques may be used. The branch conditions are specified in the disk-resident table and are implemented by a pseudo-instruction interpreter. The system can thus avoid asking unnecessary questions of the user and can also ask further questions to get more detail upon specific user responses. Commands give the user some control over the system and permit him to repeat queries, to reinitialize the system, to change query format, and to invoke features of the system that speed data entry.

The file management software is written in such a way that, if the system fails before completion of file linkage alterations, a check-pointed record will be written into its original place when the system is restarted, restoring the file to its original condition. At most, one transaction will be lost.

Each query group or record description table may be protected with a coded password which restricts access to and entry of records described by the table.

Additional user routines are available to interface programs to the file. Programs which access the file also have access to the file of record description tables that identify fields within the record. A number of batch programs are available for user jobs. Programs also exist for file restoration, error recovery, file analysis, repair of file linkages, and transaction logging.

TIRRIS is run as one of many programs that can be handled by the Baylor Executive System for Teleprocessing.[5] Essentially, BEST handles all of the terminal I/O message routing and queuing; TIRRIS processes messages from the terminal. After a record has been completed, it is stored in the TIRRIS file and is then available for use by other user programs. Under control of the user, TIRRIS may also retrieve information from the file and display it at the terminal.

User programs may be batch programs or teleprocessing programs. Each user program that accesses the TIRRIS file does so through a file interface routine. BEST handles the teleprocessing I/O for all user teleprocessing programs and permits them to have access to both video display and typewriter terminals.

The file is also interfaced to a general purpose conversational retrieval program. This program allows the user to browse through the accumulated medical and other data using logical relational statements as the search question. This program is particularly useful in responding to physicians' queries about their past patients without necessitating the frequent writing of new programs.

With the advent of more powerful minicomputers, TIRR now has under way a project to implement a similar, although altered and simplified, data management system on a small computer with particular concern for its use in the medical environments.

F. PROJECT ORGANIZATION AND MANAGEMENT

The organization structure for the TIRR Computer Applications Department makes use of two kinds of organization: *functional* for large scale projects, and *project* for smaller projects or those that do not have a large EDP component. The intention is to use functional organization to develop general methods (especially EDP and evaluation techniques) that can be applied to more than one project and to use the project organization where it is necessary to have ongoing support on a full-time basis. It will be found, therefore, that the functional organization will be used in developmental projects to a greater degree than in projects that have reached the operational stage.

1. Planning Committee

The Planning Committee is composed of the director of TIRR, the Director of Computer Applications, Project and Group Leaders, the Director of

Patient Care, the Assistant Director for Program Coordination and Management Support, and an Advisory Group (consisting of consultants and other persons affiliated with other organizations and working in related projects). The Committee reviews the specific aims of projects and sets priorities for action in the projects. These priorities are provided to the Program Coordinator for scheduling and assignment of tasks.

2. Technical Advisory Committee

This committee is composed of many of the same persons serving on the Planning Committee but is concerned with *operational* details of tasks requiring special expertise (e.g., evaluation techniques).

3. Assistant Director for Program Coordination and Management Support (Program Coordinator)

The Program Coordinator has the responsibility and authority to follow through to ensure that the plans generated at the Planning Committee meetings are carried out efficiently. He generates and maintains an integrated departmental task time line which shows the major tasks, their starting times, and their duration (a PERT or a Gantt Chart) and monitors the progress of each task through consultation with the Project and Group Leaders.

4. Group and Project Leaders

The Group and Project Leaders participate in the planning and Technical Advisory Committees and, in cooperation with the Program Coordinator, frequently generate their major tasks. On receipt of the agreed upon task schedule from the Program Coordinator, they are responsible and have the authority for ensuring that the tasks are carried out on schedule by their group or project staff.

G. SUBSYSTEMS

There are several operational modules in the TIRR Hospital Data Management System. Table 1 presents a list of all the modules which were operational as of March 1972.[6]

1. Patient Medical Record

A significant portion of the information directly related to diagnostic and therapeutic activities of the individual patient is processed by the com-

Table 1.   Modules of TIRR hospital data management system

(A)	Patient admission	
	1. Preadmission information	(On-line)
	2. Patient admission system	(On-line)
	3. Daily census	(On-line)
	4. Identification	(On-line)
(B)	Problem identification	
	1. Disability profile	(On-line/Batch)
(C)	Physician ordering and coordinating activities	
	1. Rehabilitation care planning	(On-line/Batch)
	2. Care event time and performance structuring	(On-line/Batch)
	3. Patient independence level and self care status	(On-line/Batch)
	4. Transportation planning	(On-line/Batch)
(D)	Performing activities	
	1. Blood gas calculation, interpretation and reporting	(On-line)
	2. Pulmonary function calculation, interpretation and reporting	(On-line/Batch)
	3. Clinical laboratory result reporting	(Batch)
	4. Evaluation of personal independence	(Batch)
	5. Muscle function capacity reporting	(Batch)
(E)	Patient discharge	
	1. Discharge medical data abstracting	(Batch)
	2. Statistical reports of hospital utilization	(Batch)
(F)	Resources and fiscal management	
	1. Patient equipment order monitoring	(Batch)
	2. Service department activity reporting	(Batch)
	3. Rehabilitation cost and resource forecasting	(Batch)
	4. Institutional performance statistics package	(Batch)
	5. Patient billing accounts receivable	(Batch)
	6. Staff payroll	(Batch)
	7. General ledger	(Batch)
	8. Departmental budget performance	(Batch)
	9. Accounts payable	(Batch)
	10. Inventory and depreciation	(Batch)

puter. This includes such data as (a) patient descriptors and demographic data; (b) medical problems represented by description of pathology, resulting functional impairments and associated complications; (c) detailed care plans which facilitate the coordination of care events ordered in response to the patient's needs; (d) results of all laboratory and functional capacity tests, details of types and quantities of various forms of therapy; and finally (e) the abstracted information prepared from the complete hospitalization record following discharge. All of these types of information are handled by separate, specific programs designed for efficient processing and computer file usage. These programs range from weekly batch processing functions for updating historical information to teleprocessing programs which provide immediate results for certain laboratory tests in which the timeliness of the results is crucial to patient care decisions. Because of the wide variations in volume of data and acceptable delays in accessing it, there is nothing in the way of a computer file structure which could be construed to constitute an "integrated patient record." All of the frequently required information maintained on the computer is presented to the patient care staff in the form of individual computer-printed documents which form part of the regular patient chart. While there is no single computer file which contains all the integrated patient care information, the individual data can be readily extracted and combined with other information as the need arises. All the data entered from teleprocessing terminals or available for retrieval through the terminals are maintained in a random-access partially inverted disk file by standardized record creation, modification, deletion, and retrieval routines. This makes the data classes included in this file (consisting of patient descriptors, care plans and schedule, impairments and complications, blood gas analyses, pulmonary functions results, surgery history, and discharge data) immediately available to any batch or teleprocessing program without additional batch file processing. Special purpose, one time analysis of these data is facilitated by a general purpose, interactive, teleprocessing data retrieval program which is interfaced with this file.

A new file structure is being designed to provide a more efficient way of handling the care planning activities.

A simplified conceptual model of an ideal care-event organizing system for a single patient can be visualized as a two-dimensional matrix (Figure 20–1) where the columns are labeled with the different operational services (e.g., nursing, laboratory, x-ray, physical therapy, occupational therapy, and vocational counseling, or an even finer operational breakdown), and the rows are labeled with the different patient problems. Each square, then, contains the events performed by a specific operational service for a specific patient problem. These separate patient plans can be considered to be stacked into a three-dimensional cube, whch would then be the care plan for the entire group of patients.

If this model is considered as a file structure, it is apparent that the operational departments can retrieve data by column and will see the patient care plan and schedule as it relates to their department. Care planners who retrieve by row would be able to answer the question "What are we doing about this problem?"

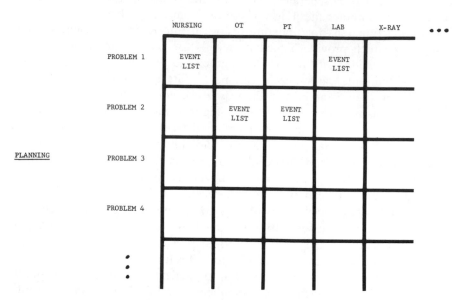

Figure 20–1. Care Planning Event Organization. This structure depicts the manner in which the events related to patient care must be arranged in order to permit entry by each functional organizational unit and to permit planners to retrieve events, by problem, across functions.

2. Administrative Functions

a. Patient registration and identification.

(1) Registration system. At the time of the admitting interview, the admitting clerk collects and enters into the computer data typically found on the face sheet, including the usual demographic data, payors, admitting diagnosis, program of care, and attending physician. The record thus created is the basic identification record for the patient and is used as well by the census, utilization, and occupancy programs.

(2) Admissions and discharge system. Admissions and daily census reports provide all departments with a concise profile of the patient's location, diagnosis, programs of rehabilitation, and onset date. The census report is listed several different ways (e.g., alphabetically or by hospital location) to suit the needs of the various departments. These programs generate keypunched cards which become input to the Accounts Receivable program for daily service charges for inpatients, the Medical Records Statistical program to produce monthly reports, and the Occupancy report on hospital utilization. The Utilization Review Committee finds the census report very useful because it indicates the number of days each patient has been in the hospital at each admission. (Figure 20–2).

DAILY CENSUS FOR 4/18/72   FIRST OF THREE PAGES

PT.NO	NAME	ROOM	BIRTH	SEX	DISABILITY (AS INDICATED BY ATTENDING PHYSICIAN)	REASON FOR ADMISSION	ADM DT	DAYS	ONSET DT	DR
STATION 1										
21741	ALA	1LT	08/11	M	CERE.THROM,R.HEMIPLEGIA	COMP.REHAB.	04/11/72	7	03/16/72	CAMP
21604	BAS	1LT	04/38	M	LEFT HEMIPARESIS	COMP.REHAR.	02/29/72	49	01/19/72	CAMP
2168R	HAW	1LT	10/26	M	CEREBRAL THROMOSIS	COMP.REHAR.	03/27/72	22	03/03/72	CAMP
21657	JAW	1LT	05/4	M	LEFT HEMIPLEGIA	COMP.REHAB.	03/16/72	33	05/00/71	CAMP
21692	KLA	1LT	08/13	M	RIGHT HEMIPARESIS	COMP.REHAB.	03/28/72	21	03/05/72	CART
21700	LFP	1LT	03/5	M	HEAD INJURY,L.HEMIPLEGIA	COMP.REHAR.	03/30/72	19	02/16/72	CART
21664	WOM	1PT	04/4	F	LEFT HEMIPLEGIA	COMP.REHAR.	03/20/72	29	02/15/72	CAMP
10130	DIK	1PT	09/33	F	PARAPLEGIA	HEMATURIA & DEHYDRATION	03/27/72	22	01/27/56	WRIG
21165	GRA	1PT	01/55	F	IDIOPATHIC SCLIOSIS	SPINAL INSTRU.& FUSION	03/29/72	20	00/00/59	DICK
10111	HUP	1PT	04/4	F	POST POLIO,SCOL.RESP.	RESP.EVALUATION	04/16/72	2	10/06/55	DICK
11211	JOH	1PT	01/55	F	ATELECTASIS OF LEFT LUNG	ATELECTASIS OF LEFT LUNG	03/31/72	18	CONGENIT	HARR
21611	LAN	1PT	05/56	F	C5-6 QUADRIPLEGIC	COMP.REHAB.	03/02/72	47	02/27/72	CART
21729	ROR	1RT	09/25	M	PARAPLEGIC	COMP.REHAB.	04/10/72	8	04/02/72	CAMP
21695	WII	1RT	01/45	F	T-6 PARAPLEGIC	ACUTE PYELONEPHRITIS	03/29/72	20	10/00/71	WRIG
STATION 2-RESPIRATORY CENTER AND ICU(2LT)										
11144	MTO	A-143	04/55	F	PNEUMONIA BILATERALLY	PNEUMONIA BILATERALLY	04/14/72	4	CONGENIT	HARR
13316	TIT	A-143	08/50	F	PNEUMONIA	PNEUMONIA	04/16/72	2	CONGENIT	HARR
19962	CHR	A-144	02/51	M	L.HEMIPARESISCHEMIPLEGIA	COMP.REHAR.	03/22/72	27	02/07/72	MART
21562	MAD	A-144	08/59	F	T-6 PARAPLEGIA	COMP.REHAB.	03/10/72	39	03/18/70	PELO
21395	CAL	2LT	04/56	F	GUILLAIN-RARRE SYNDROME	PLASTIC SURGERY	02/15/72	63	01/00/72	MART
2115C	CNN	2LT	08/38	F	C5-6 QUADRIPLEGIA	COMP.REHAB.	12/06/71	134	12/01/71	CART
21603	HAN	2LT	04/7	F	PARAPLEGIA,SEVERE SCOL.	SPINAL INSTRU.& FUSION	04/12/72	6	00/00/45	DICK
21192	HIN	2LT	01/16	M	QUADRIPARESIS	COMP.REHAR.	02/29/72	49	01/14/72	CAMP
11181	HOC	2LT	07/57	F	C-5 QUAD.	COMP.REHAR.	09/08/71	223	08/17/71	CART
18594	RAL	2LT	05/67	M	BILATERAL PNEUMOTHPAX	RILATERAL PNEUMOTHROAX	04/14/72	4	CONGENIT	HARR
21606	GAF	2RT	12/55	F	SPINA BIFIDA SCOLICSIS	PHYSICAL REHABILITATION	03/08/72	41	CONGENIT	MART
20135	LED	2RT	02/65	F	OSTEOGENESIS IMPERFCTA	POSTER.REPAIR OSTEO.ANTER-FUS	03/22/72	27	11/25/60	MART
13286	PAT	2RT	01/50	F	MORQUIOS DISEASE	ORTH.SURG(OSTEOT.R.TIBIA)	12/00/71	120	12/00/71	LANE
20377	PIN	2RT	03/69	F	CHR.BRONCHITIS,RILATERAL	MORQUIOS DISEASE	12/20/71	22	12/00/71	CART
1596R	ROW	2RT	02/64	F	PAPAPLEGIA,EPIDURAL LUM-	CHR.BRONCHITIS,BILATERAL	03/27/72	1	01/15/71	MART
21722	THO	2RT	12/68	F	REYES SYNDROME	ORTHOPEDIC SURGERY	03/09/72	12	03/09/72	MART
20689	TRA	2RT	02/71	M	SPINA BIFIDA	PNEUMONIA	04/10/72	8	CONGENIT	HARR
STATION 3-SPINAL CORD CENTER										
16390	REN	A-139	09/44	M	NEUROFIBROMATOSIS,PARA.	PLASTIC SURGERY	03/26/72	23	11/00/63	CAMP
18547	JEN	A-139	07/49	M	C-7 QUADRIPLEGIA	PLASTIC SURGERY	03/26/72	23	03/26/68	PELO
21752	MTI	A-139	10/37	M	L.FORFQUARTER,L.AK.AMPUT.	COMP.REHAB.	04/17/72	1	02/15/72	PELO
21701	GOR	3LT	05/29	M	C6-7 QUADRIPLEGIA,INC.	COMP.REHAB.	03/30/72	19	02/23/72	CART
21670	HAT	3LT	03/27	M	C-6 QUADRIPLEGIA,INCOMP.	COMP.REHAB.	03/22/72	27	03/09/72	PELO
21551	LAM	3LT	09/52	M	C-5 QUADRIPLEGIA	COMP.REHAB.	02/08/72	70	10/03/71	CART
21589	LOW	3LT	08/96	M	C-5 INCOMPLTE QUAD.	COMP.REHAB.	02/24/72	54	01/15/72	HARR
21364	STF	3LT	10/56	M	C-6 QUADRIPLEGIA	COMP.REHAB.	11/18/71	152	09/30/71	CART
21649	WIL	3RT	05/56	M	T-9 PARAPLEGIA	COMP.REHAB.	03/16/72	33	03/04/72	CART
21632	RIS	3RT	11/48	M	T-4 PAPA,FX.FEMUR	COMP.REHAB.	03/09/72	40	01/29/72	CART
21721	CRO	3RT	09/54	M	C5-6 QUADRIPLEGIA	COMP.REHAB.	04/06/72	12	02/20/71	CART
14453	MAT	3RT	07/53	M	C5,C6 QUADRIPLEGIA	COMP.REHAB.	02/25/72	53	01/11/72	CART
17397	MOY	3RT	06/49	M	C-7 QUAD,INCOMPLETE	R & F	08/04/71	252	06/22/71	CART
21609	RIV	3RT	07/45	M	C-5-6 QUADRIPLEGIA,COMPLETE	COMP.REHAB.	03/01/72	48	02/13/72	PELO

Figure 20-2. Detailed report of the Daily Census. This listing is the first of three pages which contains the list of all patients in the hospital on a given day. A summary report is presented on the last page and includes such elements as the total number of patients, the number of admissions, and the summary number of discharges.

A secondary use of the Admissions-Discharge System is to provide discharge documents which are distributed to the patient's medical chart, the Director of Patient Care, and the Business Office. Basic patient information also appears on schedule reports and disability profile reports. Automatic update of the patient name and number file is provided through the census file.

(3) Patient name-number system. The patient name-number system maintains an up-to-date file of all Institute patients, past and present, and their patient numbers and allows retrieval of this information via teleprocessing terminals. The Admissions Office uses the system daily to retrieve a patient's number when only the name is known or a patient's name when only his number is known. The Scheduling Office uses it to retrieve patient numbers. Ward clerks use it daily for number retrieval, and on weekends they file new admissions with dummy numbers to be used until real numbers can be assigned.

b. Billing, accounting and payroll.   A complete cost-centered accounting system has been in operation at TIRR since 1959; it handles all accounts payable and receivable, billing, depreciation and inventory, general ledger, and payroll.

c. Medical records statistical systems.   The major function of the medical records statistical program consists of the storage, arrangement, and consolidation of administrative data regarding each patient's admission or clinic visit. The Institute has a major problem with consolidation of records since the same patient is usually admitted and discharged numerous times over a period of years.

The primary use of this system is for the purpose of medical record statistics. Several reports are produced which list primary diagnoses, age, residency, condition and impairment (Figure 20–3), clinic visits, and patient status at discharge. The statistical usage summary (Figure 20–4), monthly and year-to-date, includes data most commonly required by the Joint Commission on Accreditation of Hospitals. These data are used administratively to project budgets to coincide with probable future utilization. Budget accuracy has improved to better than 90% of estimated figures. Besides the usual statistical reports, the medical records history file is used extensively for research.

3.   Service Units

a. Clinical laboratory.   The clinical laboratory reporting system edits clinical lab data, stores data for research purposes, produces cumulative

STATISTICAL REPORT OF CONDITION
AND IMPAIRMENT
APRIL, 1972

CODE	CONDITION AND IMPAIRMENT	MONTH			YEAR TO DATE		
		IN PAT	OUT PAT	TOT	IN PAT	OUT PAT	TOT
00	SCOLIOSIS, IDIOPATHIC	2	10	12	12	45	57
08	ASTHMA AND ALLERGIES	0	16	16	0	43	43
09	OTHER CHRONIC RESPIRATORY CONDITIONS (NOT ELSEWHERE COVERED)	10	17	27	33	48	81
10	ARTHRITIS AND THE RHEUMATISMS	0	16	16	2	24	26
11	CEREBRAL PALSY (PERINATAL CENTRAL NERVOUS SYSTEM INVOLVEMENT)	0	8	8	1	16	17
13	PARAPLEGIA (SPINAL CORD LESION)	29	20	49	55	54	109
14	QUADRIPLEGIA (SPINAL CORD LESION)	32	26	58	65	54	119
15	HEMIPLEGIA DUE TO STROKE	10	3	13	17	27	44
16	HEMIPLEGIA DUE TO OTHER CAUSES	2	6	8	9	17	26
19	POLIOMYELITIS	4	32	36	9	87	96
20	PERIPHERAL NERVE DISORDERS	2	1	3	2	5	7
21	DEMYELINATING DISEASES (SUCH AS MULTIPLE SCLEROSIS)	0	19	19	0	44	44
22	OTHER CENTRAL NERVOUS SYSTEM DISORDERS (NOT ELSEWHERE COVERED, E.G., PARKINSONISM)	1	5	6	3	14	17
23	MUSCULAR DYSTROPHY AND OTHER DEGENERATIVE AND INFLAMMATORY DISEASES OF ORGANS OF MOVEMENT	5	22	27	9	60	69
24	LOWER BACK AND CERVICAL SPINE SYNDROME (POSTERIOR NECK SYNDROME)	0	0	0	0	2	2
27	ABSENCE/LOSS, ALL OR PART, ONE OR BOTH (UPPER EXTREM-	0	2	2	0	7	7
29	ABSENCE/LOSS, ALL OR PART, (UPPER AND LOWER EXTREMITIES)	1	1	2	1	3	4
30	CONGENITAL MALFORMATIONS (NOT ELSEWHERE COVERED)	13	49	62	37	97	134
32	CHRONIC SPRAINS, SOFT TISSUE INJURIES	0	0	0	0	1	1
35	OTHER CONDITIONS NOT ELSEWHERE COVERED	1	3	4	2	6	8
98	EVALUATION ONLY (RESEARCH, ETC.)	0	2	2	0	3	3
99	UNKNOWN CONDITIONS AND IMPAIRMENTS	0	1	1	0	5	5
	TOTALS	115	266	381	264	689	953

Figure 20–3. Statistical report of condition and impairment. This report is prepared on a monthly basis for the Medical Records Department. It provides tallies of the types of impairments or problems encountered at the Institute.

STATISTICAL SUMMARY

01/01/72 TO 04/30/72

	04/01/72 TO 04/30/72	01/01/72 TO 04/30/72
REMAINING FROM LAST PERIOD	62	40
ON LOA AT BEGINNING OF PERIOD	9	19
ADMISSIONS	44	234
DISCHARGES	52	230
REMAINING AT END OF PERIOD	58	58
ON LOA AT END OF PERIOD	5	5
DAILY CENSUS		
MAXIMUM	66	71
MINIMUM	56	41
PATIENT DAYS	1826	7280
AVERAGE OCCUPANCY	61	60
PERCENTAGE OF OCCUPANCY	75	74
DAYS CARE TO DISCHARGED PATIENTS	1582	6325
AVERAGE DAYS STAY	30	28
STATUS OF DISCHARGED PATIENTS		
MALE	31	142
FEMALE	21	88
ADULT	41	166
PEDIATRIC	11	64
ANALYSIS OF PROGRAMS AT DISCHARGE		
NEW EMERGENCY	2	11
NEW ELECTIVE	18	75
EMERGENCY READMISSIONS	11	55
ELECTIVE READMISSIONS	21	89
RESEARCH ONLY	0	0
CONSULTATIONS ON PATIENTS DISCHARGED	42	164
PATIENTS HAVING CONSULTATIONS	20	88
PCT. OF PATIENTS HAVING CONSULTATIONS	38	38
RESPIRATORY STATUS OF DISCHARGED PATIENTS		
RESPIRATORY	6	16
NON-RESPIRATORY	42	204
POST-RESPIRATORY	4	10
RESULTS		
IMPROVED	40	197
UNIMPROVED	3	6
EVALUATION ONLY	9	24
LEFT AGAINST ADVICE	0	0
DEATHS, GROSS	0	3
OVER 48 HOURS AFTER ADMISSION	0	3
UNDER 48 HOURS AFTER ADMISSION	0	0
AUTOPSY		
NUMBER OF AUTOPSIES	0	1
PERCENTAGE OF AUTOPSY	0	33
*INPATIENTS TREATED	115	264
*OUTPATIENTS TREATED	283	821
*ALL PATIENTS TREATED	381	953
OUTPATIENT CLINIC VISITS	350	1592
INPATIENT CLINIC VISITS	191	1285
DAY CARE	0	27
OCCUPATIONAL THERAPY OUTPATIENT VISITS	9	81
PHYSICAL THERAPY OUTPATIENT VISITS	66	560

* NOT INCLUDING THOSE SEEN ONLY IN PT AND/OR OT.

Figure 20–4. Statistical summary prepared for the Medical Records Department. This report is prepared on a monthly basis and presents information as to hospital utilization. Input information is provided from the face sheet of the medical record and from the discharge sheet of the medical record.

reports for the patient's chart, enters charges into patient's billing file, and generates reports of selected statistics. Cumulative reports of laboratory tests reorganized in chronological order are generated for routine urinalyses, spinal fluid, hematology, blood chemistry, bacteriology, urine chemistries, and fecal analyses.

The chronological history of lab tests provides an organized and aggregated summary of laboratory test results that are useful to the physician in tracking changes in the patient's physiological reaction over time (Figure 20–5). Because the laboratory test results are known, the fact that a laboratory test has been performed is also known and charge records for that test and documents summarizing those charges are generated for the Business Office. A statistical summary of the tests is generated regularly by the computer and is used by the clinical laboratory as an aid to order sup-

CBC

DATE	TIME	EXAM. BY	HEMOG GM/ 100ML	HCT VOLS PCT	WBC THOUS CU.MM	NEUTR SEG- MNTD	NEUTR BAND FORMS	LYM- PHCY PLUS	MON- OCYT PLUS	EOSIN OPHI PLUS
01/20/69	C3:50PM		11.0	35	15.3	36	0	54	5	5
01/29/69	03:30PM		11.7	37	19.7	24	0	69	3	4
01/30/69	C4:00PM		13.9	43						
01/31/69	10:15AM		11.4	36						
06/16/69	11:25AM		11.5	36	22.1	45	0	47	5	3
12/22/69	1C:25AM		13.0	39	16.5	41	0	50	6	2
04/17/70	09:05AM	PL	12.7	39	12.1	33		53	11	2
04/18/70	08:05AM	LS	11.7	35						
04/20/70	07:25AM	RL	12.0	37	16.5	23		64	6	7
04/22/70	07:35AM	BL	11.9	36	16.2	27		63	2	8
05/01/70	11:45AM	YS	10.9	35	15.4	30	2	55	4	9
05/15/70	10:50AM	YS	10.2	32	19.5	62	2	27	7	2
05/18/70	C4:20PM	YS	10.5	35	22.7	23	1	68	4	4
05/26/70	07:35AM	YS	11.7	37	18.5	30	1	57	2	10
08/26/70	10:35AM	RL	12.7	37	17.5	26		63	3	8
08/31/70	C4:00PM	LS	12.7	40						
09/01/70	C7:40AM	RL	10.1	32						
09/03/70	C7:40AM	BL	9.7	30	8.8	47		33	6	14
09/11/70	C4:00PM	BL	10.4	32	15.6	39		46	4	11
09/14/70	04:00PM	DB	12.0	35						
09/15/70	11:30AM	BL	10.2	32						
09/16/70	07:20AM	BL	10.4	36						
09/17/70	07:35AM	BL	10.4	32						
09/24/70	C7:20AM	BL	12.5	38	12.4	38		44	5	13
11/27/70	C8:00AM	LD	12.7	39	19.9	72		24	4	
12/02/70	11:20AM	BL	13.3	40	12.0	24		65	7	4
12/03/70	C6:00PM	LS	17.0	52						
12/04/70	07:30AM	BL	19.2	61						
12/07/70	09:19AM	BL	15.3	50	6.5	38		51	7	4
12/11/70	11:35AM	RL	16.4	51	14.2	62	4	26	7	1
12/15/70	07:45AM	BL	15.0	51	10.9	58		29	7	6
02/05/71	07:15AM	BL	14.3	44	13.6	43		45	9	3
02/11/71	C7:20AM	BL	13.0	40	10.5	38		52	7	3
05/19/71	C9:50AM	MC	13.0	40	10.1	30		62	5	3
05/19/71	09:50AM	MC	13.0	40	10.1	30		62	5	3
05/25/71	C9:00AM	LD	12.8	37	12.8	45		48	5	2
05/31/71	11:00AM	LD	13.8	39						
06/11/71	C7:10AM	MC	13.5	40	13.4	37		52	2	9
08/07/71	07:20PM	DB	11.5	34	14.3	73	5	22		
08/09/71	C9:00AM	MC	13.0	38	9.4	79		20	1	
09/29/71	01:30PM	AH	11.7	36	15.2	70	6	21	2	1
11/23/71	C2:30PM	BL	13.0	43	8.8	58		28	6	8
12/24/71	11:45AM	AH	13.3	40	9.5	79		24	1	

HEMATOLOGY, TIRR   I   1██2   P██ K██████ 8██   PAGE   1
         06/26/72   STATN 2

Figure 20–5. Hematology report. The report presents a dense chronological listing of the results of hematology tests carried out on a patient.

1972 LAB 13 CHARGES   PAGE 1
MARCH 1972

	MONTH	CHARGE	YEAR	CHARGE
HEMOGLOBIN	395	782.00	1399	2776.00
HEMATOCRIT	398	788.00	1429	2794.00
RBC INDICES	5	40.00	12	96.00
RETICULOCYTE	8	24.00	20	60.00
WBC	349	350.00	1221	1227.00
DIFFERENTIAL	4	7.00	13	21.00
PLATELET COUNT	16	48.00	49	147.00
SEDIMENTATN RATE	1	5.00	10	45.00
COAGULATION TIME	24	88.00	37	140.00
L.E. CELL PREP	1	10.00	3	10.00
SICKLE CELL PREP	1	5.00	4	20.00
CAPILLARY CLOT X	1	3.00	1	3.00
EOSINOPHILE SMEAR	0	0.00	1	3.00
RBC FRAGILITY	0	0.00	1	10.00
MALARIA SMEAR	0	0.00	1	5.00
1334	5	25.00	13	65.00
LAB 13 TOTALS	1208		4214	

This is one of 14 pages of monthly statistical reports of laboratory tests performed and their costs in $.

Figure 20–6. Statistical summary of laboratory tests and their cost, This report is prepared on a monthly basis. The input information is provided from the computer data file of the laboratory test results.

plies and to determine staffing needs, since test frequency is a good indicator of this kind of resource demand (Figure 20–6).

b. Pharmacy.   The Institute has not engaged in the development of pharmacy information systems. However, recently it has implemented a program to maintain an inventory of drugs being used in the Institute, to maintain an inventory of such drugs in the pharmacy, and to perform analysis on frequency of prescription.

c. Clinical physiology.

(1) Pulmonary functions program. The pulmonary functions program performs calculations on raw data derived during pulmonary evaluation testing from spirometers and other equipment used in the cardiopulmonary laboratory. It evaluates the results of lung compartment measurements, forced expiratory efforts, and nitrogen washout. The results of these cal-

culations are expressed in percentage of normal. Also, the program provides an automatic interpretation of these results with a few statements which indicate the clinical significance of the findings for the patient. Essentially the logic of the physician in evaluating these results has been built into the program. Both batch and teleprocessing versions are available, the batch version used to generate a more carefully prepared report (Figure 20–7) and the teleprocessing version used to obtain results rapidly.

(2) Arterial blood gas analysis. The analysis of arterial blood gases has become a routine procedure to assess the respiratory and metabolic condition of patients with respiratory insufficiency. Inasmuch as the arterial pH is a function of respiratory and metabolic factors, it is crucial to measure as many of these factors as possible in order to study adequately the pathophysiology of respiratory insufficiency in a given patient and to establish whether or not artificial ventilation is being administered effectively. The blood gas program assists the technician by providing an automatic interpretation of the clinical significance of the numerical results as well as recommending the amount of buffer base necessary to correct acidosis if acidosis is present[7] (Figure 20–8).

d. Physical therapy (PT) and occupational therapy (OT).

(1) Reports of services provided. Both the PT and OT departments maintain records of the type and duration of each modality of therapy that they provide to each patient. A distinction is also made between testing and evaluation, individual patient treatment, and treatment of patients in groups. Daily, the therapists maintain these records of their activities on source documents which are subsequently keypunched and processed by the computer.

Different reports are generated from the data contained on these documents. Updated chronological history reports of the treatments provided to each patient are generated by a table-driven program (to allow for the addition of new modalities) and are placed in the patient's chart. The computer-generated reports are much denser than were the manually maintained records and aggregate all of the treatment events on a few pages, which not only reduces chart size but also saves searching for data and permits easy tracking of the treatment procedure and experience.

Monthly statistical reports are prepared from these data and provide the department heads with data as to how departmental man-hours were distributed in delivering the various modalities. Frequency-of-use data for the modalities suggest the staffing requirements and justify or deny need for additional therapy equipment.

(2) Physical therapy patient status reports. A set of programs have also been implemented to measure treatment outcome. Among these are the

SUPINE

```
*                  UNASSISTED          * TANK              * WITH CUIRASS     *
**********************************************************************************
*                  OBSERVED  PERCENT  * OBSERVED PERCENT  * OBSERVED  PERCENT*
*                  VALUE     OF NORM  * VALUE    OF NORM  * VALUE     OF NORM*
**********************************************************************************
*
* VENTILATION  MEASUREMENTS   IN LITERS BTPS
*
*    TIDAL VOL            .51           *    .64           *    .53
*    FREQUENCY         25               * 17               * 17
*    MINUTE VOL        12.89            * 10.96            * 9.13
*    O2 CONS  ATPS        .10           *    .09           *    .15
*
* LUNG  COMPARTMENTS   IN LITERS BTPS
*
*    INSP CAP             .99           *                  *
*    EXP RES              .05           *                  *
*    VITAL CAP          1.05      23    *                  *
*    INFL CAP           1.68           *                  *
*    FUNCT RES CAP      1.12      37    * 1.07      35     *    .88       29
*    TOTAL CAP          2.12           *                  *
*    INFL CAP  GPB                      *                  *
*
* DISTRIBUTION  MEASUREMENTS   NITROGEN WASHOUT
*
*    N EQUIV           17.2      143    * 12.7      106    * 30.5      254
*    FAST COMP                          *                  *
*    SLOW COMP                          *                  *
*    SLOW COMP                          *                  *
*    FINAL N2 CONCENTR    .9 PERCENT    *    .7 PERCENT    *    .9 PERCENT
*
* FORCED  VENTILATION  MEASUREMENTS  IN  PERCENT  OF  V.C.  TIMED VC
*
*    FEV .5 SEC        57               *                  *
*    FEV 1  SEC        78        93     *                  *
*    FEV 2  SEC        94               *                  *
*    FEV 3  SEC                         *                  *
*    TOTAL TIME        2.9 SECONDS      *                  *
**********************************************************************************
INTERPRETATION

   SEVERE RESTRICTIVE IMPAIRMENT AND THE INFLATION CAPACITY SUGGESTS
      GOOD COMPLIANCE
   SEVERE DECREASE IN FRC
   MODERATE IMPAIRMENT IN DISTRIBUTION AND MIXING IN UNASSISTED BREATHING
   SEVERE IMPAIRMENT IN DISTRIBUTION AND MIXING IN WITH CUIRASS BREATHING

   DATE      WT.        HT.       AGE     SEX
   6/15/66   62.29 KG   172.7CM   32 YR   M                C. VALLBONA M.D.


PULMONARY FUNCTIONS REPORT    PATIENT  1583   R■■■  D■■■  C■■■
```

Figure 20–7. Pulmonary Functions report. This report is prepared on a batch basis for interpretation and becomes part of the medical record. The interpretation is provided automatically according to an interpretation algorithm designed by the Director of the Cardiopulmonary Laboratory. The same report is available online in three separate frames when needed.

ACID/BASE BALANCE REPORT

```
NAME:SEC    .M              PAT.#:11124 WT: 80.00 AMBO2: 50.00
  SAMPLE:A    DATE:70/08/19  TIME: 345    TECH:AC
```

DERIVED DATA	VALUE	NORMAL VALUES		UNIT
		MEAN	RANGE	
PH	7.083	7.400	7.370-7.430	UNIT
PCO2	91.9	40	35-45	MM HG
PO2	91.0	95	80-110	MM HG
O2 SATURATION OF HB	92.6	97	95-99	%
ACTUAL BICARBONATE	26.5	24	22-28	MEQ/L PLASMA
TOTAL CO2	29.3	25	23-29	MMOL/L PLASMA
ALVEOLAR-ARTERIAL				
PO2 GRADIENT	198.6			MM HG
BASE EXCESS	-4.6	0	-3-(+2)	MEQ/L BLOOD
BICARBONATE REQUIRED	310.1	0		MEQ
THAM REQUIRED	1034.11	0		ML OF 0.3M SOLUTION

```
INTERPRETATION:
  ACIDOSIS, RESPIRATORY--UNCOMPENSATED
  SEVERE HYPERCARBIA
HYPOXEMIA.


GRAPH? (Y OR N)y
```

Figure 20–8. Computer report of the results of Arterial Blood Gas Analysis. This report is available online, and also displays graphically the nomogram of the Acid Base Balance.

muscle test and grip strength reports used by the PT department. Therapists evaluate and grade some 94 different muscle groups of the patient, and the computer algorithm computes the total score for different body parts as well as the whole patient. Essentially, "normal" is the highest possible score (a total of 1,000). Quadriplegics will frequently have scores from 50–200 depending on the level of the lesion and progress through the phases of rehabilitation. Test results performed at different times are listed four to a page in chronological order to facilitate tracking patient response over time and planning therapy changes. For research purposes, the reports provide a process of selecting a somewhat similar group of patients, at least with respect to ability. Grip strength measurements are similarly processed.

(3) Evaluation of personal independence reporting system. The evaluation of personal independence involves a series of patient functional tests that are performed jointly by the Occupational and Physical Therapy Departments. The system generates a report and profile that represent concisely the patient's capability to perform basic tasks related to normal living. These activities are grouped into the broad categories of bed activities, dressing, hygiene, and locomotion. These reports, which become part of the patient's chart, are used by therapists and physicians to assess the patient's functional abilities. The system provides: a graphic representation of functional ability with sufficient detail for the therapists; details on patient status, prognosis, and effectiveness of appliances for program planning by the physicians; a method for patient motivation; general knowledge of the patient's functional status for the medical, nursing, and social service staffs; a guide to home and vocational planning; an additional measurement for overall study and classification of patients; and a quick numerical reference for case histories and presentation where the entire test cannot or need not be used (Figure 20–9).

e. **Vocational unit services and activity reports.** A series of computerized programs have been developed to provide a current, ongoing analysis of several aspects of vocational unit services and activities. The output reports and their primary use are as follows:

(1) Texas Rehabilitation Commission requisition reports. The program is run biannually and is used by administration in reporting and determining fees. Individual and summary reports are given for the areas of vocational evaluation, work adjustment, transportation, driving program, and the programmer training course.

(2) Vocational unit client population description. The job is run as needed and generates reports reflecting the entire vocational unit population descriptions including socio-economic, medical, vocational, and psychiatric status. Descriptions of subsets of the population are also available. The reports are used by administration in structuring the vocational unit and in preparing unit descriptive reports.

(3) Vocational unit time distribution log. The time distribution log program is run monthly and collects client directed time by service, counselor, and disability, generating billing and summary reports reflecting these data. Reports are used by administration, counselors, and the business office (Figure 20–10).

(4) Vocational unit client employment reports. These programs are run as needed. They generate reports describing characteristics of employed vocational unit clients, and are used to determine likely job types for clients.

(5) Vocational unit driving program. This job is run as needed and

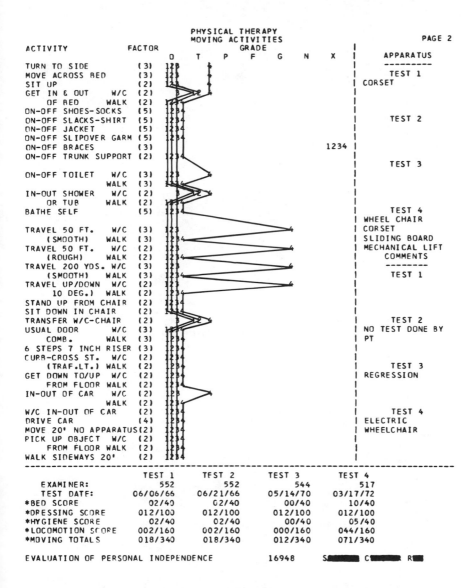

Figure 20–9. Report of evaluation of personal independence. The results of four consecutive tests are presented in a profile as well as in aggregate scores which indicate the progress or regression of a patient's ability to perform moving and stationary activities.

T.I.R.R. VOCATIONAL UNIT REPORT

STATISTICS CONCERNING PATIENT DIRECTED SERVICES

SERVICE	MONTH OF MAR 1 '72 THRU MAR 31 '72				YEAR TO DATE			
	TOTAL HRS.	NO. CLIENTS	% TIME	AVG TIME	TOTAL HRS.	NO. CLIENTS	% TIME	AVG TIME
PRE-SERV (VOC)	4.75	6	0.5	0.0	24.25	34	0.7	0.0
SOCIAL (VOC)	44.50	37	4.5	1.0	175.25	164	4.9	1.0
PSYCHOMETRCS(VOC)	149.50	16	15.2	9.0	470.50	57	13.2	8.0
WORK SAMPLE (VOC)	372.00	17	37.8	21.0	1259.00	60	35.3	20.0
WORK TLRNC (VOC)	0.00	0	0.0	0.0	32.00	3	0.9	10.0
WORK ADJ (VOC)	24.00	1	2.4	24.0	108.00	4	3.0	27.0
COUNSELING (VOC)	58.75	56	6.0	1.0	218.25	202	6.1	1.0
GROUP PROG (VOC)	42.25	19	4.3	2.0	124.00	61	3.5	2.0
PLACEMENT (VOC)	51.75	17	5.3	3.0	277.75	77	7.8	3.0
FOLLOW-UP (VOC)	10.50	13	1.1	0.0	57.75	51	1.6	1.0
REPORTING (VOC)	13.25	20	1.3	0.0	70.50	102	2.0	0.0
INTER-AGY (VOC)	4.00	10	0.4	0.0	25.25	53	0.7	0.0
STAFF CONF (VOC)	14.00	43	1.4	0.0	67.50	188	1.9	0.0
DRIVING PROG(VOC)	153.50	23	15.6	6.0	570.75	99	16.0	5.0
OTHER SERV (VOC)	41.00	1	4.2	41.0	85.75	8	2.4	10.0

Figure 20-10. Report of services provided by vocational unit. Both monthly and year-to-date statistics as to the distribution of departmental staff man-hours across various services provided by the department are presented for use by the department manager.

collects and reports descriptions of clients who have completed a driving course. Administration uses the reports in forming guidelines for the driving program.

4. Clinical Units

a. **Nurses' station system.**   We do not believe that an appropriate nursing station terminal has been designed. There are many terminals on the market, each of which has certain desirable features, but there is no single terminal available that combines them. Initially, TIRR began using the IBM 2260 series terminals driven by a control unit hooked up remotely through telephone lines to the computer system at Baylor College of Medicine. These have since been replaced with a different one manufactured by Four-Phase Systems Incorporated. This system, while marketed as a replacement for the IBM 2848 controller and 2260 terminals, is actually a rather powerful minicomputer, and a large variety of I/O devices can be attached to its CPU. Its memory is expandable to 76K bytes, and it comes with a rather broad range of software. The terminals of this system are very similar to those from IBM—that is, they consist of a cathode ray tube display of twelve 81-character lines and a standard typewriter keyboard. Across the top of the keyboard there are twelve function keys, the actions of which can be coded into programs. It is thus possible, with one keystroke, to implement a very complex action. The terminals lack the ability to read badges, which would be a desirable feature for protecting the system against unauthorized access. Another desirable feature is being developed at the University of Southern California, which has installed a device on the CRT Face that permits the terminal operator to indicate the selection of an item displayed on the screen by touching it with his finger. TIRR advocates the principle of data entry with as few key strokes as possible and is actively pursuing a method for selection of items from lists to simplify data entry and to overcome some of the hardware complexities that currently face the noncomputer-oriented operator.

b. **Computer-assisted care planning.**   The end result of the nursing care planning system at TIRR is a report that lists, at the top, the major goals that the staff intended to achieve for the patient and, toward the bottom of the report, lists the specific activities which were specified to achieve these goals (Figure 20–11). The event-list is arranged in chronological order for a 24-hour period and indicates which department is responsible for the performance of each task (Figure 20–12).[8]

For each event, the report shows the approximate time of day when the event is to be performed, the location in the hospital (the responsible

```
PRIVILEGED INFORMATION:

    27.CENSUS INFO      A.DISABILITY. C5-6 QUADRIPLEGIA
                        AGE OF PATIENT. 22YRS  0MOS
                        CURRENT PROGRAM. COMP.REHAB
                        B.ADM. REASON. COMP.REHAB

-------------------------------------------------------------------------------------

INFORMATION PERTINENT TO PATIENT CARE:

            00.CARE CATEGORY     CATEGORY 1-P - POST-OPERATIVE              SINCE- 04/12/72
    T*****
            01.SPEC.EVENTS       A.*PATIENT FASTING FOR BLOOD CHEMISTRY THIS A.M.       02
    T*****
                                 A.PATIENT SCHEDULED FOR A SHAMPOO AND A HAIRCUT TODAY  03
    T*****
                                 C.PATIENT SCHEDULED FOR HEMATOLOGY THIS A.M.           04

            02.INDEPND LEV       DO FOR. BRUSH TEETH,COMB HAIR,WASH HANDS AND FACE, EAT 17
                                 DO FOR. DRESS, BATHE, COMMODE, TRANSFER, TRANSPORT     02
                                 HELP.  MEDICATIONS                                     39

            03.HYGIENE           A.BATH QON (SURGI-LIFT) USE LOC (HOLD) - (BED BATH)    33
                                 B.HYGIENE BID                                          06
                                 C.NAIL CARE WEEKLY .                                   04
                                 D.SHAMPOO HAIR WEEKLY                                  32

            06.LOCOMOTION        *BED REST ONLY-DO NOT FLEX HIPS OR KNEES               49

            07.SITTING           PT. MAY SIT 9.30-2.00 AND 5.00 -7.00                   22

            09.TRANSFER          3 MAN LIFT                                             08

            11.POSITIONING       *******NOT TO GO PRONE********                         13
                                 ******STANDING IN P.T.                                 11


    T* = TEMPORARY CHANGE IN THE SCHEDULE (1 DAY ONLY)
         SOCIAL WORKER:TESTA
         REHAB. NURSING SPECIALIST: CAMPION            M███, D█████ JR.
         PATIENT SCHEDULE                              PATIENT   21097
         04/19/72                                      STATION   3 ROOM   3RT

         THIS IS THE FIRST OF 3 PAGES PROVIDING GENERAL NURSING CARE INFORMATION ON THIS PATIENT.
```

Figure 20–11. Computer report of Plan of Care for a patient. This is the first of three pages and describes items of general information pertinent to patient care, essentially: goals, orders, and general patient status.

department), the activity itself, and comments that clarify or explain the nature of the activity. Where applicable, the schedule will also indicate who is to be involved in the event (either by skill level or, in the case of physical and occupational therapy, the name of the therapist) and the position of the patient (as in a wheelchair at 50°). As an example, at 1:30 PM, the schedule might show that the patient, Mr. Smith, was to be in the physical therapy department for an hour of treatment under the direction of the therapist, Miss Williams, and that the patient should be taken to the therapy department in a wheelchair.

The same information may be reorganized by merging the schedules of all of the patients and listing them by nursing station. The result is a report showing, chronologically, all of the events on a nursing station for all patients. Thus, the nursing staff on a particular station can easily see the activities that they must perform during a particular time period.

By selecting only the physical therapy activities, it is possible to prepare appointment lists for that department. Similar reports can be produced for any location or department.

The care planning process involves the entire hospital staff. At admis-

TIME	LOCATION	DURATN	ACTIVITY	COMMENT	BY WHOM	POSITION - METHOD	SEQ
T***** 7.00AM	NURSING UNIT		*FASTING	BLOOD CHEMISTRY			02
T*****			BLOOD CHEMISTRY	SEE SOURCE DOCUMENT		LABORATORY PERSONNEL	01
T*****			HEMATOLOGY	SEE SOURCE DOCUMENT		LABORATORY PERSONNEL	03
T***** 7.30AM			*DELAYED BREAKFAST	BLOOD CHEMISTRY			01
		15-26	BREAKFAST		DO FOR		01
8.00AM		05-08	MEATUS CARE				R10
		04-07	VITAL SIGNS				RG7
		03-06	1 SURFAK CAP				09
8.15AM		02-03	HYGIENE				01
8.20AM		11-18	DRESS		DO FOR		01
8.30AM		C8-13	BLOW BOTTLES				R01
9.30AM			APPLY COCK-UP ORTHOS	9.30-10.30	DO FOR		04
		45-75	PUT IN W/C	9.30 -2.00	DO FOR		03
T*****			SHAMPOO + HAIRCUT			BED	01
10.30AM		04-07	REMOVE ORTHOSIS		DO FOR		01
			TURN-BACK				03
	PHYS. THERAPY	06C	(HOLD)	10.30-11.30	ROGERS	PST	02
11.30AM	NURSING UNIT	15-26	LUNCH		DO FOR		01
12.30PM		C8-13	BLOW BOTTLES				R01
		45-75	PUT IN W/C	12.30-1.30	DO FOR	ON SIDE	01
1.00PM	OCC. THERAPY	060		1.00-2.00	BEARD	W/C	03

T* = TEMPORARY CHANGE IN THE SCHEDULE (1 DAY ONLY)
SOCIAL WORKER:TESTA
REHAB. NURSING SPECIALIST: CAMPION
PATIENT SCHEDULE
04/19/72

M█████.D█████ JR.
PATIENT 21097
STATION 3 ROOM 3RT

THIS IS THE SECOND OF 4 PAGES OF A DETAILED 24-HOUR SCHEDULE OF ACTIVITIES PROGRAMED FOR THIS PATIENT.

Figure 20–12. Chronological Listing of Scheduled Activities for a patient. The inset of this figure indicates the actual activities related to the inset of special events shown in Figure 20–11.

sion, the major problems of the patient and his care program are known, which permits the staff in the scheduling office to create a primary plan of care for the patient by selecting, from a file of basic standard plans, the ideal plan for the patient's specific diagnosis and additional subplans for the complications that he may have. These plans and subplans are merged by the computer into a single plan. When the patient arrives at the nursing station, his basic plan of care (and the activities involved) is ready, and care may begin immediately. The doctor's involvement at this point is the specification of the diagnosis, the complications, and the care program. This information is typically known prior to admission. It has been shown at TIRR that this automated process reduced by as many as three days the time lag between the admission of a patient and the start of his care plan.

During a patient's stay, this basic plan is updated with orders written by the physician, the nurse, and the therapists, and becomes individualized to fit the patient's specific needs and the doctor's particular mode of practice. Other departments add their activities to the patient's activity list, which becomes an event schedule in addition to being a care plan. At the Institute, some orders are entered by the department staff themselves, while orders written by doctors and the nurses are entered by clerical staff supplied by the Computer Applications Department. In the latter case, the orders, whether new or modifications of old ones or deletions, are written on a special two-part form in the chart. Every two hours, the scheduling clerks make rounds of the nursing stations to pick up any new orders that have been written, assemble carbon copies of the orders, and return to the scheduling office where they enter the additions, changes, and deletions into the computer. At 8:30 PM, when the last orders have been entered into the computer, a program is run to print out the care plans for the next twenty-four hour period. These forms are delivered to the nursing stations and are distributed to the patients' charts at midnight. Schedules for the non-nursing departments are picked up by the departments in the morning when they start their normal working day or are delivered in the morning mail.

The reports and CRT displays generated from the care plans and schedules are used daily by all professionals involved in patient care, including the nurses, aides, orderlies, ward clerks, clinic personnel, social workers, laboratory technicians, vocational counselors, social service counselors, x-ray technicians, dietician, transportation personnel, and therapists.

Having this kind of information available permits many studies that otherwise would not be possible. For example, it is possible to investigate the work load at a nursing station during a particular time period or during an entire day. Histograms of man-hours of care at each of the nursing stations may be produced. Similar profiles can be generated for particular skill levels. Such information is useful for rescheduling events to smooth out peaks in the workload.

It is also possible to investigate different staff loading patterns for the various nursing stations. This knowledge allows the administration of the hospital to plan staffing levels and to allocate resources as the characteristics of the inpatient population change.

As problems are defined and plans are created, it is possible to abstract from the care plans for similar problems of individual patients a standard plan for a specific problem and to add it to the care plan library. This standardization process facilitates patient care by making the knowledge of experienced physicians readily available to other physicians who have not yet acquired expertise in the management of disabling conditions. The attending physician thus starts with the minimal plans that physicians agree should be used. Thus, a kind of prospective care quality assurance takes place when the patient has the potential to benefit. This is in contrast to care quality evaluation done retrospectively.

c. Disability profile. A patient's disability profile presents, in a concise form, his primary pathology with its related impairments and complications, giving onset dates, expected outcome, etiology, and circumstances. Secondary pathologies are similarly presented. Operative procedures, giving date, location, and significant past history are also included (Figure 20–13.

Disability profiles are maintained on all Spinal Cord Center patients in the Institute (approximately 60% of the inpatients). Once the basic profile is obtained from physician dictation, it is entered via a CRT terminal by a data clerk. Output can be via teleprocessing typewriter terminals or by a batch job run on the high-speed printer. The physicians review their patients' profiles weekly, bringing them up to date by adding new complications or indicating termination or continuation of existing conditions. Entries requiring the physician's attention are flagged by the program.

The data constituting the disability profile are analyzed on request by the staff to answer a wide variety of questions concerning cumulative medical experience with the patient population.

d. Outpatient clinic. Computer developments at TIRR have been targeted, for the most part, to the inpatient facility. Nevertheless, over 4,400 outpatient visits occur annually; and in the next several years, further work is planned in this phase of operations. At present, records are maintained of each clinic visit, the reason for it, the problem of the patients and which clinic the patient attended (e.g., urology, respiratory). Monthly and year-to-date reports of visit and problem frequency are generated for management and administration. While there are as yet no algorithms in

```
REPORT DATE: 04/05/72            DISABILITY  PROFILE

PATIENT: M      ,J      P         TIRR# 21598  ATT.PHY.: PELOSOF      ADM.DT.: 02/28/72  BIRTH: 04/21/33

PRIMARY DISABILITY    QUES/CONF    ETIOLOGY      CIRCUMSTANCES       ONSET DATE    EVOLUTION-DATE
------------------    ---------    --------      -------------       ----------    --------------

PATHOLOGY
  COMP.FX L1                       TRAUMA        INDUSTRIAL ACCIDENT  01/31/72      TERM 01/31/72
  SPIN.CD LES.AT L1                COMP FX L1    TRAUMA               01/31/72      PERM

MAJOR IMPAIRMENTS
  MTR PARAL.BEL.L1,COMP                                               01/31/72      PERM
  SENS.ANES.BEL.L1,COMP                                               01/31/72      PERM
  BOWEL INCONTINENCE                                                  01/31/72      PERM
  URINARY INCONTINENCE             SHOCK BLADDER  FOLEY CATHETER      01/31/72      TRAN 03/29/72*

COMPLICATIONS
  HEMOTHORAX,RT.                   TRAUMA                             01/31/72      TERM 02/07/72
  THROMB.,LT.DEEP FEM                                                 03/14/72      TRAN 04/10/72

SIGNIFICANT PAST HISTORY
  FX LT.ANKLE                      TRAUMA        INDUSTRIAL ACCIDENT  01/31/72
  LAC.VERTEX OF SCALP              TRAUMA        INDUSTRIAL ACCIDENT  01/31/72
  RUPTURED SPLEEN                  TRAUMA        INDUSTRIAL ACCIDENT  01/31/72      TERM 01/31/72

                              * PLEASE COMPLETE OR VERIFY
************************************************************************************************

OPERATIVE PROCEDURES                    DATE      LOCATION             COMMENTS
--------------------                    ----      --------             --------

LAMINECTOMY & FUSION T12-L1             01/31/72  MEM.CITY HOSPITAL
INSERTION OF CHEST TUBE,RT.             01/31/72  MEM.CITY HOSPITAL
SPLEENECTOMY                            01/31/72  MEM.CITY HOSPITAL
REMOVAL OF RT.CHEST TUBE                02/08/72  MEM.CITY HOSPITAL
```

Figure 20-13. Computer print-out of a Disability Profile of a patient with a spinal cord injury. The profile presents the primary pathology complications, impairments, and operative procedures of one patient.

operation that are used during the outpatient encounter, during 1973 a follow-up system will be designed to replace and extend the current manual procedure in order to give more prompt and timely attention to patients who have left the Institute after rehabilitation but who still require an intensive program of home care for several years. Also, because of the chronic problems involved, the Institute intends periodic review, at least by correspondence with patients who have left, both for the benefit of the patient and for the evaluation of the entire rehabilitation process over long periods.

H. EDUCATION AND RESEARCH

1. Computer-Assisted Instruction

There is an extensive CAI system at Baylor. The system consists of programs creating courses, presenting the courses to students, maintaining records of their performance, and analyzing the performance of a group of students on individual courses to assist in course editing and update. It has been used most extensively in pathology, encompassing such subjects as concepts of inflammation and repair, circulatory disturbances, anemia, leukemia, and self-evaluation review of general pathology.

The system capabilities have also been expanded to allow presentation of *clinical simulations*. One simulation concerns a patient with paroxysmal nocturnal hemoglobinuria. The student is asked to make both diagnostic and therapeutic decisions and, in turn, he receives comments upon his performance. The format of this exercise requires the student first to establish a diagnosis and then institute appropriate therapy. Another case was written by a medical student who had previously been introduced to Dr. Lawrence Weed's system of problem oriented record keeping. In this case simulation, the problems are extracted from the available information and then more data is obtained in order to combine nonspecific problems and ultimately to reach a diagnosis.

The CAI program has steadily evolved since its origin in 1970 and now consists of a family of computer programs, some of which may be used from remote terminals (those which deal with writing and modifying the courses, the teaching program proper, and the student record program) and others which enable the courses to be evaluated on paper and individual student responses to be analyzed. Unlike other institutions' systems which often use computers whose total capacity is dedicated to CAI, the Baylor computer system is used primarily for other purposes. The CAI program is experimental. There is at present no computer-assisted instruction laboratory or central facility devoted to this purpose.

The Baylor CAI system can store multiple courses and can be used simultaneously by as many as 15 students. The courses may be of any length and may consist of linear or branching programmed material or clinical-style case presentations in which the student selects appropriate diagnostic or therapeutic procedures and receives either comments upon the appropriateness of his choice or an indication of the patient's response to such procedure. A reference feature enables the student to obtain a literature reference for frames he sees. A definition feature allows him to ask for definitions of unfamiliar words or phrases. An individual record is maintained for each student indicating the course he is taking, the last question he answered in that course, and the list of review questions to be asked him during the next session. Individual instructional frames may consist of statements, multiple-choice questions, and constructed response questions in which the student types in a word and phrase.

To assist the author in creating a course, a program is available which lists the entire course or segments thereof on the high-speed printer. The program provides several options so that the course can be listed as it would appear to the student in pathway sequence with branch questions below the pathway questions or in straight sequential order by frame number. The author can request two reports as needed while students are using the course. One lists data on student performance and includes incorrect answers, current location in the course, time spent, and average error rate for each student. The other report lists courses in question number sequence with all incorrect answers as well as error rate to assist in revising ambiguous questions.

2.   Computer Research Applications

There has been wide utilization of the TIRR Hospital Data Management System for research purposes. A large data base of clinical data has been entered in the computer files since 1959. Thus, clinical investigators at TIRR have accessed the files for a variety of retrospective studies. In addition, the flexibility of the file and retrieval system has been a useful tool for prospective studies. In the following paragraphs, we provide brief descriptions of illustrative research activities that have been facilitated by the TIRR computer system.

THE TIRRIS software has been adapted for use at Baylor by the Institute of Computer Science. A general purpose Boolean retrieval program (BROWSE) has been interfaced to the TIRRIS file and data definition tables. These programs are available on-line to all the investigators of the College. The Department of Virology and the Institute of Lipid Research utilize these programs extensively.

The most extensive prospective study is the scoliosis project, which has built a data base on several hundred patients with idiopathic and paralytic scoliosis. The data file includes serial measurements of biomechanics of the spine, results of cardiopulmonary function studies, laboratory data, and clinical changes following spinal instrumentation with the Harrington technique.[9]

A large data base of hospital statistics and financial information has been gathered since 1959. This has given opportunity to the director of the institution and to his administrative staff to carry out numerous analyses of the long-term utilization of the institution[10] and of the cost of providing rehabilitation services to patients with a variety of disabling conditions.

An important need in rehabilitation is to define in quantitative terms the formal various parts of the body and possible alterations resulting from disability. Biostereometric techniques are particularly helpful because they provide an opportunity for exact measurements. Dr. Herron and associates[11] have developed a computerized technique to analyze these measurements and reproduce automatically three-dimensional models of the form of any object. The design of artificial limbs or prosthetic or orthotic devices can be greatly enhanced by this process.[12]

Dr. Cardus has developed a program for automatic analysis of the results of work tolerance tests carried out in patients with cardiac disability.[13] Exercise tests are continuously monitored from the standpoint of ECG, tidal volume, and instantaneous measurements of partial pressures of oxygen and carbon dioxide by means of a mass spectrometer and a flow meter. The analog signals are processed with a digital computer and the computer analysis of the data is displayed on a CRT located in the laboratory while the subject is under evaluation. At the end of the test, the computer prepares a report for the physician and for the patient. The reports include an evaluation of the patient's maximum capacity for physical exercise and classifies the individual according to tables applicable to the general population.

Another important area of research has been in the development of mathematical models for predicting outcome of rehabilitation. A specific example is the program to predict the degree of the recovery of patients with polyneuritis and poliomyelitis based on the results of three consecutive muscle tests carried out in the early stages of recovery following the acute onset of illness.[14]

I. HARDWARE AND SOFTWARE

1. Hardware

Development and routine operations of the hospital computer application modules are supported by a medium-scale general purpose computer (an IBM 360/50), which handles both batch and teleprocessing. The computer is housed at the Baylor College of Medicine and is also used by medical researchers at the College.

Twelve cathode ray tube display terminals, their associated controller (actually a minicomputer made by Four-Phase Systems, Inc.), and four IBM 2740 typewriter terminals are located at strategic points in the hospital and are connected by telephone lines to the computer at Baylor. Twenty additional terminals are connected to the computer for use by the various research departments at the College. One of these terminals is located at Menorah Medical Center at Kansas City, Missouri and communicates via telephone lines through a dial-up entry port.

The central processing unit has 128K of high-speed memory plus one megabyte of Ampex extended core memory and is connected through the selector channel to five dual-density Ampex disk drives, two IBM tape drives, one nine-track and one seven-track, and the local CRT displays. In addition to the 1403 printer and the card read/punch, the multiplexor channel also serves the remote CRT displays and the typewriter terminals. An IBM 1627 incremental plotter is also on-line (Figure 20–14).

2. Software

The basic systems software is provided by the IBM operating system using multiprogramming with a fixed number of tasks (OS/MFT) and HASP, the Houston Automatic Spooling Priority System. Teleprocessing is supported by the Baylor Executive System for Teleprocessing (BEST), a teleprocessing supervisor written by the Baylor systems staff.[5] Core memory is partitioned into two batch partitions and one large teleprocessing partition in which BEST runs the various user teleprocessing programs.

General purpose applications software is also available to the terminal users:

TIRRIS, a general purpose table-driven data collection and file maintenance system;

BROWSE, a general Boolean retrieval program to retrieve data from TIRRIS-maintained files and to perform elementary statistical analyses;

RASS, remote access statistical routines to perform statistical analyses of data subsets either created by BROWSE or entered directly by the user;

DCALC, to perform job entry support through BEST and HASP;

BMDRJE, to enter data, control cards and job control cards for executing programs from the Bio-Medical statistical package (developed at U.C.L.A.);

CAI, a table-driven computer-assisted instruction algorithm for which instructors may prepare courses.

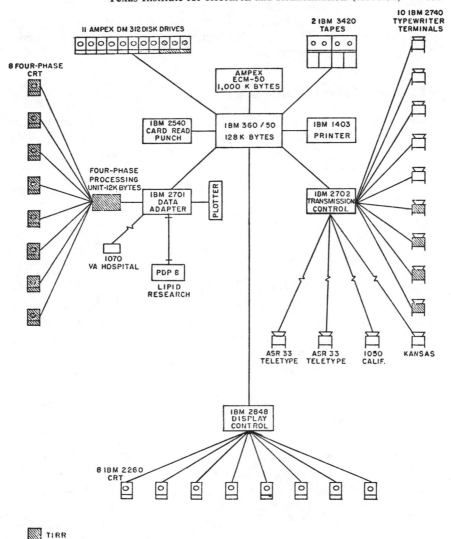

Figure 20–14. Configuration of the Baylor Computer System. This system supports users at six institutions with thirty-two terminals.

J. EVALUATION

Evaluation of the impact of the automated procedures at TIRR on patient care activities included assessment of the effectiveness and efficiency of the automated procedures, analysis of the impact of the computer system on the functional performance of the Institute, and documentation of hardware and software usage statistics. Methods used included time studies, questionnaires, accounting procedures, interviews, and descriptive analysis. The major findings of these studies are as follows:

1.   Patient Scheduling Procedure

The system has increased patient goal agreement among nursing personnel and is rated favorably by representatives of all disciplines involved in rehabilitation and by the patients themselves. From the standpoint of efficiency, there has been a 33% increase in the number of scheduled activities that were actually carried out, and the time required to implement initial orders after admission decreased from approximately two hours to several minutes.[15]

2.   Admissions and Daily Census

Using the computer versus the manual procedure has resulted in a 26% decrease in the time spent for the steps required for admission and daily census processing. The personnel involved express a favorable opinion because mistakes can be corrected more easily on the terminal; also, since data are saved, when the patient is readmitted only a few entries need to be made to update the old record. A saving of approximately 1500 characters has been estimated for each readmission.

3.   Pulmonary Function Studies

The pulmonary function studies program is estimated to have decreased the interval from scheduling of a patient for a study to the time the report is ready for the physician from approximately five days to thirty minutes. A major reason for this decrease is that the interpretation is now done completely automatically, whereas the manual system required the physician to interpret the results, which caused a delay from five minutes (if done immediately) to five days (if done routinely).

4.   Acid Base Balance Study

The results of a comparison between manual and computer methods of calculating, interpreting, and reporting blood gas analysis show an 88% decrease in time using the computer system (i.e., from twenty-five minutes to three minutes. In addition, the users of the system feel it has a favorable impact in improving accuracy and completeness of information which is needed for clinical management of the patient. This is due primarily to the fact that there is an automatic interpretation of results and therapy recommendations.

5. Time and Cost of the System

Since the computer system at TIRR is supported by a federal grant, a fixed amount of money is budgeted each year and the costs of each procedure are distributed according to the percent of time required. Statistics for cost required for personnel, teleprocessing, and batch processing for all computer procedures are collected on a routine basis. The time required has been rather high due to the initial cost of research and development, but a plateau has been reached.

The evaluation of the system points to the following general conclusions:

(1) The automated system offers great potential in providing an organized, coordinated, and concise profile of the medical, physiological, psychological, and socioeconomic needs of the patient.

(2) When technological innovations are well accepted, personnel have a tendency to depend exclusively on the automated system at the expense of verbal communications.

(3) Because of the ease and convenience for medical professionals to work independently of one another when using automated procedures, care must be taken not to oversaturate the patient's tolerance to activity.

(4) Automated activity may decrease or eliminate clerical duties but simultaneously create new responsibilities for higher-paid professionals. This may have net adverse effects unless the benefits of quality of care provided surpass the additional time required by professionals.

(5) The initial costs of developing automated health systems is large, particularly due to hardware expenses. However, a steady state has been reached in many of the automated patient care activities, and the cost of the routine operation of these systems has been assumed by the Institute.

An estimation of the cost per patient day is complicated by the fact that the system is developmental and research-oriented. A minimal hardware configuration with enough staff to keep the various systems operating would not cost as much as the present effort. For example, dividing the total cost of the project for, say 1970 ($343,164), by the number of patient days for that year (17,000) gives a per-patient-day cost of $20.07, which includes, of course, a large component for extra systems analysis and programming staff as well as extra hardware that facilitate research and development. Adjusting these figures to compensate for the extra staff but keeping essentially the same hardware configuration, we arrive at a figure of $14.47 per patient day, still quite high. The denominator, patient days, must also be adjusted since the Institute had only 56 beds in 1970 and 200 beds could easily be supported with the present system. The resulting increase in the number of patient days in such a large institution would bring the cost per patient day down to $4.20.

During 1973, several of the systems will be implemented on a mini-computer and will be able to function independently of the IBM 360/50, reducing the cost for these systems still further, even though the minicom-puter will also be linked to the 360 to support the research effort and to provide distributed processing ability.

K. SUMMARY

The TIRR Hospital Data Management System which has evolved over a period of thirteen years utilizes extensively an online computer facility. The major objectives of the system are to: (a) expedite the flow of infor-mation, (b) enhance efficiency in hospital management, (c) provide data for studies of hospital performance, (d) improve the outcome of disability, and (e) facilitate utilization of data for clinical research.

The system has been developed following a modular concept. All the modules can be classified in the following major categories: (a) patient admission, (b) problem identification, (c) physician ordering and coordi-nating activities, (d) performing activities, (e) patient discharge data, and (f) resources and fiscal management. At present, there are a total of 25 operational modules.

The TIRR System uses the computer facilities of the Institute of Com-puter Science of Baylor College of Medicine. The software developed for the TIRR System (TIRRIS) has great flexibility and transferability and it is used at Baylor for a variety of computer education and research activities.

An extensive evaluation of the TIRR computer system has been carried out. It has been found that the modules most accepted have been the patient scheduling procedure (standard plans of care), admissions and daily census, processing of physiological test data, and reports of services provided by the various departments of the hospital. Many modules have become operational and are being supported by the hospital.

The staff of the Computer Applications Department of TIRR is currently engaged in a program of transferring concepts, procedures, and, where possible, modules of the TIRR system to a wide range of rehabilitation institutions and extended care facilities in the U.S. and abroad.

ACKNOWLEDGMENTS

Contributions to this chapter were also made by Robert L. Baker, M.S.; Susan Beggs, M.P.H., M.S.; Charles L. Moffet, M.D. and Allan H. Levy, M.D., from the Departments of Rehabilitation, Community Medicine and the Institute of Computer Science of Baylor College of Medicine, Houston, Texas.

The authors are indebted to the patient care staff of the Texas Institute for Rehabilitation and Research for their enthusiastic cooperation with this project throughout the years. Special credit must be given to Dr. R. E. Carter, Director of Patient Care; Miss Sudie Cornell, Director of Nursing Education; Miss Miriam Partridge, Director of Physical Therapy; Miss Mary Joyce Newsom, Director of Occupational Therapy; Miss Diane Bertrand, Director of Clinical Laboratory; Mr. Dan Hrna, Director of Pharmacy; Mr. Charles Poor, Director of Vocational Services; Miss Mary Catherine Stubbs, Director of Medical Records; and Mr. Nicholas Hott, Business Manager.

The programming staff of the Computer Applications Department deserves recognition, especially Mrs. Judy Carrick, Miss Bonnie Burnett, Mrs. Kathy Tuer, and Miss Mary Jane Walton. In particular, we acknowledge the cooperation of Mr. Thurmon Williams, Data Processing Technician, whose daily efforts have been responsible for the success of the operational programs. We are most indebted to Mrs. Lois Westrich and Mrs. Eleanore Grefe for their exemplary dedication in the preparation of the manuscript.

REFERENCES

1. Spencer, W. A., and Vallbona, C. "Digitation of Clinical and Research Data in Serial Evaluation of Disease Processes." *IRE Trans Med. Electronics* ME—7: (1960):296–308.
2. Vallbona, C.; Blose, W. F.; and Spencer, W. A. "System for Processing Clinical Research Data. I. Experience and Problems." *Proc 6th IBM Med. Sympos.* (1964):437–462.
3. Vallbona, C.; Spencer, W. A.; Geddes, L. A.; Blose, W. F.; and Canzoneri, J. "Experience with On-line Monitoring in Critical Illness." *IEEE Spectrum.* 3(1966):136–140.
4. Vallbona, C.; Spencer, W. A.; Levy, A. H.; Baker, R. L.; Liss, D. M.; and Pope, S. G. "An On-line Computer System for a Rehabilitation Hospital." *Meth. Inform. Med.* 7(1) (1968):31–39.
5. Hobbs, W. F.; Levy, A. H.; and McBride, J. "The Baylor Medical School Teleprocessing System." *Am. Fed. of Inform. Processing Societies Conf. Proceedings.* 32(1968):31–36.

6. Spencer, W. A.; Baker, R. L.; and Moffet, C. L. Hospital Computer Systems— A Review of Usage and Future Requirements After a Decade of Overpromise and Underachievement. (in press).

7. Vallbona, C.; Pevny, E.; and McMath, F. "Computer Analysis of Blood Gases and of Acid Base Status." *Comp. and Biomed. Res.* 4 (1972) : 623–633.

8. Gotcher, S. B.; Carrick, J.; Vallbona, C.; Spencer, W. A.; Carter, R. E.; and Cornell, S. "Daily Treatment Planning with an On-line Shared Computer System." *Meth. Inform. Med.* 8 (4) (1969) : 200–205.

9. Harrington, P. R. "Technical Details in Relation to the Successful Use of Instrumentation in Scoliosis." *Sympos. on Current Pediatric Problems.* 3 (1) (1972) : 49–67.

10. Vallbona, C.; Gotcher, S. B.; Libman, C.; Spencer, W. A.; and Stubbs, M. C. "Ten Year Analysis of Duration of Hospitalization of Disabled Patients." *Med. Care.* 8 (6) (1970) : 48–50.

11. Herron, R. E. "Stereophotogrammetry in Biology and Medicine." *Photogr. Applications in Science Technology and Medicine.* 5 (1970) : 26.

12. Cardus, D. "Computerized Unit for a Cardiac Rehabilitation Program." *Arch. of PM & R.* 52 (1971) : 416.

13. Vallbona, C.; Iddings, D.; and Zeigler, R. K. "Recovery of Strength in Acute Polyneuritis and Poliomyelitis." *Arch. Phys. Med.* 50 (1969) : 512–521.

14. Beggs-Gotcher, S.; Vallbona, C.; Spencer, W. A.; Jacobs, F. M.; and Baker, R. L. "Evaluation of a System for On-line Computer Scheduling of Patient Care Activities." *Comp. and Biomed. Res.* 4 (1971) : 634–654.

CHAPTER TWENTY-ONE

Kaiser-Permanente Hospital Computer System (San Francisco)

by Edmund E. Van Brunt, Lou S. Davis, & Morris F. Collen

A. MEDICAL CARE ENVIRONMENT

The Kaiser-Permanente Medical Care Program is based upon a complementary relationship between (a) a nonprofit prepayment health insurance program (Kaiser Foundation Health Plan) and (b) a regionalized system of hospitals and ambulatory care facilities (Kaiser Foundation Hospital), together working in each region in conjunction with an independent multispecialty group of physicians (Permanente Medical Group). The Northern California Region is the largest of the regions and is the seat of origin and headquarters of the medical care program. It is physically located within an approximately 100-mile radius of the city of San Francisco and consists of 1,100,000 Health Plan members, 1,200 physicians, and 16 ambulatory care clinics, 11 of which are physically adjacent to and function jointly with a general hospital. The locations of the facilities, together with selected operating characteristics, are depicted in Figure 21–1.

The San Francisco Medical Center is one of 11 in the region. It is a 304-bed acute care general hospital with adjacent multispecialty outpatient officers and ambulatory care services. The Health Plan subpopulation served by the San Francisco facility numbers 130,000 and resembles closely the racial, cultural, and socio-economic distributions in the general population in and around San Francisco County. Medical and surgical specialty services available are listed in Table 1 together with the corresponding number of physicians. Selected operational data are listed in Table 2. An active postgraduate training program includes 51 resident physicians across

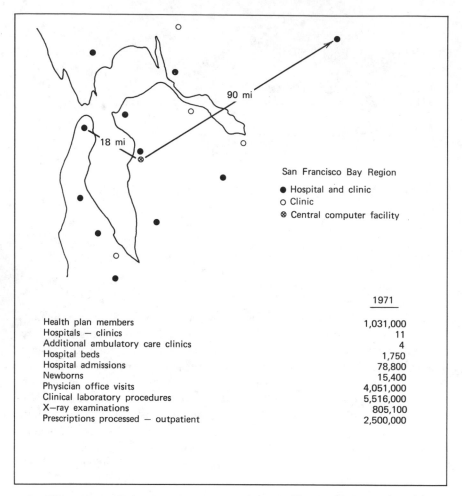

Figure 21–1.   Kaiser-Permanente—Northern California Region selected operational characteristics.

all major specialties, 28 interns, and a senior medical student training program in affiliation with the University of California School of Medicine.

Selected Health Plan, Hospitals, and Medical Group administrative services are provided by Permanente Services, Inc., including automated data processing services for administrative functions such as Health Plan membership, payroll, personnel, billing, etc.

Research and development medical data processing functions are conducted in the Department of Medical Methods Research (MMR), which is jointly administered by the Permanente Medical Group (Northern California) and the Kaiser Foundation Research Institute.

Table 1. Specialty Departments—San Francisco Facility

Specialty department	Number of full-time physicians
Dermatology	5
Emergency medicine	3
General and thoracic surgery*	9
General medicine	7
Industrial/occupational medicine	2
Internal medicine	44
Obstetrics and gynecology	10
Opthalmology	6
Optometry	8
Orthopedics	6
Otolaryngology	5
Pathology and clinical pathology	3
Pediatrics	20
Physical medicine	2
Psychiatry	3
Radiology	6
Urology	3

* Neurological Surgery is centralized in an adjacent Kaiser Medical Center (Redwood City, California).

Table 2. Operational Data—San Francisco Facility, 1971

Hospital admissions	13,520
Emergency room visits	33,253
Physician office visits	711,021
Deliveries	2,550
Clinical laboratory tests	908,800
X-ray tests	130,670
ECG	18,440
EGG (including EMG)	1,450
Isotopy	3,380
Prescriptions dispensed	322,026
Surgical pathology specimens	14,542
Cytology specimens	80,952

There are four characteristics of the overall program which deserve mention because of their influence not only on planning, policy, and the like, but also on intermediate and short-term decisions and objectives. They are:

1. The regional Health Plan members (1,100,000) may request care at any of the medical facilities. As might be expected in any geographically defined region, therefore, it is not unusual that an individual may seek care

at one facility although he had previously been treated at another. Studies of patients who had undergone multiphasic health testing, for example, revealed that approximately 18% had had one or more such experiences.

2. Although the medical care program is implemented in multiple facilities, the principles of administration and professional objectives are shared throughout. The significance is that planning of services and major alterations in procedure and developmental programs while aiming at specific goals must be consistent with the general interests of a multifacility medical care program. This is progressively important as one views the national trend to subregional and regional organization of medical services. These considerations are reflected later in this section and correctly suggest that we are in accord with Harmon's view that "large systems" technological planning is of utmost importance to future medical care.[1]

3. Patients are encouraged to select the physician(s) of their choice. It is often that two or more physicians will contribute to the management of an individual patient—e.g., an internist and a gynecologist. For a given patient, there exists but a single continuous medical record within a given facility; thus, all professional notes, test data, and other appropriate information are recorded in or obtained from the individual patient file (with certain exceptions, e.g., psychiatry notes).

4. Some facilities provide selected "central" services. For example, the San Francisco Clinical Laboratory routinely provides bacteriological studies and other analyses of specimens submitted by nearby centers, while most patients who are to receive neurosurgical treatment are referred to a different facility in the region.

B. DEFINITIONS AND OBJECTIVES

In recent years, the notion that information processing accounts for a large fraction of the cost of medical care has received documented support. The conclusion of several studies conducted in hospitals indicated that the magnitude is of the order of one-third of *per diem* costs; there is no reason not to believe that significant costs obtain also in the area of ambulatory care. In fact, such cost statements may be misleading, for it is likely that information availability and communications account for a larger fraction of those *needs* of physicians, nurses, and technicians that relate directly to patient care than can be accounted for by cost analysis alone.

Spurred on in part by these considerations, in part by awareness of the deficiencies in traditional methods of handling medical data, further by recognition of the rapid increase in volume of medical information, and finally by the dramatic advances of electronic data processing technology in nonmedical applications, a number of workers have begun the task of adapting modern data processing methods to selected aspects of medical care.

The rationale is that modern data processing methods can be expected to improve the accuracy, reliability, and speed with which medical data is handled and, if not reduce the absolute cost, at least make more data manageable for the same cost. While these expectations seem rational, they have yet to be realized at a level of sophistication that will satisfy the requirements of professional workers who are dedicated to even traditional concepts of good quality medical care. Further, and in spite of the experiences in those centers where the level of achievement is sufficient to breed confidence that such a goal is feasible, one continues to see underestimates of the magnitude of resources required to accomplish seemingly simple changes to traditional medical data processing procedures. Thus, many questions that were posed years ago are still unresolved: Will the new medical data processing technology prove eventually to cost less than, the same as, or greater than traditional methods? Will the new modalities effectively alter the validity, reliability, availability, and thereby utility of patient-related information? What are the data essential to good quality care? By what standards will we evaluate developmental costs of computer-supported medical data systems? How shall we evaluate the relationship of the new methodology to such aspects of the quality of care as professional performance and patient outcome?

So the arguments and questions have gone for several years, and so they continue today. After a decade of efforts, the applications of data processing technology to medical practice must still be classed as applied research and development or evolution—for the extraordinary variation in the specific technological applications which are being considered and tried, the approaches and methods used, the anticipated outcomes (including objectively unmeasurable outcomes), the differences in scope, etc., sorely strain one's concept of orderly development.

This is not critical in any negative sense. The highly complex social structure sometimes referred to as the health care industry is a constantly shifting blend of scientific enterprise and cultural bias (folklore). We must expect frequent changes for years to come and, as has been pointed out, we must plan for changing requirements and early obsolescence.[2] Nor is change limited to the health care process. The explosive changes in the computing industry render all but the most immediate planning and cost analyses highly unstable. The "modular approach" (to implementation of the new technology) that is espoused by many, including ourselves, is not an option—it is categorically forced upon us by the complexities noted.

The long-term objective of our program has been described before.[3] Basically, it is the development of a multifacility computer-based medical information communication system which will support the medical care operations outlined above. It is recognized that one cannot specify with precision the requirements of a system of this scale. It has therefore been necessary to approach this distant objective in smaller "subsystem" or component steps.*

Thus, the near-term objective was completion of the San Francisco Medical Data System, a pilot system which was being developed in a single medical center for implementing and testing the collection, retrieval, and communication of a representative spectrum of both inpatient and outpatient medical data.

This was further partitioned into component parts, or functions. We feel that it is vital, however, not to lose sight of long-term goals, especially at the level of early development, where basic strategies are adopted. If there is substance to the concept that emphasis on subsystem development leads to suboptimization of the larger system, then one must strive to minimize such effects by constant attention to large system objectives—i.e., by employing or developing those basic tools upon which the larger system will depend.

In Chapter One, a hospital computer system was defined as "one which utilizes electronic data processing and communications equipment to provide on-line and off-line processing of patient data with real-time responses within the hospital and its outpatient department, including ancillary services such as laboratory, x-ray, etc."

---

* This pilot system was developed, over a period of years, with the primary financial support and research interests of the U.S. H.E.W. Food and Drug Administration and the National Center for Health Services Research and Development. An added requirement, therefore, was large scale epidemiological research in addition to direct medical care support. The model was clearly defined, consisting of a single medical center data collection and reporting system linked to a central computer-supported communications system, which was, in turn, capable of supporting ten medical centers. This chapter describes the status of the project as of spring, 1973. The Federal research funds were curtailed at the end of 1973. Accordingly, the Kaiser-Permanente administration is in the process of extensive review of the regional data system projects, their relative levels of development, the extent of services rendered directly in support of patient care, proposed expansion and the related costs.

The feasibility of the central computer system and integrated data base (medical record management system) has been clearly demonstrated. However, the costs of maintaining a regional system for even short term support of a single medical center are high. The time required to implement successive facilities—two to four years—renders the initial central costs excessively high on a relative scale. Thus, while retaining the concept of modular development of a multifacility medical data system, it was decided that, in the interests of primary patient care support (data base research being at second level priority), we would discontinue the central data management system. Instead, we would expend our resources on the development of several newly designed direct patient-care modules (multiphasic laboratory, clinical laboratory, etc.) of lower unit operating cost, and program for later integration into a regional data system.

The specific objectives of our pilot data system included:

(1) Acquisition of diagnoses and clinical "visit" data on all patients visiting the San Francisco Kaiser Foundation outpatient medical offices and of data relating to all drugs dispensed from the outpatient pharmacies.

(2) Acquisition and reporting of the full spectrum of clinical laboratory data for all inpatients and outpatients.

(3) Development of communication and reporting services, such as real-time reporting of essential medical data to medical staff to expedite patient care—e.g., variable on-line retrieval of computer medical record data via interactive terminals in the emergency room or at the hospital or clinic nursing stations.

(4) Testing of an admissions-census system.

(5) Testing of acquisition of physician diagnoses and orders and nurses' drug administration data on a pilot hospital service (pediatrics), with a view to eventual expansion to other hospital services.

(6) Acquisition of additional selected hospital medical and administrative data such as pediatric ward procedures (lumbar puncture, marrow aspiration, etc.), hospital utilization data such as length of stay, changes of hospital service or primary physician, type of discharge, etc.

This communication system (real-time data acquisition and reporting) had been designed to collect these data and store them in an integrated computer record where they were retrievable in a variety of ways for medical care support (service-oriented retrieval) and health services research.

A further immediate objective was to develop and implement an evaluation program, some of the results of which will be used to guide the design and implementation of additional elements of the pilot system as well as second and future medical facilities. This program has been described previously.[4] Selected findings are discussed in Chapter Thirteen.

C. GENERAL SYSTEM CONCEPTS

The principles underlying the development of the pilot system included:

(1) Utilization of integrated, continuing, computer-stored medical records in which all data outlined above is chronologically ordered (See section E.1., this chapter).

(2) Utilization of a multi-purpose central computer facility for storage and maintenance of a single integrated record for each patient in the Northern California health plan, including all patients seen at the San Francisco pilot facility.

(3) Establishing telecommunications with the medical center data system composed of the data input and output devices used by medical personnel.

(4) Study and development of a multipurpose system of on-line real-time and batch retrieval and reporting programs for medical services support.

(5) Maximizing reliability and minimizing error production by assigning responsibility for data input to those individuals best qualified—for example, physicians for entering hospital diagnoses, pharmacist clerks for prescription data, laboratory technologists for laboratory data, etc.—and by implementing appropriate data quality-control programs.

(6) Minimizing parallel or redundant data collection and communication procedures which require medical staff involvement in order to increase utility and acceptability.

We hold that any data system whose primary purpose is the support of patient care must emulate at least two fundamental characteristics of current manual methods of processing medical information: storage of relevant data, and timely and effective communication of the data to a variety of providers of care. These two seemingly simple conditions require: (a) knowledge of what data is relevant to continuing medical care, (b) the existence of a data base in which individual patient medical records can be assessed, either directly or in a time that is appropriate to the clinical need, (c) that the data contained in the records be retrievable by category of data (e.g., by patient visit parameters, diagnoses, test results) and by time of event(s), whether recent or remote, and (d) that there exist real-time telecommunications facilities sufficient to permit access by different types of terminals at physicially discreet locations, at any one of which, for a given time segment, the retrieval requirements may differ.

There are two general approaches to achieving these objectives: (a) treat each medical facility as an independent entity, with data processing support limited and 'tailored' to local or internal operations; (b) treat each hospital-clinic complex as a 'terminal station,' serviced by a single "regional" data processing center in which are maintained computerized medical records, general reporting and communication facilities, etc. The latter has been adopted as a basic strategem for the regional (long-term) system defined by the Northern California Kaiser-Permanente Health Care Program.

Central to the concept of a regional medical data processing system is the existence of a data base consisting of the essential medical information for all patients in the region (See also Chapter Four). Regulating access to the data base is a system of telecommunications control; data quality control; and input, retrieval, and output processing. This data management and control system in turn interfaced with peripheral data subsystem functions —data collection, report generation and distribution, visual displays, printed production, data analyses, etc. It is these peripheral subsystems which can be developed and tested in a variety of environments but whose expansion and modification is truly modular—i.e., essentially independent of the central data base data management system. These relationships can be represented schematically as:

User functions†	Peripheral (terminal) data subsystem functions	Central data management systems functions‡	Data base §

Medical care
—SF MDS
   Admitting
   Nurse stations
   Laboratory
   Clinics
—AMHT
—Other facilities,
   functions
Research
—Health services
—Evaluation
	Data collection
	Quality control
	Inquiries to data base
	Report generation/
	   Distribution
	—Displays
	—Printed production
	Data analysis
		MFCS-Telecommuni-
		   cation control
		—Data quality
		   control
		—Input
		   processing
		—Retrieval
		   processing
		—Output
		   processing
		Operating system
			PCMR's
			
			sets
			Other
			data

† SF MDS—San Francisco Medical Data System
  AMHT—Automated Multiphasic Health Testing
‡ MFCS—Medical Function Control System
§ PCMR—Patient Computer Medical Record

1.   Medical Information Communication

The essential process in patient care is the eliciting of information which can form a rational basis for action. Some information is elicited directly from the patient by interview and by physical examination; other information is obtained indirectly by inquiry to persons who harbor certain knowledge—e.g., a laboratory technologist or admitting clerk—or indirectly from the medical record.

The common purpose is the acquisition of information. The recording of information is a phenomenon engaged in by anyone who feels that the recorded data will be sufficiently useful for future reference to justify the effort, or whose work requirements demand record keeping. This simple observation clarifies the concept that a data system whose intended use is in the support of patient care must have the primary objective of permitting retrieval of relevant information by the use at a time and place where it will be useful, and the concomitant objective of facilitating relevant data entry.

The extent to which the retrieval/communication aspect of a data system is beneficial determines system use. Sufficiently high use value will generate a high level of acceptability and permit a wide variation in the efficiency of data entry methods. Based on this concept, a further basic objective of this project is to attempt continually to broaden the capability to maximize medical data availability—i.e., to maximally facilitate communication between the base of medical data and the physician/paramedical personnel who constitute the "final common pathway" in patient care.

D. PROJECT ORGANIZATION AND MANAGEMENT

The Department of Medical Methods Research is located adjacent to the Kaiser Foundation Hospital in Oakland, California. It is the site of two general classes of activities, (1) applied research and development in medical technological systems, and (2) health services and epidemiological research projects which utilize the medical data base.

The Medical Data System Project comprises three groups: The first consists of a "core" computer center staff of programmers, engineers, analysts, and operating staff under the direction of a computer center manager. The second group consists of a physician-nurse-analyst team whose functions include establishing the medical "system" specifications for the hospital and clinic data processing applications and interfacing with the facility professional and administrative personnel for data processing consultation, education, and training. A third group, functioning independently of the project team, conducts evaluation studies with the primary objective of measuring the effects of new data processing developments upon facility and departmental operations, personnel, costs, etc.

1. Education and Training

A post-doctoral program was established in 1969 in conjunction with the graduate division of the University of California at Berkeley, in which trainees may work toward M.S., M.P.H., or Ph.D. degrees in various related fields. Several members of the department staff hold teaching appointments at either the Berkeley or San Francisco (School of Medicine) campuses of the University of California. Also, since 1969, a one-month training program has been made available to interested physicians who had elective time during their year of internship at the Oakland Kaiser Foundation Hospital. A description of this program has been published elsewhere.[5]

Funding for our research activities has been by means of federal grants and contracts in addition to internal support by the Kaiser Foundation Research Institute.

Our experience has shown that any significant change in the processing of information in a medical center will have an effect upon the activity and performance of nearly every individual within the center, will influence most other systems within the hospital, and will alter in some respect most procedures. Based on experience to date, if data communication terminals are to be used successfully in the management of medical information, whether it be in the hospital or the clinic environment, it is necessary to integrate the planning and implementation of the data system into each department's operation. Accordingly, all planning and decision-making has been and continues to be with the support and concurrence of administrative and medical professional personnel. To facilitate interdisciplinary communication and maximize acceptance of alterations in data management procedures, we have trained and continue to train administrative and medical personnel at several levels in selected aspects of data processing technology and its role in interfacing different physical and functional areas of hospital operations.

The amount of time involved in such interdisciplinary communication is highly variable, from a few hours to several months for a given individual or department.

2. Documentation

Careful documentation of the central computer system and applications software and operating procedures has been a fundamental requirement of our technological development policy and has accurately reflected the status of the core center's development.

Documentation for peripheral applications has been developed as far as possible within the resource constraints that usually obtain for such activities. A pilot documentation control system has been developed for data system medical applications and is currently being tested for expandability, as a general method, to several other projects. Especially in research and development work it is desirable to have available a system of documenting developmental programs so as to maximize "transferability" to other projects and minimize redundant expenditure of resources.

E. SUBSYSTEMS

1. Patient Medical Records

The patient computer medical record (PCMR) and the Medical Function Control System (MFCS) that constitute the heart of the medical data system have been described in detail elsewhere[6,7] and form part of the basis for Chapter Four. In order to support the large number of input-output and processing functions, the Medical Function Control System was developed. This system of programs comprises numerous general and special routines which operate under control of the IBM [370-155] "Operating System, allowing Multiprogramming with a Variable number of Tasks" (OS/MVT). The essential function of MFCS is to maintain the numerous data sets that constitute the medical record files. Five groups of programs comprise the MFCS: medical record manipulation routines; encoding and translation routines; medical language routines; medical functions routines; and a medical function control program. These routines include direct-access storage and handling of remote terminals as well as the usual input and output devices.

Summarized, each PCMR is an integrated tree-structured file designed to harbor all identification and medical data for a single patient, regardless of the data source, or time or method of data entry, for an indefinite period of time. We have adhered to the concept of a single "lifetime" record for each patient for our initial development for the following reasons:

a.   Unpredictable future data needs.   The practice of medicine (individual and group patient care and disease prevention and detection) may be viewed as "problem oriented," as discussed in some of the recent literature.[8,9] Problem orientation refers to the relation of the responses of medical care personnel to the perceived needs, or problems, of individuals seeking medical care. The process of care inevitably begins with the acquisition of data directly (from the patient) or indirectly (from, for example, other persons, tests, and from retrieval of antecedent information from the medical record). As far as the medical record is concerned, its value is a function of the data it contains and its availability (retrievability and communicability) to the patient care situation. Retrieval and communication, then, are the primary raisons d'être of the medical record. The retrieval need is expressed as a professional's need for information as he attempts to deal with the clinical problem. While the medical information retrieval requirements for many clinical problems can be anticipated—e.g., routine annual checkup of well-baby visit—many problems can be defined only at time of need (i.e., at retrieval-output time)—e.g., in non-appointment clinics, emergency rooms, and in day-to-day inpatient care.

It follows that the data base (medical record) from which the retrieved information is compiled and the system which maintains it, must have certain capabilities: it must permit the physician to request either routine or predictable sets of data from the medical record (e.g., multiphasic summary reports) or, as indicated above, request that data relevant to new or unanticipated situations be retrieved in real-time under program control.

We feel that this latter capability will be essential to a successfully operating medical information retrieval system since, as is true in most cases today, the retriever cannot anticipate all of his information requirements in advance, and in any case does not always know the current content of a given medical record.

It is therefore necessary that the retriever be able to indicate specific data items or sets of data as a function of time and that he be able to accomplish this in accord with the clinical situation—i.e., in real-time but with variable priority (in accord with relative urgency of the patient problem, type of information requested, etc.).

b. Study of operational requirements. The above considerations lead to many questions concerning management of medical data, for which there are not ready answers. To achieve the above capabilities, how much data must be stored? How much data can be stored at reasonable cost, and in what form or mode? What hierarchical storage schemes will permit adequately rapid access to essential medical data? What data qualifies as essential?

It appears likely that answers to such questions will be derived operationally. Accordingly, we are developing a retrieval-oriented system into which are being entered data which most medical professionals feel would qualify as members of any set defined as essential (e.g., patient identification, clinical diagnoses, clinical laboratory test results, drugs dispensed or administered, and selected "visit" parameters such as name of primary physician, dates of visits or hospitalizations, department or service name, etc.). By long-term study of data system utilization and its effect upon clinic and hospital personnel and functions, it is felt that operational answers to many questions will become apparent and help to define functionally satisfactory and cost-effective means of improvement.

We have defined certain capabilities required of the data base (medical record) from which information is retrieved. It is therefore apparent that the record must be so structured as to store all classes of patient-related data: identification, administrative, and medical. It must be continuously updatable, capable of accepting the variable timing, quantity, and formats of data input, and monitored by reliable error detection and recovery routines. An operational computer medical record system which meets these requirements has been under development since 1964.[7]

c. Confidentiality of computer medical records. The following regulations have been established by the Department of Medical Methods Research governing the release of data from the medical data base:

(1) Each PCMR in the computer center is subject to the same regula-

tions governing release, privacy, and confidentiality as is a record in the hospital medical chart room. Dial-up access to the data base is categorically prohibited.

(2) Any Permanente Medical Group (PMG) physician, upon verbal or written request or upon entering his identification number into an on-line (non-dial-up) terminal, may have access to standard reports from the record (excluding psychiatric department data) of any individual patient by medical record number.

(3) Any PMG physician may have access to the records of any patients specifically defined in a funded research grant for which he is the Principal or Co-Principal Investigator, or Project Chief, upon his completion of a data retrieval form. Each such request requires explicit definition of the data and patients for each retrieval run.

(4) Any PMG physician may have access to the records of any patient not contained within (2) or (3) above, upon signed approval of both his Physician-in-Chief and the Director of Medical Methods Research. (This restriction is primarily to protect research data belonging to other principal investigators).

(5) Any PMG Chief of Service may have access to the records of any patients who have any visits to his Service, upon completion of a data retrieval form and approval of the Physician-in-Chief.

(6) Any PMG Physician-in-Chief may have access to the records of any patients who have any visits to his facility, upon completion of a data retrieval form.

(7) Any Kaiser-Permanente Entity Head may obtain nonmedical data (administrative, scheduling, or visit data), upon completing a data retrieval form.

(8) Requests for PCMR information on any specific patient from outside sources should be referred to the appropriate facility record room for routine processing and releases. Information requested will then be provided to the record room upon completion of a data retrieval form by the medical record librarian.

(9) Psychiatry department data of any individual patient will be released only to PMG psychiatrists. Other PMG physicians will require signed approval of the chief of his Psychiatry Department and of his Physician-in-Chief or the Director of Medical Methods Research.

A special system facility provides programmers with a listing of any PCMR in the format and structure in which it is stored. However, unless proper authorization is obtained and a "password" used to the program, the patient's identification will not be printed. After the computer operator inputs the requestor's name, then that name and the name of the patient whose record is being printed will be listed in the system log. No PCMR listings will be provided for unauthorized users without signed approval from the Data Base Administrator or the Director of Medical Methods Research.

d.   Interface with manual chart.   Computer medical records will not replace manual records completely for yet a long time. The replacement process will evolve as progressively more computer-produced components of the record (test reports, summary statements, etc.) are substituted for their manually-produced counterparts.

At the San Francisco and Oakland Kaiser-Permanente facilities, the replacement process began in the outpatient clinic. The first document was the multiphasic summary report. This computer printout is produced shortly following the patient's visit to the multiphasic laboratory and entered into the chart so that it is available to the physician at the time of the patient's follow-up office visit (Figures 21–2a, 2b, 2c, 2d). Two important features of this report are (1) the summarization of abnormal findings on the first page, and (2) the presentation of information in a time-oriented array, permitting the physician to compare the patient's current medical data with results of previous checkups. This basic capability—comparing data through time—assists the phsician to evaluate more accurately any normal, marginal, or frankly abnormal findings and materially influences the management of patients undergoing periodic health examination. Approximately 50,000 such reports are produced annually.

The second type of document was the physician office visit "encounter" form, which served both as a source document for data entry and a chart record of selected aspects of the office visit. Each of the specialty clinics assisted in development by specifying the medical data content of the form each would use, while accepting selected standard structures for patient identification and other standard visit variables. An example of the medical clinic form is shown in Figure 21–3. These forms are periodically updated and tend to contain progressively higher density of data. Thus, the new pediatric form, currently under revision, contains a section for well-baby visit data, including selected digital data—e.g., weight, head circumference, immunization names and dates, etc.

Computer-produced laboratory reports have been more recently implemented. Outpatient and inpatient reports were programmed for distribution to doctors' offices and inclusion in the patients' charts. For inpatient records, summary reports are produced at the conclusion of hospitalization. Figure 21–4 is an example of the chart copy of a hospital laboratory report (see Section E.3a).

The nursing station functions, scheduled for testing on the pediatric

```
                    PERMANENTE MEDICAL GRCUP - OAKLAND          PAGE 1
        MCDS FINAL REPORT - MULTIPHASIC HEALTH CHECKUP (MHC) - (9/20/72)

TEST, PATIENT              RETIRED                  REFERRED: SELF
MR:2258590 J1      AGE 50     FEMALE    DIVORCED           LAST MHC 6/16/70
DISABILITY: PARTIALLY LIMITED           OAKL. DR. SMITH
REASON FOR VISIT:   # HEART TROUBLE
                    # CHEST PAIN
                    DIZZY SPELLS OR BLACKCUTS
      #=SEE SECOND LEVEL RESPONSE SECTION FOR ADDITIONAL HISTORY(PG 2)

SUMMARY OF POSSIBLE ABNORMALITIES:
     **(TEST)            (NORMAL)    (THIS MHC)  (LAST MHC)  (RANGE PRIOR MHCS)
    B.P.SUPINE(GODART): UNDER 160/90   164/100     154/88     190-150/ 86-108
    HEMOGLOBIN GM.:      12.0- 16.0      9.2        11.2       13.1 - 13.9
    MHC MCMCG:           26.0- 34.0     20.6        TND        TND -    TND
    MCHC %:              32.0- 38.0     25.6        TND        TND -    TND
    GLUCOSE 2HR PC MG%   UNDER- 170      332         234        212 -    247
    ALK PTASE KA UNITS   UNDER- 15.0    26.0        12.0       TND -    TND
    VDRL                   NEG           POS         NEG        NEG -    NEG
    QUANTITATIVE VDRL:                 RRWWWN
    CLINITEST:             NEG           3+          NEG        NEG -    NEG
    ACETONE :              NEG           POS         TNI        TNI -    TNI
    EKG:               LVH - SAME/LAST MHC
    HEARING:           CLINICALLY IMPAIRED HEARING LEFT - DIFFERENT LAST MHC
    CHEST X-RAY:       CARDIAC ENLARGEMENT - DIFFERENT LAST MHC
    PHYSICAL EXAM:     HEART: MURMUR, SYSTOLIC, AORTIC, GRADE 3 - DIFFERENT LAST MH(
                       ABDOMEN: ENLARGED LIVER, 4CM - SAME LAST MHC

PATIENT RECEIVED FOLLOWING ADVICE RULE DIRECTIONS:
HGB 9.0-10.5, PT. MENOPAUSAL
   -HGB, HCT, MORPH. ORDERED AND SMEAR SAVED FCR HEMATOLOGIST
2-HR GLUC ABNL, NOT UNDER RX FOR DIAB, CIET TAKEN
   -2-HR GTT ORDERED
VDRL POSITIVE
   -FTA ORDERED
-REFERRED TO PHYSICIAN FOR EARLY APPTMT.

                   --DOCTOR'S DIAGNOSES LAST MHCS--
        6/16/70                          9/20/69
HYPERTENSIVE HT DIS-NEW          HYPERTENSION-NEW
ANGINA PECTORIS-IMPROV.          HYPERCHOLESTEROLEMIA-NEW
HYPERCHOLESTEROLEMIA-OLD

                      --MEDICAL HISTORY--
--DRUGS TAKEN REGULARLY IN PAST YEAR     --SPECIAL DIETS IN PAST YEAR
     DIGITALIS TYPE MEDICINE              LOW CHOLESTEROL
     HIGH BP MECICINE                     OTHER (SEE QUESTIONNAIRE)
     MEDICINE TO LOSE WATER

PAST MEDICAL HISTORY:
     PATIENT REPORTED MEDICAL CONDITIONS IN THE PAST YEAR:
        HIGH BLOOD PRESSURE - NOW UNDER RX

**=CONSIDER POSSIBLE ABNORMAL            REPORT PRINTED:   9/25/72-11:57
SEE LAST PAGE FOR ADDITIONAL FOOTNOTES                     - CONTINUED
```

Figure 21–2a. Multiphasic summary report—Page 1.

service in mid–1973 (see section E.4), include entry of physicians' orders and nurse verification of drug administration; each of these functions involve data entry to the PCMR via an on-line terminal, and the production of a computer produced hard copy for chart entry. In addition, printed evidence of patient admissions, transfers and discharges will be merged with standard manually recorded nursing notes.

```
TEST, PATIENT              MR:2258590 J1    FEMALE      9/20/72      PAGE 2

    SURGICAL HISTORY:
     APPENDIX - BEFORE 1 YR AGO
     GALLBLADDER - BEFORE 1 YR AGO & IN THE PAST YR

    DAYS HOSPITALIZED IN PAST YEAR:  9-10

    SERIOUS ILLNESS OR INJURY IN PAST YEAR:  WHIP LASH

 REVIEW OF SYSTEMS FOR PAST 6-12 MONTHS--YES RESPONSES
        #=SEE SECOND LEVEL RESPONSE SECTION FOR ADDITIONAL HISTORY

    SKIN:      NONE
    EENT:      NONE
    RESP:      #COUGHED UP BLOOD
    C-V:       **#REPEATED EXERTIONAL CHEST DISTRESS MADE YOU STOP WALKING
               **#OFTEN LEG PAIN MAKING YOU STOP WALKING, RELIEVED BY REST
    GI:        NONE
    GU:        NONE
    GYN:       NONE
    MUS-SKEL:  NONE
    CNS:       * BAD HEADACHES NOT HELPED BY ASPIRIN, EMPIRIN, ETC.
    NEURO-     SPELLS OF SHAKING OR TREMBLING ALL OVER
    MENTAL:    SPELLS OF BEING COMPLETELY WORN OUT
    MISC:      DOCTOR SAID HAD THYROID SWELLING OR GOITER
               BAD REACTION TO PENICILLIN
    HABITS:    NOW SMOKING, HAS BEEN FOR 6-10 YRS, 1-2 PACKS A DAY
    SOCIAL:    CURRENTLY HAVING SERIOUS PROBLEM WITH JOB OR EMPLOYMENT

 # SECOND LEVEL RESPONSE HISTORY:
    RESP:     COUGHED UP BLOOD:  FOR MANY YEARS, OCCURRING A FEW TIMES A MONTH, NO
              HISTORY OF CHRONIC BRONCHITIS, HAS HAD OTHER SYMPTOMS SUCH AS FEVER,
              WEIGHT LOSS OR CHEST PAIN, NO CHRONIC COUGH DUE TO HEART DISEASE,
              BEEN GETTING WORSE, REQUEST MEDICAL ADVICE AT THIS TIME.

    C-V:      HEART TROUBLE: FOR ABOUT 1 YEAR, OCCURRING A FEW TIMES A YEAR, NOT
              NOW UNDER TREATMENT BY A DOCTOR, WAS TREATED IN THE PAST BY A DOCTOR,
              BEEN GETTING WORSE, LOSS OF TIME FROM WORK OR SERIOUSLY INTERFERED
              WITH ACTIVITIES, REQUEST MEDICAL ADVICE AT THIS TIME.

              CHEST PAIN:  FOR THE PAST FEW WEEKS, OCCURRING A FEW TIMES A WEEK,
              NOT WHEN RESTING OR SITTING, MOSTLY DURING PHYSICAL ACTIVITY, LASTS
              LESS THAN A MINUTE, VARIES IN SEVERITY FROM TIME TO TIME, REQUEST
              MEDICAL ADVICE AT THIS TIME.

              LEG PAIN:  FOR PAST FEW YEARS, OCCURRING A FEW TIMES A YEAR, DOES
              NOT OCCUR WHEN RESTING OR SITTING, IS RELIEVED QUICKLY BY RESTING,
              IS MOSTLY IN THE CALVES OF LEG(S), BEEN GETTING BETTER, NOT
              TROUBLESOME.


 *=PATIENT ANSWERED YES ON THIS MHC AND NO ON LAST MHC
 SEE LAST PAGE FOR ADDITIONAL FOOTNOTES                        -CONTINUED
```

Figure 21–2b.   Multiphasic summary report—Page 2.

2.   Administrative Functions

a.   **Patient registration and identification.**   Each individual enrolled in the Kaiser Foundation Health Plan is assigned a unique medical record number by the administrative services organization (Permanente Services, Inc.), which maintains the primary Health Plan membership files. Periodically, "update" tapes are made available to the medical computer center

```
TEST, PATIENT              MR:2258590 J1   FEMALE      9/20/72      PAGE 3

     (TEST)                (NORMAL)    (THIS MHC)  (LAST MHC)  (RANGE PRIOR MHCS)
     HEIGHT  IN.:                       63.8         64.0      63.5 - 63.9
     WEIGHT  LB.:          UNDER 160    133.5        132.0     131.5 -133.5
     TRICEPS SKINFOLD MM.: UNDER 43.0   23.0         18.0      19.0 - 20.0
   CIRCULATORY:
 **B.P.SUPINE (GODART):    UNDER 160/90 164-100      154/88    190-150/ 86-108
     RAD.PULSE SUPINE:        60-  95   68           76        68 -   74
   RESPIROMETRY:
     FEV 1 SEC L.:         OVER-  1.2   2.1          2.0       1.9 -  2.3
     FEV 2 SEC L.:                      2.4          2.5       2.2 -  2.6
     TOTAL FEV L.:         OVER-  2.1   2.8          2.7       2.5 -  2.9
     PEAK FLOW L.:                      4.1          4.0       3.9 -  4.4
   ACHILLES REFLEX MS.:     250-  400   290          270       280 -  310
   HEMATOLOGY:
     WBC /CU MM.:          3500-12000   7700         6600      5500 - 7700
     RBC MILLIONS/CU MM.:  4.0-   5.5   4.5          TND       TND -  TND
 **HEMOGLOBIN GM.:         12.0- 16.0   9.2          11.2      13.1 - 13.9
     HEMATOCRIT:           35.0- 49.0   36.0         TND       TND -  TND
     MCV CU MICRONS:       80-   100    80           TND       TND -  TND
 **MHC MCMCG:              26.0- 34.0   20.6         TND       TND -  TND
 **MCHC %:                 32.0- 38.0   25.6         TND       TND -  TND
 ¬BLOOD CHEMISTRIES:       DRAWN 6 HRS. SINCE LAST FOOD
                           75 GM CARBOHYDRATE DIET TAKEN
     SODIUM MEQ/L:         133-  145    142          TND       TND -  TND
     POTASSIUM MEQ/L:      3.0-  5.0    3.7          TND       TND -  TND
     CALCIUM MG%:          8.0- 10.5    9.9          9.5       9.0 - 10.8
 **GLUCOSE 2 HR PC MG%     UNDER- 170   332          234       212 -  247
     BUN MG.:              UNDER-22.0   15.2(C)      TND       TND -  TND
     CREATININE MG%:       UNDER- 1.4   .9(C)        .9        .8 -  1.2
     URIC ACID MG%:        2.0-  7.3    3.5(C)       TND       2.2 -  5.4
     BILIRUBIN TOT MG%:    UNDER- 1.5   .9           TND       TND -  TND
 **ALK.PTASE KA UNITS:     UNDER-15.0   26.0         12.0      TND -  TND
     SGOT RF UNITS:        UNDER-  40   36(C)        25        23 -   38
     LDH UNITS:            UNDER- 225   25(C)        TND       TND -  TND
     CHOLESTEROL MG%:      90-  330     275(C)       200       195 -  220
 **VDRL:                   NEG          POS          NEG       NEG -  NEG
 **QUANTITATIVE VDRL:                   RRWWWN
   BLOOD GROUP:                         0
   URINE:
     PH:                                6            7         7 -   7
 **CLINITEST:              NEG          3+           TNI       TNI -  TNI
 **ACETONE:                NEG          POS          TNI       TNI -  TNI
     PROTEIN:              NEG          NEG          NEG       NEG -  NEG
     BLOOD:                NEG          NEG          NEG       NEG -  NEG
     URINE BACILLI:        NEG          NEG          NEG       NEG -  NEG


 ¬ONE-HOUR SERUM CHYLOUS: (C) INDICATES TEST MAY BE AFFECTED


 SEE LAST PAGE FOR DESCRIPTION OF FOOTNOTES                      -CONTINUED
```

Figure 21–2c. Multiphasic summary report—Page 3.

and the Identification Section of the patient computer medical record (PCMR) is changed accordingly.

Any patient who registers for an outpatient office visit, or for hospitalization, presents a plastic card with his medical record (MR) number, name, and other data inscribed upon it. This data is imprinted onto appropriate registration documents. In the case of a physician office visit, the number is imprinted on the encounter form. When the form is completed, it is processed for data entry by a clerk using an on-line data terminal. The clerk

```
TEST, PATIENT                    MR:2258590 J1    FEMALE    9/20/72    PAGE 4


(TEST)
CHEST X-RAY           NO SIGNIFICANT CHANGE FROM PRIOR X-RAY
        1970:        NO SIGNIFICANT CHANGE FROM PRIOR X-RAY
¬BREAST X-RAY:        FIBROCYSTIC DIFFUSE CHANGES
        1970:        NO SIGNIFICANT CHANGE FROM PRIOR X-RAY
ECG:                 NO SIGNIFICANT CHANGE FROM PRIOR ELECTROCARDIOGRAM
        1970:        NO SIGNIFICANT CHANGE FROM PRIOR ELECTROCARDIOGRAM
**HEARING:           CLINICALLY IMPAIRED HEARING LEFT
        1970:        CLINICALLY IMPAIRED HEARING LEFT
VISUAL ACUITY:       L.E. 20/40 OR BETTER, R.E. 20/40 OR BETTER
        1970:        L.E. 20/40 OR BETTER, R.E. 20/40 OR BETTER
OCULAR TENSION:      LEFT EYE NORMAL, RIGHT EYE NORMAL
        1970:        LEFT EYE NORMAL, RIGHT EYE NORMAL


NURSE PRACTITIONER PHYSICAL FINDINGS:
  SKIN:              NEGATIVE
  EENT & NECK:       NEGATIVE
  BREASTS:           NEGATIVE
  LUNGS:             NEGATIVE
**HEART:             HEART MURMUR,SYSTOLIC,AORTIC,GRADE 3
**ABDOMEN:           ENLARGED LIVER, 4CM.
  GENITALS/RECTAL:   NEGATIVE
  BACK & SPINE:      NEGATIVE
  EXTREMITIES:       NEGATIVE
  NEUROLOGICAL:      NEGATIVE




                                          PRT  = PT. REFUSED TEST
        TND = TEST NOT DONE                TNI  = TEST NOT INDICATED
        BND = BLOOD NOT DRAWN              -    = DATA NOT AVAILABLE
        **  = CONSIDER POSSIBLE ABNORMAL   UNSAT= TEST UNSATISFACTORY
        NSA = NO SIGNIFICANT ABNORMALITY   ¬    = NOTE
```

Figure 21–2d.   Multiphasic summary report—Page 4.

enters the MR number; under program control, the corresponding PCMR is located and the patient's name, sex, and birthdate (month and year) are returned for immediate verification. In this manner, positive patient identification is achieved prior to entry of medical data to any PCMR. A conceptually similar process is followed for laboratory test, prescription, and hospital admission data—i.e., on-line entry of the MR number and return display (video or printed) of secondary patient identifiers.

HB-8-72 (REVISED)

MEDICAL CLINIC – PERMANENTE MEDICAL GROUP – DIAGNOSIS RECORD

PLEASE INDICATE THE STATUS OF CONDITIONS, FINDINGS OR EVENTS RELEVENT TO TODAY'S VISIT BY INSCRIBING ONE OF THE FOLLOWING LETTERS IN THE APPROPRIATE BOXES:

N - NEW DIAGNOSIS, FINDING OR EVENT
R - RECURRENCE
C - CONTINUING: ESSENTIALLY UNCHANGED
I - IMPROVED
W - WORSENING OR EXACERBATION
O - OLD - NO LONGER ACTIVE OR PRESENT
D - DELETE CONDITION NO LONGER VALID
P - PROVISIONAL

NFS = NOT FURTHER SPECIFIED

PATIENT'S GENERAL CONDITION TODAY IS ASSOCIATED WITH THE FOLLOWING LIMITATION IN HIS USUAL ACTIVITIES.

NONE	3
MILD	
MODERATE	
SEVERE	6
COMPLETE	

M.R. NO.
NAME:
BIRTHDATE:
SEX:
ADDRESS:
CITY:
PHONE:

CODE:
GROUP:

CATEGORY OF SERVICE
PHYSICIAN NAME CODE

APPOINTMENT	
NON-APPOINTMENT	
MHC FOLLOW-UP	
CANCEL	1
NO SHOW	2

DATE OF VISIT
MONTH   DAY   YEAR
TIME OF VISIT   A.M.   P.M.

GENERAL

NO SIGNIF ABNORMALITY 8
UNCHANGED DX & STATUS
NO DIAGNOSIS MADE 10
IMMUNIZATION ONLY
PRESCRIPTION REFILL
ADVERSE DRUG REACTION
CANCER NFS
FATIGUE CHRONIC 15
FEVER NFS
LUPUS ERYTH SYSTEMIC
OBESITY
SARCOIDOSIS
SYPHILIS LATENT 20
SYPHILIS PRIMARY
SYPHILIS SECONDARY
WEIGHT LOSS

TRAUMA
ABRASION-CONTUSION
BITE-STING INSECT 25
HEAD INJURY
LACERATION
PUNCTURE WOUND

UPPER EXTR 29
LOWER EXTR
BACK
NECK 34

S S
P T
R R
A A
I I
N N

SKIN

ACNE VULGARIS
CANCER NFS 65
CELLULITIS
CYST

DERMATITIS
CONTACT
MEDICAMENTOSA
NEURO 70
RHUS
SEBORRHEIC
STASIS
DERMATITIS NFS

ECZEMA 75
FUNGUS INFECTION
FURUNCLE
HERPES SIMPLEX
HERPES ZOSTER
KERATOSIS 80
LIPOMA
PEDICULOSIS
PITYRIASIS ROSEA
PRURITUS
PSORIASIS 85
SUNBURN
URTICARIA
XANTHELASMA

EYE

RESPIRATORY

ASTHMA BRONCHIAL 122
BRONCHIECTASIS
BRONCHITIS ACUTE
BRONCHITIS CHRONIC 125
CANCER LUNG PRIMARY
METAST TO LUNG
EMPHYSEMA 130
HEMOPTYSIS
INFLUENZA SYNDROME
PLEURAL EFFUSION
PLEURISY ACUTE 135

PNEUMONIA
ATYPICAL 136
BACTERIAL
PNEUMONIA NFS

TUBERCULOSIS
ACTIVE
INACTIVE 140
ACT. UNCERTAIN
CONVERTER
NON-PULMONARY

ETIOLOGY UNKNOWN
CHEST PAIN
COUGH 145
DYSPNEA
INTERSTITIAL DISEASE
LESION (S)

PERIPHERAL VASCULAR

ARTERIOSCL DISEASE NFS 181
BLOOD PRESS LABILE
CAROTID BRUIT

HYPERTENSION
ESSENTIAL 185
RENAL
HYPERTENSION NFS
HYPOTENSION ORTHOST
EDEMA NFS
RAYNAUD 190
THROMBOPHLEBITIS
VARICOSE VEINS
VASCULITIS 195

GASTROINTESTINAL

GENERAL
ABDOMINAL PAIN NFS
HERNIA ING-FEM 197
HERNIA UMBIL-VENTR
MASS 200
NAUSEA
TENDERNESS
VOMITING

UPPER GI
BLEEDING UPPER GI
DUODENAL ULCER 205
ESOPH HIATUS HERNIA

BREAST

ABSENT
CANCER 240
FIBROCYSTIC DISEASE
NODULE(S) 244

GENITO - URINARY

GENERAL
AZOTEMIA-UREMIA 246
BACTERIURIA ASYMPT
CALCULUS NFS
HEMATURIA
URINARY TRACT INF NFS 250

UPPER GU
ARTERIOL-NEPHROSCLER
GLOMERULO CHRONIC
NEPHROTIC SYNDROME
PYELO ACUTE
PYELO CHRONIC 255

LOWER GU
CYSTITIS
DYSURIA
EPIDIDYMITIS
GONORRHEA 260
INCONTINENCE
IMPOTENCE
HYDRO-SPERMATOCELE
PROSTATE BPH 265
PROSTATE CANCER

NERVOUS SYSTEM

BELL PALSY 303
CEREBRO-VASC INSUFF
CHRONIC BRAIN SYNDR 305
CVA RESIDUAL NFS
DIZZINESS

HEADACHE
MIGRAINE
TENSION
HEADACHE NFS 310

NEUROPATHY
DIABETIC
NUTRITIONAL
NEUROPATHY NFS
PARESTHESIA NFS
PARKINSONISM 315
SEIZURE DISORDER
SYNCOPE
TUMOR NFS
VERTIGO

PSYCHOLOGICAL

ALCOHOLISM ACUTE 320
ALCOHOLISM CHRONIC
ANXIETY
DEPRESSION
DRUG DEPENDANCE
HYPERVENTIL SYNDR 325
HYSTERIA

ENDOCRINE METABOLIC

- DIABETES MELLITUS 35
- GLYCOSURIA RENAL
- HYPERCALCEMIA
- HYPERCHOLESTEROLEMIA
- HYPERLIPIDEMIA
- HYPERURICEMIA 40
- HYPOGLYCEMIA

THYROID
- ENLARGED DIFFUSE
- HYPER
- HYPO 45
- NODULES
- THYROIDITIS 48

HEMATOLOGY

ANEMIA
- FE DEFICIENCY
- PERNICIOUS 50
- ANEMIA NFS
- HEMOGLOBIN A - S
- HEMOGLOBINOPATHY NFS
- HODGKIN DISEASE
- INFECTIOUS MONO 55
- LEUKEMIA CHRON LYMPH
- LEUKEMIA OTHER
- LYMPHADENOPATHY
- LYMPHOSARCOMA
- MULTIPLE MYELOMA 60
- POLYCYTHEMIA
- SARCOMA RETIC CELL
- THROMBOCYTOPENIA

- ARCUS SENILIS
- CATARACT 90
- CONJUNCTIVITIS
- FOREIGN BODY 94
- GLAUCOMA
- STYE 98

RETINOPATHY
- DIABETIC
- HYPERTENSIVE 100
- RETINOPATHY NFS

ENT

EAR
- CERUMEN
- HEARING LOSS 104
- MENIERE SYNDROME
- OTITIS EXTERNA
- OTITIS MEDIA 109
- TINNITUS

NOSE
- EPISTAXIS 112
- RHINITIS ALLERGIC
- RHINITIS NFS
- SINUSITIS ACUTE 115

MOUTH-PHARYNX
- DENTAL DISORDER
- LARYNGITIS-TRACHEITIS
- PHARYNGITIS BACTERIAL
- PHARYNGITIS NFS 119
- STOMATITIS APHTHOUS
- TONSILLITIS

- RALES 150
- RESTRICT PULM DISEASE
- UPPER RESP INF

CARDIAC

- ANGINA PECTORIS
- AORTIC INSUFFICIENCY 155
- AORTIC STENOSIS

ARRHYTHMIA
- ATRIAL FIBRILLATION
- ATRIAL FLUTTER
- PAROXYSMAL TACHY
- PHEMATURE CONTR'NS 160
- SINUS TACHYCARDIA
- ARRHYTHMIA NFS
- ARTERIOSCL HEART DIS
- COR PULMONALE
- HEART DISEASE NFS 165
- HEART FAILURE CONGEST
- HYPERTENSIVE HRT DIS
- MITRAL INSUFFICIENCY
- MITRAL STENOSIS
- MURMUR SYST NFS 170
- MYOCARDIAL INFARCT
- MYOCARDOPATHY-ITIS
- PACEMAKER NORMAL FUNCT'N
- PACEMAKER MALFUNCTION
- PERICARDITIS 175
- RHEUMATIC HEART DIS
- SEPTAL DEFECT ATRIAL
- SEPTAL DEFECT VENTR
- VALVE PROSTHESIS
- WPW 180

- GASTRIC CANCER
- GASTRIC ULCER
- GASTROENTERITIS
- POST GASTRECTOMY STATE
- PYROSIS 211
- GALL BLADDER DISEASE
- HEPATITIS
- LIVER CIRRHOSIS
- LIVER ABN FUNCT TESTS 215
- PANCREATITIS

LOWER GI
- COLITIS GRANULOMATOUS
- COLITIS ULCERATIVE
- COLON CANCER
- CONSTIPATION 220
- DIARRHEA
- DIVERTICULOSIS-ITIS
- IRRITABLE COLON
- HEMORRHOIDS
- MELENA 225
- POLYP (S)
- PRURITUS ANI
- RECTUM BLEEDING
- RECTUM CANCER
- REGIONAL ENTERITIS 230

GYN
- AMENORRHEA
- DYSMENORRHEA
- MENO-METRORRHAGIA
- MENOPAUSAL SYNDROME
- PREGNANCY 235
- PREMENSTRUAL TENSION
- VAGINITIS

- PROSTATITIS
- TESTIS ABS ATROPHIC
- URETHRITIS NFS 270

MUSCULO-SKELETAL

ARTHROSES
- ARTHRALGIA
- ANK SPONDYLITIS
- GOUT
- OSTEOARTHRITIS
- RHEUMATOID ARTHR 275
- BACK PAIN NFS
- BACK PAIN POSTURAL
- BURSITIS-TEND HIP 278
- BURSITIS-TEND SHOULD
- CARPAL TUNNEL SYND
- CHE T ... LL PAIN
- DISC DIS CERVICAL 285
- DISC DIS LUMBAR
- DUPUYTREN CONTR
- EPICOND ELBOW 289
- GANGLION
- JOINT EFFUSION NFS
- KYPHOSIS-SCOLIOSIS
- MUSCLE CRAMPS 295
- MUSC-SKEL PAIN NFS
- MYALGIA NFS
- MYOPATHY NFS
- OSTEOPOROSIS
- SPONDYLOSIS CERV 300
- SPONDYLOSIS LUMBAR
- TORTICOLLIS

- INSOMNIA
- PERSONALITY DISORDER
- PSYCHOTIC BEHAVIOR

DRUGS ADMINISTERED

- ADRENALIN 330
- AMYL NITRITE
- ATROPINE
- BENADRYL
- BSP
- CYTOSAR 335
- CYTOXAN
- DECADRON
- DECADRON-XYLOCAINE
- DEMEROL
- 5 FU 340
- H STALOG
- HYDELTRA TBA
- HYDROCORTISONE
- LIDOCAINE
- NEMBUTAL SOD 345
- PONTOCAINE
- SILVER NITRATE
- VALIUM
- VELBAN

POSSIBLE INDUSTRIAL 350

DISPOSITION:

	REFERRED TO	
ALLERGY	HOSPITAL	PHYS MED
DERMATOL	MEDICAL	PSYCHIATRY
EMERG RM	MULTIPHASIC	SOC SERVICE
ENT	NEUROLOGY	SURGERY
HOME CARE	NEURO SURG	UROLOGY
	NON-APPT	
	OB GYN	
	OPHTHAL-MOL	
	ORTHOPEDIC	
	PEDIATRIC	

RETURN:
- DAY(S) 375
- WEEK(S)
- MONTH(S)
- PRN 378

PRINT CONDITIONS PRESENT TODAY AND NOT LISTED ABOVE

COPYRIGHT 1972

99138 (7-72)

Figure 21-3. Encounter record for medical clinic—San Francisco.

```
                PERMANENTE MEDICAL GROUP LABORATORY
                  2425 GEARY BLVD., SAN FRANCISCO, CALIFORNIA               CHIN    3
                          M. L. BASSIS, M.D. DIRECTOR


                         INPATIENT  -   CHART REPORT
                           15:45 HR   26 JAN 73  (026)


                               MR :              DR .


        026161  SPEC. URINE    RECVD:  0928
            ACETONE (TITER)                          NEGATIVE
            GLUCOSE (QUAL)                            TRACE
            HEMOGLOBIN (QUAL)                           3+
            PH (QUAL)                                    6
            PROTEIN (QUAL)                              1+
            SEDIMENT EXAM
                  CELL TYPE                          LEUKOCYTES
                      COUNT (/HPF)                   LOADED
                  CELL TYPE                          ERYTHROCYTES
                      COUNT (/HPF)                       5
                  CELL TYPE                          EPITHELIAL
                      COUNT (/LPF)                   RARE


        026221  SPEC. URINE    RECVD:  1210
            ACETONE (TITER)                          NEGATIVE
            GLUCOSE (QUAL)                            NEGATIVE
            HEMOGLOBIN (QUAL)                           4+
            PH (QUAL)                                    5
            PROTEIN (QUAL)                              1+
            SEDIMENT EXAM
                  CELL TYPE                          LEUKOCYTES
                      COUNT (/HPF)                   LOADED
                  CELL TYPE                          ERYTHROCYTES
                      COUNT (/HPF)                      10
                  CELL TYPE                          EPITHELIAL
                      COUNT (/LPF)                   RARE
```

Figure 21–4. Inpatient chart copy of computer-produced laboratory report.

b. Billing, accounting, and payroll. All major administrative support in these categories is provided by Permanente Services, Inc. As noted earlier, the PCMR Administrative Data Section contains only that data required for group, coverage, and eligibility checking.

3. Service Units

a. Clinical laboratory. A three-phase implementation was scheduled for the clinical laboratory data collection and reporting subsystem:

Phase 1. A manual, punched card-oriented, backup system was developed and implemented in 1969 and has been fully operational since that time. While the first requirement of the laboratory data processing subsystem must be to acquire data accurately and reliably, it must maximize error detection and correction capabilities while providing to physicians and other medical personnel, as rapidly as possible, the information they need in the care of patients. Since data systems, or their components, inevitably experience failures, it is essential that the clinical laboratory can execute its responsibilities without computer system support. It is immaterial whether a data system terminal, communication line, disk track, or central processing unit is out of order; if the period of unavailability is significant in terms of the local work environment activities, then alternative procedures must be at hand and easily implementable until such time as the data system again becomes available. Since full redundancy of all elements of medium or large-scale data systems is currently economically impractical, it becomes mandatory that appropriate manual and/or semi-automated backup procedures be available.

Phase 2. A computer-supported laboratory backup and interim primary laboratory data collection and reporting system was designed in 1970. All elements of the subsystem have been tested individually, have been tested for short periods of full scale operation early in 1972, and were placed in routine operation toward the end of 1972.

Phase 3. The clinical laboratory system was integrated with the primary hospital (nursing station subsystem) computer-supported communication network. This phase was in development and was to be tested following implementation of the pediatrics data collection procedures (see section E.4).

During the design and development periods of 1969 and 1970, the decision was made to implement the various laboratory subdepartments sequentially. It was clear that, to minimize operational error and maximize hospital acceptance, adequate error detection and correction methods must be completed prior to operation in the laboratory. These methods, involving real-time patient, specimen, and test result identification and verification, have been completed.

There are three functional laboratory subsystems: LOGIN, DATA COLLECTION, and REPORTING.

(1) LOGIN.

(a) Test requisition procedure. Requests for laboratory testing originate on one of four requisitions provided in doctors' offices and nursing units: one for blood specimens, one for nonblood specimens, one for those specimens with special requirements, and the fourth for the special considerations of blood banking and the administration of blood products. Figure 21–5 is an example of the blood specimen requisition form. Copies of these documents are provided so that, in the backup mode, the results of tests which have been completed can be transcribed to the requisitions and released to the physicians as they become available.

(b) Receipt of samples in laboratory—LOGIN. Specimens arriving with their requisitions are reviewed by a receiving clerk for appropriate identification. The LOGIN process consists of six steps which, summarized, consist of assigning accession numbers to specimens and compiling a set of appropriately identified prepunched test cards. The decks of cards are then read into a card reader "home" terminal.

(c) Computer LOGIN and bookkeeping. The LOGIN function of the computer reads the cards, creates tables for each accession number, and cross references the tables by medical record number. It retrieves the patient's name and secondary identifiers from the PCMR and returns these data to the home terminal for verification. The cards are then machine-sorted into departmental categories which match those into which the specimens were sorted at the receiving station. Specimens and test cards are then delivered to the appropriate department for analysis. A technologist inscribes test results on the appropriate card. At intervals during the day and in accord with several priority schemes, she inputs into the computer terminal the data from the accumulated test cards.

(2) DATA COLLECTION. Automated (direct analog to digital) computer input of the laboratory test data does not now exist in our laboratory; this capability is planned for implementation in 1974. Test results are therefore entered by a technologist into one of several data input terminals. Three basic modes of data input are used: machine readable data—e.g., for those hematology tests which have been performed on a model S Coulter Counter, the punched cards are read into the card reader, subjected to validity checking, and, if acceptable, stored in the PCMR; tests for

which there are standard formats and structured answers—e.g., discrete, closed set answers of the form "positive," "negative," etc.—are sorted according to the results and read into the card reader. Each card set is preceded by a "lead" card which defines the result and followed by an "end" card; test results input via "overlay" keyboard terminals (IBM 1092–1093)—when a technologist is prepared to input test results, he or she chooses the proper keymat (or set of keymats), places it on the keyboard, and enters the data following the usual identification verification procedure.

(3) REPORTING. Of the many uses to which laboratory test result data and the corresponding reports are put, the primary one directly influences the care of patients. First, the report is generated in the clinical laboratory at a point in time, then delivered as soon as possible to the physician who requested the test. This sequence directly influences physician decision-making and patient management. The second use is when, at a later point in time, a physician or other professional calls for another report of the same test data, perhaps in a new context and format—e.g., arrayed in a chronological listing of all results of similar tests done on the patient in question. This process, performed manually today with high frequency by physicians is time-consuming and error-prone.

Three types of routine report production have been successfully tested.

(a) "Activity reports." These include test answers for any specimens which have been subjected to the basic activities of logging in and data analysis and entry. These reports may thus include test results from several specimens which have been subjected to activities "today," although the specimens may have been collected over a period of several days. Reports are generated for the physician's office (outpatient) or for the hospital chart (inpatient).

(b) Inpatient reporting. Each inpatient chart will, when appropriate, have one laboratory report for each hospital day, containing only those tests for which there were results that day. As indicated above, when an inpatient is discharged, a computer-produced chronological summary report of all laboratory work will be directed to the record room.

(c) Outpatient reporting. In addition to "activity" reports, which are directed on a daily basis to the physicians' offices, a final report will be distributed to the physicians upon completion of all tests for any given outpatient specimen; a duplicate final report will be directed to the chart room. The outpatient record will thus be concerned only with completed reports rather than sets of partially complete reports.

(d) Stat reports. The printing of priority reports out of the normal

☐ ANTIOCH ☐ SAN FRANCISCO
☐ HAYWARD ☐ SOUTH SAN FRAN.
☐ NAPA ☐ SAN RAFAEL
☐ OAKLAND ☐ SANTA CLARA
☐ REDWOOD C. ☐ SUNNYVALE
☐ RICHMOND ☐ VALLEJO
☐ SACRAMENTO ☐ WALNUT CREEK

WRITE ACCESS NO.   ACCESS NO. LABEL

PERMANENTE MEDICAL GROUP LABORATORY
2425 GEARY BLVD., SAN FRANCISCO, CALIF.
M. L. Bassis, M.D., Director

BLOOD SPECIMEN LABORATORY REPORT

☐ FASTING SPECIMEN
☐ I.V. RUNNING
☐ STAT. - EXT. TO CALL

INPATIENT ROOM #	OUTPATIENT CLINIC LOC.

DATE AND TIME TO BE COLLECTED ☐ A.M. ☐ P.M.

SPECIAL HANDLING
☐ LAB SUPERVISOR TO BE NOTIFIED
☐ PATIENT IS ON ANTIBIOTICS, X-RAY
AND/OR IMMUNOSUPPRESSIVE THERAPY

PHYSICIAN'S NAME   DATE

PHYSICIAN'S COMMENTS AND INSTRUCTIONS

O/P REVENUE SLIP NO.	AMOUNT $	☐ CASH ☐ CHARGE ☐ CDT.

PATIENT'S TELEPHONE NO.

PATIENT'S ADDRESS

HEMATOLOGY

☐ PRE OP/ADMIT (HCT, WBC). SURG. DATE
☐ HEMATOCRIT (MICRO) %
☐ HEMATOCRIT (COULTER) %
☐ RBC ____ X10⁶/MM³
☐ INDICES
  MCV. ____ μ³
  MCH. ____ μμG
  MCHC ____ GM%
☐ HEMOGLOBIN ____ GM%
☐ W B C. ____ /MM³
  (DIFF AUTOMATIC <5 >10'000)
☐ DIFFERENTIAL IN NORMAL RANGE
☐ RBC MORPHOLOGY (SLIDE)

☐ EOSINOPHIL COUNT ____ /MM³
☐ FETAL HGB. ____ %
* ☐ HAM TEST
* ☐ HEINZ BODY
☐ HGB. E'PHOR.

CHEMISTRY

☐ ACETONE
☐ ACID P'TASE (QUAL.)
☐ ALK P'TASE ____ K.A.U.
☐ ALK P'TASE ISOZYMES
☐ AMYLASE ____ u
☐ BILIRUBIN TOT. ____ MG%
  ☐ DIRECT BILI ____ MG%
☐ BUN (UREA N.) ____ MG%
☐ CREATININE ____ MG%
☐ CALCIUM ____ MG%
☐ CHOLESTEROL ____ MG%
☐ ELECTROLYTES, IN MEQ/L
☐ SODIUM
☐ POTASSIUM
☐ CHLORIDE
☐ BICARBONATE
☐ G-6PD

☐ ALDOLASE ____ MU/ML
☐ BARBITURATE (QUAL.)
☐ BLOOD GASES
  ☐ ART ☐ VEN ☐ CAP
  ☐ pH
  ☐ PCO₂ ____ mmHg
  ☐ PO₂ ____ mmHg
  ☐ O₂ SAT ____ %
  ☐ ACT. BICARB ____ MEQ/L
  ☐ BASE EXCESS
☐ BROMIDES ____ MG%
☐ CAROTENE ____ MCG%
☐ CHOLINESTERASE
☐ CPK ____ MU/ML
☐ COMPLEMENT C3 ____ MG%
☐ DILANTIN ____ MLG/ML
☐ FOLIC ACID
  IMMUNO DIFFUSION IN MG%
  ☐ IGA
  ☐ IGG

IMMUNOHEMATOLOGY

☐ BLOOD GROUP AND TYPE (SEE FOOTNOTE A)
  ☐ ABO
  ☐ Rh.
☐ BLOOD ANTIBODIES (AB)
  ☐ AB. SCREEN
  ☐ AB. IDENT
  ☐ ANTIBODY TITER
  ☐ ABO
  ☐ Rh
  ☐ OTHER

☐ PRENATAL
  CURRENT SERUM POS 1:
  PREVIOUS ____ POS 1: DATE

☐ DIRECT COOMBS
☐ HDN WORKUP
  (SEND SAMPLES MOTHER AND BABY)
  ☐ PHENOTYPE

☐ A.N.A.
☐ ASO ____ TODDU

COAGULATION

HGB. QUANT A2 ____ %
* L'CYTE ALK P'TASE
PARASITE SMEARS
PLATELET COUNT ____ X10³/MM³
RBC FRAGILITY:
* INCUBATED
OSMOTIC
RETIC COUNT ____ %
SED RATE ____ MM
SICKLE PREP
VISCOSITY

COAGULATION

BLEEDING TIME ____ MIN ____ SEC
CLOT LYSIS
CLOT RETRACT ____
FIBRINOGEN ____ MG%
THROMBIN TIME ____ SEC
PROTIME ____ SEC
____ %
CONTROL ____ SEC
P.T.T. ____ SEC
CONTROL ____ SEC
* APPT. REQ'D UNLESS LAB COLLECTS

GLUCOSE, IN MG%
FAST
RANDOM
MICRO
IRON ____ µG%
LIPIDS, TOTAL ____ MG%
PHOSPHOROUS ____ MG%
PROTEIN, TOTAL ____ GM%
ALBUMIN ____ GM%
PROTEIN E'PHOR, IN%
ALBUMIN ____
ALPHA 1 ____
ALPHA 2 ____
BETA ____
GAMMA ____
SGOT ____ u
SGPT ____ u
TIBC ____ µG%
T-3 ____ % UPTAKE
T-4 (COL) ____ MCG%
T-4 (MUR-PAT) ____ MCG%
(CALL LAB)
URIC ACID ____ MG%

IGM
IGD
IGE
IMMUNO E'PHOR
LACTIC ACID ____ MG%
LDH ____ u
LDH ISOZYMES
LEAD ____ MCG/100 ML
LIPASE
LIPOPROTEIN PHENOTYPE
(CHOLEST, TRIGLYC E'PHOR)
CHYL O
B-LIPO
PRE-B-LIPO
ALPHA
LITHIUM ____ MEQ/L
MAGNESIUM ____ MG%
METHEMOGLOBIN ____ % SAT
OSMOLALITY ____ mOs/Kg
PHOSPHOLIPIDS ____ MG%
PYRUVIC ACID ____ MG%
QUINIDINE ____ MG/L
SALICYLATE ____ MG%
SULFHEMOGLOBIN
TRIGLYCERIDES ____ MG%
TESTOSTERONE

* COLD AGGLUT
CRP
* CRYOGLOBULIN
* CRYOFIBRINOGEN
FEBRILE AGGLUT
BRUCELLA
PARA-A
PARA-B
PROT OX K
PROT OX 19
TULARENSIS
TYPHOID H
TYPHOID O
PROT OX 2
α FETOGLOBIN
HETEROPHILE
(RA) LATEX AGGLUT
RUBELLA
(TITER REQUIRES 2 REQUISITIONS)
SCREEN AT 1:10
TITER, 1ST SPEC.
TITER, 2ND SPEC.
TOXOPLASMA
VDRL
CORD BLOOD PREMAR PRENAT
FTA
* APPT. REQ'D UNLESS LAB COLLECTS

DIFFERENTIAL:

SEGS	BANDS	LYMPHS	MONO	EOS	BASO	ATYP LYMPH	REACT LYMPH
BLASTS	PROLYM	PROMYELO	MYELO	METAMY	NORMO	NORMO	

RBC MORPHOLOGY: NORMAL

PLATELETS: NORMAL | INCREASED | DECREASED
† NOT USED IN DIFFERENTIAL CALCULATION
99020 (REV. 8-72)

CHART COPY

A STATE LAW REQUIRES THAT THE WOMEN TESTED BE INFORMED AS TO THE RHESUS Rh TYPING TEST RESULTS.

Figure 21-5. Clinical laboratory test requisition form—blood specimens.

sequence is generated immediately upon completion of the corresponding tests. They are delivered out of the routine delivery times, directly to the appropriate ward or clinic as soon as printed.

In-laboratory services include the capability for the technologist to request listings of tests ordered, by category, and a concomitant listing of tests completed in order that he may determine after a given time period whether there are outstanding tests remaining to be reported; labels are also produced for identifying aliquots of specimens where more than one laboratory sub-department is involved in the analytic process.

b.   Pathology.   Acquisition of surgical pathology data has been planned on a region-wide scale, to be implemented in 1974. The method consists of 4 steps:

(1)   The pathologist reports the results of his findings in a traditional manner in each facility.

(2)   Copies of the reports, containing standardized patient identification data, are forwarded to a single pathology department.

(3)   A data clerk with surgical pathology training reviews the report and encodes the conclusions of the report (the descriptive text is bypassed) in SNOP (Systematized Nomenclature of Pathology).

(4)   By means of an on-line keyboard terminal, the data clerk retrieves the PCMR, identifies the patient, and enters the SNOP-encoded findings.

Within each facility, standard reports are distributed in the traditional manner. Listings of diagnoses by location and by SNOP category (topology, morphology, etc.) will be made available to each facility or analyzed for the region, as required.

It is envisioned that autopsy findings will be managed similarly. Direct (from the pathologist) automated input, is not planned in the next term.

c.   X-ray.   At the time of testing of the input of physician orders on the pediatric service (see Section E.4), an order for a given x-ray test generated at a nursing station terminal will result in a computer-produced facsimile of a requisition on a printer in the x-ray department. Much interesting work has been done in recent years on the problem of acquiring, directly from the radiologist, the conclusions to his findings.[10] We are currently exploring, although at a lower priority, the possibility of acquiring the conclusions of x-ray examination in a manner similar to that outlined for surgical pathology above; however, use of an alternative method of encoding will have to be explored.

d.   Pharmacy.   The San Francisco outpatient pharmacy data subsystem has been operational on a continuous basis for approximately three and one half years, in both the outpatient clinic building and in the outpatient portion of the hospital building. Prescriptions presented to the pharmacist are processed in accord with standard pharmacy procedures but in such a manner that, for every drug dispensed, the date, time, and drug data are entered into that patient's computer medical record. This is accomplished in "real time" by means of on-line IBM 2740 electric typewriter terminals which are connected by telephone lines to the central computer facility. Four terminals are located in the clinic building and the fifth in the hospital pharmacy. By means of these five terminals, data on approximately 1200 prescriptions per day are entered into the medical data base. About two-thirds are new prescriptions; one-third are refills.

Following entry of appropriate patient identification and drug data into the terminal, the computer responds by producing two labels, the first to be dispensed with the medication and the second to be maintained in the pharmacy for audit purposes. After visual verification of the accuracy of the computer-produced labels (Figure 21–6), the pharmacist activates the computer storage of the data.

e. Clinical Physiology. On-line monitoring of analog representations of physiologic functions—e.g., electrocardiogram, electroencephalogram, pulmonary function measures, etc.—is not scheduled prior to 1975. Studies are currently under way to implement programmed interpretation of screening electrocardiograms in 1974 (see Chapter Ten for a detailed discussion of this subject).

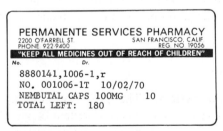

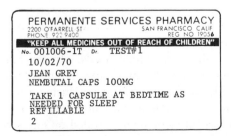

Figure 21–6. Pharmacy labels.

f. Automated multiphasic screening. A multiphasic health-testing laboratory has been in operation in the San Francisco facility since 1964. This laboratory occupies approximately 10,000 square feet of floor space in the outpatient offices building and is functionally very similar to a "twin" laboratory operating in the Oakland Kaiser-Permanente outpatient offices. Its development, operation, and evaluation as an independent methodology in medicine has been described elsewhere in the literature.[11-13] Approximately 25,000 patients receive multiphasic screening each year in San Francisco. Scheduling and patient appointments are handled under program control. In the course of approximately two and one half hours, each patient is processed through 20 phases, or stations, at which a comprehensive series of tests are performed and data from a variety of forms is acquired—e.g., history data from self-administered questionnaires and sorting of preprinted and prepunched questionnaire cards; x-ray data (70 millimeter chest), breast x-ray (in women over age 47); electrocardiogram; ocular tension; visual acuity and audiometry; and a variety of hematologic, blood chemical, and urine analyses. (See also Chapter Eleven).

At the conclusion of the 20 stations, the compiled data is communicated on-line via telephone lines to the computer center where preliminary programmed screening of selected tests is carried out and programmed "advice" or "consider" rules are communicated immediately to the nurse in charge of the multiphasic laboratory. Subsequent testing may then be performed as indicated prior to the patient leaving the laboratory. Prior to the follow-up office visit with the physician, a summary report is printed and dispatched to the appropriate medical record room for inclusion in the patient's chart.

4. Clinical Units

a. Nursing station system. The nurse station terminal system (NSTS) is a computer-supported communication system of visual display terminals designed to permit direct communication between hospital and medical personnel and the system of central patient computerized medical records. It has already been demonstrated that physicians and nurses will use interactive terminal modes of communication for purposes of retrieving data which is relevant to their immediate needs. (In the San Francisco Kaiser Hospital Emergency Room an interactive typewriter terminal has been used actively by both physicians and nurses during a test implementation.) However, day-to-day collection of patient information directly from physicians and nurses has yet to be demonstrated on any significant scale. Our objective is that professional personnel enter a small set of basic medical data (diagnoses, physician orders, and nurses' drug administration) which will be compatible with concomitant use of the manual chart for other classes of data such as progress notes, nurses' "graphics," etc. Data input may thus be accomplished at a number of locations in the hospital (e.g., nursing stations, nursery, admitting, etc.) by means of an electronically active "light-pen" or typewriter keyboard, which enables the user to engage directly in a dialogue with computer stored medical record information.

Data output is in the form of visual display and/or permanent copy produced by the printer associated with many of the data terminals.

The basic hospital data subsystem test configuration consists of a small processor linked by telephone lines to the central computer facility (see Section G). The processors are the Honeywell DDP 516 and 416 with a total of 40K core memory. These access six data disk drives which have a total capacity of approximately 4,700,000 characters. A noninterruptable reserve power system, consisting of a constant voltage current-limited battery, storage batteries, static inverter and a diesel generator, insures against data loss due to ac power failure. The processors drive 24 terminals (Sanders Associates), each terminal being defined as a visual display unit with associated light-pen sensor, keyboard, card-reader unit, and low-speed electronic printer (40 cps). The terminals are deployed throughout patient care areas of the hospital, including all nursing stations, nursery, intensive care unit, emergency room, and admitting department. This configuration, and its functional relationship to the other data processing applications in the San Francisco facility, are diagrammed in Figure 21–7.

All nursing station subsystem application programs are written in a "JOSS"-type re-entrant interpretive compiler language which was provided by Sanders Associates (File Oriented Programming System—FOPS). The general capabilities of this type of language have been discussed by Greenes et al.[14]

As can be seen, the pilot system configuration has no built-in redundancy. Our experience with this prototype system is that the full scale hospital operation (3 shifts per day, 7 days per week), which we had originally considered to be possible, is not realistic. During the past year, when the hospital data system applications had progressed sufficiently, analysis of disk storage and telecommunications requirements coupled with measured system performance revealed that revisions in the planned implementation sequence would be necessary. Basically, the revisions included reduction to one and one-half shift operation and testing of applications on a single representative hospital service.

Hardware performance was evaluated in accord with a specific protocol for six months in 1971. Malfunctions of any element of the hospital-resi-

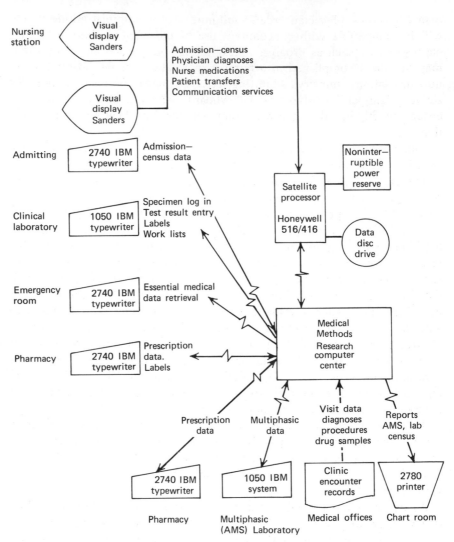

Figure 21–7. Pilot Medical Data System Hardware Configuration.

dent hardware were recorded and analyzed. Based on expected system availability (a function of the number of terminals, hours to be used per day, days per working month, etc.) there was approximately one hardware malfunction for every 43 terminal hours; extrapolated to the entire system, these data would lead to an expected four hardware malfunctions per nursing shift. While many of these malfunctions resulted in but a few minutes loss of system time, and some would have been abolished by redundancy of certain equipment elements, others resulted in down-times measured in hours. Our experience indicates that in a real-time environment a certain amount of equipment redundancy is essential at present day performance levels.

Analysis of the software malfunctions (applications errors) revealed that a significant software error (defined as one that requires system restart) occurred about every 150 terminal hours. A number of these errors occurred in the process of writing and modifying new applications programs; it was thus expected and subsequently realized that the number of restarts would reduce significantly when the system was tested in a "closed" environment—i.e., when applications programs were exercised without introduction of new programs to the system.

These considerations led to a revised implementation schedule following completion of system installation in the San Francisco facility in January 1972.

The first step consisted of operating the Admissions/Census application and message retrieval services on a hospital-wide basis, including patient admission and discharge, inquiries for patient location, data retrieval from the central patient computer medical record (e.g., laboratory test data, etc.), and interpersonnel message services.

Implementation of data collection applications was then tried, first on the pediatrics and newborn services. The rationale is that these locations contain a representative patient mix to insure an adequate test of all the medical data system applications; there is a reasonably large number of staff and house staff physicians who will interact with the data system; the locations and personnel are such that the backup and restart problems associated with scheduled and nonscheduled "down times" will provide experience sufficient to facilitate implementation into other areas of the hospital.

Terminal activation and "sign-on" procedure: The procedure for "signing on" to a terminal is identical for all categories of terminal users. Rigid plastic wallet-sized identification (ID) cards are issued for this purpose. Each card has punched holes in some or all of twelve columns, creating a unique code which identifies its holder by name, department or medical function, permissible level of access to the patient files, and whether or not the current card number is valid. Thus, for example, should a user lose his card, a new one is issued with the version digit incremented by one, thus permitting the system to recognize that the previous card was no longer valid. Standard procedures have been developed for the issuing of ID numbers and cards, and control is exercised by the facility administrator. The sign-on procedure consists of inserting the ID card into the card-read slot on the face of the terminal and depressing the signature function key on the terminal keyboard. The computer searches its files to verify identification, then displays the user name, date, and time of access to the terminal and confronts him with a series of interactive options which permit him to proceed to one of the variety of indices or data lists available for the purpose of retrieving or inputting data.

b. Admission/census. The admissions application is a relatively straightforward interactive method of maintaining an up-to-date hospital inventory of patients. At the San Francisco hospital, there are approximately 40 patients admitted and discharged each day, in addition to an average of 75 patient transfers from one bed or station location to another. The relevance of an accurate current census data set to such data processing procedures as distribution of completed laboratory test results is obvious. It is of interest that initial testing of the real time system provided a tangible, even dramatic demonstration to the nursing and admissions staff of the high degree of interdependence that exists between these two groups.

The admission report programs consist of listings of daily admissions, discharges, daily census (alphabetic listing by patient last name), physician-service census (alphabetic listing of patients by last name, per physician by alphabetically by last name, per department). Appropriate summaries are tabulated for each of the above categories, and a series of computations are executed under program control in order to facilitate error detection and correction by the medical users of the reports.

c. Medical information processing.

(1) Diagnosis data collection. In order to maximize quality of data entered, it is desirable that the physician be responsible for the input of diagnosis data via the NSTS. In general, in order to input a diagnosis, the physician is asked to identify the patient from a census display, then to proceed to a series of indices and data pages and, by appropriate sequential light-pen selections of displayed data, indicate a diagnosis term, a chronological or severity modifier, whether the diagnosis was related to an adverse drug effect, and other data he deems appropriate. At the conclusion of his selections, he verifies the selected data; the data is then stored in the patient's computer medical record, both locally (in the satellite computer) for a transient period and in the central computer data base for permanent storage. In addition, his selections are printed at the local nursing station for subsequent inclusion in the patient chart. Figure 21–8 is a facsimile of the first-level index to physician data entry and data retrieval applications. Within the sequences for diagnosis (and, in general, other classes of data) are light-pen-selectable control items which permit the user to manipulate the displays at subindex levels in order to avoid repetitive selection of the same data and also error correction capabilities which allow cancellation or alteration of items he deems appropriate.

·PHYSICIAN INDEX·

DIAGNOSIS   WARD PROCEDURES

SIGNS AND SYMPTOMS   CONSULTATION REQUEST

·ORDERS·

    COMMON ORDERS
    DISCHARGE ORDERS

    GENERAL NURSING   DIRECTORY -PATIENT
    MEDICATIONS   -STAFF
    TRANSFER
                                    PCMR REVIEW

·TESTS·

    ECG
    ISOTOPES

    LABORATORY
    NEUROLOGICAL

    X-RAY
    OTHER (KEY)

LOCAL CENSUS   SEND MESSAGE

CENSUS INDEX   WORKPAGE

GENERAL INDEX

Figure 21–8.   First level index to physician data entry. Center-dot brackets indicate non-selectable words. (Nursing station terminal system (NSTS) display.)

The diagnosis lists upon which the programs operate were established by physicians from all specialty divisions in the San Francisco medical facility. No single diagnosis terminology classification has been followed; Current Medical Terminology (CMT), International Classification of Disease Adapted (ICDA), and Systematized Nomenclature of Pathology (SNOP) principles have served as guidelines where possible. Frequency counts of diagnoses in the San Francisco hospital served as the basis for many entries.

(2) Physician orders. The decision to acquire physician orders derived from an antecedent decision to acquire essential data concerning drugs administered (or not administered) to hospitalized patients. It followed that the method by which a nurse may indicate that a drug has or has not

been administered to a patient is contingent on the existence of appropriate data sets in the computer which she can manipulate by means of a visual display terminal. The logical data would be the set of physicians' drug orders. In order to avoid redundant procedures, therefore, it appeared necessary to provide the capability of acquiring all physician orders. While current planning has it that the bulk of these will be deleted at the time the patient is discharged from the hospital, the essential drug administration information will have been stored in the patient's computer medical record.

Physician orders have been indexed at the first level as general nursing orders, test requisitions, and medications. A fourth category is "common" orders. While the general capability must exist that any specific physician order be relatively easily constructed via the interactive visual display terminal, he will first be presented with lists of prestructured "common" orders which, instead of requiring sequences of light-pen selections, may be selected as entire order statements, or sets by one or two selections. Common order sets have been developed by the physicians and nurses in the Department of Pediatrics, structured on the basis of general clinical conditions. Preprinted common order sets have been developed and implemented for routine manual use on a trial basis in the Pediatrics Department. These serve the dual purpose of educating the pediatric personnel and being a link in the error recovery procedures.

General nursing orders are categorized at the first index level into vital signs and observations, activity, diet, and a variety of treatments, including respiratory care, skin care, management of intracavitary tubes, traction devices, etc., (Figure 21–9). Subindices and data lists permit specification of time intervals, frequencies, specific measures (e.g., numeric upper limit for blood pressure), etc.

Requisitioning of laboratory, x-ray and other test procedures utilizes similar multilevel indexing techniques. In all sequences, there exists the capability to append special instructions and, for x-ray, to enter the clinical indications for requested examinations.

Drugs and intravenous solutions; drug administration. Drug orders can be entered by the physician, or by the nurse acting as his agent, with as high a degree of precision as necessary. (A nurse ID card will access physician order displays but, under program control, will require that she identify the physician on whose behalf she is acting—the subsequent printout will identify both her and the physician for that transaction). A computational capability has been incorporated which permits the pediatrician, in the process of constructing a drug order, to request that the precise drug dosage be computed automatically as a function of the child's body weight.

(3) Drug administration. Periodically through the day, the nurse will

·GENERAL NURSING ORDERS·

VITAL SIGNS AND OBSERVATIONS-ROUTINE

       SPECIAL VITAL SIGNS
       NEUROL SIGNS
       TEMPERATURE CONTROL
       WARD TESTS-URINE AND FECES
       WEIGHT - I/O

ACTIVITY-UP AD LIB

       ACTIVITY LIMITS
       ISOLATION
       RESTRICTIONS (VISITORS, TV, ETC)

DIET-REGULAR FOR AGE

       SPECIAL DIETS   INFANT FORMULAS
                              TUBE FEEDINGS

·TREATMENTS·

       ENEMAS
       RESPIRATORY (OXYGEN, IPPB, ETC)
       SKIN CARE-COMPRESSES-DRESSINGS
       TUBES,-DRAINS,-SUCTION
       TRACTION

·MISCELLANEOUS·

       EQUIPMENT REQUESTS
       PATIENT/PARENT INSTRUCTION
       PHYSICAL THERAPY

PHYSICIAN INDEX   ERROR

                                      WORKPAGE

Figure 21–9.   Index to general nursing orders.

call for drug-dispensing schedules to be printed at her local nursing station terminal printer. She may carry the work schedules on her medication rounds as she administers drugs to appropriate patients and, following drug administration, will return to the visual display terminal and proceed through a sequence of displays which enable her to indicate the drugs given, whether or not in the proper dose or on time and, if not given, the reason why.

(4) Hospital discharge. From the point of view of system implementation, generating an order to discharge a patient from the hospital can be a very simple process which will establish in the patient's computer record

the date and time of the discharge order in addition to date and time of check out of the patient from the hospital. However, such a procedure would fall short of providing a potentially useful service to the outpatient followup physician, namely, making available to him a succinct summary of the patient's hospitalization. Accordingly, under development is a method by which the physician may develop the elements of a hospitalization summary in the course of generating a discharge order. By means of multilevel indexing and branching techniques, and utilizing many of the same displays that exist for purposes of diagnosis, test, and drug data entry, the user can be lead through a sequence that will permit the acquisition of:

(1) Date and time of hospital admission (already in file)
(2) Date and time of hospital discharge
(3) Destination
(4) Discharge Orders (including medication)
(5) Follow-up appointment data (physician name or specialty clinic, and date)
(6) Outstanding test data (data unavailable at time of patient discharge
(7) Test(s) to be performed prior to the follow-up visit
(8) Major procedures during hospitalization
(9) Final diagnoses

It is planned that these data be stored in a logical set where they will be available for subsequent retrieval on either a routine or an "on demand" interactive basis, as may be required.

d. Hospital information services. Several communication services have been programmed and will be tested during the initial implementation of the pilot hospital data system.

(1) Message routing. The relaying of messages between staff and resident physicians, interns, nurses, nursing stations, and paramedical agencies is characteristically a time-consuming process, frequently resulting in over-burdening of available telephone and manual message routing facilities.

A message "file" has been created for each authorized user of the data system (holder of an authorized ID card). Each time the user "signs-on" to the terminal, he is greeted with a display of the contents of his message file. Only his card will access that file. He may read the messages and, by appropriate action with the light-pen, ignore them and continue on to a different interaction with the terminal—for example, send message or other action—or, alternatively, he may initiate local printing of the contents of the message file. In both instances, the file is deleted, preventing excessive accumulation through time of disk-stored information.

The "send message" capability includes sending "reminders" to oneself.

Potential uses of this subsystem are listed in Figure 21–10. Approximately 40 nurses used the feature during a three-month test period.

(2) Patient location. In view of the high rate of change of patient location, knowledge of the patients' whereabouts becomes a significant tactical problem. Authorized card holders may, therefore, by means of the census index and local census files, quickly access data concerning the residents of any of the hospital beds, at any of the nursing station locations, from any terminal.

(3) Other retrieval services. Real-time inquiry for status of laboratory tests, review of physician orders, and review of antecedent data stored in

GENERAL	Suggestion Box Personal messages Reminder to self Perusal of all directories for correct name spelling, classifications, physicians' clinic telephone extensions, etc.
PHYSICIANS	Consultation (via Physician Index) Department Chief to Department members; Broadcast communication to staff members. On-Call MD to on-coming staff Instruction to other category of staff Inhalation Therapy Physical Therapy, RN on all shifts
NURSING	Reminders to physicians Communication to off duty personnel Head Nurse to all shift personnel Reports to other shifts
DIRECTOR OF NURSING	Broadcast communication to staff members. Arrange meetings, cancellations, etc. Communication to off duty personnel
UNIT MANAGER WARD CLERKS	Communication to off duty personnel Reports to other shifts

HOSPITAL ADMINISTRATION
AND SERVICES
    Admitting
    Business Office
    Dietitian
    ECG
    Housekeeping
    Inhalation Therapy
    Lab
    Medical Records
    Pharmacy
    Social Service
    X-ray
	Communication to appropriate administrative and professional personnel and departments; person to person and department to department communication.
	Service and scheduling reminders, cancelling of procedures, patient condition and physical plant information, etc.

Figure 21–10.   Medical data system—San Francisco. Potential uses of the message application set.

the computer medical records is an integral part of the implementation objectives for the data system, as outlined in earlier parts of this section.

e. Outpatient clinics.

(1) Physician office visits. Outpatient data are collected from those sources primarily responsible for the specific subclasses of data involved, such as receptionists for registration data, nurses for certain procedures, etc. Diagnoses are derived directly from the physician at the time of the visit. Two data collection methods were originally considered: machine readable forms and keypunch forms. Advantages and disadvantages of each were considered; machine readable forms (IBM 1232) were selected for initial implementation because of the advantage of being similar to forms to which many physicians already had been accustomed. "Diagnosis" (encounter) forms were then developed sequentially for all specialty departments. The lists of prestructured diagnoses varied in accord with the particular needs of each department. While no formal diagnosis classification scheme was followed, CMT, ICDA, and SNOP were chosen as primary references, as noted for inpatient diagnoses.

The machine-readable documents proved to require excessive numbers of personnel for handling and were associated with excessively high inscription error rates for the required marking of the seven-digit medical record number and other selected visit data. Revised forms (See Figure 21–3) which are read by a clerk and the data entered by an on-line electric typewriter have resulted in less cost, more information per form, higher physician acceptance, and lower error rates.

Data on approximately 2,000 office visits per day are being collected. The distribution of visits by department is shown in Table 3. For each visit, standard registration data are collected, consisting of patient identification, date and time of visit, category of service (appointment, nonappointment, etc.), facility location (San Francisco), department (medicine, surgery, etc.), and name of primary physician. Variable data which may be collected for each visit include diagnoses, selected procedures, referrals, nonprescription drug information, and return interval. All of these data are stored in the patients' individual computer medical records.

Work is currently in progress which will lead to implementation of diagnosis data collection in three additional outpatient areas: Prenatal clinic, injection clinic (adult immunization data), and emergency room. Pediatric immunization and well baby developmental data are currently being designed into an expanded pediatric clinic diagnosis form. In addition, a modification in data entry procedures, to be implemented in the near future will permit on-line data entry directly from the pediatric clinic and further improvement in data quality control.

(2) Data quality control. Specific quality control steps that have been

Table 3. Distribution of Outpatient Physician Office Visits for the Major Departments, San Francisco

Department	Percent
Allergy	3.9
Dermatology	4.5
Ear, Nose and Throat	4.4
Ophthalmology	5.9
Medicine	33.4
Neurology	0.4
OB/GYN	11.2
Orthopedics	8.8
Pediatrics	16.3
Physical Medicine	0.4
Psychiatry	0.8
Surgery	7.9
Urology	2.0

implemented include: (a) correction of diagnostic blanks; (b) correction of machine errors; (c) return of uncorrectable errors to source (physician) for correction; and (d) return of selected correctable errors to appropriate receptionist and nursing personnel. Another component of quality control involves computer-programmed checking for possible patient identification errors prior to entry of medical data into the computer records. By this technique, medical data cannot be entered into individual records unless there is a precise correspondence between the patient's unique medical record number and his secondary characteristics of month and year of birth, last name, and sex. Thus, when the clerk identifies the patient with a primary identifier (medical record number), the computer can reference the appropriate record and return the secondary identifiers for immediate verification. Accuracy of diagnosis data is verified in a similar manner. A trained clerk can enter data from between 400 and 500 visits per working day.

Data collection forms currently are processed as follows:

(a) A diagnosis form is initiated by the receptionist for each patient. Patient identification, time, date, and physician identification are stamped mechanically, eliminating the previously encountered (machine-readable form) transcription errors. The form accompanies the patient's record to the physician who, upon completion of the examination, enters the appropriate medical data.

(b) The form is inspected by a nurse for any obvious omissions, then is dispatched with the medical record to the chart room where the forms are inspected by clerks for completeness and legibility of identifying data. All forms with "write-in" diagnoses are held for review by a physician (or, where appropriate, a medical records librarian) for legibility, spelling, and designation of the status of any diagnosis marked. When errors are detected, the form is returned either to the reception area or to the primary physician for correction of registration or medical data respectively. Approximately 6% of the forms received in the record room have required further handling for such errors.

(3) Hospital emergency room. In clinical medicine, the need for essential data of historical nature (prior responses to medical questions, diagnoses, immunization, and laboratory test result data, etc.) is well recognized. Accordingly, an approach to on-line real time reporting of "essential" medical information has been formulated, and a basic set of retrieval and data handling programs, collectively termed REPORTER, developed. A low-speed typewriter terminal has been installed in the emergency room.

An authorized user (physician, physician assistant, nurse, etc.) can request sets of stored general medical data from the patient computer medical record (PCMR) on-line and in real time. There are some constraints—e.g., while psychiatry clinic visit data (date, location, department, category of service, physician's name) can be requested by any authorized user, the medical information within that visit cannot be accessed except by an authorized member of the department of psychiatry. An inquiry is initiated by means of entering the requestor's MPID (Medical Personnel Identification) number, following which the system responds with nominal identification. (A heavy underline indicates the user action; all other lines are printed under program control, in "dialogue" fashion. See Figures 21–11, General Format, and 21–12, a specific report.) The patient's unique medical record number is then entered; under program control, the computer immediately returns the date and time of inquiry, patient name, sex, birth month and year (thus assuring accurate patient identification), and data concerning the number of visits in the PCMR, and their distribution, where CLIN = an office visit (any specialty), PHAR = a pharmacy visit; LAB and MHC are self-explanatory. The response continues through the last visit date and, when appropriate, displays stored immunization and possible drug sensitivity data, then waits for a "request" code from the user. The request code simultaneously functions as a verification of patient identification. Following input of the request code, the appropriate data is formatted and printed.

Request codes are designed to permit the following retrievals:

(1) MOST RECENT VISIT: any department, location.

(2) MOST RECENT VISIT TO (DEPARTMENT NAME, LOCATION NAME).

```
ENTER MPID NO. RBDAA*  PHYSICIAN NAME, MD
ENTER MR NO. 1234567

MM/DD/YY           TTTT  HR
PATIENT NAME    SEX   BR.MO.  BR.YR.
TOTAL VISITS SINCE YYYY:  NNN (CLIN=NN,PHAR=NN,LAB=NN,MHC=N)
LAST VISIT: MM DD YY

IMMUNIZATIONS:  DATE(S)              NAME(S)
                Recent               Name 1
                                     Name 2
                                       .
                                       .
                                       .
                Remote               Name n
HX POSS SENSITIVITY:  DRUG NAME(S)
                      Drug 1
                      Drug 2
                        .
                        .
                        .
                      Drug n

REQUEST (CODE)

MM/DD/YY  LOCATION   DEP'T  CATEGORY-SERV.   DR. LAST NAME
                     CLIN:  Reason for visit
                            Diagnoses
                            Procedure name(s)
                            Functional capacity
                            Referral
                            Return interval
                     PHAR:  Drug Name(s), Form, Dose, Units Dispensed
                     LAB:   Accession number
                            Specimen name(s)
                            Date Specimen received
                            Test name(s)
                            Test result
                            Comments -Physician
                                     -Technologist

NONE


ENTER MPID NO.
```

*Heavy underline = user entry. All other data are computer-generated.

Figure 21–11.   On-line PCMR visit summary general format.

(3) LAST *n* VISITS to (DEPARTMENT NAME, LOCATION NAME) *n* = 1 to 99.

(4) LAST *n* VISITS: last *n* visits, and department, any location.

(5) ALL VISITS: any department, any location. If MHC (AMS) visit, then list only MHC, LOCATION, DATE, PHYSICIAN NAME (physician scheduled for follow-up examination).

(6) LAST MHC: summary of final report, or preliminary report if final not available.

```
ENTER MPID NO. ░░░░░* PHYSICIAN NAME, MD
ENTER MR NO. 0123456

09-10-71    12:15 HR
DOE, MARY  B    FEMALE    BORN: 08-68
TOTAL VISITS SINCE 1969: 12 (CLINIC=9, LAB=2, PHAR=2, OTHER=0).
LAST VISIT: 09-04-71

IMMUNIZATIONS:  NO PCMR RECORD
HX POSS SENSITIVITY:  PENICILLIN

REQUEST:  CLIN.3.PED**

09-04-71    SF PED NON-APPT                              DR JONES
            RUBEOLA

09-02-71    SF PED NON-APPT                              DR BROWN
            FEVER UNDETERMINED ORIGIN

09-01-71    SF PED NON-APPT                              DR BROWN
            NO DIAGNOSIS MADE

REQUEST:  LAB.1***

09-02-71    SF LAB
            SPEC BLOOD         ACC NO. 246432
            HEMATOCRIT (%)                 38
            WBC (/ CU MM)               8,400
            DIFFERENTIAL SEGS              31
                       LYMPHS             69

            SPEC URINE         ACC NO. 246612
            PROTEIN                     TRACE
            GLUCOSE                     0
            ACETONE                     TRACE
            SP GR                       1.012

REQUEST: +


*Underline=user action.  All other data is computer generated.
**Last 3 visits to Pediatric Clinic.
***Last visit to clinical laboratory.
+Enter next request code, or NONE (finish).
```

Figure 21–12. Example of on-line iterative retrieval of visit data. In the Total Visit statement, 2 visits to the clinical laboratory are indicated, the most recent of which is the substance of the second request.

At the test level, acceptance of these reports has been encouraging, and useful "feedback" information has been received from the emergency room physicians and nurses. A second test terminal is to be implemented in the pediatric outpatient clinic in 1973.

Two additional retrieval capabilities are under development:

(1) Specific DATA ITEMS, or specifically named groups of items, within visits as a function of time [e.g., prior to date 1, subsequent to date 1, in the interval (date 1-date 2), etc.].

(2) ALL VISITS or MOST RECENT VISITS CONTAINING ANY MEMBERS OF THE FOLLOWING: Tables A, B, C . . . n.

Tables A,B,C . . . n represent sets of clinically relevant data, defined as those sets of data which have been specified as relevant to defined clinical "situations," or problems. Clinical problems may in turn be defined as a function of several different variables, including location (where information is to be output or input), relative urgency (patient condition and user's need to know), time of terminal interaction, classes of data requested, etc. It can be seen that the number of such tables potentially is limitless; however, a finite number may be established for named clinical situations. Thus, Table 4a might represent possible PCMR-stored information, the presence or absence of any member of which would be meaningful to an emergency room physician confronted with a stuporous or comatose patient. Similarly, Table 4b data would be useful to "screen" the medical record for problems related to intestinal bleeding.

F. EDUCATION AND RESEARCH

1. Medical Education

No computer-supported educational applications are in operation now. One of the first such applications we plan is a combined real-time, on-line, and off-line drug interaction alerting and informational subsystem to be interfaced with both the outpatient pharmacy terminals and hospital nursing

Table 4a.   Coma/Obtundation

1.	Alcoholism
2.	Cancer
3.	Congestive heart failure
4.	Diabetes mellitus
	Drugs dispensed:
5a.	Dilantin
5b.	Phenobarbital
5c.	Reserpine
5d.	Valium
5e.	Etc.
6.	Drug habituation
7.	Epilepsy
8.	Hypertension
9.	Seizure disorder NFS
10.	Skull trauma
11.	Etc.

Table 4b.   Gastrointestinal Bleeding

1.	Anemia
2.	Cancer colon
3.	Cancer stomach
4.	Diverticulosis-itis
5.	Duodenal ulcer
	Drugs dispensed:
6a.	Ascriptin
6b.	Darvon CPD
6c.	Ecotrin
6d.	Reserpine
6e.	Etc.
7.	Gastric ulcer
8.	Gastritis
9.	GI bleeding NFS
	Lab:
10a.	HCT < 38 (Male)
10b.	< 34 (Female)
10c.	Etc.
11.	Rectum-polyp (s)
12.	Sigmoidoscopy (date-conclusion)
13.	Ulcerative colitis
14.	Etc.

station terminals. Modular addition of the interaction routines to existing software is not a major problem for our system. More difficult is the definition and maintenance of the special base of drug interaction data. Important problems in this area include the realiability and accuracy (and thereby the utility) of drug interaction data, the interpretation of drug interaction literature, and the establishment of decision rules for inclusion of specific information in the data base. Work has been in progress in this area in the recent past, however, and tests of model systems probably can be expected in the relatively near future.[15,16]

2.   Research

A broad group of research projects have progressed in parallel with developmental activities; however, as noted earlier, the medical data system is itself an applied research program.

a.   Health services and epidemiological research.   Projects utilizing the medical data base, that are either in progress or recently concluded include:

Regulated patient flow

Drug-diagnosis studies

Time trends in diagnoses or events
Predisposing factors for myocardial infarction
Computer simulation of epidemics
New medical care delivery system project
Automated multiphasic health testing questionnaires
Characteristics of smokers and nonsmokers
Kidney high-risk indicator study

In addition, work has been published in the areas of drug surveillance,[17-20] multiphasic evaluation and related studies,[21-23] and automated diagnosis.[24-26,27]

Table 5.

	Word 1	Word 1	Word 1
	2		2
		2	3
	3		4
	4	3	5
			6
	5	4	7
	6		8
		5	9
	7		10
	8	6	11
			12
	9	7	13
	10		14
		8	15
	11		16
	12	9	17
			18
	13	10	19
	14		20
Relative error rate:	Low	Low	High
Relative scan speed:	High	High	Low
Relative density:	Medium	Low	High

b. Computer and information science studies. A constant stream of both formal and informal investigations have been conducted in recent years. Outstanding areas of interest include large data base structure, hierarchical storage of medical data, quality control, medical data utility, user-terminal interaction, etc.

For example, in the course of studying the relation of the format (presentation) of data on a visual display screen to user scanning speed and light-pen selection error rates, it was found that columnar presentation of data in paired rows (Table 5) resulted in reduced scan times and reduced error rates while permitting relatively high density of displayed data.[27]

G. HARDWARE AND SOFTWARE

1. Hardware

The hardware system configuration (in 1973) is that of a central computer facility, designed for both on-line and off-line processing of large volumes of all categories of medical data, linked in telecommunication mode with terminals and satellite processors in remote locations. The central computer facility has an IBM 370/155 computer with a 2 million byte monolithic memory unit from Advanced Memory Systems. Also included are direct-access disk drives (IBM 3333 and 3330's) for storage of the patient computer medical records. The central computer system is shown in Figure 21–13. The telecommunications network consists of an IBM 2701 Control Unit and a Memorex 1270 Control Unit. The IBM unit interfaces the hospital system (Figure 21–7) via two 2400 bps full duplex telephone lines. The Memorex unit interfaces the remainder of the terminals via other telephone lines.

2. Software

The computer system is controlled by the IBM OS/MVT (Operating System allowing Multiprogramming with a Variable number of Tasks). Because the information flow between the terminals, the application programs, the computer medical records, etc., in the on-line medical system are unique to our requirements, we have a medical control program supervisor operating under the IBM OS/MVT. This control program provides a command language with which the computer operators control the medical system from the main computer console. This command language includes the ability to start and stop applications, monitor the status of the system, interchange terminals when necessary, direct output to local or remote terminals, etc., and also to effect backup and recovery procedures.

Many system services are provided by the control system for use by the application programmers. These include several medical record manipulation services. To obtain all or part of a record, all the application programmer needs do is specify the medical record number and other record specifications in a parameter list. The system services use an automatically macro-invoked program to find the record, move it to appropriate

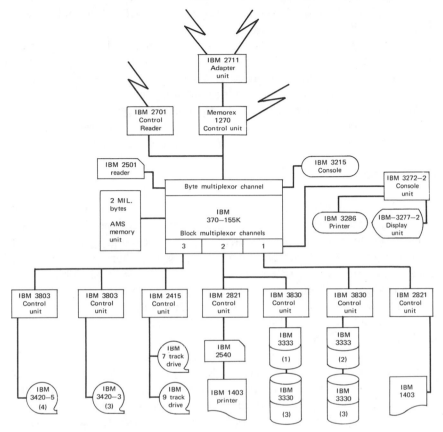

Figure 21-13. Medical methods research computer/teleprocessing equipment (1973).

devices, and return the requested portion of the record to the application program. A description of the computer medical record itself is contained in Chapter Four.

Other system services include input and output aids. Application programmers need not be concerned with input and output hardware, nor with the great difficulty in telecommunication programming, with its technical vagaries of telephone lines and remote terminal "hello/goodbye" line requirements. No actual hardware terminal addresses are used; rather, symbolic terminal addressing is used to allow greater flexibility in directing data to and from alternate terminals in case of breakdown. A comprehensive data control program is provided as a service to the application programmers. By stating various requirements in a simple parameter list, the sending and receiving of messages to and from terminals is automatically handled.

Another important service is the availability of a higher-level language for describing input data. This not only provides a standardized way of describing input data but also produces a standardized transformed internal format for input to the medical record updating routine.

An additional service for processing selected inputs from interactive terminals has also been developed and implemented. This program features the describing of input data forms in a table format so that no programming is involved and is used primarily for input of data from outpatient encounter forms.

To aid research applications, two generalized retrieval routines are available. The first is a search routine which returns variable length subrecords of specified research data for those patients who meet the selection criteria. These requests are specified via a simple language. The investigator's output is a data set on magnetic tape which then can be processed by analysis programs written in the IBM PL/I language. This general search routine is now in its second version of implementation and has been working for about one year. Newer versions will be necessary only if there is a demand for additional capabilities for establishing selection criteria.

Another service, only realized as a need after original system design and specifications, was for work table requirements. Many applications require, for their own use, keeping track of data processed. For example, the clinical laboratory has to keep an account of the specimens and daily work for internal laboratory control. These work lists are generally maintained in the form of tables, with capability of table look-up based on medical record number, accession number, transaction number, etc.

Over 150 additional service macros have been provided for use by the application programmers. These allow the programmer to be more concerned with the logic of his application and less about the actual coding techniques and hardware requirements; hence, programming and debugging time are reduced. Mandatory use of many of the service macros results in improved standardization.

H.   IMPACT AND EVALUATION

Longitudinal evaluation studies have been implemented with the objective of determining the effects of the medical data system on operations, personnel, and costs of the subsystems involved. The evaluation group is maintained separately from the development-implementation group. A general description of the evaluation program has been published[4] (See also Chapter Thirteen). One of the more dramatic outcomes to date has been the observation, based upon a study of process errors involving the San Francisco Hospital Clinical Laboratory over the period 1969 to 1971, that the implementation of the punched-card-oriented back-up system in the laboratory resulted in a 63% decrease in error production. [The major types of errors studied were: (a) record of laboratory order in chart but work not done; (b) no record of laboratory order in chart but work done and result in chart; (c) record of order in chart, work done, no result in chart; (d) no record of order in chart, work done, no result in chart; and (e) duplicate work ordered and done.]

Periodic assessement of the performance and effects of the data subsystems is a continuing program. Results of such studies are expected to serve as rational guides to the inevitable modifications of the data system that operational experience will demand and assist in such difficult areas as determination of effects on quality of patient care and the relation to costs.

I. SUMMARY

The Kaiser-Permanente Medical Data System is a long-term program of applied research and development. Its major objective is the development of data processing and communication methodologies which can (a) be adapted continuously to the differing requirements of the patient care process; (b) be progressively expandable—to multi-department, then multi-facility scale—so as to remain concordant with the growing trend in multi-facility and regionalized medical care; and (c) achieve these goals while supporting high-quality patient care and research at reasonable cost.

A basic premise is that the essential tool with which to pursue these objectives is a centralized computer-supported system of medical data storage and communications control. Such a tool has now been developed and is the vehicle which supports the progressive development and operation of a pilot medical data communication (collection and reporting) system in both the outpatient and inpatient areas of the San Francisco Kaiser-Permanente Medical Center.

Most observers of the growth and development process find it to be slow and initially very expensive. A complicated new technology, itself undergoing rapid change, is being applied to the vigorously dynamic and intricate world of medical practice. The promise of millisecond decision-making, of quick and accurate scanning of ponderous data lists, of easy manipulation of large numbers of variables, of "instant" communication, and of extraordinary consistency and reproducibility is all too exciting. Yet the novitiate is not alone in tending to underestimate the efforts required to bring these attributes to fruition. Structure, standardization, and simplicity are demanded by a fledgling information science. At the same time, the requirements for and uses of medical information are becoming progressively more complex. The costs of attempting to rationalize these conditions and the differences in understanding and experience that exist between the data processing technologist and the medical practitioner are high.

It would seem that the most rational way in which the question of cost justification can be approached is by evaluation of data processing capabilities in a manner that is appropriate to the design objectives of the system in question as these capabilities develop in the medical environment. Guidelines for evaluation have been set forth. Yet, very few formalized evaluation efforts have been initiated. That there is need for improved systematization, efficiency, and effectiveness in the medical care process is beyond question. In spite of the many problems posed, it now appears highly probable that the attempts to use information and communication technology in the support of medical care will result in a gradual realization of these improvements.

REFERENCES

1. Harmon, L. D. "Some Problems and Priorities in Health-Care Technology." *Proceedings, Conference on Technology and Health Care Systems in the 1980's.* January, 1972. San Francisco: U.S. Government Printing Office, in press.
2. Collen, M. F. "Reasons for Failures and Factors Making for Success." *Symposium on the Development of Hospital Computing Systems.* World Health Organization, Toulouse, June 1971.
3. Van Brunt, E. E. "The Kaiser-Permanente Medical Information System." *Comp. and Biomed. Res.* 3,5 (1970) : 477–487.
4. Richart, R. "Evaluation of a Medical Data System." *Comp. and Biomed. Res.* 3,5 (1970) : 415–425.
5. Woodward, K. M. "Computer Education for Physicians: A Computer Service in an Internship Program." *J. Med. Educ.* 45 (1970) : 531–534.
6. Davis, L. S. "Prototype for Future Computer Medical Records." *Comp. and Biomed. Res.* 3,5 (1970) : 539–554.
7. Davis, L. S.; Collen, M. F.; Rubin, F. L.; and Van Brunt, E. E. "Computer Stored Medical Record." *Comp. and Biomed. Res.* 1,5 (1968) : 452–469.
8. Weed, L. L. "Medical Records, Medical Education and Patient Care." *Case Western Reserve.* Cleveland: Univ. Press, 1971.

9. Hurst, J. W., and Walker, H. K. (eds.) "The Problem-Oriented System." New York: Medcom Press, 1972.

10. Lodwick, G. S. "Information Management in Radiology." *Hospital Computer Systems.* John Wiley and Sons, 1974.

11. Collen, M. F.; Kidd, P. H.; Feldman, R.; and Cutler, J. L. "Cost Analysis of a Multiphasic Screening Program." *New England. J. Med.* 280 (1969) : 1043–1045.

12. Collen, M. F. "Guidelines for a Multiphasic Health Checkup." *Arch. Int. Med.* 127 (1971) : 99–100.

13. Collen, M. F. "Preventive Medicine and Automated Multiphasic Screening." *Ninth IBM Medical Symposium, Burlington, Vermont* (1969), 81–97.

14. Greenes, R. A.; Pappalardo, A. N.; Marble, C. W.; and Barnett, G. O. "Design and Implementation of a Clinical Data Management System." *Comp. and Biomed. Res.* 2 (1969) : 469–485.

15. Garten, S.; Rowland, L. R.; Morse, S.; Stewart, W. B.; and Lindberg, D. A. B. "Drug Information: Data Base Organization and Access." *Proceedings of the Fifth Hawaii International Conference on System Sciences* (1972) 220–222.

16. Cohen, S. Stanford University. Personal Communication.

17. Kodlin, D., and Standish, J. "A Time Response Model for Drug Surveillance." *Comp. and Biomed. Res.* 3 (1970) : 620–636.

18. Friedman, G. D.; Collen, M. F.; Harris, L. E.; Van Brunt, E. E.; and Davis, L. S. "Experience in Monitoring Drug Reactions in Outpatients." *JAMA* 217 (1971) : 567–572.

19. Friedman, G. D. "Screening Criteria for Drug Monitoring." *J. Chr. Disease* 25 (1972) : 11–20.

20. Friedman, G. D., and Collen, M. F. "A Method for Monitoring Adverse Drug Reactions." *Sixth Berkeley Symposium on Mathematical Statistics and Probability.* Edited by J. Neyman, University of California Press, 6 (1971).

21. Allen, C. M.; Mitz, J. R.; and Shinefield, H. R. "Test Development in the Pediatric Multiphasic Program." *Pediatric Clinics of North America* 18 (1971) : 169–178.

22. Kodlin, D. "Cost Benefit Problem in Screening for Breast Cancer." *Methods Info. Med.* 11. 4 (1972) : 242–247.

23. Collen, M. F.; Friedman, G. D.; Dales, L.; and Feldman, R. "A Current Evaluation of Multiphasic Health Testing." *AMA Convention San Francisco, June 20, 1972.*

24. Kodlin, D. "Two Studies on Automated Diagnosis in: Automated Multiphasic Health Testing." *Engineering Foundation.* New York, New York, 1971.

25. Gleser, M., and Collen, M. F. "Towards Automated Medical Diagnoses." *Comp. and Biomed. Res.* 5 (1972) : 180–189.

26. Kodlin, D., and Collen, M. F. "Automated Diagnosis in Multiphasic Screening." *Sixth Berkeley Symposium on Mathematical Statistics and Probability* Edited by J. Neyman, Ed., University of California Press, 6 (1971).

27. Van Brunt, E. E., and Tolan, G. 1970, unpublished data.

Index